Debating the Earth

Debating the Earth

The Environmental Politics Reader

Edited by John S. Dryzek and David Schlosberg

Second Edition

OXFORD
UNIVERSITY PRESS

OXFORD
UNIVERSITY PRESS

Great Clarendon Street, Oxford OX2 6DP

Oxford University Press is a department of the University of Oxford.
It furthers the University's objective of excellence in research, scholarship,
and education by publishing worldwide in

Oxford New York

Auckland Cape Town Dar es Salaam Hong Kong Karachi
Kuala Lumpur Madrid Melbourne Mexico City Nairobi
New Delhi Taipei Toronto Shanghai

With offices in

Argentina Austria Brazil Chile Czech Republic France Greece
Guatemala Hungary Italy Japan South Korea Poland Portugal
Singapore Switzerland Thailand Turkey Ukraine Vietnam

Published in the United States
by Oxford University Press Inc., New York

British Library Cataloguing in Publication Data

Data available

Library of Congress Cataloging in Publication Data

Data available

ISBN-13: 978-0-19-927629-5
ISBN-10: 0-19-927629-3

10 9 8 7 6 5 4 3

Typeset by Laserwords Private Limited, Chennai, India

Printed in Great Britain
on acid-free paper by
Antony Rowe Ltd, Chippenham

Acknowledgements

For the first edition:

This reader represents our conception of what a core set of readings in environmental politics should look like. Our judgements have been informed by many people who shared with us their ideas, suggestions, and syllabi: notably, Jane Bennett, David Carruthers, Robert Garner, Adolf Gundersen, Robert Goodin, Tim Hayward, Andrew Light, Albert Matheny, Michael McGinnis, James O'Connor, Daniel Press, Bob Taylor, Bron Taylor, and Leslie Theile. Tim Barton of Oxford University Press helped to guide this project from conception to fruition. Graduate Assistant Paul Vaughn is to be commended for his editorial assistance. Finally, we thank our students at the University of Oregon, Northern Arizona University, and the University of Melbourne, upon whom many of these readings have been field tested.

For the second edition:

Many people offered suggestions for revisions and updates to this reader. We especially appreciate the thorough input of Terry Ball, John Barry, and John Meyer, along with a number of contributors to the Environmental Political Theory e-discussion list. Thanks to Ruth Anderson, our editor with Oxford this time around. And finally, once again, we wish to thank the subjects of our field tests of many of the new essays—students at the University of Melbourne, Northern Arizona University, and the London School of Economics and Political Science.

J.S.D. and D.S.

Contents

List of Figures

List of Tables

Introduction

John S. Dryzek and David Schlosberg

The Rise of Environmental Politics

Environmental politics is about how humanity organizes itself to relate to the nature that sustains it. Thus it encompasses matters of how people deal with the planet and its life, and how they relate to each other through the medium of the environment. It impinges on other areas of political concern such as those related to poverty, social justice, education, race, the economy, international relations, and human rights inasmuch as what happens in these areas affects our environment (and vice versa). Environmental politics has in the past 40 years come from nowhere to constitute what is now a large, lively, burgeoning and diverse field, which we survey in this reader.

The issues which we now group under the environmental heading emerged sporadically in the first six decades of the twentieth century. Early German ideas about conservation biology crossed the Atlantic to inform the development of a doctrine of resource conservation, which developed alongside a very different American tradition of reverence for wilderness. Meanwhile, concern grew over health and cleanliness in cities and workplaces. Europeans too concerned themselves with issues of public health, and tended to emphasize access to open space rather than wilderness, of which they had none.

'The environment' as a collective name for all these concerns arrived in the 1960s, which dates the beginning of environmental politics as such. Since then, the growth of environmental literature has matched the growth of environmental concern, which has spread to the developing world and the global system itself. Particular concerns have featured energy shortages, toxic wastes, air and water pollution, the hazards of nuclear power, biotechnology, species extinction, biodiversity, pesticides, animal rights, wilderness protection, climate change, and inequality in the distribution of environmental risks and benefits. Environmental politics today encompasses discussions of the various political, social, and economic causes of ecological problems and crises; the ethics of our relationship with the natural systems that sustain us; our environmental relationships with our fellow-humans; environmental movements; and designs for alternative, more sustainable forms of political organization.

We present here a text that highlights the diversity of political responses to environmental crisis. We look at the various definitions of environmental crisis (including its denial), its causes and effects, and institutional, policy, lifestyle, and community organizing responses to environmental problems.

Environmental politics has a broad scope. For the purposes of this reader, we delimit it a bit more precisely. This is not a reader on environmental policy as such, though numerous policy issues—including land and river basin management, pollution control, environmental impact assessment, wilderness protection, hazardous waste management, and corporate accountability—will enter the discussion. Nor is this a reader on environmental philosophy or ethics, though discussions of ecocentric values, deep ecology, social ecology, and ecofeminism are included, with a view to their political ramifications. And this is not a reader on environmental economics, though issues of economic sustainability, resource privatization, and the environmental implications of capitalism will be discussed—again with an eye to their political aspects. Thus the realms of environmental policy, ethics, and economics are integral parts of our coverage, though mainly in their political dimensions and consequences.

Organization of this Collection

Our readings are organized in a way that highlights the differences and debates between the various schools of thought on environmental affairs. The reader is divided into five parts, representing five key axes of environmental debate. Each part is then broken down further into sections.

We begin in Part One with the debate over the reality and severity of the environmental crisis itself, which has now raged for more than three decades. Obviously, the kind of environmental politics we do or should get depends a lot on the nature and severity of this crisis. In section I we visit some classic and contemporary claims about the severity of global ecological limits to human activity, which have catastrophic consequences should we hit them. Section II covers counter-arguments to the effect that there are no limits which human ingenuity cannot overcome, such that in truth there is no environmental crisis, only a few environmental problems that can be dealt with quite easily.

Part Two covers two kinds of reformist response to environmental issues. Section III focuses on the administrative management of the environment; while a less spectacular debate than that over global limits, this sort of management represents much if not most of what has actually been done by governments in the recent decades of environmental concern. Section IV focuses on attempts to involve public participation in environmental politics and management within the liberal democratic framework that characterizes most developed nations.

Part Three moves to the links between the environment and the economy, and how politics mediates and affects this link. Section V covers arguments to the effect that the free market is in truth the best protector of the environment, provided only that governments can arrange an appropriate specification of private property rights in natural resources and other environmental goods. Section VI represents recent claims about the compatibility of economic growth, environmental protection, and social justice, provided that these values are subsumed under the concept of sustainable development. Adding precision to such claims, Section VII looks at the idea of ecological modernization, under which a re-tooling of the economy along ecological sound lines proves beneficial to business and the economy as a whole.

In Part Four we look at some more radical interpretations of environmental crisis and what might be done about it. Section VIII covers deep ecology and bioregionalism, which trace the cause of environmental crisis to human alienation from nature, and offer solutions in the form of a deeper environmental consciousness, which will in turn require political change in the form of new kinds of human community. Section IX covers social and socialist ecology, which are inclined to see both causes and solutions in the realm of social, economic, and political structure, rather than contenting themselves with questions of deep consciousness. Section X on environmental justice looks at the fastest-growing part of the environmental movement in North America, examining its political critiques, principles, and practices, which turn on the unequal distribution of environmental risks. Section XI examines challenges to established ways of looking at interlinked issues of environment, development, and justice that come from the developing world and indigenous peoples.

Finally, Part Five addresses the possibilities for environmental action beyond the boundaries of the liberal state. Section XII looks at examples of green movement activities in civil society, a realm of political action that keeps its distance from state structures. We conclude in Section XIII with an examination of the radical democratic potential of ecological politics.

In keeping with our emphasis on the debates in the field of environmental politics, we have in most of the sections included a critique of the line of argument represented therein. So in Section II Tom Burke criticizes the Promethean caricature of environmental concern and argues that its denial of environmental crisis rests on bad science. In Section III Mary O'Brien opposes technocratic administrative techniques; in Section IV William P. Ophuls and A. Stephen Boyan, Jr. offer a scathing critique of liberal democracy; in Section V Robert E. Goodin equates market instruments with selling indulgences to sin; and in Section VI David Carruthers highlights the problematic history of sustainable development. But debates rage across the sections as well as within them. Thus the liberal democratic proposals of Section IV emerge as correctives to perceived deficiencies in the administrative rationalism of Section III. The more radical democracy of Section XIII and its associated movements discussed in Section XII expose the deficiencies of administrative rationalism and liberal democracy alike. The radical ecologies of Sections VIII and IX share this critique, and also have little time for the economic orientation of Sections VI and VII.

The way we have chosen to carve up the field corresponds to what we believe are the key fault-lines in environmental politics. But we do not claim this is the only way to organize these debates. For example, we decided that ecofeminism does not fit neatly into one box, and indeed there are good reasons not to make a ghetto of it. Thus our ecofeminist selections are spread across four debates to which ecofeminist writings have contributed, rather than gathered under a single heading. Additionally, some of our authors might make a case for different company from that which we have assigned to them. For example, Andrew Dobson's discussion of ecological citizenship which we have put in Section XIII on ecological democracy also speaks to green action in liberal democracy as discussed in Section IV. Thomas Poguntke's article on green parties captures a key part of the environmental movement, which is why we place it in Section XII. But such parties now help constitute governments in many liberal democracies, so it too connects to Section IV.

Finally, while we have aspired to a degree of comprehensiveness in our coverage, the sheer size and diversity of the environmental politics field means that we have had to leave out many valuable contributions to the literature. Such is the nature of a reader of this sort. To compensate for these exclusions, in the introduction to each section we have included suggestions for further reading that extends or responds to the themes of the section. Beyond these suggestions, we highly recommend two journals: *Environmental Politics* and *Global Environmental Politics*.

PART ONE

Feast or Famine? The Severity of Environmental Problems

Environmental issues have long histories. But the atmosphere of general environmental crisis first perceived in the 1960s and its associated social movements precipitated an avalanche of environmental writing. From Rachel Carson's *Silent Spring* in 1962 to Lois Gibbs's *Dying from Dioxin* (1995) and beyond, many writers have addressed the ways in which the modern industrial world has encountered environmental crises, ranging from resource exhaustion to species extinction to endangered human health to catastrophic climate change. But one thing is constant in the realm of environmental politics: where there are critiques and doomsayers, there are sure to be counter-arguments and cornucopians. Part One offers some classic and contemporary arguments in this long debate about the severity of environmental problems—the necessary precursor to arguments about political responses to environmental crisis.

Section I: Limits and Survivalism

The 1970s are known to both supporters and critics of environmentalism as the 'Doomsday Decade'. With a growing interest in the effects of growth and industrialization, a number of gloomy publications came out during this period—books with titles like *The Last Days of Mankind* (1974), *The Death of Tomorrow* (1972), *Terracide* (1970), *The Doomsday Syndrome* (1972), *The Doomsday Book* (1970), *The Coming Dark Age* (1973), *This Endangered Planet* (1972), etc. A quote from *Blueprint for Survival* (1972) gives an example of the mood of the time: 'If current trends are allowed to persist, the breakdown of society and the irreversible disruption of the life-support systems on this planet, possibly by the end of the century, certainly within the lifetimes of our children, are inevitable.'

Most of these works are full of serious, full-scale attacks on the various practices of modern economic life in the advanced industrialized countries, especially land and resource use, pollution, and various types of waste. The basic argument is simple: modern economic life assumes that growth and expansion can go on without limits, while the planet is made up of systems of finite resources that are threatened and carrying capacities that we are in danger of overshooting. All three of our selections in this section argue that, unless changed, modern patterns of growth and development will lead to ecological collapse.

The first of the selections here, from the Club of Rome's classic *Limits to Growth* (1972), is not a product of the stereotypical environmental activists of the late 1960s; rather, the research was conducted by an international research team at MIT, using complex computer modelling techniques. The piece we have chosen focuses on the concept of *exponential* growth, in order to demonstrate the quickly increasing nature of environmental problems—including the growth of population and the depletion of natural resources. The argument here is that limits are looming: either the continuation of existing patterns of industrialization and growth will lead to ecosystem collapse, or we need to develop self-imposed restraints on our actions to avoid such a catastrophe.

Like the Club of Rome, Garrett Hardin's essay, 'The Tragedy of the Commons', also argues that business as usual in regard to natural resources and the environment will lead to a collapse of ecosystems. But rather than focus on the nature of growth, Hardin's critique centres on how the rational self-interested actions of individuals lead to devastating collective consequences. While many have criticized Hardin's lack of understanding of the communitarian nature of true commons management, his argument holds true to the ways natural resources are currently treated in the market economy. Hardin is well known not only for this commons analysis, but also for his suggested solution: 'mutual coercion mutually agreed upon'. His authoritarian prescriptions are a precursor to some later critiques of democratic management of environmental problems.

Concern with catastrophic ecological collapse is not something left behind in the Doomsday Decade. The annual *State of the World* volumes put out by Lester Brown and the Worldwatch Institute continue to remind us about indicators of economic catastrophe. We include a 2003 piece by Lester Brown, which emphasizes imminent crisis in the global food supply.

The doomsayers were eventually joined from an unlikely direction. In 2003 the US Department of Defense commissioned a report, 'An Abrupt Climate Change Scenario and its Implications for United States National Security', on the security consequences of climate change. This report projected numerous catastrophes and attendant violent conflict in coming decades (available at <http://www.ems.org/climate/pentagon_climate_change.html>).

Further Reading

In addition to the original *Limits To Growth* (and its 1992 update, *Beyond the Limits*), the *Blueprint for Survival* (1972), by Edward Goldsmith and the other editors of Britain's *The Ecologist* magazine, is one of the classic doomsday critiques of the modern industrial order's effects on ecological stability. It is also one of the few works in the limits literature that proposes a decentralized political approach to the crisis. In the USA, the 1981 *Global 2000 Report to the President* (at that time the equally gloomy Jimmy Carter) finished the doomsday decade with a prediction of ecological collapse 'if present trends continue...'. William Catton's *Overshoot* (1980) also stands out as one of the classics of the era. Finally, as noted above, the Worldwatch Institute's *State of the World* updates dire ecological indicators annually. The *Limits to Growth* thesis met an early trenchant critique in H. S. D. Cole et al., *Models of Doom: A Critique of the Limits to Growth* (1973). Unrepentant survivalists writing in the 1990s include Robert Heilbroner, *An Inquiry into the Human Prospect: Looked at Again for the 1990s* (1991) and Garrett Hardin, *Living Within Limits: Ecology, Economics, and Population* (1993).

A concern with carrying capacity as a limit to economic growth pervades the field of ecological economics (not to be confused with the more conventional field of environmental economics, which makes an appearance in Section V). The field has its own journal, *Ecological Economics*. Representing the field, Kenneth Arrow and his co-authors, in a 1995 *Science* article entitled 'Economic Growth, Carrying Capacity, and the Environment', argue that all economic activity ultimately depends on the health of the environment in which it is embedded. In order to avoid the collapse of both economy and ecology, institutions must be designed to protect the latter. The origins of ecological economics may be found in Nicholas Georgescu-Roegen's *Energy and Economic Myths* (1976) and Herman Daly's *Toward a Steady-State Economy* (1973), which is updated in his *Valuing the Earth* (1993).

While touched on here briefly by both the Club of Rome and the Brown selections, population growth is one of the key issues of the limits literature. The classic work is Paul Ehrlich's *Population Bomb* (1968). That book, and the response by Francis Moore Lappé and Joseph Collins in *Food First* (1977), spawned the continuing argument (which we return to in Part Four) over whether it is population per se, or the social organization and condition of that population, that leads to the threat of ecological collapse. Many have criticized Hardin's understanding of the management of the commons; the most thorough is Elinor Ostrom's *Governing the Commons* (1990), which lays out more cooperative and discursive methods of commons management, in contrast to Hardin's focus on the need for central power to squash individual interest.

The most forceful criticisms of the literature of limits, however, are to be found in the writings of the Prometheans and cornucopians, who deny the reality of ecological limits. We will turn to these authors in the Section II.

1   The Nature of Exponential Growth

Donella H. Meadows, Dennis L. Meadows, Jørgen Randers, and William H. Behrens III

People at present think that five sons are not too many and each son has five sons also, and before the death of the grandfather there are already 25 descendants. Therefore people are more and wealth is less; they work hard and receive little.

(Han Fei-Tzu, c. 500 BC)

All five elements basic to the study reported here—population, food production, industrialization, pollution, and consumption of nonrenewable natural resources—are increasing. The amount of their increase each year follows a pattern that mathematicians call exponential growth. Nearly all of mankind's current activities, from use of fertilizer to expansion of cities, can be represented by exponential growth curves (see Figures 1.1 and 1.2). Since much of this book deals with the causes and implications of exponential growth curves, it is important to begin with an understanding of their general characteristics.

The Mathematics of Exponential Growth

Most people are accustomed to thinking of growth as a *linear* process. A quantity is growing linearly when it increases by a constant amount in a constant time period. For example, a child who becomes one inch taller each year is growing linearly. If a miser hides $10 each year under his mattress, his horde of money is also increasing in a linear way. The amount of increase each year is obviously not affected by the size of the child nor the amount of money already under the mattress.

A quantity exhibits *exponential* growth when it increases by a constant percentage of the whole in a constant time period. A colony of yeast cells in which each cell divides into two cells every 10 minutes is growing exponentially. For each single cell, after 10 minutes there will be two cells, an increase of 100 percent. After the next 10 minutes there will be four cells, then eight, then sixteen. If a miser takes $100 from his mattress and invests it at 7 percent (so that the total amount accumulated increases by 7 percent each year), the invested money will grow much faster than the linearly increasing stock under the mattress (see Figure 1.3). The amount added each year to a bank account or each 10 minutes to a yeast colony is not constant. It continually

From Donella H. Meadows, Dennis L. Meadows, Jørgen Randers, William H. Behrens III, *The Limits to Growth* (New York: Universe Books, 1972), 25–44. Reprinted with permission of Universe Publishing.

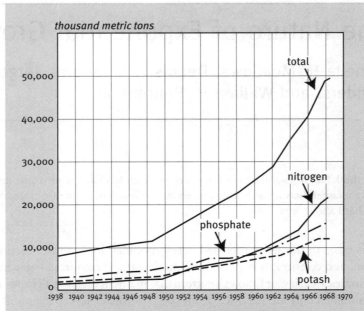

Fig. 1.1 World fertilizer consumption. World fertilizer consumption is increasing exponentially, with a doubling time of about 10 years. Total use is now five times greater than it was during World War II.

Note: Figures do not include the USSR or the People's Republic of China.
Source: UN Department of Economic and Social Affairs, *Statistical Yearbook 1955*, *Statistical Yearbook 1960*, and *Statistical Yearbook 1970* (New York: United Nations, 1956, 1961, and 1971).

increases, as the total accumulated amount increases. Such exponential growth is a common process in biological, financial, and many other systems of the world.

Common as it is, exponential growth can yield surprising results—results that have fascinated mankind for centuries. There is an old Persian legend about a clever courtier who presented a beautiful chessboard to his king and requested that the king give him in return 1 grain of rice for the first square on the board, 2 grains for the second square, 4 grains for the third, and so forth. The king readily agreed and ordered rice to be brought from his stores. The fourth square of the chessboard required 8 grains, the tenth square took 512 grains, the fifteenth required 16,384, and the twenty-first square gave the courtier more than a million grains of rice. By the fortieth square a million million rice grains had to be brought from the storerooms. The king's entire rice supply was exhausted long before he reached the sixty-fourth square. Exponential increase is deceptive because it generates immense numbers very quickly.

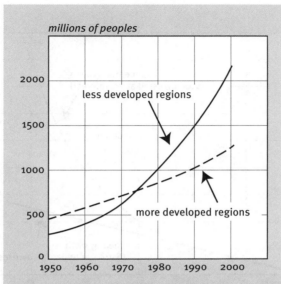

Fig. 1.2 **World urban population. Total urban population is expected to increase exponentially in the less developed regions of the world, but almost linearly in the more developed regions. Present average doubling time for city populations in less developed regions is 15 years.**

Source: UN Department of Economic and Social Affairs, *The World Population Situation in 1970* (New York: United Nations, 1971).

A French riddle for children illustrates another aspect of exponential growth—the apparent suddenness with which it approaches a fixed limit. Suppose you own a pond on which a water lily is growing. The lily plant doubles in size each day. If the lily were allowed to grow unchecked, it would completely cover the pond in 30 days, choking off the other forms of life in the water. For a long time the lily plant seems small, and so you decide not to worry about cutting it back until it covers half the pond. On what day will that be? On the twenty-ninth day, of course. You have one day to save your pond.[1]

It is useful to think of exponential growth in terms of *doubling time*, or the time it takes a growing quantity to double in size. In the case of the lily plant described above, the doubling time is 1 day. A sum of money left in a bank at 7 percent interest will double in 10 years. There is a simple mathematical relationship between the interest rate, or rate of growth, and the time it will take a quantity to double in size. The doubling time is approximately equal to 70 divided by the growth rate, as illustrated in Table 1.1.

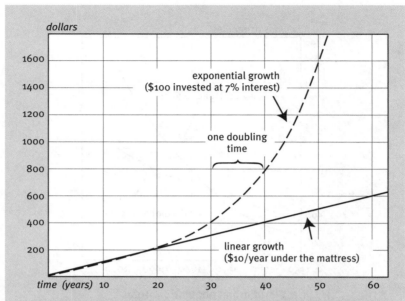

Fig. 1.3 **The growth of savings. If a miser hides $10 each year under his mattress, his savings will grow linearly, as shown by the lower curve. If, after 10 years, he invests his $100 at 7 percent interest, that $100 will grow exponentially, with a doubling time of 10 years.**

Table 1.1 **Doubling time**

Growth rate (% per year)	Doubling time (years)
0.1	700
0.5	140
1.0	70
2.0	35
4.0	18
5.0	14
7.0	10
10.0	7

Models and Exponential Growth

Exponential growth is a dynamic phenomenon, which means that it involves elements that change over time. In simple systems, like the bank account or the lily pond, the cause of exponential growth and its future course are relatively easy to understand. When many different quantities are growing simultaneously in a system, however, and when all the quantities are interrelated in a complicated way, analysis of the causes of growth and of the future behavior of the system becomes very difficult indeed. Does population growth cause industrialization or does industrialization cause population growth? Is either one singly responsible for increasing pollution, or are they both responsible? Will more food production result in more population? If any one of these elements grows slower or faster, what will happen to the growth rates of all the others? These very questions are being debated in many parts of the world today. The answers can be found through a better understanding of the entire complex system that unites all of these important elements.

Over the course of the last 30 years there has evolved at the Massachusetts Institute of Technology a new method for understanding the dynamic behavior of complex systems. The method is called System Dynamics.[2] The basis of the method is the recognition that the *structure* of any system—the many circular, interlocking, sometimes time-delayed relationships among its components—is often just as important in determining its behavior as the individual components themselves. The world model described in this book is a System Dynamics model.

Dynamic modeling theory indicates that any exponentially growing quantity is somehow involved with a *positive feedback loop*. A positive feedback loop is sometimes called a "vicious circle." An example is the familiar wage-price spiral—wages increase, which causes prices to increase, which leads to demands for higher wages, and so forth. In a positive feedback loop a chain of cause-and-effect relationships closes on itself, so that increasing any one element in the loop will start a sequence of changes that will result in the originally changed element being increased even more.

The positive feedback loop that accounts for exponential increase of money in a bank account is represented in Figure 1.4.

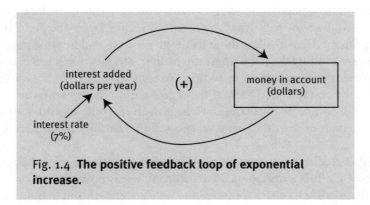

Fig. 1.4 **The positive feedback loop of exponential increase.**

Suppose $100 is deposited in the account. The first year's interest is 7 percent of $100, or $7, which is added to the account, making the total $107. The next year's interest is 7 percent of $107, or $7.49, which makes a new total of $114.49. One year later the interest on that amount will be more than $8.00. The more money there is in the account, the more money will be added each year in interest. The more is added, the more there will be in the account the next year causing even more to be added in interest. And so on. As we go around and around the loop, the accumulated money in the account grows exponentially. The rate of interest (constant at 7 percent) determines the gain around the loop, or the rate at which the bank account grows.

We can begin our dynamic analysis of the long-term world situation by looking for the positive feedback loops underlying the exponential growth in the five physical quantities we have already mentioned. In particular, the growth rates of two of these elements—population and industrialization—are of interest, since the goal of many development policies is to encourage the growth of the latter relative to the former. The two basic positive feedback loops that account for exponential population and industrial growth are simple in principle. We will describe their basic structures in the next few pages. The many interconnections between these two positive feedback loops act to amplify or to diminish the action of the loops, to couple or uncouple the growth rates of population and of industry. These interconnections constitute the rest of the world model and their description will occupy much of the rest of this book.

World Population Growth

The exponential growth curve of world population is shown in Figure 1.5. In 1650 the population numbered about 0.5 billion,[3] and it was growing at a rate of approximately 0.3 percent per year.[4] That corresponds to a doubling time of nearly 250 years. In 1970 the population totaled 3.6 billion and the rate of growth was 2.1 percent per year.[5] The doubling time at this growth rate is 33 years. Thus, not only has the population been growing exponentially, but the rate of growth has also been growing. We might say that population growth has been "super"-exponential; the population curve is rising even faster than it would if growth were strictly exponential.

The feedback loop structure that represents the dynamic behavior of population growth is shown in Figure 1.6. On the left is the positive feedback loop that accounts for the observed exponential growth. In a population with constant average fertility, the larger the population, the more babies will be born each year. The more babies, the larger the population will be the following year. After a delay to allow those babies to grow up and become parents, even more babies will be born, swelling the population still further. Steady growth will continue as long as average fertility remains constant. If, in addition to sons, each woman has on the average two female children, for example, and each of them grows up to have two more female children, the population will double each generation. The growth rate will depend on both the average fertility and the length of the delay between generations. Fertility is not necessarily constant, of course.

There is another feedback loop governing population growth, shown on the right side of the diagram in Figure 1.6. It is a *negative feedback loop*. Whereas positive feedback loops generate runaway growth, negative feedback loops tend to regulate growth and to hold a system in some

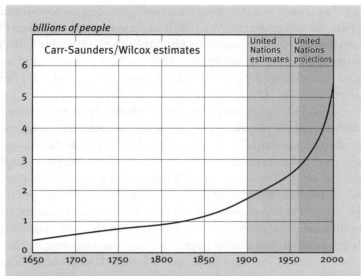

Fig. 1.5 **World population. World population since 1650 has been growing exponentially at an increasing rate. Estimated population in 1970 is already slightly higher than the projection illustrated here (which was made in 1958). The present world population growth rate is about 2.1 percent per year, corresponding to a doubling time of 33 years.**

Source: Donald J. Bogue, *Principles of Demography* (New York: John Wiley and Sons, 1969).

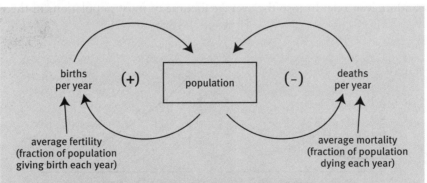

Fig. 1.6 **The feedback loop structure representing the dynamic behavior of population growth.**

stable state. They behave much as a thermostat does in controlling the temperature of a room. If the temperature falls, the thermostat activates the heating system, which causes the temperature to rise again. When the temperature reaches its limit, the thermostat cuts off the heating system, and the temperature begins to fall again. In a negative feedback loop a change in one element is propagated around the circle until it comes back to change that element in a direction *opposite* to the initial change.

The negative feedback loop controlling population is based upon average mortality, a reflection of the general health of the population. The number of deaths each year is equal to the total population times the average mortality (which we might think of as the average probability of death at any age). An increase in the size of a population with constant average mortality will result in more deaths per year. More deaths will leave fewer people in the population, and so there will be fewer deaths the next year. If on the average 5 percent of the population dies each year, there will be 500 deaths in a population of 10,000 in one year. Assuming no births for the moment, that would leave 9,500 people the next year. If the probability of death is still 5 percent, there will be only 475 deaths in this smaller population, leaving 9,025 people. The next year there will be only 452 deaths. Again, there is a delay in this feedback loop because the mortality rate is a function of the average age of the population. Also, of course, mortality even at a given age is not necessarily constant.

If there were no deaths in a population, it would grow exponentially by the positive feedback loop of births, as shown in Figure 1.7(a). If there were no births, the population would decline to zero because of the negative feedback loop of deaths, also as shown in Figure 1.7(b). Since every real population experiences both births and deaths, as well as varying fertility and mortality, the dynamic behavior of populations governed by these two interlocking feedback loops can become fairly complicated.

What has caused the recent super-exponential rise in world population? Before the Industrial Revolution both fertility and mortality were comparatively high and irregular. The birth rate generally exceeded the death rate only slightly, and population grew exponentially, but at a very slow and uneven rate. In 1650 the average lifetime of most populations in the world was

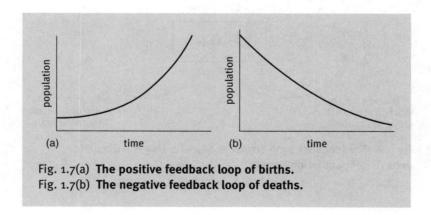

Fig. 1.7(a) **The positive feedback loop of births.**
Fig. 1.7(b) **The negative feedback loop of deaths.**

only about 30 years. Since then, mankind has developed many practices that have had profound effects on the population growth system, especially on mortality rates. With the spread of modern medicine, public health techniques, and new methods of growing and distributing foods, death rates have fallen around the world. World average life expectancy is currently about 53 years[6] and still rising. On a world average the gain around the positive feedback loop (fertility) has decreased only slightly while the gain around the negative feedback loop (mortality) is decreasing. The result is an increasing dominance of the positive feedback loop and the sharp exponential rise in population pictured in Figure 1.5.

What about the population of the future? How might we extend the population curve of Figure 1.5 into the twenty-first century? For the moment we can safely conclude that because of the delays in the controlling feedback loops, especially the positive loop of births, there is no possibility of leveling off the population growth curve before the year 2000, even with the most optimistic assumption of decreasing fertility. Most of the prospective parents of the year 2000 have already been born. Unless there is a sharp rise in mortality, which mankind will certainly strive mightily to avoid, we can look forward to a world population of around 7 billion persons in 30 more years. And if we continue to succeed in lowering mortality with no better success in lowering fertility than we have accomplished in the past, in 60 years there will be four people in the world for every one person living today.

World Economic Growth

A second quantity that has been increasing in the world even faster than human population is industrial output. Figure 1.8 shows the expansion of world industrial production since 1930, with 1963 production as the base of reference. The average growth rate from 1963 to 1968 was 7 percent per year, or 5 percent per year on a per capita basis.

What is the positive feedback loop that accounts for exponential growth of industrial output? The dynamic structure, in Figure 1.9, is actually very similar to the one we have already described for the population system.

With a given amount of industrial capital (factories, trucks, tools, machines, etc.), a certain amount of manufactured output each year is possible. The output actually produced is also dependent on labor, raw materials, and other inputs. For the moment we will assume that these other inputs are sufficient, so that capital is the limiting factor in production. (The world model does include these other inputs.) Much of each year's output is consumable goods, such as textiles, automobiles, and houses, that leave the industrial system. But some fraction of the production is more capital—looms, steel mills, lathes—which is an investment to increase the capital stock. Here we have another positive feedback loop. More capital creates more output, some variable fraction of the output is investment, and more investment means more capital. The new, larger capital stock generates even more output, and so on. There are also delays in this feedback loop, since the production of a major piece of industrial capital, such as an electrical generating plant or a refinery, can take several years.

Capital stock is not permanent. As capital wears out or becomes obsolete, it is discarded. To model this situation we must introduce into the capital system a negative feedback loop

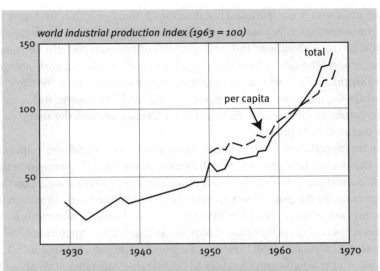

Fig. 1.8 **World industrial production. World industrial production, relative to the base year 1963, also shows a clear exponential increase despite small fluctuations. The 1963–8 average growth rate of total production is 7 percent per year. The per capita growth rate is 5 percent per year.**

Sources: UN Department of Economic and Social Affairs, *Statistical Yearbook 1956* and *Statistical Yearbook 1969* (New York: United Nations, 1957 and 1970).

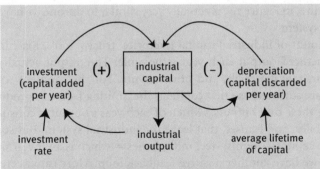

Fig. 1.9 **Positive feedback loop accounting for exponential growth of industrial output.**

accounting for capital depreciation. The more capital there is, the more wears out on the average each year; and the more that wears out, the less there will be the next year. This negative feedback loop is exactly analogous to the death rate loop in the population system. As in the population system, the positive loop is strongly dominant in the world today, and the world's industrial capital stock is growing exponentially.

Since industrial output is growing at 7 percent per year and population only at 2 percent per year, it might appear that dominant positive feedback loops are a cause for rejoicing. Simple extrapolation of those growth rates would suggest that the material standard of living of the world's people will double within the next 14 years. Such a conclusion, however, often includes the implicit assumption that the world's growing industrial output is evenly distributed among the world's citizens. The fallacy of this assumption can be appreciated when the per capita economic growth rates of some individual nations are examined (see Figure 1.10).

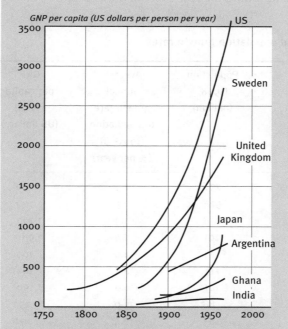

Fig. 1.10 **Economic growth rates. The economic growth of individual nations indicates that differences in exponential growth rates are widening the economic gap between rich and poor countries.**

Source: Simon Kuznets, *Economic Growth of Nations* (Cambridge, Mass.: Harvard University Press, 1971).

Most of the world's industrial growth plotted in Figure 1.8 is actually taking place in the already industrialized countries, where the rate of population growth is comparatively low. The most revealing possible illustration of that fact is a simple table listing the economic and population growth rates of the ten most populous nations of the world, where 64 percent of the world's population currently lives. Table 1.2 makes very clear the basis for the saying, "The rich get richer and the poor get children."

It is unlikely that the rates of growth listed in Table 1.2 will continue unchanged even until the end of this century. Many factors will change in the next 30 years. The end of civil disturbance in Nigeria, for example, will probably increase the economic growth rate there, while the onset of civil disturbance and then war in Pakistan has already interfered with economic growth there. Let us recognize, however, that the growth rates listed above are the products of a complicated social and economic system that is essentially stable and that is likely to change slowly rather than quickly, except in cases of severe social disruption.

It is a simple matter of arithmetic to calculate extrapolated values for gross national product (GNP) per capita from now until the year 2000 on the assumption that relative growth rates of

Table 1.2 **Economic and population growth rates**

Country	Population (1968) (million)	Average annual growth rate of population (1961−8) (% per year)	GNP per capita (1968) (US dollars)	Average annual growth rate of GNP per capita (1961−8) (% per year)
People's Republic of China[a]	730	1.5	90	0.3
India	524	2.5	100	1.0
USSR[a]	238	1.3	1,100	5.8
United States	201	1.4	3,980	3.4
Pakistan	123	2.6	100	3.1
Indonesia	113	2.4	100	0.8
Japan	101	1.0	1,190	9.9
Brazil	88	3.0	250	1.6
Nigeria	63	2.4	70	−0.3
Federal Republic of Germany	60	1.0	1,970	3.4

[a] The International Bank for Reconstruction and Development qualifies its estimates for China and the USSR with the following statement: 'Estimates of GNP per capita and its growth rate have a wide margin of error mainly because of the problems in deriving the GNP at factor cost from net material product and in converting the GNP estimate into US dollars.' United Nations estimates are in general agreement with those of the IBRD.

Source: *World Bank Atlas* (Washington, DC: International Bank for Reconstruction and Development, 1970).

Table 1.3 **Extrapo-Lated GNP for the year 2000**

Country	GNP per capita (in US dollars[a])
People's Republic of China	100
India	140
USSR	6,330
United States	11,000
Pakistan	250
Indonesia	130
Japan	23,200
Brazil	440
Nigeria	60
Federal Republic of Germany	5,850

[a] Based on the 1968 dollar with no allowance for inflation.

population and GNP will remain roughly the same in these ten countries. The result of such a calculation appears in Table 1.3. The values shown there will almost certainly *not* actually be realized. They are not predictions. The values merely indicate the general direction our system, as it is currently structured, is taking us. *They demonstrate that the process of economic growth, as it is occurring today, is inexorably widening the absolute gap between the rich and the poor nations of the world.*

Most people intuitively and correctly reject extrapolations like those shown in Table 1.3, because the results appear ridiculous. It must be recognized, however, that in rejecting extrapolated values, one is also rejecting the assumption that there will be *no change* in the system. If the extrapolations in Table 1.3 do not actually come to pass, it will be because the balance between the positive and negative feedback loops determining the growth rates of population and capital in each nation has been altered. Fertility, mortality, the capital investment rate, the capital depreciation rate—any or all may change. In postulating any different outcome from the one shown in Table 1.3, one must specify which of these factors is likely to change, by how much, and when. These are exactly the questions we are addressing with our model, not on a national basis, but on an aggregated global one.

To speculate with any degree of realism on future growth rates of population and industrial capital, we must know something more about the other factors in the world that interact with the population-capital system. We shall begin by asking a very basic set of questions.

Can the growth rates of population and capital presented in Table 1.3 be physically sustained in the world? How many people can be provided for on this earth, at what level of wealth, and for how long? To answer these questions, we must look in detail at those systems in the world which provide the physical support for population and economic growth.

Notes

1. We are indebted to M. Robert Lattes for telling us this riddle.
2. A detailed description of the method of System Dynamics analysis is presented in J. W. Forrester's *Industrial Dynamics* (Cambridge, Mass.: MIT Press, 1961) and *Principles of Systems* (Cambridge, Mass.: Wright-Allen Press, 1968).
3. The word "billion" in this book will be used to mean 1,000 million, i.e. the European "milliard."
4. A. M. Carr-Saunders, *World Population: Past Growth and Present Trends* (Oxford: Clarendon Press, 1936), 42.
5. US Agency for International Development, *Population Program Assistance* (Washington, DC: Government Printing Office, 1970), 172.
6. *World Population Data Sheet 1968* (Washington, DC: Population Reference Bureau, 1968).

2   The Tragedy of the Commons

Garrett Hardin

At the end of a thoughtful article on the future of nuclear war, Wiesner and York concluded that:

Both sides in the arms race are . . . confronted by the dilemma of steadily increasing military power and steadily decreasing national security. It *is our considered professional judgment that this dilemma has no technical solution*. If the great powers continue to look for solutions in the area of science and technology only, the result will be to worsen the situation.[1]

I would like to focus your attention not on the subject of the article (national security in a nuclear world) but on the kind of conclusion they reached, namely that there is no technical solution to the problem. An implicit and almost universal assumption of discussions published in professional and semipopular scientific journals is that the problem under discussion has a technical solution. A technical solution may be defined as one that requires a change only in the techniques of the natural sciences, demanding little or nothing in the way of change in human values or ideas of morality.

In our day (though not in earlier times) technical solutions are always welcome. Because of previous failures in prophecy, it takes courage to assert that a desired technical solution is not possible. Wiesner and York exhibited this courage; publishing in a science journal, they insisted that the solution to the problem was not to be found in the natural sciences. They cautiously qualified their statement with the phrase "It is our considered professional judgment." Whether they were right or not is not the concern of the present article. Rather, the concern here is with the important concept of a class of human problems which can be called "no technical solution problems," and, more specifically, with the identification and discussion of one of these.

It is easy to show that the class is not a null class. Recall the game of tick-tack-toe. Consider the problem "How can I win the game of tick-tack-toe?" It is well known that I cannot, if I assume (in keeping with the conventions of game theory) that my opponent understands the game perfectly. Put another way, there is no "technical solution" to the problem. I can win only by giving a radical meaning to the word "win." I can hit my opponent over the head; or I can drug him; or I can falsify the records. Every way in which I "win" involves, in some sense, an abandonment of the game, as we intuitively understand it. (I can also, of course, openly abandon the game—refuse to play it. This is what most adults do.)

The class of "no technical solution problems" has members. My thesis is that the "population problem," as conventionally conceived, is a member of this class. How it is conventionally conceived needs some comment. It is fair to say that most people who anguish over the population problem are trying to find a way to avoid the evils of overpopulation without relinquishing any of the privileges they now enjoy. They think that farming the seas or developing new strains of wheat will solve the problem—technologically. I try to show here that the solution they seek cannot be found. The population problem cannot be solved in a technical way, any more than can the problem of winning the game of tick-tack-toe.

What Shall We Maximize?

Population, as Malthus said, naturally tends to grow "geometrically," or, as we would now say, exponentially. In a finite world this means that the per capita share of the world's goods must steadily decrease. Is ours a finite world?

A fair defense can be put forward for the view that the world is infinite; or that we do not know that it is not. But, in terms of the practical problems that we must face in the next few generations with the foreseeable technology, it is clear that we will greatly increase human misery if we do not, during the immediate future, assume that the world available to the terrestrial human population is finite. "Space" is no escape.[2]

A finite world can support only a finite population; therefore, population growth must eventually equal zero. (The case of perpetual wide fluctuations above and below zero is a trivial variant that need not be discussed.) When this condition is met, what will be the situation of mankind? Specifically, can Bentham's goal of "the greatest good for the greatest number" be realized?

No—for two reasons, each sufficient by itself. The first is a theoretical one. It is not mathematically possible to maximize for two (or more) variables at the same time. This was clearly stated by von Neumann and Morgenstern,[3] but the principle is implicit in the theory of partial differential equations, dating back at least to D'Alembert (1717–1783).

The second reason springs directly from biological facts. To live, any organism must have a source of energy (for example, food). This energy is utilized for two purposes: mere maintenance and work. For man, maintenance of life requires about 1,600 kilocalories a day ("maintenance calories"). Anything that he does over and above merely staying alive will be defined as work, and is supported by "work calories" which he takes in. Work calories are used not only for what we call work in common speech; they are also required for all forms of enjoyment, from swimming and automobile racing to playing music and writing poetry. If our goal is to maximize population it is obvious what we must do: We must make the work calories per person approach as close to zero as possible. No gourmet meals, no vacations, no sports, no music, no literature, no art. . . . I think that everyone will grant, without argument or proof, that maximizing population does not maximize goods. Bentham's goal is impossible.

In reaching this conclusion I have made the usual assumption that it is the acquisition of energy that is the problem. The appearance of atomic energy has led some to question this assumption. However, given an infinite source of energy, population growth still produces an inescapable problem. The problem of the acquisition of energy is replaced by the problem of its dissipation, as J. H. Fremlin has so wittily shown.[4] The arithmetic signs in the analysis are, as it were, reversed; but Bentham's goal is still unobtainable.

The optimum population is, then, less than the maximum. The difficulty of defining the optimum is enormous; so far as I know, no one has seriously tackled this problem. Reaching an acceptable and stable solution will surely require more than one generation of hard analytical work—and much persuasion.

We want the maximum good per person; but what is good? To one person it is wilderness, to another it is ski lodges for thousands. To one it is estuaries to nourish ducks for hunters to shoot; to another it is factory land. Comparing one good with another is, we usually say, impossible because goods are incommensurable. Incommensurables cannot be compared.

Theoretically this may be true; but in real life incommensurables *are* commensurable. Only a criterion of judgment and a system of weighting are needed. In nature the criterion is survival. Is it better for a species to be small and hidable, or large and powerful? Natural selection commensurates the incommensurables. The compromise achieved depends on a natural weighting of the values of the variables.

Man must imitate this process. There is no doubt that in fact he already does, but unconsciously. It is when the hidden decisions are made explicit that the arguments begin. The problem for the years ahead is to work out an acceptable theory of weighting. Synergistic effects, nonlinear variation, and difficulties in discounting the future make the intellectual problem difficult, but not (in principle) insoluble.

Has any cultural group solved this practical problem at the present time, even on an intuitive level? One simple fact proves that none has: there is no prosperous population in the world today that has, and has had for some time, a growth rate of zero. Any people that has intuitively identified its optimum point will soon reach it, after which its growth rate becomes and remains zero.

Of course, a positive growth rate might be taken as evidence that a population is below its optimum. However, by any reasonable standards, the most rapidly growing populations on earth today are (in general) the most miserable. This association (which need not be invariable) casts doubt on the optimistic assumption that the positive growth rate of a population is evidence that it has yet to reach its optimum.

We can make little progress in working toward optimum population size until we explicitly exercise the spirit of Adam Smith in the field of practical demography. In economic affairs, *The Wealth of Nations* (1776) popularized the "invisible hand," the idea that an individual who "intends only his own gain" is, as it were, "led by an invisible hand to promote . . . the public interest."[5] Adam Smith did not assert that this was invariably true, and perhaps neither did any of his followers. But he contributed to a dominant tendency of thought that has ever since interfered with positive action based on rational analysis, namely, the tendency to assume that decisions reached individually will, in fact, be the best decisions for an entire society. If this assumption is correct it justifies the continuance of our present policy of laissez-faire in reproduction. If it is correct we can assume that men will control their individual fecundity so as to produce the optimum population. If the assumption is not correct, we need to reexamine our individual freedoms to see which ones are defensible.

The Tragedy of Freedom in A Commons

The rebuttal to the invisible hand in population control is to be found in a scenario first sketched in a little-known pamphlet in 1833 by a mathematical amateur named William Forster Lloyd (1794–1852).[6] We may well call it "the tragedy of the commons," using the word "tragedy" as the philosopher Whitehead used it: "The essence of dramatic tragedy is not unhappiness. It resides in the solemnity of the remorseless working of things." He then goes on to say, "This inevitableness of destiny can only be illustrated in terms of human life by incidents which in fact involve unhappiness. For it is only by them that the futility of escape can be made evident in the drama."[7]

The tragedy of the commons develops in this way. Picture a pasture open to all. It is to be expected that each herdsman will try to keep as many cattle as possible on the commons. Such an arrangement may work reasonably satisfactorily for centuries because tribal wars, poaching, and disease keep the numbers of both man and beast well below the carrying capacity of the land. Finally, however, comes the day of reckoning, that is, the day when the long-desired goal of social stability becomes a reality. At this point, the inherent logic of the commons remorselessly generates tragedy.

As a rational being, each herdsman seeks to maximize his gain. Explicitly or implicitly, more or less consciously, he asks, "What is the utility to me of adding one more animal to my herd?" This utility has one negative and one positive component.

1. The positive component is a function of the increment of one animal. Since the herdsman receives all the proceeds from the sale of the additional animal, the positive utility is nearly +1.

2. The negative component is a function of the additional overgrazing created by one more animal. Since, however, the effects of overgrazing are shared by all the herdsmen, the negative utility for any particular decision-making herdsman is only a fraction of −1.

Adding together the component partial utilities, the rational herdsman concludes that the only sensible course for him to pursue is to add another animal to his herd. And another; and another. . . . But this is the conclusion reached by each and every rational herdsman sharing a commons. Therein is the tragedy. Each man is locked into a system that compels him to increase his herd without limit—in a world that is limited. Ruin is the destination toward which all men rush, each pursuing his own best interest in a society that believes in the freedom of the commons. Freedom in a commons brings ruin to all.

Some would say that this is a platitude. Would that it were! In a sense, it was learned thousands of years ago, but natural selection favors the forces of psychological denial.[8] The individual benefits as an individual from his ability to deny the truth even though society as a whole, of which he is a part, suffers. Education can counteract the natural tendency to do the wrong thing, but the inexorable succession of generations requires that the basis for this knowledge be constantly refreshed.

A simple incident that occurred a few years ago in Leominster, Massachusetts, shows how perishable the knowledge is. During the Christmas shopping season the parking meters downtown were covered with plastic bags that bore tags reading: "Do not open until after Christmas. Free parking courtesy of the mayor and city council." In other words, facing the prospect of an increased demand for already scarce space, the city fathers reinstituted the system of the commons. (Cynically, we suspect that they gained more votes than they lost by this retrogressive act.)

In an approximate way, the logic of the commons has been understood for a long time, perhaps since the discovery of agriculture or the invention of private property in real estate. But it is understood mostly only in special cases which are not sufficiently generalized. Even at this late date, cattlemen leasing national land on the western ranges demonstrate no more than an ambivalent understanding, in constantly pressuring federal authorities to increase the head count to the point where overgrazing produces erosion and weed dominance. Likewise, the oceans of the world continue to suffer from the survival of the philosophy of the commons. Maritime nations still respond automatically to the shibboleth of the "freedom of the seas." Professing to believe in the "inexhaustible resources of the oceans," they bring species after species of fish and whales closer to extinction.[9]

The national parks present another instance of the working out of the tragedy of the commons. At present, they are open to all, without limit. The parks themselves are limited in extent—there is only one Yosemite Valley—whereas population seems to grow without limit. The values that visitors seek in the parks are steadily eroded. Plainly, we must soon cease to treat the parks as commons or they will be of no value to anyone.

What shall we do? We have several options. We might sell them off as private property. We might keep them as public property, but allocate the right to enter them. The allocation might be on the basis of wealth by the use of an auction system. It might be on the basis of merit, as defined by some agreed-upon standards. It might be by lottery. Or it might be on a first-come, first-served basis, administered to long queues. These, I think, are all the reasonable possibilities. They are all objectionable. But we must choose—or acquiesce in the destruction of the commons that we call our national parks.

Pollution

In a reverse way, the tragedy of the commons reappears in problems of pollution. Here it is not a question of taking something out of the commons, but of putting something in—sewage, or chemical, radioactive, and heat wastes into water; noxious and dangerous fumes into the air; and distracting and unpleasant advertising signs into the light of sight. The calculations of utility are much the same as before. The rational man finds that his share of the cost of the wastes he discharges into the commons is less than the cost of purifying his wastes before releasing them. Since this is true for everyone, we are locked into a system of "fouling our own nest," so long as we behave only as independent, rational, free enterprisers.

The tragedy of the commons as a food basket is averted by private property, or something formally like it. But the air and waters surrounding us cannot readily be fenced, and so the tragedy of the commons as a cesspool must be prevented by different means, by coercive laws or taxing devices that make it cheaper for the polluter to treat his pollutants than to discharge them untreated. We have not progressed as far with the solution of this problem as we have with the first. Indeed, our particular concept of private property, which deters us from exhausting the positive resources of the earth, favors pollution. The owner of a factory on the bank of a stream—whose property extends to the middle of the stream—often has difficulty seeing why it is not his natural right to muddy the waters flowing past his door. The law, always behind the times, requires elaborate stitching and fitting to adapt it to this newly perceived aspect of the commons.

The pollution problem is a consequence of population. It did not much matter how a lonely American frontiersman disposed of his waste. "Flowing water purifies itself every ten miles," my grandfather used to say, and the myth was near enough to the truth when he was a boy, for there were not too many people. But as population became denser, the natural chemical and biological recycling processes became overloaded, calling for a redefinition of property rights.

How to Legislate Temperance?

Analysis of the pollution problem as a function of population density uncovers a not generally recognized principle of morality, namely: *the morality of an act is a function of the state of the system at the time it is performed.*[10] Using the commons as a cesspool does not harm the general public under frontier conditions, because there is no public; the same behavior in a metropolis is unbearable. A hundred and fifty years ago a plainsman could kill an American bison, cut out only the tongue for his dinner, and discard the rest of the animal. He was not in any important sense being wasteful. Today, with only a few thousand bison left, we would be appalled at such behavior.

In passing, it is worth noting that the morality of an act cannot be determined from a photograph. One does not know whether a man killing an elephant or setting fire to the grassland is harming others until one knows the total system in which his act appears. "One picture is worth a thousand words," said an ancient Chinese; but it may take 10,000 words to validate it. It is as tempting to ecologists as it is to reformers in general to try to persuade others by way of the photographic shortcut. But the essence of an argument cannot be photographed: it must be presented rationally—in words.

That morality is system-sensitive escaped the attention of most codifiers of ethics in the past. "Thou shalt not ..." is the form of traditional ethical directives which make no allowance for particular circumstances. The laws of our society follow the pattern of ancient ethics, and therefore are poorly suited to governing a complex, crowded, changeable world. Our epicyclic solution is to augment statutory law with administrative law. Since it is practically impossible to spell out all the conditions under which it is safe to burn trash in the back yard or to run an automobile without smog control, by law we delegate the details to bureaus. The result is administrative law, which is rightly feared for an ancient reason—*Quis custodiet ipsos custodes?*—"Who shall watch the watchers themselves?" John Adams said that we must have "a government of laws and not men." Bureau administrators, trying to evaluate the morality of acts in the total system, are singularly liable to corruption, producing a government by men, not laws.

Prohibition is easy to legislate (though not necessarily to enforce); but how do we legislate temperance? Experience indicates that it can be accomplished best through the mediation of administrative law. We limit possibilities unnecessarily if we suppose that the sentiment of *Quis custodiet* denies us the use of administrative law. We should rather retain the phrase as a perpetual reminder of fearful dangers we cannot avoid. The great challenge facing us now is to invent the corrective feedbacks that are needed to keep custodians honest. We must find ways to legitimate the needed authority of both the custodians and the corrective feedbacks.

Freedom to Breed Is Intolerable

The tragedy of the commons is involved in population problems in another way. In a world governed solely by the principle of "dog eat dog"—if indeed there ever was such a world—how many children a family had would not be a matter of public concern. Parents who bred too exuberantly would leave fewer descendants, not more, because they would be unable to care adequately for their children. David Lack and others have found that such a negative feedback demonstrably controls the fecundity of birds.[11] But men are not birds, and have not acted like them for millenniums, at least.

If each human family were dependent only on its own resources; *if* the children of improvident parents starved to death; *if*, thus, overbreeding brought its own "punishment" to the germ line—*then* there would be no public interest in controlling the breeding of families. But our society is deeply committed to the welfare state,[12] and hence is confronted with another aspect of the tragedy of the commons.

In a welfare state, how shall we deal with the family, the religion, the race, or the class (or indeed any distinguishable and cohesive group) that adopts overbreeding as a policy to secure its own aggrandizement?[13] To couple the concept of freedom to breed with the belief that everyone born has an equal right to the commons is to lock the world into a tragic course of action.

Unfortunately this is just the course of action that is being pursued by the United Nations. In late 1967, some thirty nations agreed to the following:

The Universal Declaration of Human Rights describes the family as the natural and fundamental unit of society. It follows that any choice and decision with regard to the size of the family must irrevocably rest with the family itself, and cannot be made by someone else.[14]

It is painful to have to deny categorically the validity of this right; denying it, one feels as uncomfortable as a resident of Salem, Massachusetts, who denied the reality of witches in the seventeenth century. At the present time, in liberal quarters, something like a taboo acts to inhibit criticism of the United Nations. There is a feeling that the United Nations is "our last and best hope," that we shouldn't find fault with it; we shouldn't play into the hands of the archconservatives. However, let us not forget what Robert Louis Stevenson said: "The truth that is suppressed by friends is the readiest weapon of the enemy." If we love the truth we must openly deny the validity of the Universal Declaration of Human Rights, even though it is promoted by the United Nations. We should also join with Kingsley Davis[15] in attempting to get Planned Parenthood—World Population to see the error of its ways in embracing the same tragic ideal.

Conscience Is Self-Eliminating

It is a mistake to think that we can control the breeding of mankind in the long run by an appeal to conscience. Charles Galton Darwin made this point when he spoke on the centennial of the publication of his grandfather's great book. The argument is straightforward and Darwinian.

People vary. Confronted with appeals to limit breeding, some people will undoubtedly respond to the plea more than others. Those who have more children will produce a larger fraction of the next generation than those with more susceptible consciences. The difference will be accentuated, generation by generation.

In C. G. Darwin's words: "It may well be that it would take hundreds of generations for the progenitive instinct to develop in this way, but if it should do so, nature would have taken her revenge, and the variety *Homo contracipiens* would become extinct and would be replaced by the variety *Homo progenitivus*."[16]

The argument assumes that conscience or the desire for children (no matter which) is hereditary—but hereditary only in the most general formal sense. The result will be the same whether the attitude is transmitted through germ cells, or exosomatically, to use A. J. Lotka's term. (If one denies the latter possibility as well as the former, then what's the point of education?) The argument has here been stated in the context of the population problem, but it applies equally well to any instance in which society appeals to an individual exploiting a commons to restrain himself for the general good—by means of his conscience. To make such an appeal is to set up a selective system that works toward the elimination of conscience from the race.

Pathogenic Effects of Conscience

The long-term disadvantage of an appeal to conscience should be enough to condemn it; but it has serious short-term disadvantages as well. If we ask a man who is exploiting a commons to desist "in the name of conscience," what are we saying to him? What does he hear?—not only at the moment but also in the wee small hours of the night when, half asleep, he remembers not merely the words we used but also the nonverbal communication cues we gave him unawares? Sooner or later, consciously or subconsciously, he senses that he has received two communications, and that they are contradictory: (1, the intended communication) "If you don't do as we ask, we will openly condemn you for not acting like a responsible citizen"; (2, the unintended communication) "If you *do* behave as we ask, we will secretly condemn you for a simpleton who can be shamed into standing aside while the rest of us exploit the commons."

Everyman then is caught in what Bateson has called a "double bind." Bateson and his coworkers have made a plausible case for viewing the double bind as an important causative factor in the genesis of schizophrenia.[17] The double bind may not always be so damaging, but it always endangers the mental health of anyone to whom it is applied. "A bad conscience," said Nietzsche, "is a kind of illness."

To conjure up a conscience in others is tempting to anyone who wishes to extend his control beyond the legal limits. Leaders at the highest level succumb to this temptation. Has any President during the past generation failed to call on labor unions to moderate voluntarily their demands for higher wages, or to steel companies to honor voluntary guidelines on prices? I can recall none. The rhetoric used on such occasions is designed to produce feelings of guilt in noncooperators.

For centuries it was assumed without proof that guilt was a valuable, perhaps even an indispensable, ingredient of the civilized life. Now, in this post-Freudian world, we doubt it. Paul Goodman speaks from the modern point of view when he says: "No good has ever come from feeling guilty, neither intelligence, policy, nor compassion. The guilty do not pay attention to the object but only to themselves, and not even to their own interests, which might make sense, but to their anxieties."[18]

One does not have to be a professional psychiatrist to see the consequences of anxiety. We in the Western world are just emerging from a dreadful two-centuries-long Dark Ages of Eros that was sustained partly by prohibition laws, but perhaps more effectively by the anxiety-generating mechanisms of education. Alex Comfort has told the story well in *The Anxiety Makers*;[19] it is not a pretty one.

Since proof is difficult, we may even concede that the results of anxiety may sometimes, from certain points of view, be desirable. The larger question we should ask is whether, as a matter of policy, we should ever encourage the use of a technique the tendency (if not the intention) of which is psychologically pathogenic. We hear much talk these days of responsible parenthood; the coupled words are incorporated into the titles of some organizations devoted to birth control. Some people have proposed massive propaganda campaigns to instill responsibility into the nation's (or the world's) breeders. But what is the meaning of the word responsibility in this context? Is it not merely a synonym for the word conscience? When we use the word responsibility in the absence of substantial sanctions are we not trying to browbeat a free man in a commons into acting against his own interest? Responsibility is a verbal counterfeit for a substantial *quid pro quo*. It is an attempt to get something for nothing.

If the word responsibility is to be used at all, I suggest that it be in the sense Charles Frankel uses it.[20] "Responsibility," says this philosopher, "is the product of definite social arrangements." Notice that Frankel calls for social arrangements—not propaganda.

Mutual Coercion Mutually Agreed upon

The social arrangements that produce responsibility are arrangements that create coercion, of some sort. Consider bank robbing. The man who takes money from a bank acts as if the bank were a commons. How do we prevent such action? Certainly not by trying to control his behavior solely by a verbal appeal to his sense of responsibility. Rather than rely on propaganda we follow Frankel's lead and insist that a bank is not a commons; we seek the definite social arrangements that will keep it from becoming a commons. That we thereby infringe on the freedom of would-be robbers we neither deny nor regret.

The morality of bank robbing is particularly easy to understand because we accept complete prohibition of this activity. We are willing to say "Thou shalt not rob banks," without providing for exceptions. But temperance also can be created by coercion. Taxing is a good coercive device. To keep down-town shoppers temperate in their use of parking space we introduce parking meters for short periods, and traffic fines for longer ones. We need not actually forbid a citizen to park as long as he wants to; we need merely make it increasingly expensive for him to do so. Not prohibition, but carefully biased options are what we offer him. A Madison Avenue man might call this persuasion; I prefer the greater candor of the word coercion.

Coercion is a dirty word to most liberals now, but it need not forever be so. As with the four-letter words, its dirtiness can be cleansed away by exposure to the light, by saying it over and over without apology or embarrassment. To many, the word coercion implies arbitrary decisions of distant and irresponsible bureaucrats; but this is not a necessary part of its meaning. The only kind of coercion I recommend is mutual coercion, mutually agreed upon by the majority of the people affected.

To say that we mutually agree to coercion is not to say that we are required to enjoy it, or even to pretend we enjoy it. Who enjoys taxes? We all grumble about them. But we accept compulsory taxes because we recognize that voluntary taxes would favor the conscienceless. We institute and (grumblingly) support taxes and other coercive devices to escape the horror of the commons.

An alternative to the commons need not be perfectly just to be preferable. With real estate and other material goods, the alternative we have chosen is the institution of private property coupled with legal inheritance. Is this system perfectly just? As a genetically trained biologist I deny that it is. It seems to me that, if there are to be differences in individual inheritance, legal possession should be perfectly correlated with biological inheritance—that those who are biologically more fit to be the custodians of property and power should legally inherit more. But genetic recombination continually makes a mockery of the doctrine of "like father, like son" implicit in our laws of legal inheritance. An idiot can inherit millions, and a trust fund can keep his estate intact. We must admit that our legal system of private property plus inheritance is unjust—but we put up with it because we are not convinced, at the moment, that anyone has invented a better system. The alternative of the commons is too horrifying to contemplate. Injustice is preferable to total ruin.

It is one of the peculiarities of the warfare between reform and the status quo that it is thoughtlessly governed by a double standard. Whenever a reform measure is proposed it is often defeated when its opponents triumphantly discover a flaw in it. As Kingsley Davis has pointed out, worshippers of the status quo sometimes imply that no reform is possible without unanimous agreement, an implication contrary to historical fact.[21] As nearly as I can make out, automatic rejection of proposed reforms is based on one of two unconscious assumptions: (1) that the status quo is perfect; or (2) that the choice we face is between reform and no action;

if the proposed reform is imperfect, we presumably should take no action at all, while we wait for a perfect proposal.

But we can never do nothing. That which we have done for thousands of years is also action. It also produces evils. Once we are aware that the status quo is action, we can then compare its discoverable advantages and disadvantages with the predicted advantages and disadvantages of the proposed reform, discounting as best we can for our lack of experience. On the basis of such a comparison, we can make a rational decision which will not involve the unworkable assumption that only perfect systems are tolerable.

Recognition of Necessity

Perhaps the simplest summary of this analysis of man's population problems is this: the commons, if justifiable at all, is justifiable only under conditions of low population density. As the human population has increased, the commons has had to be abandoned in one aspect after another.

First we abandoned the commons in food gathering, enclosing farm land and restricting pastures and hunting and fishing areas. These restrictions are still not complete throughout the world.

Somewhat later we saw that the commons as a place for waste disposal would also have to be abandoned. Restrictions on the disposal of domestic sewage are widely accepted in the Western world; we are still struggling to close the commons to pollution by automobiles, factories, insecticide sprayers, fertilizing operations, and atomic energy installations.

In a still more embryonic state is our recognition of the evils of the commons in matters of pleasure. There is almost no restriction on the propagation of sound waves in the public medium. The shopping public is assaulted with mindless music, without its consent. Our government is paying out billions of dollars to create supersonic transport which will disturb 50,000 people for every one person who is whisked from coast to coast three hours faster. Advertisers muddy the airwaves of radio and television and pollute the view of travelers. We are a long way from outlawing the commons in matters of pleasure. Is this because our Puritan inheritance makes us view pleasure as something of a sin, and pain (that is, the pollution of advertising) as the sign of virtue?

Every new enclosure of the commons involves the infringement of somebody's personal liberty. Infringements made in the distant past are accepted because no contemporary complains of a loss. It is the newly proposed infringements that we vigorously oppose; cries of "rights" and "freedom" fill the air. But what does "freedom" mean? When men mutually agreed to pass laws against robbing, mankind became more free, not less so. Individuals locked into the logic of the commons are free only to bring on universal ruin; once they see the necessity of mutual coercion, they become free to pursue other goals. I believe it was Hegel who said, "Freedom is the recognition of necessity."

The most important aspect of necessity that we must now recognize is the necessity of abandoning the commons in breeding. No technical solution can rescue us from the misery of overpopulation. Freedom to breed will bring ruin to all. At the moment, to avoid hard decisions many of us are tempted to propagandize for conscience and responsible parenthood. The temptation must be resisted, because an appeal to independently acting consciences selects for the disappearance of all conscience in the long run, and an increase in anxiety in the short.

The only way we can preserve and nurture other and more precious freedoms is by relinquishing the freedom to breed, and that very soon. "Freedom is the recognition of necessity"—and it is the role of education to reveal to all the necessity of abandoning the freedom to breed. Only so can we put an end to this aspect of the tragedy of the commons.

Notes

1. J. B. Wiesner and H. F. York, *Scientific American*, 211: 4 (1964), 27. Offprint 319.
2. G. Hardin, *Journal of Heredity*, 50 (1959), 68; S. von Hoernor, *Science*, 137 (1962), 18.
3. J. von Neumann and O. Morgenstern, *Theory of Games and Economic Behavior* (Princeton: Princeton University Press, 1947), 11.
4. J. H. Fremlin, *New Science*, 415 (1964), 285.
5. A. Smith, *The Wealth of Nations* (New York: Modern Library, 1937), 423.
6. W. F. Lloyd, *Two Lectures on the Checks to Population* (Oxford: Oxford University Press, 1833), reprinted (in part) in G. Hardin (ed.), *Population, Evolution, and Birth Control*, 2nd edn. (San Francisco: W. H. Freeman and Company, 1969), 28.
7. A. N. Whitehead, *Science and the Modern World* (New York: Mentor, 1948), p. 17.
8. Hardin, *Population, Evolution, and Birth Control*, 46.
9. S. McVay, *Scientific American*, 216: 8 (1966), 13. Offprint 1046.
10. J. Fletcher, *Situation Ethics* (Philadelphia: Westminster, 1966).
11. D. Lack, *The Natural Regulation of Animal Numbers* (Oxford: Clarendon Press, 1954).
12. H. Girvetz, *From Wealth to Welfare* (Stanford, Calif.: Stanford University Press, 1950).
13. G. Hardin, *Perspectives in Biology and Medicine*, 6 (1963), 366.
14. U. Thant, *International Planned Parenthood News*, 168 (February 1968), 3.
15. K. Davis, *Science*, 158 (1967), 730.
16. S. Tax (ed.), *Evolution after Darwin* (Chicago: University of Chicago Press, 1960), ii. 469.
17. G. Bateson, D. D. Jackson, J. Haley, J. Weakland, *Behavioral Science*, 1 (1956), 251.
18. P. Goodman, *New York Review of Books*, 10: 8 (23 May 1968), 22.
19. A. Comfort, *The Anxiety Makers* (London: Nelson, 1967).
20. C. Frankel, *The Case for Modern Man* (New York: Harper, 1955), 203.
21. J. D. Roslansky, *Genetics and the Future of Man* (New York: Appleton-Century-Crofts, 1966), 177.

3 A Planet Under Stress

Lester Brown

As world population has doubled and as the global economy has expanded sevenfold over the last half-century, our claims on the earth have become excessive. We are asking more of the earth than it can give on an ongoing basis, creating a bubble economy.

We are cutting trees faster than they can regenerate, overgrazing rangelands and converting them into deserts, overpumping aquifers, and draining rivers dry. On our cropland, soil erosion exceeds new soil formation, slowly depriving the soil of its inherent fertility. We are taking fish from the ocean faster than they can reproduce.

We are releasing carbon dioxide (CO_2) into the atmosphere faster than nature can absorb it, creating a greenhouse effect. As atmospheric CO_2 levels rise, so does the earth's temperature. Habitat destruction and climate change are destroying plant and animal species far faster than new species can evolve, launching the first mass extinction since the one that eradicated the dinosaurs 65 million years ago.

Throughout history, humans have lived on the earth's sustainable yield—the interest from its natural endowment. But now we are consuming the endowment itself. In ecology, as in economics, we can consume principal along with interest in the short run, but in the long run it leads to bankruptcy.

In 2002, a team of scientists led by Mathis Wackernagel, an analyst at Redefining Progress, concluded that humanity's collective demands first surpassed the earth's regenerative capacity around 1980. Their study, published by the U.S. National Academy of Sciences, estimated that our demands in 1999 exceeded that capacity by 20 percent. We are satisfying our excessive demands by consuming the earth's natural assets, in effect creating a global bubble economy.[1]

Bubble economies are not new. American investors got an up-close view of this when the bubble in high-tech stocks burst in 2000 and the NASDAQ, an indicator of the value of these stocks, declined by some 75 percent. Japan had a similar experience in 1989 when the real estate bubble burst, depreciating stock and real estate assets by 60 percent. The bad-debt fallout and other effects of this collapse have left the once-dynamic Japanese economy dead in the water ever since.[2]

The bursting of these two bubbles affected primarily people living in the United States and Japan, but the global bubble economy that is based on the overconsumption of the earth's natural capital assets will affect the entire world. When the food bubble economy, inflated by

From *Plan B: Rescuing a Planet Under Stress and a Civilization in Trouble* (Earth Policy Institute, 2003), 3–19.

the overpumping of aquifers, bursts, it will raise food prices worldwide. The challenge for our generation is to deflate the economic bubble before it bursts.

Unfortunately, since September 11, 2001, political leaders, diplomats, and the media worldwide have been preoccupied with terrorism and, more recently, the invasion of Iraq. Terrorism is certainly a matter of concern, but if it diverts us from the environmental trends that are undermining our future until it is too late to reverse them, Osama Bin Laden and his followers will have achieved their goal of bringing down western civilization in a way they could not have imagined.

In February 2003, U.N. demographers made an announcement that was in some ways more shocking than the September 11th attack: the worldwide rise in life expectancy has been dramatically reversed for a large segment of humanity—the 700 million people living in sub-Saharan Africa. The HIV epidemic has reduced life expectancy among this region's people from 62 to 47 years. The epidemic may soon claim more lives than all the wars of the twentieth century. If this teaches us anything, it is the high cost of neglecting newly emerging threats.[3]

The HIV epidemic is not the only emerging mega-threat. Numerous countries are feeding their growing populations by overpumping their aquifers—a measure that virtually guarantees a future drop in food production when the aquifers are depleted. In effect, these countries are creating a food bubble economy—one where food production is artificially inflated by the unsustainable use of groundwater.

Another mega-threat—climate change—is not getting the attention it deserves from most governments, particularly that of the United States, the country responsible for one fourth of all carbon emissions. Washington wants to wait until all the evidence on climate change is in, by which time it will be too late to prevent a wholesale warming of the planet. Just as governments in Africa watched HIV infection rates rise and did little about it, the United States is watching atmospheric CO_2 levels rise and doing little to check the increase.[4]

Other mega-threats being neglected include eroding soils and expanding deserts, which are threatening the livelihood and food supply of hundreds of millions of the world's people. These issues do not even appear on the radar screen of many national governments.

Thus far, most of the environmental damage has been local: the death of the Aral Sea, the burning rainforests of Indonesia, the collapse of the Canadian cod fishery, the melting of the glaciers that supply Andean cities with water, the dust bowl forming in northwestern China, and the depletion of the U.S. Great Plains aquifer. But as these local environmental events expand and multiply, they will progressively weaken the global economy, bringing closer the day when the economic bubble will burst.[5]

Ecological Bills Coming Due

Humanity's demands on the earth have multiplied over the last half-century as our numbers have increased and our incomes have risen. World population grew from 2.5 billion in 1950 to 6.1 billion in 2000. The growth during those 50 years exceeded that during the 4 million years since we emerged as a distinct species.[6]

Incomes have risen even faster than population. Income per person worldwide nearly tripled from 1950 to 2000. Growth in population and the rise in incomes together expanded global economic output from just under $7 trillion (in 2001 dollars) of goods and services in 1950 to $46 trillion in 2000, a gain of nearly sevenfold.[7]

Population growth and rising incomes together have tripled world grain demand over the last half-century, pushing it from 640 million tons in 1950 to 1,855 million tons in 2000. To satisfy this swelling demand, farmers have plowed land that was highly erodible—land that was too dry or too steeply sloping to sustain cultivation. Each year billions of tons of topsoil are being blown away in dust storms or washed away in rainstorms, leaving farmers to try to feed some 70 million additional people, but with less topsoil than the year before.[8]

Demand for water also tripled as agricultural, industrial, and residential uses climbed, out-stripping the sustainable supply in many countries. As a result, water tables are falling and wells are going dry. Rivers are also being drained dry, to the detriment of wildlife and eco-systems.[9]

Fossil fuel use quadrupled, setting in motion a rise in carbon emissions that is overwhelming nature's capacity to fix carbon dioxide. As a result of this carbon-fixing deficit, atmospheric CO_2 concentrations climbed from 316 parts per million (ppm) in 1959, when official measurement began, to 369 ppm in 2000.[10]

The sector of the economy that seems likely to unravel first is food. Eroding soils, deteriorating rangelands, collapsing fisheries, falling water tables, and rising temperatures are converging to make it more difficult to expand food production fast enough to keep up with demand. In 2002, the world grain harvest of 1,807 million tons fell short of world grain consumption by 100 million tons, or 5 percent. This shortfall, the largest on record, marked the third consecutive year of grain deficits, dropping stocks to the lowest level in a generation.[11]

Now the question is, Can the world's farmers bounce back and expand production enough to fill the 100-million-ton shortfall, provide for the more than 70 million people added each year, and rebuild stocks to a more secure level? In the past, farmers responded to short supplies and higher grain prices by planting more land and using more irrigation water and fertilizer. Now it is doubtful that farmers can fill this gap without further depleting aquifers and jeopardizing future harvests.[12]

In 1996, at the World Food Summit in Rome, hosted by the U.N. Food and Agriculture Organization (FAO), 185 countries plus the European Community agreed to reduce hunger by half by 2015. Using 1990–92 as a base, governments set the goal of cutting the number of people who were hungry—860 million—by roughly 20 million per year. It was an exciting and worthy goal, one that later became one of the U.N. Millennium Development Goals.[13]

But in its late 2002 review of food security, the United Nations issued a discouraging report: "This year we must report that progress has virtually ground to a halt. Our latest estimates, based on data from the years 1998–2000, put the number of undernourished people in the world at 840 million...a decrease of barely 2.5 million per year over the eight years since 1990–92."[14]

Since 1998–2000, world grain production per person has fallen 5 percent, suggesting that the ranks of the hungry are now expanding. As noted earlier, life expectancy is plummeting in sub-Saharan Africa. If the number of hungry people worldwide is also increasing, then two key social indicators are showing widespread deterioration in the human condition.[15]

Farmers Facing Two New Challenges

As we exceed the earth's natural capacities, we create new problems. For example, farmers are now facing two new challenges: rising temperatures and falling water tables. Farmers currently on the land may face higher temperatures than any generation since agriculture began 11,000 years ago. They are also the first to face widespread aquifer depletion and the resulting loss of irrigation water.

The global average temperature has risen in each of the last three decades. The 16 warmest years since recordkeeping began in 1880 have all occurred since 1980. With the three warmest years on record—1998, 2001, and 2002—coming in the last five years, crops are facing heat stresses that are without precedent.[16]

Higher temperatures reduce crop yields through their effect on photosynthesis, moisture balance, and fertilization. As the temperature rises above 34 degrees Celsius (94 degrees Fahrenheit), photosynthesis slows, dropping to zero for many crops when it reaches 37 degrees Celsius (100 degrees Fahrenheit). When temperatures in the U.S. Corn Belt are 37 degrees or higher, corn plants suffer from thermal shock and dehydration. They are in effect on sick leave. Each such day shrinks the harvest.[17]

In addition to decreasing photosynthesis and dehydrating plants, high temperatures also impede the fertilization needed for seed formation. Researchers at the International Rice Research Institute in the Philippines and at the U.S. Department of Agriculture have together developed a rule of thumb that each 1-degree-Celsius rise in temperature above the optimum during the growing season reduces grain yields by 10 percent.[18]

These recent research findings indicate that if the temperature rises to the lower end of the range projected by the Intergovernmental Panel on Climate Change, grain harvests in tropical regions could be reduced by an average of 5 percent by 2020 and 11 percent by 2050. At the upper end of the range, harvests could drop 11 percent by 2020 and 46 percent by 2050. Avoiding these declines will be difficult unless scientists can develop crop strains that are not vulnerable to thermal stress.[19]

The second challenge facing farmers, falling water tables, is also recent. With traditional animal- or human-powered water-lifting devices it was almost impossible historically to deplete aquifers. With the worldwide spread of powerful diesel and electric pumps during the last half-century, however, overpumping has become commonplace.

As the world demand for water has climbed, water tables have fallen in scores of countries, including China, India, and the United States, which together produce nearly half of the world's grain. Water tables are falling throughout the northern half of China. As the water table falls, springs and rivers go dry, lakes disappear, and wells dry up. Northern China is literally drying out. Water tables under the North China Plain, which accounts for a fourth or more of China's grain harvest, are falling at an accelerating rate.[20]

In India, water tables are also falling. As India's farmers try to feed an additional 16 million people each year, nearly the population equivalent of another Australia, they are pumping more and more water. This is dropping water tables in states that together contain a majority of India's 1 billion people.[21]

In the United States, the third major grain producer, water tables are falling under the southern Great Plains and in California, the country's fruit and vegetable basket. As California's population expands from 26 million to a projected 40 million by 2030, expanding urban water demands will siphon water from agriculture.[22]

Scores of other countries are also overpumping their aquifers, setting the stage for dramatic future cutbacks in water supplies. The more populous among these are Pakistan, Iran, and Mexico. Overpumping creates an illusion of food security that is dangerously deceptive because it enables farmers to support a growing population with a practice that virtually ensures a future drop in food production.

The water demand growth curve over the last half-century looks like the population growth curve, except that it climbs more steeply. While world population growth was doubling, the use of water was tripling. Once the growing demand for water rises above the sustainable yield of an aquifer, the gap between the two widens further each year. As this happens, the water table starts to fall. The first year after the sustainable yield is surpassed, the water table falls very little, with the drop often being scarcely perceptible. Each year thereafter, however, the annual drop is larger than the year before.

In addition to falling exponentially, water tables are also falling simultaneously in many countries. This means that cutbacks in grain harvests will occur in many countries at more or less the same time. And they will occur at a time when the world's population is growing by more than 70 million a year.[23]

These, then, are the two new challenges facing the world's farmers: rising temperatures and falling water tables. Either one by itself could make it difficult to keep up with the growth in demand. The two together provide an early test of whether our modern civilization can cope with the forces that threaten to undermine it.

Ecological Meltdown in China

In the deteriorating relationship between the global economy and the earth's ecosystem, food is the most vulnerable economic sector, but geographically it is China that is on the leading edge. A human population of 1.3 billion and their 400 million cattle, sheep, and goats are weighing heavily on the land. Huge flocks of sheep and goats in the northwest are stripping the land of its protective vegetation, creating a dust bowl on a scale not seen before. Northwestern China is on the verge of a massive ecological meltdown.[24]

Since 1980, the Chinese economy has expanded more than fourfold. Incomes have also expanded by nearly fourfold, lifting more people out of poverty faster than at any time in history. Like many other countries, China is exceeding the carrying capacity of its ecosystem—overplowing its land, overgrazing its rangelands, overcutting its forests, and overpumping its aquifers. In its determined effort to be self-sufficient in grain, it cultivated highly erodible land in the arid northern and western provinces, land that is vulnerable to wind erosion.[25]

While overplowing is now being partly remedied by paying farmers to plant their grainland in trees, overgrazing is destroying vegetation and increasing wind erosion. China's cattle, sheep, and goat population more than tripled from 1950 to 2002. The United States, a country with comparable grazing capacity, has 97 million cattle, while China has 106 million. For sheep and goats, the figures are 8 million versus 298 million. Concentrated in the western and northern provinces, sheep and goats are destroying the land's protective vegetation. The wind then does the rest, removing the soil and converting productive rangeland into desert.[26]

China is now at war. It is not invading armies that are claiming its territory, but expanding deserts. Old deserts are advancing and new ones are forming, like guerrilla forces striking unexpectedly, forcing Beijing to fight on several fronts. And worse, the growing deserts are gaining momentum, occupying an ever-larger piece of China's territory each year.

China's expanding ecological deficits are converging to create a dust bowl of historic dimensions. With little vegetation remaining in parts of northern and western China, the strong winds of late winter and early spring can remove literally millions of tons of topsoil in a single day—soil that can take centuries to replace.

For the outside world, it is these storms that draw attention to the dust bowl forming in China. On April 12, 2002, for instance, South Korea was engulfed by a huge dust storm from China that left residents of Seoul literally gasping for breath. Schools were closed, airline flights were cancelled, and clinics were overrun with patients having difficulty breathing. Retail sales fell. Koreans have come to dread the arrival of what they now call "the fifth season"—the dust storms of late winter and early spring. Japan also suffers from dust storms originating in China. Although not as directly exposed as Koreans are, the Japanese complain about the dust and the brown rain that streaks their windshields and windows.[27]

Each year, residents of eastern Chinese cities such as Beijing and Tianjin hunker down as the dust storms begin. Along with the difficulty in breathing and the dust that stings the eyes, there is the constant effort to keep dust out of homes and to clean doorways and sidewalks of dust and sand. Farmers and herders, whose livelihoods are blowing away, are paying an even heavier price.

Desert expansion has accelerated with each successive decade since 1950. China's Environmental Protection Agency reports that the Gobi Desert expanded by 52,400 square kilometers (20,240 square miles) from 1994 to 1999, an area half the size of Pennsylvania. With the advancing Gobi now within 150 miles of Beijing, China's leaders are beginning to sense the gravity of the situation.[28]

The fallout from the dust storms is social as well as economic. Millions of rural Chinese may be uprooted and forced to migrate eastward as the deserts claim their land. Desertification is already driving villagers from their homes in Gansu, Inner Mongolia (Nei Monggol), and Ningxia provinces. A preliminary Asian Development Bank assessment of desertification in Gansu Province reports that 4,000 villages risk being overrun by drifting sands.[29]

The U.S. Dust Bowl of the 1930s forced some 2.5 million "Okies" and other refugees to leave the land, many of them heading west from Oklahoma, Texas, and Kansas to California. But the dust bowl forming in China is much larger, and during the 1930s the U.S. population was only 150 million—compared with 1.3 billion in China today. Whereas the U.S. migration was measured in the millions, China's may measure in the tens of millions. And as a U.S. embassy report entitled *The Grapes of Wrath in Inner Mongolia* noted, "unfortunately, China's twenty-first century 'Okies' have no California to escape to—at least not in China."[30]

Food: A National Security Issue

The ecological deficits just described are converging on the farm sector, making it more difficult to sustain rapid growth in world food output. No one knows when the growth in food production will fall behind that of demand, driving up prices, but it may be much closer than we think. The triggering events that will precipitate future food shortages are likely to be spreading water shortages interacting with crop-withering heat waves in key food-producing regions. The economic indicator most likely to signal serious trouble in the deteriorating relationship between the global economy and the earth's ecosystem is grain prices.

Food is fast becoming a national security issue as growth in the world harvest slows and as falling water tables and rising temperatures hint at future shortages. More than 100 countries import part of the wheat they consume. Some 40 import rice. While some countries are only marginally dependent on imports, others could not survive without them. Iran and Egypt, for example, rely on imports for 40 percent of their grain supply. For Algeria, Japan, South Korea, and Taiwan, among others, it is 70 percent or more. For Israel and Yemen, over 90 percent. Just six countries—the United States, Canada, France, Australia, Argentina, and Thailand—supply 90 percent of grain exports. The United States alone controls close to half of world grain exports, a larger share than Saudi Arabia does of oil.[31]

Thus far the countries that import heavily are small and middle-sized ones. But now China, the world's most populous country, is likely to soon turn to world markets in a major way. When the former Soviet Union unexpectedly turned to the world market in 1972 for roughly a tenth of its grain supply, following a weather-reduced harvest, world wheat prices climbed from $1.90 to $4.89 a bushel. Bread prices soon rose too.'[32]

If China depletes its grain reserves and turns to the world grain market to cover its shortfall, now 40 million tons per year, it could destabilize world grain markets overnight. Turning to the world market means turning to the United States, presenting a potentially delicate geopolitical situation in which 1.3 billion Chinese consumers with a $100-billion trade surplus with the United States will be competing with American consumers for U.S. grain. If this leads to rising food prices in the United States, how will the government respond? In times past, it could have restricted exports, even imposing an export embargo, as it did with soybeans to Japan in 1974. But today the United States has a stake in a politically stable China. With an economy growing at 7–8 percent a year, China is the engine that is powering not only the Asian economy but, to some degree, the world economy.[33]

For China, becoming dependent on other countries for food would end its history of food self-sufficiency, leaving it vulnerable to world market uncertainties. For Americans, rising food prices would be the first indication that the world has changed fundamentally and that they are being directly affected by the growing grain deficit in China. If it seems likely that rising food prices are being driven in part by crop-withering temperature rises, pressure will mount for the United States to reduce oil and coal use.

For the world's poor—the millions living in cities on $1 per day or less and already spending 70 percent of their income on food—rising grain prices would be life-threatening. A doubling of world grain prices today could impoverish more people in a shorter period of time than any event in history. With desperate people holding their governments responsible, such a price rise could also destabilize governments of low-income, grain-importing countries.[34]

When I projected in 1995 in *Who Will Feed China?* that China would one day turn abroad for part of its grain, the U.S. National Intelligence Council, the umbrella over all the U.S. intelligence agencies, launched the most detailed assessment of China's food prospect ever undertaken. The council was concerned precisely because such a move by China could drive up world grain prices and destabilize governments in developing countries. An interdisciplinary team led by Michael McElroy, Chairman of Harvard's Department of Earth and Planetary Sciences, conducted this extraordinarily ambitious study. Relying on an interdisciplinary approach and a vast array of resources, including 35 years of CIA satellite data on land use and the Sandia National Laboratories to model the water supply-demand balance of every river basin in China, the team concluded in its "most likely" scenario that China would one day have to import massive quantities of grain.[35]

The team then decided that the world would not have any difficulty in supplying grain on such a vast scale. The shortcoming of this conclusion, in my opinion, was that it relied too heavily on extrapolating late twentieth-century grain production trends into the twenty-first century, failing to take into account emerging constraints on harvests, such as aquifer depletion and rising temperatures.

When grain prices began to climb in 1972–74, it did not take long for a politics of food scarcity to emerge. Pressure from within grain-exporting countries to restrict exports in order to check the rise in domestic food prices was common.[36]

More recently, the Canadian Wheat Board, which handles the nation's wheat exports, announced in early September 2002 that it had no more to sell. This abrupt withdrawal from the market—even before that year's drought-reduced harvest was complete—illustrates the kind of action that exporters can take when confronted with scarcity. Instead of letting the world market allocate scarce supplies of high-quality wheat, the Board decided that it would protect domestic supplies, then sell only to traditional clients, leaving other importers to fend for themselves. In late October, Australia—also experiencing a severe drought—announced that it would ration wheat and barley exports among its best customers, excluding all other potential buyers.[37]

Historically, the world had two food reserves: the global carryover stocks of grain and the cropland idled under the U.S. farm program to limit production. The latter could be brought into production within a year. Since the U.S. land set-aside program ended in 1996, however, the world has had only carryover stocks as a reserve.[38]

Food security has changed in other ways. Traditionally it was largely an agricultural matter. But now it is something that our entire society is responsible for. National population and energy policies may have a greater effect on food security than agricultural policies do. With most of the 3 billion people to be added to world population by 2050 being born in countries already facing water shortages, childbearing decisions may have a greater effect on food security than crop planting decisions. Achieving an acceptable balance between food and people today depends on family planners and farmers working together.[39]

Climate change is the wild card in the food security deck. It is perhaps a measure of the complexity of our time that decisions made in the Ministry of Energy may have a greater effect on future food security than those made in the Ministry of Agriculture. The effect of population and energy policies on food security differ in one important respect: population stability can be achieved by a country acting unilaterally. Climate stability cannot.

The Case for Plan B

Thus far, this chapter has focused primarily on how environmental changes can affect the food prospect, but there could be other wake-up calls, including more destructive storms or deadly heat waves.

Unless we quickly reverse the damaging trends that we have set in motion, they will generate vast numbers of environmental refugees—people abandoning depleted aquifers and exhausted soils and those fleeing advancing deserts and rising seas. In a world where civilization is being squeezed between expanding deserts from the interior of continents and rising seas on the periphery, refugees are likely to number not in the millions but in the tens of millions. Already we see refugees from drifting sand in Nigeria, Iran, and China.[40]

We are now looking at the potential wholesale evacuation of cities as aquifers are depleted and wells go dry. Sana'a, the capital of Yemen, and Quetta, the capital of Pakistan's Baluchistan province, may become the early ghost towns of the twenty-first century.[41]

A reversal of the basic trends of social progress of the last half-century has long seemed unthinkable. Progress appeared inevitable. But now we are seeing reversals. As noted earlier, the number of hungry may be increasing for the first time since the war-torn decade of the 1940s. And a rise in life expectancy—a seminal measure of economic and social progress—has been interrupted in sub-Saharan Africa as a result of the HIV epidemic. As millions of able-bodied adults die, families are often left with no one to work in the fields. The disease and spreading hunger are both weakening immune systems and reinforcing each other, something epidemiologists had not reckoned on.

The failure of governments to deal with falling water tables and the depletion of aquifers in the Indian sub-continent could be as disruptive for the 1.3 billion living there as the HIV epidemic is for the people in sub-Saharan Africa. With business as usual, life expectancy could soon begin to fall in India and Pakistan as water shortages translate into food shortages, deepening hunger among the poor.[42]

The world is moving into uncharted territory as human demands override the sustainable yield of natural systems. The risk is that people will lose confidence in the capacity of their governments to cope with such problems, leading to social breakdown. The shift to anarchy is already evident in countries such as Somalia, Afghanistan, and the Democratic Republic of the Congo.

Business as usual—Plan A—is clearly not working. The stakes are high, and time is not on our side. Part I details the mounting evidence that our modern civilization is in trouble. The good news, as outlined in Part II of this book, is that there are solutions to the problems we are facing. The bad news is that if we continue to rely on timid, incremental responses, our bubble economy will continue to grow until eventually it bursts. This book argues for a new approach—for Plan B—an urgent reordering of priorities and a restructuring of the global economy in order to prevent that from happening.

Notes

1. Mathis Wackernagel et al., "Tracking the Ecological Overshoot of the Human Economy," *Proceedings of the National Academy of Sciences* (9 July 2002), 9266–71.

2. Steven Pearlstein, "How the Bubble Economy Burst," *Washington Post*, 13 November 2002; Thomas F. Cargill, Michael M. Hutchinson, and Takatoshi Ito, *The Political Economy of Japanese Monetary Policy* (Cambridge, MA: The MIT Press, 1997).

3. United Nations, *World Population Prospects: The 2002 Revision* (New York: February 2003); Joint United Nations Program on HIV/AIDS (UNAIDS), *Report on The Global HIV/AIDS Epidemic 2002* (Geneva, July 2002), 44.

4. G. Marland, T. A. Boden, and R. J. Andres, "Global, Regional, and National Fossil Fuel CO_2 Emissions," in *Trends: A Compendium of Data on Global Change* (Oak Ridge, TN: Carbon Dioxide Information Analysis Center, Oak Ridge National Laboratory, 2002).

5. U.N. Environment Programme, *Afghanistan: Post-Conflict Environmental Assessment* (Geneva: 2003), 60; Forest Watch Indonesia (FWI) and Global Forest Watch (GFW), *The State of the Forest: Indonesia* (Bogor, Indonesia, and Washington, DC: 2002), xii; Canadian cod fishery from Clyde H. Farnsworth, "Cod are Almost Gone and a Culture Could Follow," *New York Times*, 28 May 1994; melting glaciers in Andean region from Lonnie G. Thompson, "Disappearing Glaciers Evidence of a Rapidly Changing Earth," American Association for the Advancement of Science annual meeting proceedings, San Francisco, CA, February 2001; United Nations, "China's Experience With Calamitous Sand-Dust Storms," in Yang Youlin, Victor Squires, and Lu Qi, eds.,

Global Alarm Dust and Sandstorms from the World's Drylands (Bangkok: Secretariat of the U.N. Convention to Combat Desertification, September 2002), 215–53; U.S. aquifer depletion from U.S. Department of Agriculture (USDA), *Agricultural Resources and Environmental Indicators 2000* (Washington, DC: February 2000), chapter 2.1, p. 6.

6. United Nations, *World Population Prospects*.

7. Erik Assadourian, "Economic Growth Inches Up," in World-watch Institute, *Vital Signs 2003* (New York: W.W. Norton & Company, 2003), 44–5.

8. USDA, *Production, Supply, and Distribution*, electronic database, updated 13 May 2003.

9. Water demand from Peter H. Gleick, *The World's Water 2000–2001* (Washington, DC: Island Press, 2000), 52.

10. C. D. Keeling, T. P. Whorf, and the Carbon Dioxide Research Group, "Atmospheric Carbon Dioxide Record from Mauna Loa," Scripps Institution of Oceanography, University of California, 13 June 2002, at <cdiac.esd.ornl.gov/ftp/ndp001/maunaloa.co2>.

11. USDA, *World Agricultural Supply and Demand Estimates* (Washington, DC: 12 May 2003), 6.

12. Population added each year from United Nations, *World Population Prospects*.

13. World Food Summit from U.N. Food and Agriculture Organization (FAO), *The World Food Summit Goal and the Millennium Goals*, Rome, 28 May–1 June 2001, at <www.fao.org/docrep/meeting/003/Yo688e.htm>; FAO, *The State of Food Insecurity in the World 2002* (Rome: 2002), 4.

14. FAO, *State of Food Insecurity*.

15. Grain production per person based on USDA, *Production, Supply, and Distribution*.

16. Goddard Institute for Space Studies, NASA Goddard Space Flight Center Earth Sciences Directorate, "Global Temperature Anomalies in .01 C," at <www.giss.nasa.gov/data/update/gistemp/GLB.Ts.txt>, viewed 15 April 2003.

17. Effect of higher temperatures from John E. Sheehy, International Rice Research Institute, Philippines, e-mail to Janet Larsen, Earth Policy Institute, 2 October 2002.

18. Ibid.

19. U. Cubasch et al., "Projections of Future Climate Change," in Intergovernmental Panel on Climate Change, *Climate Change 2001: The Scientific Basis. Contribution of Working Group I to the Third Assessment Report of the Intergovernmental Panel on Climate Change* (New York: Cambridge University Press, 2001).

20. Grain from USDA, *Production, Supply, and Distribution*; World Bank, *China: Agenda for Water Sector Strategy for North China* (Washington, DC: April 2001), vii, xi; water tables falling from Sandra Postel, *Last Oasis* (New York: W.W. Norton & Company, 1997), 36–7.

21. United Nations, *World Population Prospects*; Postel, *Last Oasis*.

22. USDA, *Agricultural Resources*; U.S. Bureau of the Census, *Projections of the Total Population of States: 1995–2025*, at <www.census.gov>, updated 2 August 2002.

23. David Seckler, David Molden, and Randolph Barker, "Water Scarcity in the Twenty-First Century," *Water Brief 1* (Colombo, Sri Lanka: International Water Management Institute, 1999); population from United Nations, *World Population Prospects*.

24. Population from United Nations, *World Population Prospects*; livestock population from FAO, *FAOSTAT Statistics Database*, at <apps.fao.org>, with livestock data updated 9 January 2003.

25. Chinese economic expansion from International Monetary Fund (IMF), *World Economic Outlook Database*, at <www.imf.org/external/pubs/ft/weo>, updated April 2003.

26. Livestock population from FAO, *FAOSTAT Statistics Database*.

27. Howard W. French, "China's Growing Deserts Are Suffocating Korea," *New York Times*, 14 April 2002.

28. Wang Tao, "The Process and Its Control of Sandy Desertification in Northern China," seminar on desertification in China, Cold and Arid Regions Environmental & Engineering Institute, Chinese Academy of Sciences, Lanzhou, China, May 2002.

29. Ibid.

30. California population from U.S. Bureau of the Census, *1930 Fact Sheet*, at <www.census.gov>, revised 28 March 2002; U.S. Embassy, *Grapes of Wrath in Inner Mongolia* (Beijing: May 2001).

31. Grain trade from USDA, *Production, Supply, and Distribution*.

32. Ibid.; IMF, *International Financial Statistics Yearbook 2001* (Washington, DC: August 2001), p. 184.

33. Annual shortfall from USDA, *Production, Supply, and Distribution*; U.S. soybean embargo on Japan from David Rapp, "Farmer and Uncle Sam: An Old, Odd Couple," *Congressional Quarterly Weekly Report*, 4 April 1987, 598–603; Chinese trade surplus with the United States from U.S. Census Bureau, "U.S. Trade Balance with China," at <www.census.gov/foreign-trade/balance/c5700.html>, updated 13 May 2003; Chinese economic growth from IMF, *World Economic Outlook* (Washington, DC: September 2002), 36.

34. People living on $1 a day from World Bank, *World Development Report 2000/2001* (New York: Oxford University Press, 2001), 3.

35. Lester R. Brown, *Who Will Feed China?* (New York: W.W. Norton & Company, 1995); Michael McElroy et al., *China Agriculture: Cultivated Land Area, Grain Projections, and Implications* (Washington, DC: National Intelligence Council, November 1997).

36. Lester R. Brown and Erik P. Eckholm, *By Bread Alone* (New York: Overseas Development Council, 1974), 69–72.

37. "Wheat Board Pulls Out of Market," *Canadian Press*, 6 September 2002; "Drought

Threat to Australian Summer Crops," *Financial Times*, 27 November 2002.

38. U.S. farm program from USDA, *Agricultural Resources and Environmental Indicators 1996–97* (Washington, DC: July 1997), 255–327; carryover stocks from USDA, *Production, Supply, and Distribution.*

39. Population estimates from United Nations, *World Population Prospects.*

40. China from U.S. Embassy, "Desert Mergers and Acquisitions," *Beijing Environment, Science, and Technology Update* (Beijing: 19 July 2002); Nigeria from "Combating Desertification and Deforestation," *Africa*

News Service, 23 April 2002; IRNA (Iranian News Agency), "Official Warns of Impending Desertification Catastrophe in Southeast Iran," *BBC International Reports*, 29 September 2002.

41. Christopher Ward, "Yemen's Water Crisis," based on a lecture to the British Yemeni Society in September 2000, July 2001; "Pakistan: Focus on Water Crisis," *U.N. Integrated Regional Information Networks*, 17 May 2002.

42. Figure of 1.3 billion from UNAIDS, *Report on The Global HIV/AIDS Epidemic 2002.*

Section II: The Promethean Response

One response to the doomsaying of Section I is a literature that denies that there is an environmental crisis either present or looming. This literature is often categorized as cornucopian or Promethean, and embodies two main arguments. First, this school argues that environmental conditions and indicators are much better than documents like *Limits to Growth*, the *Global 2000 Report*, and the annual Worldwatch Institute *State of the World* reports claim. Secondly, it has unlimited confidence in the ability of humans—especially in their technologies and their social organization in markets—to overcome any obstacles they encounter, including supposed limits. Approaching scarcities serve only to inspire human minds to devise innovations and solutions. These minds are to Julian Simon *The Ultimate Resource* (1981). Simon and others in this camp believe that there is an infinite supply of the natural resources we need—and if we start to run out, we'll find something else to use. Thus, continued innovation, growth, and technology are the solution to any problem that may be produced by *past* innovation, growth, and technology.

We include here the leading representatives of two generations of the Promethean/cornucopian literature. The introduction to Julian L. Simon and Herman Kahn's *The Resourceful Earth: A Response to Global 2000* makes the point quite radically and forcefully. Simon and Kahn take on the limits arguments point by point, arguing generally that either the problems laid out by *Global 2000* and others simply do not exist, or that all relevant environmental indicators are improving. It remains one of the best representations of the Promethean position.

Bjorn Lomborg now carries Simon's torch, and we include here a brief summary of his view published at greater length—and to great controversy—elsewhere. Lomborg is criticized in the selection by Tom Burke for caricaturing the views of environmentalists and highly selective use of evidence.

Further Reading

Julian Simon was the dean of the Prometheans. His works include *The Resourceful Earth* (1984), *The Ultimate Resource* (1981), and *The State of Humanity* (1995). He debates the survivalist Norman Myers in Myers and Simon, *Scarcity or Abundance: A Debate on the Environment* (1994). By 2001 Simon was eclipsed by Bjorn Lomborg, whose book *The Skeptical Environmentalist* (2001) immediately became an international bestseller, as well as the target of hostility from environmentalists and biological scientists. The most comprehensive critique of Lomborg, 'Misleading Math About the Earth', appeared in *Scientific American*, January 2002.

Greg Easterbrook's mammoth *A Moment on the Earth: The Coming Age of Environmental Optimism* (1995) argues that all the problems the doomsayers point out are short-lived and ephemeral—minor annoyances in the great journey of the natural world. Easterbrook claims that all pollution problems will be solved in our lifetimes. Economists appear prominently in the Promethean literature, beginning with Harold Barnett and Chandler Morse's *Scarcity and Growth* (1963). Oxford economist Wilfred Beckerman makes an early argument in *In Defence of Economic Growth* (1974), which he revisits in the bluntly titled *Small is Stupid: Blowing the Whistle on the Greens* (1995). Aaron Wildavsky's *But Is It True? A Citizen's Guide to Environmental Health and Safety Issues* (1995) argues that the risks which energize environmentalists are revealed by a close examination of the underlying science to be in truth non-existent. The Prometheans' own science is criticized in Paul and Anne Ehrlich's *Betrayal of Science and Reason* (1996), which argues that the politics of the 'brownlash' movement pollutes its science, and vice versa.

4 Introduction to *The Resourceful Earth*

Julian L. Simon and Herman Kahn

Executive Summary

The original 1980 *Global 2000 Report to the President* (*Global 2000* hereafter) is frightening. It received extraordinarily wide circulation, and it has influenced crucial governmental policies. But it is dead wrong. Now *The Resourceful Earth*, a response to *Global 2000*, presents the relevant reliable trend evidence which mainly reassures rather than frightens.

Two paragraphs summarize the "Major Findings and Conclusions" of *Global 2000* on its page 1:

If present trends continue, the world in 2000 will be more crowded, more polluted, less stable ecologically, and more vulnerable to disruption than the world we live in now. Serious stresses involving population, resources, and environment are clearly visible ahead. Despite greater material output, the world's people will be poorer in many ways than they are today.

For hundreds of millions of the desperately poor, the outlook for food and other necessities of life will be no better. For many it will be worse. Barring revolutionary advances in technology, life for most people on earth will be more precarious in 2000 than it is now—unless the nations of the world act decisively to alter current trends.

To highlight our differences as vividly as possible, we restate the above summary with our substitutions in italics:

If present trends continue, the world in 2000 will be *less crowded* (though more populated), *less polluted, more stable ecologically*, and *less vulnerable to resource-supply disruption* than the world we live in now. Stresses involving population, resources, and environment *will be less in the future than now* ... The world's people will be *richer* in most ways than they are today ... The outlook for food and other necessities of life will be *better* ... life for most people on earth will be *less precarious* economically than it is now.

The high points of our findings are as follows:

(1) Life expectancy has been rising rapidly throughout the world, a sign of demographic, scientific, and economic success. This fact—at least as dramatic and heartening as any other in human history—must be fundamental in any informed discussion of pollution and nutrition.

From Julian L. Simon and Herman Kahn, *The Resourceful Earth* (New York: Basil Blackwell, 1984), 1–27. Reprinted with permission.

(2) The birth rate in less developed countries has been falling substantially during the past two decades, from 2.2 percent yearly in 1964–5 to 1.75 percent in 1982–3, probably a result of modernization and of decreasing child mortality, and a sign of increased control by people over their family lives.

(3) Many people are still hungry, but the food supply has been improving since at least World War II, as measured by grain prices, production per consumer, and the famine death rate.

(4) Trends in world forests are not worrying, though in some places deforestation is troubling.

(5) There is no statistical evidence for rapid loss of species in the next two decades. An increased rate of extinction cannot be ruled out if tropical deforestation is severe, but no evidence about linkage has yet been demonstrated.

(6) The fish catch, after a pause, has resumed its long upward trend.

(7) Land availability will not increasingly constrain world agriculture in coming decades.

(8) In the US, the trend is toward higher-quality cropland, suffering less from erosion than in the past.

(9) The widely-published report of increasingly rapid urbanization of US farmland was based on faulty data.

(10) Water does not pose a problem of physical scarcity or disappearance, although the world and US situations do call for better institutional management through more rational systems of property rights.

(11) The climate does not show signs of unusual and threatening changes.

(12) Mineral resources are becoming less scarce rather than more scarce, affront to common sense though that may be.

(13) There is no persuasive reason to believe that the world oil price will rise in coming decades. The price may fall well below what it has been.

(14) Compared to coal, nuclear power is no more expensive, and is probably much cheaper, under most circumstances. It is also much cheaper than oil.

(15) Nuclear power gives every evidence of costing fewer lives per unit of energy produced than does coal or oil.

(16) Solar energy sources (including wind and wave power) are too dilute to compete economically for much of humankind's energy needs, though for specialized uses and certain climates they can make a valuable contribution.

(17) Threats of air and water pollution have been vastly overblown; these processes were not well analyzed in *Global 2000*.

We do not say that all is well everywhere, and we do not predict that all will be rosy in the future. Children are hungry and sick; people live out lives of physical or intellectual poverty, and lack of opportunity; war or some new pollution may do us in. *The Resourceful Earth does* show that for most relevant matters we have examined, aggregate global and US *trends* are improving rather than deteriorating.

In addition we do not say that a better future happens *automatically* or *without effort*. It will happen because men and women—sometimes as individuals, sometimes as enterprises working for profit, sometimes as voluntary non-profit making groups, and sometimes as governmental agencies—will address problems with muscle and mind, and will *probably* overcome, as has been usual throughout history.

We are confident that the nature of the physical world permits continued improvement in humankind's economic lot in the long run, indefinitely. Of course there are always newly arising local problems, shortages and pollutions, due to climate or to increased population and income. Sometimes temporary large-scale problems arise. But the nature of the world's physical conditions and the resilience in a well-functioning economic and social system enable us to overcome such problems, and the solutions usually leave us better off than if the problem had never arisen; that is the great lesson to be learned from human history.

We are less optimistic, however, about the constraints currently imposed upon material progress by political and institutional forces, in conjunction with popularly-held beliefs and attitudes about natural resources and the environment, such as those urged upon us by *Global 2000*. These constraints include the view that resource and environmental trends point towards deterioration rather than towards improvement, that there are physical limits that will increasingly act as a brake upon progress, and that nuclear energy is more dangerous than energy from other sources. These views lead to calls for subsidies and price controls, as well as government ownership and management of resource production, and government allocation of the resources that are produced. To a considerable extent the US and the rest of the world already suffer from such policies (for example, on agriculture in Africa), and continuation and intensification could seriously damage resource production and choke economic progress. In particular, refusal to use nuclear power could hamper the US in its economic competition with other nations, as well as cause unnecessary deaths in coal mining and other types of conventional energy production. We wish that there were grounds to believe that a shift in thinking will take place on these matters, but we do not find basis for firm hope. So in this respect we are hardly optimistic.

We also wish to emphasize that though the global situation may be reasonably satisfactory or improving in some given respect, there are likely to be areas in which there are severe difficulties which may be on the increase. Such local problems may be due to local mismanagement, or they may be due to natural catastrophe which the larger community may not yet have been able to help mitigate. Such local problems should not be glossed over in any global assessment.

Background

More than one million copies of the original *Global 2000 Report to the President of the United States* have been distributed. It has been translated into five major languages. Other countries such as Germany have commissioned studies imitating *Global 2000*.

Global 2000 also underlies important US policy pronouncements. For example, the following paragraphs, and the rest of the full speech at the Alpbach European Forum in 1980, which was an official "American perspective on the world economy in the 1980s," were founded squarely on *Global 2000*:

Defying the generally buoyant mood, Richard Cooper, U.S. under secretary of state for economic affairs, delivered a grim message. If present trends continue, he said, the world population will swell to five billion by 1990 from four billion at present, leading to "open conflict, greater terrorism and possibly localized anarchy," as well as "congestion, famine, deforestation."

The decade's population growth would equal "nearly half the total world population when I was born," he said. Even then, he added ominously, "some political leaders were calling for more lebensraum" (or living space). (*The Wall Street Journal*, 15 September 1980, 32)

Before *Global 2000* was even completed, President Carter had discussed its conclusions with other world leaders at an economic summit held in Italy. Immediately upon receiving the Report, the President established a task force to ensure that *Global 2000* received priority attention. The task force included the Secretary of State, the director of the Office of Management and Budget, the President's Assistant for Domestic Affairs, and the director of the Office of Science and Technology Policy. Secretary of State Edmund Muskie used *Global 2000* as the centre-piece for an address to the UN General Assembly. The Joint Economic Committee of Congress launched a series of hearings on the Report. The President instructed the State Department to arrange an international meeting of environmental and economic experts to discuss population, natural resources, environment, and economic development, the subjects of *Global 2000*. Finally, in his farewell address to the nation, President Carter referred to the subject of *Global 2000* as one of the three most important problems facing the American people (the other two being arms control and human rights). And *Global 2000*'s effect did not disappear with the change of administration. It continues to be cited as support for a wide variety of forecasts by governmental agencies.[1]

The press received *Global 2000* with great respect and enormous attention. *Time* and *Newsweek* ran full-page stories, and *Global 2000* made front-page newspaper headlines across the country as an "official" government study forecasting global disaster. Though the Report included some qualifications, it was interpreted by all as a prediction of gloom-and-doom. For example, *Science*'s story title was: "Global 2000 Report: Vision of a Gloomy World."[2] *Time*'s title was "Toward a Troubled 21st Century: A Presidential Panel Finds the Global Outlook Extremely Bleak."[3] *Newsweek*'s title was "A Grim Year 2000."[4] The typical local paper in central Illinois had this banner across the top of the front page: "U.S. Report Says World Faces Ecological Disaster."[5] And its story began:

Mass poverty, malnutrition and deterioration of the planet's water and atmosphere resources—that's a bleak government prediction that says civilization has perhaps 20 years to act to head off such a worldwide disaster.

A full-page advertisement for the volume in *The New York Review of Books* was headed:

Government Report as follows: Poisoned seas, acid rain, water running out, atmosphere dying.

However—and seldom can there have been a bigger "however" in the history of such reports—the original *Global 2000* is totally wrong in its specific assertions and its general conclusion. It is replete with major factual errors, not just minor blemishes.[6] Its language is vague at key points, and features many loaded terms. Many of its arguments are illogical or misleading. It paints an overall picture of global trends that is fundamentally wrong, partly because it relies on non-facts and partly because it misinterprets the facts it does present. (In partial defense of the writers who prepared the *Global 2000* work, the summary Volume I—which was the main basis for the news stories—egregiously mis-stated, for reasons which we can only surmise,[7] many analyses and conclusions in the working-paper Volume II, thereby turning optimistic projections into pessimistic ones.)

Our statements about the future in *The Resourceful Earth* are intended as unconditional predictions in the absence of an unforeseeable catastrophe such as nuclear war or total social breakdown. We feel no need to qualify these predictions upon the continuation of current policies, as *Global 2000* claimed to do, and in fact we believe that such a qualification is not meaningful. Throughout history, individuals and communities have responded to actual and expected shortages of raw materials in such fashion that eventually the materials have become more readily available than if the shortages had never arisen. These responses are embodied in the observed long-run trends in supply and cost, and therefore extrapolation of such trends (together with appropriate theoretical attention) takes into account the likely future responses.

Aside from this Introduction and one section in most of the chapters, *The Resourceful Earth* is not primarily an evaluation or criticism of *Global 2000*. (For evaluation and criticism, see Clawson 1981; Dubos 1981; Kahn and Schneider 1981; Simon 1981.) It is a compendium of careful, authoritative, independent studies of many of the topics dealt with by *Global 2000* plus some others, by writers selected by the editors because their claim to the label "expert" is as strong as any such claim can be. Taken together, the chapters are intended to be a fair assessment of the trends together with an analysis of what the trends portend for the future. We hope that *The Resourceful Earth* will also serve as a reference volume of first resort for persons seeking knowledge on these topics. This introduction summarizes the findings of the technical chapters. It also offers some general observations about *Global 2000*, global modeling, and policy recommendations. The findings express the views of the authors of the individual chapters. The editors are responsible for the general observations, though the individual chapter authors have commented upon these general observations. We have also included a section at the end of the volume where individual authors may express their disagreements with any of these general views.

The Resourceful Earth chapters were produced without a penny's added cost to the public. The chapters are presented here exactly as written, with the authors having final authority over their chapters without bureaucratic tampering. This process is in contrast to the largely staff-written and politically edited *Global 2000*; more details are given below about the process of financing, writing, and editing *Global 2000* and *The Resourceful Earth*.

The Specific Conclusions

We now briefly summarize the main issues raised by *Global 2000* as covered by our topical chapters. For convenience, the order will be the same as in the *Global 2000* summary quoted above for the topics mentioned there, followed by the other central issues raised in their summary volume.

"MORE CROWDED"

There surely will be more people on earth in the year 2000 than there are now, barring a calamity. But a growing population does not imply that human living on the globe will be more "crowded" in any meaningful fashion. As the world's people have increasingly higher incomes, they purchase better housing and mobility. The homes of the world's people progressively have more floorspace, which means people dwell in less-crowded space with more privacy. The United States, for which data are readily available, illustrates the trends in developed countries. In 1940, fully 20.2 percent of households had 1.01 or more persons per room, whereas in 1974 only 4.5 percent were that crowded (US Department of Commerce 1977: 90). (Also relevant: in 1940 44.6 percent of housing units lacked some or all plumbing facilities; but in 1974 only 3.2 percent were lacking. In 1940, 55.4 percent had all plumbing facilities, whereas in 1974, 96.8 percent had all plumbing; US Department of Commerce, 1977: 91). The world's people are getting better roads and more vehicles; therefore they can move around more freely, and have the benefits of a wider span of area. In the US, paved highways have increased from zero to over 3 million miles since the turn of the century. Natural park areas have been expanding (Figure 4.1). And trips to parks have increased to an extraordinary degree (Figure 4.2). These trends mean that people increasingly have much more space available and accessible for their use, despite the increase in

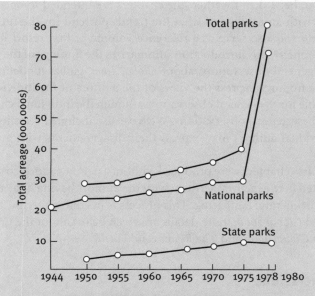

Fig. 4.1 **Land in public parks, 1944–80.**

Source: Statistical Abstract of the US 1973: 202; 1980: 242 for 1950–79; *Information Related to the National Park System*, US Department of the Interior, National Park Service, 30 June 1944: 35 for 1944.

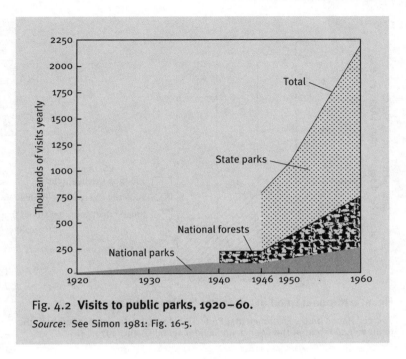

Fig. 4.2 **Visits to public parks, 1920–60.**

Source: See Simon 1981: Fig. 16-5.

total population, even in the poorer countries. All this suggests to us that the world is getting less crowded by reasonable tests relevant to human life.

"MORE POLLUTED"

Global 2000 asserts that the world is getting more polluted. But it cites no systematic data for the world or even for regions. It is certainly reasonable to *assume* that man-made industrial pollutions increase as the most backward countries begin to modernize, get somewhat less poor, and purchase pollution-creating industrial plants. The same is true of consumer pollution—junked cars, plastic bags, and pop tops of beverage cans. But it is misleading to suggest that there are *data* showing that such pollution is a major problem.

In the early stages of industrialization, countries and people are not yet ready to pay for cleanup operations. But further increases in income almost as surely will bring about pollution abatement. (At the same time, biological disease pollution has been declining, even in the poor countries, at a rate far outweighing any hazardous effect of man-made pollution, as seen in increased life-expectancy.)

In the richer countries there is solid evidence that hazardous air pollution has been declining. Figure 4.3 shows the Council on Environmental Quality's new Pollutant Standard Index for the US, and Figure 4.4 shows one key measure of air quality for which data are available since 1960; the benign trend has been under way for quite a while, and does not stem only from the onset of the environmental movement around 1970.

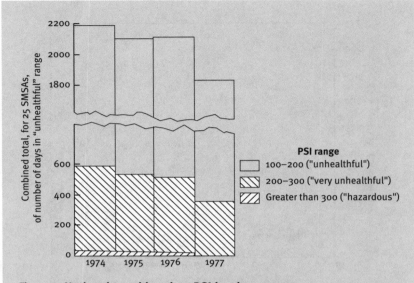

Fig. 4.3 **National trend in urban PSI levels, 1974–7.**

Source: Based on US Environmental Protection Agency data, reproduced from the tenth annual report of the Council on Environmental Quality 1979: 39.

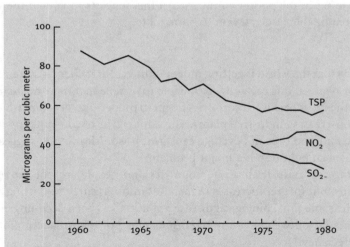

Fig. 4.4 **National ambient concentrations of total suspended particulates, nitrogen dioxide, and sulfur dioxide, 1960–80. Data may not be strictly comparable.**

Source: US Environmental Protection Agency.

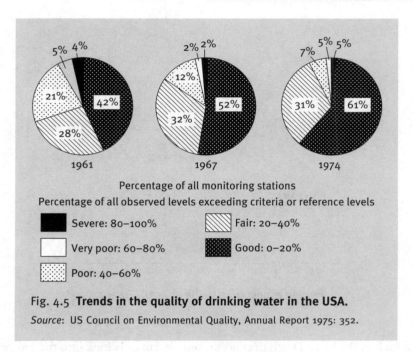

Fig. 4.5 **Trends in the quality of drinking water in the USA.**

Source: US Council on Environmental Quality, Annual Report 1975: 352.

Water quality too, has improved in the richer countries. Figure 4.5 shows the improvements in drinkability of water in the US since 1961. Such alarms of the 1960s and 1970s as the impending "death" of the Great Lakes have turned out totally in error; fishing and swimming conditions there are now excellent. (Ironically, the "death" that was warned of is really a condition of too much organic "life", and is therefore self-curing as soon as people stop adding so much nutrient to the water.) In the developing countries the proportion of the urban population served by a safe water supply rose modestly in the 1970s, and rose markedly among the rural population (but from 14 percent to only 29 percent; Holdgate et al. 1982: 135).

The long-run historical record, to the extent that there are data, offers examples upon which one may seize to argue almost any shade of opinion about pollution. But many of the oft-cited series that purportedly show "deterioration" prove, upon inspection, to be the result of forces other than recent human activities.

"LESS STABLE ECOLOGICALLY, AND MORE VULNERABLE TO DISRUPTION"

These concepts are so diffuse that we have no idea how one would measure them directly. *Global 2000* gives no relevant trend data.

Perhaps *Global 2000* had in mind that there is more danger of disruption as humankind's capacity to alter the ecosystem increases. In itself, this must be true. But at the same time, humankind's ability to restore imbalances in the ecosystem also increases. And the trend data on pollution, food (discussed below), and life expectancy suggest that the life-supporting capacities have been increasing faster than the malign disturbances. Of course some unprecedented

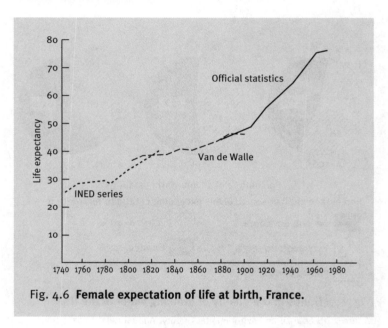

Fig. 4.6 **Female expectation of life at birth, France.**

catastrophe such as the Black Death may occur, but we can only look into the future as best we can, and conclude that no such catastrophe is in view. The one crucial exception is war, which is outside our scope here, and which is not a matter of the natural resource constraints that depend upon the nature of the physical world.

"SERIOUS STRESSES INVOLVING POPULATION, RESOURCES, AND ENVIRONMENT . . ."

This *Global 2000* phrase sounds ominous, but like many other *Global 2000* warnings it is hard to pin down. If it means that people will have a poorer chance of survival in the year 2000 than now, due to the greater number of people, the trends in life expectancy suggest the contrary. Declining mortality and improving health have accompanied unprecedented population growth in the world (as well as in the US, of course). Figure 4.6 shows the long-run trend of life expectancy in the more-developed world, a pattern toward which the less-developed countries are converging. For example, life expectancy in less-developed regions rose from 43 years in 1950/55 to 53 years in 1970/75 (the rise in Asia being even greater), a much bigger jump than the rise from 65 years to 71 years in the more-developed regions (Gwatkin 1980).

If the phrase "serious stresses" implies that along with more people in the year 2000 will come more costly resources and a deteriorated environment, the trends suggest the opposite, as noted above for the environment, and as discussed next for resources. If the phrase means that life expectancy, resource availability, and the quality of the environment could be even better in the year 2000 with fewer people than are expected, *Global 2000* has not even attempted to demonstrate such a complex causal correction. The existing research on the subject does not suggest to us that such would be the case.

"...RESOURCES..."

Global 2000 projected a 5 percent yearly increase in the real price of non-fuel minerals until the year 2000. There has always been "serious stress" in the sense that people have to pay a price to get the resources they want. But the relevant economic measures of "stress"—costs and prices—show that the long-run trend is toward less scarcity and lower prices rather than more scarcity and higher prices, hard as that may be for many people to believe. The cost trends of almost every natural resource have been downward over the course of recorded history.

An hour's work in the United States has bought increasingly more of copper, wheat, and oil (which are representative and important raw materials) from 1800 to the present (see, for example, Figure 4.7). The trend is less dramatic in the poorest countries, but the direction of the trend is unmistakable there, too, because per person income has been rising in poor countries as well as rich ones. The same trend has held throughout human history for such minerals as copper and iron (Clark 1957: appendix). Calculations of expenditures for raw materials as a falling proportion of total family budgets make the same point even more strongly.

These trends mean that raw materials have been getting increasingly available and less scarce relative to the most important and most fundamental element of economic life, human work-time. The prices of raw materials have even been falling relative to consumer goods and the Consumer Price Index. All the items in the Consumer Price Index have been produced with increasingly efficient use of labor and capital over the years, but the decrease in cost of raw materials has been even greater than that of other goods. This is a very strong demonstration of progressively decreasing scarcity and increasing availability of raw materials. The trend of raw material prices relative to consumer goods, however, has much less meaning for human welfare than does the trend of resource prices relative to the price of human time—a trend which is decidedly benign, as we have seen. Even if raw materials were rising in price relative to consumer goods, there would be no cause for alarm as long as it takes progressively less effort, and a smaller proportion of our incomes, to obtain the service from raw materials that we need and want.

Moreover, the observed fall in the prices of raw materials understates the positive trend, because as consumers we are interested in the services we get from the raw materials rather than the raw materials themselves. We have learned to use less of given raw materials for given purposes, as well as to substitute cheaper materials to get the same services. Consider a copper pot used long ago for cooking. The consumer is interested in a container that can be put over heat. After iron and aluminium were discovered, quite satisfactory cooking pots—with advantages as well as disadvantages compared with pots of copper—could be made of those materials. The cost that interests us is the cost of providing the cooking service, rather than the cost of the copper.

A single communications satellite in space provides intercontinental telephone connections that would otherwise require thousands of tons of copper. Satellites and microwave transmission and the use of glass fibers in communications are dramatic examples of how a substitute process can supply a service much more cheaply than copper.

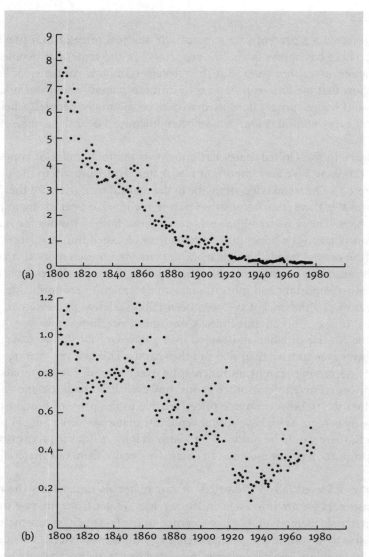

Fig. 4.7 The scarcity of copper (a) as measured by its price relative to wages and (b) as measured by its price relative to the consumer index. The diagrams are typical of the pattern for each of the metals (see Simon 1981: appendix).

"THE WORLD'S PEOPLE WILL BE POORER IN MANY WAYS ..."

The Global 2000 qualifying phrase "in many ways" could imply that a decrease in the number of elephants, or the deaths of some elderly beloved persons, are ways in which the world's people will be poorer in the future than now; if so, the statement is logically correct. But if we consider more general and economically meaningful measures, the world's people have been getting richer rather than poorer, and may be expected to be richer in the future. Measured in conventional terms, average income for the world's population has been rising. Particularly noteworthy, and contrary to common belief, income in the poorer countries has been rising at a percentage rate as great or greater than in the richer countries since World War II (Morawetz 1978). Another vivid proof of the rise in income in poorer countries is the decline in the proportion of the labor force devoted to agriculture—from 68 percent to 58 percent between 1965 and 1981 in the developing countries, consistent with the trend in developed countries where the agricultural labor force has plummeted to, for example, well below 3 percent in the US. The rising average income in poorer countries combined with the rough stability of their internal income-distribution shares suggests that the poorer classes of representative countries have been participating in this income rise along with the richer classes.

"THE OUTLOOK FOR FOOD ... WILL BE NO BETTER"

Consumption of food per person in the world is up over the last 30 years (Figure 4.8). And data do not show that the bottom of the income scale is faring worse, or even has failed to share in the general improvement, as the average has improved. Africa's food production per capita is down, but no one thinks that has anything to do with physical conditions; it clearly stems from governmental and other social conditions. Famine deaths have decreased in the past century even in absolute terms, let alone relative to population. World food prices have been trending lower for decades and centuries (Figure 4.9), and there is strong reason to believe that this trend will continue. This evidence runs exactly counter to *Global 2000*'s conclusion that "real prices for food are expected to double." If a problem exists for the US, it is a problem caused by abundance. Food production in the US is now so great that farmers are suffering economically. Food stocks in the world are so high that they are causing major problems (Figure 4.10). Agricultural yields per hectare have continued to rise in such countries as China, France, and the US. These gains in production have been accomplished with a decreasing proportion of the labor force—the key input for and constraint upon the economic system.

   Careful study of the quantities of actual and potential agricultural land in various countries, plus possibilities for irrigation and multicropping together with yields already routinely reached in the developed countries, suggests that agricultural land will not be a bottleneck in the foreseeable future, even without new technological breakthroughs. And the supply of water for agriculture (which is by far the largest use of water) poses even fewer problems arising from purely physical conditions. Physical measurements of water withdrawal in the world as a whole provide no relevant information. The possibility of the world as a whole running out of water is zero. The supply of water is always a local or regional issue within a country (or occasionally at the border of two countries). The key constraints upon the supply of water arise from

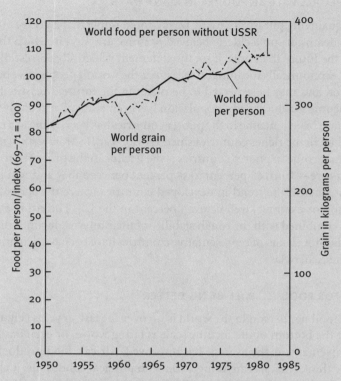

Fig. 4.8 **World grain and food production per person.**

Sources: USDA, FAS, FG-8-82 (3-15-82); Brown, *Building a Sustainable Society* (Norton, 1981), 81 (with authors' extrapolation of 1981 and 1982 population). The Food index includes all food commodities—including grain, pulses, oil-seeds, vegetables, and fruit; it excludes the PRC. Source of index USDA, ERS, Statistical Bulletin No. 669, July 1981; USDA, personal communication, Dr Patrick M. O'Brien (1980, 1981 index).

institutional and political conditions, and especially the structure of property rights to water and the price structure for water, rather than mere physical availability.

The issue of a well-constituted system of property rights—the absence of which often leads to "the tragedy of the commons"—arises sharply with respect to water rights; but appropriate rules for private property are also of fundamental importance in many other natural resource and environmental situations. Drilling rights in oil basins, rights to pollute the air and water, and hunting rights for wild animals, are but three dramatic examples. A sound set of social rules with respect to property can go far to ensure a satisfactory supply of resources and an acceptably clean environment. On this there is ever-growing agreement among naturalists, economists, geologists, and others concerned with these matters.

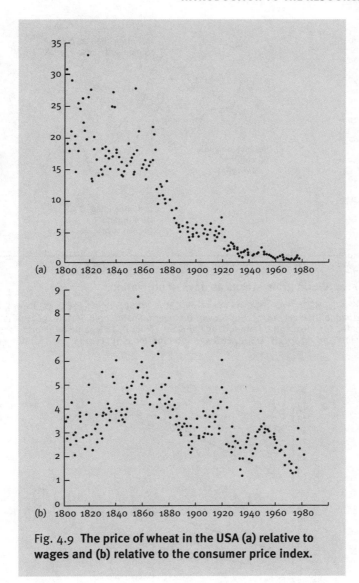

Fig. 4.9 **The price of wheat in the USA (a) relative to wages and (b) relative to the consumer price index.**

"SIGNIFICANT LOSSES OF WORLD FORESTS WILL CONTINUE OVER THE NEXT 20 YEARS"

According to *Global 2000*, "by 2000 some 40 percent of the remaining forest cover in LDCs will be gone." If nonsense is a statement utterly without factual support, this is nonsense. Forests are not declining at all in the temperate regions. In the US, for example, the total quantity of trees has been increasing, and wood production has been increasing rapidly (Figure 4.11). The rate of deforestation in tropical areas has been far slower than suggested by *Global 2000*. The

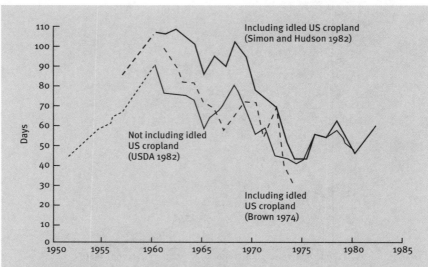

Fig. 4.10 **World grain stocks as days of utilization.**

Sources: (1) USDA, FAS, FG-8-82 (3-15-82); USDA, WASDE-133 (5-11-81); (2) Brown, *By Bread Alone* (Praeger, 1974), 60; Brown, *Building a Sustainable Society*, 96; authors' estimates for 1961, 1982. Data for 1952 and 1957 from D. Gale Johnson, *World Food Problems and Prospects*; USDA, ERS 479, *US Corn Industry*, February 1982, table 46.

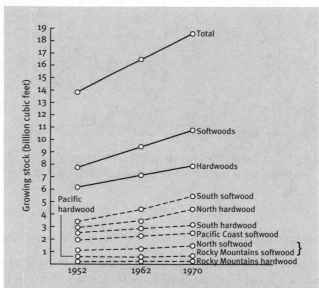

Fig. 4.11 **Forest resources in the USA, 1952–70.**

Source: *Perspectives on Prime Lands* (US Department of Agriculture, 1975).

prospects for world wood production to meet demand without grave deforestation are excellent, especially because plantations which require only small land areas have just begun to make the major contribution to total world production of which they are capable.

"ARABLE LAND WILL INCREASE ONLY 4 PERCENT BY 2000. . . . SERIOUS DETERIORATION OF AGRICULTURAL SOILS WILL OCCUR WORLDWIDE, DUE TO EROSION"

Arable land has been increasing at a rate very much faster in recent decades than the rate *Global 2000* projected for coming decades—an increase which we can approximate at fully 16 percent over the 20-year period from 1950 to 1975 for which there are good data (Table 4.1). There is no apparent reason why in the next decades the increase should fall anywhere nearly as low as the 4 percent *Global 2000* suggests. A comprehensive assessment of the earth's land resources for agriculture by an authoritative President's Science Advisory Committee suggested that arable land will not be a key constraint upon food production in the world, and our findings agree. Rather, social and economic conditions are the key constraints on the amount of land brought into production.

In the United States, the conversion of farmland to urbanized land is proceeding at about the same rate as in recent decades, rather than at three times that rate, as was widely reported recently by a now-discredited agency of the US Department of Agriculture (the National Agricultural Lands Study), the source of the *Global 2000* statement on the subject. Furthermore, each year more (and better) new land is being brought into cultivation by irrigation and drainage than is being urbanized and built upon.

Concern about the "loss" of cropland to new housing, and the resulting governmental regulations that have constrained housing starts and raised the price of new homes, especially in California, does not square with contemporary federal policies for reducing planted acreage to meet the problem of "overproduction" of grain. In 1983 perhaps 39 percent of US crop acreage was kept idle by federal subsidy programs, at an unprecedented high cost to US taxpayers of $18.3 billion (compared to an original estimate of $1.8 billion for the year; *New York Times*, 31 January 1983, 5). The argument is sometimes made that governments must act to save cropland for future generations, but this argument lacks support from either economic analysis or technological considerations. The driving motive behind urging government action to "preserve" farmland seems to be more aesthetics than economics.

Soil erosion is not occurring at a dangerous pace in most parts of the United States, contrary to much recent publicity. In most areas top soil is not being lost at a rate that makes broad changes in farming practices economical from either the private or public standpoint, though recent advances in tillage may change the picture somewhat. Regulating or subsidizing particular tillage practices portends greater social cost than benefit in the long run. The largest social cost of soil erosion is not the loss of top soil, but rather the silting-up of drainage ditches in some places, with consequent maintenance expenses. In the aggregate, just the opposite of land ruination has been taking place, as the soil of American farms has been improving rather than deteriorating, and as fewer rather than more crop acres suffer from severe erosion over the decades since the 1930s. The continuing advance in agricultural productivity per acre is consistent with the improvement in the quality of farmland.

Table 4.1(a) **Changes in land use, 1950–60**

	Arable land as a percentage of total area		Percentage of arable land that is cultivated		Cultivated land as a percentage of total land		Agricultural land (arable and pasture) as a percentage of total area	
	(1)	(2)	(3)	(4)	(1 × 3) and (2 × 4)			
	1950	1960	1950	1960	1950	1960	1950	1960
Africa	14.27	15.30	36.21	42.72	5.2	6.5	46.50	49.02
Middle East	12.87	13.91	52.11	57.88	6.7	8.1	13.06	17.34
Asia	19.03	20.78	82.06	86.17	15.6	17.9	46.35	49.60
North and South America, USSR, Australia, New Zealand	6.88	7.75	82.75	82.96	5.7	6.4	34.27	38.59
Europe	30.79	30.98	89.02	90.06	27.4	27.9	45.63	46.10
ALL REGIONS	10.73	11.73	82.74	83.99	8.9	9.9	37.35	41.07

Source: Kumar 1973: 107.

Table 4.1(b) **Changes in land use, 1961–5 to 1975**

	Arable land as a percentage of total area				Agricultural land (arable and pasture) as a percentage of total area			
	1961–5	1966	1970	1975	1961–5	1966	1970	1975
Africa	6.28	6.50	6.76	6.96	32.88	32.96	33.13	33.29
Middle East	6.25	6.38	6.54	6.79	21.91	22.12	22.32	22.62
Far East	28.87	29.37	29.88	30.73	33.08	33.62	33.80	34.56
North America	11.50	11.43	12.17	13.08	26.10	25.85	25.88	25.50
USSR	10.24	10.24	10.39	10.37	26.83	27.34	27.09	26.97
Latin America	5.64	5.97	6.43	6.82	29.56	30.29	31.29	32.41
Western Europe	27.21	26.55	25.97	25.04	46.35	45.08	44.83	43.72
ALL REGIONS	10.41	10.58	10.93	11.25	33.13	33.38	33.71	33.99

Source: UN Food and Agriculture Organization 1976.

"EXTINCTIONS OF PLANT AND ANIMAL SPECIES WILL INCREASE DRAMATICALLY. HUNDREDS OF THOUSANDS OF SPECIES—PERHAPS AS MANY AS 20 PERCENT OF ALL SPECIES ON EARTH—WILL BE IRRETRIEVABLY LOST AS THEIR HABITATS VANISH, ESPECIALLY IN TROPICAL FORESTS"

This assertion by *Global 2000* is remarkably unsupported by statistical evidence. The only scientific observations cited in support of a numerical estimate of future species extinction are (*a*) between 1600 and 1900 perhaps one species every 4 years was extinguished, and (*b*) between 1900 and 1980 perhaps one species every year was extinguished. The leap to *Global 2000*'s estimate of 40,000 species extinguished each year by the year 2000 is based on pure guesswork by the *Global 2000* writers and the source upon which they draw (Myers 1979). We do not neglect the die-off of the passenger pigeon and other species that may be valuable to us. But we note that extinction of species—billions of them, according to Mayr (1982)—has been a biological fact of life throughout the ages, just as has been the development of new species, some or many of which may be more valuable to humans than extinguished species whose niches they fill.

"ATMOSPHERIC CONCENTRATIONS OF CARBON DIOXIDE AND OZONE-DEPLETING CHEMICALS ARE EXPECTED TO INCREASE AT RATES THAT COULD ALTER THE WORLD'S CLIMATE AND UPPER ATMOSPHERE SIGNIFICANTLY BY 2050"

The longest available records of climatic variations reveal very wide temperature swings, much or all of which may be thought of as random. In that context, recent changes in temperature may reasonably be viewed as normal oscillation rather than as a structural change induced by man's activity, including changes in CO_2.

The CO_2 question is subject to major controversy and uncertainty—about the extent of the buildup, about its causes, and especially about its effects. It would not seem prudent to undertake expensive policy alterations at this time because of this lack of knowledge, and because problems that changes in CO_2 concentration might cause would occur far in the future (well beyond the year 2000). Changes in the CO_2 situation may reasonably be seen, however, as an argument for increased use of nuclear power rather than fossil fuel. Continued research and monitoring of the CO_2 situation certainly is called for.

If it is considered desirable to reduce the amount of CO_2 released into the atmosphere by human activity, on the grounds that atmospheric change with unknown effects carries undesired risks, only two possibilities are feasible: reduce total energy consumption, or increase energy production from nuclear power plants. Reduction in total world energy consumption below the level determined by prices reflecting the production cost of energy is clearly unacceptable to most nations of the world because of the negative effects on economic growth, nutrition and health, and consumer satisfaction. This implies an inverse tradeoff relationship between CO_2 and non-fossil (especially nuclear) power.

"ACID RAIN . . ."

There is trend evidence that the pollution of acid rain has been getting more intense, and that it has some ill effects on fresh water lakes and their fish, upon perhaps forests, and hence upon people's ability to enjoy nature. Emissions from combustion of fossil fuels are undoubtedly a partial cause, although natural sources also contribute. There is some evidence of limited local ecological damage, but no proven threat to agriculture or human life. The trend deserves careful monitoring. The consensus of recent official committee reports (with which we agree) questions the use of high-sulfur coal for power production. This squares with our general advocacy of nuclear electricity generation. Whether any tighter pollution controls are warranted, economically or otherwise, has not been established. Fighting acid-rain effects on fish by liming lakes does not generally seem economically feasible. The acid-rain issue increases the comparative advantage of nuclear power plants relative to coal-burning plants. As with CO_2, then, there is an inverse tradeoff relationship between nuclear power and acid rain.

"REGIONAL WATER SHORTAGES WILL BECOME MORE SEVERE"

In the previous decade or so, water experts have concluded that the "likelihood of the world running out of water is zero." The recent UN Report of the World Environment, for example, tells us not to focus upon the ratio between physical water supply and use, as *Global 2000* does nevertheless, and emphasizes making appropriate social and economic as well as technological choices. From this flows "cautious hope from improved methods of management." That is, an appropriate structure of property rights, institutions, and pricing systems, together with some modicum of wisdom in choosing among the technological options open to us, can provide water for our growing needs at reasonable cost indefinitely.

Moreover, *Global 2000*'s statements about the world's future water situation are completely inconsistent with—in fact, are completely opposed to—*Global 2000*'s own analysis of what can reasonably be said about the world's water resources. It develops a sound analysis that finds that no reasonable or useful forecasts can be made about the world's water supply, but then proceeds to offer frightening forecasts totally inconsistent with its analysis. This inconsistency should be more than sufficient grounds to reject *Global 2000*'s gloomy conclusions out of hand.

"ENERGY . . ."

The prospect of running out of energy is purely a bogeyman. The availability of energy has been increasing, and the meaningful cost has been decreasing, over the entire span of humankind's history. We expect this benign trend to continue at least until our sun ceases to shine in perhaps 7 billion years, and until exhaustion of the supply of elemental inputs for fission (and perhaps for fusion).

Barring extraordinary political problems, we expect the price of oil to go down. Even with respect to oil, there is no basis to conclude that the price will rise until the year 2000 and beyond, or that humankind will ever face a greater shortage of oil in economic terms than it does now; rather, decreasing shortage is the more likely, in our view. For the next decade or two, politics—especially the fortunes of the OPEC cartel, and the prevalence of war instability—are likely to be the largest element in influencing oil prices. But no matter what the conditions, the market for oil substitutes probably constitutes a middle-run ceiling price for oil not much above what it is now; there could be a short-run panic run-up, but the world is better protected from that now than in the 1970s. And if free competition prevails, the price will be far below its present level.

Electrical power from nuclear fission plants is available at costs as low or much lower than from coal, depending upon the location, and at lower costs than from oil or gas. Even in the US, where the price of coal is unusually low, existing nuclear plants produce power more cheaply than from coal. Nuclear energy is available in unlimited quantity beyond any conceivable meaningful human horizon. And nuclear power gives every evidence of costing fewer lives per unit of energy produced than does coal or oil. The main constraints are various political interests, public misinformation, and cost-raising counter-productive systems of safety regulation. Nuclear waste disposal with remarkably high levels of safeguards presents no scientific difficulties.

Energy from sources other than fossil fuel and nuclear power, aside from hydropower where it is available, do not hold much promise for supplying the bulk of human energy elements, though solar power can be the cheapest source of power for heating buildings and water in certain geographic locations. The key defect of solar power, as well as with its relatives such as power from waves, is that it is too dilute, requiring very large areas and much capital to collect the energy.

"RAPID GROWTH IN WORLD POPULATION WILL HARDLY HAVE ALTERED BY 2000 ... THE RATE OF GROWTH WILL SLOW ONLY MARGINALLY FROM 1.8 PERCENT A YEAR TO 1.7 PERCENT"

Population forecasting involving fertility is notoriously unreliable. The birth rate can go down very rapidly, as numerous countries have demonstrated in the past few decades, including a country as large as China. (The rate can also go up rapidly, as the baby boom in the U.S. following World War II demonstrated.) Therefore, confidence in any such forecast for a matter of decades would be misplaced. The passage of only a handful of years already seems to have knocked the props out from under *Global 2000*'s forecast quoted above. The world's annual growth rate, which was 2.2 percent less than two decades ago in 1964–5, is down to 1.75 percent (US Department of Commerce News, 31 August 1983), a broad decline over the bulk of all the poorer and faster-growth nations. Though the growth rate may have stabilized in the last few years, these data alone seem inconsistent with the *Global 2000* forecast. The author of that forecast acknowledges that we have already moved from their "medium" forecast to their "low" forecast.

Even the apparently sure-fire *Global 2000* forecast that "in terms of sheer numbers, population will be growing faster in 2000 than it is today" might very well turn out to be wrong. Because the total population will be larger in 2000 than now, the fertility rate would have to be considerably smaller than it is now to falsify that forecast. But the drop would have to be only of the magnitude of the drop during the past two decades for that to come about, which would not seem beyond possibility.

More generally, the *Global 2000* forecasts of a larger population are written in language that conveys apprehension. But viewing the long sweep of human history, larger population size has been a clear-cut sign of economic success and has accompanied improvement in the human lot. The growth in numbers over the millennia, from a few thousands or millions living at subsistence to billions living well above subsistence, is proof positive that the problem of sustenance has eased rather than intensified. And the increase in life expectancy, which is the main cause of the increase in population size, is not only a sign of success in agriculture and public health, but also is the fundamental human good.

In the long run, human beings are the only possible source of human progress. Therefore, we consider *Global 2000*'s choice of language to describe population developments to be inappropriate and misleading.

Our positive statements about the recession of the physical constraints upon human progress are based primarily upon presently known progress, not taking into account possible or even likely advancements in technology. If we were to take into account such possibilities as the resources available to us in space and other such advances—even those possibilities which are already solidly worked out scientifically—our assessment would be much more "optimistic" than it is.

Notes

1. Paragraph adapted from Kahn and Schneider (1981). Various other material adapted from Simon (1981).
2. Carter (1980: 575–6).
3. *Time*, 4 August 1980, 54.
4. *Newsweek*, 4 August 1980, 38.
5. Champaign-Urbana *News Gazette*, 24 July 1980, 1.
6. For additional material on *Global 2000*'s factual errors and internal inconsistencies, see Simon (1981).
7. Ned Dearborn, one of the three *Global 2000* staff writers, stated in the abstract of a public

talk he gave at the 1982 meeting of the American Association for the Advancement of Science:

> By deliberate political choice, only part of the *Global 2000 Report to the President* was featured in the Report's summary volume and press releases—the part containing the Report's projections. The other part, while not suppressed, was barely mentioned in the official material receiving the widest distribution.

References

Ascher, William (1978), *Forecasting* (Baltimore: Johns Hopkins Press).

Barney, Gerald O. (1982), "Improving the Government's Capacity to Analyze and Predict Conditions and Trends of Global Population Resources and Environment," manuscript dated 24 March.

Carter, Luther, J. (1980), "Global 2000 Report: Vision of a Gloomy World," *Science*, 209 (1 August): 575–6.

Champaign-Urbana *News Gazette*, 24 July 1980, 1.

Clark, Colin (1957), *Conditions of Economic Progress*, 3rd edn. (New York: Macmillan).

Clawson, Marion (1981), "Entering the Twenty-First Century—The Global 2000

Report to the President," *Resources*, 66 (Spring): 19.

Council on Environmental Quality, United States Department of State (1981), *Global Future: Time to Act*, January: 1–209.

Dearborn, Ned (1982), Address to American Association for the Advancement of Science, January.

Dubos, Rene (1982), "Half Truths about the Future," *Wall Street Journal*, 8 May, editorial page.

Global 2000 Report to the President, i, ii, and iii (Washington, DC: US Government Printing Office, 1980).

Gwatkin, Davidson R. (1980), "Indications of Change in Developing Country Mortality

Trends: The End of an Era?", *Population and Development Review*, 6 (December); 615–44.

Hamilton, C. F. (1982), Memo from Command and Control Technical Center, Defense Communications Agency.

Holdgate, Martin W., Kassas, Mohammed and White, Gilbert F. (1982), *The World Environment, 1971–1982* (Dublin: Tycooly).

Kahn, Herman, and Schneider, Ernest (1981), "Globaloney 2000" *Policy Review*, Spring: 129–47.

Kumar, Joginden (1973), *Population and Land in World Agriculture* (Berkeley: University of California Press).

Mayr, Ernst (1982), *The Growth of Biological Thought: Diversity and Inheritance* (Cambridge, Mass.: Belknap Press of Harvard University Press).

Morawetz, David (1978), *Twenty-Five Years of Economic Development 1950–1975* (Baltimore: Johns Hopkins).

Myers, Norman (1979), *The Sinking Ark* (New York: Pergamon).

Myrdal, Gunnar (1975), *Against the Stream—Critical Essays on Economics* (New York: Vintage Books).

New York Times, 31 January 1983, 5.

Newsweek, 4 August 1980.

Simon, Julian L. (1981), "Global Confusion, 1980: A Hard Look at the Global 2000 Report," *Public Interest*, 62 (Winter): 3–21.

Time, 9 August 1980.

US Department of Commerce, Bureau of the Census (1977), *Social Indicators: 1976* (Washington, DC: US Government Printing Office).

US Department of the Interior, National Park Service (1944), *Information Relating to the National Park System*, 30 June.

Wall Street Journal, 15 September 1980, 32.

Wall Street Journal, 1 April 1983, 13.

Willson, Pete (1982), Memorandum, Alan Guttmacher Institute, 17 September.

5 The Truth About the Environment

Bjorn Lomborg

Ecology and economics should push in the same direction. After all, the "eco" part of each word derives from the Greek word for "home", and the protagonists of both claim to have humanity's welfare as their goal. Yet environmentalists and economists are often at loggerheads. For economists, the world seems to be getting better. For many environmentalists, it seems to be getting worse.

These environmentalists, led by such veterans as Paul Ehrlich of Stanford University, and Lester Brown of the Worldwatch Institute, have developed a sort of "litany" of four big environmental fears:

- Natural resources are running out.
- The population is ever growing, leaving less and less to eat.
- Species are becoming extinct in vast numbers: forests are disappearing and fish stocks are collapsing.
- The planet's air and water are becoming ever more polluted.

Human activity is thus defiling the earth, and humanity may end up killing itself in the process.

The trouble is, the evidence does not back up this litany. First, energy and other natural resources have become more abundant, not less so since the Club of Rome published "The Limits to Growth" in 1972. Second, more food is now produced per head of the world's population than at any time in history. Fewer people are starving. Third, although species are indeed becoming extinct, only about 0.7% of them are expected to disappear in the next 50 years, not 25–50%, as has so often been predicted. And finally, most forms of environmental pollution either appear to have been exaggerated, or are transient—associated with the early phases of industrialisation and therefore best cured not by restricting economic growth, but by accelerating it. One form of pollution—the release of greenhouse gases that causes global warming—does appear to be a long-term phenomenon, but its total impact is unlikely to pose a devastating problem for the future of humanity. A bigger problem may well turn out to be an inappropriate response to it.

From *The Economist*, 2001; online at <www.economist.com/science/displayStory.cfm?Story_ID= 718860>

Can Things Only Get Better?

Take these four points one by one. First, the exhaustion of natural resources. The early environmental movement worried that the mineral resources on which modern industry depends would run out. Clearly, there must be some limit to the amount of fossil fuels and metal ores that can be extracted from the earth: the planet, after all, has a finite mass. But that limit is far greater than many environmentalists would have people believe.

Reserves of natural resources have to be located, a process that costs money. That, not natural scarcity, is the main limit on their availability. However, known reserves of all fossil fuels, and of most commercially important metals, are now larger than they were when "The Limits to Growth" was published. In the case of oil, for example, reserves that could be extracted at reasonably competitive prices would keep the world economy running for about 150 years at present consumption rates. Add to that the fact that the price of solar energy has fallen by half in every decade for the past 30 years, and appears likely to continue to do so into the future, and energy shortages do not look like a serious threat either to the economy or to the environment.

The development for non-fuel resources has been similar. Cement, aluminium, iron, copper, gold, nitrogen and zinc account for more than 75% of global expenditure on raw materials. Despite an increase in consumption of these materials of between two- and ten-fold over the past 50 years, the number of years of available reserves has actually grown. Moreover, the increasing abundance is reflected in an ever-decreasing price: *The Economist*'s index of prices of industrial raw materials has dropped some 80% in inflation-adjusted terms since 1845.

Next, the population explosion is also turning out to be a bugaboo. In 1968, Dr Ehrlich predicted in his best selling book, "The Population Bomb", that "the battle to feed humanity is over. In the course of the 1970s the world will experience starvation of tragic proportions—hundreds of millions of people will starve to death."

That did not happen. Instead, according to the United Nations, agricultural production in the developing world has increased by 52% per person since 1961. The daily food intake in poor countries has increased from 1,932 calories, barely enough for survival, in 1961 to 2,650 calories in 1998, and is expected to rise to 3,020 by 2030. Likewise, the proportion of people in developing countries who are starving has dropped from 45% in 1949 to 18% today, and is expected to decline even further to 12% in 2010 and just 6% in 2030. Food, in other words, is becoming not scarcer but ever more abundant. This is reflected in its price. Since 1800 food prices have decreased by more than 90%, and in 2000, according to the World Bank, prices were lower than ever before.

Modern Malthus

Dr Ehrlich's prediction echoed that made 170 years earlier by Thomas Malthus. Malthus claimed that, if unchecked, human population would expand exponentially, while food production could increase only linearly, by bringing new land into cultivation. He was wrong. Population growth has turned out to have an internal check: as people grow richer and healthier, they have smaller families. Indeed, the growth rate of the human population reached its peak, of more than 2% a year, in the early 1960s. The rate of increase has been declining ever since. It is now 1.26%,

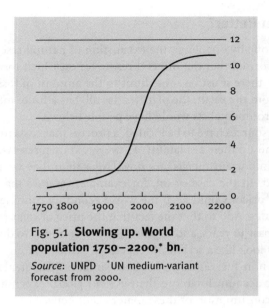

Fig. 5.1 Slowing up. World population 1750–2200,* bn.

Source: UNPD   *UN medium-variant forecast from 2000.

and is expected to fall to 0.46% in 2050. The United Nations estimates that most of the world's population growth will be over by 2100, with the population stabilising at just below 11 billion (see Figure 5.1).

Malthus also failed to take account of developments in agricultural technology. These have squeezed more and more food out of each hectare of land. It is this application of human ingenuity that has boosted food production, not merely in line with, but ahead of, population growth. It has also, incidentally, reduced the need to take new land into cultivation, thus reducing the pressure on biodiversity.

Third, that threat of biodiversity loss is real, but exaggerated. Most early estimates used simple island models that linked a loss in habitat with a loss of biodiversity. A rule-of-thumb indicated that loss of 90% of forest meant a 50% loss of species. As rainforests seemed to be cut at alarming rates, estimates of annual species loss of 20,000–100,000 abounded. Many people expected the number of species to fall by half globally within a generation or two.

However, the data simply does not bear out these predictions. In the eastern United States, forests were reduced over two centuries to fragments totalling just 1–2% of their original area, yet this resulted in the extinction of only one forest bird. In Puerto Rico, the primary forest area has been reduced over the past 400 years by 99%, yet "only" seven of 60 species of bird has become extinct. All but 12% of the Brazilian Atlantic rainforest was cleared in the 19th century, leaving only scattered fragments. According to the rule-of-thumb, half of all its species should have become extinct. Yet, when the World Conservation Union and the Brazilian Society of Zoology analysed all 291 known Atlantic forest animals, none could be declared extinct. Species, therefore, seem more resilient than expected. And tropical forests are not lost at annual rates

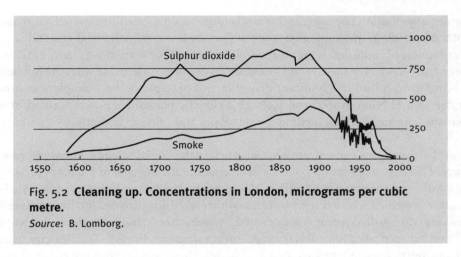

Fig. 5.2 Cleaning up. Concentrations in London, micrograms per cubic metre.
Source: B. Lomborg.

of 2–4%, as many environmentalists have claimed: the latest UN figures indicate a loss of less than 0.5%.

Fourth, pollution is also exaggerated. Many analyses show that air pollution diminishes when a society becomes rich enough to be able to afford to be concerned about the environment. For London, the city for which the best data are available, air pollution peaked around 1890 (see Figure 5.2). Today, the air is cleaner than it has been since 1585. There is good reason to believe that this general picture holds true for all developed countries. And, although air pollution is increasing in many developing countries, they are merely replicating the development of the industrialised countries. When they grow sufficiently rich they, too, will start to reduce their air pollution.

All this contradicts the litany. Yet opinion polls suggest that many people, in the rich world, at least, nurture the belief that environmental standards are declining. Four factors cause this disjunction between perception and reality.

Always Look on the Dark Side of Life

One is the lopsidedness built into scientific research. Scientific funding goes mainly to areas with many problems. That may be wise policy, but it will also create an impression that many more potential problems exist than is the case.

Secondly, environmental groups need to be noticed by the mass media. They also need to keep the money rolling in. Understandably, perhaps, they sometimes exaggerate. In 1997, for example, the Worldwide Fund for Nature issued a press release entitled, "Two-thirds of the world's forests lost forever". The truth turns out to be nearer 20%.

Though these groups are run overwhelmingly by selfless folk, they nevertheless share many of the characteristics of other lobby groups. That would matter less if people applied the same degree of scepticism to environmental lobbying as they do to lobby groups in other fields. A trade organisation arguing for, say, weaker pollution controls is instantly seen as self-interested.

Yet a green organisation opposing such a weakening is seen as altruistic, even if a dispassionate view of the controls in question might suggest they are doing more harm than good.

A third source of confusion is the attitude of the media. People are clearly more curious about bad news than good. Newspapers and broadcasters are there to provide what the public wants. That, however, can lead to significant distortions of perception. An example was America's encounter with El Niño in 1997 and 1998. This climatic phenomenon was accused of wrecking tourism, causing allergies, melting the ski-slopes and causing 22 deaths by dumping snow in Ohio.

A more balanced view comes from a recent article in the *Bulletin of the American Meteorological Society*. This tries to count up both the problems and the benefits of the 1997–98 Niño. The damage it did was estimated at $4 billion. However, the benefits amounted to some $19 billion. These came from higher winter temperatures (which saved an estimated 850 lives, reduced heating costs and diminished spring floods caused by meltwaters), and from the well-documented connection between past Niños and fewer Atlantic hurricanes. In 1998, America experienced no big Atlantic hurricanes and thus avoided huge losses. These benefits were not reported as widely as the losses.

The fourth factor is poor individual perception. People worry that the endless rise in the amount of stuff everyone throws away will cause the world to run out of places to dispose of waste. Yet, even if America's trash output continues to rise as it has done in the past, and even if the American population doubles by 2100, all the rubbish America produces through the entire 21st century will still take up only the area of a square, each of whose sides measures 28km (18 miles). That is just one-12,000th of the area of the entire United States.

Ignorance matters only when it leads to faulty judgments. But fear of largely imaginary environmental problems can divert political energy from dealing with real ones. The table below (5.1), showing the cost in the United States of various measures to save a year of a person's life, illustrates

Table 5.1 **The price of a life. Cost of saving one year of one person's life (1993$)**

Passing laws to make seat-belt use mandatory	69
Sickle-cell anaemia screening for black new-borns	240
Mammography for women aged 50	810
Pneumonia vaccination for people aged over 65	2,000
Giving advice on stopping smoking to people who smoke more than one packet a day	9,800
Putting men aged 30 on a low-cholesterol diet	19,000
Regular leisure-time physical activity, such as jogging for men aged 35	38,000
Making pedestrians and cyclists more visible	73,000
Installing air-bags (rather than manual lap belts) in cars	120,000
Installing arsenic emission-control at glass-manufacturing plants	51,000,000
Setting radiation emission standards for nuclear-power plants	180,000,000
Installing benzene emission control at rubber-tyre manufacturing plants	20,000,000,000

Source: T. Tengs et al., *Risk Analysis*, June 1995

the danger. Some environmental policies, such as reducing lead in petrol and sulphur-dioxide emissions from fuel oil, are very cost-effective. But many of these are already in place. Most environmental measures are less cost-effective than interventions aimed at improving safety (such as installing air-bags in cars) and those involving medical screening and vaccination. Some are absurdly expensive.

Yet a false perception of risk may be about to lead to errors more expensive even than controlling the emission of benzene at tyre plants. Carbon-dioxide emissions are causing the planet to warm. The best estimates are that the temperature will rise by some 2°–3°C in this century, causing considerable problems, almost exclusively in the developing world, at a total cost of $5,000 billion. Getting rid of global warming would thus seem to be a good idea. The question is whether the cure will actually be more costly than the ailment.

Despite the intuition that something drastic needs to be done about such a costly problem, economic analyses clearly show that it will be far more expensive to cut carbon-dioxide emissions radically than to pay the costs of adaptation to the increased temperatures. The effect of the Kyoto Protocol on the climate would be minuscule, even if it were implemented in full. A model by Tom Wigley, one of the main authors of the reports of the UN Climate Change Panel, shows how an expected temperature increase of 2.1°C in 2100 would be diminished by the treaty to an increase of 1.9°C instead. Or, to put it another way, the temperature increase that the planet would have experienced in 2094 would be postponed to 2100.

So the Kyoto agreement does not prevent global warming, but merely buys the world six years. Yet, the cost of Kyoto, for the United States alone, will be higher than the cost of solving the world's single most pressing health problem: providing universal access to clean drinking water and sanitation. Such measures would avoid 2m deaths every year, and prevent half a billion people from becoming seriously ill.

And that is the best case. If the treaty were implemented inefficiently, the cost of Kyoto could approach $1 trillion, or more than five times the cost of worldwide water and sanitation coverage. For comparison, the total global-aid budget today is about $50 billion a year.

To replace the litany with facts is crucial if people want to make the best possible decisions for the future. Of course, rational environmental management and environmental investment are good ideas—but the costs and benefits of such investments should be compared to those of similar investments in all the other important areas of human endeavour. It may be costly to be overly optimistic—but more costly still to be too pessimistic.

6 Ten Pinches of Salt: A Reply to Bjorn Lomborg

Tom Burke

Introduction: Ten Pinches of Salt

'The Sceptical Environmentalist', by Professor Bjorn Lomborg, is published by the Cambridge University Press this week. Professor Lomborg is a statistician and political scientist and, by his own assertion, an environmentalist.

The book has received widespread advance notice in the press—a half page article in the Observer; an invited essay in the Economist; a series of three articles by the author in the Guardian and additional articles in both the Evening Standard and the New York Times.

Professor Lomborg's argument is that 'environmentalists' are responsible for creating a widely held illusion that the 'environment is in poor shape here on Earth.' They have accomplished this result by the repetition of a series of false propositions he calls 'the Litany'. He sets out the Litany on page four:

The population is ever growing, leaving less and less to eat. The air and water are becoming ever more polluted. The planet's species are becoming extinct in vast numbers—we kill off more than 40,000 each year. The forests are disappearing, fish stocks are collapsing and the coral reefs are dying.

We are defiling our Earth, the fertile topsoil is disappearing, we are paving over nature, destroying the wilderness, decimating the biosphere, and will end up killing ourselves in the process. The world's ecosystem is breaking down. We are fast approaching the absolute limits of viability, and the limits to growth are becoming apparent.

The repetition of this Litany combines with four other factors to cause 'a disjunction between perception and reality'. These four factors are: lopsided scientific research; the need of environmental groups to generate funds; the media's preoccupation with bad news and 'poor individual perception'. Taken together, the Litany and these four factors lead to 'faulty judgements' in the allocation of resources, the most significant example of which, as least as judged by page length, is climate change.

In the Professor's view these 'environmental exaggerations' make us 'scared ... and more likely to spend our resources and attention solving phantom problems while ignoring real and pressing (possibly non-environmental) issues.'

Critique of Lomborg; online at <www.green-alliance.org.uk/Documents/Reports/ten%20pinches%20of%20salt.pdf>

This briefing offers ten considerations, the 'pinches of salt', to bear in mind as you read the 352 pages and 2,930 footnotes.

1. Professor Invents Caricature

No major environmental organisation anywhere in the world subscribes to the views outlined in Professor Lomborg's Litany. This might explain why the references used to support this assertion come from two magazines and a pair of science fiction writers. Science fiction writers and magazine editors are, of course, entitled to their opinions and are fair game for criticism, but they can hardly be taken to be representative of an environmental community with some tens of millions of professional and volunteer members and a vast array of informational outputs—outputs that could readily have been surveyed to discover what today's 'environmentalists' actually think. As a statistician, Professor Lomborg has the skills to have done so.

What is an influential idea within the environmental community is the idea that there are limits to the extent to which we can degrade biological systems and still go on benefiting from the goods and services they offer. There is a wide consensus, not just within the environmental community, but also within governments and inter-governmental organisations, that the ecological foundations of the economy are being degraded in an increasing number of places, beyond the point at which it is economically or biologically possible to replace that lost productivity with inputs of fossil fuels or non-fossil minerals. This is why 124 nations agreed in Rio de Janeiro in 1992 that the world must make a transition to sustainable development.

It may be that Professor Lomborg, like many other propagandists, has exaggerated for effect. This is a much used literary device and is, generally, well understood by most readers. But its use is, to say the least, somewhat odd in a book that rounds quite so aggressively on others for deploying the same device.

2. Unoccupied Position Successfully Stormed

Professor Lomborg devotes 13 pages to demonstrating that 'we are not having an energy crisis'. He is right. It is true that we are not having an energy crisis. What is not true is that 'environmentalists' think that we are having an energy crisis. To support his belief that an energy crisis is part of the Litany, the Professor cites a CNN report and a magazine called E magazine. He does not cite an environmental organisation or even a leading environmental personality as believing in an energy resource crisis, for the simple reason that none do. Professor Lomborg has waged a powerful attack on a position that no serious person in the environmental world holds. His success is guaranteed, but his purpose is a mystery.

There was a period in the early 1970s when many environmentalists did believe in an energy resource crisis, but they were hardly alone. Just about every government, business and media outlet in the world also believed that we would soon run out of oil. It was actually leading environmental thinkers who led the counter-challenge, arguing persuasively that we had all the energy resources we could ever need, but we were not using the right technologies to convert them into services useful to people. This case was first set out by Amory Lovins in his book, 'Soft

Energy Paths', published when Professor Lomborg was 11 years old. It was derided at the time for proposing that energy efficiency improvements and technology changes would reduce global demand for fossil fuels well below what was then projected. Global primary energy demand only reached his 'soft path' level in the year 2000.

The only people that have argued strongly that there is an energy resource crisis of any kind in recent times have been the President and Vice-President of the United States and their allies. Opinion polls suggest that they have not yet managed to persuade their fellow Americans that they are correct. The current evidence from the movement of key prices is that the American people are right.

3. Dead Dragon Slain—Again!

Environmentalists do not believe that 'natural resources are running out'. There has been no such unqualified statement from major environmental organisations individually or collectively, nor, as far as I can recall in any influential environmental book or journal, in the past twenty years. The Club of Rome did make this argument in 1972, and did indeed attract considerable attention to it for a few years. But even they had begun to modulate this position by 1974. Paul Erlich did make, and lose, his famous wager with Julian Simon. This tells you that whilst Erlich knew a lot about ecology he knew somewhat less about economics, a fault he has in common with much of the human race. It is hard to see what is gained in 2001 by resurrecting a long dead argument only to kill it all over again.

It is a common mistake, often made by environmentalists, to argue too quickly from the particular to the general. In so far as there is any concern with things 'running out' in the contemporary discussion of environmental and resource issues, it is biological not mineral resources that are in focus. The term 'natural resources' does of course cover both, but it is clear from the author's claim that 'energy and other natural resources have become more abundant', and from the other evidence he cites in his book, that what he actually has in mind are mineral resources.

Were Professor Lomborg a natural scientist he would understand that it is either ignorant or a sloppy exaggeration to claim that even these resources have become 'more abundant', when what he really means is that our knowledge of the availability of such resources in the earth's crust, and our technological ability to gain access to them, have grown. It is inconsistent to accuse others of lack of rigour and then to be quite so cavalier with the laws of conservation of mass and energy.

4. Did He Say *That?*

Professor Lomborg focuses his most excoriating criticisms on the publications of the Worldwatch Institute, and in particular on the views of its former President, Lester Brown. He identifies Mr Brown, and Professor Paul Erlich, a Stanford University ecologist, as the high priesthood of environmental doom. It is they who 'keep on telling us that food production is going down the tubes'. Professor Erlich did predict in his book 'The Population Bomb', published 23 years

ago, that 'In the course of the 1970s the world will experience starvation of tragic proportions—hundreds of millions of people will starve to death'. He was, as we all too often witnessed
from the comfort of our living rooms, right. They did starve—though it might be difficult to
give an exact count of how many millions actually died from hunger or hunger related disease
since accurate record keeping was hardly a high priority at the time. But I cannot recall, and
Professor Lomborg does not cite, another occasion on which he made this prediction.

Lester Brown did write in 1965 that 'the food problem emerging in the less developing regions
maybe one of the most nearly insoluble problems facing man over the next few decades.' This
is, indeed, an argument he has consistently advanced in subsequent years. And he, too, was
right—it has been a nearly insoluble problem. In 1974, Henry Kissinger promised the World
Food Conference that by 1984 no-one would go to bed hungry. In 1996, governments at the
World Food Summit in Rome cut this target in half, and doubled the time it would take to reach
it. Three years later it was agreed that even this goal was unlikely to be achieved.

Professor Lomborg rightly points out that food production has greatly increased and the
proportion of people starving has gone down, but the absolute number of people starving has
remained almost constant because of population growth. Brown's actual point is that there are
now growing signs that the world may not be able in future to sustain such a high rate of growth
in food production. In this context, Professor Lomborg's argument that Brown only looks at
short term trends is irrelevant. What is at issue is whether the long term trend, which Brown
has frequently recognised, will continue or not. Brown and Lomborg disagree, but this is a
legitimate difference of interpretation of the facts, not a conspiracy to mislead. In any case, most
of Brown's key data sets cover four decades, raising the interesting question of when exactly a
short term trend becomes long term.

The notion that there is anything resembling a real world price for grain, containing significant
information about the availability of food supplies to those who need them, in a market place as
distorted as that for food commodities, is simply naive. Furthermore, as has often been pointed
out, most people starve not because there is no food, but because they have no money.

5. Simon Says

Professor Lomborg's penchant for shooting sharp statistical arrows at the wrong targets is most
strikingly evident in his chapter on wastes. If you are not careful, you could miss this discussion
of one of the most widely-researched environmental issues—it covers all of three and a half
pages, precisely one per cent, of the volume. Nevertheless, it is revealing—though more about
Professor Lomborg than about the environment. His dismissal of the issue leans heavily on data
from his mentor, Julian Simon, to show that US production of waste has only increased 45 per
cent over the past four decades but, since US population has also increased, this only amounts
to a 13 per cent per capita increase—so we need not worry about finding space to put it all.

In a series of dazzling calculations, Professor Lomborg goes on to demonstrate that all of
America's municipal waste for the whole of the 21st century would fit into an 18 mile square, 100
feet high. This, we are informed, would occupy just 26 per cent of the land area of Woodward
County in the state of Oklahoma, which would be less than 0.5 per cent of the state's area and

a mere 0.009 per cent of the area of the 'entire US landmass.' Woodward County may be an entirely suitable site for a landfill for the whole of the US, though the logistical problems do appear daunting, but so what?

Lomborg fails to mention of toxic or hazardous wastes, nothing is said about industrial wastes or the problems of large volume wastes from the mining industry. Radioactive wastes do not get a mention, nor do agricultural wastes. The rest of the world seems to have no waste management problems at all, for all the attention they get. The environmental critique of waste management policies has been primarily about the wastage of resources that go into producing such large volumes of municipal wastes, and the nature of many of our industrial wastes and their impact on the environment and, in the case of radioactive wastes, human health for millennia to come.

Finding enough space is a secondary issue—it has been largely local government officials who have worried about finding space to put municipal waste. This may explain why the environmental authorities Professor Lomborg finds to cite as his source for this spatial anxiety are our two science fiction writers and a casual reference by Al Gore, another favourite in the Lomborg green demonology.

6. 'Let Them Eat Cake'

Professor Lomborg boldly announces in his Economist essay that 'pollution also is exaggerated'. His argument on pollution is again guilty of many of the very same faults he is decrying in environmentalists. He is correct to point out that air quality has improved greatly in London—this was hardly a secret—though, given his views elsewhere on the difficulties of modelling atmospheric dynamics, it is hard to see how he can come so confidently to the conclusion that it is better than at any time since 1585, on the basis of one model. The rest of his argument relies heavily on US experience, focuses on a limited range of pollutants and contains the following extraordinary, and unsubstantiated sentence: 'Of course there are many other substances we could also have investigated, such as VOCs, dioxins and heavy metals, but for one thing, far fewer data are available on these, and for another, they probably pose less of a danger to human beings.'

No one contests that emissions of sulphur dioxide and some other pollutants have declined in the developed world in recent years. But, as the current debates in the US make clear, these declines in emissions still leave a very great many cities and tens of millions of people with air quality that does not meet legal standards, especially with regard to particulates and aromatic hydrocarbons. This picture that is repeated in the EU, where some 70–80 per cent of the 105 cities with populations of more than 500,000 people have air pollution that exceeds WHO standards for one or more pollutants. Such progress as has been made would not have occurred without the powerful and sustained intervention of the environmentalists he attacks.

Air pollution in the rest of the world, where two thirds of humanity live, need not be considered, in Professor Lomborg's view, because this will cease automatically as they get richer. This confuses cause and correlation, not a mistake you would expect from a statistician. Although national wealth and the state of a nation's environment are observably associated to some extent, the relationships are complex and not at all well understood. To set this somewhat callow opinion in context, it is worth considering the following comment about the Asia-Pacific region: 'Environmental degradation in the region is pervasive, accelerating, and unabated. At risk are people's health and livelihoods, the survival of species and ecosystem services that are the basis for long-term economic development. Economic development and poverty reduction are increasingly constrained by environmental concerns, including degradation of forestry and fisheries, scarcity of freshwater, and poor human health as a result of air and water pollution.'

The irresponsible, environmental exaggerator making this judgement is the Asian Development Bank, and the judgement was published this year, not thirty years ago. The thrust of the argument is that the people of the Asia-Pacific region may never get 'sufficiently rich' for their pollution to be reduced by Professor Lomborg's micawberish optimism. The alternative to the apocalypse school of environmentalism appears to be that of Marie Antoinette.

7. 'Lies, Damned Lies and Statistics'

Forests are another area in which Professor Lomborg has no fear of wielding his sturdy statistical sword. His confidence stems in part from his belief in the efficacy of 'official sources'. As he points out, 'the most important thing is that there is no doubt about the credibility of my sources. For this reason. . . most of the statistics come from official sources, which are widely accepted by the majority of people involved in the environmental debate.' Having witnessed the blatant efforts of a succession of British governments to massage the unemployment figures by changing the basis on which they were calculated, you might be forgiven for being sceptical about the wisdom of such reliance. Furthermore, it is hardly a secret that most international agencies simply report the numbers that national governments report to them without any right, let alone capacity, to challenge their veracity. Only very recently, with the advent of satellite monitoring, has it become possible to provide an independent check on some geographical data.

This makes a comparison of past estimates of forest cover, with a very high degree of unreliability, difficult to compare with much more reliable current estimates. Improved data quality is to be welcomed but it provides no justification for Professor Lomborg's accusation that some, perhaps most, environmentalists have deliberately misled the public. Simply having a better set of geographical data still leaves open a huge realm within which judgements may legitimately differ.

One reason it is so notoriously difficult to estimate the area of tropical forest is because there is a very wide range of different types of forest that are classified as 'tropical', and not all classifiers agree on what should and should not be counted. Furthermore, there is no agreed definition of what counts as 'loss', although here again there is a very vigorous technical debate on the subject. In these circumstances, it is difficult to attach much significance to a dispute over the difference in the estimate of 1.95 per cent, as it is likely that the whole argument falls well within the current bounds of error.

Furthermore, argument about the amount of forest is far less important than argument about the quality of forest. Covering Kalimantan with palm oil plantations may leave you with no net loss of forest cover, but what you have now is not what you had before, from the point of view of either biodiversity or of the people who depend on the forest for their livelihood.

8. 'Kill Not the Moth nor Butterfly . . .'

One of the more emotional issues in the environmental debate is that surrounding the loss of species. The advent of television, perhaps more than anything else, has generated a huge public awareness of, and concern for, the fate of the so-called charismatic species such as tigers, pandas and whales. Not that a concern for the fate of our fellow creatures is a new phenomenon. It is powerfully captured in literature by William Blake's poem 'Auguries of Innocence', from which the quote in the title is taken. The scientific debate on biodiversity, however, devotes itself to somewhat more prosaic and less well known species such as insects or amphibians.

There is a wholly unresolved scientific debate about how many living species there actually are, and over the rate at which we are losing species. Estimates vary widely. Professor Lomborg is particularly scathing about the estimate of losses of 40,000 species a year, made by Norman Myers in a book published 22 years ago. Other estimates have actually been larger. E.O. Wilson, widely regarded as the intellectual founder of modern ecological science, estimated that it might be between 27,000 and 100,000 species a year. Paul Erlich, whose professional discipline is ecology, estimated that it might be as many as 250,000.

Mathematical modelling of species dynamics is, to be generous, primitive. This is largely because, contrary to one of Professor Lomborg's other assertions, there are a very great many problems that have failed to attract large sums of either public or private research funds. Among the most important of those are precisely those to do with research on ecosystem quality and viability—research that would allow more reliable estimates of the ecological consequences of human activities. Clearly, biodiversity policy would be much more soundly based if we know more than we do currently. But where the best is not to hand, we must do the best we can.

In these circumstances, Professor Lomborg is perfectly entitled to choose to believe the work of some rather less well known ecologists who estimate much lower rates of extinction. What he is not entitled to do, in a book that is separating reality from myth, is to fail to explain why, in his judgement, these estimates are so much better, other than that they are later, and perhaps more importantly for him, smaller.

9. Cool Views

On climate change, Professor Lomborg is arguing beyond the boundaries of his professional competence, despite having increased the number of pages devoted to the issue from the original 33 in the Danish edition to the current 66. Of the 66 pages, almost two-thirds are devoted to an extended rehearsal of the widely recognised scientific difficulties of forecasting the future climate, and the possible impacts of climate change on the human environment. Yet the scientists involved in the Intergovernmental Panel on Climate Change (IPCC) process have made no attempt to duck the fact that, on many of the most urgent issues, there are only uncertain answers.

This, too, is a normal part of the human condition, and one that we are well used to dealing with. We do not postpone major economic decisions simply because economists disagree and economic models produce results that are uncertain. In these instances, judgement must be exercised—and democracy is the process by which we choose who should make those judgements. As Winston Churchill pointed out, this is a far from reliable method, it is just better than all the others. Lomborg's recitation of the science identifies in a clear and accessible way all the points where his judgement differs from that of the majority of the climate scientists in the IPCC process. He is entitled to his opinion; we are entitled to wonder about its authority.

Where he is not on such firm ground is in making the assertion that 'economic analyses clearly show that it will be far more expensive to cut carbondioxide emissions radically than to pay the costs of adaptation to the increased temperatures'. The state of knowledge of the impacts of climate change, as has been often pointed out by many of the critics of the IPCC, is currently so low that no-one is in a position to make a reliable estimate of the costs, either of the temperature rises or of any adaptations that might be made to those rises. Calculating the true costs of things in the past is very difficult, as William Nordhaus pointed out in a widely read essay in The Economist. Doing so into the future is even more so.

Furthermore, the whole art of economic modelling is, as yet, so immature as to make such estimates relatively useless as a guide to public policy. A World Resources Institute study, for example, found that different modellers using different assumptions, estimated the impact of tackling climate change on the US economy as ranging from +3% of GDP to −7%. It is often overlooked that, for all their well documented difficulties, models of the climate are like Rolls-Royces when compared to those of the economy. Interestingly, Lomborg's entire economic argument relies heavily on the outputs of an economic model developed by the same William Nordhaus who pointed out how difficult it was to estimate costs that had occurred in the past. His work has been widely criticised in the technical literature for exaggerating the costs and ignoring the benefits of acting on climate change—something Lomborg omits to mention—and which was pointed out to Professor Lomborg by his Danish colleagues some time ago. It is inconsistent to fail to apply the same test of intellectual rigour to one part of an argument but not to another.

The most egregious element of Professor Lomborg's climate change argument is the proposition that the world faces a choice between spending money on mitigating climate change and providing clean access to clean drinking water and sanitation. We must and can do both, and indeed, that is exactly where the world's environmental community actually stands. Such artificial choices may be possible in an academic ivory tower, where ideas can be arranged to suit the prejudices of the occupant, but they are not available in the real world.

10. First Stone Thrown?

The paradox of Professor Lomborg's book is that in making the case for a more rational debate on the environment, he has committed all of the offences for which he attacks environmentalists. He exaggerates for effect, substitutes forceful assertion for weight of argument, sometimes makes sweeping generalisations from particular instances, presents false choices and is somewhat select-ive in his use of evidence and quotation. These are the familiar features of all polemics—they are only illegitimate in scholarship.

All that renders this book dishonest is only its claim to tell you the real truth about the state of the world—its pretence to scholarship. Were it presented more directly as a forthright expression of the author's opinions—which is what it is—it would be a more valuable contribution. There is undoubtedly too much sanctimony, self-righteousness and, indeed, self-satisfaction within the environmental community. Disagreement and debate are an essential feature of democracy which withers their absence. Unchallenged ideas eventually become tired and irrelevant.

It is undoubtedly true that there is a large gap between perception and reality within the public at large. This is not a new or previously unremarked phenomenon, and it is certainly not confined to the environment. This does often lead to a considerable wastage of financial resources when compared to some idealised optimum. We could solve this problem, and many others, if we could first find a way to invent better people and then persuade them to conform their behaviour more closely with the dictates of economic rationality. Unfortunately, we are stuck with the people we have got and we must stick with them.

It is also true that some environmentalists exploit, sometimes aggressively, the gap between perceptions and reality, playing on people's fears in order to generate headlines and revenues. In doing so, they are primarily following an example set by, and deploying techniques developed by, the business community and by those in the political world seeking office: when did you last see a tiger get out of a petrol tank, and just how big was the famous Kennedy missile gap? It would be better if we lived in a world with a more rational and judicious realm of public discourse. Were Professor Lomborg's book a contribution to building that world, there would be little to quarrel with him about.

The idea that the environmental community has collaborated in some implicit conspiracy with the mass media to gull most people into to thinking the environment is in a much worse state than it actually is, is not convincing. There is indeed a litany, and it is a litany of tragedy. It reads DDT, Bhopal, Torrey Canyon, thalidomide, CFCs, Seveso, Flixborough, Minimata, Exxon Valdez, Love Canal, Chernobyl. These are not words that people have written, but events that have happened. These events, and many more, were brought to the public's attention by the carelessness or ignorance of businesses and governments, not by environmentalists. In my thirty years as an environmentalist I have never, to my regret, had as much influence on public opinion. Journalists and environmentalists, and professors too, spend more time riding waves than making them.

PART TWO

REFORMIST RESPONSES

The survivalists and Prometheans surveyed in Part One have generated plenty of heat and perhaps some light, but not a great deal in the way of public policy or political reform. In Part Two we turn to less obviously apocalyptic pronouncements that relate more closely to the real world of environmental politics and policy-making as it has unfolded in recent decades. That world features attempts to extend the capacities of both the administrative state and liberal democracy in an environmental direction.

Section III: Administrative Rationalism

Environmental problems arise in human dealings with ecological systems. Ecological systems are complex; so are human social systems. One should therefore expect environmental problems to be doubly complex. Complex problems demand the application of expertise, be it in ecology, engineering, economics, biochemistry, climatology, nuclear physics, epidemiology, or hydrology. The most established way to put expertise to use in the service of solving complex problems, concerning the environment no less than elsewhere, is to organize experts into administrative bureaucracies. Aside from specialists with the relevant substantive expertise, such bureaucracies contain experts in management, whose specialization is converting general statements of policy principle (in favour of, say, pollution reduction, or wilderness preservation) into specific actions on the ground (say anti-pollution regulations). Along the way these managers will need to harness the appropriate substantive knowledge. Such an arrangement, according to the German sociologist Max Weber (writing in the early twentieth century), constitutes the pinnacle of rationality in collective human problem-solving. Today's world is well populated by Weberian bureaucracies. Until around 1970 these were few and small in the environmental area. But the wave of environmental concern that engulfed the developed world in the late 1960s soon produced a wide range of such bureaucracies: environmental protection agencies, ministries and departments of the environment, expert advisory commissions, and so forth. Indeed, the repertoire of institutional responses to environmental crisis in that era was remarkably similar in different countries. The character of those responses was essentially administrative, and their legacy remains.

Now, very few people actually claim to like bureaucracy, least of all the people who operate it. The fact that there is a lot of it about, notwithstanding this general dislike, is testimony perhaps to the truth of Weber's opinion concerning its problem-solving effectiveness. But what of the effectiveness of such administrative mechanisms in the environmental area? Can bureaucracies be made to operate in environmentally benign fashion? Our selections by Robert V. Bartlett and Kai N. Lee suggest that they can, though in quite different ways. Bartlett argues that the main function of one particular landmark piece of legislation—the United States National Environmental Policy Act of 1970—has been to insinuate environmental values into the entire range of agencies of the US federal government and their operations. In so doing, he believes that the Act has advanced the cause of ecological rationality in government, acting as a counterweight to more established economic and political rationality.

While Bartlett believes that environmental laws can change the way bureaucrats think, Lee's emphasis is more structural, entailing the redesign of bureaucracies themselves. To fit ecological specifications, administrative processes need to involve adaptive management, open to learning from both natural processes and political pressures from the people living in or concerned with an ecosystem.

Charles Sabel, Archon Fung, and Bradley Karkkainen depart still further from the Weberian ideal. They want to open environmental administration into flexible and cooperative relationships with stakeholders and communities in what they call 'rolling rule regulation', elements of which can now be found in the United States. Mary O'Brien is equally critical of narrow administrative rationalism, in her case when it comes to administrators who apply technocratic methods such as risk assessment. She argues for a more participatory process that assesses policy options from a variety of perspectives, with a full range of social and environmental concerns in mind.

Further Reading

Herbert Kaufman's *The Forest Ranger* (1960) is an early classic in how individuals working in resource management bureaucracies can assimilate a common set of professional values. Samuel Hays, in *Beauty, Health, and Permanence: Environmental Politics in the United States, 1955–1985* (1987), chronicles the subsequent rise of the 'environmental professional'. An elaboration of Kai Lee's work on ecosystem management, social learning, and civic science can be found in his *Compass and Gyroscope: Integrating Science and Politics for the Environment* (1993), with a case study of the Columbia River Basin. Bruce A. Ackerman and William T. Hassler, in *Clean Coal, Dirty Air* (1981), offer an entertaining cautionary tale of what can happen when environmental bureaucracies do become overly politicized, and argue for more autonomous expert agencies insulated from direct political control. Steven Yaffee's *The Wisdom of the Spotted Owl* (1994) examines politicization in the US Forest Service, and how it hampered objective evaluations of the state of an endangered species in the Pacific Northwest. Walter Rosenbaum, in *Environmental Politics and Policy* (1985), offers another American perspective on the consolidation and strengthening of autonomous administrative agencies in the environmental area. Timothy Doyle and Aynsley Kellow, in *Environmental Politics and Policy Making in Australia* (1995), have similar hopes for Australia. A good critical collection on the limits of environmental administration is Robert Paehlke and Douglas Torgerson, eds., *Managing Leviathan II: Environmental Politics and the Administrative State* (2004). Many of the limitations of administration as they appear in the 'old' (i.e., 1970s) politics of pollution are exposed in Albert Weale's *The New Politics of Pollution* (1992), which has a more European flavour. Another good comparative study is David Vogel's *National Styles of Regulation: Environmental Policy in Great Britain and the United States* (1986). John Braithwaite and Peter Drahos, in *Global Business Regulation* (2000), show how regulation can be practised in the international system—though in creative ways that move beyond administrative bureaucracies. Martin Jänicke and Helmut Weidner, eds., *National Environmental Policies* (1996), develops the idea that the key to policy success is building 'capacity'—including administrative capacity.

7 Rationality and the Logic of the National Environmental Policy Act

Robert V. Bartlett

Ideals pass into great historic forces by embodying themselves in institutions.
(Rashdall 1936)

Science is a multifaceted field of inquiry which in many of its aspects is involved with the procedures that have become known as environmental impact analysis and assessment (EIA). The idea behind the information gathering, analysis, and synthesis activities that constitute EIA originated with the National Environmental Policy Act of 1969 (NEPA).[1] The rationale underlying NEPA has never been easily explained, although many have tried. The legislation was itself influenced by scientific concepts, particularly ecology and systems theory, and reflected the intent of its authors that science be used as an integral tool in developing and administering a national policy for the environment. NEPA, however, is more than a law that uses science in a complex and interesting way. NEPA was a policy Act written in such a manner that its implementation would depend not on establishment of a new agency, nor on the continuing interest of a chief executive, nor on the goodwill of disparate bureaucracies. Implicit in NEPA and its science aspects is a form of rationality relatively new to government and having significance beyond the more obvious features of the Act.

Science and the Legislative Intent of NEPA

Although a casual reading of this brief law would reveal only three instances of the word "science" or its derivatives, science nevertheless is pervasive in nearly every section of NEPA, reflecting the significant influences that the environmental sciences had in the genesis of the Act (Caldwell 1982). Scientific concepts are implicit, for example, in NEPA's statement of purpose:

To declare a national policy which will encourage productive and enjoyable harmony between man and his environment; to promote efforts which will prevent or eliminate damage to the environment and bio-sphere and stimulate the health and welfare of man; to enrich the understanding of the ecological systems and natural resources important to the Nation; and to establish a Council on Environmental Quality.

The principal link provided by NEPA between science and administrative decisionmaking is Section 102(2)(C). Unquestionably the best-known provision of NEPA, Section 102(2)(C)

From *The Environmental Professional*, 8 (1986), 105–11. Reprinted by permission of Blackwell Science, Inc.

institutionalized environmental impact analysis by requiring preparation of environmental impact statements (EISs) for federal agency actions significantly affecting the human environment. The specified content of these "detailed statements" obviously necessitated recourse to science; otherwise, the required discussions of "environmental impact," "irreversible and irretrievable commitments of resources," and "the relationship between local short-term uses of man's environment and the maintenance and enhancement of long-term productivity" could be little more than collections of empty phrases.

Section 102(2)(C) was added to NEPA relatively late in the legislative process, although after much deliberation, expressly to provide an "action-forcing" mechanism for the Act (Finn 1972; Andrews 1976; Liroff 1976; Caldwell 1978; Dreyfus and Ingram 1976). Because of the significant political and economic ramifications of this procedural provision, and the significant bureaucratic reforms that it required, it is not surprising that subsequent attention focused overwhelmingly on the environmental impact statement, to the neglect of the more substantive policies enunciated in the legislation.

The EIS indeed forced action, but the action to be taken was described elsewhere in NEPA, a fact often lost on many who somehow saw the EIS as an end in itself and NEPA as essentially a procedural Act. The EIS requirement could only be understood and appropriately implemented if interpreted within the context of the rest of NEPA, a point officially acknowledged in 1978 with issuance, under presidential executive order, of the first regulations for implementing NEPA.[2] These regulations, promulgated by the Council on Environmental Quality (CEQ), emphasized and reinforced the science-dependent components of the Act.

The influence of scientific ideas can be easily discerned throughout Title I of NEPA, which constitutes the declaration of national policy with provisions for implementation. The impact of human activity on the interrelations of all components of the natural environment is recognized, as is the importance of restoring and maintaining environmental quality for the overall welfare and development of man. Six precepts are provided in Section 101(b) as guides to future action: (1) each generation as trustee of the environment for succeeding generations (drawing from and depending upon the sciences with a distant time horizon); (2) assurance of safe, healthful, productive, and aesthetically and culturally pleasing surroundings (necessitating reliance on a broad range of sciences and technical knowledge, particularly the biological, social, and behavioral sciences and the environmental design arts); (3) attainment of the widest range of beneficial uses of the environment without undesirable and unintended consequences (requiring the capacity to ascertain limits and to adequately predict the consequences of complex actions); (4) preservation of important historic, cultural, and natural aspects of the national heritage and maintenance of an environment supporting diversity and variety of individual choice (using knowledge and methodologies from archeology, cultural anthropology, cultural history, geography, and ecology); (5) achievement of a balance between population and resource use permitting high living standards and wide sharing of life's amenities (possible only with knowledge from ecology, economics, geography, sociology, agronomy, geology, and numerous other sciences); and (6) enhancement of the quality of renewable resources and maximum recycling of depletable resources (requiring application of a developed materials science, resource economics, recycling engineering, and environmental management science). In short, this part of the Act provides goals or directions that derive from the sciences and demand the advancement and application of a broad range of scientific and technical knowledge.

Section 102, which follows, contains more than the EIS requirement. Section 102(2)(A) is pivotal: it directs that all agencies of the federal government shall "utilize a systematic, interdisciplinary approach which will insure the integrated use of the natural and social sciences and the environmental design arts in planning and in decisionmaking which may have an impact on man's environment." In other provisions of significance, federal agencies are directed to: (B) "identify and develop methods and procedures . . . which will insure that presently unquantified environmental amenities and values may be given appropriate consideration in decision-making along with economic and technical considerations"; (F) "lend appropriate support to initiatives, resolutions, and programs designed to maximize international cooperation in anticipating and preventing a decline in the quality of mankind's world environment"; and (H) "initiate and utilize ecological information in the planning and development of resource oriented projects."

Title II, establishing the Council on Environmental Quality, reflects the intent of Congress to assure the adequacy of science for the policies it sought to declare and implement through Title I.[3] Clearly, science and science-related concepts were crucial in the development of NEPA and were embodied in the text; moreover, the logic of the Act meant that science would necessarily be indispensable in the implementation of both the substantive policy provisions and the mandated procedural requirements. NEPA unmistakably implies the use of science through its use of such surrogate terms as information, plant and animal systems, studies, surveys, research, and analyses, none of which would have meaning within the context of the Act unless backed by scientific content and methodology. Thus, beyond the explicit statement of intent in Section 102(2)(A), one effect of NEPA has been to revise and extend the ways in which the federal agencies are required to use science in their decision processes.

NEPA and Decisionmaking

Intended by its designers to force action to achieve greater rationality in governmental decisionmaking, NEPA constitutes a far-reaching attempt to influence decisions—and thus to alter the substantive outcomes of government activities—by changing the rules and premises for arriving at legitimate decisions. Federal agencies were henceforth required to undertake a particular kind of analysis, to incorporate this analysis into regular decision processes, and to make public a justiciable document (the EIS) demonstrating compliance. In essence, the EIS requirement was expected to lead to at least partial accomplishment of the general policy goals specified in NEPA by institutionalizing a kind of mandatory, continuing, systematic, integrated, science-based policy analysis, henceforth to be undertaken before a final decision was reached on any proposed action that would significantly affect the quality of the human environment. One of the most deceptively sweeping measures ever passed into law by the Congress of the United States, NEPA represented a far-reaching innovation, not only in environmental policy and management, but also in the design of policy processes and institutions.

NEPA did not employ as a primary strategy either of the two traditional approaches to changing bureaucratic behavior: (1) reorganization and budgetary redistribution, or (2) detailed, administratively enforced rules and standards. Instead, NEPA sought to influence government activities by changing—subtly and yet profoundly—the decision structures and evaluative standards of all federal agencies. Recognizing that decisions do not emerge from a black box, but are shaped and channeled before they are officially "made," NEPA's designers sought to alter the processes and procedures by which decisions that might significantly affect the human environment were actually shaped, channeled, and made. NEPA sought to affect decisionmaking by extending, legitimating, and mandating particular choice criteria and by requiring consideration of a different set of factual premises.

In short, NEPA is quintessential policy legislation—"a set of rules for realizing some outcome"—which has been recognized only belatedly and still inadequately by scholars, administrators, and politicians. NEPA represents an ambitious and idealistic effort at policy design—the formulation, adoption, and implementation of "a decision that governs and affects future decisions" (Boulding 1981). In spite of its brevity and apparent simplicity, NEPA is a complex, elusive, and subtle piece of legislation. Environmental values are typically—as the designers of NEPA knew—precarious values, and the natural bias of most organizations goes "against their realization unless protected by special arrangements" (Taylor 1984).

Serge Taylor points out that there were three other systematic failings of government decision processes that were addressed by NEPA: (1) advantage was not being taken of long planning periods to search for possible impacts and to explore design options, (2) important early choice points in agency decision processes were not visible or accessible to other agencies or the public, and (3) there were only weak norms of analysis underlying the creation, sharing, and criticism of empirical information (Taylor 1984). NEPA addressed these failings by mandating, and requiring the disclosure of, pre-decision analyses emphasizing environmental values and consequences. The justiciable disclosure document was the environmental impact statement—the primary action-forcing mechanism of the Act. Through the EIS requirement, and the emphasis on analysis in other substantive provisions, NEPA's designers sought to institutionalize a kind of policy analysis in the decision processes of the federal bureaucracy.

There have been, of course, other attempts to institutionalize analysis in government—notable examples being cost-benefit analysis, required planning studies, and various budget reforms such as program budgeting and zero-base budgeting (Wildavsky 1983; Andrews 1982). Thus the new policy enacted through NEPA was not without considerable antecedent. But the policy analysis mandated by NEPA had several distinctive features. First and foremost, requiring government agencies to undertake environmental impact analysis involved an attempt to establish a "feedforward" mechanism to inform a particular category of decisions, namely decisions about actions expected to have a significant impact on the human environment (Dryzek 1982). Characteristic of (but not unique to) this category of action are consequences that are often irreversible and impacts that may be geographically or temporally dispersed or may appear at the end of a long causal sequence. Some environmentally important outcomes will only result if a (usually unknown) threshold is exceeded. Sometimes actions have effects that would be unremarkable if the action occurred independently in isolation, but are noteworthy as the product of more than one action (that is, cumulative, interactive, and synergistic effects). The expected presence of these kinds of substantial consequences makes reliance on decomposition, trial-and-error learning, incremental decisionmaking, or system feedback less appropriate.

Such problems, if substantial, necessarily call for a degree of "thinking big" in policy design and analysis. An obvious strategy involves basing decisions upon careful consideration of the future through a sort of strategic feedforward mechanism such as environmental impact analysis (Dryzek 1982; Dryzek 19883b; Simon 1981). NEPA thus attempts to institutionalize a measure of protection against what Alfred E. Kahn has labeled "the tyranny of small decisions" (Kahn 1966).

In essence, NEPA is more than a policy Act; it embodies meta-policy or meta-design—the design of a policy process (Dryzek 1982). NEPA's designers sought to declare and establish a national policy for the environment, but because a coherent environmental policy was necessarily very inclusive, it entailed changing the premises, choice criteria, and procedures under which all sorts of other decisions and policies could in the future be formulated and executed. Not only does NEPA provide a procedural reform—the EIS requirement—to force agencies to undertake environmental impact analyses, but NEPA also amends the statutory mandates of all federal agencies. Section 105 of NEPA states, "The policies and goals set forth in this Act are supplementary to those set forth in existing authorizations of Federal agencies." Thus, in addition to requiring that agencies undertake decision-focused analyses and disclose a summary of these analyses to other agencies and the public, NEPA changed the legislative authorization of each and every federal agency. The EIS is a mechanism to force observance of NEPA's policy goals and to obtain compliance with its other directives, including those pertaining to unquantified environmental amenities and values and the use of science in agency planning and decisionmaking.

Unlike cost-benefit analysis or other analytical approaches that often pretend to be value neutral, environmental impact analysis makes no such pretense; the EIS requirement can only be understood in the context of the rest of NEPA. The EIS requirement was intended to lead toward realization of the general policy goals specified in NEPA by institutionalizing a kind of science-based policy analysis. Implementation of NEPA would be advanced by the availability of judicial enforcement of its substantive and procedural mandate; by the persuasive appeal of NEPA's precepts and declarations; by opening agency decision processes to external influences from Congress, other agencies, and the public; by contributing to a shift in the prevailing values of agency personnel through learning and changes in hiring patterns; and by stimulating the generation of new information that would be incorporated into and focused through a revised approach to planning and decisionmaking.

NEPA and Ecological Rationality

Recourse to science is indispensable to implementation of NEPA; as discussed earlier, science is explicit and implicit throughout both the language and the logic of NEPA. In part, science is important simply because information is important—science, is, after all, a particular approach, perhaps the best we have, to reducing the ambiguity of evidence (Boulding 1981). Also, and more important, a tacit objective of NEPA is the introduction of scientific precepts and canons into the policy process:

We believe that scientists have a more fundamental contribution to make. At their best, scientists bring to impact assessment a process of thought, and habits of inquiry, that stress understanding of changes and consequences rather than touting progress; and that stress honest recognition of preconceived courses of action.

The principal contributions that scientists can make to impact assessment are the scientific method of inquiry, a method which has all too often been sorely lacking, and the concept of probability of occurrence of natural events (Andrews et al. 1977).

Indeed, Serge Taylor has undertaken a detailed analysis of NEPA viewed "as an attempt to import 'scientific' norms and procedures into a political setting of often intense conflict" (Taylor 1984). NEPA, of course, is a great deal more than an attempt to impose science-like norms and procedures on bureaucratic decision processes. To be sure, scientific methods and ways of thinking are often held up as the paradigm of rationality, and it is apparently widely believed by scientists and laymen alike that the world could be vastly improved if only politics were made more like science (Gunnell 1981). Perhaps some of NEPA's designers did subscribe in part to that naive view, but there is no evidence to that effect. NEPA does not preempt the political or administrative roles of government decisionmakers. NEPA was not merely or even primarily an attempt to force bureaucracies to use science-like analysis as a basis for policies and decisions. It was not just any science that NEPA mandated in 1969, but a systematic, interdisciplinary, integrated use of the natural and social sciences, with an emphasis on ecology. NEPA is best understood as an attempt to force greater rationality in government decisionmaking through an experiment in institutional and policy design. But again, it is not just any conception of rationality that underlies NEPA—not some superficial and simplistic view of scientific rationality, nor some warmed over and disguised revisitation of the rational-comprehensive decisionmaking model of classical public administration. Rather, NEPA provides a "constitutional" charter for government use of a particular form of reasoning distinct from other legitimate historical forms: ecological rationality.

The National Environmental Policy Act is best understood and evaluated if it is viewed as an exercise in policy and institutional design—a "natural experiment" in the institutionalization of rationality in government organizations and, indeed, in a whole society. The enactment and implementation of NEPA constitute an effort to structure situations to achieve certain results. Other analysts have perceived that NEPA was intended to force rationality, or to induce rationality (Andrews 1976; Friesema and Culhane, 1976; Fairfax 1978; Culhane et al. 1978). But a narrow conception of rationality can constrain the criteria used to evaluate the natural experiment. Recognition of ecological rationality as a functional and critical kind of reasoning with unique characteristics distinguishing it from other forms of rationality is necessary in order to understand the rationale of, and evaluate the success or failure of, the National Environmental Policy Act (Diesing 1962; Dryzek 1983a; Bartlett 1984a).

The thrust of the declaration of national environmental policy comprising much of Section 101 of NEPA is one of ecological rationality: "to create and maintain conditions under which man and nature can exist in productive harmony." The ultimate test for judging NEPA is whether the society and government to which it applies exhibit functional ecological rationality.

Has the nation been able, in the words of NEPA, to "attain the widest range of beneficial uses of the environment without degradation, risk to health or safety, or other undesirable or unintended consequences" and to "enhance the quality of renewable resources and approach the maximum attainable recycling of depletable resources"? Whether achievement of functional ecological rationality is somewhat closer, in part because of NEPA, is the important determination.

With respect to individual actions or decisions, NEPA also presents a standard of ecological rationality. According to NEPA, "it is the continuing responsibility of the Federal Government to use all practicable means . . . to improve and coordinate Federal plans, functions, programs, and resources" consistent with six precepts of Section 101, discussed earlier. Moreover, "to the fullest extent possible," all agencies of the federal government are required by NEPA, before undertaking "action significantly affecting the quality of the human environment," to consider any unavoidable adverse environmental effects, the "relationship between local short-term uses of man's environment and the maintenance and enhancement of long-term productivity," and any "irreversible and irretrievable commitments of resources. All agencies are further required to "recognize the worldwide and long-range character of environmental problems." Thus NEPA specifies several attributes of ecological rationality.

But ecological rationality cannot be achieved by mere declaration; without some attention to processes—whatever the specific mechanisms or resources—no legislation can ever be more than symbolic incantation, the spell of which is likely not to be powerful or lasting. Rather than attempt to achieve ecological rationality through directed reorganization, dictated resources redistribution, or the promulgation of sweeping detailed rules and standards, the designers of NEPA sought to change the procedures used to arrive at and to justify agency choices. Decisions would be affected not only because balances of political influence would be shifted, not only because a different set of incentives would henceforth bear on bureaucratic decisionmakers, but also because a new way of thinking would thereafter be required of bureaucratic agents. Federal agencies were required by NEPA to improve, coordinate, consider, and recognize commitments, relationships, and environmental effects, and they were required to do so in a certain way. That is, agencies were required to "initiate and utilize ecological information," to "utilize a systematic, interdisciplinary approach which will insure the integrated use of the natural and social sciences and the environmental design arts in planning and in decisionmaking," and to "identify and develop methods and procedures . . . which will insure that presently unquantified environmental amenities and values may be given appropriate consideration in decisionmaking." In short, through NEPA, Congress ordered all agencies of the federal government to begin using procedural ecological reasoning in their planning and decisionmaking.

That is not to say that NEPA ignores other, more established realms of rationality. Rather, NEPA emphasizes the integration of other forms of rationality with ecological rationality. Economic as well as social rationality are acknowledged in NEPA's declaration that it is the continuing policy of the federal government "to use all practical means and measures . . . in a manner calculated to . . . fulfill the social, economic, and other requirements of present and future generations of Americans." Economic and social rationality are not ignored or denigrated; rather, their dependence on, and hoped-for consistency with, ecological rationality is emphasized. For example, one of the important six precepts of Section 101 states that it is the continuing responsibility of the federal government to "achieve a balance between population and resource use which will permit high standards of living and a wide sharing of life's amenities." Title II of NEPA, which establishes the Council on Environmental Quality, at several points instructs the CEQ to be conscious of and responsive to social and economic needs, interests, and goals. Section 102(2)(B) directs that methods and procedures be developed to insure that unquantified environmental amenities and values be given appropriate consideration "along with economic and technical considerations." And Section 102(2)(A) requires a systematic, interdisciplinary, integrated use of the social sciences and environmental design arts, along with the natural sciences. Economic cost-benefit analyses are compatible with NEPA-mandated environmental impact analyses, as subsequent CEQ regulations have made clear, and the contemporary techniques collectively known as social impact analysis (SIA) can actually be traced back to NEPA's provisions (Porter et al. 1980; Daneke and Priscoli 1979; Finsterbusch 1980).

Legal rationality is not irrelevant to NEPA either. Section 102(2)(C) of the Act, requiring environmental impact statements, got the attention it did from courts and law journals precisely because it involved modification of a system of rules governing bureaucratic and judicial behavior.

And, except for ecological rationality, it is political rationality that is most important to the logic of NEPA. Diesing writes:

Political decisions are necessary whenever an organization, or society, or person is faced with a political problem; that is, whenever there is a deficiency in its decision structure. The deficiency may be some form of narrowness, in that the structure is not receptive to an adequate range of facts, or that it is not able to break away from well-known formulas in its estimates of problems and suggestions for action, or that it is insufficiently self-critical and slow to admit error, or that its procedures are excessively rigid and thus shut out novelty. (Diesing 1962)

NEPA is, in effect, the result of a political decision that addressed a basic and increasingly critical deficiency in the decision structure of the United States. With respect to various dimensions of environmental quality and ecological life-support, the governmental decision structure had not been receptive to an adequate range of facts, had not been able to break away from well-known formulas, and had been insufficiently critical and excessively rigid. NEPA and environmental impact analysis represent one effort to deal with this political problem, through a process that is overtly and intentionally political, "a process of reasoned deliberation, argument, and criticism rather than a pragmatic calculus" (Anderson 1979).

Ecological rationality as embodied in NEPA has implications for policy formation and implementation well beyond this statute. NEPA provides an important and rich example of an attempt to foster and institutionalize ecological rationality, but by no means is it the only such example. Indeed, the many laws and procedures inspired by NEPA make up a sizable subset of such efforts since 1970—including, among others, federal forest and land management laws and the environmental policy and impact analysis arrangements established by state and local governments and by other nations.

NEPA is, in summary, a manifestation of both ecological and political rationality, which can readily be seen if the Act is analyzed in terms of the "good" achieved by this sort of rationality, namely, practical intelligence. By practical intelligence Diesing is referring not to an intellectual ability to deal with mathematical and linguistic abstractions, but to intelligence which in Dewey's sense is "the ability of the whole society or personality to effectively solve the problems confronting it" (Diesing 1962; Dewey 1930).[4] The intent of NEPA—against which judgments about its achievements or lack thereof must ultimately, but even now can only tentatively, be made—is to advance and foster social intelligence with respect to the human environment (Caldwell et al. 1983; Bartlett 1984b).

Notes

1. The general idea of assessing environmental impacts before acting was not new, nor are all assessment techniques and methodologies of recent origin. As early as the 1870s the Army Corps of Engineers had developed techniques for assessing environmental impacts (Rowe 1978). In the 1920s and 1930s, community and natural resource planners often tried to provide for explicit consideration of environmental impacts (Stein 1957; Spreiregen 1971).

2. These regulations replaced guidelines that had previously been issued (40 CFR 1500–1508).

3. The science-related provisions of Title II of NEPA borrowed heavily from the proposed Ecological Research and Survey Act, introduced in 1965 by Senator Gaylord Nelson of Wisconsin. The objective of that bill was to advance development of the science of ecology through federal policy commitment and funding. As enacted, the potential of Title II of NEPA has been largely unrealized—a consequence of lack of significant congressional or presidential support.

4. Diesing continues: "In the hierarchy of values, intelligence (or freedom) is the supreme value. It is supreme, even absolute, because it is instrumental to all other values.... No excessive pursuit of intelligence is possible, because intelligence makes all other values achievable" (Diesing 1962). Dewey writes that "our intelligence is bound up ... with the community of life of which we are a part." Dewey's conception of reason is consistent with and relevant to ecological rationality:

   "Demand for consistency, for 'universality,' far from implying a rejection of all consequences, is a demand to survey consequences broadly, to link effect to effect in a chain of continuity. Whatever force works to this end *is* reason. For reason, let it be repeated is an outcome, a function, not a primitive force. What we need are those habits, dispositions which lead to impartial and consistent foresight of consequences. Then our judgements are reasonable; we are then reasonable creatures" (Dewey 1930).

References

Anderson, C. W. (1979), "The Place of Principles in Policy Analysis," *American Political Science Review*, 73: 722.

Andrews, R. N. L. (1976), *Environmental Policy and Administrative Change: Implementation of the National Environmental Policy Act* (Lexington, Mass.: Lexington Books).

——et al. (1977), *Substantive Guidance for Environmental Impact Assessment: An*

Exploratory Study (Washington, DC: The Institute of Ecology).

Andrews, R. N. L. (1982), "Cost-Benefit Analysis as Regulatory Reform," in D. Swartzman, R. A. Liroff, and K. G. Croke (eds), *Cost-Benefit Analysis and Environmental Regulations: Politics, Ethics, and Methods* (Washington, DC: The Conservation Foundation).

Bartlett, R. V. (1984a), "Institutionalizing Ecological Rationality," presented at Western Social Science Association meeting, San Diego, Calif.

——(1984b), "Rationality and Science in Public Policy: The National Environmental Policy Act," Ph.D. diss. (Indiana University, Bloomington).

Boulding, K. (1981), *Evolutionary Economics* (Beverly Hills, Calif.: Sage).

Caldwell, L. K. (1978), "The Environmental Impact Statement: A Misused Tool," in R. K. Jain and B. L. Hutchings (eds.), *Environmental Impact Analysis: Emerging Issues in Planning* (Urbana, Ill.: University of Illinois Press).

——(1982), *Science and the National Environmental Policy Act: Redirecting Policy Through Procedural Reform* (University, Ala.: University of Alabama Press).

——et al. (1983), *A Study of Ways to Improve the Scientific Content and Methodology of Environmental Impact Analysis* (PB222851; Springfield, Va.: National Technical Information Service).

Culhane, P. J., et al. (1978), "The Effectiveness of NEPA" (letters), *Science*, 202: 1034–1041.

Daneke, G. A., and Priscoli, J. D. (1979), "Social Assessment and Resource Policy: Lessons from Water Planning," *Natural Resources Journal*, 19: 363.

Dewey, J. (1930), *Human Nature and Conduct: An Introduction to Social Psychology* (New York, NY: Modern Library).

Diesing, P. (1962), *Reason in Society: Five Types of Decisions and their Social Conditions* (Urbana, Ill.: University of Illinois Press).

Dreyfus, D. A., and Ingram, H. M. (1976), "The National Environmental Policy Act: A View of

Intent and Practice," *Natural Resources Journal*, 16: 243–62.

Dryzek, J. S. (1982), "Policy Design in an Uncertain World," presented at Southern Political Science Association meeting, Atlanta, Ga.

——(1983a), "Present Choices, Future Consequences: A Case for Thinking Strategically," *World Futures*, 19: 1–19.

——(1983b), "Don't Toss Coins in Garbage Cans: A Prologue to Policy Design," *Journal of Public Policy*, 3: 345–68.

Fairfax, S. K. (1978), "A Disaster in the Environmental Movement," *Science*, 199: 744–5.

Finn, T. T. (1972), "Conflict and Compromise: Congress Makes a Law—The Passage of the National Environmental Policy Act," Ph.D. diss. (Georgetown University, Washington, DC).

Finsterbusch, K. (1980), *Understanding Social Impacts: Assessing the Effects of Public Projects* (Beverly Hills, Calif.: Sage).

Friesema, H. P., and Culhane, P. J. (1976), "Social Impacts, Politics and the Environmental Impact Statement Process," *Natural Resources Journal*, 16: 339–56.

Gunnell, J. G. (1981), "Encounters of a Third Kind: The Alienation of Theory in American Political Science," *American Journal of Political Science*, 25: 442.

Kahn, A. E. (1966), "The Tyranny of Small Decisions: Market Failures, Imperfections, and the Limits of Economics," *KYKLOS: International Review for Social Science*, 19: 23–45.

Liroff, R. A. (1976), *A National Policy for the Environment: NEPA and its Aftermath* (Bloomington: Indiana University Press).

Porter, A. L., et al. (1980), *A Guidebook for Technology Assessment and Impact Analysis* (New York: Elsevier North Holland).

Rashdall, H. (1936), *The Universities of Europe in the Middle Ages* (New York: Oxford University Press).

Rowe, P. G., et al. (1978), *Principles for Local Environmental Management* (Cambridge, Mass.: Ballinger).

Simon, H. A. (1981), *The Sciences of the Artificial*, 2nd edn. (Cambridge, Mass.: MIT Press).

Spreiregen, R. D. (1971), "Perspectives on Regional Design," *American Institute of Architects Journal*, 56: 20–2.

Stein, C. S. (1957), *Toward New Towns for America* (New York: Reinhold).

Taylor, S. (1984), *Making Bureaucracies Think: The Environmental Impact Statement Strategy of Administrative Reform* (Stanford, Calif.: Stanford University Press).

Wildavsky, A. (1983), *The Politics of the Budgetary Process*, 4th edn. (Boston: Little, Brown).

8   Appraising Adaptive Management

Kai N. Lee

Introduction

Adaptive management (Holling 1978, Walters 1986) — implementing policies as experiments — is a methodological innovation in resource management. Like any method, the adaptive approach implies revised ends as well as novel means: as its name implies, adaptive management promotes learning to high priority in stewardship. This essay considers the difficulties of realizing the promise of adaptive management in natural resource management and biodiversity conservation. I write as a social scientist and erstwhile decision-maker who sought to use adaptive management; I am an outsider to the technical practice, and my observations are meant to complement those of Walters and Holling (1990) by emphasizing the organizational and human dimensions of learning while doing. The questions proposed at the end of this essay invite critique from insiders as well as NGOs, managers, and others for whom the uncertainties of the natural world imply opportunity as well as concern.

The adaptive approach is an important component of a search for a new meaning for conservation—a meaning that is *bioregional* in scope, and *collaborative* in governance, as well as adaptive in managerial perspective. Conservation of this kind is emerging from two forces: the realization that highly valued ecological processes and species can only be preserved in large ecosystems; and the recognition that many ecosystems high in biodiversity are and will continue to be inhabited by humans. These factors inform a redefinition of conservation in a way that points towards an ambitious goal: reconciling conservation biology with sustainable development—that is, bringing together two of the principal themes of environmentalism. I return to that grand aspiration below.

Appraisal

Adaptive management, like other policy innovations, can be appraised using a framework devised by Garry Brewer (1973). Brewer proposed that appraisal be done by considering four dimensions of a policy design:

- Conceptual soundness: is the idea sensible?
- Technical: is the idea translated into practice well?

From *Conservation Ecology*, 3: 2 (1999), 1–9; extracted from online version, <http://www.consecol.org/vol3/iss2/art3>

- Ethical: who loses and who wins?
- Pragmatic: does it work?

Appraisal examines questions that are obvious—though not so obvious that they are considered automatically or even often.

CONCEPTUAL SOUNDNESS: LEARNING BY EXPERIMENTING

Adaptive management has been much more influential as an idea than as a way of doing conservation so far. Given that influence, consider theory first: why should one do adaptive management at all? (cf. Holling 1978)

Adaptive management is grounded in the admission that humans do not know enough to manage ecosystems. Managing is different from exploiting, which requires knowledge of how to capture or harvest. Harvest is a formidable task, but it is not management; managing is closer to cultivation or agriculture. Yet cultivating an ecosystem in order to foster its wild state is paradoxical. This paradox has been resolved by turning around the objective: to think of ecosystem management as managing the *people* who interact with the ecosystem. This focus for management raises questions to which there are few reliable answers, but they can be explored, among other ways, by experimentation.

Adaptive management, from this perspective, formulates management policies as experiments that probe the responses of ecosystems as people's behavior in them changes. (This experimental emphasis is called "active" adaptive management in Walters and Holling (1990).) In conducting these experiments we aim to learn something about the ecosystem's processes and structures, and we seek both to design better policies and to contrive better experiments. Note that the goal is to learn *something*: experiments can surprise the experimenter, and one mark of a good scientist is that she recognizes surprise and pursues its implications. This has not been considered the mark of a good manager, however, who is rewarded instead for steadfast pursuit of objectives.

Experimentation is not the only way to learn; indeed, an adaptive approach is often not the obvious way, as shown in Table 8.1 (also see Marcot 1998).

Many public policies are grounded in anecdotal knowledge, especially those enacted by legislatures, referenda, and general-purpose governments. From this perspective trial and error is an unusually systematic way to learn. In that light, one can reasonably ask how much of the scientific rigor of the laboratory is attainable in the field setting of adaptive management.

The adaptive approach rests on a judgment that a scientific way of asking questions produces reliable answers at lowest cost and most rapidly; this may not be the case very often. As Carl Walters has emphasized, adaptive management is likely to be costly and slow in many situations (e.g., Walters, Goruk, and Radford 1993), so those involved in stewardship need to think through whether the scientific approach is worthwhile in specific cases. In particular, it is important to spell out how much difference in management might result if adaptive learning proceeds as envisioned (Walters and Green 1997).

A research-based approach can be reasonable when one takes into consideration the complexity and subtlety of natural systems, including those that have been driven far from their undisturbed state by human utilization. The complexity suggests that even simple steps may yield

Table 8.1 **Modes of learning**

Each mode of learning	makes observations ...	and combines them ...	to inform activities ...	... that accumulate into usable knowledge	Example
Laboratory Experimentation	Controlled observation to infer cause	Replicated to assure reliable knowledge	Enabling prediction, design, control	**Theory** (it works, but range of applicability may be narrow)	*Molecular biology & biotechnology*
Adaptive Management (Quasi-Experiments in the Field)	Systematic monitoring to detect surprise	Integrated assessment to build system knowledge	Informing model-building to structure debate	**Strong inference** (but learning may not produce timely prediction or control)	*Green Revolution agriculture*
Trial & Error	Problem-oriented observation	Extended to analogous instances	To solve or mitigate particular problems	**Empirical knowledge** (it works but may be inconsistent & surprising)	*Learning by doing in mass production*
Unmonitored Experience	Casual observation	Applied anecdotally	To identify plausible solutions to intractable problems	**Models of reality** (test is political, not practical, feasibility)	*Most statutory policies*

Political conflict tends to weigh more heavily than scientific debate as one moves downward in the table. Cf. "Scientific uncertainty can be high so long as acceptability is high." (Walters and Holling 1990, 2067).

Environmental *policy* has been formulated in response to unmonitored experience (e.g., disappearance of valued species), but environmental *management* assumes one of the other modes of learning is possible (e.g., maximum sustainable yield).

surprising outcomes—and science is an efficient way of recognizing and diagnosing surprise. In principle, the scientific approach leads to reliable determination of causes; in practice, that means being able to learn over time how management does and does not affect outcomes. The complexity of the ecosystems and human behavior in the situations discussed here implies, however, that causal understanding is likely to emerge slowly, perhaps more slowly than the long struggle to understand the causal mechanisms of economic policy (Stein 1996, Hall 1989). The slow emergence of an economic policy paradigm reflects the fact that, to be effective, learning must become *social*—knowledge that informs public policy and collective choice (Parson and Clark 1995, Heclo 1974).

Reliable knowledge of natural systems used by humans is essential if a sustainable economy is to be achieved. An experimental approach may be costly and onerous in the near term, but it is probably the only way to root out *superstitious* learning—erroneous connections between cause and effect. As Walters has stressed, management of natural systems takes place against a dynamic background, and it is usually impossible to sort out the effects of management from those of concurrent changes in the natural environment (e.g., Walters and Holling 1990). The field is profoundly different from a laboratory in this respect. Yet the designs needed to distinguish treatment from background tend to be more costly and slower than non-experimental analyses of the past (what Walters called "passive" adaptive management).

So it is important to remember the value of explicit experimentation, which also addresses two other social misdirections of learning. The first is regression to the mean. Most environmental and resource problems come to notice in extreme situations, such as the decline of a commercial fishery. Yet in a dynamic, mutable world, extreme situations are usually followed by less-extreme ones: there is regression to the mean, not because something has been remedied but simply because the mix of fluctuating causal factors has changed. This is fertile ground for erroneous inferences. Second, as Levitt and March pointed out, superstitious learning is also enhanced when "evaluations of success are insensitive to the actions taken" (1988, 326); the mechanism is related to regression to the mean. In competitive situations, for instance, one contestant may be slightly ahead of the others for reasons that are not under the competitors' control. Yet as every athlete knows, contestants who are striving mightily are convinced of their own explanations for success or failure. Many of these do not stand up to scientific scrutiny. The more that resource managers are held to standards that have no grounding in ecological science, the more likely it is that accountability itself will induce superstitious learning. The rigors of experimentation provide a cure, but it is usually not an inexpensive one.

Experimentation has three components: a clear hypothesis, a way of controlling factors that are (thought to be) extraneous to the hypothesis, and opportunities to replicate the experiment to check its reliability. These guide the selection of treatments applied to test hypotheses, and the selection of techniques that define what is being controlled and which measurements are being replicated. Hypothesis, controls, and replicates are all important to reliable knowledge but none is easily achieved in conservation practice.

Adaptive management is learning while doing. Adaptive management does not postpone action until "enough" is known but acknowledges that time and resources are too short to defer *some* action, particularly actions to address urgent problems such as human poverty and declines in the abundance of valued biota. Adaptive management emphasizes, moreover, that our ignorance of ecosystems is uneven. Management policies should accordingly be chosen in light of the assumptions they test, so that the most important uncertainties are tested rigorously and early. This too is a criterion that managers have not valued. Management responds to problems and opportunities, and that is different from an experimental scientist's desire to explore a phenomenon systematically. Accordingly, there is no reason to think that adaptive management will work smoothly, that it will be easy to coordinate.

In theory, adaptive management recapitulates the promise that Francis Bacon articulated four centuries ago: to control nature one must understand her. Only now, what we wish to control is not the natural world but a mixed system in which humans play a large, sometimes dominant role. Adaptive management is therefore experimentation that affects social arrangements and how people live their lives. The conflict encountered in doing that is discussed below; that conflict is a central reason that adaptive management has had more influence as an idea than as a way of doing conservation.

TECHNICAL: COST OF INFORMATION

The essence of managing adaptively is having an explicit vision or model of the ecosystem one is trying to guide (Walters 1986). That explicit vision provides a baseline for defining surprise. Without surprise, learning does not expand the boundaries of understanding.

The technology of the geographic information system (GIS) now provides a ready template for assembling models. Into a GIS one can import physiographic and topographic databases, natural history observations, scientific measurements, and social and economic data.

Assembling information, attaching spatial coordinates and dates to the data, and preparing maps is a rapid, powerful way to create a shared view of the landscape. Figure 8.1 brings together a wide-ranging literature review by Eric Dinerstein and his colleagues at the World Wildlife Fund

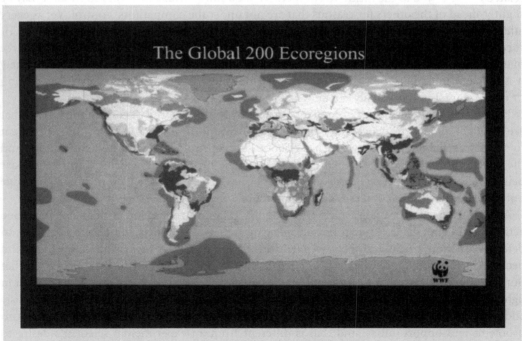

Fig. 8.1 **Global 200 ecoregions, proposed by World Wildlife Fund.**

(Olson and Dinerstein 1998). Its identification of 200 regions of key importance to preserving representative species and ecosystem processes has catalyzed an international commitment to conservation at large spatial scales.

Maps provide a vivid portrayal of how geography matters to a threatened species or ecosystem function. Environmental concerns often have a crucial geographic dimension, and the power of maps to motivate non-biologists to act is a valuable tool in struggles that often seem abstract or remote from everyday life. Still, maps are only one element of the analytical toolkit needed for conservation or resource management.

Three cautions, at least, are important. First, any map emphasizes static structure rather than dynamic processes, although one may of course use a sequence of maps to show changes such as shrinking forest area. But a map is so engaging that one can easily forget that it is by itself static. Ecosystems are dynamic: what matters to learning is whether one can see policy-induced changes in the behavior of the ecosystem. For this, it is essential to ask whether the manager-experimenter *expects* to see a measurable difference due to manipulation of the experimental variables (Walters and Green 1997). This is a question for which a model is needed even to speculate sensibly; a map is not a model, in this important respect.

A second caution is that relatively little significant information is now available in geo-referenced form. As a result, measurements made at particular locations are often attributed to much wider areas. Maps, like statistics, can easily mislead—indeed, any good map should make a clear point, which means that the map-maker is deliberately leaving out a lot.

Third and most important, having an explicit vision of an ecosystem does *not* mean having a complete or detailed or even correct baseline suite of data. Adaptive management is about urgency, acting without knowing enough, and learning. One can be surprised by one's own ignorance—and one can learn from it. The focus should be on learning, not on getting ready to learn. A map is not an end in itself but a means.

(To be sure, a good baseline is desirable—so much so, Walters (1997) suggests, that some resource managers are using models to *infer* parameters, as a substitute for actual measurements in the field. This is of course logically incorrect, compounding the errors in the information that went into the model in the first place.)

There is a broader theme here. Information is expensive. Scientists know this well, since they work hard for each data point. But scientifically trained professionals, who know something about statistical significance and error, have been slow to face a pressing problem in adaptive management: how to get information cheaply and with as few organizational and procedural hassles as possible. Unfortunately, would-be adaptive managers have often jumped too quickly to thinking of information gathering as monitoring. That *is* what an adaptive approach leads to, but it should emerge from a skeptical appraisal of what kinds of information one can afford to collect (Rogers 1998). The model of rapid assessment in conservation biology is worth remembering; the value of information needs to be balanced against the human and environmental values one is seeking to protect. Action guided by imperfect information is often—though not invariably—better than action guided by no information at all. (I do not, of course, suggest replacing monitoring with rapid assessment, a family of methods aimed taking an approximate inventory of the biodiversity of a place.)

The issue is the cost-effective testing of hypotheses. Adaptive management is not laboratory science, where the burden of proof is tilted toward highly reliable findings by rules such as $p < 0.05$, the notion that one's inferences should be reliable 95 percent of the time. In public policy and the world of action, the usual test is "more likely than not"—that is, $p < 0.5$. (There is also an important difference between methods that control for Type I errors, the kind discussed here, and the problem of Type II errors, which is often more germane to adaptive management of ecosystems (Anderson 1998).) The findings that emerge from such roughshod hypothesis testing will not be as reliable as academic science (see Walters and Green 1997). But that is the point: adaptive management is likely to be worthwhile when laboratory style precision seems infeasible but trial-and-error seems too risky. And that's much of the time in conservation.

ETHICAL: BEAR IN MIND AMBIGUITY

Adaptive management is an unorthodox approach for people who think of management in terms of command. Learning is information-intensive and requires active participation from those most likely to be affected by the policies being implemented (see Margoluis and Salafsky 1998). Those who operate the human infrastructures of harvest—farmers, ranchers, dam operators, loggers, fishers—are usually those who know most, in a day to day sense, about the condition of the ecosystem. Their reports constitute much of the information that can be obtained at reasonable cost. Harvesters also see themselves as stewards of the resources upon which they rely, a claim that frequently turns out to be well-founded (McCay and Acheson 1987, Ostrom 1990, Getz et al. 1999).

Those who would preserve species and ecosystems propose to alter the behavior of just these user-stewards. Change is normally resisted. Moreover, when conservation is the objective of management, environmental decline has become apparent, and those who have been users, owners, or governors of an ecosystem are already under fire from critics. Under these conditions, it makes sense to have low expectations. First, adaptive management will often be resisted or sabotaged. Second, when adaptive management works it will usually be the tool of those who want to affect how an ecosystem's human inhabitants earn their living; moreover, inhabitants of protected areas in the developing world are often vulnerable and poorly represented in official deliberations. Win or lose there is ethical ambiguity.

It is tempting to ignore this ambiguity but important not to do so because it usually emerges as conflict. Conflict is an essential element of governance. Differences are inevitable, and an orderly approach to resolving those differences is essential; over the time periods needed to establish conservation practices, conflict and turbulence must be expected and should be welcomed. But conflict needs to be bounded—disputes should be conducted within the boundaries of a social process that the disputing parties perceive as legitimate. Unbounded conflict can tear apart the social fabric, thwarting learning. The difficulty is that conflict is a situation in which control of the rules of engagement are themselves contested. When the conflict is between sovereign powers like national governments, there is no superior authority able to impose a bounded process. In practice, even parties with little power can delay the resolution of conflicts enough to frustrate experimentation and learning.

A surprising aspect of the ethical ambiguity is that environmentalists have often been unwilling to confess the ignorance upon which adaptive management is founded. Armed with legal mandates such as the Endangered Species Act in the U.S., environmentalists often act to force reluctant authorities to obey their own laws. This is essential when environmental activists seek recognition as legitimate stakeholders: forcing action demonstrates power. Yet when environmentalists exercise power they often do so by denying that the natural world is uncertain. This forestalls the learning that will be needed if a sustainable policy is to be devised.

Another ethical challenge of adaptive management lies in the fact that knowledge is a public good: once discovered, knowledge can be transferred at much lower cost than was necessary to make the initial discovery. For this reason, an agency or property-owner carrying out adaptive management faces a situation of increasing but not well-controlled transparency. What is learned from the adaptive process reveals not only the way the ecosystem responds but also what the managers are doing, whether it works, and whose interests it serves. Because information needs to be gathered, usually from a variety of sources in the ecosystem, it is hard to keep what is being learned from diffusing outward via the communication channels through which data are collected.

Undertaking an experimental approach presents the manager with two faces of learning. There are benefits from increasing understanding of the social and natural interactions—the usual justification for an adaptive approach. But there are costs, which Walters has pioneered in estimating (Walters and Green 1997). Perhaps more important than quantifiable costs, there are risks of disclosure of activities which look inappropriate in the eyes of one or more stakeholders. The balance between the uncertain future benefits of increased understanding and the risks of inconvenient disclosure, which may come soon or by surprise, is necessarily subjective. This means that the judgments applied in initiating and sustaining adaptive management are volatile. Moreover, the scope of the cooperation needed to gather information for adaptive management means that many besides the official manager or owner need to maintain a commitment to the learning process, each weighing anticipated benefits against costs and risks. It is likely in such a setting that some members of the coalition will waver or resist participating.

These frailties underscore the importance of leadership in making adaptive management work. The obvious leader is the manager herself, since the manager usually controls the flow of benefits of harvest from or protection of the ecosystem, a key role in motivating those whose cooperation is essential for information gathering, analysis, and diagnosis of surprises. When the manager is a public official, the balance between benefits and risks of learning is likely to be measured in political metrics. Thus, using the term "adaptive management" as a buzzword—when what is happening is much less likely to lead to disruptive disclosures than truly active adaptive learning—is a temptation hard to resist.

In Table 1 the Green Revolution is used as an example of successful learning by focused experimentation. It is useful to bear in mind that the benefits of increased rice, corn, and wheat harvest were visible in a short time, and that the sponsors of the learning initially were private donors who were removed from needing to please diverse stakeholders. Moreover, the controversies that came to beset the Green Revolution arose well after the process of breeding new varieties was well-established as an economic strategy. For all these reasons, the Green

Revolution is both a clear model and a hard one to follow in the realm of natural resource management and conservation. (Bruton (1997, 142) stimulated the observations above with a remark that the Green Revolution is also an unusual example of direct transfer from science to agrarian practice. His comment is also a caution for adaptive management: the discoveries that result from learning may not be readily applied by all or even any of the stakeholders.)

PRAGMATIC: MAKING A DIFFERENCE

The pragmatic question is simple—does adaptive management work? We do not know yet. We do not know for two reasons. First, the battle for control of ecosystems is not decided in a lot of places. So the learning process that adaptive management organizes is subverted or ignored if it is even attempted. Second, the time scales for ecosystem response are typically long, and it is too early to know how or even if changes in human management policies have made an unambiguous difference. Most natural indicators yield one data point a year; even a simple trend takes patience in a world with a 24-hour news cycle, quarterly profit reports, and congressional elections every other year.

The high-water mark, so far, in adaptive management practice appears to be a careful series of management experiments conducted in ground fisheries by Keith Sainsbury of the Australian CSIRO in Tasmania. Beginning in 1988 Sainsbury designed an adaptive management regime for a declining groundfish fishery off northwest Australia (Peterman and Peters 1998). Using a decision analysis framework to organize hypotheses and available information, Sainsbury analyzed the value of additional information to be gathered by an experimental program. He showed in that situation that the expected value of catch could be quadrupled by carrying out one set of management experiments. This was done, with results indicating that one of the four hypotheses had strong support. Fisheries regulation has now been altered in response to these findings. The adaptive learning program took about a decade to yield practical results in fisheries management.

In the U.S., adaptive management was initially adopted in 1984 by the Northwest Power Planning Council, as a way of organizing the council's activities to protect and enhance Pacific salmon in the Columbia River basin (Lee 1993, chap. 2). Those efforts were diverted in 1990 by litigation under the Endangered Species Act, so that the experimental phase of the Columbia basin program did not get very far (Volkman & McConnaha 1993, National Research Council 1996).

Adaptive management has been implemented in several other settings (see Gunderson, Holling, and Light 1995, Walters and Green 1997). Three recent instances are noteworthy. First, the U.S. Forest Service has attempted to forge a consensus management plan for its Pacific coastal forests in California, Oregon, and Washington (FEMAT 1993). These have included the definition of Adaptive Management Areas "for land managers, researchers and communities [to] work together to explore new methods of doing business" (Olympic National Forest 1998). The Forest Service's definition of adaptive management does not emphasize experimentation but rather rational planning coupled with trial and error learning. Here "adaptive" management has become a buzzword, a fashionable label that means less than it seems to promise.

Second, the Plum Creek Timber Company (1998), a major landowner in Washington State, adopted a habitat conservation plan for its Cascade region lands in 1996, enabling harvest in a landscape where endangered species are found. Plum Creek has made specific commitments to experimental methods in the way it will carry out the conservation plan (see also Plum Creek 1999). Also in 1996 the U.S. Department of the Interior sought to rebuild riparian habitat in the Grand Canyon by deliberately releasing large quantities of water from Glen Canyon Dam (Glen Canyon Environmental Studies 1996, Grand Canyon Monitoring and Research Center 1998, see also Barinaga 1996). This spring flood was accompanied by a substantial monitoring effort, and it has been followed by research studies now being reviewed by a committee of the National Academy of Sciences.

None of these efforts has been as systematic as Sainsbury's decision analysis in Australia. That is probably appropriate to the state of the art: decision analysis assumes there is a single decision-maker, with a rationally structured set of preferences. In an economically significant fishery, it makes sense to measure preferences via the value of catch as Sainsbury did. But when conventionally measured economic value conflicts with environmental values, as in the U.S. cases, the fundamental premise that a non-controversial optimal decision can be identified is not plausible. (Walters and Green (1997) propose a way to estimate the economic value of non-market attributes. Although their method is less cumbersome than the elicitation methods developed for decision analysis, its practical utility remains to be shown.)

In sum, adaptive management is an idea highly attractive to the scientifically sophisticated, who understand how little is really known about the behavior of modified ecosystems that continue to be used by humans. Its requirements for patient record-keeping and clear-headed assessment turn out to be hard to muster where there is conflict—that is, in all the important cases. This practical reality has not seemed to dim the luster of the idea itself (e.g., National Research Council 1996). I am unsure whether to worry or to take comfort in that impression, but the uneven success of adaptive management is one indication of how far from realization is the "new social contract" (Lubchenco 1998) that thoughtful leaders have urged upon the scientific community and the society it serves.

References

Anderson, J. L. (1998), "Errors of Inference," in V. Sit and B. Taylor (eds), *Statistical Methods for Adaptive Management Studies*, Lands Management Handbook no. 42. (Ministry of Forests, Research Branch, Victoria, British Columbia, Canada), 69–87.

Barinaga, M. (1996), A Recipe for River Recovery? *Science*, 273: 1648–50.

Brewer, G. D. (1973), *Politicians, Bureaucrats, and the Consultant. A Critique of Urban Problem Solving* (New York: Basic Books).

Bruton, H. J. (1997), *On the Search for Well-being* Ann Arbor: (University of Michigan Press).

Forest Ecosystem Management Assessment Team (FEMAT) (1993), *Forest Ecosystem Management: An Ecological, Economic, and Social Assessment*. Appendix A of draft supplemental environmental impact statement on management of habitat for late-successional and old-growth forest related species within the range of the Northern spotted owl (Federal Interagency SEIS Team, Portland, Oregon, July).

Getz, W. M., Fortmann, L., Cumming, D., du Toit, J., Hilty, J., Martin, R., Murphree, M., Owen-Smith, N., Starfield, A. M., Westphal M. I. (1999), "Sustaining Natural and Human

Capital: Villagers and Scientists," *Science*, 283: 1855–6.

Glen Canyon Environmental Studies (1996), "Floods in the Grand Canyon," available at: <http://www.usbr.gov/gces/rod.html>.

Grand Canyon Monitoring and Research Center (1998), "Programs and Announcements," available at: <http://www.usbr.gov/gces/prog.htm>.

Gunderson, L. H., Holling, C. S., and Light, S. S. (1995) (eds), *Barriers and Bridges to the Renewal of Ecosystems and Institutions* (New York: Columbia University Press).

Hall, P. A. (1989) (ed.), *The Political Power of Economic Ideas: Keynesianism Across Nations* (Princeton: Princeton University Press).

Heclo, H. (1974), *Modern Social Politics in Britain and Sweden* (New Haven: Yale University Press).

Holling, C. S. (1978) (ed.), *Adaptive Environmental Assessment and Management* (New York: John Wiley & Sons).

Lee, K. N. (1993), *Compass and Gyroscope. Integrating Science and Politics for the Environment* (Washington, D.C.: Island Press).

Levitt, B., and March, J. G. (1988), "Organizational Learning," *Annual Review of Sociology*, 14: 319–40.

Lubchenco, J. (1998), "Entering the Century of the Environment: A New Social Contract for Science," *Science*, 279: 491–7.

Marcot, B. G. (1998), "Selecting Appropriate Statistical Procedures and Asking the Right Questions: A Synthesis," in V. Sit and B. Taylor (eds), *Statistical Methods for Adaptive Management Studies*. Lands Management Handbook no. 42. (Ministry of Forests, Research Branch, Victoria, British Columbia, Canada), 129–43.

Margoluis, R., and Salafsky, N. (1998). *Measures of Success. Designing, Managing, and Monitoring Conservation and Development Projects* (Washington, D.C.: Island Press).

McCay, B. J., and Acheson, J. M. (1987) (eds), *The Question of the Commons* (Tucson: University of Arizona Press).

National Research Council (1996), *Upstream: Salmon and Society in the Pacific Northwest.* Report of the Committee on the Protection and Management of Pacific Northwest Anadromous Salmonids (Washington, D.C.: National Academy Press).

Olson, D. M., and Dinerstein, E. (1998), "The Global 200: A Representation Approach to Conserving the Earth's Most Biologically Valuable Ecoregions," *Conservation Biology*, 12: 502–15.

Olympic National Forest (1998), "The Olympic Adaptive Management Area," available at: <http://www.fs.fed.us/r6/olympic/ecomgt/nwfp/adaptman.htm>.

Ostrom, E. (1990), *Governing the Commons. The Evolution of Institutions for Collective Action* (Cambridge: Cambridge University Press).

Parson, E. A., and Clark, W. C. (1995), "Sustainable Development as Social Learning: Theoretical Perspectives and Practical Challenges for the Design of a Research Program," in L. H. Gunderson, C. S. Holling, and S. S. Light (eds), *Barriers and Bridges to the Renewal of Ecosystems and Institutions* (New York: Columbia University Press), 428–60.

Peterman, R. M., and Peters, C. N. (1998), "Decision Analysis: Taking Uncertainties into Account in Forest Resource Management," in V. Sit and B. Taylor (eds), *Statistical Methods for Adaptive Management Studies*. Lands Management Handbook no. 42. (Ministry of Forests, Research Branch, Victoria, British Columbia, Canada), 105–27.

Plum Creek Timber Co., L.P. (1998), "Cascade Region Habitat Conservation Plan" (web summary), available at: <http://www.plumcreek.com/eleader/initiatives01.htm>.

Plum Creek Timber Co., L.P. (1999), "Plum Creek Native Fish Habitat Conservation Plan" (web summary), available at: <http://www.plumcreek.com/eleader/initiatives05.htm>.

Price, D. K. (1965), *The Scientific Estate*, (New York: Oxford University Press).

Rogers, K. (1998), "Managing Science/Management Partnerships: A Challenge of Adaptive Management," *Conservation Ecology*, 2(2): R1; available at: <http://www.consecol.org/vol2/iss2/resp1>.

Stein, H. (1996), *The Fiscal Revolution in America: Policy in Pursuit of Reality* (Washington, D.C.:

AEI Press). Second revised edition of the 1969 version.

Volkman, J. M., and McConnaha, W. E. (1993), "Through a Glass, Darkly: Columbia River Salmon, the Endangered Species Act, and Adaptive Management," *Environmental Law*, 23: 1249–72.

Walters, C. (1986), *Adaptive Management of Renewable Resources* (New York: Macmillan).

Walters, C. (1997), "Challenges in Adaptive Management of Riparian and Coastal Ecosystems," *Conservation Ecology*, 1(2): 1; available at: <http://www.consecol.org/vol1/iss2/art1>.

Walters, C., Goruk, R. D., and Radford, D. (1993), "Rivers Inlet Sockeye Salmon: An Experiment in Adaptive Management," *North American Journal of Fisheries Management*, 13: 253–62.

Walters, C., and Green, R. (1997), "Valuation of Experimental Management Options for Ecological Systems," *Journal of Wildlife Management*, 61: 987–1006.

Walters, C. J., and Holling, C. S. (1990), "Large-Scale Management Experiments and Learning by Doing," *Ecology*, 71: 2060–8.

9 Beyond Backyard Environmentalism: How Communities are Quietly Refashioning Environmental Regulation

Charles Sabel, Archon Fung, and Bradley Karkkainen

From California habitats to Massachusetts toxics, the United States is in the midst of a fundamental reorientation of its environmental regulation, one that is as improbable as it is unremarked. Minimally, the new forms of regulation promise to improve the quality of our environment. At a maximum, they suggest a novel form of democracy that combines the virtues of localism and decentralization with the discipline of national coordination.

In substance and spirit, this new approach to regulation grows out of the tradition of backyard environmentalism. For two decades, residents of Woburn, Love Canal, and countless other communities across the country have organized to reclaim authority over their lived environment. These pioneers of citizen environmental activism typically fought to keep harmful activity out of their neighborhoods—hence the acronym NIMBY, for "Not In My Backyard." In their struggles to protect themselves and their children from poisoned air, soil, and water, ordinary citizens have often been pitted against certified experts from corporations, government, and even big environmental organizations.

Recent developments in environmental regulation go beyond the first generation in two closely related ways. First, citizens now face the daunting task of determining what *should* occur in their backyards—what kinds of activity are productive, yet acceptably sustainable. Second, they must transform their traditionally antagonistic relationships with experts into partnerships for environmental protection; to determine what the tolerable activities are, given continuous change in the nature of risks and our understanding of how to respond to them, they need to fuse the broad experience of professional practitioners with the contextual intelligence that only citizens possess. If the lesson of the first generation of backyard environmentalism was that citizens living near polluting firms, or drawing on contaminated watersheds, will not be overrun by distant corporate and governmental bureaucracies, the lesson of the succeeding generation is that citizens with their new allies can fundamentally reshape regulatory systems, for the good of democracy and the environment.

From *Boston Review*, 1999; online at <http://bostonreview.mit.edu/BR24.5/sabel.html>, 1–17.

The new relationship is founded on an exchange between local units and higher level authorities. The local units might, for example, be groups of neighbors on the same tributary planning together to reduce the polluting runoff from their homes and farms; or they might be teams of workers and managers planning to reduce the use and leakage of toxics in their plant. The higher-level authorities might be a state department of the environment, a regional or national office of the Environmental Protection Agency (EPA), or a field office of the Fish and Wildlife Service (FWS). Within broad limits the local units set their own environmental performance targets and devise the means to achieve them. In return, they provide detailed reports on actual performance and possible improvements to public authorities. The resulting framework replaces regulation based on central commands with a combination of local experimentation and centralized pooling of experience. In this new architecture—we will call it a *rolling-rule regime*—regulators use reports on proposals and outcomes to periodically reformulate minimum performance standards, desirable targets, and paths for moving from the former to the latter. In pursuing these targets as they see best, local actors provide the information necessary for regulators to revise their standards and goals, and receive information on the performance of others that guides further experimentation. Thus the new framework forces continuous improvements in both regulatory rules and environmental performance while heightening the accountability of the actors to each other and the larger public.

The rolling-rule regime should not be confused with voluntarism, if that term is understood to imply the abdication of public authority and responsibility to private actors, singly or in groups. Nor is it merely devolution of authority from the federal government to smaller units. For while the rolling-rule regime radically expands the bounds of local autonomy and demands deep participation by private as well as public actors as, it also requires accountability. Central authorities ensure that local units live up to their commitments by coordinating their activities, monitoring their performance, pooling their experiences, and enforcing feasible standards that emerge from their practice. But unlike conventional, hierarchical forms, in which subordinate parts answer to the center's authoritative command, rolling-rule regulation creates a collaborative and mutual accountability of center to parts, parts to center, parts to other parts, and all to the whole enterprise—and to the public generally.

This re-orientation is little noticed because of the sheer improbability of its success, given current assumptions about interest-group politics and failed public institutions. Environmentalists are taken to be inveterate opponents of industrialists or real-estate developers, just as officials of federal, state, and local government are taken to be natural adversaries. How can all of these cooperate continuously, for the long term, under rapidly shifting conditions and even more rapidly evolving knowledge of the world?

We will argue that this emergent regulatory regime owes its success precisely to a counterintuitive but durable form of practical deliberation between and among environmentalists, developers, farmers, industrialists, and officials from distinct, perhaps competing, subdivisions of government—parties who are conventionally thought to be antagonists. In this problem-solving process, disciplined consideration of alternative policies leads protagonists to discover unanticipated solutions provisionally acceptable to all. Further deliberation leads to successive re-definitions of self-interest that permit robust collaborative exploration, including revision of institutional boundaries, procedures, and even ideas of what is feasible. In avoiding the notorious inflexibility of centralized command systems and the problems of information-gathering associated with market-based mechanisms, the rolling-rule regime achieves levels of cooperation and environmental performance beyond the reach of either. At the limit, the practical successes of this form of deliberation in solving problems suggest the possibility of a directly deliberative form of participatory democracy in environmental regulation—and elsewhere as well.

A New Architecture

We start where many of these reforms began: with the frustration of environmental activists, managers of regulated firms, ordinary citizens, and regulators with the shortcomings of centralized command regulation on one hand and at the impracticality of market-based correctives on the other.

COMMAND AND MARKET

The distinguishing feature of centralized regulation is its claim to a modest omniscience. Though regulators renounce the pretension to complete knowledge of a complex and changing world, they nonetheless attempt to determine enduring solutions to well-specified problems. The result of this combination of confidence and self-deprecation is regulation that, piece by piece, attempts too little and too much.

There is too little regulation in the world of centralized command because detailed regulation requires sharp boundaries between what is regulated, and what is not (otherwise, rule making would require plain old, immodest omniscience). But under complex and changing conditions, problems just outside the regulated zone will frequently turn out to be just as significant as those within it. For example, the Endangered Species Act (ESA) applies only to species nearing extinction. But it may be immeasurably harder to save a species once it is sufficiently imperiled to qualify than when it is merely in decline. Similarly, the Clean Water Act (CWA) regulates gross and concentrated emissions of a handful of pollutants by large and conspicuous polluters such as factories and waste treatment facilities. The more varied and diffuse effluents of households and farms, though less obvious and harder to measure, may cause greater damage overall, but remain essentially unregulated.

But where it does aim for more definitive solutions, centralized command often regulates too much. The best available solution at the moment of adoption may have long-term, unintended consequences that outweigh early gains. Or the very successes of the best current solution may hinder the search for better ones. Even when the parties to the original rule suspect that they have been overtaken by events, fear of re-opening discussions may prevent them from taking advantage of new opportunities. Those who broadly speaking favor regulation worry that confessing error opens the door to backsliding and jeopardizes their authoritative claims. Those who generally oppose regulation worry that new rules may expose them to even greater costs than the old. For example, some rules prescribe the use of specific ''best'' technologies to trap pollutants before they are introduced into the air or water—despite the possibility of improvements in these technologies, or the possibility that others could prevent the production of pollutants in the first place.

The 1980s brought two kinds of market-simulation proposals that promised to correct these defects. One focused on trades among polluting units. The other, cost-benefit analysis, focused on methods for analyzing the trade-offs implicit in competing regulatory proposals. Both approaches recognize that effective centralized regulation requires more knowledge than it can summon, and therefore would leave crucial choices to decentralized actors. But neither approach delivered on its promises of orderly decentralization.

To see why, consider the first and most familiar of these two proposals: to create "tradable emissions permits" that allow firms to pollute specified quantities of specified substances. In such a system, a central regulator identifies the regulated substance and establishes an overall cap on emissions based on the harm it causes and an estimate of reasonably attainable reductions. The regulator then assigns initial permit allotments to current polluters, creates trading rules and a compliance-monitoring regime, and lets the magic of the market do the rest. Polluters facing low costs of abatement will reduce their emissions and sell their excess permits at a profit to higher-cost abaters, who find it more economical to purchase permits than to make reductions themselves. As trades continue, the costs of abating a unit of pollution will stabilize around a market price. Thus every dollar spent to protect the environment from the regulated substance will ultimately buy as much protection as every other dollar, and society will achieve a goal of which the social planner can only dream: efficient allocation of the resources spent on pollution reduction.

Despite their modest claims to knowledge, market-simulating mechanisms ultimately share with centralized command regulation a demand for information they cannot satisfy. All markets—including those in pollution permits, water rights, and land—require extraordinary quantities and varieties of information. Among these are precise definitions and allocations of ownership rights, costs and other terms for their transfer, as well procedures for *re*-setting prices or *re*-distributing rights when initial allocations prove too generous, or too niggardly. Ordinary markets work because most of this information is amassed from decentralized actors. In artificial markets, created from the center, the information must first be accumulated (or specified) by the regulator. Before issuing permits that create these commodities, regulators must know how much of the pollutant is being emitted in the aggregate and by individual sources, how much environmental harm results from various levels of emissions, and what reductions are feasible. Moreover, because markets depend on secure ownership rights, there are limits on post-hoc program corrections and thus excessive expectations of inhuman foresight from all-too-human regulators.

Nor is simple deregulation a viable alternative to centralized command or market simulation. The wave of environmentalism that produced the EPA and Clean Air and Water Acts has evolved into a robust popular movement that insists on public supervision of environmental hazards. Environmentalism, as a commitment to public stewardship of the biosphere, is now a securely established political fact. The only live debate is about the appropriate level of environmental protection, and how best to achieve it.

NOVELTY?

This abiding commitment to environmental protection has begun to weave bits of the old programs and a few innovations into a novel regulatory framework. This framework discounts the possibility of central, panoramic knowledge more steeply than either centralized command or market-simulating regulation, and it puts a higher premium on collaborative processes that allow central and local actors to learn from one another and from their actions in the world. It would use these surprises to revise the rules that frame collaboration, then seek further discoveries under guidance of the more capable frame, and so on. The philosophy of this architecture is pragmatist: while it rejects immutable principles, it keeps faith with the idea that we can always institutionalize better ways of learning from the inevitable surprises that experience offers us.

The new framework embraces local autonomy and broad accountability. Local actors—firms, local governments, local representatives of federal agencies, or representatives of all these acting together in composite entities—are given the responsibility, subject to general guidelines, to devise suitable measures within a broad policy area: say, the management of a watershed or habitat, or the reduction of toxics. Moreover, they devise measures by which they will assess their progress toward the goals they have set and mechanisms for correcting practice in light of actual performance.

In return for this autonomy, local actors agree to pool information on their performance, plans, and metrics—on how they are doing, how they plan to improve, and what standards they use to assess performance—typically by reporting them to a central monitor. The central monitor uses these data, in consultation with local actors, to determine minimally acceptable levels of performance, plausible targets for improvement, generally acceptable methods for assessing it, as well as acceptable and preferred methods of organizing participation in subsequent discussion of goals and measures. Interim standards and general measures become benchmarks. Referring to these, local units then re-assess their own performance. Local criticism and national scrutiny disciplines laggards. Local actors are accountable to each other, within any one locality, and to the nation as a whole. National institutions are exposed to the informed gaze of the collectivity of localities. The next round of experimentation takes account of the feedback from these results, and leads, through further comparisons, to revisions in the standards and measures, as well as national and local procedures. Because the emphasis throughout is on measurement, evaluation, and continuous improvement of performance, we will call this new architecture *performance-based*.

The performance-based framework emphasizes the continuing importance of local knowledge, and thus requires broader and deeper local participation in environmental regulation than earlier regimes contemplated. Indeed, it assumes that its predecessors failed in part because they ignored the knowledge diffused among the broader public. Its own success will therefore depend on organizing participation that systematically taps this information even as it places additional demands and confers new powers on citizens. Already, as we will see, work teams within firms are beginning to engage in pollution-reduction efforts directly linked to the reorganization of production. Similarly, as a result of growing attention to non-point source pollution, small farms and households whose run-off influences conditions in local tributaries are being asked to engage in (and authorized to implement) the kind of self-assessment and pollution-reduction planning once presumed to be within the reach only of large firms.

But this broader participation must also be deeper than traditional forms. Voting, comment in public hearings, or advocacy in environmental movements—the familiar varieties of direct participation—are occasions for making citizens' voices count in public decision making. In a performance-based regime, the citizen is called on not merely to express an opinion—or demand a solution—but to help formulate and implement solutions. The idea is to exercise joint responsibility, not simply to defend group interests. In this process, the new institutions may transform the identities of the users themselves. To underscore these transformative possibilities we will speak of *deep use* and *deep users* to distinguish participation and participants in the new regime from the old.

So the pragmatist architecture promises regulation that is more effective than current arrangements, and more democratic—which sounds too good to be true. To see just how much truth there is in this promise, let's consider how things work in practice.

Performance-Based Regulation

A diverse set of recent innovations in environmental regulation shows how crucial components of this architecture are feasible in a wide array of settings, even if none of these settings contains all the relevant elements. On one side this incompleteness is a vulnerability: each of these programs must eventually address its unanswered questions. On the other side, the fact that these experiments have been able to substitute novel components for the traditional ones in piecemeal fashion, displays the adaptability of the overall architecture. It is hard to imagine that these programs could ever be built if each of its key components depended simultaneously upon the implementation of all the others.

For convenience we group the cases by policy area. Thus the Toxics Release Inventory (TRI), the Massachusetts Toxics Use Reduction Act of 1989 (TURA), and Responsible Care control industrial pollutants, while the Chesapeake Bay Program and HCPs aim to regulate watersheds and other ecosystems.

INFORMATION MATTERS

The Toxics Release Inventory (TRI) is a federal "right-to-know" measure that forces some 30,000 facilities to publicly report their releases of toxic chemicals. Enacted in response to the catastrophic 1984 explosion of a Union Carbide facility in Bhopal, India, its roots lie in a broad domestic movement against environmental hazards. That movement dates to the Love Canal scandal of 1978, when large amounts of toxic industrial chemicals were found to have been buried on a site where a local elementary school was later built. The resulting anger and activism connected the battle for information—what chemicals were present in what quantities, and what were the health risks—to defense of home, family, and neighborhood, and set the tone for a new style of local, lunch-pail environmentalism. Hundreds of communities organized to demand clean-ups of toxic waste disposal sites, and to receive information under the banner of the community's "right-to-know." That movement represented an extension of earlier efforts focused on the workplace, where activists had been seeking the "right-to-know" about job-related toxic exposures since the early 1970s. By the mid 1980s, locally-based movements had already won right-to-know laws in at least 30 states and 65 cities and counties. Popular participation created a political atmosphere in which Congress, faced with the fears crystallized by Bhopal, reacted swiftly, and with little regard for the niceties of conventional administration.

TRI requires only that private and government-run facilities meeting statutory size requirements report estimates of the amounts of some 650 chemicals transferred off-site, or routinely or accidentally released. Since passage of the Pollution Prevention Act of 1990, facilities must also report transfers of listed chemicals within the plant and efforts at pollution reduction and recycling. The data are publicly available via print and the Internet in both raw form and as tables comparing amounts released by substance, facility, industry, and location. Though failure to file a required report may result in penalties, inaccurate reporting does not. While the EPA does little to verify the accuracy of emissions reports, citizens may sue firms for failure to comply with TRI's disclosure provisions. Data they obtain can then be used to establish violations of other, substantive statutory obligations, or as a lever by which to apply public pressure for improvements.

From the standpoint of the traditional regulatory regime, TRI is environmental "regulation," in the minimal sense of formally requiring disclosure of a body of information from which environmental rules and standards, fixed or rolling, might eventually be fashioned or enforced. Its operation therefore constitutes a rough test, under admittedly favorable circumstances, of whether benchmarking in general—and benchmarking of "alarming" information in particular—can play the central role that we have attributed to it in synchronizing performance-improving efforts.

The effects of TRI strongly suggest that it can. First, the collection and publication of TRI data immediately disciplines polluting private actors. Public comparisons of polluters compiled by journalists or community activists from TRI data also lead to significant declines in the share value of publicly traded firms that show poorly. These reputational and financial market penalties give managers strong incentives to either reduce their toxics emissions or shade their reporting estimates to appear cleaner than they are.

As the EPA itself has noted, in making possible comparisons across regions and facilities, the release of information about toxics has allowed federal, state, and local governments to cooperate with the public and industry to "evaluate existing environmental programs, establish regulatory priorities, and track pollution control and waste reduction progress." In particular, states such as Massachusetts, Oregon, New Jersey, Washington, and Minnesota are using this collaborative redirection of regulatory activity to refine reports on the use of toxics and improve the pooling of the resulting information. Of these more developed pooling programs, the most established, comprehensive, and influential was created by TURA, the Massachusetts toxics reduction act.

TURA both broadens and extends TRI. It broadens by requiring firms to report not only toxic releases, but also use or generation of toxics in any stage of production. TURA further requires that these reports be connected to biannual Toxics Use Reduction Plans. Sometimes these plans are formulated by managers or process engineers alone, but frequently they are produced by problem solving teams that include production workers as well. On the basis of such benchmarking surveys of possibilities, firms specify in the plan particular measures to be adopted, the schedule for implementing them, and two- and five-year reduction targets. Although TURA establishes the general goal of reducing use of toxics in Massachusetts by 50 percent by 1997, and penalizes "willful" violations of the reporting and planning requirements, the act sets no more specific performance standards, nor does it penalize failure to act on reduction plans. Thus, rather than fix objectives and compel their attainment, TURA furthers the TRI strategy of using the obligation for self-monitoring to induce firms and citizens to acquire information that reveals problems and helps formulate their solution.

At the same time, TURA extends and helps formalize industry efforts at improved environmental performance both by creating a peer inspectorate to review the usage reduction plans and by providing technical consulting services. TURA requires that Plans be certified by toxics-use-reduction planners. Planner certification in turn requires individuals to complete various training programs and classes. The act accordingly establishes a Toxics Use Reduction Institute (TURI) at the Lowell campus of the University of Massachusetts to develop the curricula and provide these courses, inform industry or the public of developments in this area, and conduct research necessary to these activities. It also establishes an Office of Technical Assistance to assist firms (particularly small, first-time filers) in meeting their TURA obligations, and to help coordinate the provision of relevant services by the public and private sectors. Taken together, plans, planners, TURI, and the Office of Technical Assistance create an inspection system in which current conditions in individual firms or industrial segments can be compared with each other and with academic understanding of best practices, even as that understanding improves through exposure to innovative firms. Finally, TURA provides a high-level governance structure that periodically suggests modifications of the new state services and reporting requirements in the light of its evaluation of progress towards the Act's original reduction target.

This apparatus seems to work. From 1990 to 1995, the production-adjusted use of toxic chemicals fell by 20 percent in Massachusetts and the generation of toxic byproducts by 30 percent. Furthermore, the toxics use planning requirement has enabled firms to discover significant net benefits of pollution prevention and increase their support for the public institutions that facilitate this process. Nor were these benefits offset for the firms by the costs of preparing reports and plans; 86 percent of all respondents said they would continue to plan even absent legal requirements.

THE NEED FOR A PUBLIC ROLE

Responsible Care is a Chemical Manufacturers' Association (CMA) program to reduce pollution through disciplined error detection and elimination by its member firms. The program, which started in 1988, effectively accepts the key assumptions of rolling-rule regulation. This is a vast undertaking: the CMA's roughly 200 members account for about 95 percent of domestic production of basic chemicals, and the chemical sector as a whole accounts for half of the six billion pounds of toxics generated each year in the United States. But the CMA attempts to implement these mechanisms solely through private parties, with no government coordination and no public use of the relevant data. The core of Responsible Care consists of six "disciplines" that oblige firms to link pollution prevention efforts to their production processes. The program sets target dates for installing the new disciplines, advises member firms to monitor progress towards their goals, and helps document and disseminate best practices.

The results of Responsible Care are so far inconclusive; and the reason is close at hand in the configuration of the CMA. On the one side, as a trade association, the CMA depends on a consensus of its members for the authority to act. On the other, the sincere implementation of Responsible Care requires it to act as regulatory authority that can sanction members who do not discipline themselves. Whenever these sanctions threatens members' separate interests to the point of menacing consensus, the CMA vacillates, and Responsible Care risks degenerating into a public-relations maneuver.

The new architecture we have outlined suggests that greater transparency and public accountability can resolve this overcome this stalemate. We find supportive evidence in the evolution of earlier, strikingly similar efforts at private regulation in the nuclear power generating industry housed in the Institute of Nuclear Power Operations (INPO). These efforts succeeded only when the system of self-monitoring was placed under the aegis of public institutions and authority.

Like Responsible Care, INPO grew out of a public relations crisis: it was formed in 1979, nine months after the Three Mile Island disaster. Like Responsible Care, INPO was designed as a private effort, and was financed by the utilities.

From the outset INPO's chief activities consisted of pooling the industry's operating experience, establishing benchmarks to distill the lessons there, and then evaluating individual power plants according to their ability to meet those benchmarks. Operating information is gathered initially through the Significant Event Evaluation Information Network. INPO officials sift event reports to distinguish harmless disruptions of operations from dangerous ones. They then circulate analyses of the causes of the dangerous disruptions and ways to prevent them in Significant Operating Experience Reports. Industry Operating Experience Reviews are then conducted periodically to assess the ability of particular plants to make effective use of the information provided by the reports.

This collection and dissemination of information to the immediate actors did not produce large, improvements in performance. By the mid- 1980s, it became clear that the effectiveness of INPO as a new center for performance improvement through information pooling depended crucially on its ability to divulge what it learned about the industry and individual firms to broader circles of participants. These would have to include high-level managers, boards of directors, and ultimately the Nuclear Regulatory Commission (NRC).

The broader diffusion began in late 1984, when INPO began to rank plants, and make the results available to the CEO of the utility operating the power plant, the utility's board of directors, and the responsible public service commissions and NRC. The NRC, in effect, retains the formal authority to promulgate regulations, but either adopts the standards in training, maintenance, and other matters elaborated by INPO, or simply acknowledges best practices defined by the institute without formalizing them. In addition to peer discipline and the authority derived from close cooperation with the NRC, INPO can suspend uncooperative member utilities. Thus, although there are no civil or criminal penalties for noncompliance with INPO standards, the institute found means to resolve the problems that now plague Responsible Care and thereby achieve notable safety improvements.[1]

DIFFUSE PROBLEMS

The Chesapeake Bay Program, responsible for protecting and restoring the largest estuarine system in the United States, is at once the most extensive, mature, institutionally complex, and successful of the ecosystem regimes emerging in the new regulatory framework. The Program grew up along side of the nascent EPA: while the Clean Water Act regulated point-source polluters such as factories and power plants, it did not regulate pollution—more threatening to the Bay—that derived from non-point sources such as farms, construction sites, lawns, landfills, septic tanks, and city streets. The Program's exemplary accomplishment has been to address this latter, more diffuse problem amidst radically changing ideas of the exact nature of the threat, and how, ecologically and institutionally, to respond to it. Such is the attractive power of its example that the EPA is currently trying to model new programs on the Chesapeake experience, with the apparent intent of eventually reconfiguring regulation under the CWA itself.

The Chesapeake Bay Program emerged from a broad citizen movement, concerned with the degradation of a beautiful but fragile ecosystem that to this day evokes widespread pride and vigilance from residents, farmers, and business people alike. In 1966—four years before Earth Day and six years before the passage of the CWA—these citizens formed the Chesapeake Bay Foundation as an advocacy organization to "Save the Bay." At the behest of this group, among others, congressional leaders funded a major six-year EPA study in 1973 to determine the status and causes of decline of the ecosystem. The report revealed a complex web of interrelated causes and alarming symptoms—such as declining fish and shellfish stocks—that spanned several states in the Bay region.

In response to this report and continuing investigations, a multi-state, inter-agency Chesapeake Bay Agreement was signed in 1983 "to improve and protect water quality and living resources in the Chesapeake Bay ecosystem."[2] The agreement—whose signatories included US Environmental Protection Agency, the governors of Maryland, Virginia, and Pennsylvania, and the mayor of the District of Columbia—established the core institutional framework for future cooperative efforts. It created an Executive Council and an implementation committee that would develop ecosystem restoration plans in conjunction with state and federal environmental agencies.

A second Chesapeake Bay Agreement, signed in 1987, marked the next evolutionary phase of the program. Much more concrete than previous efforts, this accord established a regime of biological monitoring as the bedrock of future management efforts. It identified the "productivity, diversity, and abundance" of the Bay's living resources as "the best ultimate measures of the Chesapeake Bay's condition," and set ambitious performance targets, including reduction of nutrient loadings by 40 percent by the year 2000. When further studies revealed that loadings in various tributaries had differential impacts on water quality in the bay itself, parties revised their system-wide goals and codified them in a 1992 commitment to develop tributary-specific nutrient reduction targets, strategies, and implementation tools. The 1992 amendments also established a specific, quantifiable biological monitoring regime, and Executive Council directives have added progressively more detailed commitments in such areas as a basin-wide toxic reduction strategy, habitat restoration, wetlands protection, and agricultural non-point source reduction.

All these arrangements and rearrangements are, however, the public face of deeper, less visible changes in the understanding of environmental regulation that have come to shape the strategic reflections of the program's leading protagonists. First, there is the realization that the more we learn about the ecology of the Bay, the more surprising new findings will be. The second and third cumulative changes in the program's self-understanding are procedural. One concerns govern-ance. The various agreements and the entities that they establish constitute an institutional chassis for forming and re-forming governance mechanisms as changing conditions warrant. In practice, the Chesapeake Bay Program has employed a grab bag of regulatory techniques, legal instruments, and voluntary measures. Above all, it has experimented with legal forms. Many of its policies build concerted packages from disparate administrative and legislative measures in typically segregated arenas such as "land use," "air pollution," "water pollution," "public lands management," "fisheries management," and "wildlife conservation." More specifically, many actions of the Chesapeake Executive Council advancing such packets take the form of "directives." These are joint executive decrees of dubious legal pedigree and status. Yet they are regarded as, at a minimum, morally binding commitments on the part of each executive to use all available powers and authorities to carry out the stated commitments.

These arrangements work well enough for adjusting program activities within broadly-agreed-upon boundaries. But more traditional forces come into play in larger re-definitions of purpose. In such moments, the very fluidity of the internal governance of the program becomes a liability, as external interlocutors seek, in vain, to determine *the* authoritative voice of an institutional ensemble that adjusts precisely by not having one.

The other change concerns citizen participation. Through the 1960s and early '70s, participa-tion in the program meant conventional public education through publications, public meetings, hearings, and mass media. When it became clear that the level of monitoring required to man-age the Bay and its tributaries was beyond the technical and financial capacity of government alone, emphasis shifted to more active, deeper forms of participation—essentially, teaching large numbers of volunteers to mimic the monitoring and reporting protocols developed by scientific experts, so as to produce a larger volume of reasonably reliable monitoring data. In the process, ordinary citizens would become quasi-experts by imitation. In the 1980s, the program explicitly equated participation with the emulation of expert knowledge.

The recent emergence of a "tributary strategy" emphasizing the need for stream-specific goals and implementation measures, marks the third re- conceptualization of citizens' roles and their relationship experts. Continuing surprises to expert judgment have led, reasonably enough, to the conclusion that the required level of specificity in planning and implementation is now beyond the capacity of experts alone. Nor can the necessary measures be developed by the lay public simply by following precise routines or protocols defined by the experts. Instead, responsibility is devolved to semi-autonomous "tributary teams" comprising government officials, scientific experts, agricultural and industry representatives, and citizen volunteers. As a group they become experts with regard to their own tributaries, drawing on a unique mix of local knowledge, expert science (adapted to local needs), and basin-wide experience to become the authors and implementers of the tributary strategy. Because measures can be tailored to the local circumstances of each watershed part, the tributary teams are simultaneously more effective and equitable in the burdens they impose than uniform statewide measures. Together, these changes lend plausibility to the idea of broad, continuing, and deeply informed citizen participation in environmental affairs that, unlike the first wave of backyard environmentalism, constructs as much as it obstructs.

PUTTING THE PIECES TOGETHER

Among the most dynamic and supple prototypes of the new regulatory architecture is the HCP, which ironically emerged out of one of the most rigid of all environmental laws: the Endangered Species Act. Section 9 of the act prohibits the "taking" of listed wildlife species. "Take" includes both direct injury and habitat modification that "kills or injures wildlife by significantly impairing essential behavior patterns, including breeding, feeding or sheltering."[3] In application, this simple language becomes a sweeping, inflexible rule with the potential to bar a broad range of land development and resource extraction activities wherever endangered species have been identified. Not surprisingly, landowners, industries, and communities complain that they are unfairly singled out under a harsh and arbitrary rule that provides dubious species protection benefits.

In 1982, Congress responded by authorizing the issuance of permits to "take" listed species if the taking is "incidental to, and not the purpose of" an otherwise lawful activity. To secure a permit, the applicant must produce an HCP, and demonstrate that the taking will not appreciably reduce the likelihood of the species' survival and recovery. The Fish and Wildlife Service (FWS) retains broad discretionary authority to add any terms and conditions it deems necessary to ensure species survival. By April 1999, 254 plans—regulating more than 11 million acres—had been approved and 200 more were in various stages of development.[4]

Bruce Babbitt, appointed Secretary of the Interior in 1993, and his staff favored the HCP process. They saw it as an opportunity to bring landowners and environmentalists together to hammer out conservation plans that might provide greater ecosystem protection than strict application of Section 9-without halting development and economic growth. To demonstrate the workability of this approach to the public, regulated communities, and even to their own field agents, Babbitt and his associates would have to intervene in local HCP processes to elaborate a real and attractive alternative to traditional ESA enforcement.

Opportunities to do just this arose in San Diego and Orange Counties, where urban sprawl had already reduced much of the coastal sage scrub ecosystem to tract housing, shopping malls, and office parks. This, in turn, had shrunk and badly fragmented the habitat of native species like the California gnatcatcher, a songbird endemic to the southern California coastal region. Yet when the gnatcatcher was proposed for listing under the ESA, Section 9's prohibition against "taking" threatened to bring lucrative development in fast-growing San Diego and Orange Counties to an abrupt halt.

Compared to such listing, almost any alternative seemed reasonable to landowners, developers, and state and local government officials. The ESA allowed them to use the HCP process as a framework for negotiation. A California statute, the Natural Communities Conservation Planning Act, linked motive to framework by providing for a process (initially voluntary) that brought together landowners, state and local officials, conservationists, and other interested parties to develop integrated, regional-level ecosystem protection plans. They negotiated the first of a new generation of participatory and performance-based landscape-scale, multi-species HCPs in San Diego, Orange, and Riverside Counties.

Jointly formulated by developers, public officials, conservationists, and scientists, these plans require landowners to dedicate large tracts of land for exclusive use as habitat reserves for unlisted as well as listed species. They restrict development in buffer zones adjacent to the reserves to provide additional habitat benefits. Biological and environmental monitoring regimes, governance institutions, and funding mechanisms are put in place, and a range of "adaptive management" measures are specified, allowing adjustments to be made and contingency plans to kick in, based on the results of monitoring, new scientific information, and changes in conditions. In return, landowners are awarded "incidental take" permits that allow them to develop their remaining lands in accordance with the overall plan. The agreements are controversial among environmentalists,[5] some of whom prefer strict application of Section 9, and among landowners and developers, some of whom see the HCP process as legalized extortion. But many leading environmentalists, landowners, public officials, and scientists contend that, on the whole, these agreements produce more, better, and more sophisticated ecosystem management regimes than would emerge from even the strictest application of Section 9.

The inclusiveness and sophistication of these Southern California HCPs illuminate the promise of the new regulatory regime and offer a scalable example for the almost 500 plans that are in development or have already been approved. While many of these are quite limited in scope, others are far more ambitious in their measures and goals and innovative in their internal architecture. Increasingly, HCPs are formulated by diverse affected parties and move beyond basic land use planning approaches to embrace water quality and stream flow measures, ecosystem restoration projects, forestry and agricultural "best management practices," and a variety of other implementation measures.[6]

But these Southern California successes are slow to diffuse to all HCPs because the emergent nationwide conservation planning regime is by and large unable to pool the information generated by local projects or to systematically learn from innovative developments, trends, successes, and errors. Such pooling as does occur is done mainly by the Fish and Wildlife Service,[7] whose highly decentralized internal structure has so far proved far better at dispersing authority to local decision makers than at reviewing the ensuing decisions. The result is nearly unsupervised local autonomy with correspondingly wide variations in the performance of HCPs from one place to another. Thus local circumstance, seldom corrected by national discipline, determines whether an HCP monitors its progress well or poorly,[8] or whether its decision-making is accessible not only to local deal-makers, but also to independent scientists, conservationists, and generally informed citizens. Often, in fact, HCPs amount to an agreement between a permit seeker and a service field agent. Where the experience of the Chesapeake tributary teams shows that open participation and good science may be mutually reinforcing, this kind of involution—especially in the absence of rigorous monitoring—can lead to self-deluding celebrations of expert powers and so to under-estimation of the combined political, scientific, and practical complexity of large-scale ecosystem management.[9] At the worst, it can undermine the democratic legitimacy of HCPs by transforming them into unprincipled backroom deals between regulators and the regulated.[10]

In response to such concerns two measures—a new FWS guidance and the Endangered Species Recovery Act of 1999 (HR960, or the Miller Bill)—have been proposed to create a minimal informational infrastructure for the coordination of the HCPs, and thereby to improve performance of individual plans with respect to monitoring and accessibility. As concerns monitoring, the guidance directs the Service to create a database that tracks basic plan features such as permit duration, acreage covered, species and habitat details, authorized take, and permitted activity. It may also record monitoring programs, actual take, operational adjustments, and field visit reports.[11] Similarly, the Miller Bill directs bilateral monitoring of the implementation of HCPs and their biological outcomes; permit holders would be required to report publicly on actions taken in accordance with the plan, status of jeopardized species, and progress toward objective, measurable biological goals, while the Secretary would be required to report on the implementation and quantitative biological progress of each plan every three years.

As concerns accessibility, the FWS guidance responds tepidly by extending the Administrative Procedure Act's after-the-fact "notice and comment" period from 30 to 60 days and offering the only slightly more ambitious proposal to add advisory and informational committees in cases of large-scale HCPs. The Miller Bill goes further, instructing the department to take steps to ensure balanced public participation in the development of large scale, multiple landowner, and multi-species plans. Without better institutionalizing the distinctive contributions that the public can make to ecosystem governance—information, monitoring capacity, oversight, and democratic legitimacy—reformers risk losing elements critical to a successful process. On an optimistic reading these measures, or something like them, will lay the groundwork for a TRI-style, information-based pooling system whose own initial shortcomings will be incrementally corrected even as the emergent infrastructure makes it possible to begin overcoming, locale by locale, the defects of disjointed decentralized ecosystem management.

Weaving The Whole

Does this tale of environmental reorientation merit further elaboration, beyond recounting these illustrations? On one interpretation, the independent emergence of this architecture in diverse settings attests to its robustness across local environments and political regimes. Formulating a comprehensive regulatory design might then be unnecessary because some groups will eventually discover it, or unhelpful because it would shackle novel local experimentation to half-baked and half-replicable experiences.

This incremental view is too optimistic, and in any case has already been overtaken by events: Federal agencies are extending and elaborating the emergent principles of innovation by undertaking large projects that aim to replicate the kinds of regulatory successes we have been examining. The piecemeal decentralization of authority from federal to subnational authorities has excited the interest of the states. And crucially, Congress is noticing the anomalies of the new regimes as viewed in the light of the legislation from which their authorization is derived.

Like it or not, debate about the legitimacy of the performance-based systems is about to be on the agenda. At the core of that debate will be a fundamental question: how can directly deliberative, problem-solving regimes co-exist with the institutions of pluralist democracy? This question arises, we will now see, as much when the reformers aim for self-limiting modesty, as when they are more ambitiously expansive. Precisely because the problem is ubiquitous, consolidation of the new architecture will, we believe, in the end depend on an open validation—probably through Congress—of the changes that have emerged as much outside the current order as within.

To illustrate the vulnerability of administrative reform not backed by law, consider the recent HCP experience. High officials in the Department of the Interior argued that under conditions of modern complexity, government can at most reveal the possibilities of new forms of collective problem solving through a discrete politics of the deed. Once working models of the alternative have proved their worth, the equilibrium mechanisms of pluralist society ensure that the incipient experiments develop in ways society judges fair and effective. With regard to the HCPs, for instance, local "under-enforcement" that threatened vulnerable species would be registered by national environmental groups, who would press the authorities for corrective action; "over-enforcement" would conversely provoke protests by local property owners, and move *their* national representatives to corresponding interventions. Aggressive advocates of more comprehensive strategies misunderstand what government under modern conditions can do, and imperil what has been done by bringing it to the attention of busybodies.

This peculiar optimism seems misplaced. Why assume that the dueling political powers produce an exquisite balance, rather than a welter of clashing rules, or a self-canceling swing of policy from "too much" to "too little" protection of endangered species or prosecution of other goals? In recent decades, in policy area after policy area, this, not harmony, has been the outcome. The introduction of forms of direct deliberation at the local levels will, if anything, make pluralist interest balancing at the highest levels less practicable than before. Institutions such as HCPs work precisely by uncovering, through experimentalist investigation, potential solutions initially unknown even to the local actors. How, and on the basis of which incentives, will the pluralist rule-makers at the center come to know of the local discoveries? If they knew, what solutions would they in turn support? But if higher-ups predictably rule in ignorance, indifference, or hostility to these innovations, why should local actors engage in experimentalist exploration at all?

The Miller Bill could furnish an elegant resolution to this clash between directly deliberative and pluralist decision-making in the case of HCPs. The proposed Bill in effect carries forward the careful environmentalist criticism of the promise of HCPs. It aims to solve much of the problem simply by requiring the Department of the Interior to respect minimum HCP conditions. Thus, to be recognized as valid, the HCPs must incorporate objective, measurable biological goals aimed at species recovery, a regime to monitor the biological status of each covered species, regularized reporting, and appropriate adaptive management measures. Development of large-scale HCPs involving multiple landowners or multiple species would require substantial public participation, and to ensure consistency, transparency, and accountability within individual HCPs and throughout the system as a whole, the Secretary would be required to review each HCP triennially and recommend such adjustments as be necessary to ensure species recovery, and publish an annual report on the status of all HCPs.

Thus Congress, if it passed the Miller Bill, would subtly modify both its own legislative role and that of the administrative agency. Congress's role would shift from the familiar one of setting some relatively circumscribed public goal—protecting endangered species—and delegating responsibility for achieving it to a federal rule maker, to authorizing and conferring pluralist political legitimacy on the constitutive framework under which citizens as local agents can experimentally determine how to pursue a presumptively broad and changing project—protecting and restoring habitats. The role of the Department of the Interior would shift from relying on its own expertise and judgment to help craft the agreements and determine their acceptability, to rigorously policing a framework within which a broad and open circle of participants, local and national, can determine for themselves whether particular HCPs, and the institution taken as a whole, are meeting the goals it sets for itself. Familiar fights will of course continue, but the rules for adjudicating them will change.

None of this is likely to happen immediately. But the very variety of ways in which deep users are prospectively combining the current, imperfect buildings blocks suggests that there will also be many opportunities to crystallize this democratic regulatory reorientation in political discussion, and so to insert a promising new item on the reform agenda.

Democratic Reform

The great dilemma for twentieth-century democrats has been the conflict between efficiency and the values of fairness and self-determination served when citizens rule themselves. The mainstream view is simply that markets are the most efficient instruments for allocating resources and hence that any democratically inspired adjustments to market operations or redirection of their proceeds induces inefficiency. Even the great currents of American popular reform—such as Jacksonianism, populism, and Progressivism, which shared a deep fear of the predatory power of economic elites—themselves treat private ordering as a kind of precious nature preserve, easily disrupted by excesses of democratic participation.

Jacksonians, populists, and their contemporary descendants, Reagan-era monetarists and supply-siders, sought to reform finance once and for all. They aimed to re-make the market so that the everyday transactions by which citizens effected their economic advancement would not result in accumulations of wealth and influence that might then be turned against their freedom. Through these movements runs the thread of the characteristically American distinction between well-ordered markets as the instrument and guarantee of legitimate self-assertion and perverted ones as the tool of domination.

The Progressive impulse, in contrast, seeks redress not in a once-and-for-all institutional reform, but rather in an enduring and self-reinforcing shift of authority away from contending class interests and towards the trusteeship of a circle of technically versed experts. The hope—in the turn-of-the-century struggle against trusts and corrupt political machines as well as in recent battles with cigarette makers, pharmaceutical companies, and drug dealers—is to attenuate the destructive contest between elite and mass by interposing stewards of the common good who would themselves be disciplined by rigorous inquiry.

The environmental reforms discussed above arose within these channels, but overflowed their original banks. They commingle these streams of reform and reveal in their novel course the most improbable of possibilities: that participation of a directly deliberative kind, far from being a charge against efficiency, may be today a precondition for it. The profusion of participation that makes backyard environmentalism work springs from our traditional ideas of reform, yet holds promise of freeing us from deep limits to our idealism.

The inspiration of TRI and, more diffusely, of the Chesapeake Bay Program, was the Jacksonian or populist notion that occulted powers were literally poisoning the people in pursuit of private gain. The remedy was to use government authority to force transparency—to require the disclosure to local communities of the additional information they needed to defend themselves from those who would poison them. Both had the distinctly Jacksonian flavor of efforts to re-order markets, not attack market order as such. Opponents of both programs disparage the ability of common people to digest and responsibly respond to the disclosures in terms that recall the nineteenth-century patrician fear and disdain of the tempestuous mob. Moreover, because both programs were launched with the intent of creating self-contained and self-enforcing mechanisms, neither anticipated the need, soon manifest, for higher-order mechanisms continuously to adjust the frame of intervention itself according to the findings of initial investigations.

TURA, Responsible Care, and HCPs, in contrast, were Progressive. All depend on the active participation of experts—toxics use reduction planners, conservation biologists—whose disciplining presence on *both* sides of the bargaining table is said to make the bargains possible and manageable once struck. The chief limitation of these programs has accordingly been the tension they create between the circle of experts, exchanging information openly amongst themselves, and the concentric circles of the more or less engaged public who are not formally included in the discussion but by virtue of their information and experience eventually move toward its center.

To establish these continuities between past and present is not, of course, to foretell a continuation of the old errors of Jacksonianism and Progressivism. On the contrary, the confluence of expertise and market ordering of both traditions in the new regime holds the promise of transcending their separate limitations. Thus the successes of TRI, as well as many aspects of the operation of certain HCPs or of INPO, shame the Progressives in their deference to expertise and vindicate the Jacksonian faith in the capacity of citizens to govern their own affairs. Above all, the self-transformative successes of the Chesapeake Bay Program reveal the needless limitations of the Jacksonian faith in once-and-for-all solutions to problems of social order and vindicate the confidence of many Progressives that the public could respond to its problems through institutionalized, deeply informed self-scrutiny in a way that John Dewey—the boldest of them all—could himself scarcely imagine. The common lesson is that expertise without local participation remains ignorant of crucial detail, while localism unprovoked by expertise remains haplessly parochial.

To be sure, some parts of the established environmental movement continue to prefer the insider's game of pluralist grappling for influence at power centers. But other parts are reorganizing to take advantage of the local participatory possibilities of the emergent regime. For example, largely self-directed chapters of the Nature Conservancy and other, often ad hoc groupings of conservation-minded citizens are stepping forward on their own initiative to lead ambitious ecosystem-management projects, loosely coordinated by the flow of information to national conservation organizations and government agencies, and back again to other local projects. In these efforts, distinctions between the public sphere and the private begin to blur, as the citizen-authors of public policy come to view government at all levels as a partner to be recruited into a broadly collaborative effort, rather than as master rule-maker or ultimate arbiter before whom they must come as supplicant or subject.[12]

Even at the pinnacle of the Washington environmental establishment, some see the need for self-redefinition and democratic renewal. The National Wildlife Federation, for one, candidly acknowledges that with habitat conservation programs now dominant in endangered species policy, decision-making authority has already shifted from the center to localities. Consequently, they say environmentalists' emphasis must also shift. No longer able to influence the substantive rules directly, the national organizations must instead work to ensure a deeply participatory local process, both by influencing the overall design of the regulatory architecture and by encouraging and supporting citizen participation in HCP planning, locality-by-locality.[13] The national organizations thus begin to reinvent themselves as independent monitors of local performance and poolers of best practices, in effect becoming a separate and parallel repository for the rich flow of information generated by the new regime.[14] In this way, they position themselves simultaneously to monitor and offer informed critiques of the regime's design and performance overall and in the local particulars, and to provide local citizens an independent channel of information to guide, assist, and empower them in local efforts. Thus do participation, coordinated decentralization, and the open flow of information merge over time into a self-reinforcing system of deep use, and in so doing enrich our democratic polity.

Whatever the immediate outcomes of the struggles over environmental reform, backyard environmentalism has progressed far enough to make us insist on exploring the possibilities for augmenting and transforming our democracy before continuing to settle for less and less of it.

Notes

1. The two measures are the number of "scrams," or rapid reactor shutdowns, and the number of safety system actuations. Both represent a gauge of the frequency of emergencies and are therefore inversely correlated with overall reactor safety. Between 1980 and 1990, the number of scrams per unit decreased by 80 percent. The number of safety system actuations decreased by 60 percent between 1985 (the first year such measures were taken) and 1990.

2. The Chesapeake Bay Agreement of 1983, signed by the United States EPA, the governors of Maryland, Virginia, and Pennsylvania, and the mayor of the District of Columbia.

3. 50 C.F.R. 17.3. The Supreme Court has upheld this regulation as a valid interpretation of the statutory prohibition against "taking" of listed wildlife. See Babbitt v. Sweet Home Chapter of Communities for a Great Oregon, 115 S.Ct. 2407 (1995).

4. U.S. Fish and Wildlife Service, Division of Endangered Species, "Status of Habitat Conservation Plans" (April 23, 1999). An electronic version of this document can be obtained at <http://www.fws.gov/r9endspp/hcp/hcptable.pdf>.

5. John Kostyack, "Habitat Conservation Planning: Time to Give Conservationists and Other Concerned Citizens a Seat at the Table," Endangered Species UPDATE 14 (July–August 1997), 51–5.

6. An effective system must be an adaptive one because even the best science gets better: "There is never enough information" to allow timeless determinations of fixed rules, and "[n]o key ecosystem management decision ever gets made in a setting of adequate information." See George Frampton, "Ecosystem Management in the Clinton Administration," Duke Environmental Law and Policy Forum 7 (1996), 39. Frampton was, at the time he wrote these words, Assistant Secretary for Fish, Wildlife, and Parks in the Department of the Interior, overseeing the Fish and Wildlife Service and its endangered species program.

7. In interviewing FWS and Interior officials in July, 1998, the authors learned that no one in Washington had even collected the HCPs that had already been negotiated up until that point—much less read them, or attempted to absorb any generally-applicable lessons that might be learned from them.

8. Peter Kareiva et al., *Using Science in Habitat Conservation Plans* (Santa Barbara: National Center for Ecological Analysis and Synthesis, 1998).

9. Frampton describes how the FWS's traditional emphasis on purely science-based decision making stands at odds with the inherently political nature of ecosystem management.

10. For a thoughtful and textured environmentalist critique of the shortcomings of public participation in HCP planning, see Kostyack, "Habitat Conservation."

11. See *Federal Register*, 64: 45 (March 9, 1999), 11488. A first draft of this database can be obtained on the Internet at: <http://www.fws.gov/r9endspp/hcp/hcptable.pdf>.

12. See Lee P. Breckenridge, "Reweaving the Landscape: The Institutional Challenges of Ecosystem Management for Lands in Private Ownership," *Vermont Law Review*, 19 (1995), 363.

13. See Kostyack, "Habitat Conservation."

14. Tellingly, the Washington office of the National Wildlife Federation made itself a central repository for Habitat Conservation Plans before it occurred to anyone in the Department of the Interior that such a thing might be useful. In addition, NWF convened the first national conference to assess HCP policy and practice, and has produced thoughtful and detailed critiques of many HCPs that will undoubtedly inform future ones.

10 Goal: Replace Risk Assessment with Alternatives Assessment

Mary O'Brien

The goal of this book is to help replace risk assessment of a narrow range of options with public assessment of a broad range of options. The book is based on a set of values, principles, and understandings, as well as on scientific and factual information.

Imagine a woman standing by an icy mountain river, intending to cross to the other side. A team of four risk assessors stands behind her, reviewing her situation. The toxicologist says that she ought to wade across the river because it is not toxic, only cold. The cardiologist says she ought to wade across the river because she looks to be young and not already chilled. Her risks of cardiac arrest, therefore, are low. The hydrologist says she ought to wade across the river because he has seen other rivers like this and estimates that this one is not more than 4 feet deep and probably has no whirlpools at this location. Finally, the EPA policy specialist says that the woman ought to wade across the river because, compared to global warming, ozone depletion, and loss of species diversity, the risks of her crossing are trivial.

The woman refuses to wade across. "Why?" the risk assessors ask. They show her their calculations, condescendingly explaining to her that her risk of dying while wading across the river is one in 40 million.

Still, the woman refuses to wade across. "Why?" the risk assessors ask again, frustrated by this woman who clearly doesn't understand the nature of risks.

The woman points upstream, and says "Because there is a bridge."

The risk assessors in this story are evaluating the risks of only one option: wading across an icy river. The woman is evaluating her alternatives, one of which involves crossing the river on a bridge. The woman doesn't really care whether getting wet in the icy stream will kill her or not, because it doesn't make sense to her to even become chilled in light of her options. This is the fundamental difference between risk assessment and alternatives assessment.

Now contemplate another story—one in which risk assessment takes place after, rather than before, a hazardous activity has begun.

Imagine a company whose air emissions coalesce during rain into heavy, baseball-size clumps. The balls hurt when they hit someone on the head. Occasionally the pollution balls cause concussions, but they rarely kill someone.

From *Making Better Environmental Decisions* (Cambridge, MA: MIT Press, 2000), 2–15.

A team is hired by the company (or the county, or the federal government) to calculate how often someone's head is hit, how soon the pain generally goes away, how often a concussion is mild and how often severe, and which people seem particularly susceptible to death when hit by the pollution balls.

This team would be doing a risk assessment.

You might say to yourself that this is an absurd story. People would not simply stand by and do a risk assessment in such a situation. The company would not be allowed to emit pollutants that could ball up. They would be forced to change their production practices so pollution balls wouldn't be hitting people in the head.

When we do risk assessments, however, we do the precise equivalent of this, "standing by" and analyzing possible damages while people (company bosses, landowners, farmers, consumers, legislators) and the materials they use, create, and discard (in factories, on farms and ranches, in forests, in towns, in cities, at government installations) unnecessarily inflict stress, harm, or even death on both living things and natural processes. Thus, humans—ourselves, our children, and future generations—are affected, along with animal and plant life and the natural elements (such as ground-water and the ozone layer) that help support life. The activities that inflict harm include emitting toxic chemicals or particulates,[1] draining an underground water supply, allowing sediments to wash into a river, erecting dams that block salmon from returning home to spawn, draining wetlands to build developments, or killing trees with acid rain.

The process of estimating damages that may be occurring, or that may occur if an activity is undertaken, is called risk assessment.

Example: A large incinerator in East Liverpool, Ohio, burns hazardous wastes. Because the incinerator doesn't completely burn all of the toxic chemicals and doesn't burn toxic metals that are present in the wastes, it emits some highly toxic chemicals and metals into the air. The incinerator is located 400 yards from an elementary school. This school is up on a bluff, approximately level with the incinerator's stack. The toxic chemicals that leave the stack are carried in the wind over to the school, where the children are hit by them every day. They breathe the toxic chemicals into their lungs, they absorb them on their skin, they pick some up on their fingers in the schoolyard, and they ingest some whenever they stick their fingers in their mouths or eat their food.

Industry consultants and government employees calculate how much WTI, the corporation that runs the incinerator, shall be allowed to hit the elementary school children with toxic chemicals and metals (Hazardous Waste Facility Approval Board 1984; EPA Deputy Administrator Robert Sussman, letter to Terri Swearingen of Tri-State Environmental Council, July 16, 1993). They have decided, for instance, that the incinerator's managers can annually send 9400 pounds of lead, 2560 pounds of mercury, and 157,400 pounds of fine particles out of the 150-foot incinerator stack (Montague 1992).

These people are doing risk assessment.

Most of the activities assessed in risk assessments produce some commercial benefit, or supposedly "solve" some problem, such as what to do with toxic wastes. The real or perceived benefits are generally considered justification for the activity being evaluated. For instance, providing jobs or competing in the global economy may be a benefit assumed for the commercial facilities that are bringing their toxic wastes to the WTI incinerator. An assumed benefit of the incinerator itself may be that it avoids the construction of new hazardous-waste landfills. The risk assessment will then focus on particular potential "risks" caused by incinerator operations, such as asthma or cancer from the toxic chemicals and metals escaping from the incinerator stack.

Thus, a risk-benefit or a cost-benefit analysis is implicit in a decision-making process involving risk assessment, even if the actual existence or extent of the benefits (e.g., jobs or waste disposal) is not explicitly examined in a formal risk-benefit or cost-benefit analysis.

The thinking and the processes of risk assessment currently pervade policy decision making throughout many industrialized societies. The most basic, unstated goal of risk assessment, however, is to provide permission for undertaking some amount or form of the activity whose risks are being assessed.

It would be more helpful to the school children of East Liverpool if, instead of simply writing permits for "acceptable" exposure of the children to lead, mercury, and particulates from the WTI incinerator, we encouraged reduction of toxic-waste production by those industries that haul their wastes to the WTI incinerator. Similarly, we might be more helpful to the children if we worked with industries to help them develop and use alternative technologies that don't depend on using toxic chemicals. We could develop laws that require industries to keep their toxic wastes to themselves (for instance, by storing the wastes on their property in large, above-ground containers). Having to store their own wastes on their own property would give the companies incentives to reduce their production of wastes and to develop technologies that detoxify certain toxic chemicals.

If industry consultants, the government employees, or the communities and states involved in the WTI case examined the risks and benefits of these potentially helpful options alongside the risks and benefits of the proposed WTI incinerator operations, they would be doing alternatives assessment.

Fundamental Principles

Before plunging into my arguments, I want to lay out the principles on which both this book and the concept of alternatives assessment are based. These principles, or bases for conduct, come out of particular values and biases. (For each, I have indicated how risk assessment is based on different values and biases.)

Adherence to the following principles requires decision making based on diverse public participation and consideration of numerous social and technical options. In other words, the following principles require public-based alternatives assessment.

1. It is not acceptable to harm people when there are reasonable alternatives.

Harm can be wrought by hunger, emotional abuse, noise, toxic chemicals, radiation, loss of open spaces, or other stresses, as well as by physical violence.

Risk assessment generally focuses on a particular activity, hazardous substance, or project. Alternatives to these activities, substances, or projects are rarely considered or pursued in a meaningful way.

2. It is not acceptable to harm non-humans when there are reasonable alternatives.

I am not talking about hunting here, although some people would (Kerasote 1997). I'm talking about the type of harm involved in polluting wildlife with toxic, chlorinated organic compounds (organochlorines) that weaken or kill them.[2]

I am talking about the type of harm involved in building more roads in the last areas where wild wolves (e.g., eastern timber wolves) survive. Humans often kill wolves when they see them from roads. Wolves are wary of raising pups near people and cars and roads. In general, wolves will have trouble surviving if there is more than one mile of road in a square mile of land where they are living (USFWS 1992).

While people differ on the value they place on providing health and habitat for non-human beings, such as wolves, butterflies, or fish, this book is based on the assumption that, for their own well-being and that of all living things, human beings need to share the Earth with as broad a diversity of living beings as possible.

Alternatives assessments could technically consider benefits and damages of particular activities only as they would affect human beings. However, many people acknowledge their personal, cultural, spiritual, physical, psychological, and/or economic dependence on a biologically and ecologically diverse world. Many people also recognize a deep connection with the non-human world and feel fully human only when they respect the needs of their non-human co-inhabitants of the Earth. This book is based on such respect.

Again, risk assessments rarely involve serious consideration of viable alternatives.

3. Nobody is able to define for someone else what damage is "acceptable".

Alabama State Attorney General Jimmy Evans has explained this well in relation to the chemical called "dioxin" (Kipp 1991):

The risk assessment technologies . . . say people will die as a result of dioxin emissions. Then they say that is perfectly acceptable. . . . That is really, really—to me—outrageous and bizarre. It reflects an elitism, a plantation mentality. I think it amounts to a confession. It is very, very simple to me. It is a moral issue. They have said people will die, and we are supposed to accept that. As attorney general of this state, I can't.

Some of the laws and regulations we have developed in the United States require government regulators to determine "acceptable" damage: "acceptable" levels of drinking-water contamination, "acceptable limits of change" on public lands, "acceptable" numbers of cancers that will be caused by some activity like producing or using some toxic, "acceptable daily intakes" of toxic pesticides, and so on. This does not alter the fact that what they have regulated as being "acceptable" may in fact *not* be acceptable to you, to your unborn child, to your community or tribe, or to Florida panthers or wood ducks.

What is acceptable to any person is a matter of personal judgment, but the word is used by risk assessment's promoters as if it were something concrete that could be measured by others, or as if it were something about which everyone must surely agree. This is not accurate. For instance, while a state's Department of Environmental Quality may call some amount of toxic

Box 10.1   Dioxin, dioxin-like chemicals, and organochlorines

The term "dioxin" refers to a group of 75 different chlorinated organic chemicals that contain two "rings" of carbon atoms, two oxygen atoms joining the two rings, and chlorine atoms attached to certain carbon atoms on the carbon rings. Sometimes "dioxin" is used to refer to the most toxic known dioxin, 2,3,7,8-tetra-chlorodibenzo-p-dioxin, which is also referred to as 2,3,7,8-TCDD.

Certain (but not all) dioxins cause particular toxic effects in numerous living organisms. These toxic effects include cancer, immune-system damage, imbalance of sexual hormones, nervous-system damage, reproductive failure, birth defects, kidney damage, and skin defects.

"Dioxin-like chemicals" refers to a larger group of chemicals that elicit the same toxic effects as does 2,3,7,8-TCDD in numerous living organisms. These chemicals include certain other dioxins (i.e., those that have a chlorine atom at each of the 2, 3, 7, and 8 positions on the carbon rings, but also have chlorines at other positions on the carbon rings), furans, polychlorinated biphenyls (PCBs), polybrominated biphenyls (PBBs), and polychlorinated naphthalenes (PCNs). The source of nearly all dioxins and dioxin-like chemicals present in the environment is human manufacture, use, and disposal of chlorinated organic (i.e., carbon-containing) compounds.

The dioxin-like chemicals elicit the same toxic effects as 2,3,7,8-TCDD because they attach to the same receptor in cells and lead to production of the same enzymes and toxic chemical reactions in living organisms as 2,3,7,8-TCDD. They do this in weaker fashion, however. Some dioxins and furans, for instance, are one-half or one-thousandth as "potent" as dioxin at eliciting the toxic effects. These "weaker" dioxins and furans, however, may be present as pollutants in the environment in much larger amounts than dioxin. They can thereby cause large amounts of dioxin-like damage.

Chemical compounds that contain carbon are called "organic compounds," and organic compounds that contain chlorine atoms are called "organochlorine compounds" or "chlorinated organic compounds."

Source: O'Brien 1990

pollution of well water acceptable, a person who actually drinks this well water may not find *any* unnecessary pollution acceptable.

The alternatives-assessment approach is based on the concept that foisting any risk or damage on an unconsenting, unwilling, non-speaking living being or ecosystem must not be labeled acceptable if there are reasonable alternatives to causing that damage, or that much damage.

Decision makers and industry frequently use risk assessment to justify their decisions, as it appears to consist of scientific information (data or assumptions) objectively plugged into mathematical models that supposedly document the minimal, insignificant, or acceptable risk of their proposed activities.

4. Most private behavior has environmental consequences for the public, so it isn't actually private.

If someone stood on his front porch and shot at children walking to or from school, that person would not be able to claim that he can do what he wants on his private property. He may be standing on his own property when he pulls the trigger, but the impact of the bullet will occur somewhere else.

When WTI releases lead (and other toxic metals and chemicals) from its incinerator, it is, in reality, "shooting" at children required to attend and play at the neighborhood school. Lead damages children's brains, kidneys, and blood-forming organs (National Research Council 1993). The National Research Council[3] notes that "there is growing evidence that even very small exposures to lead can produce subtle effects in humans" and admits that the current "standard" of "acceptable" exposure, 10 micrograms of lead per deciliter of blood, may not protect people (National Research Council 1993).[4] The WTI incinerator is permitted to send 9400 pounds of lead into the air of East Liverpool each year (Montague 1992).

In other words, WTI is a private company that is polluting children's bodies with lead, without the children's knowledge or consent. WTI is impinging on the lives and fates of children whose lives and fates WTI does not own. This behavior of WTI cannot accurately be called "private" behavior, because it contaminates and endangers the public. The public therefore has a right to participate in decision making about whether particular consequences of WTI's activities will be permitted.

Risk assessments tend to involve citizens only as commenters, if at all. In addition, risk assessments are generally difficult for the public to participate in or understand.

5. We humans inevitably cause environmental damage; the only way we will cause the least damage is to consider options for causing the least damage and restoring environmental health when possible.

With our numbers, our technologies, and our consumption, we humans have not proven "safe" for one another, for other animals, or for plants. For instance, few grizzly bears remain in the lower 48 states, where they once were abundant. Less than 50 percent of the wetlands that once flourished in the lower 48 states remain (Noss et al. 1995). The ability of numerous children to remember numbers and words has been damaged because, prior to pregnancy and/or while breast feeding, their mothers ate some fish (about two to three salmon or lake trout meals per month) from the Great Lakes, which have become polluted with toxic chemicals. Among the toxic chemicals these mothers ingested by eating these fish were PCBs,[5] which can damage the brains of developing embryos. The PCBs passed through the mothers' umbilical cords and breast milk to their children when the children were embryos and infants, still developing their brains (Jacobson et al. 1990).

The damage we do, however, can be less dramatic than manufacturing and using highly persistent toxic compounds such as PCBs. Most of us, for instance, have contributed to destruction of the intellectual power of children and other beings by disposing of plastics, toxic household chemicals, or toxic paints in bulging landfills, which occupy land that was once home to wildlife and where water runoff was once clean.

It is not a matter of *whether* we cause damage to each other and other living organisms. Instead, it is a matter of *how much* damage we cause. The major question is whether we and our social institutions (e.g., corporations and legislatures) will approach the world recklessly, causing or permitting as much damage as we can get away with; or carefully, causing or permitting as little damage as possible. If we are going to try to cause as little damage as possible, we (and our social institutions) have to systematically examine options for least damage.

6. It is difficult for many people to think of alternatives to business as usual. Also, it is in the interests of some people (and some corporations) to pretend there are no better ways of behaving, so that they need not change their current behaviors.

Sometimes we are hardly aware that the damage we are causing is unnecessary.

Example: If a father has always killed prairie dogs on his family's cattle ranch because he is convinced that prairie dogs compete with the cattle for forage (edible plants), it may be hard for others in the family to know or acknowledge that they could maintain both prairie dogs and cattle on their ranch, as some ranchers do. Because relatively few prairie-dog towns have been allowed to continue on range land, black-footed ferrets, which eat only prairie dogs, have become among the rarest animals on Earth (Kenworthy 1992). Keeping prairie dogs on a ranch can help with recovery of black-footed ferrets.[6]

Example: We may not be aware that if instead of buying white paper we bought cream-colored paper made without using chlorinated compounds we would be causing less damage to the environment. A paper mill that uses chlorine gas, chlorine dioxide, or hypochlorite to whiten pulp produces and dumps at least half a ton of chlorinated wastes a day into the river or lake from which it draws water. These chlorinated wastes contain as many as 1000 different organochlorines, many of which are known to be toxic to fish, to fish-eating wildlife, and to humans. A pulp mill that does not use any chlorine compound to pulp dumps virtually zero toxic organochlorines into its river or lake (Kroesa 1990).

Part of the reason we allow the environment to be harmed in numerous ways, then, is that we may have only one side of the story. When a corporation sets out to sell products that are made using harmful practices, it tries to convince customers that it has to make the products the way it does, and that the customer really needs and wants those products.

Public consideration of options for environmentally sound behavior destroys the claims that environmentally damaging activities, such as killing prairie dogs or using chlorine compounds to produce paper, are necessary.

By assessing the risks of hazardous activities and concluding that some level of the activity poses no or insignificant risks of damage, the risk-assessment process generally attempts to obviate consideration of serious alternatives to those activities or substances.

7. It is difficult to change many of our habits and behaviors.

It is hard for an individual, a company, or a government agency to change habits. Habits include thinking in certain ways, following certain bureaucratic processes, selling to certain markets, using certain equipment or manufacturing processes, or even listening only to certain people. We tend to be creatures of habit. As the writer Terry Tempest Williams said to me when we were temporarily "lost" in the snow on a small butte where I had hiked many times, "once you step out of your ordinary track, you don't know where you are at all."

Change is often scary, economically or socially disruptive (at least temporarily), anxiety-producing, or technically difficult. All strategies for improving human approaches to the environment ought to take into account the economic, political, structural,[7] psychological, and emotional bases of resistance to change.

For the most part, risk assessments are used to justify business as usual and to marginalize calls for change.

8. We have no choice but to gain practice in changing our environmentally bad habits everywhere.

Most people are aware of numerous environmental problems, many of which we suspect will only get worse in the future, such as population growth and excessive consumption, loss of wildlife habitat, water shortages, and global warming. We know we have to deal with these issues, but none can be resolved until we change certain ways we behave. Therefore, we have to change how we behave.

For the most part, risk assessments are used to claim that change is not necessary.

9. One of the most essential prerequisites for political change is understanding that there are alternatives.

Democratic processes for change have always been triggered when some people have become convinced that undesirable conditions are not inevitable and that a better approach is possible. These democratic processes for change include writing laws, passing initiatives, exerting community pressure on local businesses, litigation, boycotts, market pressures, incentives, and protests. Once people learn about attractive alternatives, there are many democratic routes to their implementation.

We need to establish public procedures that ensure that alternatives for treating the world and each other better will be publicly discussed and considered. We need to publicly discuss both the benefits and the drawbacks of each alternative.

By claiming on a supposedly objective basis that current activities pose little if any risk of damage, risk assessors generally downplay the need to even consider alternatives.

10. Changes in the damaging behaviors and habits of other people (and corporations) must be accomplished through political action.

Ultimately, we need to implement environmentally protective and socially respectful alternatives through democratic processes that communities, states, nations, and the international community have created for enabling people to protect themselves, the public health, and the environment.

Changes do not come easily when powerful entities benefit from the status quo. Change is accomplished through political action, and political action is the responsibility of citizens in a democracy if they are truly to govern themselves. Citizens include scientists, parents, bureaucrats, teachers, physicians, judges, workers, and children.

As Frederick Douglass wrote in 1857:

If there is no struggle, there is no progress. Those who profess to favor freedom, and yet deprecate agitation, are men who want crops without plowing up the ground, they want rain without thunder and lightning. They want the ocean without the awful roar of its many waters.

This struggle may be a moral one, or it may be a physical one, and it may be both moral and physical, but it must be a struggle. Power concedes nothing without a demand. It never did and it never will.

Risk assessment is an extremely flexible and powerful tool for dispelling calls for change.

Notes

1. Particulates are small particles suspended in the atmosphere, especially pollutants.

2. An organic compound is a chemical that contains carbon and some other atoms. A chlorinated organic compound is a chemical that contains both carbon and chlorine; it may also contain other atoms, such as hydrogen and oxygen. Chlorinated organic compounds, sometimes called organochlorines, are rarely made in nature. Most of them are produced by humans, and most are toxic in some way to most living organisms.

3. The National Research Council is an organization of scientists, engineers, and other professionals serving as volunteers on approximately 900 study committees. It serves as an independent advisor to the federal government on certain scientific and technical questions deemed to be of national importance (Jaszczak 1997). Its address is 2101 Constitution Ave NW, Washington, DC 20418.

4. A gram is about a thirtieth of an ounce; a microgram is a millionth of a gram. A liter is approximately equal (depending on the liquid) to a kilogram, or 2.2 pounds; it is slightly larger than a U.S. quart. A decilitre is a tenth of a liter. Ten micrograms of lead per decilitre of blood is approximately 100 parts of lead per billion parts of blood.

5. Polychlorinated biphenyls (PCBs) are a group of human-made chemicals that consist of rings of carbon atoms to which are attached chlorine and hydrogen atoms. They were once produced industrially for use in plasticizers, adhesives, hydraulic fluids, and electrical transformers. They persist in air, soil, water, and sediments, and can now be found in the tissues of organisms throughout the Earth, even in polar regions far from industrial sources (Tanabe 1988). They are attracted to fats (i.e. are lipophilic) and become increasingly concentrated as they are transferred up through food webs. PCBs are transferred to developing embryos through the placenta in humans and to nursing infants through fatrich human milk. PCBs cause skin diseases, reduced birth size, altered motor behavior, and reductions in short-term memory and certain types of learning (Jacobson et al. 1990).

6. Many ranchers in the western U.S. are convinced that prairie dogs compete with cattle for forage (edible plants), although scientific studies indicate that forage competition is minimal and that plant regrowth after prairie-dog foraging is of higher nutritional quality, preventing losses in cattle weight (O'Melia et al. 1982; Hansen and Gold 1977). However, because of an

undocumented 1901 Bureau of Biological Survey statement that forage competition was major (Merriam 1901), most prairie-dog towns on grasslands of the West have been poisoned and eliminated. As a result, black-footed ferrets, which eat only prairie dogs, are among the most endangered mammals on Earth (Kenworthy 1992). Some ranchers privately acknowledge that prairie dogs are compatible with cattle on their ranch, causing little or no impact, but hesitate to differ publicly with the multi-generational habit of eliminating

prairie-dog towns upon which ferrets depend (personal communication, Jonathan Proctor, Prairie Dog Ecosystem Campaign Coordinator, Predator Project, Missoula, Montana, July 2, 1999).

7. Examples of structural bases of resistance include current corporate decision-making processes, separation of regulatory specialists from alternative-technology specialists in government agencies, and legal privileges that protect business as usual.

References

Douglass, Frederick (1857), "The Significance of Emancipation in the West Indies," in J. Blassingane (ed.), *The Frederick Douglass Papers. Series one. Speeches, Debates and Interviews*, vol. 3 (Yale: Yale University Press, 1979).

Hansen, R., and Gold, I. (1977), "Black-tailed Prairie Dogs, Desert Cottontails, and Cattle Trophic Relations on Short Grass Range," *Journal of Range Management*, 30: 210–14.

Hazardous Waste Facility Approval Board of the State of Ohio (1984), Written opinion and final order approving application for hazardous waste facility installation and operation permit (16 February). Case 82-NF-0589.

Jacobson, Joseph, Jacobson, Sandra, and Humphrey, Harold (1990), "Effects of *in utero* Exposure to Polychlorinated Biphenyls and Related Contaminants on Cognitive Functioning in Young Children," *Journal of Pediatrics*, 116: 38–45.

Jaszczak, Sandra (1997) (ed.), *Encyclopedia of Associations* (Farmington Hills, MI: Gale).

Kenworthy, Tom (1992), "The Lesson of the Black-footed Ferret: Grazing and Conservation Compatible, Preaches Wyoming Cattleman," *Washington Post*, August 2.

Kerasote, Ted (1997), *Heart of Home* (New York: Villard Books).

Kipp, Stephen (1991), "Evans Will Ask EPA for Tougher Dioxin Standards," *Birmingham* (Alabama) *Post Herald*, October 28.

Kroesa, Renate (1990), *The Greenpeace Guide to Paper* (Greenpeace International).

Merriam, C. (1901), "The Prairie Dog of the Great Plains," *Yearbook of the Department of Agriculture*, 257–70.

Montague, Peter (1992), "The Breakdown of Morality," *Rachel's Environment and Health Weekly*, 287: 1–2.

National Research Council (1993), *Measuring Lead Exposure in Infants, Children, and Other Sensitive Populations* (Washington, D.C.: National Academy Press).

Noss, Reed, LaRoe, Edward, and Scott, Michael (1995), *Endangered Ecosystems of the United States: A Preliminary Assessment of Loss and Degradation* (National Biological Service, U.S. Department of the Interior).

O'Brien, Mary (1990), "A Crucial Matter of Cumulative Impacts: Toxicity Equivalency Factors," *Journal of Pesticide Reform*, 10(2): 23–7.

O'Melia, M., Knops, F., and Lewis, J. (1982), "Some Consequences of Competition Between Prairie Dogs and Beef Cattle," *Journal of Range Management*, 35: 580.

Tanabe, Shinsuke (1988), "PCB Problems in the Future: Foresight from Current Knowledge," *Environmental Pollution* 50: 5–28.

USFWS (U.S. Fish and Wildlife Service) (1992), *Recovery Plan for the Eastern Timber Wolf*.

Section IV: Liberal Democracy

Liberal democracy survived the twentieth century as the dominant political system in the Western world. Yet liberal democracy as a system of government has always stood in tension with the administrative state's claims to harness expertise in the interests of rational problem-solving. This conflict is played out in the environmental arena no less than elsewhere. Ultimately, do we let the experts or the people decide on what is best for the environment and how to go about it? Here we look at those who argue on behalf of the people—or the people's representatives—having a decisive say not just in formulation of the goals of policy in legislatures, but also in devising the content of particular policy responses to environmental problems.

The liberal democratic approach to environmental affairs is by definition pretty much reconciled to the status quo imposed by the capitalist political economy. As we will see in Part Five, more radical democratic notions challenge this status quo.

Our selection by Mark Sagoff affirms the sovereignty of the democratic public in environmental policy. Sagoff argues that all individuals have preferences as both citizens and consumers, but that their higher citizen preferences can only be expressed through democratic means. Economists err in counting only lower consumer preferences; aside from a defence of liberal democracy, Sagoff's argument can be read as a stinging critique of economic reasoning of the sort that appears in Section V, 'Market Liberalism'. He believes that citizen preferences are far more likely to be conducive to environmental conservation values than are consumer preferences.

Sagoff says little about the detailed institutional implications of his liberal democratic argument. Robert Paehlke has much more to say on this score. He notes that the last three and a half decades of environmental concern have been accompanied not by the centralized authoritarian structures postulated in the discourse of limits and survival, but also by the exact opposite. Indeed, over these decades the environmental area has led all others in the scope and extent of democratic innovation, not just in legislative politics, but also in environmental administration and law. Such innovations include public inquiries, right-to-know legislation, alternative dispute resolution, and policy dialogues. For Paehlke, effective environmental problem-solving is democratic and open, not administrative or authoritarian.

The selection by Marcel Wissenburg operates at a more philosophical level and emphasizes the 'liberal' in liberal democracy. Against those who believe that liberal individualism is a contributing cause of environmental crisis, Wissenburg stresses that individualism can also mean individual responsibility—including 'ecoduties'. He offers a series of green amendments that would redeem liberalism for the environment.

William P. Ophuls and A. Stephen Boyan, Jr., in contrast, believe liberal democracy is irredeemable. Focusing on the United States, they allow that liberal democracy does indeed give people what they want. But unlike Sagoff, Ophuls and Boyan believe that people do not express their public-spirited citizen preferences through democratic politics. Instead, they give vent to their selfish material interests. This kind of politics therefore reinforces rather than ameliorates the environmental rapacity of the capitalist economy, and exacerbates rather than resolves the tragedy of the commons. Liberal democracy is just as addicted to permanent economic growth as is capitalism, and so equally unsustainable.

Further Reading

There are many books on how environmental politics and policy proceed in liberal democratic states. One of the best collections (emphasizing the United States) is James P. Lester, ed., *Environmental Politics and Policy: Theories and Evidence* (2nd edn., 1995). In much of Europe, green parties are now central to the practice of liberal democracy. The German greens were the pioneers, and their experience is discussed in Margit Mayer and John Ely, *The German Greens* (1998). A defence of liberal democratic deliberation as a way of coping effectively with environmental problems is made by Adolf Gundersen in his *The Environmental Promise of Democratic Deliberation* (1995). The idea that greens should pursue their goals through conventional party politics is expressed in an Anglo-American context in Robert Goodin's *Green Political Theory* (1992). Two books which combine sophisticated analysis of the possibility of extending democracy in environmental politics with an awareness of the problems and constraints involved are Bruce A. Williams and Albert R. Matheny, *Democracy, Dialogue, and Environmental Disputes: The Contested Languages of Environmental Disputes* (1995) and Daniel Press, *Democratic Dilemmas in the Age of Ecology: Trees and Toxics in the American West* (1994). The affinities of liberal democratic political systems and ecological systems are highlighted by Gus DiZerega in 'Unexpected Harmonies: Self-Organization in Liberal Modernity and Ecology', *The Trumpeter*, 10 (1993): 25–32. Douglas Amy, in *The Politics of Environmental Mediation* (1987), offers a trenchant critique of the kinds of democratic process innovations applauded by Paehlke. Marcel Wissenburg develops his argument on behalf of liberalism in *Green Liberalism* (1998), and in a collection co-edited with John Barry: *Sustaining Liberal Democracy* (2001). A more radical approach that begins with liberal democracy is developed in Avner De-Shalit, *The Environment Between Theory and Practice* (2000).

11   The Allocation and Distribution of Resources

Mark Sagoff

In a course I teach on environmental ethics, I ask students to read the opinion of the Supreme Court in *Sierra Club* v. *Morton*.[1] This case involves an environmentalist challenge to a decision by the US Forest Service to lease the Mineral King Valley, a quasi-wilderness area in the middle of Sequoia National Park, to Walt Disney Enterprises, to develop a ski resort. But let the Court describe the facts:

The final Disney plan, approved by the Forest Service in January 1969, outlines a $35 million complex of motels, restaurants, swimming pools, parking lots, and other structures designed to accommodate 14,000 visitors daily. . . . Other facilities, including ski lifts, ski trails, a cog-assisted railway, and utility installations, are to be constructed on the mountain slopes and in other parts of the valley. . . . To provide access to the resort, the State of California proposes to construct a highway 20 miles in length. A section of this road would traverse Sequoia National Park, as would a proposed high-voltage power line.[2]

I asked how many of the students had visited Mineral King or thought they would visit it as long as it remained undeveloped. There were about six hands. Why so few? Too many mosquitoes, someone said. No movies, said another. Another offered to explain in scrupulous detail the difference between chilblain and trench foot. These young people came from Boston, New York, and Philadelphia. They were not eager to subsist, for any length of time, on pemmican and rye biscuits.

Then I asked how many students would like to visit the Mineral King Valley if it were developed in the way Disney planned. A lot more hands went up. Someone wanted to know if he had to ski if he went. No; I told him if he stayed indoors, he need miss nothing. He could get snow blindness from the sour cream. He could meet Ms Right at the après-ski sauna and at encounter sessions. The class got really excited. Two students in back of the room stood on tiptoe, bent their wrists, and leaned forward, as if to ski. I hope I have left no doubt about where the consumer interests of these young people lay.

I brought the students to order by asking if they thought the government was right in giving Disney Enterprises a lease to develop Mineral King. I asked them, in other words, whether they thought that environmental policy, at least in this instance, should be based on the principle of

From Mark Sagoff, *The Economy of the Earth* (New York: Cambridge University Press, 1988), 50–73. Reprinted with permission.

satisfying consumer demand. Was there a connection between what the students as individuals wanted for themselves and what they thought we should do, collectively, as a nation?

The response was nearly unanimous. The students believed that the Disney plan was loathsome and despicable, that the Forest Service had violated a public trust by approving it, and that the values for which we stand as a nation compel us to preserve the little wilderness we have for its own sake and as a heritage for future generations. On these ethical and cultural grounds, and in spite of their consumer preferences, the students opposed the Disney plan to develop Mineral King.

Consumer and Citizen Preferences

The consumer interests or preferences of my students are typical of those of Americans in general. Most Americans like a warm bed better than a pile of wet leaves at night. They would rather have their meals prepared in a kitchen than cook them over a camp stove. Disney's market analysts knew all this. They found that the resort would attract more than fourteen thousand tourists a day, in summer and winter alike, which is a lot more people than now hike into Mineral King.[3] The tourists would pay to use the valley, moreover, while the backpackers just walk in.

You might suppose that most Americans approved of the Disney proposal; after all, it would service their consumer demands. You could ride up the mountain and get a martini or watch TV. You could buy a burger and a beer at the gondola stops. The long Kaweah River might be transformed into a profitable commercial strip. Every red-blooded American with a camper, an off-road vehicle, a snowmobile, or some snazzy clothes and a taste for a little "action" might visit the Disney playland.

You might think that the public would have enthusiastically supported the Disney plan. Yet the public's response to the Disney project was like that of my students—overwhelming opposition.[4] Public opinion was so unfavorable, indeed, that Congress acted in 1978 to prohibit the project, by making the Mineral King Valley a part of Sequoia National Park.[5]

Were the rights of the skiers and scenemakers to act freely within a market thwarted by the political action of the preservationists? Perhaps. But perhaps some of the swingers and skiers were themselves preservationists. Like my students, they may themselves condemn the likely consequences of their own consumer interests on cultural or ethical grounds.

I sympathize with my students. Like them and like members of the public generally, I, too, have divided preferences or conflicting "preference maps." Last year, I bribed a judge to fix a couple of traffic tickets, and I was glad to do so because I saved my license. Yet, at election time, I helped to vote the corrupt judge out of office. I speed on the highway; yet I want the police to enforce laws against speeding. I used to buy mixers in returnable bottles—but who can bother to return them? I buy only disposables now, but to soothe my conscience, I urge my state senator to outlaw one-way containers.

I love my car; I hate the bus. Yet I vote for candidates who promise to tax gasoline to pay for public transportation. I send my dues to the Sierra Club to protect areas in Alaska I shall never visit. And I support the work of the American League to Abolish Capital Punishment although, personally, I have nothing to gain one way or the other. (If I hang, I will hang myself.) And of course, I applaud the Endangered Species Act, although I have no earthly use for the Colorado squawfish or the Indiana bat. The political causes I support seem to have little or no basis in my interests as a consumer, because I take different points of view when I vote and when I shop. I have an "Ecology Now" sticker on a car that drips oil everywhere it's parked.

I am not alone in possessing incompatible "consumer" and "citizen" preference orderings. Economists have long been aware of the existence of these conflicting preference schedules in the average individual. Indeed, the distinction between consumer and citizen preferences has long vexed the theory of public finance. R. A. Musgrave, reporting a conversation he had with another economist, Gerhard Colm, states the problem as follows:

He [Colm] holds that the individual voter dealing with political issues has a frame of reference quite distinct from that which underlies his allocation of income as a consumer. In the latter situation the voter acts as a private individual determined by self-interest and deals with his personal wants; in the former, he acts as a political being guided by his image of a good society. The two, Colm holds, are different things.[6]

Are these two different things? Stephen Marglin suggests that they are. He writes:

The preferences that govern one's unilateral market actions no longer govern his actions when the form of reference is shifted from the market to the political arena. The Economic Man and the Citizen are for all intents and purposes two different individuals. It is not a question, therefore, of rejecting individual ... preference maps; it is, rather, that market and political preference maps are inconsistent.[7]

Marglin observes that if this is true, social choices optimal under one set of preferences will not be optimal under another. What, then, is the meaning of optimality? An efficient policy, let us say, is one that maximizes the satisfaction of preferences weighted by their intensity. If individuals possess conflicting preference-maps, however, how can we say what an efficient policy is?

Marglin jokes that economists, in order to preserve the coherence of the efficiency concept, "might argue on welfare grounds for an authoritarian rejection of individuals' politically-revealed preferences in favor of their market revealed preferences!" One might argue just the reverse as well, namely, that we may reject our market-revealed preferences to pursue politically revealed values!

Very few economists, if any, advocate an authoritarian rejection of either political or consumer preferences. Some would seek a way to combine both sorts of preferences on the same preference map. They might agree with Gordon Tullock, who observes that two assumptions about preferences are essential to modern economic theory.

One of these is simply that the individual orders all alternatives, and the schedule produced is his total preference schedule. The second is that he will be able to make choices among pairs of alternatives, unless he is indifferent between them. ... From this assumption and a further assumption, that such choices are transitive, it is possible to deduce the preference schedule, and most modern economists have taken this route.[8]

If we make these assumptions, which are essential to the theory of welfare economics, it must be possible to infer, for any individual, a "meta-ordering" of his consumer and political preferences.

Markets, to be sure, would *not* reveal this meta-ordering, for it includes politically expressed values. Yet economists, by using interview techniques and the like, might be able, at least in principle, to derive the individual's combined preference schedule and price environmental benefits on that basis.

Attempts to find a "combined" or inclusive preference ordering, however, are bound to fail. They will fail for logical, not merely practical, reasons. Individuals have a variety of often incompatible preference schedules they reveal in the contexts appropriate to each, for example, in markets, family situations, professional contexts, and political circumstances. To try to combine these preference schedules into one is to search for a single comprehensive role the individual plays, it is to ask for the individual to behave *not* as a parent, citizen, consumer, or the like but in all and none of these roles at once. The individual, in effect, must reveal himself or herself as the "rational man" of economic theory simply because economic theory demands it. As one commentator rightly points out, no such social role exists, unless it is the role of a social moron.[9]

In some roles—particularly that of a citizen or a member of a community—the individual states what he or she thinks the group should do; the individual makes a judgment that he or she would expect any member of the community to make insofar as that person reflects on the values of the community, not just on his or her own interests. In that situation, each member of the group judges, as it were, for all, and if they disagree, they must deliberate together to determine who is right and who is wrong. This way of finding the will of the community may require a vote; the vote settles a logical contradiction between beliefs, however, not necessarily a conflict among personal interests. Thus, analysts who attempt to shuffle citizen judgments and personal preferences into the same ordering commit a logical mistake. They confuse judgment with preference, that is to say, beliefs about what *we* should do with expressions of what *I* want or prefer.

Some economic analysts attack the problem of split preference-orderings in another way. They note that efficiency analysis need not take into account the concerns of social equity or justice. Thus, one might rely on an individual's self-regarding market-revealed preferences to determine efficient social policies, for instance, by cost-benefit analysis. Then one could rely upon altruistic or politically revealed preference orderings to organize the redistribution of opportunities and wealth.

This reply may be helpful insofar as consumer preferences reveal a person's interests with regard to his or her own consumption opportunities, while citizen preferences express his or her altruistic concerns about the distribution of consumption opportunities in society generally. Yet citizens advocate many ideal-regarding convictions and beliefs that are not directed to the ways consumption opportunities are distributed. Environmentalists are sensitive to the distributive effects of the policies they favor politically, but they do not necessarily support these policies for the sake of those effects.

One could speculate, indeed, that the distributive effect of environmental protection is often to make the rich richer and the poor poorer.[10] When land is removed from development, housing becomes more expensive; consumer products also cost more when corporations are required to pollute less. The rich can afford to live in environmentally protected areas and, therefore, arguably benefit more than the poor from environmental preservation. It has been very difficult for state governments to site environmentally necessary hazardous-waste treatment and landfill facilities; one often hears, however, that these tend to end up in the neighborhoods of the poor. This would be another example of the way the poor may pay the costs of environmental protection while the rich reap the benefits.

I do not think any systematic relationship exists in fact between the policies environmentalists favor and the relative well-being of the rich and the poor or, for that matter, of present and future generations. The speculations I have offered so far are just that—speculations. I know of no recent empirical study that substantiates them. They suggest, however, that equality or justice is not the only ethical or cultural goal that concerns us as citizens. We may also be concerned as citizens with education, the arts and sciences, safety and health, and the integrity and beauty of the natural environment. These concerns cannot be assimilated to the personal, arbitrary preference-maps of consumers. Nor can they be entirely analyzed in terms of equity or justice.

Allocation and Distribution

I want to approach my thesis in this chapter by way of an important distinction: that between the *allocation* and the *distribution* of resources. The allocation of resources has to do with how they are used; the distribution has to do with who uses them or benefits from their use.[11] The Mineral King Valley, as a matter of *allocation*, could be used as a ski resort, kept as a wilderness, or exploited in some other way. Some individuals or groups would be made better off as a result; some would be made worse off; the decision, in other words, would have *distributive* or *redistributive* effects. The resort, for example, would benefit skiers at the expense of hikers; it would be good for property owners in Tulare County but bad for property owners in Sun Valley. Some might argue in favor of the Disney project because it would produce tax revenues to support social welfare programs for the poor. This would be to argue in favor of an allocation because of a beneficial distributive effect.

Some economic theorists who write about the environment assume that natural resources should be used in the way a perfect market would allocate them: the way that maximizes efficiency, consumer surplus, utility, preference satisfaction, or wealth. For a given allocation, of course, questions of justice, fairness, or equality may arise with respect to the distribution of costs and benefits. Most analysts concede that ethical or political choices may have to be made concerning these distributive effects. They tell us, however, that the best way to produce wealth and the best way to divide it are separate issues best decided separately; they urge us, therefore, not to make an allocative decision on the basis of its distributive consequences.[12] Once the pie is as big as we can make it, we may distribute it in the way we then decide is just or fair.

Analysts who argue along these lines tend to collapse all discussion of regulatory policy into questions concerning efficiency in the allocation of resources and equity or fairness in the distribution of wealth. They argue, for example, that the allocation of fossil fuels should be left to the market, properly regulated for externalities. The inequalities that result may then be remedied, for instance, by a windfall profit tax used to help the poor pay their heating bills.[13]

Not all policy problems allow a neat separation between issues of allocation and issues of distribution; for example, any social transfer of wealth to the poor could increase the cost of labor and thus lead to an inefficient allocation of human resources. Many policy analysts speak, therefore, of a "trade-off" between equality and efficiency. They recommend, however, that policymakers use those two values to justify whatever decisions they make with respect to environmental and regulatory policy. Decisions that cannot be explained as rational attempts to make markets efficient, then, must be explained as attempts to distribute wealth more fairly.

Although some writers like to emphasize a "trade-off" between efficiency and equality, it is useful to recognize that these concepts complement each other and that the conflict between them, insofar as one exists, is largely overstated. Analysts who believe that efficiency is an important social value do so, in general, because they conceive of the social good as the satisfaction of preferences, weighted by their intensity, however arbitrary or contingent these preferences may be. Philosophers who emphasize the claims of justice or equity do not necessarily disagree with this conception of the good, but may in fact rely upon it. When the good is conceived in this way—when it is assimilated to the satisfaction of arbitrary preferences—then it is unsurprising that a conception of the right, that is, a conception of justice, should be prior to it. Some have argued that an adequate philosophy of right has yet to be written: one that shows how we should balance a conception of justice with a more appealing or more persuasive conception of the good than the notions of efficiency and preference-satisfaction imply.[14]

Many well-known writers (Ronald Dworkin is an example) argue that a conception of equality should be the criterion of public policy.[15] Other writers argue that the efficiency criterion should be the principal guideline. Most of the statutes and regulations that govern social policy, particularly for natural resources, public safety, and the environment, however, have fairly specific goals, like improving mine safety or protecting endangered species. These concerns of public policy stand on their own feet, as it were, and do not need to be supported by criteria or guidelines established by a priori philosophical or economic arguments.

What characterizes the debate between the "efficiency" and "equality" positions is not the touted conflict between them but the extent to which each is plausible only in comparison to the other. Both adopt the same vocabulary and conceptual framework; each assimilates all values either to essential human rights or to arbitrary personal preferences. They agree that any claim that is not based on a *right* must, then, simply state a *preference* or reveal a *want*.

Those who advocate the priority of equality find worthy opponents in those who defend the priority of efficiency.[16] They debate at length and without any apparent sense of tedium the extent to which rights "trump" interests because (1) rights go to the essence of free agency and personhood or (2) rights are justified, at a higher level of analysis, in relation to interests.[17] Once discussion takes off on this theoretical path, pitting "deontologists" against "rule utilitarians," it becomes irrelevant to officials and others who need a vocabulary adequate to the moral, aesthetic, historical, scientific, and legal considerations that matter in health, safety, and environmental policy.[18]

Congress, by rescinding the Disney lease, for example, made a decision based on aesthetic and historical considerations such as the argument that a majestic million-year-old wilderness is objectively *better* than a commercial honky-tonk. In this way, Congress responded to the opinions citizens backed up with arguments in public hearings and not to the wants individuals might back up with money in a market or the rights they might assert in court.

To speak bluntly, the problem with efficiency and equality as principles of social policy is that they have the smell of the lamp about them. Each approach assumes that academic economists and philosophers, by practicing deep thinking, discover the fundamental truths about Man, Civil Society, and the State from which the goals of social regulation may be derived. This assumption is false. The goals of social regulation are based in public values and are found in legislation.

Insofar as options are available under the law, policy decisions, often expressed in parts per billion, must be justified, as it were, from the bottom up, not from the top down. To make hard choices, public officials must organize the minute particulars involved in assessing risks, monitoring compliance, and litigating penalties. Discussions of the "trade-off" between efficiency and equality have become a useless academic pastime to which this book seeks to write an epitaph. These discussions have little to contribute to the practical and political concerns of social regulation.

The Rights of Future Generations

Some writers have suggested that the way we use the environment could change if we balanced our consumer interests with those of future generations. Some of these writers have worked hard to define a "social rate of discount"[19] to determine how we should take the interests of future consumers into account.

The rate at which we discount future preferences may make little difference, however, in the way natural resources are used. We can build resorts, highways, shopping centers, tract housing, and power lines to satisfy future as well as present demand. There are few decisions favorable to our wishes that cannot be justified by a likely story about future preferences. Even a nasty strip mine or a hazardous-waste dump produces energy that will strengthen the industrial base left to future generations.

What are future generations likely to want? Will vacationers a hundred years from now want to backpack into Sequoia National Park, or will they prefer to drive their recreational vehicles in? I think the interests of future generations will depend largely on two things. The first is education, or advertising. I suspect that the Disney resort would always be jammed with visitors because Disney knows how to run an effective advertising campaign. Through the use of advertising, corporations typically ensure demand for the goods and services they create so that the product and the market for it are developed at the same time. Since what corporations want to sell is usually a good indicator of what consumers will be trained to buy, perhaps we should let the marketing departments of the top five hundred businesses tell us how to prepare the earth for future generations. The best way to create the bars and pizza palaces and motels and strips tomorrow's consumers will want may be to bring in the bulldozers today.

Second, the tastes of future individuals will depend not only on what is advertised but on what is available. People may come to think that a gondola cruise along an artificial river is a wilderness experience if there is simply nothing to compare it with. When I moved from a rural area to an urban one, I was appalled at the changes: noise, pollution, ugliness, congestion. People said I would get used to it—that I would come to *like* the convenience stores and the fast-food stands. They were right. This is what happens. If individuals in the future have no exposure to anything that we would consider natural or unspoiled, they will not acquire a taste for such things. What they will want will be determined more or less by what we leave to them, however dreary it may be.

Derek Parfit has constructed an argument that supports the point I wish to make. He argues that any policy we adopt today will make people born in the future better off than they would have been had we made some other decision. The reason is that these people would not even exist, and therefore could not be better off, had we made the other choice.

To show this, Parfit describes two policies, which he calls "High Consumption" and "Low Consumption." He then writes:

> If we choose High rather than Low Consumption, the standard of living will be higher over the next century. . . . Given the effects of . . . such policies on the details of our lives, different marriages would increasingly be made. More simply, even in the same marriages, the children would increasingly be conceived at different times. . . . this would in fact be enough to make them different children. . . .
>
> Return next to the moral question. If we choose High Consumption, the quality of life will be lower more than a century from now. But the particular people who will then live would never have existed if instead we had chosen Low Consumption. Is our choice of High Consumption worse for these people? Only if it is against their interests to have been born. Even if this makes sense, we can suppose that it would not go as far as this. We can conclude that, if we choose High Consumption, our choice will be worse for no one.[20]

The idea is that whichever policy we choose, future generations will have nothing to complain about, because but for that choice, different marriages would have been made and different children conceived. Whatever policy decision we make, therefore, determines who shall exist, and thus the policy we choose is better for those who will be born than any other policy would have been. Because these people will be all who exist, our choice will make no one worse off. Most people would agree that a policy that is the very best for all those it affects, and that makes no one worse off, is satisfactory from the point of view of distributive justice and efficiency. Thus, whichever policy we choose will be just and efficient with respect to the generations that come after us.

Parfit's argument does not clear us of moral responsibility with respect to future generations; rather, it helps us to understand what our responsibility is. It is not—if I may put it this way—a responsibility *to* the future as much as it is a responsibility *for* the future. If Parfit is correct, the major decisions we make determine the identity of the people who follow us; this, however, is not the only, or the most morally significant, consequence. Our decisions concerning the environment will also determine, to a large extent, what future people are like and what their preferences and tastes will be.

If we leave them an environment that is fit for pigs, they will be like pigs; their tastes will adapt to their conditions as ours might when we move from the country into town. Suppose we destroyed all of our literary, artistic, and musical heritage; suppose we left to future generations only potboiler romances, fluorescent velvet paintings, and disco songs. We would then ensure a race of uncultured near illiterates. Now, suppose we leave an environment dominated by dumps, strip mines, and highways. Again, we will ensure that future individuals will be illiterate, although in another way. Surely, we should strive to make the human race better, not even worse than it already is. Surely, it is morally bad for us to deteriorate into a pack of yahoos who have lost both knowledge of and taste for the things that give value and meaning to life.

Future generations might not complain: A pack of yahoos will *like* a junkyard environment. This is the problem. That kind of future is efficient. It may well be equitable. But it is tragic all the same.

Our obligation to provide future individuals with an environment consistent with ideals we know to be good is an obligation not necessarily to those individuals but to the ideals themselves.[21] It is an obligation to civilization to continue civilization: to pass on to future generations a heritage, natural and cultural, that can be valued and enjoyed without absurdity. These ideals are aesthetic; they have to do not with the utility but with the meaning of things, not with what things are used for but what they express. The programs that preserve them, however, are morally good. The moral good involved is not distributional; for it is not the good *of* individuals we are speaking of, but *good individuals* who appreciate things that are good in themselves. The allocation of resources in environmental law need not always—it sometimes should not—be based on norms of distribution. The way we use resources may also be justified in the context of a reverence we owe to what is wonderful in nature; for in this kind of appreciation, aesthetic and moral theory find a common root.[22]

That political authority should avoid acts of paternalism has been a traditional theme of liberalism. Liberals since John Stuart Mill have argued that the state should restrict the freedom of one individual only to protect the welfare of another—not merely to prevent the individual from harming himself. Although this reluctance to interfere with a person "for his own good" is not absolute in liberalism (or even in Mill himself),[23] it is a consequence of the principle that the state should leave it to individuals to answer the moral questions and thus should not make their mistakes for them.

Yet, to protect a wilderness we may have to prohibit a resort; to provide a resort we may have to destroy a wilderness. So we must make decisions that affect the preferences or values future generations will have, not just the degree to which they can act on their own values or satisfy their preferences. To what extent should the possibility of one lifestyle be restricted to protect the possibility of another? What moral opportunities are worth providing? As we debate public policy for the environment, we must answer questions such as these. We cannot avoid paternalism with respect to future generations.[24]

Yet this paternalism, if that is what it is, is of a peculiar kind. It is not a paternalism about the welfare of future generations; for, as I have argued, whatever policy we choose is likely to be optimal for the individuals and the interests it helps to create. Rather, it is a paternalism about the character of future individuals, their environment, and their values. In short, it is a concern about the character of the future itself. We want individuals to be happier, but we also want them to have surroundings to be happier about. We want them to have what is *worthy of happiness*. We want to be able to respect them and to merit their good opinion. How may we do this except by identifying what is best in our world and trying to preserve it? How may we do this except by determining, as well as we can, what is worth saving, and then by assuming that this is what they will want?

What is worth saving is not merely what can be consumed later; it is what we can take pride in and, indeed, love. To protect wilderness and to restore the environment to meet shared ideals is not merely to show respect and concern for future generations but to show respect for ourselves as well.

To think about our moral responsibilities to future generations is to consider how resources should be used and not merely to consider who should use them. Ethics in allocation, in other words, is not a consequence of ethics in distribution. An environmental ethic cannot be derived entirely from a theory of justice.

The Conflict within Us

If an environmentalist wants to preserve parts of the natural environment for their own sake, he might do well to concede that this is his intention. The environmentalist must then argue that the principles of justice, fairness, and efficiency that may apply to the distribution of income in our society need not apply to the protection or preservation of the natural environment. The reason is that the conflict involved, for example, over Mineral King is not primarily a distributional one. It does not simply pit the skiers against the hikers. The skiers themselves may believe, on aesthetic grounds, that the wilderness should be preserved, even if that belief conflicts with their own consumer preferences. Thus, this conflict pits the consumer against himself as a citizen or as a member of a moral community.

The conflict, in other words, arises not only *among* us but also *within* us. It confronts what I want as an individual with what I believe as a citizen. This is a well-known problem. It is the conflict Pogo describes: "We have met the enemy and he is us."

The conflict is an ethical one. It is not ethical only because it raises a question about the distribution of goods to the rich or the poor, to the present or the future. The ethical question is not simply the distributional question. It concerns, rather, how we satisfy our interests and how we live by our beliefs. This sort of question could never arise in a society that made efficiency and equity in the satisfaction of consumer demand its only goals. That sort of society could deal only with the opposition between the hikers and the skiers. It could never respond to, act upon, or resolve the opposition between the skiers and themselves.

I do not want to comment on the ethical position my students, like many Americans, hold with respect to preserving the natural environment. I merely want to point out that it *is* an ethical position. It is also an opinion that is widely shared, deeply held, and embodied in legislation. I imagine that if the law were changed and the Disney resort were built, more than half the skiers in the lift line would agree, in principle, with my students. They might condemn the resort on ethical grounds. But money is money, and only money talks. The skiers would have paid a lot of money and gone to a lot of trouble to use the facilities. There could be no question—could there?—about what they want.

The problem is a general one. It arises not just because of our high regard for wilderness areas, such as Mineral King, but because of broad values we share about nature, the environment, health, safety, and the quality and meaning of life. Many of us are concerned, for example, that the workplace be safe and free of carcinogens; we may share this conviction even if we are not workers. And so we might favor laws that require very high air-quality standards in petrochemical plants. But as consumers, we may find no way to support the cause of workplace safety. Indeed, if we buy the cheapest products, we may defeat it.

We may be concerned as citizens, or as members of a moral and political community, with all sorts of values—sentimental, historical, ideological, cultural, aesthetic, and ethical—that conflict with the interests we reveal as consumers, buying shoes or choosing tomatoes. The conflict within individuals, rather than between them, may be a very common conflict. The individual as a self-interested consumer opposes himself as a moral agent and concerned citizen.

What kind of society are we? Do we admit into public consideration values of only two kinds: personal interests and distributive norms? Do we insist that the only political decisions we can make are those intended to distribute wealth or welfare, for example, by making markets more equitable and efficient, while every other choice—every allocative decision about the environment—should be left, if possible, for those markets to decide? Should we leave allocative choices to the tourist listening to his John Denver cassette as he pulls his recreational vehicle into the Automobile Reception Center at the Disney resort? Is this fellow the appropriate legislator of our common will?

Suppose *he* opens his mouth to express an ethical opinion—*horribile dictu*—about the use of the environment. Suppose he tells us that we should have kept Mickey Mouse out of the mountains. Must we shut our ears to him? Is that the kind of society we are? Is a perfectly competitive market all we wish to have?

I do not know the answers to these questions. I suspect, however, that most people are resigned, by now, to an affirmative answer to them. How else can one explain the reluctance of environmentalists to argue on openly ethical or political grounds? Why do they prefer to tell stories about the possible economic benefits of the furbish lousewort rather than offer moral reasons for supporting the Endangered Species Act? That law is plainly ethical; it is hardly to be excused on economic grounds. Why do environmentalists look for interests to defend, costs to price, benefits to enter—even if they have to go to the ludicrous extreme of counting the interests of the trees?

Americans, no matter how they shop, generally share the ideology of the environmentalists.[25] Indeed, most Americans might claim that they are environmentalists.[26] Why, then, are they reluctant to confess to themselves that they make environmental law on the basis of shared ideals rather than on the basis of individual utilities? Why do they find it hard to concede that their society is more than a competitive market and that allocative efficiency and distributional equity do not exhaust their repertoire of public values? Why is it so difficult for them to say that one may allocate resources not always as a perfect market would but on substantive, normative, and frankly ethical grounds?

I think the answers have something to do with the insecurity many of us feel when we find ourselves without "neutral" theories and criteria against which to evaluate political, ethical, and aesthetic positions. It's scary to think about problems on their own terms; it's easier to apply a methodology; it's even more tempting to think about the problems raised by the methodology or to investigate the theory itself. Besides, if one side has numbers, the other may need numbers as well. Because developers tell stories about willingness to pay for recreational opportunities at Mineral King, environmentalists tell stories about option values and amenity costs.

As a result, public officials discuss the meaning of magnificent environments using a vocabulary that is appropriate to measure the degree to which consumers may exploit them. A principal purpose of an environmental ethic may be to help policymakers find more appropriate concepts they can use to think about the goals of public policy and to address the obstacles that stand in the way of those goals. The concepts associated with the principles of allocatory efficiency and distributive equity are not especially suitable for this purpose.

Money and Meaning

The things we cherish, admire, or respect are not always the things we are willing to pay for. Indeed, they may be cheapened by being associated with money. It is fair to say that the worth of the things we love is better measured by our *unwillingness* to pay for them. Consider, for example, love itself. A civilized person might climb the highest mountain, swim the deepest river, or cross the hottest desert for love, sweet love. He might do anything, indeed, except be willing to pay for it.

The Church once auctioned off indulgences. It sold future shares in heaven at the margin with a very favorable discount rate. Was it a good idea to establish a market in salvation? Of course it was. How else can you determine how much an infinity of bliss, discounted by the probability that God does not exist, is worth?[27] The Church membership, however, grew a little disillusioned when it saw that the favors of the Lord were auctioned for silver and gold. This disillusionment was one cause of the Reformation.

The things we are unwilling to pay for are not worthless to us. We simply think we ought not to pay for them.[28] Love is not worthless. We would make all kinds of sacrifices for it. Yet a market in love—or in anything we consider "sacred"—is totally inappropriate. These things have a *dignity* rather than a *price*.[29]

The things that have a dignity, I believe, are in general the things that help us to define our relations with one another. The environment we share has such a dignity. The way we use and the way we preserve our common natural heritage help to define our relations or association with one another and with generations in the future and in the past.

Let me return, now, to the example with which I began. My students, as I said, are pulled one way when they are asked to make a consumer choice whether or not to patronize the Disney resort. That question goes to their wants and desires simply as individuals. They are pulled another way when asked to make a political decision whether the United States should turn wilderness areas into ski resorts. That decision calls upon their conception of the values we share or the principles we respect as a nation.

Should we base environmental policy on the interests individuals may act upon as consumers or on the values that they may agree upon as citizens? Our policy may be "rational" either way. We may have a "rational" policy in an economic sense if we limit the role of law to that of protecting rights and correcting market failures. We should then assume that the ends of policy-making are simply "given" in the preferences consumers reveal or would reveal in a market. Alternatively, we might suppose that a "rational" policy advances a certain conception of equality—or meets some other condition or criterion laid down in advance.

We may have a policy that is rational in what we may call a deliberative sense, however, if we strive to base law on principles and ideals that reflect our best conception of what we stand for and respect as a nation. This kind of rationality depends on the virtues of collective problem solving; it considers the reasonableness of ends in relation to the values they embody and the sacrifices we must make to achieve them. This deliberative approach respects the constitutional rights that make it possible for people to contribute as equals to the political process, but it asserts no a priori political theory about the purposes of public policy.

This approach assumes, on the contrary, that the values on which we base social policy are objects of public inquiry. They are not to be derived (as they would be in a market) by aggregating exogenous preferences, or (as they might be in a political philosophy) from metaphysical truths about the nature of persons. Thus, the general goals of public policy are to be determined through a political process in which citizens participate constrained only by rights of the kind protected by the Constitution. These goals are not known beforehand by a vanguard party of political economists or by an elite corps of philosopher-kings.

Compromise and Community

The students in the class I taught had no trouble understanding the difference between the judgments they make as citizens and the preferences they entertain as individuals. They also understood the importance of their "positive" freedom to lobby for their views politically and their "negative" freedom to pursue their personal interests without undue interference from the state.[30] Plainly, these freedoms, like these values and preferences, are bound to come into tension or conflict. If the nation preserves every mountain as a wilderness heritage, there will be no place for these young people to ski.

This tension has been a central problem for political theories of liberalism. As one historian writes: "Liberalism of all sorts [in America] is troubled by the seemingly contrary pulls of responsibility to individual and community, by the divergent demands of absolute adherence to the doctrine of individual integrity and the needs and potentials of the common life."[31]

The students in my class found it fairly easy to resolve the tension between their consumer interests and their public values with respect to the example of Mineral King. They recognized that private ownership, individual freedom of choice, and the profit motive would undoubtedly lead to the construction of the Disney paradise. They reasoned, nevertheless, that we should act on principle to preserve this wilderness, which has an enormous cultural meaning for us, since the resort, though profitable, would not serve important social ends. The students argued that because there are a lot of places for people to party, we do not need to make a ski resort of Sequoia National Park.

But what if the stakes were reversed? What if we should have to make enormous financial sacrifices to protect an environmentally insignificant landscape? Suppose industry would have to pay hundreds of millions of dollars to reduce air pollution by a small, perhaps an insignificant, amount? The students in my class, by and large, answered these questions the way they answered questions about Mineral King. Just as they rejected the dogma of the perfect market, they also rejected the dogma of the perfect environment.

The students recognized that compromise is essential if we are to act as a community to accomplish any goal, however pure or idealistic it may be. To improve air quality, for example, one needs not only a will but a way; one needs to express one's goals in parts per billion or, more generally, to deal with scientific uncertainties and technical constraints. The goal of environmental purity, like the goal of economic efficiency, can become a Holy Grail, in other words, suitable only as the object of an abstract religious quest. To make progress, we need to recognize that God dwells in the details—in parts per billion and in the minute particulars of testing, monitoring, and enforcement.

Although the students thought that social policy usually involves compromise, they kept faith with the ideals they held as citizens. They understood, moreover, that if we are to take these ideals seriously, we must evaluate them in the context of the means available to achieve them. To will the end, in other words, one must also will the means: One must set goals in relation to the obstacles—economic, political, legal, bureaucratic, scientific, technical, and institutional—that stand in the way of carrying them out. We do not become a functioning political community simply by sharing public goals and by celebrating a vision of harmony between nature and society, although ceremonies of this sort are a part of citizenship. To function as a community we must also reach the compromises necessary to move beyond incantation to political and economic achievement.

This is the reason that the Mineral King example—and the difference between citizen and consumer preferences it illustrates—may serve to introduce a course in environmental ethics, but it does not take us very far into the problems of environmental policy. The interesting problems arise when we move, in Winston Churchill's phrase, "from the wonderful cloudland of aspiration to the ugly scaffolding of attempt and achievement."[32] Then we must chasten our goals by adjusting them to economic, legal, scientific, and political realities. How can we do this and still retain the ethical and aspirational nature of our objectives? How do we keep faith with the values of the citizen while recognizing the power of the consumer?

Notes

1. 405 US 727 (1972).
2. Ibid. 729.
3. The Council on Environmental Quality wrote: "Mineral King well illustrates the issue of recreational development for the pleasure of tens of thousands of people every year versus the value of an undisturbed naturalness for fewer visitors." *Sixth Annual Report*, 2 (1975), 242. For details relating to the Disney project and its market, see John Harte and Robert Socolow, *Patient Earth* (New York: Holt, Rinehart and Winston, 1971), 168–70; Commentary, "Mineral King Goes Downhill," *Ecology Law Quarterly*, 5 (1976), 555.
4. See Arnold Hano, "Protectionists vs. Recreationists—The Battle of Mineral King," *New York Times Magazine*, 17 August 1969, 24: Peter Browning, "Mickey Mouse in the Mountain," *Harper's*, March 1972, 65–71; "Thar's Gold in Those Hills," *Nation*, 206 (1968), 260.
5. National Parks and Recreation Act of 1978, Pub. L. No. 95–625, sec. 314, 92 Stat. 3467 (codified at 16 USC sec. 45F (supp. III 1979)).

6. Richard A. Musgrave, *The Theory of Public Finance* (New York: McGraw-Hill, 1959), 87–8.

7. Stephen Marglin, "The Social Rate of Discount and the Optimal Rate of Investment," *Quarterly Journal of Economics*, 77 (1963), 98.

8. Gordon Tullock, *Toward a Mathematics of Politics* (Ann Arbor: University of Michigan Press, 1967), 3. Cf. p. 1: "In modern economics and in the political theory which is now developing out of economics, the preference schedule has substituted for the man."

9. A. K. Sen, "Rational Fools: A Critique of the Behavioral Foundations of Economic Theory," *Philosophy and Public Affairs*, 6 (1977), 317–44. Sen writes (pp. 335–6): "A person is given *one* preference ordering, and as and when the need arises this is supposed to reflect his interest, represent his welfare, summarize his idea of what should be done, and describe his actual choices and behavior. Can one preference ordering do all these things? A person thus described may be 'rational' in the limited sense of revealing no inconsistencies in his behavior, but if he has no use for these distinctions . . . , he must be a bit of a fool. The *purely* economic man is close to being a social moron. Economic theory has been much preoccupied with this rational fool decked in the glory of his *one* all-purpose preference ordering."

10. See Martin H. Krieger, "Six Propositions on the Poor and Pollution," *Policy Sciences*, 1 (1970), 311–24; and Henry Peskin, "Environmental Policy and the Distribution of Benefits and Costs," in Paul R. Portney (ed.), *Current Issues in U.S. Environmental Policy* (Baltimore: Resources for the Future, 1978), 144–63.

11. This distinction has been drawn in a somewhat different form by Henry M. Peskin and Eugene Seskin, "Introduction and Overview," in Peskin and Seskin (eds), *Cost Benefit Analysis and Water Pollution Policy* (Washington, DC: The Urban Institute, 1975), 4–5. These authors use "allocation" to mean the total amount of a resource which should be produced or otherwise made available; they use distribution the way I use the allocation–distribution distinction to mark the difference between resource management and its consequences on income. For a similar treatment, see Burton Weisbrod, "Income Redistribution Effects and Benefit-Cost Analysis," in Samuel B. Chase (ed.), *Problems in Public Expenditure Analysis* (Washington, DC: Brookings Institution, 1968), 177, 178. For the same distinction made in somewhat different language, see Otto Eckstein, *Water-Resource Development* (Cambridge, Mass.: Harvard University Press, 1958), 17.

12. "Allocation programs include measures to affect relative prices and/or the allocation of resources in an economy, motivated by considerations of economic efficiency. Distribution programs consist of efforts to alter the distribution of incomes in society, motivated by considerations of distributive equity." Edward M. Gramlich, *Benefit-Cost Analysis of Government Programs* (Englewood Cliffs, NJ: Prentice-Hall, 1981), 13.

13. See e.g. Thomas C. Schelling, "Economic Reasoning and the Ethics of Policy," *Public Interest*, 63 (1981), 37.

14. For an argument to the effect that the priority of the right to the good is trivial when the good is conceived in terms of preference satisfaction, see Michael J. Sandel, *Liberalim and the Limits of Justice* (Cambridge: Cambridge University Press, 1982). I have reviewed Sandel's arguments in "The Limits of Justice," *Yale Law Journal*, 92: 6 (1983), 1065–1081.

15. Ronald Dworkin, "Liberalism," in Stuart Hampshire (ed.), *Public and Private Morality* (Cambridge: Cambridge University Press, 1978), 112–43.

16. Some critics of liberalism, like Sandel (see n. 14), believe that liberals are doomed to carry on this empty debate. I do not believe that the efficiency-or-equality issue is *necessarily* central to the discussion of public policy within liberalism.

17. Leading examples of this literature include Ronald Dworkin, *Taking Rights Seriously* (Cambridge, Mass: Harvard University Press, 1977), and Richard Posner, *The Economics of*

Justice (Cambridge, Mass: Harvard University Press, 1985).

18. There are some court cases, for example, those involving affirmative action, to which debates of this sort are quite relevant. See e.g. Ronald Dworkin, "Reverse Discrimination," in *Taking Rights Seriously*, 223–39.

19. For discussion relating the social discount rate to environmental ethics, see J. A. Doeleman, "On the Social Rate of Discount: The Case for Macroenvironmental Policy," *Environmental Ethics*, 2 (1980), 45, and sources cited therein.

20. Derek Parfit, "Energy Policy and the Further Future," working paper, Center for Philosophy and Public Policy, University of Maryland, 23 February 1981. A slightly different version of the passage cited appears in Parfit, "Energy Policy and the Further Future: The Identity Problem," in Douglas MacLean and Peter F. Brown (eds), *Energy and the Future* (Totowa, NJ: Rowman & Littlefield, 1983), 167–79, esp. p. 17.

21. William Blackstone summarizes well my view on this point. See Blackstone, "The Search for an Environmental Ethic," in Tom Regan (ed.), *Matters of Life and Death* (Philadelphia: Temple University Press, 1980), 331.

22. Immanuel Kant, *Critique of Judgment*, trans. H. Bernard (New York: Hafner, 1951), sec. 59.

23. Mill argues in several passages that one may be legitimately compelled under certain circumstances to be a "good Samaritan." See "On Liberty," in *Collected Works*, xviii (Toronto: University of Toronto Press, 1977), 224.

24. I have argued this position more fully in "Liberalism and Law," in Douglas MacLean and Claudia Mills (eds), *Liberalism Reconsidered* (Totowa, NJ: Rowman & Littlefield, 1983), 12–24.

25. See Council on Environmental Quality, *Public Opinion on Environmental Issues* (1980).

26. Ibid. 4, 11. For more evidence, see John M. Gilroy and Robert Y. Shapiro, "The Polls: Environmental Protection," *Public Opinion Quarterly*, 50 (1986), 270–9. This excellent survey describes and summarizes many polls.

27. Pascal's wager seems to follow along these lines. "Let us weigh the gain and loss in wagering that God is. Let us estimate the two chances. If you gain, you gain all; if you lose, you lose nothing. Wager, then, without hesitation that He is." B. Pascal, *Pensées*, trans. W. Trotter (1952), sec. 233.

28. Robert Goodin extends this analysis to many goods besides environmental ones. See Goodin, *Political Theory and Public Policy* (Chicago: University of Chicago Press, 1982), chap. 6.

29. "That which is related to general human inclination and needs has a *market price*. . . . But that which constitutes the condition under which alone something can be an end in itself does not have a mere relative worth, *i.e.*, a price, but an intrinsic worth, *i.e.*, *dignity*." Immanuel Kant, *Foundations of the Metaphysics of Morals*, ed. R. Wolff, trans. L. Beck (Indianapolis: Bobbs-Merrill, 1959), 53 (emphasis in original).

30. For a general discussion of the distinction between "positive" and "negative" freedom, see Isaiah Berlin, *Four Essays on Liberty* (London: Oxford University Press, 1969), esp. the third essay and pp. xxxvii–lxiii of the Introduction; and Gerald MacCallum, "Negative and Positive Freedom," *Philosophical Review*, 76 (1967), 312–21.

31. David W. Minar, *Ideas and Politics: The American Experience* (Homewood, Ill.: Dorsey Press, 1964), 416.

32. Quoted in this context by William Ruckelshaus in "Risk, Science, and Society," *Issues in Science and Technology*, 3 (Spring 1985), 24.

12 Democracy and Environmentalism: Opening a Door to the Administrative State

Robert Paehlke

....

In the 1970s, the early days of environmentalism, bleak political and economic conclusions were frequently drawn regarding the impact of environmental realities on democratic practice. Some lamented the possible demise of democratic practice on the shoals of coming economic scarcity of "environmental" origin.[1] The suspicion was also voiced that environmentalism itself, whatever its merits, might harbor a threat to democratic institutions.[2] While these concerns were made in a theoretically cogent manner, the day-to-day practice of environmental politics and policy throughout the 1970s and 1980s had an opposite effect: democratic processes were generally enhanced. Moreover, the environmental movement itself has been at odds with the techno-cratic administrative state, environmentalists characteristically distrusting bureaucratic—and even some scientific—expertise.[3] Environmentalist organizations have all along and still today favored openness and participation in environmental administration, thereby reflecting deeply democratic impulses. Arguably, especially perhaps in today's era of global-scale environmental decision-making, the successful resolution of environmental problems is more likely in a context that is more rather than less democratic.

Environmentalism and the End of Democracy: The Theory

The pessimistic case regarding democracy in an age of environmental limits was made by both William Ophuls and Robert Heilbroner. Ophuls, a political theorist, wrote in a Hobbesian spirit; Heilbroner, an economist, offered a modern update of the Malthusian dilemma. Unlike Malthus, however, both Ophuls and Heilbroner understood many of the complexities of resource scarcity. They did not characterize the problem as simply the product of excessive population growth. Unlike Hobbes, neither unambiguously welcomed increased authority as a necessary pro-tector of commodious living; indeed they expressed profound regret regarding the undemocratic future they concluded was likely and necessary. Each came to gloomy economic and political conclusions after a quite careful review of future resource availability, food-growing capabilities,

From Robert Paehlke and Douglas Torgerson (eds), *Managing Leviathan*, 2nd edn (Peterborough, Ontario: Broadview, 2004).

likely population growth, pollution and the general environmental impacts of human economic activities, and, most important perhaps, future energy options.

As Ophuls put it:

Once relative abundance and wealth of opportunity are no longer available to mitigate the harsh political dynamics of scarcity, the pressures favoring greater inequality, oppression, and conflict will build up, so that the return of scarcity portends the revival of age-old political evils, for our descendants if not for ourselves. In short, the golden age of individualism, liberty and democracy is all but over.[4]

Similarly, Heilbroner drew this conclusion:

... given these mighty pressures and constraints we must think of alternatives to the present order in terms of social systems that offer a necessary degree of regimentation as well as a different set of motives and objectives. I must confess I can picture only one such system. This is a social order that will blend a "religious" orientation and a "military" discipline. Such a monastic organization of society may be repugnant to us, but I suspect it offers the greatest promise for bringing about the profound and painful adaptations that the coming generations must make.[5]

Both, in keeping with the view of many 1970s environmentalists, anticipated a coming era of resource scarcity and environmental limits. From this followed the need for severe political control, economic restraint, and enforced discipline uncharacteristic of liberal-democratic societies and capitalist economies.

Writing at about the same time as Heilbroner and Ophuls, but without being explicitly familiar with their particular arguments, John Passmore presents the following in seeming reply:

The view that ecological problems are more likely to be solved in an authoritarian than in ... a liberal democratic society rests on the implausible assumption that the authoritarian state would be ruled by ecologist-kings. In practice there is more hope of action in democratic societies. In the United States, particularly, the habit of local action, the capacity of individuals to initiate legal proceedings, and the tradition of public disclosure are powerful weapons in the fight against ecological destruction.[6]

But elsewhere in his argument Passmore feared that the expansion of governmental responsibilities virtually implied the "gradual emergence of a bureaucratic police state."[7] Further, Passmore at several points characterized environmentalists as possessing an enthusiasm for coercion, generally without granting the existence of a stronger tendency within the movement to precisely the opposite: popular empowerment with enhanced participation and openness.[8]

Passmore's argument, as well as those of Ophuls and Heilbroner, has in the ensuing years provided considerable fuel to those who would prefer virtually any form of economic growth to even a modicum of environmental protection, if forced to choose. These critics and editorial writers have continuously told the public that environmentalists are anti-democratic elitists. A particular point of criticism is that environmentalists are themselves usually economically comfortable and thereby for the most part unconcerned about the loss of jobs implicit in the policies they espouse; and this point has been effectively countered elsewhere.[9] However, the general allegation that environmentalism is anti-democratic has not been clearly rebutted from an environmentalist perspective. Here I offer one response to this charge.

One might claim that Ophuls and Heilbroner simply over-reacted to the implications of exponential population growth, the 1970s energy crisis, and the seemingly sudden visibility of environmental degradation. Such a conclusion may well be valid in hindsight, but is far too easy. For example, while there are now signs that global population stabilization may be possible, it remains a very long way from achievement and we still face coming declines in fossil fuel availability largely unprepared and unmindful of the extent of the challenge before us.[10] It is clear as well that grain producing capabilities can be, and indeed have been, radically expanded in most of the Third World.[11] However, this latter achievement rests in turn on radical increases in the use of water and fertilizer, and thus fossil fuel, inputs. These latter increases may both be unsustainable in the long run.[12] Whether or not this change is temporary, it is not obvious that population stabilization will be achieved before we reach the limits of ecologically sound and sustainable food production capabilities.

Finally here, though there are now signs that the economic and political systems of many developed nations can stop growth in total energy demand, there is limited evidence that the political will can be mustered to oversee any long-term reduction in that demand, however gradual.[13] Indeed, a more convincing case can be made that the future holds a long series of economic lurches created by energy supply problems dwarfing those of 1979–83. Overall one might conclude, again with the advantage of hindsight, that the economic and resource arguments lying behind the frightening political visions of the 1970s were overstated, but nonetheless may yet prove an important dimension of our long-term future.

The more serious error of Ophuls, Heilbroner, and others is their underestimation of the capabilities of democratic political institutions. At least some nations may find an answer to future economic, environmental, and resource problems in *more* rather than *less* democracy. Democracy, participation, and open administration carry not only a danger of division and conflict, but as well perhaps the best means of mobilizing educated and prosperous populations in difficult times. Indeed, the environmental issues of the 1970s have, in practice, often led to the revitalization and expansion of participatory opportunities.

Environmentalism and Democratic Practice: Opening a Door

Several important analysts of the environmental movement have noted a reasoned and principled inclination of many environmental organizations to the open administration of environmental and resource policies. To some extent this emphasis contrasts with the perspective of earlier conservationists, particularly with the faith they placed on expert administration and governmental bureaucracies as protectors of the public interest.[14] Richard Andrews noted that conservationists assumed that there was a "single public interest" that "could be discovered or determined by experts."[15] In practice, however, it was found that the very private interests that were to be controlled by public servants (acting in the public interest) came themselves to dominate the resource management agencies. Those private interests in effect came to determine the public interest jointly with those in the employ of the public bureaucracies. In response to this pattern, "[t]he solution demanded by environmentalists was open access to administrative decision processes for all interested persons."[16] Thus, with this experience and perception, environmentalists typically urged greater openness and greater public involvement in administrative decision-making.

One can link this distinctive emphasis to some important academic perceptions of the 1950s and 1960s. In the 1950s, Grant McConnell and others linked the concept of the "captured" administrative agency to conservation issues. McConnell argued that administrative decisions regarding valuable resources are never exclusively technical in nature; they are political and value-laden. As he put it in a study of the U.S. Forest Service: "Any decision that will in fact be made will be in terms of the particular set of values held by the administrator, or perhaps, by the particular set of pressures that are brought to bear on him."[17] Similarly Lynton Caldwell, writing in 1963, observed that:

Scientists may one day tell us what kinds of environment are best for our physical and mental health, but it seems doubtful if scientists alone will be able to determine the environmental conditions that people will seek. There will surely remain an element of personal judgment that cannot be relegated to the computer.[18]

In short, expertise is necessary to achieving effective environmental decision-making, but it is not sufficient. Effective decision-making, from an environmentalist viewpoint, involves both expertise and the views of those who are most affected by the decisions at hand. All views, environmentalists have consistently argued, must be aired openly. Again, as Andrews put it, it has been the view of environmentalists that "in closed or low visibility arenas the power of highly organized private interests is maximized."[19] There has all along among environmentalists been a very strong sense of the public's right to know and to be involved in the decisions that affect their lives. Rachel Carson, whom many have called the founder of environmentalism, wrote in *Silent Spring* in 1960:

It is not my contention that chemical insecticides must never be used. I do contend that we have put poisonous and biologically potent chemicals indiscriminately into the hands of persons largely or wholly ignorant of their potentials for harm. We have subjected enormous numbers of people to contact with these poisons, *without their consent, and often without their knowledge.*[20]

The early statements of McConnell, Caldwell, and Carson and early analyses of the environmental movement by Andrews, Hays, Schnaiberg, and others suggest that there is a strong link between environmentalism and enhanced democratic openness and participation.[21] This link in principle, as we shall see, was generally carried through into the early practice of environmental administration in the 1970s.

The development of participatory opportunities at the national level began in the United States with the Administrative Procedures Act of 1946. The anti-pollution bills of the 1960s revived this initial effort and a significant leap, in the view of some analysts, was made with the National Environmental Policy Act (NEPA) of 1969. NEPA, as is well known, required the preparation of environmental impact statements and open agency consideration of alternatives. Executive Order 11514, which followed, required timely public information and ("whenever appropriate") public hearings. The NEPA process also created an additional basis for litigation by environmental interest groups and citizens, and such activity increased considerably, especially in the early years of the bill.[22] More than a decade after its passage Lynton Caldwell wrote the following by way of a summary evaluation:

The genius of NEPA lies in its linkage of mandatory procedure to substantive policy criteria and in the pressure it brings on administrative agencies to consider scientific evidence in their planning and decision-making. NEPA is importantly, even though secondarily, a full disclosure or public participation law. Other statutes provide more explicitly for this procedural reform, although NEPA adds to their strength.[23]

Not all analysts of NEPA, however, have been so favorably disposed to its effectiveness, especially as a means of enhancing public involvement. Sally Fairfax, writing in *Science* in 1978, argued that NEPA locks environmental activists into an unduly formal set of procedures and reduces the effectiveness of their participation in a sea of paperwork. "While it cannot be conclusively demonstrated, the public involvement that NEPA has induced is so formal, so predictable, and so proposal-oriented that it seems to have stifled meaningful dialogue between citizens and agencies."[24] Indeed, in Fairfax's view, NEPA may well have stifled public participation in environmental decision-making which was developing well in any case prior to 1969.[25] In expressing her doubts about NEPA, Fairfax makes clear that public participation regarding environmental protection was increasing in a variety of ways prior to NEPA and continued to expand after NEPA in ways Fairfax contends were unrelated to that particular bill. As an example of this, Fairfax carefully documented the ways in which "standing" before the U.S. courts on environmental matters broadened independently from the provisions of NEPA. Although formally providing participatory procedures, she thereby suggested, the new administrative mechanism served to contain rather than expand the impulses of popular participation.

For our purposes here we do not need to resolve the debate regarding the strengths and weaknesses of this particular bill. The reality doubtless lies between Fairfax's skepticism and Caldwell's general comfort. But no one questions that citizen participation was an important part of the early stages of the environmental era. More than that, environmentalists—Fairfax among them—have consistently pressed at every opportunity for more and more effective means of involving the public in decision-making processes.

It is hardly surprising that agencies have sought to structure, and in effect control, public involvement. As Fairfax noted, they naturally want to promote the expansion of their attentive publics, their clientele. But bureaucracies, almost by definition, seek silence, and if open to participation, prefer managed participation. Max Weber observed this early in the century as he described what we have come to call the administrative state:

Every bureaucracy seeks to increase the superiority of the professionally informed by keeping their knowledge and intentions secret. Bureaucratic administration always tends to be an administration of "secret sessions": insofar as it can, it hides its knowledge and action from criticism.[26]

In effect, environmental organizations have sought to counter this tendency; indeed, the whole body of early U.S. environmental legislation was, in part, a means of opening a door to the administrative state. The expansion of democratic practice was sometimes consciously intended and sometimes simply the outcome of the fact of participation—of attempts to reverse or modify existing environmental policies by legal, democratic means. In general the partici-patory dimensions of environmental legislation both promote and place orderly bounds on participation. In so doing such legislation limits, but at the same time legitimizes, such partici-pation. Limitation is particularly important to some in decision-making agencies. Legitimation can prove to be very important to environmentalists, especially in political contexts wherein environmentalism is less favored by the political leadership of the day, or of lesser interest to the public at large.

Throughout the 1970s new environmental legislation in the United States and else-where contained provisions assuring public participation.[27] Indeed, every major piece of U.S. environmental legislation in the 1970s allowed for public participation in environmental decision-making. Environmental legislation that did not add new channels for public involve-ment was rarely, if ever, proposed and never enacted in this period.

The 1980s and Since: Closing the Open Door?

The Reagan years in the United States showed how easily public sentiment can become tentative about environmental concerns. In such a context a political leadership hostile to environmental protection can roll back earlier gains very rapidly, even if majority, but more subdued, public support still exists. But public participation provisions built into legislation can be very import-ant within a climate of relative indifference. Knowledge of what is going on and vehicles for comment and action can help to check a hostile bureaucracy. Such supports are also essential as particular issues jump into and then fade from the headlines, as the issue attention cycle continues its seemingly inevitable rhythms.[28] The Reagan administration sought to close the open door in environmental administration, but in eight years was never fully able to do so. During the Reagan years the environmental movement grew in strength rather than faded, in part because there were windows into the administrative world and in part because those put in place to close the doors were either unappealing, or dishonest, or both.

In Canada, where the tradition of cabinet government has normally led to a more closed administrative process, environmental decision-making also led to a perceived need for enhanced public involvement. However, greater governmental caution regarding openness has led, for example, to an environmental assessment process, both federal and provincial, which is gen-erally more limited. Nonetheless, Canadian environmentalists have also consistently sought more open and participatory administrative procedures.[29] For example, while decision-making regarding pesticides in Canada was historically a closed and cautious process, cautious in the sense that there has been a general absence of significant challenges to the preferences of farmers or the agricultural chemical industry, environmentalists sought to open the process to greater public scrutiny. For decades the process most often simply followed the environmental chal-lenges to pesticide use that were previously sustained in the United States. However, in the wake of the Industrial Biotest (IBT) scandals in the United States, Agriculture Canada, the responsible ministry, was pushed to revise decision procedures significantly and to increase openness and opportunities for public inputs significantly.[30] More recently citizen activism at the municipal level has blocked the cosmetic use of pesticides on lawns in several cities including Toronto.

In general though the hesitation to encourage and promote ongoing public involvement in administrative and legal decision-making in Canada stands in contrast to the extent to which normal ad hoc participatory policy instruments have been applied to environmental issues. Specifically in Canada, as in Britain and Australia, Royal Commissions were frequently appointed to deal with environmental matters. It has seemed at times, especially when environmental issues were highly prominent, as if this device of long-standing general use has been tailor-made for controversies of an environmental nature. There was a general lull in the use of this instrument through the 1990s, but a commission of inquiry was struck yet again following the events at Walkerton, Ontario (discussed below).

Even yet today though, far and away the most important single use of environmental Royal Commissions in Canada was the federal government's Mackenzie Valley Pipeline Inquiry headed by Mr. Justice Thomas R. Berger.[31] The Berger Commission (1974–7) was highly innovative as regards public involvement. Berger spent days and even weeks in each of very many, very small native villages in the remote and distant northern reaches of Canada. Hearings were as informal as necessary to make participants comfortable and television and media coverage of some of these meetings was extensive. Berger's more recent efforts in Alaska showed a similar approach and have elicited this comment:

In the inquiry process Tom Berger has created what may well become the most important invention of the Twentieth Century. We could call it a "Cross-Cultural Hearing Aid." In his second northern inquiry, Berger journeyed to 62 villages all over Alaska to listen to Eskimos, Indians, and Aleuts. The "hearing aid" quality of both efforts derived primarily from the media coverage (which differed considerably in the two cases), the provision of interpreters in Native languages, and, in the case of the MVP Inquiry, the concurrent organizing work undertaken by Dene Nation field workers.[32]

The first Berger Commission set an example of effective public participation noted worldwide. It also, to some extent, reinforced the sense of caution in Canadian governmental circles about the political risks associated with the public inquiry process. Nonetheless, numerous other inquiries followed the Berger inquiry, mostly within provincial rather than federal jurisdiction and including most notably, in Ontario, the Royal Commission on Electric Power Planning, the Royal Commission on the Northern Environment, and the Royal Commission on Matters of Health and Safety Arising from the Use of Asbestos. All of these inquiries utilized an extensive public hearing process. In addition, at least three other provinces held inquiries regarding the environmental and/or occupational health effects of uranium mining when the health effects associated with that occupation gained wide public attention and concern. In each of these cases, and many others, there has been extensive public involvement, often encouraged by intervenor funding, and generally involving participation from a wide variety of social groups.[33]

Until economic factors rendered concern regarding the expansion of nuclear energy at least temporarily moot, public involvement in environmental decision-making was probably most extensive in the case of nuclear power plants, uranium mining, and nuclear fuel processing. This was true in Canada, the United States, Australia, and most Western European countries. In Canada the environmental impact assessment process has been extensively used, as have Royal Commissions. Regular Canadian channels for decision-making regarding nuclear safety have, however, been very closed indeed.[34] In the United States the public has been far more involved in the regular decision channels regarding nuclear power. In Britain and Australia large-scale special inquiries have been used. In Continental Europe large-scale public reviews, extra-parliamentary dissent, and referenda have been commonplace in France, West Germany, Sweden, Austria, the Netherlands, Switzerland, and elsewhere. In Sweden a long process of special public discussion led, in 1979, to a halt to new reactor construction and a possible phasing out of nuclear power by 2010. Sweden previously was relatively heavily dependent on nuclear electricity.

As Nelkin and Pollack wrote, following an extended study of participation in nuclear decision-making in several European jurisdictions:

... the participatory ideology has been "contagious." Demands for increased public involvement have spread from one sector to another; the experiments in the area of nuclear policy were but a natural extension of political reforms directed to democratization in the workplace ... [and elsewhere].[35]

And:

The experiments to date surely represent more an effort to convince the public about the acceptability of government decisions than any real sharing of power. Yet even the limited increase in public discussion has influenced nuclear policies, at the very least encouraged greater caution. In the long run, the implementation of public policies concerning technology and the very legitimacy of the responsible authorities may depend on the politics of participation.[36]

These words take on new meaning in the realization that the inquiries in question in this case preceded both Chernobyl and Three Mile Island. These events suggest that the doubts of a skeptical public may have been at least as reliable as the views of the "objective" experts in the employ of governments and the nuclear industry. Following these events both public and private authorities were more wary of proceeding with nuclear or other high-risk technologies without some process of public involvement. Indeed the whole process of risk assessment, when seen as a technical (non-participatory) exercise, has faced heavy criticism within and outside the environmental movement as fundamentally anti-democratic.

The recent pattern regarding the use of public inquiries in Canada has been much more mixed. Despite considerable public concern regarding the use of genetically modified crops and a widespread desire for labeling there has been no public inquiry on this question. However, in Europe there have been innovative public participation processes regarding this and other issues. The reason for this is plain: in Europe, the level of active public concern regarding the environment, and GM crops in particular, has been higher than in North America.[37] This suggests that perhaps there is a public involvement tipping point at which the use of inquiry processes cannot be avoided.

One might even hypothesize that when the public is openly alarmed public inquiries be used. Even governments hostile to both public participation and environmental protection will still respond if they fear for their futures. That was the case with the extreme neo-conservative Harris government in Ontario in May 2000 when seven people died and thousands were sickened by contaminated tap water in Walkerton, Ontario shortly after the privatization of water testing and other related budgetary cutbacks and changes in regulatory procedures. A thorough public inquiry with widespread public participation, conducted by Judge Dennis O'Connor, laid explicit blame on both the provincial government and on malfeasant local water officials. Shortly thereafter Premier Harris resigned and in 2003 the Conservative government was defeated, suggesting that their fears were well founded.

Innovative public participation in the environmental policy arena has taken other forms as well. These would include such diverse initiatives as: (1) community right-to-know legislation, (2) internal responsibility systems regarding occupational health and safety, (3) the use of referenda in environmental matters, and (4) direct participatory interaction between environmental citizen organizations and corporations.

Community right-to-know and, as in New Jersey, for example, state right-to-know legislation became increasingly popular during the 1980s.[38] These laws, by-laws, and ordinances require the disclosure of all sites where certain hazardous chemicals are manufactured or stored and the routes on which they are transported. In some cases these disclosures complement requirements on manufacturers and industrial users to inform their employees regarding chemicals to which those workers may be exposed. Community right-to-know can be important to residential and commercial property owners and to firefighters, for obvious reasons. A right-to-know approach has also been included on at least one occasion at the federal level, in Title 3 of the superfund amendments. This basic right to know the risks to which citizens are being subjected has been established reasonably widely, but it took the passage of a quarter of a century from the time that Rachel Carson argued, with regard to pesticides, that such a right existed.[39]

An occupational health and safety internal responsibility system was established by the 1980s in several Canadian provinces, most notably Ontario, Quebec, Saskatchewan, Alberta, and British Columbia.[40] The system involves three basic rights: the right to know, the right to a union-management (or worker-management) health and safety review committee, and the right to refuse unsafe work. Here again is a legislated requirement of openness and participation, this time throughout the private sector as regards employer–employee relations in the health and safety field. The internal responsibility system provides a means whereby individuals can in principle achieve workplace safety without the need to resort to actions so drastic as plant-wide strikes. Katherine Swinton noted that many believe that this system is superior to a system wholly dependent on either management initiatives or government inspection or both:

Prevention is more likely to occur through an effective internal responsibility system and worker participation. Worker input into occupational health and safety regulation, whether in establishing programs to improve health in the workplace or in carrying out inspections utilizes the workers' experience and knowledge of the workplace. Those on the shop floor are likely to be aware of the unused machine guard or the clogged ventilation system . . . [41]

She went on to argue that especially those managers who feel that more responsibility regarding health and safety must ultimately rest with workers appreciate the educative and peer-pressure aspects of the system. But Swinton also made clear that many workers and union leaders

. . . see participation in regulating the workplace as a basic right. It is a worker's health and bodily integrity which are threatened by hazardous conditions, and he should be given sufficient information to evaluate the risks, opportunity for questioning the existence of such hazards, and a voice in their control.[42]

An internal responsibility system has considerable potential as a device for mobilizing industrial workers to a greater participatory role in workplace decision-making. This is a prospect
that has not been lost on pro-union observers in the United States. Charles Noble concluded
for this very reason that a system of this sort would be preferable to the existing practice of the
Occupational Safety and Health Administration.[43] But, one must be clear that both instruments
of protection can be made less effective in the climate created by global economic integration,
which allows for systematically exporting industrial employment.

The third in our list of techniques, the referendum, though less widely noted, has been used
in many U.S. states, particularly at one point especially for initiatives concerning refillable containers and nuclear issues.[44] In the 1980s, for example, there were referenda regarding nuclear
power, toxic chemicals, urban growth, radioactive waste dumps, and toxic waste treatment
facilities in various states.[45] A wide variety of environmental referenda have been conducted in
California since with mixed results. We might recall as well the important use of the referendum
on nuclear power in Sweden in the 1970s. In the 1990s and since this instrument has been used
less frequently with regard to environmental initiatives.

In this period there has, however, been an increase in direct interaction between corporations
and citizen organizations regarding environmental matters. This shift reflects the rising power of
corporations in the era of global economic integration and the corresponding widespread decline
in the willingness on the part of governments to challenge industries. Perhaps the first notable
example of this was the 1990–1 joint Waste Reduction Task Force struck by the Environmental
Defense Fund and the McDonald's Corporation that led to the demise of the clamshell packaging
for hamburgers. The early 1990s saw, especially in Canada, the wide use of so-called multi-
stakeholder sustainable development committees. And most recently, the World Resources
Institute has worked with utilities, business schools and directly challenged the business strategy
of U.S. auto industry as overly dependent on large vehicles that are uneconomic outside the
United States and loosing market share within. All of these initiatives involve considerable public
participation through environmental non-governmental organizations, but find government
either uninvolved or but one participant among many.

The forms of public involvement discussed here are ones that intervene in the decision-making
processes of administrative organizations. As we review the current scene of public participation
in environmental administration, one final matter should be considered. Weber pointed out
that those who sought to challenge an administrative apparatus were typically forced to adopt a
similar administrative form. As mechanisms for the articulation of interests, political parties in
particular have tended to follow the path of bureaucratization. The issue that arises here, then,
is the organizational form adopted by environmentalists for the mobilization of environmental
opinion.

What we find among environmental organizations is ambivalence and diversity: there is at
times some amount of bureaucratization, but there is also strong resistance to this tendency.
This resistance has become especially clear when environmentalists have organized political
parties. Here we might note in particular the matter of party organization in the early days of
the German Green Party. The German Greens made several notable participatory innovations.
The party's federal assembly met annually and half of the membership of the party's federal

board of directors was newly elected each year and only one re-election to the same position was permitted. There were even efforts to rotate holders of elected office within their terms, but the party backed off from this as too destabilizing.

Nonetheless, it was expected in those early days that few if any officeholders would seek re-election to avoid the entrenchment of particular individuals in power. As the party came nearer to a share of power (and then entered government) this rule went by the boards, but efforts remain to decentralize control of the party and to actively involve a maximum proportion of the membership involved in party governance. In power as part of a national coalition government and governing outright on the municipal level, German Greens have worked to enhance public participation in the wider society.[46] Other Green parties are structured in a more participatory fashion than are other political parties or, for that matter, many environmental NGOs. Notably as well the Green electoral breakthrough in San Francisco in 2003 was rooted in one of the most highly participatory electoral efforts in recent U.S. history, especially at the municipal level.

Conclusion

In sharp contrast to the theoretical views noted at the outset, environmentalism has in practice widely and consistently led to (or at least sought) an expansion of democratic opportunities and an opening of administrative decision-making to public participation. Environmentalists have highly valued both the protection and the further development of democratic institutions. Even the emphasis on potential threats to democracy in the writings of Ophuls and Heilbroner can be interpreted as further evidence of such concern, however pessimistic their overall conclusions. With the advantage of hindsight, we might now conclude that both Ophuls and Heilbroner were looking too widely, and perhaps too early, to see the consistency of the pattern set out in this essay. It does not necessarily follow, of course, that the potential next wave of resource limitations on economic prosperity will not seriously weaken the democratic hopes and efforts of today's environmentalists.[47] What needs rethinking is the character of the relationship between the quality of democratic institutions and processes and the actuality of resource and environmental limitations.

One important dimension of this rethinking is the relationship between elites, masses, and economic growth. Volkmar Lauber and Mark E. Kann, without apparently being aware of each other's work, argued that it is elites—particularly economic elites in the case of Kann and political elites in the case of Lauber—that pursue economic growth to the detriment of the environment.[48] The general public, both maintain, would be relatively more open to accepting restraints on such forms of economic growth. As Kann put it: "There are no guarantees that people will make wise decisions, but they have an incentive to do so: they must live with the consequences."[49] This is, of course, too simple: some populations can export some of the environmental costs of their economic gains to other jurisdictions and/or impose them on future generations. Nonetheless, Kann's central assertion may remain valid: "My thesis is that to the extent that the environment has been influenced in the United States it has mainly been influenced by elites who exercise concentrated power on their own behalf."[50] Lauber's proffered cure, moreover, is one with which both Kann and I would be comfortable: "power today is too closely linked with growth. Under those circumstances it seems more promising to restrain and limit power. For that purpose, liberal democracy is rather well fitted; it is one of the problems for which it was designed."[51]

Lauber, Kann, Ophuls, and Heilbroner could not have imagined in detail the world in which we have arrived in the early part of this new millennium. However, they anticipated the spirit of what we are seeing—an administration in Washington that not only does not hold public hearings on energy policy but which is prepared to go to the Supreme Court to protect its perceived right to not even disclose the names of those that attended such meetings. That policy it turns out all but ignores the possibility of taking energy conservation seriously. That administration is also prepared to throw fiscal caution to the winds to assure short-term economic growth and to go to war to assure, or attempt to assure, a dominant position in the oil-producing regions of the world. This is elite-driven economic growth with a vengeance.

In the future, environmental protection may well mandate economic restraint. What sorts of economic restraints are likely to arise in a world where, for example, conventional energy resources are more limited than they are today? Will adequate environmental protection require economic restraints that a democratic majority could not be persuaded to actively insist upon? That is perhaps the heart of the dilemma that all societies may well soon face. This problem cannot be solved here, but it is important to recognize it sooner now rather than later.[52]

What can be ventured are some limited observations. First, democracy may well be the best political tool humankind has developed for mobilizing populations, especially educated and at least moderately prosperous ones.[53] Environmentalists have, at least implicitly, sensed this. Since they often call for significant changes in socio-economic organization, and even socio-economic goals, innovative democratic means may be the best, if not the only, means of achieving their goals. This may be particularly true as global economic integration advances. In this context democratic innovation must be carried through to the international level lest all nations be forced to compete with ever-lower taxation, as well as ever less stringent social and environmental standards.

One understanding of the relationship between resource limitations, environmentalism, and democracy different from and more suited to an age of globalization than that of Ophuls, Heilbroner, and Passmore, is that of Richard J. Barnet. Barnet reviewed the same range of issues that Ophuls and Heilbroner considered. He came to similarly pessimistic conclusions regarding future resource prospects typical of the late 1970s, but explicitly rejected both their neo-Malthusian and neo-Hobbesian conclusions: "In today's world," he first noted, "the heirs of Malthus preach what they call 'lifeboat ethics,' claiming the same monopoly on realism that fortified the dismal preacher when he pronounced his death sentence for the poor."[54] And he went on to add this: "Despairing of human altruism to subordinate the quest for personal enrichment to the common good, the heirs of Hobbes have seized upon the dangers of ecological catastrophe to legitimate the modern-day Leviathan."[55] In stark contrast to both these views, Barnet noted the importance of democracy as an educational and mobilizing tool:

Democracy is under severe attack at the moment when gathering evidence suggests that popular participation is a survival value. Major structural changes cannot take place in any country without the mobilization of the whole people. The solution to the energy crisis in the U.S., for example, requires a degree of public understanding and participation which our political institutions do not know how to achieve.[56]

This conclusion is even more apt now twenty-five years after it was written. Even Barnet, however, may have underestimated to some extent the potential power of effective democratic institutions. Goldrich's analysis of the process that followed on the Northwest Power Act of 1980 is a case in point, as are many of the examples already noted above. Both the Northwest Power Planning Council, an official planning body, and the Northwest Conservation Act Coalition, a citizen body, sought "to integrate the values of environmental enhancement, citizen participation in government decision-making, and economic development."[57] The point is that all things environmental do not necessarily involve bleak economic and political scenarios.

A wide variety of environmental measures, including recycling and sustainability-oriented industrial redesign, household energy conservation, the separation of household wastes, sustainable agriculture and forestry, and enhanced use of public transportation, require active public involvement, but also generally produce more rather than fewer employment opportunities. However, most such measures may involve economic dislocations, economic costs for someone to bear, and, in some cases, induced inconveniences. But the general public, polls suggest, is not unwilling to make sacrifices to achieve environmental protection. Political participation can help make the necessary effort as well as the attendant redistribution of costs and benefits fairer and more widely understood. Democratic mobilization is essential to the achievement of such policies in the face of the opposition of vested interests that such policies frequently engender.

In conclusion, I would stress what I think is obvious: environmental politics, especially in North America, must be a centrist and democratic politics. To achieve this, environmentalists must be constantly mindful of the socio-economic impacts of whatever measures they propose and must counter those that claim that environmental rollbacks, or access other nation's resources, are somehow essential to our 'way of life'. Environmentalists should continue to emphasize the positive side of their program—sustainable and decentralized economic development and employment opportunities.[58] Finally, environmentalism cannot be successful in the long run without a continuous enhancement of opportunities for democratic participation.

Notes

1. William Ophuls, *Ecology and the Politics of Scarcity* (San Francisco: W. H. Freeman, 1977); Robert L. Heilbroner, *An Inquiry into the Human Prospect* (New York: W. W. Norton, 1974). A thoughtful response to this literature from a perspective similar to that in this chapter is David W. Orr and Stuart Hill, "Leviathan, the Open Society and the Crisis of Ecology," in David W. Orr and Marvin S. Soroos (eds), *The Global Predicament: Ecological Perspectives on World Order* (Chapel Hill: University of North Carolina Press, 1979). I came upon this excellent article shortly after the original publication of an earlier version of this essay in *Environmental Ethics*, 10 (Winter, 1988), 291–308.

2. John Passmore, *Man's Responsibility for Nature* (London: Duckworth, 1974). Passmore's case was made against what he saw as dangerous tendencies within environmentalism; the arguments of Ophuls

and Heilbroner focused on the political implications of environmental and resource scarcity. Passmore might well regard Ophuls and Heilbroner as examples of that which he feared. Passmore's work has, of course, been seen as problematic in several regards. See, e.g., Robin Attfield, *The Ethics of Environmental Concern* (Oxford: Basil Blackwell, 1983); Val Routley, "Critical Notice of John Passmore, *Man's Responsibility for Nature*," *Australasian Journal of Philosophy*, 53 (1975), 171–85.

3. It is this environmentalist distrust of "established" science that seems to disconcert Passmore. Passmore concentrated perhaps too much on extreme statements of this distrust and did not appreciate that such doubts, rather than being a threat to democratic values, could support more participatory forms of decision-making. Further, one might add that the recognition that in some contexts science and values become inextricably linked can also result in better science.

4. Ophuls, *Ecology and the Politics of Scarcity*, 145.

5. Heilbroner, *Inquiry into the Human Prospect*, 161.

6. Passmore, *Man's Responsibility for Nature*, 183.

7. Ibid. 193–4.

8. Ibid. 60–1, 96, and 99. To his credit Passmore does allow the possibility that environmentalism may turn out to be an "anti-bureaucratic" force (see p. 183 n.).

9. Regarding the net positive effect on employment opportunities associated with pro-environmental policies see, for example, the numerous studies cited in Frederick H. Buttel, Charles C. Geisler, and Irving W. Wiswall (eds), *Labor and the Environment* (Westport, CT: Greenwood Press, 1984) and in David B. Brooks and Robert Paehlke, "Canada: A Soft Path in a Hard Country," *Canadian Public Policy*, 6 (1980), 444–53. Also of interest here is Richard Kazis and Richard L. Grossman, *Fear at Work: Job Blackmail, Labor, and the Environment* (New York: The Pilgrim Press, 1982).

10. The United Nations now projects that global population stability will be achieved over the next century at perhaps a total of ten billion souls, roughly twice the present population. However, given the fact that until the 1970s population growth had done little but accelerate for centuries this new projection is as much hope as certainty.

11. For an overinterpretation of this new reality see Peter Drucker, "The Changed World Economy," *Foreign Affairs*, 64 (1986), 768–91.

12. That is, not only will it be difficult to achieve further increases, but those that have occurred may be at least in part temporary. Obviously we cannot count on long-term supplies of those fertilizers that are obtained from fossil fuels. Some irrigation water as well is drawn from nonreplenishing sources and most irrigation affects soil salinity. Biotechnology may find ways around some of these limits, but gains without costs can hardly be assumed.

13. That is, the early 1980s saw a halt to energy demand growth, but the mid-1980s have witnessed a considerable and unwarranted relaxation of attention to this issue.

14. I discuss this theme more extensively in "Participation in Environmental Administration: Closing the Open Door?" *Alternatives*, 14: 2 (1987), 43–8. Indeed the conservation movement often seemed to assume that public bureaucracies could somehow objectively determine the "public interest."

15. Richard N. L. Andrews, "Class Politics or Democratic Reform: Environmentalism and American Political Institutions," *Natural Resources Journal*, 20 (1980), 228.

16. Ibid. 237.

17. Grant McConnell, "The Conservation Movement—Past and Present," *Western Political Quarterly*, 7 (1954), 471.

18. Lynton K. Caldwell, "Environment: A New Focus for Public Policy?" *Public Administration Review*, 23 (1963), 139.

19. Andrews, "Class Politics or Democratic Reform," 237.

20. Rachel Carson, *Silent Spring* (Greenwich, CT: Fawcett Publications, 1962), 22.

21. Sources not thus far cited are Samuel Hays, "From Conservation to Environment: Environmental Politics in the United States Since World War Two," *Environmental Review*, 6: 2 (1982), 14–41; and Allan Schnaiberg, *The Environment: From Surplus to Scarcity* (New York: Oxford University Press, 1980).

22. Lettie McSpadden Wenner, "The Misuse and Abuse of NEPA," *Environmental Review*, 7 (1983), 229–54; on this point see esp. 229–31.

23. Lynton K. Caldwell, *Science and the National Environmental Policy Act* (Tuscaloosa: University of Alabama Press, 1982), 74. A quite effective, pro-NEPA argument is also made by Serge Taylor in *Making Bureaucracies Think: The Environmental Impact Assessment Strategy of Administrative Reform* (Stanford: Stanford University Press, 1984).

24. Sally K. Fairfax, "A Disaster in the Environmental Movement," *Science*, 199 (1978), 746.

25. For example, Fairfax dates the origins of greater participatory involvement in administration to the Administrative Procedures Act of 1946.

26. Max Weber, "Bureaucracy," in *From Max Weber: Essays in Sociology* (New York: Oxford University Press, 1946), 233.

27. This generalization holds for the Clean Air Acts of 1970 and 1977, the 1972 amendments to the Federal Water Pollution Control Act, the Toxic Substances Control Act (TSCA) of 1976, the Resource Conservation and Recovery Act (RCRA) of 1976, and the Comprehensive Environmental Response, Compensation, and Liability Act of 1980, the so-called "superfund" legislation.

28. Cf. Robert Paehlke and Douglas Torgerson, "Toxic Waste and the Administrative State: NIMBY or Participatory Management," in idem (eds), *Managing Leviathan* (Lewiston, NY: Broadview Press, 1990); and Walter A. Rosenbaum, "The Politics of Public Participation in Hazardous Waste Management," in James P. Lester and Ann O'M. Bowman (eds), *The Politics of Hazardous Waste Management* (Durham, NC: Duke University Press, 1983).

29. Regarding both the cautiousness and the call for reform see Robert B. Gibson and Beth Savan, *Environmental Assessment in Ontario* (Toronto: Canadian Environmental Law Research Foundation, 1986); G. E. Beanlands and P. N. Duinker, *An Ecological Framework for Environmental Impact Assessment in Canada* (Halifax: Dalhousie University Institute for Resource and Environmental Studies, 1983); Evangeline S. Case et al. (eds), *Fairness in Environmental and Social Impact Assessment Processes* (Calgary: University of Calgary Law School, 1983); and J. B. R. Whitney and V. W. Maclaren (eds), *Environmental Impact Assessment: The Canadian Experience* (Toronto: Institute for Environmental Studies, University of Toronto, 1985).

30. See *National Workshop on Risk-Benefit Analysis* (Ottawa: Pesticides Directorate, Environment Canada, 1985); and William Leiss, *The Risk Management Process* (Ottawa: Pesticides Directorate, Agriculture Canada, October 1985). Regarding IBT see Samuel Epstein, *The Politics of Cancer* (San Francisco: Sierra Club Books, 1978).

31. See the final report of this commission, *Northern Frontier/Northern Homeland*, 2 vols. (Ottawa: Supply and Services Canada, 1977); for a lucid commentary see Douglas Torgerson, "Between Knowledge and Politics: Three Faces of Policy Analysis," *Policy Sciences*, 19 (1986), 33–59.

32. Walt Taylor and Peggy Taylor review of Thomas R. Berger's *Village Journey: The Report of the Alaska Native Review Commission*, *Alternatives*, 14 (1987), 35.

33. For a good overview of the use of the inquiry process see Liora Salter and Debra Slaco, *Public Inquiries in Canada* (Ottawa: Science Council of Canada, 1981).

34. See G. Bruce Doern, "The Atomic Energy Control Board," in G. Bruce Doern (ed.), *The Regulatory Process in Canada* (Toronto: Macmillan Company of Canada, 1978).

35. Dorothy Nelkin and Michael Pollack, "The Politics of Participation and the Nuclear

Debate in Sweden, the Netherlands, and Austria," *Public Policy*, 25 (1977), 333–57.

36. Ibid. pp. 356–7. See also Dorothy Nelkin and Michael Pollack, *The Atom Besieged* (Cambridge, MA: The M.I.T. Press, 1981).

37. See Christopher Rootes, ed., *Environmental Process in Western Europe* (Oxford: Oxford University Press, 2003).

38. Mary Louise Adams, "Right to Know: A Summary," *Alternatives*, 11: 3/4 (1983), 29–36. For a discussion of the extent to which recent federal initiatives in this area have been an attempt to preempt state and local efforts see P. R. Tyson, "The Preemptive Effect of the OSHA Hazard Communication Standard on State and Community Right to Know Laws," *Notre Dame Law Review*, 62 (1987), 1010–23, and Albert R. Matheny and Bruce A. Williams, "The Crisis of Administrative Legitimacy: Regulatory Politics and The Right-to-Know," in R. Paehlke and D. Torgerson (eds), *Managing Leviathan* (Lewiston, NY: Broadview Press, 1990).

39. See note 20 above. In that statement Carson went on to say, "If the Bill of Rights contains no guarantee that a citizen shall be secure against lethal poisons distributed by either private individuals or by public officials, it is surely only because our forefathers, despite their considerable wisdom and foresight, could conceive of no such problem."

40. See, e.g., G. B. Reshenthaler, *Occupational Health and Safety in Canada* (Montreal: Institute for Research on Public Policy, 1979) and Katherine E. Swinton, "Enforcement of Occupational Health and Safety Legislation: The Role of the Internal Responsibility System," in Kenneth Swan and Katherine E. Swinton (eds), "Studies in Labour Law" (Toronto: Butterworths, 1982).
T. F. Schrecker, *Workplace Pollution* (Ottawa: Law Reform Commission of Canada, 1986). The term *internal responsibility system* was first used by Dr. James Ham, head of the Ontario Royal Commission on the Health and Safety of Workers in Mines (1976).

41. Swinton, "Enforcement," 146.

42. Ibid. 146–7.

43. Charles Noble, *Liberalism at Work* (Philadelphia: Temple University Press, 1986).

44. See, e.g., William U. Chandler, *Materials Recycling: The Virtue of Necessity* (Washington, DC: Worldwatch Institute, 1983).

45. See *Environmental Action*, 18: 4 (1987), 6.

46. Gerd Langguth, *The Green Factor in German Politics* (Boulder, CO: Westview Press, 1986), 47–9.

47. That is, how solid are the participatory structures that have been established? Would they withstand, for example, another wave of oil price shocks? Would we not see environmental impact analysis by-passed in any future "crisis" mentality? Or indeed would environmental protection itself stand up in the face of the economic fall-out that may yet result from the last price shock (namely the current debt crisis induced in large part by the flood of petrodollars)?

48. Mark E. Kann, "Environmental Democracy in the United States," in Sheldon Kamienniecki, Robert O'Brien, and Michael Clarke (eds), *Controversies in Environmental Policy* (Albany: SUNY Press, 1986), 252–74 and Volkmar Lauber, "Ecology, Politics, and Liberal Democracy," *Government and Opposition*, 13 (1978), 199–217.

49. Kann, "Environmental Democracy," 253.

50. Ibid.

51. Lauber, "Ecology, Politics, and Liberal Democracy," 217.

52. For further discussion, see Robert Paehlke, *Environmentalism and the Future of Progressive Politics* (New Haven: Yale University Press, 1989) and *Democracy's Dilemma: Environment, Social Equity and the Global Economy* (Cambridge, MA: MIT Press, 2003).

53. There has been an extensive literature regarding the relationship between democracy, socio-economic development, and political mobilization—particularly work in the 1960s by J. P. Nettl, Karl Deutsch, Phillips Cutright, S. M. Lipset, Karl de Schweinitz, Jr., Lyle W. Shannon, and Deane Neubauer.

54. Richard J. Barnet, *The Lean Years: Politics in the Age of Scarcity* (New York: Simon and Schuster, 1980), 297–8.
55. Ibid. 302.
56. Ibid. 313.
57. Daniel Goldrich, "Democracy and Energy Planning: The Pacific Northwest as Prototype," *Environmental Review*, 10 (1986), 211.
58. By decentralization I do not mean to suggest that the geographic dispersion of populations is environmentally appropriate. On the contrary environmentalists, in my view, have significantly underestimated the technical and political links between environmental protection and urbanism. See Robert Paehlke, *Bucolic Myths: Towards a More Urbanist Environmentalism* (Toronto: Institute for Urban and Community Studies, University of Toronto, 1986).

13 Sustainability and the Limits of Liberalism

Marcel Wissenburg

Introduction

Whatever liberalism is taken to mean, it has a bad name when it comes to matters of ecology and the environment. Liberalism values individual freedom, particularly freedom of thought and religion, freedom of lifestyle, the freedom to live the life of one's own choosing. Care for the environment is usually seen as interfering in the genesis of individual preferences, which seems taboo for liberalism—their development is a purely private affair. At the level of state and market, a critic might say, liberalism is about satisfying (strictly human) preferences rather than educating people; it thus allows and to a degree even encourages the satisfaction of environmentally harmful preferences. For some Americans, liberalism is a meddlesome ideology, hand in glove with government inefficiency and ineffectiveness. For most Europeans, liberalism is identified with a laissez-faire state and the free market, the latter being held responsible for the exploitation of nature. Philosophical liberalism, in European eyes often including libertarianism, is seen as the conscience of economic and political liberalism and is as such guilty by association.

In this chapter I shall argue, against these all too easy judgements, that there are ways in which existing mainstream liberal political philosophy is or can be enriched with the kind of premises that allow it to sensibly discuss environmental issues and translate environmental concerns into political principles. Since liberalism is ultimately about taking one's individual responsibility seriously, this implies that it can also prescribe individual 'ecoduties'. In fact, I shall argue that philosophical liberalism is already an ecology-conscious and environmentally friendly theory, so to speak, 'by nature'—it is just that most of its past interpreters failed to realize liberalism's green potential, or had no reason to do so. What I shall *not* say is that liberalism's bad name in green circles is undeserved, that it is all an unfortunate misunderstanding or that the environmental dimension of liberalism fits in easily with the rest of the theory. We should, after all, not confuse 'is' and 'ought', or 'is' and 'might have been'.

I shall first discuss in the next section two ways of protecting the environment as an *object* of liberal concern by improving the democratic element in liberal thought and by revising the so-called Lockean provisos used to justify private property. In the third section, the focus changes

From Marcel Wissenburg and John Barry (eds), *Sustaining Liberal Democracy* (London: Palgrave, 2001), 192–204.

to ways in which the liberal concern extends to include new *subjects*: animals or nature as a whole, and future generations. This is followed by arguments for considering environmental care to be based on duties, or mutual individual obligations, first as an aim of liberal justice and as a side-constraint in the form of a savings principle in the fourth section and then, in the fifth section, my own invention, as an environmental side-constraint on the attribution of rights in society via the restraint principle.

Although these seven green 'amendments' to liberalism represent the most important recent developments in liberal political philosophy, I do not pretend that this list is complete. It is a representative selection of arguments based on obligations and duties, not of other sources of green 'preferences'. Several contributors to this book [John Barry and Marcel Wissenburg (eds) *Sustaining Liberal Democracy* (2001)], for instance, discuss a number of other ways of greening liberalism: Hayward who considers constitutional protection, Attfield who deals with individual preferences, considered and other, and Oksanen who considers the effects of privatizing nature. Green consumerism, green production (Anderson and Leal, 1991), eco-taxes and ecological modernization (Weale, 1992) will also be disregarded. Nor will any of the amendments proposed in this chapter ensure that real-world liberalism, liberal-democratic society, becomes green. Greening philosophical liberalism is a necessary but not a sufficient condition for a greener world. The points I want to make are these: there *can* be such a thing as green liberalism (cf. Wissenburg, 1998); it can be based on moral duties rather than sheer preferences; and the appeal to duty and individual responsibility even seems the most promising way of greening liberalism.

Preferences and Liberalism

Liberalism, some critics say, would care less about educating than about satisfying preferences and promoting economic growth (e.g. Opschoor, 1994; Achterhuis, 1994). It is important to note that we are dealing with a two-headed monster here: a critique of liberal democracy and one of economic liberalism. The two are not Siamese twins. Capitalism is not a necessary condition for the existence of the political structure and liberties associated with liberal democracy (cf. Lauber, 1978); the free market existed before liberal democracy evolved. Nor is political liberalism predestined to take a laissez-faire attitude towards the market (cf. Stephens, 1996), or to hold that life is all about making profits or the satisfaction of material self-interest. It sees trade and commerce as one way of life, one means to the realization of a plan of life, among others (cf. Holmes, 1993, p. 212). The critique of economic liberalism must therefore be judged on its own merits and cannot reflect on political liberalism.

There is no such thing as a society without a free market; even in the direst of times and under the most oppressive political systems, something called 'the black market' operates—and operates on the same principles as the free market: demand and supply. If 'the' free market is to be blamed for environmental problems, it cannot be blamed because of its being a *free* market; it is because there are consumers and producers who are looking for a market. The free market is only instrumental in satisfying environmentally harmful preferences; it is in the preferences that the problem originates.

At this point, we encounter the first and weakest of our seven revisionist proposals. In recent years, a number of political theorists have argued for more and better democracy, both in politics and in other social spheres (e.g. the economy). Inspired by classic Republican thinkers, they argue that deliberation, public debate and discussion can change preferences and can change them for the (environmentally) better (cf. several contributions to, for example, Doherty and de Geus, 1996; cf. also Beckman 2001). The opposite, however, cannot be excluded: democracy as a decision-making process is and remains a process that selects the most favoured, not necessarily the morally or environmentally best, solution. Developing or expanding the democratic aspect of liberalism, both in politics and in other social spheres, including those where consumers' preferences, are conceived, does not therefore make liberalism necessarily green; like economic liberalism, it remains preference-neutral.

A more promising way of defending philosophical liberalism against the charge that its attempted preference-neutrality prevents it from being or becoming green is to focus on inter-pretations of liberal democracy as a system that seeks to protect typically 'liberal' values of which democracy is only one—and one that can be overruled or outweighed by a higher value where they seem to conflict.

One of these values which might be, and on libertarian views usually is, prior to democracy is the institution of private property. It has been argued that private ownership of natural resources can contribute to environmental sustainability (see Dobson, 1998; see also Oksanen 2001). One line of thought on this focuses on John Locke's classic defence of the legitimacy of property. Building forth on, medieval (mainly Thomistic) arguments, Locke argued that one cannot just grab any previously unowned good from nature and use it at will. The act of grabbing ('original acquisition') is justified only if 'enough and as good' is left for others and if whatever is taken from nature is used for basic needs, subsistence or the greater good of the community, but never when it is taken to stock and rot (Locke, 1965). In a finite world, the 'enough and as good' proviso poses severe limits to the exploitation of nature, according to some even too severe. Hence, Robert Nozick (1974), for instance, amended Locke's proviso: rather than demanding that enough and as good be left, we should allow original acquisition as long as others can be adequately compensated for being excluded from some resource X.

Unfortunately, the Lockean road to environmental sustainability is insecure. One objection to Nozick's and similar amendments is that it begs the question of what exactly could count as adequate compensation, since some goods may be unsubstitutable (Dobson, 1998). Additionally, no amendment to Locke's conditions can protect natural resources against 'pure' waste: waste is only waste if people appreciate a resource and would prefer it not to be wasted. If no one but i is interested in X, i can take as much of X as he or she wants—neither proviso applies here.

Nature as a Subject of Justice

The idea that private properly is an inviolable pre-social right is not widely shared; most modern liberals like Rawls, Barry and Ackerman defend private property as a social convention. Their primary interest lies in establishing how *any* distribution of goods, opportunities, liberties and rights (including that to private property) can be defended. On this perspective, democracy and social convention can only be overruled by (whatever follows from) the categorical liberal imperative of impartiality with regard to the plans of life of individuals. Among the many possible ways in which authors have tried to adapt these mainstream theories of distributive justice to the green agenda (most recently Rowlands, 1998), two deserve special mention: the inclusion of parts of nature and of future generations as subjects of justice who have, up to now, been unjustly excluded from the community of justice (for more detailed discussions see Wissenburg, 1998, 1999).

Even if they only aim to include animals, the problem with proposals of this kind—usually presented in the format of a contract theory—is that part of the support for any impartial theory of justice must stem from the real-life reader; he or she must be convinced that impartiality obliges one to see animals as contracting partners. Yet it is highly questionable whether we can identify in this sense with a contract situation where we would have to put ourselves (or our impartial representatives) in the position of, say, the common house fly, and it is probably impossible to imagine an animal in our own position (cf. Wissenburg, 1993). What is even more troubling is that a construction of this sort seems to presuppose the conclusion, namely that animals have an interest in human justice. It may go too far to demand that to apply the term 'justice' to a human's relation with another creature, the latter must stand in a reciprocal relation to others, as Brian Barry (1989) once argued, or that it can communicate, as Bruce Ackerman (1980) suggested. It does not seem to be a necessary condition; we do not demand it of comatose humans either. Yet as long as humans can argue for the existence of relevant differences between themselves and animals, the status of animals as subjects cannot a priori be taken as part of our considered judgements.

Introducing future generations of humans in a contract setting or in any other way as subjects of justice seems less problematical at first sight. At least humans are humans: we do not have to imagine them or ourselves as basically alien beings. Yet the fact that future individuals by definition do not exist (yet) creates some mind-boggling problems.

For one, future generations do not need to exist; we can choose not to procreate any further. In this respect one could argue that future individuals and the interests they might have are the creation of present generations, hence in fact interests of present generations—making the introduction of future generations in a contract setting redundant.

Even assuming that future generations should be allowed to represent their own interests, and assuming that I am responsible for your offspring, it is not clear what exactly future generations can claim from us, that is what exact obligations we have towards them and which interests they may legitimately voice. It makes a difference for our obligations and for our choice of principles of justice whether we do or do not owe them more, rather than that we do not make their lives unbearable (cf. Narveson, 1973). Again, we cannot presume conclusions that may not be part of our considered judgements.

Further objections to 'over-inclusion', which I can only mention in passing here, are that we simply would not know how many of future humans there will or should be, nor to which degree we can be held accountable for the welfare of our most distant descendants, nor where their interests lie. Since their interests and plans are the product of a dialectic between the self and its environment, one might even argue that there is no sense in talking about the plans of life of future individuals. As long as neither they nor their environment exist, there simply are no plans of life.

Mutual Obligations

If making future humans and non-humans subjects of justice seems a risky route to take, two alternatives are left. One is to argue that we have obligations to our direct descendants and that we can even hazard to guess where these obligations lie. Another is the more direct approach: the claim that impartial decision-makers would opt for an environmentally sustainable society, regardless of whom they represent.

It is the latter alternative in which Brian Barry (Barry, 1995) believes: in his view, the discovery that people actually do have (various and diverging) interests in (various and diverging interpretations of) a clean and healthy environment obliges us to take environmental interests into account. However, this solution lacks a reflective moment. If the current plans of life of currently existing people determine the outcome of the contract, and if the current shape of society influences these plans, then it is the shape of society—culture and structure—that dictates limits to the possible outcome of negotiations. The degree of greenness of such a society thus depends at least on existing preferences, at worst on the existing structure of society, but certainly not on what reasonable individuals freed from the bonds and prejudices of their specific society would presume that a just society *should* look like.

Hence, we are thrown back at the idea that we have ecological obligations to currently existing younger generations. The perhaps easiest method of greening liberalism follows this line of thought and builds forth on an idea introduced by John Rawls (1971): that we have an obligation to 'save' on behalf of future generations. On this new interpretation (Rawls, 1993), which is originally David Gauthier's (1986), future generations can be introduced without making them subjects or including them in contractual negotiations, thus avoiding many of the problems discussed above. Rawls now states that contracting parties in the original position (Rawls's version of a state of nature) will 'agree to a savings principle subject to the further condition that they must want all previous generations to have followed it' (Rawls, 1993, p. 274).

Rawls makes one important improvement on the orthodox understanding of justice between generations: they exist next to each other, not one after the other: 'society is a system of co-operation between generations over time' (Rawls, 1993, p. 274). It is this fact that makes an intergenerational savings principle mutually beneficial; *regardless* of whether one has or wants or likes children, the savings principle guarantees that no generation is made worse off relative to any previous generation, that is, relative to the circumstances in which each generation lives. It would be irrational to reject it, and thereby step out of society and lose the advantages of intergenerational cooperation. Moreover, defection destroys the basis of trust on which society is built. Others can perhaps go on as before in their cooperative venture, but they will have learned that no one can be trusted—a lesson that cannot be too healthy for the survival of society.

Note that the possible existence of as yet non-existent future generations is irrelevant to the Rawlsian argument. There is no way to protect them directly against 'thieves'—stealing from them is easier than stealing candy from a baby. Instead, they are protected indirectly at any given moment by a principle that means to protect the interests of existing generations.

The beauty of this new interpretation of the savings principle is its simplicity: it is a simple combination of rationality and mutual advantage. This is not to say that there are no problems. For one (for others see Wissenburg, 1998), every change in the structure of a society, every move towards a more just society, is made by a first generation that will (ideally) judge its own performance in relation to what people in the original position would decide. If the latter cannot represent a situation which the former experience on a regular basis, a choice situation that will influence their well-being—then there may well be something wrong with the design of the original position.

The Restraint Principle

The last path to a greener liberalism which I want to discuss in this chapter again makes use of the concepts of duties and rights. However, it does not refer to any substantial rights that subjects of justice might have or any obligations we have: it requires a purely formal conception of rights.

At the basis of this greening strategy lies the observation that the effects of principles of justice, or more generally the effects of implementing liberal key values, can always in some way be represented as permissions and negations of permissions. In their most simple form, these permissions apply to one individual only, at one place and one moment in time, for one 'basic act', one distinct action (for more details see Wissenburg, 1998). On the basis of these 'molecules', formal rights can be designed: *molecular* rights referring to one person (me), one basic act (cutting down a tree to warm my house), one point in time and space alone (here and now), as well as *complex* rights to series of basic acts, wider areas or longer periods. And of course these rights can be of several types: permissions to do x, permissions to do not-x, liberties to choose to do x or not-x, duties to do x and not do not-x, and so on. Formal rights are composible (cf. Steiner, 1994); no single molecular right can be assigned twice, hence no complex right can ever contradict another. Ideally, moral systems and legal codes meet this condition—though of course nobody is perfect, including the legislator. Apart from more general advantages (Wissenburg, 1998, 1999), formal rights allow us to indicate first that, and secondly where, rights are limited as a matter of principle.

To start with the first bit: rights in the everyday sense of the word can be limited, given certain assumptions. First, rights, even 'natural' or 'divine' rights, do not fall from the skies. They have to be recognized, and recognition is the prerogative of human beings. Only those who can follow a law can give it, only those who can be moral can design criteria of morality. Next, we need to assume that there is always a material aspect to rights, so that rights become rights to *goods*, to material things. Without stone, we cannot create a sculpture; without a tongue, we cannot speak; without the right to use one's brain, even the right to freedom of thought becomes void.

Now goods can be individuated: they can be the subject of individual (or group or collective) rights. They can be acquired, sold, granted and taken away. There are very few physical objections to the acquisition or transfer of rights: I can take an apple from a tree as easily as I can give it to you, and I can give you the apple almost as easily as my labour, my thoughts or an arm. In short, ownership rights are *physically* alienable, and that raises the question of the *moral* justification for each particular right. We have, for instance, no reason to believe that there can be ownership rights to everything, nor, more importantly, that an ownership right to x implies that one can do everything one likes with x, i.e. that ownership is an unconditional right, one with which no one may interfere: absolute sovereignty.

Since rights need to be recognized, claims to rights have to be defended. Many rights thus become conditional: no matter how scarce or abundant they may be, as long as they are alienable, claims to them can be compared, evaluated and ordered. Even in the absence of competing claims a claim need not become a right: that only one person applies for, say, a subsidy is not enough reason to give it; we also need a positive reason to recognize her claim as valid. Hence, *arguments* determine whether a particular attribution of rights is justified.

Principles for the attribution of rights can be of two kinds: one determines what is to be distributed, the other how. The first puts side-constraints on distribution, the second defines allocation aims. The latter are the kind of principles to which liberal theorists refer as 'principles of justice' in a strict sense. Both can offer ways towards an environmentally sane society. On the one hand, green interests *may* perhaps be satisfied more by one scheme for the allocation of resources than another, and liberalism *may* support such a scheme, but there is no reason to assume beforehand that either thesis is true. On the other hand, there can be side-constraints to the distribution of rights to natural resources that ensure, say, sustainability regardless of the way in which resources will be allocated, so that we can worry a little less about the environmental effects of liberal principles of justice.

It is the latter type of principle that generates what I have called the restraint principle, a principle that demands that conditional rights to (in a physical sense) scarce goods be distributed in such a way that they remain, within the limits of necessity, available for redistribution. This is done by excluding from any (individual's or collective's) set of rights to a good x, at least in principle, the right to destroy x:

No goods shall be destroyed unless unavoidable and unless they are replaced by perfectly identical goods; if that is physically impossible, they should be replaced by equivalent goods resembling the original as closely as possible; and if that is also impossible, a proper compensation should be provided.

Where does this principle come from? The attribution of rights is a matter of arguments. Because liberals have no yardstick for the ultimate truth or validity of principles, they have to accept, firstly, that any conditional right (any good) that can physically be withdrawn (alienated) can also be withdrawn morally should a stronger argument come along, and secondly, that a right to x is not a right to x-plus—a right to pluck apples is not a right to cut down trees.

The recognition of (formal) rights to each separate basic act (see above) requires, in principle, a separate argument. It is simply not true that an argument p that would convince us that I should have the freedom to type or not type 'e' next will convince us that I therefore also deserve the right to vote. An argument p may support rights to more than one basic act, but p does not support my right to do x_2 merely *because* it supports my right to do x_1. By the same token, and other things being equal, a valid argument for picking fruit from trees here and now justifies only those acts that are necessary to that purpose. It is not necessary to cut down the tree to get hold of the fruit, therefore a right to possess or take possession of the fruit does not entitle one to cut down the tree. Arguments in favour of a specific set of complex rights can only bring one so far and no further.

If an ownership right to x does not imply that one can do everything one likes with x, it becomes possible to say that there are specific molecular rights to x that simply cannot be granted. As a matter of fact, a case can be made for the thesis that there is at least one such right that can never be granted: the right to destroy the object of x, thus turning ownership rights into rights to use rather than (absolutely) possess x.

Conditional ownership depends on reasons, but reasons are as fallible as those who articulate them. The soundness of reasons may change over time or depending on the information we have. Others may turn out to have better claims to goods than I have—they merely have not yet made those claims, have not been able to do so or have not been heard. They may even be unaware of their own good reasons, as it takes time to grow up and develop or discover one's plan of life. A first-come or finders-keepers principle is not a warrant for justice—my claim may be prior in time without being prior in terms of urgency or need. In sum: whenever there is a choice between on the one hand destroying a good, depriving others of options, limiting their freedom and thus harming them, or on the other merely using it without limiting other people's options, we have a duty to chose the latter.

In theory then, no argument can justify that we destroy anything that could be used by anyone else for a better reason. Theory is often an impractical thing. Following a general duty not to destroy anything means starving or thirsting or freezing to death—whichever comes first. No environmentalist who values the lives of subjects (humans or other) and no liberal who values the liberty of life could ever accept this. Hence, both will agree that this duty to restraint can be overruled by necessity, i.e. by the quest for survival or, in liberal terms, by the quest for a life worth living. Although necessity overrules the duty to restraint, it does not annul the rights and claims of others. In general, your valid claim to x does not make it a duty for us to make an alternative for x available to you, yet it does not prohibit it either. If x is vital to my survival or to my liberty of life, it can also be vital for you. There may be reasons why my survival is less important than yours. Which reasons exactly are not important here: they could be that 'you' are a whole people and that I am a mouse or that I love you and we both value your life more than mine. The point is that your claim to x can be stronger than mine, only your claim has not been recognized for the same reasons that supported the duty to restraint. In circumstances like these, the freedom to replace x turns into a duty to replace—with the same proviso: unless necessity prohibits it.

The demand that nothing be destroyed 'unless necessary' forms a weak spot in the restraint principle. Its 'greening' potential depends on where exactly a specific theory of justice draws the border between necessity and indulgence—or rather, since few liberals have touched on this question, where it *should* be drawn. One part of this problem is to decide if it makes sense at all to distinguish between what I call basic needs and further wants (cf. Wissenburg, 1999); some liberals, after all, do not: they never question the moral equivalence of preferences. This may well be the simpler problem. We do make distinctions like this in everyday life, and there may be ways to justify it, using the idea that some but not all goods, acts, rights, etc. are necessary conditions for a tolerable life and necessary but not sufficient preconditions for a morally good, rewarding or full life (cf. Barry's (1995) conception of crucial goods). Even the terms need and want are not sacred: a similar distinction can be made in terms like use and abuse or (perhaps more to the green taste) symbiotic and parasitic (cf. Barry, 1999).

Philosophically slightly less interesting yet practically far more disturbing is the second question: if it makes sense to distinguish between need and want, where should we draw the border? The fact that defining such a criterion is difficult cannot count against the validity of the distinction between needs and wants or the symbiotic and parasitic itself, but it does imply that a prima facie limitation of the right to exploit and destroy nature is not yet enough to guarantee that liberal democracy and environmental sustainability are compatible. Given that even liberals who use the concept of preferences as a black box make a distinction between the more and less 'needed' (preferred) and an implicit distinction between need (preference) and the insignificant, defining a border between need and want is, or must be, essential for all liberal theories.

Conclusion

In the previous sections, I have tried to describe ways in which liberal philosophy can and actually does try to make room for the environment. None of these solutions was perfect, all typically require 'further research', yet two interesting conclusions can be drawn.

First, some of the proposals discussed can be combined to generate theoretically broader versions of green liberalism. This appears to be true, in particular, for the restraint principle. Note, for example, that the restraint principle protects more than humans only: it also incorporates non-human nature. Let us assume for a moment that animals are not subjects but mere objects, livestock. Now even a merely instrumentally valuable object can be irreplaceable. The restraint principle demands that, unless there is no way to avoid it, no rock, animal or plant should be destroyed, no species made extinct. There can hardly be more protection for 'natural objects' like animals. It also demands that if this is impossible, the most similar possible alternative should be made available: nature should be replaced by nature, not by concrete. Like the precautionary principle, it puts the onus of proof for the legitimacy of environmentally harmful acts on the bad guys. At this point, it can link up with green debates on animal rights, on the intrinsic value of nature and on the substitutability of natural capital, as well as strengthen attempts to introduce animals and other parts of nature in liberal theories as morally relevant entities.

The restraint principle can, furthermore, be incorporated in, or incorporate, an amended Lockean view on the legitimacy of property—and it can be combined with contractarian theories of justice. Being a logical implication of a formal understanding of rights, it would be rational for impartial contracting parties to accept it. It also offers a second elegant solution to a problem discussed in both liberal and green theory: that of justice between generations, particularly between existing and therefore morally relevant generations and non-existing and not necessarily relevant generations. It protects the interests of future generations implicitly by protecting those of present generations.

In short: a combination of the arguments discussed here can mend some of the shortcomings of each of the arguments separately: the need to refer to absurd premises in order to reach desirable conclusions with regard to the protection of animals and the environment; the need to rely on the preferences of current individuals only; the dangers involved in a conservative attitude towards present institutions.

The second conclusion to be drawn is that, regardless of current political practices, liberalism as a political theory is not incompatible with green intentions and theories. At the very least, it is not a necessary or sufficient precondition of an unsustainable society—perhaps (see the Conclusion of this book) it is even more. Although it can never support one and only one theory of the good as the exclusive way to ecological salvation, its core values offer enough room for green rules and duties to take liberalism seriously as an environment in which notions of sustainability are likely to flourish. Whether they do depends not in the first instance on institutions but on individuals and their appreciation of the environment. Perhaps, then, critics of the past have misconstrued the problem: perhaps it is not so much a question of squaring liberalism with sustainability, but of discovering where liberals can find the moral courage to become greener liberals.

References

Achterhuis, H. (1994), 'The Lie of Sustainability', in W. Zweers and J. Boersema, *Ecology, Technology and Culture: Essays in Environmental Philosophy* (Knapwell: White Horse Press), 198–203.

Ackerman, B. (1980), *Social Justice in the Liberal State* (New Haven, CT: Yale University Press).

Anderson, T. and Leal, D. (1991), *Free Market Environmentalism* (San Francisco: Pacific Research Institute for Public Policy).

Barry, B. (1995), *Justice as Impartiality* (Oxford: Oxford University Press).

—— (1989), *A Treatise on Social Justice. Volume I: Theories of Justice* (London: Harvester-Wheatsheaf).

Barry, J. (1999), *Rethinking Green Politics: Nature, Virtue and Progress* (London: Sage).

Beckman, L. (2001), 'Virtue, Sustainability, and Liberal Values', in John Barry and Marcel Wissenburg (eds), *Sustaining Liberal Democracy* (New York: Palgrave).

Dobson, A. (1998), *Justice and the Environment: Conceptions of Environmental Sustainability and Theories of Distributive Justice* (Oxford: Oxford University Press).

Doherty, B. and de Geus, M. (1996), 'Introduction', in B. Doherty and M. de Geus (eds), *Democracy and Green Political Thought* (London: Routledge), 1–15.

Gauthier, D. (1986), *Morals by Agreement* (Oxford: Clarendon Press).

Holmes, S. (1993), *The Anatomy of Antiliberalism* (Cambridge, MA: Harvard University Press).

Lauber, V. (1978), 'Ecology, Politics and Liberal Democracy', *Government and Opposition*, 14: 199–217.

Locke, J. (1965), *Two Trentises of Government* (New York: Cambridge University Press).

Narveson, J. (1973), 'Moral Problems of Population', *Monist* 57: 199–217.

Nozick, R. (1974), *Anarchy, State, and Utopia* (New York: Basic Books).

Oksanen, Markku (2001), 'Privatizing Genetic Resources: Biodiversity, Communities and Intellectual Property Rights', in John Barry and Marcel Wissenburg (eds), *Sustaining Liberal Democracy* (New York: Palgrave).

Opschoor, H. (1994), 'Market Forces as Causes of Environmental Degradation', in W. Zweers and J. Boersema (eds), *Ecology, Technology and Culture. Essays in Environmental Philosophy* (Knapwell: White Horse Press), 175–97.

Rawls, J. (1971), *A Theory of Justice* (Cambridge, MA: Harvard University Press).

_____ (1993), *Political Liberalism* (New York: Columbia University Press).

Rowlands, M. (1998), *Animal Rights: A Philosophical Defence* (London: Macmillan).

Steiner, H. (1994), *An Essay on Rights* (Oxford: Blackwell).

Stephens, P. (1996), 'Plural Pluralisms: Towards a More Liberal Green Political Theory', in I. Hampsher-Monk and J. Stanyer (eds), *Contemporary Political Studies 1996*, vol. 1 (Oxford: PSA), 369–80.

Weale, A. (1992), *The New Politics of Pollution* (Manchester: Manchester University Press).

Wissenburg, M. (1993), 'The Idea of Nature and the Nature of Distributive Justice', in A. Dobson and P. Lucardie (eds), *The Politics of Nature* (London: Routledge), 3–20.

_____ (1998), *Green Liberalism: The Free and the Green Society* (London: UCL Press).

_____ (1999), *Minimal Justice: An Outline of a Liberal Theory of Social Justice* (London: UCL Press).

14 The American Political Economy II: The Non-Politics of Laissez Faire

William P. Ophuls with A. Stephen Boyan, Jr.

The invisible hand is no longer to be relied on for social decisions; we shall be obliged to make explicit political choices in order to meet the challenges of ecological scarcity. This is an embarrassing conclusion, for we Americans have never had a genuine politics—that is, something apart from economics that gives direction to our community life. Instead, American politics has been but a reflection of its laissez-faire economic system.

The Political Functions of Economic Growth

From our earliest colonial beginnings, rising expectations have been a fundamental part of the American credo, each generation expecting to become richer than the previous one. Thanks to this expectation of growth, the class conflict and social discontent typical of early nineteenth-century Europe were all but absent in America; politics was accordingly undemanding, pragmatic, and laissez-faire. Thus, said Alexis de Tocqueville in his classic study of American civilization *Democracy in America*, we were indeed a "happy republic."

Growth is still central to American politics. In fact, it matters more than ever, for the older social restraints (the Protestant ethic, deference, isolation) have all been swept away. Growth is the secular religion of American society, providing a social goal, a basis for political solidarity, and a source of individual motivation. The pursuit of happiness has come to be defined almost exclusively in material terms, and the entire society—individuals, enterprises, the government itself—has an enormous vested interest in the continuation of growth.

The Economic Basis of Pragmatic Politics

Growth continues to be essential to the characteristic pragmatic, laissez-faire style of American politics, which has always revolved around the question of fair access to the opportunity to get on financially. Indeed, American political history is but the record of a more or less amicable squabble over the division of the spoils of a growing economy. Even social problems have been handled by substituting economic growth for political principle, transforming non-economic

From William P. Ophuls with A. Stephen Boyan, Jr., *Ecology and the Politics of Scarcity Revisited: The Unraveling of the American Dream* (New York: W. H. Freeman, 1992), 237–53. © 1992 by W. H. Freeman & Company. Reprinted with permission.

issues into ones that could be solved by economic bargaining. For example, when labor pressed its class demands, the response was to legitimize its status as a bargaining unit in the division of the spoils. Once labor had to be bargained with in good businesslike fashion, compromise, in terms of wages and other costable benefits, became possible. In return for labor's abandonment of uncompromising demands for socialism, others at the economic trough "squeezed over" enough for labor to get its share. Similarly, new political demands by immigrants, farmers, and so on were bought off by the opportunity to share in the fruits of economic growth. The only conflict that we failed to solve in this manner was slavery and its aftermath, and it is typical that once the legitimacy of black demands was recognized in the 1960s, the reflex response was to promote economic opportunity via job training, education, "black capitalism," and fair hiring practices—that is, the wherewithal to share the affluence of the envied whites. If blacks prosper economically, says our intuitive understanding of politics, racial problems will vanish.

As a political mode, economic reductionism has many virtues. Above all, it is a superb means of channeling and controlling social conflict. Economic bargaining is a matter of a little more or a little less. Nobody loses on issues of principle, and even failure to get what you want today is tolerable, for the bargaining session is continuous, and the outcome of the next round may be more favorable. Besides, everybody's share is growing, so that even an unfair share is a more-than-acceptable bird in the hand. Most people understand that in a growth economy, individuals or groups have more to gain from increases in the size of the enterprise as a whole than from any feasible change in distribution. Furthermore, people have gotten what was of primary interest to them—access to income and wealth—and with their chief aim satisfied, they were able to repress desires for community, social respect, political power, and other values that are not so easily divisible as money.

This characteristic style of conflict resolution presupposes agreement on the primacy of economics and a general willingness to be pragmatic and to accept the bargaining approach to political and social as well as economic issues. Unfortunately, the arrival of ecological scarcity places issues on the political agenda that are not easily compromisable or commensurable, least of all in terms of money. Trade-offs are possible, of course, but environmental imperatives are basically matters of principle that cannot be bargained away in an economic fashion. Environmental management is therefore a role for which our political institutions are miscast, because it involves deciding issues of principle in favor of one side or another rather than merely allocating shares in the spoils. Worse, a cessation or even a slowing of growth will bring opposing interests into increasingly stark conflict. Economic growth has made it possible to satisfy the demands of new claimants to the spoils without taking anything away from others. Without significant growth, however, we are left with a zero-sum game, in which there will be winners and losers instead of big winners and little winners. Especially in recent years, growth has become an all-purpose "political solvent" (Bell 1974: 43), satisfying rapidly rising expectations while allowing very large expenditures for social welfare and defense. Without the political solvent of growth to provide quasi-automatic solutions to many of our domestic social problems, our political institutions will be called on to make hard choices about how best to use relatively scarce resources to meet a plethora of demands. More important, long-suppressed social issues can now be expected to surface—especially the issue of equality.

Ecological Scarcity versus Economic Justice

To state the problem succinctly, growth and economic opportunity have been substitutes for equality of income and wealth. We have justified large differences in income and wealth on the grounds that they promote growth and that all members of society would receive future advantage from current inequality as the benefits of development "trickled down" to the poor. (On a more personal level, economic growth also ratifies the ethics of individual self-seeking: You can get on without concern for the fate of others, for they are presumably getting on too, even if not so well as you.) But if growth in production is no longer of overriding importance, the rationale for differential rewards gets thinner, and with a cessation of growth it virtually disappears. In general, anything that diminishes growth and opportunity abridges the customary substitutes for equality. Because people's demands for economic betterment are not likely to disappear, once the pie stops growing fast enough to accommodate their needs, they will begin making demands for redistribution.

Even more serious than the frustration of rising expectations is the prospect of actual deprivation as substantial numbers of people get worse off in terms of real income as a result of scarcity-induced inflation and the internalization of environmental costs. Indeed, the eventual consequence of ecological scarcity is a lower standard of living, as we currently define it, for almost all members of society. One does not need a gloomy view of human nature to realize that this will create enormous political and social tension. It is, in fact, the classic prescription for revolution. At the very least, we can expect that our politics will come to be dominated by resentment and envy—or "emulation," to use the old word—just as it has many times in the past in democratic polities.

To make the revolutionary potential of the politics of emulation more concrete, let us imagine that the current trend toward making automobile ownership and operation more expensive continues to the point where the car becomes once again a luxury item, available only to "the carriage trade." How will the average person, once an economic aristocrat with his or her own private carriage but now demoted to a scooter or a bicycle, react to this deprivation, especially in view of the fact that the remaining aristocrats will presumably continue to enjoy their private carriages?

Of course, such an extreme situation is probably a long way off (although many would be priced out of the market today if all the social costs attributable to the automobile were internalized). Yet it is toward such a situation that the rising costs due to ecological scarcity are pushing us. Already, in striking contrast to the not-too-distant past, the price of a detached house in the most populous areas of the country is more than the average family can afford to pay. Also, as the cost of food and other basic necessities continues to increase, less disposable income will be left for the purchase of automobiles and other highly desired goods. In sum, deprivation is inevitable, even in the short term.

This point has not been lost on advocates for the disadvantaged, who have already protested vehemently against the regressive impact of even modest increases in the cost of energy (through increased gasoline taxes, for example) and goods.[1] More generally, they fear that lessened growth will tend to restrict social mobility and freeze the status quo, or even turn the clock back in some areas, such as minority rights.

The political stage is set, therefore, for a showdown between the claims of ecological scarcity on the one hand and socioeconomic justice on the other. If the impact of scarcity is distributed in a laissez-faire fashion, the result will be to intensify existing inequalities. Large-scale redistribution, however, is almost totally foreign to our political machinery, which was designed for a growth economy and which has used economic surplus as the coin of social and political payoff. Thus the political measures necessary to redistributing income and wealth such that scarce commodities are to a large degree equally shared will require much greater social cooperation and solidarity than the system has exhibited in the past.

They will also require greater social control. Under conditions of scarcity, there is a trade-off between freedom and equality, with perfect equality necessitating almost total social control (as was attempted in Maoist China). However, even partial redistribution will involve wholesale government intervention in the economy and major transfers of property rights, as well as other infringements of liberty in general, that will be resisted bitterly by important and powerful interests.

Thus either horn of the dilemma—laissez faire or redistribution—would toss us into serious difficulties that would strain our meager political and moral resources to or beyond capacity. American society is founded on competition rather than cooperation, and scarcity is likely to aggravate rather than ameliorate the competitive struggle to gain economic benefits for oneself or one's group. Similarly, our political ethic is based on a just division of the spoils, defined almost purely in terms of fair access to the increments of growth; once the spoils of abundance are gone, little is left to promote social cooperation and sharing. As Adam Smith pointed out, the "progressive state" is "cheerful" and "hearty"; by contrast, the stationary state is "hard," the declining state "miserable" (Smith 1776: 81). How well will a set of political institutions completely predicated on abundance and molded by over 200 years of continuous growth cope with the "hardness" of ecological scarcity?

The Non-Politics of Due Process

This dilemma is only a specific instance of a more general problem. In many areas, the American government will be obliged to have genuine policies—that is, specific measures or programs designed to further some particular conception of the public interest. This will require radical changes, because in our laissez-faire political system, ends are subordinated to political means. In other words, we practice "process" politics as opposed to "systems" politics (Schick 1971). As the name implies, process politics emphasizes the adequacy and fairness of the rules governing the process of politics. If the process is fair, then, as in a trial conducted according to due process, the outcome is assumed to be just—or at least the best that the system can achieve. By contrast, systems politics is concerned primarily with desired outcomes; means are subordinated to predetermined ends.

The process model has many virtues. Keeping the question of ends out of politics greatly diminishes the intensity of social conflict. People debate the fairness of the rules, a matter about which they find it relatively easy to agree, and they do not confront each other with value demands, which may not be susceptible to compromise. However, by some standards, the process model hardly deserves the name of politics, for it evades the whole issue of the common interest simply by declaring that the "will of all" and the "general will" are identical. The common interest is thus, by definition, whatever the political system's invisible hand cranks out, for good or ill.

Of course, we have found that pure laissez-faire politics, like pure laissez-faire economics, produces outcomes that we find intolerable, but our instinct has always been to curb the social costs of laissez faire by reforms designed to preserve its basic features: We check practices that prevent the efficient or fair operation of the market rather than converting to a planned economy; we promote equal opportunity rather than redistributing wealth or income. Planning with certain ends in mind does take place in such a political system. Each separate atom or molecule in the body politic (individuals, corporations, government agencies, advisory commissions, and supreme courts) plans in order to maximize its own ends, and the invisible hand produces the aggregated result of action on these private plans. But the central government does not plan in any systematic way, even though its ad hoc actions—VA and FHA home loans, tax breaks for homeowners, and the like—do in a sense constitute a "plan" for certain outcomes—in this case, suburban sprawl.

In reality, "the American political system" is almost a misnomer. What we really have is congeries of unintegrated and competitive subsystems pursuing conflicting ends—a non-system. And our overall policy of accepting the outcome of due process means that in most particulars we have non-policies. Now, however, just as in economics, the externalities produced by this laissez-faire system of non-politics have become unacceptable. Coping with the consequences of ecological scarcity will require explicit, outcome-oriented political decisions taken in the name of some conception of an ecological, if not a political and social, common interest. What likelihood is there of this happening?

Who Dominates The Political Marketplace?

Critics of the American political system almost never question the necessity (or superiority) of process politics. If bad outcomes are generated, it must be because powerful interests dominate the political marketplace and prevent the will of the majority from being fully and fairly translated into outcomes. There has been, say the critics, a wholesale expropriation of the public domain by private interests (Lowi 1969; McConnell 1966). Nevertheless, although much of this criticism is incontrovertible, the general preferences of the American people are in fact quite well reflected in political output. People want jobs, economic opportunities, and a growing economy. Indeed, to the extent that the system has had a guiding policy goal at all, it has been precisely to satisfy the rising expectations of its citizens. Even if special interests have benefited disproportionately from the measures taken to promote this end, most of the benefit has been transmitted to the vast majority of the population. The problem, then, is not that our political institutions are unresponsive to our wills but that what we desire generates the tragedy of the commons.

Naturally, to the extent that our government is largely a brokerage house for special interests, the situation is much worse, because such interests have an even bigger stake in continued economic growth. But within a process system of politics, government decisions that consistently favor producer over consumer interests are all but inevitable, for the political marketplace is subject to the public-goods problem. For example, those who have a direct and substantial financial interest in legislation and regulation are strongly motivated to organize, lobby, make campaign contributions, advertise, litigate, and so forth in pursuit of their interests. By comparison, the great mass of the people, who will be indirectly affected and whose personal stake in the outcome is likely to be negligible, have very little incentive to organize in defense of their interests. After all, the "right" decision may be worth $10 million to General Motors but will cost each individual only a few pennies. Thus those who try to stand up to special interests on environmental issues find themselves up against superior political resources all across the board.

The gross political inequality of profit and nonprofit interests is epitomized by the favorable tax treatment accorded the former. By law, tax-deductible donations cannot be used for lobbying or other attempts to influence legislation (for example, by advertising). Thus the nonprofit organizations that depend very heavily on donations are severely handicapped; if they lobby, they undercut their financial support. Businesses, by contrast, can deduct any money spent for the same purpose from their taxable income and pass on the remaining expense in the form of higher prices. The public, both as consumers and as taxpayers, therefore subsidizes one side in environmental disputes. Moreover, the law is self-protecting, for public-interest groups cannot even lobby to have it changed without losing their tax-exempt status.

Thus the outcome of the process of American politics faithfully reflects the will of the people and their desire for economic growth. However, just as in the economic marketplace, the public suffers from certain negative externalities as a result of the inordinate political power of producer interests; political power tends to be used to ratify and reinforce, rather than countermand, the decisions of the economic market. In sum, the American political system has all the drawbacks of laissez faire, wherein individual decisions add up to an ecologically destructive macro-decision, as well as a structural bias in favor of producers that tends to make this macro-decision even more destructive of the commons than it would otherwise be.

The Ecological Vices of Muddling Through

The logic of the commons is enshrined in a system of process politics obedient to the demands of both consumer and producer for economic growth. The ecological vices of this system are further intensified by the decision-making style characteristic of all our institutions—disjointed incrementalism or, to use the more honest and descriptive colloquial term, "muddling through."

Incremental decision making largely ignores long-term goals; it focuses on the problem immediately at hand and tries to find the solution that is most congruent with the status quo. It is thus characterized by comparison and evaluation of marginal changes (increments) in current policies, not radical departures from them; by consideration of only a restricted number of policy alternatives (and of only a few of the important consequences for any given alternative); by the adjustment of ends to means and to what is "feasible" and "realistic"; by serial or piecemeal treatment of problems; and by a remedial orientation in which policies are designed to cure obvious immediate ills rather than to bring about some desired future state. Moreover, analysis of policy alternatives is not disinterested, for it is carried out largely by partisan actors who are trying to improve their bargaining position with other partisan actors.

Muddling through is therefore a highly economic style of decision making that is well adapted to a pragmatic, laissez-faire system of politics. Moreover, it has considerable virtues. Like the market itself, disjointed incrementalism promotes short-term stability by minimizing serious conflict over ultimate ends, by giving everybody something of what they want, and by bringing bargained compromises among political actors, satisfying their needs reasonably well at minimal intellectual and financial cost. At the same time, it promotes the consensus and legitimacy needed to support public policy. It is also basically democratic; like the economic market, it reflects the preferences of those who participate in the political market (assuming that all legitimate interests can participate equally, which is not always the case). Disjointed incrementalism is also con-servative in a good sense: It does not slight traditional values, it encourages appreciation of the costs of change, and it prevents overly hasty action on complex issues. It may also avoid serious or irreversible mistakes, for an incremental measure that turns out to be mistaken can usually be corrected before major harm has been done. Under ideal circumstances, disjointed incremen-talism therefore produces a succession of policy measures that take the system step by step toward the policy outcome that best reflects the interests of the participants in the political market.

Unfortunately, muddling through has some equally large vices. For example, it does not guarantee that all relevant values will be taken into account, and it is likely to overlook excellent policies not suggested by past experience. In addition, disjointed incrementalism is not well adapted to handling profound value conflicts, revolutions, crises, grand opportunities, and the like—in other words, any situation in which simple continuation of past policies is not an appropriate response. Most important, because decisions are made on the basis of immediate self-interest, muddling through is almost guaranteed to produce policies that will generate the tragedy of the commons. It is perfectly possible to come up with a series of decisions that all seem eminently reasonable on the basis of short-term calculation of costs and benefits and that satisfy current preferences but that yield unsatisfactory results in the long run, especially because the future is likely to be discounted in the calculation of costs and benefits. In fact, that is just how we have gotten ourselves into an ecological predicament. Thus the short-term adjustment and stability achieved by muddling through is likely to be achieved at the expense of long-term stability and welfare.

A perfect illustration of the potential dangers of muddling through is our approach to global warming. As a result of millions of separate decisions made by industry and individuals, 6 billion tons of carbon dioxide are emitted into the atmosphere each year, and emissions are increasing by 3% annually. Yet no real congressional debate has occurred on whether to control these private decisions in order to reduce carbon emissions. Even worse, the executive branch blithely ignores the problem and advocates a more aggressive pursuit of the traditional energy and growth policies that have brought about the rise in carbon dioxide emissions. As a result, we go on unwittingly pursuing business as usual, making short-term calculations of costs and benefits, and bring upon ourselves the greenhouse effect almost by default.

Indeed, in its purest form, muddling through *is* policy making by default instead of by con-scious choice—simply an administrative device for aggregating individual preferences into a "will of all" that may bear almost no resemblance to the "general will." Unfortunately, the contrasting synoptic, or outcome-oriented, style of decision making cannot be fully achieved in the real world because of limits to our intellectual capacities (even with computers), lack of information (plus the cost of remedying it), uncertainty about our values and conflicts between them, and time constraints, as well as many lesser factors. Moreover, in its pure form, synoptic decision making could lead to irreversible and disastrous blunders, obliviousness to people's values, and the destruction of political consensus. Thus some measure of muddling through is a simple administrative necessity in any political system.

However, we Americans have taken muddling through, along with laissez faire and other prominent features of our political system, to an extreme. We have made compromise and short-term adjustment into ends instead of means, have failed to give even cursory consideration to the future consequences of present acts, and have neglected even to try to relate current policy choices to some kind of long-term goal. Worse, we have taken the radical position that there can be no common interest beyond what muddling through produces. In brief, we have elevated what is an undeniable administrative necessity into a philosophy of government, becoming in the process an "adhocracy" virtually oblivious to the implications of our governmental acts and politically adrift in the dangerous waters of ecological scarcity.

Disjointed incrementalism, then, provides an almost sufficient explanation of how we have proceeded step by step into the midst of ecological crisis and of why we are not meeting its challenges at present. As a normative philosophy of government, it is a program for ecological catastrophe; as an entrenched reality with which the environmental reformer must cope, it is a cause for deep pessimism. At the very least, the level or quality of muddling through must be greatly upgraded, so that ecology and the future are given due weight in policy making. But goal-oriented muddling through comes close to being a contradiction in terms (especially within a basically democratic system). Moreover, incrementalism is adapted to status-quo, consensus politics, not to situations in which policy outcomes are of critical importance or in which the paradigm of politics itself may be undergoing radical change (Dror 1968: especially pp. 300−4; Lindblom 1965; Schick 1971: especially p. 158). Thus steering a middle course will be difficult at best, and it may not be possible at all during the transition to a steady-state society.

Policy Overload, Fragmentation, and Other Administrative Problems

Disjointed incrementalism is not the only built-in impediment to an effective response to ecological scarcity. In the first place, the growing scale, complexity, and interdependence of society make the decision-making environment increasingly problematic, for the greater the number of decisions (and, above all, the greater the degree of risk they entailed), the greater the social effort necessary to make them. Given the size and complexity of the task of environmental management alone, especially with the declining margin for ecological or technological error, there would be a danger of administrative overload. But the crisis of ecological scarcity is only one crisis among many—part of a crisis of crises that will afflict decision makers in the decades ahead (Platt 1969). An allied crisis of priorities also impends, as burgeoning demands for environmental cleanup, more and better social services, and so on compete for the tiny portion of government resources remaining after the "fixed" demands of defense, agricultural supports, and other budgetary sacred cows are satisfied, so that decision makers will simply lack sufficient funds to act effectively across the board. (In the United States, this has been true throughout the 1980s and early 1990s.) In addition, there may be critical shortfalls in labor power, especially technical and scientific labor power. In short, the problems are growing faster than the wherewithal to handle them, and political and administrative overload is therefore a potentially serious problem for the future, if not right now.

A second serious problem is fragmented and dispersed administrative responsibility. The agency in charge of decisions on air pollution, for example, usually has no control over land-use policy, freeway building, waste disposal, mass transit, and agriculture! Also, some elements of policy are handled at the federal level, whereas others belong to the state and local governments; the boundaries of local governments, especially, have no relationship to ecological realities. As a result, it frequently happens that one agency or unit of government works at cross-purposes with another, or even with itself, as in the old Atomic Energy Commission, which was charged with both nuclear development and radiation safety.[2] Furthermore, each agency has been created to perform a highly specialized function for a particular constituency, which leads to a single-mindedness or tunnel vision that deliberately ignores the common interest. In brief, we have as many different policies as we have bureaus and it is difficult to get them to pull together.

A third major defect of our policy-making machinery is that decisions inevitably lag behind events—usually far behind. In part, the problem is that the decision makers' information and knowledge are deficient and out of date. Owing to the complexity and scope of the problems of environmental management, these deficiencies are either impossible to remedy or too costly. Thus, even if they are inclined to be forward-looking, decision makers are virtually obliged to muddle through critical problems with stopgap measures that provoke disruptive side effects. Much the larger part of the time-lag problem, however, is that the procedural checks and balances built into our basically adversary system of policy making can subject controversial decisions to lengthy delays. For example, Congress in 1977 amended the Clean Air Act to protect visibility in large national parks and wilderness areas; it took until 1990, however, for the EPA to issue draft regulations to implement the law. Thereafter, before the EPA issued its final regulations, the White House weakened them, sacrificing two-thirds of the visibility reductions that the EPA had proposed (Rauber 1991: 28). The matter may still end up in court. By presidential decree, the White House Office of Management and Budget subjects all EPA regulations to cost-benefit analysis. But the 1977 law requires power plants to install "the best available retrofit technology" to eliminate the air pollution impairing visibility in the parks. Opponents argue that insofar as cost-benefit analysis causes regulations to be issued that do not require the use of the best available technology, the use of such analysis is illegal. They also argue a proper cost-benefit analysis, in any event, supports the original EPA draft regulations—that OMB simply manipulated the data to weaken them. This example suggests that the best we can expect in most cases is long wars of legal attrition against environmental despoilers. However, the adversary legal system is already having difficulty coping with environmental issues,[3] and there is some risk that environmental policy making may simply bog down in a morass of hearings, suits, counter-suits, and appeals, as government agencies, business interests, and environmentalist groups use all the procedural devices available to harass each other. And even if total stalemate is avoided, there are bound to be significant delays—an ominous prospect now that an anticipatory response to problems has become essential for their solution.

Additional hindrances to effective environmental decision making abound. The narrowly rationalistic norms and *modus operandi* of bureaucracies, for example, are at odds with the ecological holism needed for the task of environmental management. History also shows that regulatory agencies tend to be captured by the interests they are supposed to be regulating, so that they rapidly turn into guardians of special interest instead of public interest. In addition, the institutions charged with environmental management are frequently so beholden to their own institutional vested interests or so dominated by sheer inertia that they actively resist change, employing secrecy, special legal advantages available to government agencies, and other devices to squelch the efforts of critics and would-be reformers (for example, Lewis 1972). In recent years, environmental decision making has been hindered by nonstatutory mechanisms established in the White House. The President's Council on Competitiveness, for example, is a non-statutory body that, after closed meetings with industry, has repeatedly forced the Environmental Protection Agency to rewrite regulations to make them hospitable to industry interests. As of this writing, the Council has successfully forced the EPA to gut four major provisions—some say the "pillars"—of the 1990 Clean Air Act (Weisskopf 1991: A1).[4] These difficulties suggest that the problem is not simply to overcome inertia and vested interest but rather to arrest that the problem is not simply to overcome inertia and vested interest but rather to arrest the institutional momentum in favor of growth created by two centuries of prodevelopment laws, policies, and practices. This will require across-the-board institutional reform, not merely new policies.

In sum, administrative overload, fragmented and dispersed authority, protracted delays in making and enforcing social decisions, and the institutional legacy of the era of growth and exploitation are likely to obstruct timely and effective environmental policy making.

How Well Are We Doing?

None of the tendencies and trends we have just considered inspires much optimism that our political institutions at any level are adequate to the challenges of dealing with ecological scarcity. Although the final verdict is not yet in, this conclusion is certainly reinforced by the quality of their performance so far.

Energy policy is a good illustration. Despite a consensus that a coherent national energy policy is absolutely essential to avoid economic and social turmoil, a menacing international trade deficit, and even the compromise of its political independence, the United States has no genuine policy, much less a coherent one. Instead, the past decade has seen almost continual dithering and muddle and devotion to business as usual. In 1989 President Bush called for a long-term comprehensive policy, but what he proposed in 1991 was a mere grab-bag of favored projects of the oil, coal, gas, and nuclear power industries. Among these was more off-shore oil drilling, drilling in environmentally pristine areas, and the doubling of nuclear power capacity by 2030. The President proposed few conservation measures, only a minuscule increase in research on renewable energy, and support only for selected alternative fuels (ethanol and methanol but not for hydrogen, fuel cells, or electric vehicles). He proposed nothing to combat greenhouse gas emissions, except as an incidental consequence of his support for nuclear power.

When the Reagan administration made similar proposals during its years in office, it and Congress fought each other to a stalemate on energy conservation, environmental protection, and the relative support for renewable energy and fuels versus the support for fossil fuel and nuclear energy development. For example, a majority in Congress has thus far rejected oil drilling in the Arctic and other wilderness areas; instead it favors raising automobile fuel-efficiency standards to 40 miles per gallon by 2001, which would save 5 to 10 times the oil expected to be produced by oil drilling in the Arctic. But the Congressional majority is not veto-proof and the result is a stalemate. Continued stalemate, regrettably, sets the stage for an eventual general collapse of our energy economy because of either rising costs of petroleum or intolerable levels of pollution.

Similarly, our political institutions have so far conspicuously failed to meet the challenge represented by the automobile. The decline in air quality was sufficiently alarming to cause Congress to pass the Clean Air Act in 1970. For all its faults, this was a landmark piece of environmental legislation, and acting under the law's authority, government agencies forced emission control on a reluctant automobile industry. However, Detroit several times succeeded in winning delayed compliance. Moreover, the air-quality standards mandated by Congress in the 1970 Clean Air Act simply could not be achieved through technology alone. Yet when the Environmental Protection Agency tried to impose on key municipalities pollution-control plans that would have penalized or restricted car use (through gas rationing and parking sur-charges, for instance), the resulting political ruckus soon forced the EPA into retreat, and all pretense of meeting the original standards was abandoned. At the same time, Congress tried to control emissions through Corporate Fuel Economy Standards (CAFE). A 1975 law required manufacturers to raise the average efficiency of the cars they sold to 27.5 miles per gallon by 1985. Again, the executive branch granted the automobile industry many delays in complying with the law, and by 1990, efficiency standards had reached only 26.5 miles per gallon (which meant that the hoped-for reduction in pollution was nullified by a doubling, since the law was passed, of the number of vehicle miles driven). The 1990 Clean Air Act does tighten emission standards further and hopes to achieve its objectives via technological changes such as the use of reformulated gasoline in the nine most polluted metropolitan regions by 1995. But although the 1990 law will help, cleaning up the air and reducing greenhouse gas emissions cannot be achieved by more stringent emissions standards alone, because improvements in clean-air tech-nology are more than eaten up by growth in the automobile fleet and increases in vehicle miles driven. In short, Americans must simply drive much less than they do now (with much more efficient vehicles) and use mass transit much more. Unfortunately, having allowed the automobile so completely to dominate our lives that to restrict its use would produce instant economic and social crisis, we are repeatedly reduced to the desperate hope that some kind of technological fix will turn up in time to prevent natural feedback mechanisms—extreme price rises, national bankruptcy, intolerable levels of air pollution—from taking matters out of our hands.

Thus in these and other critical areas we are failing to meet the challenges. Everybody wants clean air and water, but nobody wants to pay the price. Nor do we wish to give up the appurtenances of a high-energy style of life or to accept the major restructuring of the economy and society that would be needed to reduce greenhouse-gas emissions significantly. Even modest invasion of sacrosanct private property rights—for example, in the form of vitally needed land-use law—has also proved to be well beyond our current political capacity. In fact, since the beginning of the 1980s there has been considerable backlash and backsliding on environmental issues, leading to relaxed standards and blatant denial of problems. In short, although there has been genuine progress since environmental issues first became a matter for political concern, our political institutions have so far largely avoided the tasks of environmental management and have for the most part done too little too late in those efforts they have undertaken.

As we have seen, the basic institutional structure and *modus operandi* of the American political system are primarily responsible for this. Nevertheless, the lack of courage and vision displayed by the current set of political actors should not escape notice. Neither Congress nor the executive branch has provided real leadership or faced up to crucial issues. To the extent that they have acted, as in the area of pollution control, they have acted faintheartedly or, what is almost worse, expediently rather than effectively. Say what one will about the institutional impediments and the difficulty of the problems, it is hard to conclude that our political leaders are doing the job they were elected to do. But of course, the inability or reluctance of our political officials to act simply reflects the desires of the majority of the American people, who have so far evinced only modest willingness to make minor sacrifices (for example, to support and engage in recycling) for the sake of environmental goals, but no willingness to accept fundamental changes in their way of life (for example, to restrict development to areas where public transit is available, or to support and use public transit and drive less). Our public officials can hardly be expected to commit political suicide by forcing unpopular environmental measures on us. Until the will of the people ordains otherwise or fundamental changes are quite literally forced on us, the best we can expect is piecemeal, patchwork, ineffective reform that lags ever farther behind onrushing events.

The Necessity for Paradigm Change

Our political institutions, predicated almost totally on growth and abundance, appear to be no match for the mounting challenges of ecological scarcity. This is a shocking conclusion about a political system that was once regarded, even by many foreigners, as marvelously progressive. For all its faults, the virtues of the American political system are undeniable: It worked well for nearly two hundred years, and it was eminently just and humane by any reasonable historical standard. Unfortunately, the problems of scarcity that confront the system today are problems that *it was never designed to handle.* Many of its past virtues are therefore irrelevant; what we must now address are its equally undeniable failings in the face of ecological scarcity.

Efforts to patch up the current paradigm of politics with new modes of decision making and planning—or even with new policies—will not succeed. These can only delay, and perhaps intensify, the ultimate breakdown. Only a new politics based on a set of values that are morally and practically appropriate to an age of scarcity will do. To achieve this new politics will require a revolution even more fundamental than that which created our nation in the first place, for the characteristic features of American civilization, not merely the nature of the regime, must be transformed. A great question stands before the American polity: Will we make the effort to translate our ideals of equality and freedom into forms appropriate to the new age of scarcity, or will we not even try, continuing prodigally to sow as long as we can and leaving the future to reap the consequences? Only time will tell whether the return of scarcity must inevitably presage retrogression to the classical scenario of inequality, oppression, and conflict, but one way or another, we Americans are about to find out what kind of people we really are.

Notes

1. For every $1.00 increase in the price of oil, about 78,000 jobs are lost in the United States. Yet if the gasoline tax were adjusted to pay the cost of all public subsidies to the automobile, Americans would have to pay $4.50 per gallon of gas (Schaeffer 1990: 15).
2. The Nuclear Regulatory Commission, whose mission is protection of the public from nuclear and radiation hazards, in practice also promotes nuclear energy. It has become, as do most government agencies, the captive of the industry it is charged to regulate.
3. Increased volume is only part of the problem. The traditional legal machinery for redressing civil wrongs, designed for two-party litigation, is having trouble with standing to sue and other issues that crop up in the typical

environmental suit, where society as a whole is one of the parties. Also, technology creates new situations faster than the courts can work out precedents, and much of the scientific evidence used in environmental litigation is of a probabilistic and statistical nature that ill accords with the standards of proof traditionally demanded by courts.
4. Industry and administration lobbyists had tried to persuade Congress to adopt their substitutes for all four provisions when the legislation was being considered, but Congress had refused to adopt them. Environmentalists may thus be in a strong position to challenge these regulations as illegal, but even if they prevail, implementation of the law's requirements will be substantially delayed.

References

Abelson, Philip H. (1972a), "Environmental Quality," *Science*, 177: 655.

—— (1972b), "Federal Statistics," *Science*, 175: 1315.

Bachrach, Peter (1967), *The Theory of Democratic Elitism: A Critique* (Boston: Little, Brown).

Bell, Daniel (1974), "The Public Household—On 'Fiscal Sociology' and the Liberal Society," *Public Interest*, 37: 29–68.

Brown, Harrison, Bonner, James, and Weir, John (1963), *The Next Hundred Years* (New York: Viking), esp. chaps. 14–17, which discuss manpower.

Bruce-Briggs, B. (1974), "Against the Neo-Malthusians," *Commentary*, July: 25–9.

Burch, William R., Jr. (1971), *Daydreams and Nightmares: A Sociological Essay on the American Environment* (New York: Harper and Row).

Caldwell, Lynton K. (1971), *Environment: A Challenge to Modern Society* (Garden City, NY: Doubleday).

—— and Siddiqi, Toufiq A. (1974), *Environmental Policy, Law and Administration: A Guide to Advanced Study* (Bloomington: University of Indiana School of Public and Environmental Affairs).

Carpenter, Richard A. (1972), "National Goals and Environmental Laws," *Technology Review*, 74 (3): 58–63.

Carter, Luther J. (1973*a*), "Environment: A Lesson for the People of Plenty," *Science*, 182: 1323–24.

——— (1973*b*), "Environmental Law (I): Maturing Field for Lawyers and Scientists," *Science*, 179: 1205–09.

——— (1973*c*), "Environmental Law (II): A strategic Weapon Against Degradation?," *Science*, 179: 1310–12, 1350.

——— (1973*d*), "Pesticides: Environmentalists Seek New Victory in a Frustrating War," *Science*, 181: 143–5.

——— (1974*a*), "Cancer and the Environment (I): A Creaky System Grinds On," *Science*, 186: 239–42.

——— (1974*b*), "Con Edison: Endless Storm King Dispute Adds to Its Troubles," *Science*, 194: 1353–58.

——— (1974*c*), "The Energy Bureaucracy: The Pieces Fall into Place," *Science*, 185: 44–5.

——— (1974*d*), "Energy: Cannibalism in the Bureaucracy," *Science*, 186: 511.

——— (1974*e*), "Pollution and Public Health: Taconite Case Poses Major Test," *Science*, 186: 31–6.

——— (1975*a*), "The Environment: A 'Mature' Cause in Need of a Lift," *Science*, 187: 45–8.

——— (1975*b*), *The Florida Experience: Land and Water Policy in a Growth State* (Baltimore: Johns Hopkins).

Cohn, Victor (1975), "The Washington Energy Show," *Technology Review*, 77 (3): 8, 68.

Conservation Foundation (1972), "Wanted: A Coordinated, Coherent National Energy Policy Geared to the Public Interest," *CF Letter*, No. 6–72.

Cooley, Richard A., and Wandesforde-Smith, Geoffrey (eds), *Congress and the Environment* (Seattle: Washington).

Crossland, Janice (1974), "Cars, Fuel, and Pollution," *Environment*, 16 (2): 15–27.

Dahl, Robert A. (1970), *After the Revolution?: Authority in a Good Society* (New Haven: Yale).

Davies, Barbara S., and Davies, Clarence J., III (1975), *The Politics of Pollution*, 2nd edn. (New York: Pegasus).

Davis, David H. (1974), *Energy Politics* (New York: St Martin's).

Dexter, Lewis A. (1969), *The Sociology and Politics of Congress* (Chicago: Rand McNally).

Downs, Anthony (1972), "Up and Down with Ecology—The 'Issue-Attention Cycle,'" *Public Interest*, 28: 38–50.

Dror, Yehezkel (1968), *Public Policymaking Reexamined* (San Francisco: Chandler).

Edelman, Murray (1964), *The Symbolic Uses of Politics* (Urbana: Illinois).

Forrester, Jay W. (1971), *World Dynamics* (Cambridge: Wright–Allen), esp. chaps. 1 and 7 for a radical critique of nonsystematic, incremental decision making.

Forsythe, Dall W. (1974), "An Energy-Scarce Society: The Politics and Possibilities," *Working Papers for a New Society*, 2 (1): 3–12, an excellent short analysis.

Gillette, Robert (1973*a*), "Energy: The Muddle at the Top," *Science*, 182: 1319–21.

——— (1973*b*), "Western Coal: Does the Debate Follow Irreversible Commitment?," *Science*, 182: 456–8.

——— (1975), "In Energy Impasse, Conservation Keeps Popping Up," *Science*, 187: 42–5.

Goldstein, Paul, and Ford, Robert (1973), "On the Control of Air Quality: Why the Laws Don't Work," *Bulletin of the Atomic Scientists*, 29 (6): 31–4.

Green, Charles S., III (1973), "Politics, Equality and the End of Progress," *Alternatives*, 2 (2): 4–9.

Haefele, Edwin T. (1974), *Representative Government and Environmental Management* (Baltimore: Johns Hopkins).

Hartz, Louis (1955), *The Liberal Tradition in America: An Interpretation of American Political Thought Since the Revolution* (New York: Harcourt, Brace).

Henning, Daniel H. (1974), *Environmental Policy and Administration* (New York: American Elsevier).

Hirschman, Albert O. (1970), *Exit, Voice and Loyalty* (Cambridge: Harvard), esp. chap. 8 on frontier-style decision making and problem avoidance.

Horowitz, Irving L. (1972), "The Environmental Cleavage: Social Ecology versus Political Economy," *Social Theory and Practice*, 2 (1): 125–34.

Jacobsen, Sally (1974), "Anti-Pollution Backlash in Illinois: Can a Tough Protection Program Survive?" *Bulletin of the Atomic Scientists*, 30 (1): 39–44.

Jones, Charles O. (1975), *Clean Air: The Policies and Politics of Pollution Control* (University of Pittsburgh Press).

Kohlmeier, Louis M., Jr. (1969), *The Regulators: Watchdog Agencies and the Public Interest* (New York: Harper and Row).

Kraft, Michael (1972), "Congressional Attitudes Toward the Environment," *Alternatives*, 1 (4): 27–37, congressional avoidance of the environmental issue.

—— (1974), "Ecological Politics and American Government: A Review Essay," in Nagel (1974), 139–59, the best critical review of the political science literature in the light of environmental problems.

Lecht, L. A. (1966), *Goals, Priorities and Dollars* (New York: Free Press).

—— (1969), *Manpower Needs for National Goals in the 1970's* (New York: Praeger).

Lewis, Richard (1972), *The Nuclear Power Rebellion* (New York: Viking).

Lindblom, Charles E. (1965), *The Intelligence of Democracy: Decisionmaking Through Mutual Adjustment* (New York: Free Press).

—— (1969), "The Science of 'Muddling Through,'" *Public Administration Review*, 19 (2): 79–88.

Little, Charles E. (1973), "The Environment of the Poor: Who Gives a Damn?," *Conservation Foundation Letter*, July.

Loveridge, Ronald O. (1971), "Political Science and Air Pollution: A Review and Assessment of the Literature," in Paul B. Downing (ed.), *Air Pollution and the Social Sciences* (New York: Praeger), 45–85, why we are not coping with the problem.

—— (1972), "The Environment: New Priorities and Old Politics," in Harlan Hahn (ed.), *People and Politics in Urban Society* (Los Angeles: Sage), 499–529.

Lowi, Theodore (1969), *The End of Liberalism: Ideology, Policy, and the Crisis of Public Authority* (New York: Norton).

McConnell, Grant (1966), *Private Power and American Democracy* (New York: Knopf).

McLane, James (1974), "Energy Goals and Institutional Reform," *The Futurist*, 8: 239–42.

Michael, Donald N. (1968), *The Unprepared Society: Planning for a Precarious Future* (New York: Harper and Row).

Miller, John C. (1957), *Origins of the American Revolution* (Stanford, Calif.: Stanford University Press).

Moorman, James W. (1974), "Bureaucracy v. The Law," *Sierra Club Bulletin*, 59 (9): 7–10, how agencies evade or flout their legal responsibilities.

Murphy, Earl F. (1967), *Governing Nature* (Chicago: Quadrangle).

Nagel, Stuart S. (1974) (ed.), *Environmental Politics* (New York: Praeger).

Nelkin, Dorothy (1974), "The Role of Experts in a Nuclear Siting Controversy," *Bulletin of the Atomic Scientists*, 30 (9): 29–36.

Neubaus, Richard (1971), *In Defense of People* (New York: Macmillan).

de Nevers, Noel (1973), "Enforcing the Clean Air Act of 1970," *Scientific American*, 228 (6): 14–21.

Odell, Rice (1975*a*), "Automobiles Keep Posing New Dilemmas," *Conservation Foundation Letter*, March.

—— (1975*b*), "Should Americans Be Pried Out of Their Cars?," *Conservation Foundation Letter*, April.

Pirages, Dennis C., and Paul, R. Ehrlich (1974), *Ark II: Social Response to Environmental Imperatives* (New York: W. H. Freeman and Co.).

Platt, John (1969), "What We Must Do," *Science*, 166: 1115–21.

Potter, David M. (1954), *People of Plenty: Economic Abundance and the American Character* (Chicago: University of Chicago).

Quarles, John (1974), "Fighting the Corporate Lobby," *Environmental Action*, 7 December: 3–6, how the political and other resources of corporations overwhelm the environmental regulators.

Quigg, Philip W. (1974), "Energy Shortage Spurs Expansion of Nuclear Fission," *World Environment Newsletter in SIR World*, 29 June: 21–2.

Rauber, Paul (1991), "O Say, Can You See," *Sierra*, July/August: 24–9.

Roos, Leslie L., Jr. (1971) (ed.), *The Politics of Ecosuicide* (New York: Holt, Rinehart and Winston).

Rose, David J. (1974), "Energy Policy in the U.S.," *Scientific American*, 230 (1): 20–9.

Rosenbaum, Walter A. (1973), *The Politics of Environmental Concern* (New York: Praeger).

Ross, Charles R. (1970), "The Federal Government as an Inadvertent Advocate of Environmental Degradation," in Harold W. Helfiich, Jr. (ed.), *The Environmental Crists* (New Haven: Yale), 171–87.

Ross, Douglas, and Wolman, Harold (1971), "Congress and Pollution—The Gentleman's Agreement," in Warren A. Johnson and John Hardesty (eds), *Economic Growth vs. the Environment* (Belmont, Calif.: Wadsworth), 134–44.

Schaeffer, Robert (1990), "Car Sick," *Greenpeace*, May/June: 13–17.

Schick, Allen (1971), "Systems Politics and Systems Budgeting," in Roos (1971), 135–58.

Shapley, Deborah (1973), "Auto Pollution: Research Group Charged with Conflict of Interest," *Science*, 181: 732–5.

Shubik, Martin (1967), "Information, Rationality, and Free Choice in a Future Democratic Society," *Daedalus*, 96: 771–8.

Sills, David L. (1975), "The Environmental Movement and Its Critics," *Human Ecology*, 3: 1–41.

Smith, Adam (1776), *An Inquiry into the Nature and Causes of the Wealth of Nations*, ed. Edwin Cannan (New York: Modern Library, 1937).

Smith, James N. (1974) (ed.), *Environmental Quality and Social Justice* (Washington, DC: Conservation Foundation).

Sprout, Harold, and Sprout, Margaret (1971), *Ecology and Politics in America: Some Issues and Alternatives* (New York: General Learning Press).

—— (1972), "National Priorities: Demands, Resources, Dilemmas," *World Politics*, 24: 293–317.

Weisskopf, Michael (1991), "Rule-Making Process Could Soften Clean Air Act," *Washington Post*, 21 September, A1.

White, Lawrence J. (1973), "The Auto Pollution Muddle," *Public Interest*, 32: 97–112.

Wolff, Robert Paul (1968), *The Poverty of Liberalism* (Boston: Beacon).

PART THREE

ENVIRONMENT AND ECONOMICS

Environmental values and economic values have long been treated as pointing in opposite directions. Survivalists have always claimed that economic values must yield to ecological ones; reformists have implicitly assumed that the best we could hope for is some reasonable compromise between the two opposites. In Part Three we introduce literatures that point to the essential compatibility of environment and economics. Section V focuses on the possibility of putting economic instruments (especially quasi-market schemes) to the service of environmental values. Section VI and VII deal with arguments that economic growth and environmental conservation can proceed hand-in-hand, provided that intelligent political action can redirect the structure and development of global and national political-economic systems.

Section V: Market Liberalism

While environmental policy in practice has generally featured some combination of administrative and liberal democratic procedures, environmental policy in theory has seen a great deal more of market liberalism. Market liberals believe that the key of effective resolution of environmental problems is the intelligent deployment of markets and quasi-markets. They have nothing but scorn for the kind of professional resource management advocated by administrative rationalists, and believe that liberal democratic politics is little more than licence for special interests to poke their snouts into the public trough.

Hard-line market liberals believe that all environmental problems have a common origin: the failure to specify appropriate private property rights. If it is a truism that people tend to take care of their private property much more carefully than they care for what they hold in common with others, why not, then, convert the environment into private property too? Market liberals have devoted a great deal of effort to exploring how property rights might be established in land, fisheries, air, and water. Once established, such rights can be exchanged in the market, available to the highest bidder and so to the most socially and economically beneficial use. The classic statement of this hard-line position appears in our selection from Terry L. Anderson and Donald T. Leal. Robert Stavins and Bradley Whitehead provide some examples of the use of market mechanisms in US environmental policy, also considering why such instruments have not been used more extensively.

Not all proponents of market and quasi-market schemes share the hard-line position of Anderson and Leal. As Robert E. Goodlin notes, such schemes are also attractive to a broad spectrum of environmentalists. The difference here is that these environmentalists want to keep the schemes under tight governmental control. So rather than simply turning everything into private property, quasi-market schemes would involve (say) managed markets in pollution rights, with government free to increase or decrease the number of rights available for auction. Other proposals involve the use of 'green taxes', which provide an incentive to polluters to cut back on their emissions or other environmentally damaging activities. One of the best-known such proposals is a carbon tax levied on fossil fuels in order to reduce emissions of greenhouse gases, now levied in several European countries. Market liberal schemes of all sorts are attacked by Goodin, who likens the selling of rights to pollute to the selling of indulgences to sinners by the medieval Catholic Church.

Further Reading

Anderson and Leal's *Free Market Environmentalism* (revised edition, 2001) remains the best comprehensive statement of hard-line market liberalism. This position is also developed in Richard L. Stroup and Roger E. Meiners (eds), *Cutting Green Tape: Toxic Pollutants, Environmental Regulation, and the Law* (2000). Herman E. Daly shows why environmentalists might reject this hard-line position while still making use of market-type policies in 'Free Market Environmentalism: Turning a Good Servant into a Bad Master', *Critical Review*, 6 (1992): 171–83. A comprehensive regime of green taxes is advocated in a British context in David Pearce, Anil Markandya, and Edward R. Barbier, *Blueprint for a Green Economy* (1989), updated in David Pearce and Edward R. Barbier, *Blueprint for a Sustainable Economy* (2000). A critical account of economists and their schemes, which helps to explain why many environmentalists are uneasy with them, is developed by Steven Kelman in *What Price Incentives? Economists and the Environment* (1981). Mark Sagoff's *The Economy of the Earth* (1988) is a sustained attack on environmental and natural resource economists. Elinor Ostrom, in *Governing the Commons* (1990), shows that dividing the commons into chunks of private property is not the only way to solve the tragedy of the commons. Perspective on the varieties of market liberalism and their critics is provided in Robyn Eckersley (ed.), *Markets, the State and the Environment: Towards Integration* (1995).

15 Rethinking the Way We Think

Terry L. Anderson and Donald R. Leal

John Maynard Keynes, the British economist responsible for changing the way we think about the role of government spending and taxing to even out business cycles, aptly described the impact of ideas, foretelling his own legacy:

Both when they are right and when they are wrong, the ideas of economists and political philosophers are more powerful than is commonly understood. Indeed the world is ruled by little else. Even practical men, who believe themselves exempt from intellectual influences, are usually the slaves of defunct economists. Madmen in authority, who hear voices in the air, are distilling their frenzy from academic scribblers of a few years back.[1]

In the area of environmental economics, it was another British economist, A. C. Pigou, whose scribblings left their mark on modern environmental policy.[2] Pigou argued that because not all costs are taken into account by private decision makers, political intervention is necessary to correct what he saw as failures of the market. Hence, in the case of a paper mill disposing of its wastes by dumping them into the air or water, the mill is imposing unwanted costs on the rest of society, costs for which the mill owners are not held accountable. With these costs unaccounted for by polluters, private decision makers will overuse the water and air for waste disposal, and people who want to use these resources for other purposes (e.g., swimming or breathing) will bear the costs.

To counter this market failure and maximize the value derived from natural resources, Pigou called for taxes or regulations on polluters imposed through a political process. In his words,

No "invisible hand" can be relied on to produce a good arrangement of the whole from a combination of separate treatments of the parts. It is therefore necessary that an authority of wider reach should intervene to tackle the collective problems of beauty, of air and light, as those other collective problems of gas and water have been tackled.[3]

Pigou believed that this authority should be given "to the appropriate department of central Government to order them [the polluters] to take action."[4]

Following the teaching of Pigou, economists and policy analysts have approached natural resource and environmental policy with the presumption that markets are responsible for resource misallocation and environmental degradation and that political processes can correct these problems. They assume there is a socially efficient allocation of resources that will be

From Terry L. Anderson and Donald T. Leal, *Free Market Environmentalism*, revised edn (London: Palgrave 2001), 9–26.

reached when "the appropriate department of central Government" correctly accounts for all the costs and benefits. One economist even went so far as to outline the conditions that would take society to its "bliss point."[5]

The purpose of this book is to challenge this traditional way of thinking and to provide a more realistic way of thinking about natural resource and environmental policy, thinking based on markets and property rights. This alternative recognizes and emphasizes the importance of incentives and of the costs of coordinating human actions. Rather than assuming that people are always altruistic, it presumes that self-interest prevails and asks how that self-interest can be harnessed to produce environmental goods that people demand. It does not assume that the costs of obtaining information or coordinating activities are zero or that there is perfect competition among producers. To the contrary, free market environmentalism focuses on how the costs of coordinating human actions (transaction costs, as economists label them) limit our ability to attain human goals through political processes and how markets can help overcome these costs. In this chapter, we proceed by considering the importance of incentives and transaction costs and then comparing incentives and transaction costs in market and political processes. Finally, the chapter addresses some specific arguments against free market environmentalism.

We emphasize from the outset that this way of thinking assumes that the environment's only value derives from human perceptions. Under this anthropocentric conception, the environment itself has no intrinsic value. People cannot manage natural resources for the sake of animals, plants, or other organisms because there is no Dr. Doolittle to "talk to the animals" and find out what is best for them. As long as humans have the power to alter the environment, they will do so based on human values—the only values that are ascertainable.

Incentives and Transaction Costs

In rethinking natural resource and environmental policy, two facts must be recognized. First, we cannot ignore the important role of incentives in guiding human behavior. No matter how well intended resource managers are, incentives affect their behavior. Like it or not, individuals will undertake more of an activity if the benefits of that activity are increased or if the costs reduced. This holds as much for bureaucrats and politicians as it does for profit-maximizing owners of firms or for citizens. Everyone accepts that managers in the private sector would dump production wastes into a nearby stream if they did not have to pay for the cost of their actions. Too often, however, we fail to recognize that the same elements work in the political arena. If a politician is not personally accountable for allowing oil development on federal lands or for the environmental impact of building dams on naturally-flowing rivers, we can expect too much oil development or too many dams. Moreover, when the beneficiaries—call them special interest groups—of these policies do not have to pay the full cost, they will demand more of them from their political representatives.

Once incentive effects are recognized, we can no longer rely on good intentions to generate good resource stewardship and environmental quality. Even if the superintendent of a national park believes that grizzly bear habitat is more valuable than additional campsites, his good intentions will not necessarily result in the creation of more grizzly bear habitat. Hence, Grant

Village, a tourist facility in the southern part of Yellowstone National Park, was built in the middle of prime grizzly bear habitat because politics, not science, dominated the decision.[6] In a political setting where commercial interests have more influence over a bureaucrat's budget, his peace and quiet, or his future promotions, good intentions by the bureaucrat will have to override political incentives if grizzly bear habitat is to prevail. Although possible in some cases, there is ample evidence that good intentions are not enough.

If a private resource owner believes that grizzly bear habitat is more valuable and can capture that value through a market transaction, then politics will not matter. Moreover, if those demanding the preservation of grizzly habitat are willing to pay more than those who demand campsites, then incentives and information reinforce each other.

Traditional thinking about natural resource and environmental policy has tended to emphasize incentive problems inherent in markets but to ignore them in the context of political processes. In markets profit maximizers are continually on the lookout for ways to externalize costs, but in the political process they are presumed to be on the lookout for the public interest. Consider the approach taken in one natural resource economics textbook that describes government as "a separate agent acting in the social interest when activity by individuals fails to bring about the social optimum. . . . we discuss some limits of this approach, but it permits us to abstract from the details of the political process."[7] To abstract from the details of the political process ignores incentives inherent in that process. Daniel Bromley claims that government agencies are

politically responsible to the citizenry through the system of . . . elections and ministerial direction. However imperfect this may work, the *presumption* must be that the wishes of the full citizenry are more properly catered to than would be the case if all environmental protection were left to the ability to pay by a few members of society given to philanthropy.[8]

Why must we "presume" that the "wishes of the full citizenry are more properly catered to"? Moreover, what does "full citizenry" mean? Is there unanimous consent? Does a majority constitute the "full citizenry" when voting turnout is traditionally low? Bromley also charges that "claims for volitional exchange are supported by an appeal to a body of economic theory that is not made explicit," but there is little made explicit when we "abstract from the details of the political process" by presuming "that the wishes of the full citizenry are more properly catered to" in the political process. In short, the lens of free market environmentalism forces us to realize that incentives matter everywhere.

Second, free market environmentalism focuses our attention on the costs of coordinating human activities. The scribblings of Nobel laureate Ronald Coase brought the importance of transaction costs into the forefront of policy analysis.[9] Coase's important point was that transaction costs in the marketplace and in the political arena explain why individuals may not always be able to resolve their competing uses of resources and the environment. He explained that, in a world of zero transaction costs, markets would work perfectly because producers and consumers would know all. Producers would always supply consumers with what they want, and consumers would always be able to hold producers accountable for any costs created by production. In the political arena, zero transaction costs would also yield perfect results because citizens would have no problem communicating their demands to politicians or knowing whether their demands were being met.

Of course, transaction costs are not zero in the real world. Producers do not always know what consumers want. Consumers do not always get what they expect. And people who use resources or dispose of garbage in the environment are not always held accountable for their actions. It is this lack of accountability that explains almost all concerns about natural resource stewardship and environmental quality.

Consider what happens when two people engage in a trade where one offers meat raised on private land in exchange for fish caught in the open ocean. The supplier of meat must consider the impact of his grazing cattle on the future productivity of the land. If he grazes too many cattle this year, there will be less grass next year, and possibly no grass at all. The fish supplier, on the other hand, faces a very different set of costs. Catching fish this year means those fish will not have an opportunity to grow larger and to reproduce, but in the open ocean a fish left for tomorrow will be caught by another fisher. Hence, each fisher ignores the future value of the fishery and overharvests today. After all, a fish not taken will be caught by someone else. Indeed, taking a fish today imposes costs on all fishers tomorrow because fish will be smaller and will not be reproducing, but these costs are spread among all fishers, while the benefits redound to the individual.

This problem is known as the tragedy of the commons.[10] If access to a valuable resource such as an ocean fishery is unrestricted, people entering the commons to capture its value will ultimately destroy it. Even if each individual recognizes that open access leads to resource destruction, there is no incentive for him to refrain from harvesting the fish. If he does not take it, someone else will, and therein lies the tragedy.

A similar tragedy occurs where there is open access to water as a medium for waste disposal. When consumers contract with paper producers to supply paper, some waste is inevitable, and the producers will seek the cheapest way to dispose of the waste. If they choose to dump it into the water, waste disposal will compete with other uses such as swimming. As far as swimmers are concerned, the tragedy of the commons has resulted in too much use of water for waste disposal.

The tragedy of the commons can also result in not enough production of a good thing if people can free ride on the actions of others. For example, if one individual or group sets aside land for biodiversity, the benefits of that biodiversity may redound to many people who did nothing to help provide it. As long as third parties can enjoy environmental amenities without paying for them, there is the potential for a free ride and therefore the possibility that the amenities will be underproduced. In other words, if third-party costs result in too much pollution, third-party benefits (free riding) result in too little production of environmental amenities.

All of these tragedies raise two questions: who has what rights and what are the costs associated with defining and enforcing those rights? Where rights are clearly defined and easily enforced, as in the case of surface land, there is no tragedy because entry is limited by the owner's fence. If party A dumps his garbage on party B's land, party B can enforce his right against trespass. On the other hand, where rights are not well defined or easily enforced, as with the right to clean air, trespass is much more difficult to prevent. It is much more difficult to identify who owns the fish, the water, or the air than it is to specify who owns the land, making enforcement against trespass a much tougher task. If the value of preserving wilderness is derived mainly by those who wish to hike in that wilderness, then the landowner can install pay booths at entrances and collect payment for the services he is providing. If the value is derived mainly by people who enjoy sitting in their offices thinking about the existence of wilderness, however, it will be more difficult for the owner/provider of wilderness to collect for his efforts.

Reenter transaction costs. If it were costless to organize to restrict entry into the commons, the tragedy would never occur. It does occur, however, because organizing to restrict entry is costly. People will not always know the impact of their actions until it is too late and the commons is overexploited. Even if they do recognize the potential for tragedy, the costs of organizing can be high. Bargaining to agree on who will fish and when and forming binding agreements to restrict fishing will be costly especially to the extent that detection of violators is difficult. Because these two types of costs—information costs and contracting costs—are pervasive in both market and political solutions to environmental problems, it is important that we examine them in more detail.

Information costs are the costs of articulating or measuring the values that humans place on goods and services they desire from their limited resources and of knowing how one person's actions impinge on the values of another. These are the costs that each of us incurs when trying to decide whether we would be happier spending more of our budget on housing, health care, or outdoor recreation. They are the costs companies incur in trying to determine whether there is a market for their products. They are the costs of knowing whether barbecue smoke wafting from your neighbor's yard is sufficiently carcinogenic to warrant asking your neighbor to stop polluting. They are the costs that politicians incur when deciding whether constituents would be better off with more national defense, more public lands, or lower taxes.

If all of these costs were zero, solving environmental problems would be much easier, but they are not and people must find ways of articulating and discovering information. In families and other small groups of people who care about one another, for example, intimate knowledge of one another's values may suffice to allow group members to take into account the preferences of others. Beyond such groups, we rely on communication processes in which there is far less personal knowledge of the values of others. In markets, for example, consumers will have to discover the value of goods they wish to purchase by doing research on product quality, and producers will attempt to supply information about their goods through advertising. Ultimately consumers express their values by offering money for goods and services, and suppliers decide whether these offers are sufficient to cover their costs of supplying. In a democratic political arena, we must do our research on candidates and then communicate our values by voting, protesting, letter writing, and contributing to campaigns, and the politicians must decide whether they can or want to meet the competing demands for goods and services subject to political constraints.

Even if we solve the information problem, we contract with one another to achieve our goals. These contracting costs include bargaining on the terms of the agreement and enforcing the terms of the agreement. Consumers need to ensure delivery of the goods and services for which they pay. Was the price paid commensurate with the expected quality? Were the goods or services delivered on time? Did suppliers charge more than consumers ultimately realized the product was worth? Likewise, suppliers must ensure that they are paid for services rendered. Was the payment on time? Did it cover the costs? In the political arena, did the politician deliver on his or her campaign promises? Are the citizens paying their taxes and abiding by the rules and regulations established by government? All such contracting costs make it more difficult for consumers and suppliers—whether in markets or politics—to coordinate with each other to enjoy gains from trade.

Markets and Politics Compared

Though there is a myriad of processes for coordinating human interaction in order to benefit from potential gains from trade (for example, families, clubs, or totalitarian states) and to prevent the tragedy of the commons, we compare and contrast transaction costs in the context of two—market processes and political processes. The important point is that although the information and contracting costs outlined above are endemic to both coordination processes, costs and benefits faced by decision makers differ systematically between the two and thus affect incentives and outcomes.

INFORMATION COSTS

First, consider information costs. In a world of scarce resources, private and political resource managers must obtain information about the relative values of alternative uses of everything from land to wildlife to air. When one resource use rivals another, tradeoffs must be made, and resource managers can only make these tradeoffs based on the information they receive, or on their own personal values. For example, if timber managers believe lumber is more valuable than wildlife habitat, they will cut trees. Timber managers may know how fast trees grow under different soil and climate conditions, but they cannot know the value of that growth without incurring some cost of surveying how consumers value the wood.

In the marketplace, prices provide an objective measure of subjective preferences and are therefore an important source of information about subjective values. Because each of us places different value on environmental amenities, there must be some way of quantifying and aggregating those values. Some see a forest as a place for quiet hikes, while others see it as a place for snowmobiling. Some see a rain forest as a jungle that, when cleared, can grow crops, while others see it as a source of biodiversity. Psychology can tell us a little about how these values are formed and influenced by peers, parents, advertising, genetics, and so on, but ultimately they are subjective to each individual.

Once individuals undertake market trades to achieve their desires, their bids provide an objective measure of these subjective values because bidders must give up one thing of value to obtain another. In the case of timberlands, private and public timber managers can obtain relatively comprehensive information on the value of wood from a lumberyard, where people offer money, which could be used to purchase other goods and services, for the wood products they value more highly. In the absence of markets for wildlife habitat or hiking trails, however, obtaining values is more costly. Nonetheless, private timber managers in a company such as International Paper obtain information on the value of wildlife amenities through an active market for hunting, camping, and other recreation on their private lands. When leasing its land for these activities, the company faces a tradeoff between timber harvesting, which produces revenue from wood products, and recreational land uses, which produce revenue from not cutting trees. Decisions on land use are driven by the differences in potential profit between the two activities.

Prices also allow a measure of efficiency through profits and losses. If a shareholder wants to know how well the management of his firm is performing, he can at least consult the profit and loss statement. This may not be a perfect measure of performance, but continual losses suggest that actual results differ from desired results. This can indicate to the shareholder that he should consider alternate managers who can produce the product at a lower cost or that he should reconsider the market for the product. Unlike the political sector, where the output of government is not priced and where agency performance is not measured by the bottom line, profits and losses in the private sector provide concise information with which owners can measure the performance of their agents.

In the public sector, on the other hand, there are few market prices and no profits to motivate decisions. Loggers compete in auctions for timber sales and thus provide some objective measure of market values, but recreational users of public lands generally pay little or nothing for the services they receive. Hence information on recreational values must be revealed through the political process. Special interest groups may articulate their demands through voting, campaign contributions, and letter-writing campaigns, to mention a few. In this process, lumber companies might argue that timber harvesting is the most important use of public land, while environmental groups will argue that wilderness values should trump all other values, including logging.

Hence free market environmentalism identifies systematic differences in the way information about subjective values is communicated in markets and politics. In the marketplace, prices lower information costs by converting subjective values into objective measures. In a democratic political process, the main counterpart to prices for signaling values is voting. Voting is a signal that, at best, communicates the subjective values of the median voter and, especially given that voter turnout is often low and representative of organized interest groups, communicates the subject values of special interest groups. While information costs are positive in both processes, prices offer a low-cost mechanism for articulating subjective values, and connect the person paying the price with the actual cost of the product or service.

As a solution to the information problem, some policy analysts embraced the idea of scientific management. This idea first surfaced in the United States with the formation of the U.S. Forest Service in the late nineteenth century. Ostensibly, scientific management directed at the federal level was supposed to be the answer to the perceived exploitation of U.S. forests.[11] Because the main task of the Forest Service was to manage forests for future wood fiber production in accordance with the best silva cultural techniques, there was little need to consider other values. However, as citizens have begun to demand other products and services from political lands, professional foresters have been forced, by either politics or legislation, to consider other values and to trade off between multiple uses.

Making these tradeoffs, in the economist's framework, is a simple matter of comparing the additional value of one use to the additional value of another. The calculus is simple; if the additional value of shifting a resource from one use is greater than the value in the use from which it is being taken, then reallocation will be prudent. In other words, if the marginal benefits are greater than the marginal costs, do it.

In this analysis, there are many margins for adjustments and few decisions that have all-or-nothing consequences. Put simply, neither demand nor supply is insensitive to price changes. If prices rise, then consumers will adjust by shifting consumption to the nearest substitutes, and suppliers will adjust by shifting to other inputs or technologies, or by producing other products.

The logic of this analysis combined with models and computers capable of simulating resource use can lure policy analysts into thinking that efficient resource management is simple. Unfortunately, such logic and simplification are not helpful guides because they mask transaction costs and incentives.

Consider the case of multiple-use management of the national forests, where scientific managers are required to balance timber production, wildlife habitat, aesthetic values, water quality, recreation, and other uses to maximize the value of the forest. Scientific managers, not motivated by profits or self-interest, who are armed with the economic concept of marginal analysis, are assumed to be omniscient, analytical, and impartial.[12] But as F. A. Hayek pointed out many years ago, "the economic problem of society is ... not merely a problem of how to allocate 'given resources' if 'given' is taken to mean given to a single mind which deliberately solves the problem set by these 'data.'"[13]

The problem is that obtaining the value data to make the necessary tradeoffs is no small task because of information costs. Scientific management assumes that values are known or can be discovered and, therefore, that there is also an efficient solution waiting to be discovered. Thomas Sowell describes this view of traditional resource economics as it relates to scientific management:

Given that explicitly articulated knowledge is special and concentrated ... the best conduct of social activities depends upon the special knowledge of the few being used to guide the actions of the many. ... Along with this has often gone a vision of intellectuals as disinterested advisors ... [14]

As analytical tools, economic models focus on the importance of marginal adjustments, but they cannot instruct managers in which tradeoffs to make or which values to place on a particular resource. In the absence of objective measures of subjective individual values, the marginal solutions derived by sophisticated efficiency-maximization models are unachievable ideals. Though these models add sophistication to decisions and give them an aura of authority and correctness, they cannot be effectively implemented in a world where political forces drive incentives.

No matter how rational or comprehensive the models may be, such models still necessitate obtaining costly information. Here again Hayek's insights are valuable, for he saw the allocation problem as one of "how to secure the best use of resources known to any of the members of society, for ends whose relative importance only these individuals know. Or, to put it briefly, it is a problem of utilizing knowledge not given to anyone in its totality."[15] As he well understood, subjective human values are best revealed through human action in accordance with those values. What form that action takes—for example, bidding or lobbying—will depend on incentives that in turn depend on the allocation system.

In contrast to scientific management, the market process generates information on the subjective values as individuals engage in voluntary trades. The decentralized decisions made in markets are crucial because "practically every individual has some advantage over all others in that he possesses unique information of which beneficial use might be made, but of which use can be made only if the decisions depending on it are left to him or are made with his active cooperation."[16] Once we understand that most knowledge is fragmented and dispersed, then we can understand that "systemic coordination among the many supersedes the special wisdom of the few."[17]

Traditional economic analysis has failed to recognize this fundamental point. The information necessary for "efficient" resource allocation depends on the knowledge of what Hayek called the special circumstance of time and place.[18]

CONTRACTING COSTS

Contracting costs also differ systematically between market and political processes. In a market transaction in which the Nature Conservancy purchases conservation easements to prevent land development, it must negotiate what land is involved, what uses are acceptable, and what price will be paid. At the same time the landowner must consider the opportunity cost of not developing the land and must be sure that the Nature Conservancy is not restricting development beyond an agreed upon level. These costs of measuring and monitoring private transactions will always be positive, but each party to the contract gains if he or she can reduce them.

Of course, citizens who demand goods and services from government also must measure and monitor the performance of the politicians and bureaucrats supplying them. Like a consumer displeased with food purchased from the supermarket, a citizen who is unhappy with the actions of his political representative has experienced the cost of measuring and monitoring supplier performance. Political outcomes do not always reflect citizens' desires; in the eyes of voters, the political process may, therefore, supply too many of some goods, say nuclear arms, or too few of other goods, say quality education. If sufficiently displeased, he must take action to rectify the problem or at least not support the restaurant or politician in the future.

There are several reasons that these contracting costs are likely to be systematically lower in market processes. While it may seem that self-interested individuals will always cheat if they believe they can avoid detection, there are also incentives for people to resist cheating. For example, people with a reputation for honesty are better trading partners because the costs of enforcing contracts are lower. Reputation capital becomes a valuable asset worth cultivating.

Furthermore, competition among both consumers and suppliers gives each side of the bargain alternate trading partners and therefore discourages cheating on contracts. Contracting costs will not be completely eliminated, but at least competition among buyers and sellers encourages traders to find ways to use brand names or independent rating companies to lower contracting costs.

In the political sector, if a citizen does not believe he is getting from government the goods and services he desires, he can attempt to sway a majority of the voters and elect new suppliers or he can physically move from one location to another. In either case, the costs of changing suppliers are much higher than in the private sector, where there is more competition among potential suppliers. For example, if a local supermarket does not sell what a customer desires, the customer has alternatives from which to make purchases. Even in the more complex case of corporate managers, a stockholder can change agents by selling shares in one company and purchasing shares in another. Simply, because changing suppliers in the private sector does not require agreement from a majority of the other consumers, change is less costly. This condition imposes a strong competitive discipline. In general, information through prices, internalization of costs and benefits from monitoring by individuals, and agent discipline imposed by competition reduce measurement and monitoring costs in market processes.

Measuring and monitoring the actions of political agents can be especially high at the national level.[19] At lower levels of government, the possibility of voting with one's feet and thus changing jurisdictions creates some competition among political regimes and therefore lowers contracting costs in the same way that competition among market suppliers does. Just as competition among firms encourages more attention to consumers and to production costs, competition among political units is more likely to give citizens what they want. But at the national level, the costs of moving to another country are much higher and therefore competition among political entities will be lower.[20] While a free press and free access to governmental information can reduce monitoring costs, the multitude of decisions made at various levels of government and the large number of constituents represented by each political agent continue to keep these costs high. Monitoring costs may also be reduced somewhat if the political or bureaucratic unit supplying a good or service is more dependent on user fees, as it will be more responsive to users. For example, state parks that depend on user fees offer a wide variety of services to visitors at a much lower cost than national parks that depend on general budget appropriations.[21]

Measuring and monitoring a politician's performance is exacerbated by the problem of rational ignorance. That is, on most issues, voters do not bother to become informed because the costs of becoming informed are high relative to the benefits. In the political process, voters ultimately decide who the suppliers will be. In order to make good decisions, however, voters must gather information about alternative candidates or referenda issues and vote on the basis of that information. If an individual takes the time to become informed and votes on what is best for society, he does a service for his fellow citizens. If, however, the voter is not well informed and votes for things that will harm the society, then this cost is spread among all voters. In other words, well-informed voters produce a classic public good, and as with any public good, other voters will be free riders. Many voters will underinvest in becoming informed, thus remaining rationally ignorant. By contrast, individuals in the private sector bear the costs of being informed, but they also directly reap the benefits of good choices and bear the costs of bad ones.

The counterpart to the rational ignorance effect is the special interest effect, in which well-organized special interest groups can lower the cost of information to members and use the size of their memberships to influence how a political representative views an issue. This gives political agents more leeway to respond to the desires of special interest groups whose members care about the specific policies that affect their group and receive low-cost information about policies from their group. Therefore the general public will be rationally ignorant about the specifics of legislation such as the Clean Water Act or Clean Air Act, but environmental groups and regulated companies will be better informed and will lobby for favorable treatment by legislators. If we assume that the political process works perfectly, which is the equivalent of assuming that markets work perfectly, then each opposing side's countervailing powers would internalize the benefits and costs for the decision maker. But in the absence of such perfection, special interest preferences are likely to dominate.

The combination of rational ignorance and the special interest effect explains why legislation can pass that costs each taxpayer a few pennies but provides significant benefits to special interest groups. Because politicians and bureaucrats are rewarded for responding to political pressure groups, there is no guarantee that the values of unorganized interests will be taken into account even if such interests constitute a majority of the population. Most Americans pay marginally higher prices for petroleum products because oil production is prohibited in the Arctic National Wildlife Refuge.[22] Since the cost to each individual is low and the costs of information and action are high relative to the benefits, each person remains rationally ignorant. On the other side, organized groups that favor preserving wildlife habitat in the pristine tundra gain by stopping drilling in the refuge. To the extent that those benefiting from wildlife preservation do not have to pay the opportunity costs of forgone energy production, they will demand more wildlife habitat. In the absence of a perfect political process, we must depend on good intentions to overpower the special interest incentives built into the imperfect system.

This helps explain why we often get perverse environmental results from political action. Government dams have contributed to the demise of salmon and the loss of wild rivers, and logging on national forests has reduced water quality because not all of the costs are borne by the decision makers. The nature of government funding generates another type of third-party effect by concentrating the benefits on special interest groups while diffusing the costs over a large segment of the population. In other words, the political process operates by externalizing costs and internalizing the benefits to special interest groups. When millions or billions of federal dollars are spent cleaning up a Superfund site, the construction companies that do the cleanup will receive tremendous benefits, but the costs will be diffused over a broad taxpayer base. Not surprisingly, campaign contributions from construction political action committees are more highly correlated with the amount spent on Superfund sites than is the toxicity of the site.[23]

Similarly, the uses of public lands are seldom fully paid for by the users, but are covered by general funds collected through taxes. The political agents who supply land for recreation or wilderness must divert it from other uses such as timber production, for which there is an opportunity cost. Neither consumers nor suppliers in the political process, however, directly pay that cost. The bureaucratic manager or politician who does not own the land does not face all the opportunity costs of his decisions. He takes the forgone values into account only if the political process makes him do so. In contrast, private landowners interested in maximizing the value of the resource must take this cost into account in supplying private recreational experiences. Just as external costs result in too much pollution or in overgrazing of the commons, a political process that externalizes costs can result in excessive production of public goods by distorting the real costs of actions to demanders and suppliers.

The potential to concentrate benefits on winners in the political process and to diffuse costs over a broad range of losers obviously has significant implications for how political games are played. As noted above, voting, lobbying, contributing to campaigns, letter writing, and protesting are all examples of actions designed to influence political decisions. In the political process, wealth is often redistributed rather than created, so that, at best, it is a zero-sum game. Unfortunately, as resources are invested in the redistribution, the game becomes negative sum. Economists call this "rent seeking," where "rent" refers to returns in excess of costs.[24] Whether people or groups make large campaign contributions or form voting coalitions, they do so with the expectation of collecting rents that come at the expense of other citizens. In the absence of voluntary exchange, there is no guarantee of net gains from trade in this rent-seeking process; one group's gain is another's loss. Thus the results of rent seeking are in sharp contrast to the potential gains from trade in markets.

Free Market versus Political Environmentalism

Because traditional thinking about resource and environmental policy pays little attention to the institutions that structure incentives and provide information in the political sector, practitioners often seem puzzled that efficiency implications from scientific management models are ignored in the policy arena. Efficiency is not the direct goal of private-sector decision makers either, but because profits result from decisions that move resources from lower-valued to higher-valued alternatives, there is a tendency toward efficiency in the private sector. The incentive structure in the political sector is less likely to tend toward efficiency because voters are rationally ignorant, because benefits can be concentrated and costs diffused, and because individual voters seldom (probably never) influence the outcome of elections. For these reasons, it is unlikely that elections will link political decisions to efficiency in the same way that private ownership does in the market process.[25]

With private ownership, profits and losses are the measure of how well decisions makers are managing. Even where shareholders in a large company have little effect on actual decisions, they can still observe stock prices and annual reports as measures of management's performance. In other words, private ownership gives owners both the information and the incentive to measure performance.

In the political sector, however, similar information and incentives are lacking. Annual budget figures offer information about overall expenditures and outlays, but it is not clear who is responsible and whether larger budgets are good or bad. Even when responsibility can be determined, there is no easy way for a citizen to buy and sell shares in the government. That is why citizens remain rationally ignorant about most aspects of political resource allocation and rationally informed only about issues that directly affect them. The rewards for political resource managers depend not on maximizing net resource values, but on providing politically active constituents with what they want—with little regard for cost. If political resource managers were to follow the efficiency tenets of traditional natural resource economics, it would have to be because there were honest, sincere people (professional managers) pursuing the public interest.

Anthony Fisher has provided perhaps the best summary of how markets and politics should be compared:

We have already abandoned the assumption of a complete set of competitive markets. . . . But if we now similarly abandon the notion of a perfect planner, it is not clear . . . that the government will do any better. Apart from the question of the planner's motivation to behave in the way assumed in our models, to allocate resources efficiently, there is the question of his ability to do so.[26]

If market transactions fail to encourage good natural-resource stewardship or environmental quality, it is either because the benefits received by the decision maker are low or because the costs incurred are high. For example, suppose a landowner is deciding whether to forgo commercial timber production to enhance an aesthetic quality. If the aesthetic quality involves a beautiful flower garden, a high fence may be sufficient to exclude free riders and capture the full benefits from the product. However, if the tradeoff is between cutting trees and preserving a beautiful mountainside, excluding casual sightseers might be so costly as to preclude capturing a return on production of the view.

Therefore, the key to getting the incentives right through free market environmentalism is to establish property rights that are well defined, enforced, and transferable. Consider each of these elements.

The physical attributes of the resources must be defined in a clear and concise manner if individuals are to reap the benefits of their good actions and are to be held accountable for their bad actions. The rectangular survey system, for example, allows us to define ownership rights over land and clarifies some disputes over ownership. This system may also help us define ownership to the airspace over land, but more questions arise here because of the fluidity of air and the infinite vertical third dimension above ground. If property rights to resources cannot be defined, they obviously cannot be exchanged for other property rights.

Property rights must also be defendable. A rectangular survey may define surface rights to land, but conflicts are inevitable if there is no way to defend the boundaries and prevent other incompatible uses. Barbed wire provided an inexpensive way to defend property rights on the western frontier; locks and chains do the same for parked bicycles. But enforcing one's rights to peace and quiet by "fencing out" sound waves is more difficult, as is keeping other people's hazardous wastes out of a groundwater supply. Whenever the use of property cannot be monitored or enforced, conflicts are inevitable and trades are impossible.

Finally, property rights must be transferable. In contrast to the costs of measuring and monitoring resource uses, which are mainly determined by the physical nature of the property and technology, the ability to exchange is determined largely by the legal environment. Although well-defined and enforced rights allow the owner to enjoy the benefits of using his property, legal restrictions on the sale of that property hinder the potential for trade gains. Suppose that a group of fishers values water for fish habitat more highly than farmers value the same water for irrigation. If the fishers are prohibited from renting or purchasing the water from the farmers, then gains from trade will not be realized and potential wealth will not be created. The farmer will, therefore, have less incentive to leave the water in the stream.

In sum, free market environmentalism requires well-specified rights to take actions with respect to specific resources. If such rights cannot be measured, monitored, and marketed, then there is little possibility for exchange. Garbage disposal through the air, for example, is more of a problem than solid waste disposal in the ground because property rights to the atmosphere are not as easily defined and enforced as are ones involving the Earth's surface. Private ownership of land works quite well for timber production, but measuring, monitoring, and marketing the land for endangered species habitat requires entrepreneurial imagination—especially if the species migrate over large areas.

Free market environmentalism does not assume that these property rights exist or that they are costless to create. Rather, it recognizes the costs of defining and enforcing property rights and emphasizes the role of entrepreneurs in producing new property rights when natural resources and environmental amenities become valuable. Where environmental entrepreneurs can devise ways of marketing environmental values, market incentives can have dramatic results.[27] Entrepreneurs recognize that externalities provide profit opportunities for those who successfully define and enforce property rights where they are lacking. A stream owner who can devise ways of charging fishers can internalize the benefits and gain an incentive to maintain or improve the quality of his fishing stream. The subdivider who puts covenants on deeds that preserve open space, improve views, and generally harmonize development with the environment establishes property rights to these values and captures the value in higher asset values.

The property rights approach to natural resources recognizes that property rights evolve depending on the benefits and costs associated with defining and enforcing rights. This calculus will depend on such variables as the expected value of the resource in question, the technology for measuring and monitoring property rights, and the legal and moral rules that condition the behavior of the interacting parties. At any given time, property rights will reflect the perceived costs and benefits of definition and enforcement. Therefore, the lack of property rights does not necessarily imply a failure of markets, because property rights are continually evolving. As the perceived costs and benefits of defining and enforcing property rights change, property rights will evolve.

This does not mean that there is no role for government in the definition and enforcement process or that property rights will always take all costs and benefits into account. The costs of establishing property rights are positive and can potentially be reduced through governmental institutions, such as courts. Furthermore, because transaction costs are positive, market contracts will not take all costs into account. In the case of water pollution from sources that cannot be identified (with current technology) at low costs, for example, the definition and enforcement of property rights governing water use may be impossible. In addition, excluding nonpayers from enjoying a scenic view may be costly enough that a market cannot evolve under current technologies and institutions. In these cases, there is a utilitarian argument for considering government intervention, but there is no guarantee that the results from political allocation will work any better than a market with positive transaction costs. If markets produce "too little" clean water because discharges do not have to pay for its use, then political solutions may also produce "too much" clean water because those who enjoy the benefits do not pay the cost.

Addressing the Critics

There are three main critiques of free market environmentalism: free market environmentalism considers only economic values and ignores environmental values; free market environmentalism pays too little attention to the distribution of rights; and free market environmentalism's focus on markets and politics ignores other important allocative institutions.[28]

WHICH VALUES: ECONOMIC OR ENVIRONMENTAL?

Because free market environmentalism focuses on human values, it is criticized by those who argue that saving the environment is a moral issue, not an economic one. Philosopher Mark Sagoff puts it this way:

Lange's Metalmark, a beautiful and endangered butterfly, inhabits sand dunes near Los Angeles for the use of which developers are willing to pay more than $100,000 per acre. Keeping the land from development would not be efficient from a microeconomic point of view, since developers would easily outbid environmentalists. Environmentalists are likely to argue, however, that preserving the butterfly is the right thing morally, legally, and politically—even if it is not economically efficient.[29]

Assuming that property rights to the land in question are well defined and that the environmental values can be captured, Sagoff is correct.[30] Free market environmentalism argues that the willingness of developers to outbid environmentalists tells us which values are higher. This is not to say that moral values have no place in decisions or that moral suasion is not a valuable tool for influencing human behavior. Sagoff further asserts that "environmentalists are concerned about saving magnificent landscapes and species, keeping the air and water clean, and in general getting humanity to tread more lightly on the Earth. They are not concerned . . . about satisfying preferences on a willing-to-pay basis."[31] Turning moral values into political issues and arguing that it is a matter of treading more lightly on the Earth, however, becomes another form of rent seeking, wherein people with one set of moral values get what they want at the expense of others.

WHOSE RIGHTS?

The second criticism of free market environmentalism is that it pays too little attention to the distribution of rights. The issue here is who has claims over resources and therefore who must pay whom.[32] To the extent that those wanting to save magnificent landscapes and species must pay landowners for those landscapes and habitats, distribution will be important. It is entirely possible that people with environmental preferences will not have enough wealth to act on their preferences. It is here that environmentalists like to take a page from Marx and suggest that "what is important is not the choices people *do* make but the choices people *would* make if they were free of their corrupt bourgeois ideology."[33] By this reasoning, it is easy to say that environmentalists would be willing to pay more if only they had the resources. Of course, this is not verifiable through voluntary trading and thus opens the door for political redistribution.

A related argument is that the distribution of wealth favors people with nonenvironmental preferences over those with environmental preferences.[34] In the case of public lands, making people pay for use of national parks or forests is unfair because it precludes poor people from using the parks. In the case of private land, big corporations already have the rights to use the land, and poor environmentalists cannot afford to purchase these rights from them. In response, there is the empirical question of whether poor people do, in fact, use environmental amenities such as national parks at their current low price. If they do not, what is the justification for subsidizing the environmental amenity for use by the wealthy? Second, because poor people do not have access to many amenities, there may be an argument for redistributing income in their favor, but the redistribution does not have to come in the form of in-kind services from national parks. If they had more income, they could decide how to spend it without subsidizing wealthy park visitors. Finally, is it the case that environmentalists who demand environmental goods and services are poor compared to the rest of the population? A growing body of evidence suggests that the demand for environmental quality is highly sensitive to income and that members of environmental groups have quite high incomes, thus this argument seems tenuous.[35]

IS THE CHOICE BETWEEN ONLY MARKETS AND POLITICS?

As described above, market processes and political processes are but two alternatives for addressing natural resource use and environmental quality. Even within each of these there are gradations between individual resource owners, corporate owners, town governments, and national governments. It is becoming better recognized that between markets and government are community organizations that can play a role in resource allocation.[36] These might be communities of fishers who regulate access to a fishery[37] or tribal members who restrict access to a grazing common.[38] In either case, how well the institutional arrangement works will depend on its ability to generate information on values and provide incentives for individuals to act on those values. Thought of in this way, free market environmentalism is less about markets and government and more about how various management institutions determine environmental values and how decision makers respond to that information.

Conclusion

Which institutional process is more likely to move resources from lower- to higher-valued alternatives is ultimately an empirical question. Traditional natural resource economics has generally concluded that markets do not do very well and that the political process can do better. Free market environmentalism generally comes to the opposite conclusion. As Sagoff argues with regard to markets, such conclusions often turn on the fallacy of disparate comparison:

A free market with inviolable property rights, low transaction costs, and so on, may, indeed, treat nature better than does an often bumbling and occasionally corrupt bureaucracy beset by special interests. However, this kind of argument . . . commits the fallacy of disparate comparison. It compares what the perfect market would do in theory with what imperfect governmental agencies, at their worst, have done in fact.[39]

Perhaps this is an effective debating tactic, but it is not inherent in the analytical framework described above. Traditional economic analysis stresses the potential for market failure in the natural resource and environmental arena on the grounds that externalities are pervasive. Free market environmentalism explicitly recognizes that this problem arises because it is costly to define, enforce, and trade rights in both the private and political sectors. In fact, the symmetry of the externality argument requires that specific attention be paid to politics as the art of diffusing costs and concentrating benefits. Assuming that turning to the political sector can solve externality problems in the environment ignores the likelihood that government will externalize costs. Just as pollution externalities can generate too much dirty air, political externalities can generate too much water storage, clear-cutting, wilderness, or water quality.

Free market environmentalism emphasizes the importance of market processes in getting more human value from any given stock of resources. Only when rights are well defined, enforced, and transferable will self-interested individuals confront the tradeoffs inherent in a world of scarcity. As entrepreneurs move to fill profit niches, prices will reflect the values we place on resources and the environment. Mistakes will surely be made, but in the process a niche will be created and profit opportunities will attract resource managers with better ideas. Even externalities offer profit niches to the environmental entrepreneur who can better define and enforce property rights to the unowned resource and charge the free rider. In cases in which definition and enforcement costs are insurmountable, political solutions may be called for. Unfortunately, however, those kinds of solutions often become entrenched and stand in the way of innovative market processes that promote fiscal responsibility, efficient resource use, and individual freedom.

Free market environmentalism recognizes that transaction costs are positive under all institutions. The question is which arrangements minimize these costs. Rather than falling into the fallacy of disparate comparison, the challenge for proponents of markets, politics, or other institutional arrangements is to muster the empirical evidence to support their case. Indeed, since the idea of free market environmentalism was first articulated, researchers have been uncovering a growing body of evidence showing the efficacy of market approaches to environmental problems. Let us consider some of that evidence.

Notes

1. John Maynard Keynes, *The General Theory of Employment, Interest, and Money* (New York: Harcourt, Brace & World, 1964), 383.
2. A. C. Pigou, *The Economics of Welfare* (London, England: Macmillan, 1920).
3. Ibid. 195.
4. Ibid.
5. Francis Bator, "The Simple Analytics of Welfare Maximization," *American Economic Review* (March 1957), 22–59.
6. Alston Chase, *Playing God in Yellowstone* (Boston: Atlantic Monthly Press, 1986).
7. John M. Hartwick and Nancy D. Olewiler, *The Economics of Natural Resource Use* (New York: Harper & Row, 1986), 18.
8. Daniel W. Bromley, *Property Rights and the Environment: Natural Resource Policy in Transition* (Cambridge, MA: Blackwell, 1991), 55.
9. Ronald Coase, "The Problem of Social Cost," *Journal of Law and Economics*, 3 (October 1960), 1–44.
10. Garret Hardin, "The Tragedy of the Commons," *Science*, 162 (December 1968).
11. Samuel P. Hays, *Conservation and the Gospel of Efficiency: The Progressive Conservation Movement, 1890–1920* (Cambridge, MA: Harvard University Press, 1959), 28.
12. Alan Randall, *Resource Economics: An Economic Approach to Natural Resource and Environmental Policy* (New York: Wiley, 1987), 36.
13. F. A. Hayek, "The Use of Knowledge in Society," *The American Economic Review*, 35 (September 1945), 519–20.
14. Thomas Sowell, *A Conflict of Visions* (New York: William Morrow and Company, 1987), 46.

15. Hayek, "The Use of Knowledge," 520.

16. Ibid. 521–2.

17. Sowell, *A Conflict of Visions*, 48.

18. Hayek, "The Use of Knowledge," 521.

19. See James D. Gwartney and Richard L. Stroup, *Economics: Private and Public Choice*, 8th edn. (Orlando, FL: Harcourt Brace & Company, 1997), 785–809, for a discussion of the forces that lead to higher transaction costs in government.

20. Charles M. Tiebout, "A Pure Theory of Local Expenditures," *Journal of Political Economy*, 64 (1956), 416–24.

21. See Donald R. Leal and Holly Lippke Fretwell, "Back to the Future to Save Our Parks," *PERC Policy Series*, No. PS-10 (Bozeman, MT: Political Economy Research Center, June 1997), for a comparison of state and local parks.

22. Pamela Snyder and Jane S. Shaw, "PC Oil Drilling in a Wildlife Refuge," *Wall Street Journal*, September 7, 1995, A14.

23. Thomas Stratmann, "The Politics of Superfund," in *Political Environmentalism: Going Behind the Green Curtain*, ed. Terry L. Anderson (Stanford, CA: Hoover Institution Press, 2000).

24. See Terry L. Anderson and Peter J. Hill, *The Birth of a Transfer Society* (Stanford, CA: Hoover Institution Press, 1980), for a discussion of rent seeking.

25. Gwartney and Stroup, *Economics*, 785–809.

26. Anthony Fisher, *Resource and Environmental Economics* (New York: Cambridge University Press, 1981), 54.

27. Terry L. Anderson and Donald R. Leal, *Enviro-Capitalists: Doing Good While Doing Well* (Lanham, MD: Rowman and Littlefield Publishers, 1997).

28. For several articles critiquing free market environmentalism, see Mark Sagoff, "Free Market Versus Libertarian Environmentalism," *Critical Review*, 6 (spring/summer 1992), 211–30.

29. Sagoff, "Free Market," 214.

30. The free market environmentalism argument is premised on the existence of property rights. It can always be argued that externalities exist and therefore that market exchanges won't work, but this is an efficiency argument, not a moral argument.

31. Sagoff, "Free Market," 218.

32. Coase, "The Problem of Social Cost."

33. Sagoff, "Free Market," 218.

34. Peter S. Menell, "Institutional Fantasylands: From Scientific Management to Free Market Environmentalism," *Harvard Journal of Law and Public Policy*, 15 (1992), 489, 509.

35. Jane S. Shaw, "Environmental Regulation: How It Evolved and Where It is Headed," *Real Estate Issues*, 1 (1996), 6.

36. Elinor Ostrom, *Governing the Commons: The Evolution of Institutions for Collective Action* (New York: Cambridge University Press, 1990).

37. Donald R. Leal, "Community-Run Fisheries: Avoiding the Tragedy of the Commons," *PERC Policy Series*, No. PS-7 (Bozeman, MT: Political Economy Research Center, September 1996).

38. Terry L. Anderson, "Conservation—Native American Style," *PERC Policy Series*, No. PS-6 (Bozeman, MT: Political Economy Research Center, July 1996).

39. Sagoff, "Free Market," 224.

16 Market-Based Environmental Policies

Robert Stavins and Bradley Whitehead

It is not a new idea. Using market forces instead of bureaucratic fiat as a tool of environmental policy has been proposed by economists, discussed by policymakers, and implemented on a limited scale for two decades. But the concept of putting a price on pollution has yet to live up to its proponents' promises. Is this simply a breakdown between theory and practice? Has the effort to transform environmental regulations with economic incentives been nothing more than quixotic tilting at windmills? Should we continue to rely on more established—if costly—policy mechanisms? We believe the answer is no.

Market mechanisms can work. In fact, they have worked exceptionally well in a number of areas across the United States.[1] Of course, economic instruments, as they are sometimes called, are not panaceas. We have made less progress than we might have toward getting companies and individuals to pay for environmental harms they cause because of unrealistic expectations, lack of political will, design flaws, limitations in regulators' skills, and, all too often, obstacles thrown up by those who might be affected—in industry, the environmental community, and government. All of this can be addressed. Indeed, policymakers at all levels of government, in partnership with private businesses and nongovernmental organizations, should reinvigorate their efforts to develop and implement a next generation of economic incentives.

Properly designed and implemented, market-based instruments—regulations that encourage appropriate environmental behavior through price signals rather than through explicit instructions—provide incentives for businesses and individuals to act in ways that further not only their own financial goals but also environmental aims such as reducing waste, cleaning up the air, or reducing water pollution. In most cases, market mechanisms take overall goals of some sort—say, the total reduction of emissions of a specific pollutant—and leave the choice of how to accomplish this up to the individuals or companies concerned.[2]

In contrast, conventional approaches to regulating the environment, so-called command-and-control regulations,[3] typically force everyone to implement the same pollution control strategies, regardless of the relative costs to them of this burden.[4] For example, a regulation might limit the quantity of a pollutant that a company can release into the atmosphere in a given time period or even specify, in effect, that a certain type of pollution control device must be put in place. But holding everyone to the same target or mandating the same abatement equipment can

From M. Chertow and D. Esty (eds), *Thinking Ecologically: The Next Generation of Environmental Policy* (Yale: Yale University Press, 1997), 105–15.

be expensive and, in some circumstances, counter-productive. Thus, although this command approach has often succeeded in limiting emissions, it frequently does so in an unduly expensive way. Inevitably, it fails to tailor the demands imposed to the particular circumstances of each company. There is little or no financial incentive to do better than the law requires or to develop and experiment with new technology and equipment that might lead to even greater improvements in performance. The net result is a drag on productivity and complaints about regulatory inefficiency, both of which undermine commitments to achieving environmental gains.

Market-based instruments align the financial incentives of companies with environmental objectives. They can be cost-effective and can provide a powerful impetus for companies to innovate and to adopt cheaper and better pollution control technologies.[5] This leaves more room for economic growth or for more stringent environmental standards to be adopted.

Types of Market Mechanisms

Market-based instruments used in environmental programs can be divided into six major categories:

Pollution charge systems assess a fee or tax on the amount of pollution that a company or product generates.[6] Such "green fees" should be calibrated to actual emissions rather than simply to pollution-generating activities: for example, a charge per unit of sulfur dioxide released by an electric utility, not a charge per unit of electricity generated. Consequently, it is worthwhile for the utility to reduce pollution up to the point at which the cost of doing this equals what it otherwise would pay in pollution charges or taxes. How it does this and how much it can reasonably spend until costs exceed the pollution tax will vary enormously among firms due to differences in their production designs, physical configurations, ages of assets, and other factors. The end result will be a substantial savings in the total cost of pollution control, as compared to forcing all firms to reduce pollution to exactly the same level or to employ the same equipment.

Setting the amount of the tax is, of course, not a trivial matter. Policymakers cannot know precisely how firms will respond to a given level of taxation, so it is difficult to know in advance precisely how much cleanup will result from any given charge. Nevertheless, in recent years, tax or green fee programs have been used successfully to phase out production of CFCs and other ozone-layer-harming chemicals and to promote better municipal solid waste management practices by charging people "by the bag" for the garbage they throw out.

Tradable permits get much the same results as pollution charges, but avoid the problem of trying to predict the results.[7] Under this system, policymakers first set a target of how much pollution will be allowed for an industry, an area, or a nation. Companies generating the pollution then receive (through free distribution or auction) permits allowing them a share of the total. Firms that keep their emission levels below the allotted levels can sell their surplus permits to other firms or use the allotment for one of their facilities to offset excess emissions in another one of their plants. Firms that run out of allowances must buy them from other companies or face legal penalties. In either case, it is in the financial interest of the participating firms to reduce emissions as much as they efficiently can.

There are now in place a number of successful applications of trading programs. In the 1980s, the EPA developed a lead credit program that allowed gasoline refiners greater flexibility in meeting emission standards at a time when the lead content of gasoline was being reduced to 10 percent of its previous level.[8] If refiners produced gasoline with a lower lead content than was required during any time period, they earned lead credits that could be either banked for the future or traded immediately with competitors. The EPA estimated that, compared to alternative programs, the lead banking and trading program saved the industry (and consumers) about $250 million per year and accelerated the phase-down of lead in gasoline.

A tradable permit system is the centerpiece of the acid rain provisions of the Clean Air Act Amendments of 1990. The law sets a goal of reducing emissions of sulfur dioxide (SO_2) and nitrogen oxides (NOx) by ten million tons and two million tons, respectively, from 1980 levels.[9] As discussed in more detail in chapter 14, electric utility companies annually receive tradable allowances that allow them to emit a specific amount of sulfur dioxide. Those that reduce their emissions below the level of their allowances can sell their excess permits. A robust market for the permits has emerged with savings estimated to be on the order of $1 billion annually compared to command-and-control regulatory alternatives.[10]

In another case, more than 350 companies in southern California are now participating in a tradable permit program intended to reduce nitrogen oxides and sulfur dioxide emissions in the Los Angeles area. The Regional Clean Air Incentives Market (RECLAIM) program operates through the issuance of tradable permits that specify and authorize decreasing levels of pollution over time. As of mid-1996, participants had traded more than 100,000 tons of NOx and SO_2 emissions with a permit value of more than $10 million.[11] Authorities are now considering expanding the program to allow trading between stationary sources (facilities) and mobile sources (cars and trucks).

Deposit-refund systems are familiar to many consumers because of the nine state "bottle bills" that have been implemented to reduce waste from beverage containers. Consumers pay a surcharge when purchasing potentially polluting products and get it back when the product is returned for recycling or proper disposal.[12] Although beverage-container deposits are the most common application, a few states have initiated deposit-refund systems for lead-acid batteries and other items.

Reducing market barriers can also help curb pollution. Measures that make it easier to exchange water rights, for example, promote more efficient allocation and use of scarce water supplies.[13] California, in particular, has achieved considerable improvements in water allocation by creating a market in water rights.

Eliminating government subsidies can promote more efficient and environmentally sound resource consumption and economic development. Below-cost timber sales, for instance, encourage overlogging. Similarly, federal water projects that provide below-market-cost water for farmers in California's Central Valley encourage wasteful irrigation practices and discourage water conservation. In these cases, market prices would deter waste and promote better environmental practices.

Finally, *providing public information* can improve environmental performance by allowing consumers to make more informed purchasing decisions and creating incentives for environmental care among companies. The Toxic Release Inventory, revealing emissions to air, water, and land of a large number of waste products, has emerged as a powerful tool for encouraging companies to reduce their emissions.[14] And the "dolphin-safe" label on cans of tuna fish virtually eliminated from the U.S. market tuna caught with methods that resulted in incidental, but significant, dolphin mortality.[15]

Barriers to Implementation

Notwithstanding considerable success in implementing specific programs, economic instruments represent only a small share of new regulation and a trivial portion of existing regulation. We must ask why market mechanisms seem to have achieved so little penetration. The most obvious reason is that there has not been a great deal of new environmental regulation. The Clean Air Act and Safe Drinking Water Act are the only major environmental regulations that have been reauthorized since 1990. And even when Congress has been willing to consider market-based instruments for creating *new* regulation, it has not been willing to substitute the technique for the *existing* regulations that now cover 14,310 pages of the Code of Federal Regulations. At the same time, most EPA employees were hired to oversee traditional command-and-control programs and some may be hesitant to switch courses. Traditional regulatory programs require regulators with a technical or legal-based skill-set. Market-based instruments require an economics orientation.

Many environmental organizations have also been hesitant to move regulation toward market-based instruments. Some groups worry that increased flexibility in environmental regulation will lower the overall level of environmental protection. Others believe that market mechanisms condone the "right to pollute" and that conventional government mandates thus have superior moral virtue. Finally, some environmental professionals, like their government counterparts, are simply resisting the dissipation of *their* experience and existing skills in dealing with command-and-control programs.

The ambivalence of government officials and environmentalists is mirrored by the regulated community. Many industries and companies have applauded market-based instruments in an abstract sense because of their promise of flexibility and cost-effectiveness.[16] As a practical matter, however, the vast majority of businesses have not enthusiastically lobbied for the implementation of these instruments. Much of the hesitation stems from reluctance to promote any regulation, no matter how flexible or cost-effective. Perhaps seasoned by experience, businesses fear that implementation might not prove as cost-effective as promised or that the ground rules could change after programs get under way.

From a political economy perspective,[17] private firms are likely to prefer command-and-control standards to (auctioned) permits or taxes because standards produce economic rents,[18] which can be sustainable if coupled with sufficiently more stringent requirements for new sources. In contrast, auctioned permits and taxes require firms to pay not only abatement costs to reduce pollution to a specified level but also costs of polluting up to that level.

Command-and-control standards are also likely to be preferred by legislators for several reasons: the training and experience of legislators may make them more comfortable with a direct standards approach than with market-based approaches; the time needed to learn about market-based instruments may represent significant opportunity costs; standards tend to hide the costs of pollution control while emphasizing the benefits; and standards may offer greater opportunities for symbolic politics.

Moreover, those who would differentially be affected may be expected to press for changes. For instance, several high-sulfur-coal-producing states attempted to skew the acid rain trading program by forcing companies to install high-cost scrubbers instead of shifting to more economical low-sulfur coal from other states. At the same time several midwestern coal-burning utilities demanded—and received—"bonus" allowances. Additionally, for companies that have invested tens of millions of dollars in meeting existing pollution control requirements, any change in policy might entail more expense or the writing off of capital stock now in place. Indeed, for businesses to optimize their environmental investments, regulations have to be not only flexible but also predictable over time.

Coupling concerns about consistency with the antiregulatory climate pervading the country, many corporations have concluded that it is better to argue against *any* regulation rather than for better regulation. Several environmentally sensitive industries now argue in favor of voluntary industry programs rather than compulsory regulations. The chemical industry, for example, has developed Responsible Care codes that it says obviate the need for intensive regulation. The petroleum and paper industries have similar initiatives. The energy being directed toward these programs has diverted attention away from economic incentive approaches.

Part of the problem with market mechanisms is that the benefits they bring are often invisible to consumers, while the costs they impose as fees or taxes are all too plain. It is not obvious, for example, that gasoline and electricity prices are lower than they might otherwise have been because we successfully used market-based programs rather than command-and-control mandates to phase out lead and to reduce acid rain. On the other hand, long-distance drivers will pay more with higher gas taxes—and they know it. It is difficult to generate enthusiasm for economic instruments among those for whom it clearly means money out of their pockets.

Companies, moreover, often do not have internal incentive systems in place to reward managers who take advantage of market-based instruments. In many corporations, environmental costs are not fully measured and are not charged back to the business units from which they are derived. Moreover, the focus of many corporate environmental officers has been primarily on problem avoidance and risk management rather than on the creation of opportunities to benefit competitively from environmental decisions. Until corporate culture changes, the full potential of market mechanisms' cost-effectiveness and improved incentives for technological change will not be realized.

Next-generation market mechanisms. The limited use of economic incentives to date should not cause us to abandon or deemphasize market-based instruments as a next-generation policy option. Rather, we should make price signals a central part of the environmental policy toolkit. With more than $140 billion being spent annually in the U.S. on pollution control and cleanup, environmental policymakers need to seek more effective tools to maintain and improve environmental quality in a cost-conscious manner. This need dictates that we not lose the opportunity of using programs that can reduce costs and stimulate the development of new, more efficient technologies. In the long term, public support for environmental programs depends on confidence that the money invested is delivering good returns.

The first step toward better acceptance of market mechanisms is to improve the design of the programs. This must be done to counter the resistance of private firms, to calm fears of environmental groups and others about back-sliding on results, and to ensure that the actual cost savings come closer to, if not match, predictions. Accomplishing this means recognizing that market-based instruments are not a solution to all environmental problems. Rather, they are a useful element in what should be a portfolio of policy instruments. Indeed, some environmental problems will continue to require command-and-control solutions. On the other hand, market forces acting alone or voluntary industry initiatives may be sufficient to address other problems. But when regulation is called for, getting price signals to reflect environmental harms should be the first option considered.

An overarching design goal should be to make regulatory programs based on economic instruments more predictable. This requires stable rules, careful calibration of pollution control targets, and credible commitments to keeping programs in place for the long term. In addition, market-based instruments should be designed to deliver the greatest cost savings possible. Transaction and administrative costs must be reduced. Rights bestowed under these programs must be protected. Competitive market conditions must be maintained. The incentives for participation must be clear. When knowledge about environmental harms changes or new political pressures necessitate revisions to a market-based program, the transition should be made in a manner that does not detract from the program's efficiency.

In addition to design changes, the use of market-based instruments should evolve beyond Washington to the state and local levels. Although federal spending for environmental control continues to outpace state spending (in 1991, federal spending was about $18.2 billion for environmental and natural resource programs, compared to state spending of $9.6 billion), the gap is closing.

One of the most exciting uses of market-based incentives on the state and local level has been in an area not usually regarded as environmental: the general permitting process. A great challenge for state and local governments—and a source of frustration for new and growing companies—is the time required to issue permits for activities such as zoning, construction, and pollution discharge. Some states have developed programs that incorporate incentives into the existing framework for permits and inspections. For example, expedited evaluations of permit applications are often completed for firms that choose to participate in new pollution prevention programs. Although not a market-based instrument in the strict sense, such initiatives embody the spirit of what is called for in next-generation environmental policy: a relatively simple way to give firms incentives to meet environmental goals.

Market-based instruments can also be used to address the environmental issues at which most state and local initiatives are directed: waste management, land use, and air quality improvement. At the core of most municipal solid-waste problems, for example, are price signals that fail to convey to consumers and producers the true costs of waste collection and disposal. In fact, these costs are frequently embedded in property or other taxes. Some municipalities do highlight a charge for waste collection in their semiannual property tax assessments. However, since such charges are usually flat fees that do not vary with the quantity of waste generated by individuals, there is no incentive for users to reduce the waste they create. Unit pricing corrects this. By charging households for waste collection services in proportion to the amount of refuse they leave at the curbside, unit pricing ties household charges to the real costs of collection and disposal. Households thus have an incentive to reduce the amount of waste they generate either by changing what they buy, reusing products or containers, or composting yard and garden material. Moreover, if municipalities charge extra for unseparated refuse, they can also give residents an incentive to separate the recyclable components of their trash.

Unit charges will not solve all solid-waste management problems. They are difficult to apply to apartment units. Some form of "lifeline" pricing is required for low-income families so that these households do not pay a disproportionate amount of income for trash collection. And illegal dumping can be a problem if the programs are not organized properly.[19] However, this approach combines cost-effectiveness with minimum inconvenience. The number of these programs has mushroomed from one hundred in 1989 to some three thousand today.[20]

Market-based instruments can also help balance local economic growth with environmental protection of the land. As economic and population growth continues, a larger share of environmental problems will be associated with tensions over land use. Land-oriented tradable permit programs have already been adopted in several states, including New Jersey, Florida, and California. Florida established a wetlands-mitigation banking program in 1993 that allows the state and five local water management districts to license owners of wetlands property as "mitigation bankers."[21] Private developers are asked to offset the potential environmental damage arising from a proposed development by purchasing a "credit" from the bankers, who in turn agree to preserve and often improve their wetlands. Thus, those who diminish the amount of wetlands through development provide the resources to expand wetlands elsewhere in the ecosystem. Even before the program was formally established, a group of entrepreneurs set up Florida Wetlandsbank, which sells mitigation credits for forty-five thousand dollars per acre and uses part of the proceeds to improve degraded wetlands.

While working to incorporate the use of market-based instruments on the state and local level, policymakers should also work toward adopting new incentive programs on the federal level. In the hazardous waste area, deposit-refund programs could provide incentives not only to reduce the amount of waste but also to change disposal systems. The amount of lead, mostly from batteries, that enters landfills and incinerators may still be a significant hazard, despite EPA regulation of landfill construction and incinerator operation. The number of such batteries recycled each year has been declining. More than twenty million enter the waste stream annually, and this number could increase by some 30 percent by 2000. Under a deposit-refund system, a deposit would be collected by the administering agency at the time manufacturers sell batteries to distributors or manufacturers, who would pass on the charge to vehicle purchasers.[22] In time, the used batteries would be returned to redemption centers that would refund the deposit and then be compensated by the agency. Although some states have launched these programs, federal action is preferable when a national market or scale economies argue for a single system.

Market mechanisms may also be useful at the global level, especially in response to problems arising from diffuse sources. If, for example, the United States decides to participate in a binding international agreement to reduce worldwide greenhouse gas emissions, a carbon tax may be the most effective and least costly way to meet any emissions reduction targets. By altering price signals through charges based on the carbon content of fuels and tax credits for those establishing new carbon "sinks," a market-based regulatory system would internalize the potential costs of climate change. Higher prices would reduce demand for fossil fuels, thereby reducing emissions of carbon dioxide, and would stimulate the development of new technologies that are less carbon-intensive. Moreover, a properly designed revenue-neutral tax policy, under which carbon charges are offset by the reduction or elimination of pay-roll or other taxes, could help to protect the environment, reduce distortions associated with other taxes, promote economic growth, and render the program of greenhouse gas emissions controls more politically palatable.

By shifting organizational mindsets, developing new and needed skills, and overcoming the resistance of sometimes competing interest groups, we can make market-based instruments work for our collective benefit and bring environmental policy into the twenty-first century. If cost-effective regulation is a serious priority for environmental policymakers—and it must be in our world of tight budgets, both private and public—we cannot afford to overlook the opportunity to deliver more bang for the buck by harnessing market forces to protect the environment.

Notes

1. Janet Milne and Susan Hasson, *Environmental Taxes in New England: An Inventory of Environmental Tax and Fee Mechanisms Enacted by the New England States and New York* (South Royalton: Environmental Law Center at Vermont Law School, 1996).
2. See, for example, Robert Stavins (ed.), *Project 88-Round II Incentives for Action: Designing Market-Based Environmental Strategies* (Washington, D.C.: Government Printing Office, May 1991); and Robert Stavins (ed.), *Project 88: Harnessing Market Forces to Protect Our Environment* (Washington, D.C., December 1988). Both studies were sponsored by Sen. Timothy E. Wirth, Colorado, and Sen. John Heinz, Pennsylvania.
3. There is something of a continuum from a pure market-based instrument to a pure command-and-control instrument, with many hybrids falling between. Nevertheless,

for ease of exposition, it is convenient to consider these two fundamental categories. See Robert Hahn and Robert Stavins, "Incentive-Based Environmental Regulation: A New Era from an Old Idea?" *Ecology Law Quarterly*, 18 (1991), 1–42.
4. For a detailed case-by-case description of the use of command-and-control instruments, see P. R. Portney (ed.), *Public Policies for Environmental Protection* (Washington, D.C.: Resources for the Future, 1990).
5. For an empirical analysis of the dynamic incentives for technological change under different policy instruments, see Adam B. Jaffe and Robert Stavins, "Dynamic Incentives of Environmental Regulations: The Effects of Alternative Policy Instruments on Technology Diffusion," *Journal of Environmental Economics and Management*, 29 (1995), S43–S63. This paper develops a general approach for comparing the impact

of policies on technology diffusion and applies it to the most frequently considered policy instruments for global climate change.

6. A. C. Pigou is generally credited with developing the idea of a corrective tax to discourage activities that generate externalities, such as environmental pollution. See A. C. Pigou, *The Economics of Welfare*, 4th edn. (London: Macmillan, 1938). For a modern discussion of the concept and a number of case examples, see Robert Repetto et al., *Green Fees: How a Tax Shift Can Work for the Environment and the Economy* (Washington, D.C.: World Resources Institute, 1993).

7. See Robert Hahn and Roger Noll, "Designing a Market for Tradeable Permits," in *Reform of Environmental Regulation*, ed. W. Magat (Cambridge, Mass.: Ballinger, 1982). Much of the literature on tradable permits can actually be traced to Coase's treatment of negotiated solutions to externality problems. See generally Ronald Coase, "The Problem of Social Cost," *Journal of Law and Economics*, 3 (1960), 1–44.

8. In each year of the program, more than 60 percent of the lead added to gasoline was associated with traded lead credits. See Robert Hahn and Gordon L. Hester, "Marketable Permits: Lessons for Theory and Practice," *Ecology Law Quarterly*, 16 (1989), 361–406.

9. For a description of the legislation, see Brian L. Ferrall, "The Clean Air Act Amendments of 1990 and the Use of Market Forces to Control Sulfur Dioxide Emissions," *Harvard Journal on Legislation*, 28 (1991), 235–52.

10. See Dallas Burtraw, "Cost Savings sans Allowance Trades? Evaluating the SO_2 Emission Trading Program to Date," Discussion Paper 95–130 (Washington, D.C.: Resources for the Future, September 1995); and Elizabeth M. Bailey, "Allowance Trading Activity and State Regulatory Rulings: Evidence from the U.S. Acid Rain Program," MIT-PAPER 96-002 WP (Cambridge: Center for Energy and Environmental Policy Research, MIT, 1996).

11. For a detailed case study of the evolution of the use of economic incentives in the SCAQMD, see NAPA, *The Environment Goes to Market: The Implementation of Economic Incentives for Pollution Control* (Washington, D.C.: NAPA, July 1994), chap. 2. Recent implementation problems with the RECLAIM program, however, illustrate a point we emphasize throughout the chapter: for a host of reasons, actual applications of market-based instruments tend not to perform up to the standards that the simplest analysis might anticipate.

12. See P. Bohm, *Deposit-Refund Systems: Theory and Applications to Environmental, Conservation, and Consumer Policy* (Baltimore: Published for Resources for the Future, in the Johns Hopkins University Press, 1981). Peter S. Menell, "Beyond the Throwaway Society: An Incentive Approach to Regulating Municipal Solid Waste," *Ecology Law Quarterly*, 17: 4 (1990), 655–739.

13. See W. R. Z. Willey and Thomas J. Graff, "Federal Water Policy in the United States—An Agenda for Economic and Environmental Reform," *Columbia Journal of Environmental Law* (1988), 349–51.

14. See James T. Hamilton, "Pollution as News: Media and Stock Market Reactions to the Toxics Release Inventory Data," *Journal of Environmental Economics and Management*, 28 (1995), 98–113; and EPA, 1994 *Toxic Release Inventory: Public Data Release* (Washington, D.C.: EPA, January 1996).

15. See Daniel C. Esty, *Greening the GATT* (Washington, D.C.: Institute for International Economics, 1994).

16. There have been some genuine enthusiasts for market mechanisms. See Stephan Schmidheiny with the Business Council for Sustainable Development, *Changing Course: A Global Business Perspective on Development and the Environment* (Cambridge: MIT Press, 1992).

17. See Nathaniel O. Keohane, Richard L. Revesz, and Robert Stavins, "The Positive Political Economy of Instrument Choice in Environmental Policy," paper presented at

the Allied Social Science Associations meeting, New Orleans, Jan. 4–6, 1997.

18. "Economic rent" is that part of an individual's or firm's income which is in excess of the minimum amount necessary to keep that person or firm in its given occupation. It is sometimes thought of as above-normal profits, such as those that accrue to a monopolist or the owner of a scarce resource.

19. See Don Fullerton and Thomas C. Kinnaman, "Household Responses to Pricing Garbage by the Bag," *American Economic Review*, 86 (1996), 971–84.

20. See Lisa A. Skumatz, "Beyond Case Studies: Quantitative Effects of Recycling and Variable Rates Programs," *Resource Recycling* (September 1996), 62–8.

21. See William Fulton, "The Big Green Bazaar," *Governing Magazine* (June 1996), 38.

22. See Hilary A. Sigman, "A Comparison of Policies for Lead Recycling," *RAND Journal of Economics*, 26 (1995), 452–78.

17 Selling Environmental Indulgences

Robert E. Goodin

According to a common and currently influential diagnosis, the environmental crisis has essentially economic roots. The problem is not just that there are too many people, or even that they are on average enjoying too high a standard of living. All that is true, too, of course. More fundamentally, however, problems of environmental despoliation are said to derive from skewed incentives facing agents as they pursue their various goals.

For some things, people must pay full price. For others, they pay only partially or indirectly or belatedly. To an economist, it goes without saying that the lower the costs the more people will consume of any particular commodity. Where some of the costs of their activities will be borne by others, agents looking only to their own balance sheets will over-engage in those activities. Because some of the costs are 'external' (which is to say, are borne by others, rather than themselves) agents will undertake more of those activities than they would have done, had they been forced to pay their full costs. They will do more of them than is socially optimal, taking due account of costs and benefits to everyone concerned (Pigou 1932).

Environmental despoliation poses problems of economic externalities of just that sort. Environmental inputs are typically 'common property resources'. Clean air and water, fisheries, the ozone layer, the climate are everyone's business—and no one's. No one 'owns' those things. There is no one with standing to sue you if you take them without paying; nor is there anyone you could pay for permission to impinge on them, even if you wanted to do so. That fact inevitably gives rise to a divergence between the full social costs created by your actions and the portion of those costs sheeted back to you as private costs, to be entered on your own ledger. It is, of course, only the latter sorts of costs to which economically rational agents can be expected to respond (Freeman et al. 1973; Fisher 1981; Pearce et al. 1989: see esp. p. 5).

Either of two prescriptions might follow from that economistic diagnosis of the environmental problem. Both would put government in control of—cast it in the role of 'owner' of—common property resources. Both vest in government the power to authorise the use of environmental resources, and to punish people for using them without authorisation. The two prescriptions differ, principally, over the form that those authorisations and punishments would take.

The standard 'legalistic' approach operates by manipulating rights and duties. It is essentially a command-and-control strategy, specifying what people may or must or must not do and attaching penalties to violation of those commands. The newer 'economistic' approach works by manipulating incentives. In the limiting case, nothing is required or prohibited: everything

From *Kyklos*, 47 (1994), 573–96. Reprinted with permission.

just has a higher or lower price; and so long as you are willing to pay that price, you are perfectly welcome to do just as you please. Any actual control system may well combine both modes, of course, but for analytic purposes it pays to treat them separately.

The most dramatic form of the economistic strategy is to sell transferable permits to pollute, which permit-holders can then resell to others in turn.[1] Imposing 'green taxes', conceived essentially as charges for using the environment in certain ways, constitutes a less dramatic and politically more acceptable form of the same basic strategy. In that form, economistic logic attracts the endorsement of a surprisingly wide range of political players: from, on the one side, the OECD (1975; Opschoor and Vos 1988), national Treasuries and their advisers (Pearce et al. 1989: chap. 7) and economic think tanks (Epstein and Gupta 1990; Weimer 1990); to, on the other side, various Green Parties across Europe (Die Grünen 1983: sec. IV.1; European Greens 1989: sec. 1; Spretnak and Capra 1986). The 'carbon tax' in particular is now the instrument of choice among the widest possible range of policymakers for controlling emissions of greenhouse gases.[2]

In all variations on that economistic strategy, the highest aspiration is to set the price of licenses/permits/fees/taxes at a rate that would force polluters to internalise, in their own cost calculations, the full measure of environmental damage that they do. Of course, calculating that price will never be easy; many of the complaints with these economistic strategies will amount to little more than the (often, perfectly proper) complaint that the price has been set too low (Pearce et al. 1989: chaps. 3, 4, and 7). But once we have calculated total social costs correctly, and once we have forced the creators of those costs to internalise them fully, then objections to environmental despoliation should (on the economistic diagnosis of the problem) cease. Once despoilers have been made to repay fully the environmental costs of their activities, there would be no further reason to stop them from proceeding with those activities.

From an economic point of view, that case for 'green taxes' seems well nigh indisputable.[3] Environmental economists are therefore frankly dumbfounded when such 'unassailable' proposals nonetheless come under attack from fellow environmentalists. The latter, in turn, have proven particularly inept at articulating exactly what they see wrong with green taxes, though. The exchange amounts to a veritable dialogue of the deaf (Kelman 1981, 1983; Frey 1986).

This article is thus devoted essentially to bridging a gap within environmentalist discourse. Whilst fully acknowledging all the advantages that environmental economists see in green taxes, I hope to explain in terms congenial to them what other environmentalists have against them. The running analogy which will figure centrally in my discussion is that between green taxes and medieval indulgences. The former amount, in effect, to 'selling rights to destroy nature'; the latter amount, in effect, to 'selling God's grace'.

This analogy, like all analogies, is far from perfect in various respects. Perhaps the most obvious and important point of disanalogy is just this. There is a general ban on sin: a sin is always wrong. Environmental emissions, in contrast, are not always necessarily thought to be wrong. There is, or it is generally thought there should be, no general ban on them. (On the contrary, green taxes and such like are offered as *alternatives* to bans.) Religious indulgences are set against the background assumption of a prohibition on sin, the function of indulgences there being to forgive sinners their lapses. Environmental indulgences seem to be set against the background assumption that some pollution will be permitted, the function of environmental indulgences being to allocate those permissions to particular people.

Equating environmental pollution with sin seems to suggest that zero emissions should be our ideal goal. To most practical people, that seems plainly crazy—just the sort of thing that gives philosophy in general a bad name. But it pays to pause to reflect exactly why we think that a zero emission standard is so plainly crazy. In part, that is merely because a zero emission standard seems unrealistic (so, too, are the Ten Commandments, but they are nonetheless attractive as ideal standards for that). In part, it is because some emissions—ones in certain circumstances, or below certain levels—actually do no harm. The implication there is merely that it is environmental despoliation (an outcome) rather than environmental emissions (an act) that should be counted as the sin. Finally, even some genuinely despoiling emissions seem misdescribed as sins because, though harmful, they cause harm unavoidably and in the service of some greater good. The implication of there, however, is not that certain genuinely despoiling emissions are perfectly all right. The implication is, instead, that we are there operating in the realm of 'tragedy': even if we have done 'the right thing on balance', we will nonetheless have committed a wrong.[4]

These are only preliminary remarks, designed not so much to motivate the analogy as to defuse any strong initial sense of disanalogy, between religious indulgences and environmental ones. Arguments of a more positive sort for treating (certain sorts of) environmental despoliation as akin to a sin will be offered in Section II below.[5] There it will be shown that, while less than perfect, the analogy is closer that one might initially suppose. Despite the various points of (often important) disanalogy, it nonetheless remains a telling way into this troubled debate.

The upshot of those arguments is to dash the highest hopes of economistic advocates of green taxes. As I hope will be clear from those discussions, we may not legitimately use green taxes and cognate economistic mechanisms as optimising devices in directly guiding 'policy choice'. Such techniques may nonetheless retain a secondary use as tools of 'policy enforcement'. There, they would be serving merely to provide incentives and disincentives for people to achieve certain 'target' levels of maximum permissible environmental damage—levels that have been set elsewhere, by other means, in the political system.[6] That fallback position has much to be said for it. But as shown in Section III, that more modest case for green taxes must be sharply distinguished from the other, for it amounts to falling back a very long way indeed from those bolder claims often made on behalf of green taxes.

I. Religious Indulgences: A Potted History

The function of indulgences, in Catholic theology, is to remit time to be served by a sinner in purgatory. Indulgences were granted *by* church officials (originally popes, latterly bishops). They were granted *to* those who have sinned (by definition the only ones in need of them).

The practice of *granting* such indulgences goes back to the early history of the Church. The practice of *selling* them can be traced, fairly precisely, to the need of popes to provide incentives for Crusades—in the first instance for people to participate in them, in the second instance for people to pay for them (Purcell 1975). From the eve of the Third Crusade in 1187 to the Council of Trent which finally abolished the practice in 1563, selling indulgences became an increasingly common phenomenon. Indulgences were increasingly awarded in exchange for assistance, of an increasingly crassly material sort, rendered to the church and, increasingly, its temporal allies (Boudinhon 1940).

Increasingly, in turn, the practice became the subject of controversy among theologians of all stripes. Notable critics included Jan Hus, who in 1412 crossed the King Wenceslas on the matter (Boudinhon 1940). Most famous of all was Martin Luther (1517), whose 'Ninety-five Theses' nailed to the door of the Wittenberg Cathedral were largely devoted to an attack on the practice.

This is no place for a detailed examination of either the history or the theology of the matter, though. (On that, see Eliade (1987).) Present purposes will be better served by a more stylised account of generic sorts of possible objections to the sale of indulgences. As is only to be expected, these generic styles of objections track actual Church history only very imperfectly. But this being an exercise in moral philosophy rather than in theology, still less in Church history, that is just as it should be.

II. Grounds for Objecting to the Sale of Indulgences

Surveying the many possible grounds for objecting to the sale of indulgences for sin in religious affairs, surprisingly many of them might apply, *mutatis mutandis*, to the sale of indulgences (in the form of 'green taxes' or 'pollution permits') for activities degrading the natural environment.

Many environmentalists, of course, would take a vaguely spiritual attitude toward nature (Spretnak 1986). For them, the analogy between the sacrilege of selling nature's benefice and that of selling God's grace might be felt particularly powerfully. It would be wrong, however, to think that this analogy literally works only by implicitly or explicitly giving environmental values a spiritual twist.

1. SELLING WHAT IS NOT YOURS TO SELL

One of the recurring themes in opposition to the selling of religious indulgences, even by popes, was that they were selling what was not truly theirs to sell. The item on auction was God's grace: His forgiveness. When it comes to grace and forgiveness, what is at issue is not God's commandments (which popes are indeed empowered to interpret) but rather the exercise of His discretionary powers. Those are for Him alone to exercise. It is simply presumptuous—preempting prerogatives properly reserved to Him—for others, however high their Churchly station, to act on His behalf.[7]

There are important elements of this sort of logic at work within objections to selling environmental indulgences. Those elements figure particularly importantly in the objections of those who take a vaguely mystical view of nature, of course. It is not our place to grant (much less to sell) indulgences for violations of what, on this view, would be regarded as almost literally Mother Nature's physical integrity. It would be simply presumptuous of any human agents to grant indulgences on behalf of Mother Nature. Forgiveness is the prerogative of the party who has been wronged.

There is no need to give environmental ethics a spiritual twist to find an echo of this objection to the selling of indulgences, however. Many, for example, suppose merely that we have 'stewardship' responsibilities—either toward nature, or perhaps just toward future generations and their interests in the natural environment (Passmore 1980: chaps. 4 and 5; Goodin 1985: 169–86; Barry 1989: chaps. 17–19; Sax 1970). It would be objectionable for such stewards to sell environmental indulgences in much the same way, and for much the same reason. They, too, would be selling something that is not theirs to sell. Stewards would then be permitting people to destroy irrevocably that which those stewards are duty-bound to preserve, either for its own sake or for the sake of future generations.

2. SELLING THAT WHICH CANNOT BE SOLD

The objection just canvassed deals in terms of a breach of stewardship responsibilities per se. As such, it applies with equal force whatever the reasons for allowing those responsibilities to be breached or whatever form the breach takes. Stewards are bound to protect that which indulgers would allow to be destroyed. Hence granting indulgences, for whatever reason, would seem equally illegitimate.

There is, however, a variation on that objection which applies with peculiar force to the *sale* of indulgences—to the indulging of wrongful behaviour for reason of money. The objection there is not (or not just) that the impermissible is permitted. It is instead that the impermissible is permitted for a peculiarly sordid (pecuniary) motive. The objection is to the sale of the unsaleable, more than (and, indeed, often instead of) to the permitting of the impermissible.

The spiritual analogy is again illuminating here. It is not unreasonable to suppose, someone like Luther might say, that God forgives people their sins. It is not even unreasonable for those versed in God's words and His ways to second-guess (in a way that is of course utterly non-binding on Him) the circumstances in which he might do so. What *is* unreasonable, however, is to suppose that God's grace can be bought. What counts with Him is the purity of the heart, not the size of the purse (Luther 1517: prop. 27).

By the same token in the environmental case, it might be thought that there are indeed circumstances in which it is perfectly proper for the environment to be despoiled. Suppose that were the only way of securing a decent life (or, indeed, life at all) for a great many people who would otherwise lead miserable lives or face even more miserable deaths. Then chopping down large portions of the Amazonian rain forest might well be forgivable, if nonetheless unfortunate. But what makes it forgivable has nothing to do with (or, as in the case here sketched, may even be negatively related to) the size of the purse of those chopping down the forests. Certainly permission to chop down the forests should not be publicly auctioned to the highest bidder, any more than should remission of time in purgatory for sins committed.

A religious indulgence is granted upon condition of the indulged feeling true contrition for their sins. The environmental indulgence may be granted, by the same token, upon condition of the indulged showing that they have no other choice and that they have made good-faith (albeit unsuccessful) efforts to avoid damage to the environment.[8] The objection here in view is not to conditionality as such, but rather to making the granting of the indulgence conditional upon payment of hard, cold cash. God may grant His favours freely and simply; but God cannot be

244 ROBERT E. GOODIN

bought. By the same token, we might forgive people who despoil the environment for certain sorts of reasons—but the pursuit of pure profit (as represented in 'willingness to pay' green taxes) is not one of them.

Why that should be so is an open question that admits of various different styles of answer. One might have to do with distributive justice. We might suppose that the present distribution of cash holdings is without justification or that it is positively unjustified. For that reason, we might be reluctant to let one person's environmental quality be determined, in part, by another's unwarranted riches.

Alternatively, the argument might work in terms of 'blocked exchanges'. We may think that, even if the distribution of cash is morally unexceptionable, there are nonetheless certain things that money ought not be able to buy. Why the category should exist at all is, perhaps, philosophically mysterious; what falls into it certainly is sociologically variable (Simmel 1907/1978; Tobin 1970; Douglas and Isherwood 1979; Walzer 1983). Still, that the category exists seems both sociologically undeniable and ethically (not just ethnographically) interesting.

One way of justifying the category—and of rationalising much of its sociological content—is this. It is a clear affront to practical reason to engage in an exchange that secures you cash only at the cost of depriving you of the material and nonmaterial prerequisites for making use of that cash. So selling yourself into slavery is wrong (irrational) because once a slave you will no longer have the legal capacity to dispose of the money thereby acquired. By the same token, trading all your foodstuffs for money is self-defeating insofar as without sustenance you will not survive to spend the money.

Perhaps the objection to trading environmental quality for money derives from a similar thought. If you trade away (all) the environmental prerequisites for human existence, then the money acquired in exchange for that will do you no good; the trade makes no sense, at least in that limiting case. Perhaps, by extension, it makes little sense in many other much less extreme cases for something of the same sorts of reasons. Private affluence, of certain sorts anyway, may simply be pragmatically impossible to enjoy, under circumstances of sufficiently severe public squalor (Barry 1989: chap. 20).

Another way of justifying a category of things which ought not be bought and sold is in terms of the corruption of public morals. There is a well-known tendency, firmly established in the literature of empirical social psychology, for extrinsic rewards to drive out otherwise strong intrinsic motivations to perform the same actions. The precise psychological mechanisms at work are many and varied, and the precise nature of the interactions among them is none too clear. What is nonetheless clear is that there are many worthy actions that people would originally have done 'for their own sake', but which they will no longer do simply for their own sake once extrinsic material (especially monetary) rewards are also offered for doing them. Putting certain sorts of good deeds on the auction block, so to speak, demeans them and diminishes their intrinsic value in the eyes of those initially most sensitive to such intrinsic moral values (Goodin 1981, 1982: chap. 6; Lane 1991: chaps. 19–21; Frey 1986: 552–6, 1992, 1993).

What people value in that very special way is, as I have said, sociologically variable. Still, insofar as any appreciable part of the population does regard the value of the environment in that special way—and there seem to be reasons to think both that they should and that they do (Sagoff 1988)—then there is likely to be an efficiency cost that will potentially offset any efficiency gain in offering material incentives for environmental protection. Just as in Titmuss's (1971) famous case of blood donation, so too with the 'free' supply of voluntary environmental protection: it is likely to dry up the more we pay people (those same people, or others) for undertaking the same or similar actions.

3. RENDERING WRONGS RIGHT

Environmentalists sometimes say that they have no objection to *fining* despoilers of the environment: their objection is merely to charging, licensing, or taxing them. Economists scratch their heads at that. In terms of corporate balance sheets, there is no important difference between fines, charges, and taxes. In strictly economic terms, exactly the same disincentive is provided by a $100,000 fine as a $100,000 charge as a $100,000 tax on any given activity. To careful watchers of the profit-and-loss statements, it is a distinction without a difference.

To others, however, the difference is very real. With a fine, the wrongness remains even after the payment of a fine. It is wrong to have done what you have been fined for doing; you may have 'paid your debt to society' and be a member in good standing once again after having done so; but what you did nonetheless remains wrong. Not so with a mere license fee or charge. If you buy a pollution permit, then you are permitted to do what you have paid for permission to do: there is nothing wrong with it. The same is true of a 'charge'. There is nothing wrong with people dumping wastes in a sanitary landfill, once they have paid the charge for doing so. Similarly, with a 'tax', there is nothing wrong with doing most of the things for which we are ordinarily taxed. Quite the contrary, the ordinary activities giving rise to tax liability—like turning a profit or earning a wage—are very much socially approved.[9]

The problem with green taxes or pollution charges or permits, on this model, is that they seem to say, 'It is okay to pollute, provided you pay', when the proper message is instead, 'It is wrong to pollute, even if you can afford to pay'. (The reasons that is the right message are elaborated in Section II.6 below.) On the religious analogy, this comes through very strongly. There, an indulgence is forgiveness of sins. The sins clearly remain wrong things to have done. It is the punishment that is being remitted, not the wrongness of the action that is being cancelled, by the indulgence.[10]

The bottom line, here, is that putting indulgences up for sale makes them too easy to come by. In the religious case, remission for sin is granted too easily, and consequently sins are taken insufficiently seriously (Luther 1517: prop. 40). Much the same objection applies there as in the case of selling environmental indulgences (Frey 1992: 170–2; see similarly McCarthy 1990). In both cases, the problem with being able to buy your way out of the consequences of a nefarious activity is that anyone with sufficient ready cash is consequently led to take the nefariousness of the activity insufficiently seriously.

4. MAKING WRONGS ALL RIGHT

Maybe the point of buying an indulgence is not to make a wrong right, but merely to make it all right. Advocates of environmental charges emphasise that we license and tax all sorts of things we vaguely disapprove of, including gambling, smoking, drinking. What payment of the requisite price has done is not to make wrongs right but, rather, to make them 'all right'—permissible, if still undesirable in some ideal world.[11]

Classic religious indulgences did something less than that, though. Religious indulgences granted forgiveness for sins past, on condition of penance and a genuine intention not to do it again. Indulgences once granted made it all right to *have* sinned, but that indulgence stopped well short of making it all right to *sin*. The religious formula offered a mechanism for forgiving past wrongs without encouraging future ones. Through religious indulgences, past wrongs were rendered all right but present or future ones were not.

The whole point (in religious, if not necessarily pragmatic terms) of buying a religious indulgence was backward-looking, to wipe one's slate clean of past sins. The whole point of buying an environmental indulgence is forward-looking, to secure permission to despoil the environment now and in the future. Whereas the religiously indulged are seeking merely forgiveness for things past, the environmentally indulged seek permission for future actions. If buying an environmental indulgence is tantamount to buying a permission to commit a wrong, it is continuing permission (conditional on continuing payment) to commit continuing wrongs.

The reason the wrong remains wrong, even after payment, is simply that the wrong done to the environment and to people using it is not an economic wrong. It is not as if it (or we) are 'poorer' for those acts, at least not in any way that can be made good by any transfer of financial resources. Yet while the wrong remains, even after payment of taxes, that wrong is nonetheless permitted on a continuing basis, on continuing payment of the taxes. I return to these themes in Section II.6 below.

5. INDULGING SOME BUT NOT ALL

In granting indulgences there is a further problem of fairness to confront. Crudely put, it might be thought unfair, somehow, to indulge some but not all sinners. If not all can be (or, anyway, not all will be) indulged, then perhaps it is wrong—unfair—to indulge any at all. And that unfairness might be felt to be especially strong when indulgences are being sold in situations in which some but not all are willing or able to pay the asking price. Less crudely put, it might be thought a matter of elementary fairness that if any sinners are to be indulged, then all with relevantly similar characteristics should be. Of course not all sinners should be indulged: some are unreconstructed reprobates who really ought be punished. But all who are in the same boat ought, in fairness, be treated similarly.[12]

In the religious case, the issue of fairness arguably does not arise. There, indulgences merely reflect God's grace, understood as His purely discretionary whimsy. He can choose to indulge whomsoever He pleases, without a thought for constraints of consistency (although few would be attracted to a vision of so purely capricious a God, perhaps). Insofar as we are making a *social* practice of granting indulgences (environmental or otherwise), however, the practice surely ought be grounded in principles that are more regular and publicly defensible than that.

The particular problem of fairness arises, in the environmental case, from the fact that we can often afford a few—but only a few—environmental renegades (Kennan 1970). A few countries can continue to hunt whales, for example, without causing the extinction of any species, just so long as not all do. A few countries can continue generating greenhouse gases or emitting CFCs without altering the climate or destroying the ozone layer, just so long as most countries do not. In short, nature can tolerate some but not all misbehaving (Goodin 1995: chap. 18).

In such cases, the question immediately becomes how to choose who gets to play this role of environmental renegade. Advocates of green taxes suggest that these slots should be sold to the highest bidder: others suggest other ways in which this determination might be made (Taylor and Ward 1982). Behind all such schemes, however, is an unspoken assumption that we ought make sure that all those slots are taken—that we ought allow just as many renegades as nature itself will tolerate.

Critiques couched in terms of fairness query precisely that proposition. The root idea there is that if we cannot allow everyone to do something, then we ought not allow anyone to do it. That may not appeal much as a general principle: it seems perfectly reasonable that I should be able to allow some people to share my house without allowing everyone to do so. But that principle seems considerably more apt when it comes to the exploitation of genuinely collective goods: it seems far less reasonable to allow some co-owners of a common property resource to use it in certain ways, without allowing all co-owners to use it similarly.

The impetus to economic efficiency leads us to regard such opportunities to exploit common property resources (by some but not all) as things to be allocated—somehow, to someone. The impetus to fairness leads us to regard such opportunities as things to be eschewed, rather than being allocated at all. Granting environmental indulgences, upon payment of a suitable price, is essentially an allocation device. On the fairness critique, it allocates what ought not be allocated at all. Those are efficiency gains that, in all fairness, we ought not pursue.

That rejoinder is not always compelling. Efficiency ought not always be eschewed in the interests of fairness. The fact that we do not have food enough to feed everyone does not mean that we should let such food as we do have go to waste, with the consequence that everyone starves. Rather, we ought ration scarce necessities in such a way that they do as much good as possible.

Still, in circumstances of rationing, we are characteristically highly sensitive to the precise mechanisms employed for allocating rights to use hyper-scarce, necessary resources. We generally want to ensure that the distribution of those rationed commodities is more equal than the distribution of cash holdings or of other commodities in general. That is reflected in the fact that the buying and selling of ration coupons is almost invariably prohibited: and necessarily so, if the ration coupons are to serve their social function as an independent 'second' currency, distinct from and restraining on the operation of ordinary economic forces (Tobin 1952, 1970; Neary 1987; Hirshleifer 1987: esp. chap. 1).

6. GROUNDS FOR INDULGENCE

Many of those objections ultimately turn on questions of appropriate (relevant) criteria for granting indulgences. In the religious case, and on one telling of the environmentalist case, it is an inerasable wrong that is being indulged. In the economistic telling of the environmentalist tale, it is merely a previously uncompensated external cost that is being indulged, upon condition of payment of some sum adequate to compensate those who would otherwise have to bear that cost.

In the case of religious indulgences, what is wrong with their being bought and sold is that money payments are the wrong basis for granting them. It is not how much people pay, but rather their regret for what they have done, that is there relevant. Not every penitent can afford to pay, nor are all those who can afford to pay truly penitent. Granting indulgences only to those who pay (or even to all those who pay) would result in a maldistribution of indulgences, by the only standard that is really relevant there.

What ought be the relevant standards for granting indulgences depends upon the nature of the wrong being indulged, though. The salient feature of sin, in this regard, is that it can never be undone. It is a blot that can never be erased or wiped clean. So the most we can be looking for, in deciding whether to indulge any particular sinner, is a genuinely penitent attitude: sincere regret, and a deep commitment not to sin again.

On one account, the wrong done in despoiling the environment is just like that: a presumptuous intrusion into, and destruction of, the creation of another's hand. On that view, it would be wrong for the same reasons to grant environmental indulgences to all, or to any, who were prepared to pay for them. There, as in the religious case, what we should be looking for in granting indulgences is genuine remorse and a firm commitment not to harm nature again. There, as in the religious case, granting indulgences in return for monetary payment would be to grant them for wrong (anyway, irrelevant) reasons. Worse, it would encourage the continued wronging of nature, since knowing you can always buy your way out of trouble tempts you to do it again.

Others, environmental economists conspicuously among them, take a different view of the nature of the wrong done by despoiling the environment. They would say that the wrong is an economic wrong. The wrong is the destruction, or diminution, of a collective good. It is a cost that one person's activities impose upon everyone sharing in those collective goods. Furthermore, environmental economists tend to conceive of that harm as a cost or 'welfare loss' which can in principle be recompensed.

That conjunction of attitudes carries important implications for one's view of the power of environmental indulgences to rectify wrongs. If environmental despoilers can and do fully compensate others for the harm that they have done them, then that on this view wipes the slate clean. On that view of the sort of wrong done by environmental despoilers, ability/willingness to pay for indulgences would indeed be a relevant criteria for allocating indulgences. By paying the price, despoilers would—quite literally—have undone the wrong.

Clearly, there are some deep issues at stake in deciding between these interpretations of the wrongs done by environmental despoilers. For those who view the wrong as being done to nature, righting the wrong requires recompensing nature, somehow; and if it is naturalness that is of value, most obvious forms of recompense are not viable—or anyway are not as valuable—options (Goodin 1992: 26–41). Only those who are prepared to view the wrong as one done to other people might conceivably regard paying them a suitable price in exchange for an indulgence as suitable recompense.

It is important to note, however, that not everyone who views the wrong as one done to other people would necessarily regard paying the right price as suitable recompense. That is to say, this difference of opinion does not map easily onto the difference—easily relegated to the 'too hard' basket—between deep and shallow ecologists (Devall and Sessions 1985; Sylvan 1985). Even anthropocentric analysts might regard cash transfers, of the sort entailed in buying indulgences through payment of green taxes and such like, as inadequate recompense for environmental harms. Anthropocentric analysts might, for example, have a more nuanced notion of human interests, such that people cannot be compensated for losses in one category (e.g. environmental quality) by gains in another (e.g. money, or even any of the things that money can buy) (Goodin 1989, 1995: chap. 11).

My own view of the value of nature is very much like that. The value of natural processes is to provide a context, outside of ourselves (individually, or even collectively), in which to set our lives (see similarly Hill 1983). What is wrong with environmental despoliation is that it deprives us of that context; it makes the external world more and more one of our own (perverse) creation. That is ultimately a wrong to humans, rather than to nature as such, to be sure. It is, nonetheless, a wrong that cannot be recompensed by cash payments. The humans wronged by such practices might be made better off in some sense or another by such payments. But they will be better off, if at all, in dimensions altogether different from those in which their losses have been sustained. The cash offered in payment for environmental indulgences—through green taxes and such like—cannot possibly recompense them for the loss of that context that provided meaning, of a sort, to their lives (Goodin 1992: 41–54).

III. Economistic Backtracking

From an economist's point of view, making environmental despoilers pay for indulgences might serve two quite distinct functions. The first and more modest function is one of 'policy enforcement'. The idea here is to use green taxes simply to provide a disincentive for despoiling. The higher the charges are, for whatever reason, the greater the disincentive effect: that is the end of the story (Baumol and Oates 1971). How much despoliation we want to tolerate, and how much we want to deter, is a matter for determination by other non-economistic means (by politicians, theologians, or moralists).

I shall return to that more modest version of the tale shortly. First, however, let us consider the more ambitious function that might be served by selling environmental indulgences—one of actual 'policy choice'. The aim here would be to use green taxes and associated economistic techniques to determine 'optimal' levels of despoliation. This second argument subsumes the first; the whole idea is to provide an incentive for (certain) would-be despoilers to desist. But this second argument transcends the first, in acknowledging that certain despoilers ought be allowed to persist and in providing some mechanism for determining who they should be and how much they should be allowed to despoil.

For purposes of this more ambitious argument, we are required to make the following assumptions:

(1) the price of indulgences fully reflect social costs of the activity;
(2) the activity occurs only upon payment of that price; and
(3) that payment is actually used to compensate or correct for the harm done.

Under those assumptions, environmental despoliation would be a socially optimal activity which actually ought be engaged in by anyone who can afford to pay for the indulgence out of the proceeds of that despoliation. The sense in which it would be optimal is the weak and unexceptionable Paretian sense of no one being worse off (thanks to the compensation in clause 3 above) and at least one person being better off (that is, despoilers who want to persist even after having had to pay the price of the indulgence).[13]

It is of course the latter, more ambitious defence of the sale of environmental indulgences that is the more attractive to defenders of the economistic faith. It is the selfsame defence that is the greater anathema to their detractors. What is problematic, in particular, is the presumption that money payments can ever correct or compensate for environmental despoliation.

For those who attach great importance to environmental integrity, 'correcting' environmental despoliation is simply not a feasible option. No doubt, even for them, restoration and reclamation might be preferable to letting a despoiled bit of nature remain utterly despoiled. But for those who attach great importance to authenticity, the process by which a bit of nature came to be as it is matters greatly; and restored or reclaimed bits of nature, however effective the restoration or reclamation, will necessarily be of less value than they would have been had they never been despoiled in the first place. The reason, quite simply, is that they will have come to be as they are in part through artificial human interventions rather than through more purely natural processes.[14]

Neither, many would say, can cash transfers of the sort received in payment for environmental indulgences compensate for the harms involved in environmental despoliation. If, as just argued, they cannot be used to correct the damage, they could 'compensate' if at all only by making people better off in some other respect altogether. Their environment might be worse, but their wine cellar better; and, on balance, they think themselves better off in consequence. Surely it is true that overall well-being is a composite of roughly that sort; and surely some of its components are tradeable, at the margins, for one another in just that way. The question is whether environmental quality is of that character. On at least some of the arguments canvassed above, it is not: it is more fundamental; it is a precondition for valuing, rather than merely a source of values which can be set alongside and traded against other values. If so, neither money nor anything that money can buy can compensate for its loss.[15]

Of course, there are also a great many practical difficulties in calculating (or, rather, in defending any particular calculation of) the cash value of environmental quality. More in deference to those practicalities than in deference to any matters of high principle, environmental economists are sometimes prepared (and governments are often keen) to fall back onto the first 'policy-enforcement' defence of green taxes alone.[16]

This fallback position amounts to using a 'market-based incentive system to meet preordained environmental quality standards' (Pearce et al. 1989: 165, after Baumol and Oates 1971). The basic idea goes something like this. Let there be some independent social determination of the environmental standards that we want to attain. Let those be given by the political process, rather than by any economistic calculation of 'social cost' or 'optimal' despoliation. Let us merely use the price system to enforce that standard, floating the price up or down until the desired level of environmental quality has been achieved.

There is, on this model, no independent justification of the particular price charged. It is all just a matter of what it takes to get people to cut back on their activities sufficiently to achieve our environmental targets.[17] While there is nothing special about the particular price being charged, however, there is nonetheless a good economistic reason to use price mechanisms to enforce those standards. The rationale is just that, insofar as the standards can be attained in ways that admit of partial noncompliance, pricing mechanisms evoke compliance from those whom economists would regard as the 'right' people—those who gain relatively less from environmental despoliation or whom it costs relatively less to desist from it.

This fallback position effectively insulates economists against the criticism that, in selling environmental indulgences, they are auctioning off nature's bounty too cheaply. If too much environmental despoliation is occurring, they would say, then that can only be for either of two reasons: either the price has been set too low to achieve the desired standard (and advocates of green taxes and such like would be the first to agree that it should be raised as high as necessary to achieve that goal); or else the standard has been set too low (which is the fault of politicians, and ought not be taken as criticism of the price mechanism as a way of securing compliance with the standard). Either way, the complaint seems not to touch the practice of selling environmental indulgences, as such.

Of course, efficiency gains from using the pricing mechanism even in this minimal way arise only in very particular circumstances. They presuppose that we can afford to tolerate some people, but not all people, acting as environmental despoilers. Sometimes, though, the situation is such that we cannot—or cannot be sufficiently confident that we can—afford any slackers at all. (Whaling negotiations are often like that: we do not know just how close we are to the limits of a successful breeding population, and given the real risks of destroying the whole species we do not want to take any chances.) Other times, considerations of fairness of the sort discussed in Section II.5 above would lead us to say that, purely as a matter of principle, we should not tolerate any slackers even if practicalities would allow. For reasons either of practicality or principle, we might thus set the desired standard at zero despoliation. And if that is the goal, there is no advantage to pursuing it through the price mechanism.

The more fundamental point to be made here, though, is that in retreating to this fallback position environmental economists really have given away their strongest claims on behalf of green taxes. Their proudest boast was that the buying of an environmental indulgence made despoliation not merely all right but actually right—socially optimal. But that boast was predicated on the assumption that the price was right, that it was a true reflection of the full social costs of environmental despoliation. If there is no social-cost based rationale for the particular price being set for environmental indulgences, then their sale cannot perform that role of serving as a solvent turning wrongs into rights.[18]

IV. Conclusions

How attractive we find green taxes and the 'polluter pays' principle more generally depends, in large part, upon what we see as their alternative. If, realistically, the alternative is polluters not paying, then the 'polluter pays' principle looks to be the relatively more restrictive option. Most of us would probably prefer a regime in which polluters at least be made to pay something—however inadequate that sum (or any sum) might be—if the alternative realistically in view were that otherwise they be allowed to continue polluting with gay abandon.

Suppose, however, the alternative in view were instead that polluters desist from polluting altogether. Then a rule that the 'polluter pays' looks to be the relatively more permissive option. If absent the option to pay the alternative is that people not pollute, then giving them permission to pollute upon payment is actually a mechanism for allowing more pollution than would otherwise occur. Seen in that light, many of us may well hesitate to endorse the 'polluter pays' principle that, in that other light, looked relatively attractive.

Which is the correct comparison—which, realistically, is the alternative to polluters paying (their not paying, or their not polluting)—is essentially a political question. As such, it varies according to time and place, policy arena and issue area. That in itself is an important lesson. Perhaps it is right that environmentalists should endorse green taxes, in circumstances where stronger prohibitions are not yet in sight. But they ought not turn that into blanket endorsement or an unalterable policy commitment, debarring them from the pursuit of stronger measures should they ever come politically into view.

Therein lies, perhaps, a larger lesson for green politics. True, perhaps environmentalists ought be realists. They ought not go tilting at windmills; they ought not let the best be the enemy of the good; they ought get what they can, here and now, rather than holding out in all-or-nothing fashion when doing so only guarantees that nothing will be achieved. Be all that as it may, it is nonetheless equally true that environmentalists ought not be so sensitive to current political realities as to render them insensitive to shifting political realities. Shifting alliances and provisional policy commitments—as to green taxes—ought be very much part of the environmentalist's political repertoire.[19]

Notes

1. For discussions of such proposals, see Dales (1968: 93–7); Hahn (1982); Hahn and Hester (1987, 1989); Ackerman and Stewart (1988); and Pearce et al. (1989: 165–6). Note that, by setting upper limits on the amount of allowable pollution, these permits are more limiting than charges or taxes, which in principle dictate no such upper limit on the amount of allowable pollution (although in practice, of course, they price it out at some point).

2. Elaborating such proposals, see Epstein and Gupta (1990); Weimer (1990); and Pearce et al. (1989: 165–6). On the political uptake, see Palmer (1992) and Taylor (1992).

3. This is the cumulative conclusion of, e.g., Dales (1968: chap. 6); Kneese and Schultze

(1975); Schultze (1977); Schelling (1983); Rhoads (1985: 40–56); Pearce et al. (1989: chap. 7).

4. Poisoning one person so that thousands may lives is, by most standards, the obviously right thing to do in the desperately unfortunate circumstances. But there is something obviously wrong with someone who is not even vaguely apologetic to the bereaved family for the sad necessity of that sacrifice (Nussbaum 1984).

5. See in particular Section II.2 and 6 below. Another tack, unexplored here, is Hill's (1983) observation that certain sorts of character traits hang together, so the environmentally insensitive are likely also to be morally insensitive in ways classically linked to sin.

6. That is precisely the use made of permits under the most familiar instantiation of these techniques, in the US Emissions Trading Program and the Clean Air Act and Amendments of 1990 (US EPA 1986; US Congress 1990). See Hahn and Hester (1989) for discussion of those policies and Ackerman and Steward (1988) for elaboration of the 'democratic' roots underlying their rationale.

7. In the Eastern and the older Western Church, 'the priest invoked divine forgiveness but could not himself declare the sinner to be absolved'; it was only 'after the Papal Revolution' in the eleventh century that 'a new formula was introduced in the West: *Ego te absolvo* ('I absolve you'). This was at first interpreted as the priest's certification of God's action ... In the twelfth century, however, it was interpreted as having a performative, that is, a sacramental as well as a declarative, effect' (Berman 1983: 173). Luther's (1517) fifth and sixth propositions especially hark back to this older understanding.

8. Some such 'good-faith' condition is built into the US offset policy: emissions permits can be sold only by those who have controlled their own emissions more than they are legally required to do; and potential buyers must as a precondition of purchase demonstrate that they have already installed the best available control technology, and they must buy 20 percent more permits than they will actually use (US EPA 1986; Hahn and Hester 1989).

9. Not always: see Section II.4 below.

10. Even God might not be able to make wrongs right or bads good. On the so-called 'Euthyphro argument', His will does not make things good; rather, He wills what He does because it is good independently of His will. In Socrates' formulation, 'Is what is holy holy because the gods approve it, or do they approve it because it is holy?' (Plato nd/1961: sec. 10a/p. 178).

11. This may have to do with limits of criminal sanction. Much that we regard as morally wrong remains legally permissible, because it would be wrong (inappropriate, given the limits of the criminal sanction) literally to outlaw it—so we merely tax it instead.

12. What counts as 'the same boat' comes down to a matter of what are the characteristics that would make them 'relevantly similar'. The question of fairness, posed that way, quickly transforms itself into one of appropriate (relevant) criteria for granting indulgences. That issue is taken up in Section II.6 below.

13. The more standard welfare-economic phrasing of that point would substitute hypothetical compensation for actual in clause 3 above: the test, there, is whether gainers *could* compensate losers (Kaldor 1939; Hicks 1939). Nothing is lost rephrasing the arguments of this article in those terms. Nor is anything gained by advocates of optimal despoilation, for the whole point of those opposing such optimization is that certain forms of damage could not even in principle be corrected or compensated by cash payments of any sort.

14. Elliot (1982). Humanity is part of nature, too, of course: but surely we ought not infer from that that any human intervention, however destructive of the rest of creation, is acceptable because it is just part of a natural process. Those intuitions seem firm and clear. How to justify them—and with them, any sharp distinction between human and non-human parts of nature—is less straightforward, perhaps. One way is to say that the value that humans derive from being able to set their lives in some context outside of themselves, either individually or collectively; and for this purpose, it is precisely the non-human part of nature that is crucial (Goodin 1992: chap. 2).

15. Even the OECD (1975: 28), acknowledges that 'direct controls' of a more legalistic, command-and-control sort are preferable to incentives of a 'green tax' sort as a 'means of preventing *irreversible effects or unacceptable pollution* (mercury, cadmium, etc.).'

16. Even the OECD's (1975) *Polluter Pays Principle* proceeds in this way. Its 'Guiding Principles' state that 'the polluter should bear the expenses of carrying out ... measures decided by public authorities to ensure that

the environment is in an *acceptable* state' (pp. 12–13, emphasis added). A rather confused 'Note' glossing those guidelines elaborates, 'The notion of an "acceptable state" decided by public authorities.' The 'collective choice' of what is an 'acceptable' should be made with due regard to comparative social costs of the pollution and of its abatement, but those determinations are to be made politically rather than literally economically; it therefore follows that 'the Polluter-Pays Principle is no more than an efficiency principle for allocating costs and does not (necessarily) involve bringing pollution down to an optimum level of any type' (p. 15). See further Pearce et al. (1989: 157–8; cf. chap. 3).

17. In similar vein, the US Comptroller General (1979) reported to Congress that the then-existing limits on fines that the Nuclear Regulatory Commission could impose on operators of nuclear power plants for safety violations were inadequate deterrents: allowing a maximum penalty of $5,000 for each violation up to a maximum of $25,000 for all violations over a period of 30 consecutive days is a derisory deterrent, when it would cost the operators of the power plant something on the order of $300,000 to purchase power from the grid every day it is shut down to make repairs.

18. Environmental economists, of course, see themselves retreating to this fallback position purely for reasons of pragmatism—purely because of practical difficulties in calculating costs. The imposition of 'standards' which the price mechanism is then used to enforce is nonetheless justified, at root, in terms of social costs, even if they cannot be calculated precisely. Even on this minimal understanding of why the retreat was necessary, however, paying the price still cannot right wrongs. As those environmental economists themselves would be the first to concede (indeed, insist, as a criticism of standard-setting ungrounded in hard economic calculations more generally), standards will only accidentally if at all correspond to what is socially optimal, defined as the level of environmental despoliation that would follow from a proper calculation of social costs. (See Pearce et al. 1989: chap. 7.) Hence paying a price set merely to achieve those standards will only accidentally if at all provide recompense for the damage done. The price is essentially arbitrary, even from the environmental economist's point of view; and paying an *arbitrarily* high price cannot, even from their point of view, serve to right any wrongs.

19. Earlier versions were read at the Universities of Queensland and Melbourne and at various venues around the Australian National University. I am particularly grateful for valuable comments, then and later, from John Dryzek, Patrick Dunleavy, Bruno S. Frey, René L. Frey, Daniel Hausman, Max Neutze, Alan Ryan, Rob Sparrow, and Cass Sunstein.

References

Ackerman, Bruce A., and Stewart, Richard B. (1988), 'Reforming Environmental Law: The Democratic Case for Market Incentives', *Columbia Journal of Environmental Law*, 13: 171–99.

Barry, Brian (1989), *Democracy, Power and Justice* (Oxford: Clarendon Press).

Baumol, William J., and Oates, Wallace E. (1971), 'The Use of Standards and Prices for Protection of the Environment', *Swedish Journal of Economics*, 73: 42–54.

Berman, Harold J. (1983), *Law and Revolution: The Formation of the Western Legal Tradition* (Cambridge, Mass.: Harvard University Press).

Boudinhon, A. (1940), 'Indulgences', in James Hastings (ed.), *Encyclopedia of Religion and Ethics* (Edinburgh: T. & T. Clark), vii. 252–5.

Dales, J. H. (1968), *Pollution, Property & Prices* (Toronto: University of Toronto Press).

Devall, Bill, and Sessions, George (1985), *Deep Ecology* (Salt Lake City: Peregrine Smith Books).

Die Grünen (1983), *Programme of the German Green Party*, trans. Hans Fernbach (London: Heretic Books).

Douglas, Mary, and Isherwood, Brian (1979), *The World of Goods* (London: Allen Lane).

Eliade, Mircea (1987) (ed.), *The Encyclopedia of Religion* (New York: MacMillan).

Elliot, Robert (1982), 'Faking Nature', *Inquiry*, 25: 81–94.

Epstein, Joshua M., and Gupta, Raj (1990), *Controlling the Greenhouse Effect: Five Global Regimes Compared* (Washington, DC: Brookings Institution).

European Greens (1989), *Common Statement of the European Greens for the 1989 Elections to the European Parliament* (Brussels: European Greens).

Fisher, Anthony C. (1981), *Resource and Environmental Economics* (Cambridge: Cambridge University Press).

Freeman, A. Myrick, III, Haveman, Robert H., and Kneese, Allen V. (1973), *The Economics of Environmental Policy* (New York: Wiley).

Frey, Bruno S. (1986), 'Economists Favour the Price System—Who Else Does?', *Kyklos*, 39: 537–633.

—— (1992), 'Tertium Datur: Pricing, Regulating and Intrinsic Motivation', *Kyklos*, 45: 161–84.

—— (1993), 'Motivation as a Limit to Pricing', *Journal of Economic Psychology*, 14: 635–64.

Goodin, Robert E. (1981), 'Making Moral Incentives Pay', *Policy Sciences*, 12: 131–45.

—— (1982), *Political Theory and Public Policy* (Chicago: University of Chicago Press).

—— (1985), *Protecting the Vulnerable* (Chicago: University of Chicago Press).

—— (1989), 'Theories of Compensation', *Oxford Journal of Legal Studies*, 9: 56–75.

—— (1992), *Green Political Theory* (Oxford: Polity Press).

—— (1995), *Utilitarianism as a Public Philosophy* (Cambridge: Cambridge University Press).

Hahn, Robert W. (1982), 'Marketable Permits: What's all the Fuss About?', *Journal of Public Policy*, 2: 395–412.

—— and Hester, Gordon L. (1987), 'The Market for Bads: EPA's Experience with Emissions Trading', *Regulation*, 3/4: 48–53.

—— (1989), 'Marketable Permits: Lessons for Theory & Practice', *Ecology Law Quarterly*, 16: 361–406.

Hicks, John R. (1939), 'The Foundations of Welfare Economics', *Economic Journal*, 49: 696–712.

Hill, Thomas E., Jr. (1983), 'Ideals of Human Excellence and Preserving Natural Environments', *Environmental Ethics*, 5: 211–24.

Hirshleifer, Jack (1987), *Economic Behaviour in Adversity* (Brighton: Harvester-Wheatsheaf).

Kaldor, Nicholas (1939), 'Welfare Propositions of Economics and Interpersonal Comparisons of Utility', *Economic Journal*, 49: 549–52.

Kelman, Steven (1981), *What Price Incentives? Economists and the Environment* (Boston: Auburn House).

—— (1983), 'Economic Incentives and Environmental Policy: Politics, Ideology and Philosophy', in Thomas C. Schelling (ed.), *Incentives for Environmental Protection* (Cambridge, Mass.: MIT Press), 291–332.

Kennan, George F. (1970), 'To Prevent a World Wasteland', *Foreign Affairs*, 48: 401–13.

Kneese, Allen V., and Schultze, Charles L. (1975), *Pollution, Prices and Public Policy* (Washington, DC: Brookings Institution).

Lane, Robert E. (1991), *The Market Experience* (Cambridge: Cambridge University Press).

Luther, Martin (1963), 'Ninety-five Theses' (1517), in Carl S. Meyer (trans.), *Luther's and Zwingli's Propositions for Debate* (Leiden: E. J. Brill), 3–21.

McCarthy, Eugene J. (1990), 'Pollution Absolution', *New Republic*, 3: 9.

Neary, J. Peter (1987), 'Rationing', in *The New Palgrave: A Dictionary of Economics* (London: MacMillan), iv. 92–6.

Nussbaum, Martha C. (1984), *The Fragility of Goodness* (Cambridge: Cambridge University Press).

Opschoor, J. B., and Vos, H. (1988), *The Application of Economic Instruments for Environmental Protection in OECD Member Countries* (Paris: OECD).

Organisation for Economic Co-operation and Development (1975), *The Polluter Pays Principle* (Paris: OECD).

Palmer, John (1992), 'Community Plans Carbon Fuel Tax', *Guardian Weekly*, 146(21): 11.

Passmore, John (1980), *Man's Responsibility for Nature*, 2nd edn. (London: Duckworth).

Pearce, David, Markandya, Anil, and Barbier, Edward B. (1989), *A Blueprint for a Green Economy: A Report to the UK Department of the Environment* (London: Earthscan).

Pigou, A. C. (1932), *The Economics of Welfare*, 4th edn. (London: MacMillan).

Plato, *Euthyphro*. Reprinted in E. Hamilton and H. Cairns (eds), *The Collected Dialogues of Plato* (Princeton, NJ: Princeton University Press, 1961).

Purcell, Maureen (1975), *Papal Crusading Policy, 1244–1291* (Leiden: E. J. Brill).

Rhoads, Steven E. (1985), *The Economists's View of the World* (Cambridge: Cambridge University Press).

Sagoff, Mark (1988), *The Economy of the Earth* (Cambridge: Cambridge University Press).

Sax, Joseph L. (1970), 'The Public Trust Doctrine in Natural Resource Law', *Michigan Law Review*, 68: 471–566.

Schelling, Thomas C. (1983) (ed.), *Incentives for Environmental Protection* (Cambridge, Mass.: MIT Press).

Schultze, Charles (1977), *The Public Use of Private Interest* (Washington, DC: Brookings Institution).

Simmel, Georg (1978), *The Philosophy of Money*, trans. T. B. Bottomore and D. Frisby (London: Routledge & Kegan Paul) (originally published 1907).

Spretnak, Charlene (1986), *The Spiritual Dimension of Green Politics* (Santa Fe, N. Mex.: Bear & Co).

—— and Capra, Fritjof (1986), *Green Politics: The Global Promise* (Santa Fe, N. Mex.: Bear & Co).

Sylvan, Richard (1985), 'A Critique of Deep Ecology', *Radical Philosophy*, 40: 2–12 and 41: 10–22.

Taylor, Jeffrey (1992), 'Global Market in Pollution Rights Proposed by U.N.', *New York Times*, 31 January: C1 and C12.

Taylor, Michael, and Ward, Hugh (1982), 'Chickens, Whales and Lumpy Public Goods: Alternative Models of Public-Goods Provision', *Political Studies*, 30: 350–70.

Titmuss, R. M. (1971), *The Gift Relationship* (London: Allen and Unwin).

Tobin, James (1952), 'A Survey of the Theory of Rationing,' *Econometrica*, 20: 521–53.

—— (1970), 'On Limiting the Domain of Inequality', *Journal of Law and Economics*, 13: 363–78.

United States, Comptroller General (1979), *Higher Penalties Could Deter Violations of Nuclear Regulations*, Report to the Congress number EMD-79-9 (Washington, DC: General Accounting Office).

United States, Congress (1990), Clean Air Act, Amendments, Public Law 101–549 (S.1630), 15 November 1990, *Statutes*, 104: 2399–2712.

United States, Environmental Protection Agency (1986), Emissions Trading Policy Statement, *Federal Register*, 51: 43–814.

Walzer, Michael (1983), *Spheres of Justice* (Oxford: Martin Robertson).

Weimer, David L. (1990), 'An Earmarked Fossil Fuels Tax to Save the Rain Forests', *Journal of Policy Analysis and Management*, 9: 254–9.

Section VI: Sustainable Development

As we saw in Section V, market liberals believe that economic mechanisms can serve environmental values, provided only that the appropriate set of private property rights is in place. Sustainable development too is a doctrine that believes in the integration of economic and environmental values, but in a somewhat different dimension. The era of sustainable development began in earnest on the global stage in the 1980s, when it largely displaced the more established discourse of limits and survivalism. The ecological limits stressed by the latter were in no sense disproved by sustainable development; rather, these limits were downgraded and assumed to be avoidable by intelligent action. Sustainable development begins from the contention that economic growth and environmental protection can be brought into productive harmony on a global scale, though only by concerted collective action (of the sort that horrifies market liberals). A commitment to redistribution from rich to poor now and in the future is thrown in for good measure, though this redistribution should not prove especially painful for the rich.

While sustainable development is nowhere an accomplished fact, as a concept and a framework it informs the efforts of international organizations, environmental groups, socially responsible corporations, and governments. Its hold on the global environmental imagination was confirmed in 1987 with the publication of *Our Common Future*, the report of the World Commission on Environment and Development chaired by Norwegian Prime Minister Gro Harlem Brundtland, whose basic statement we reprint here (Chapter 18). Since then it has gone from strength to strength. Perhaps its finest hour was the 1992 Earth Summit in Rio de Janeiro, where heads of state from all over the world gathered to endorse a broad global strategy for sustainable development. While the sustainable development agenda has flagged and occasionally languished in its implementation, it still has no real competitor in international environmental politics. The 2002 World Summit on Sustainable Development in Johannesburg was an even bigger gathering, but its outcomes were perhaps still more ambiguous. The key products included many partnerships between businesses, governments, and non-governmental organizations, and commitments on access to clean water and sanitation for the world's poor. The selection by James Meadowcroft charts the rise of sustainable development and its application in industrial societies from a broadly sympathetic point of view.

Sceptics charge that the popularity of sustainable development stems only from the fact that it can mean all things to all people. To the World Business Council on Sustainable Development it means mainly continued economic growth. To the international environmental groups that endorse the concept it means deeper commitment to ecological values in redesigning the world's political economy. The selection by David Carruthers recovers the deeper history of sustainable development as a radical discourse based in the Third World. He argues that Brundtland bent the idea to make it compatible with dominant currents in global capitalism. Carruthers considers how the radical edge might be regained.

Further Reading

Aside from the Brundtland report, key documents advancing the cause of sustainable development published by international organizations include the lengthy *Agenda 21* coming out of the 1992 Earth Summit, and *Caring for the Earth: A Strategy for Sustainable Living*, produced jointly in 1991 by the International Union for the Conservation of Nature, United Nations Environment Program, and World Wildlife Fund. The 2002 World Summit on Sustainable Development produced a *Plan of Implementation* of key agreements. Michael Jacobs in *The Green Economy: Environment, Sustainable Development and the Future* (1991) gives an environmentalist's account of how economics might be reoriented in the interests of sustainable development. Frank Fischer and Michael Black (eds), *Greening Environmental Policy: The Politics of a Sustainable Future* (1995) is a good collection oriented to environmental policy and politics. Stephan Schmidheiny, in *Changing Course: A Global Business Perspective on Development and the Environment* (1992), shows how sustainable development can be accommodated to the interests of large corporations. Michael Redclift's *Sustainable Development: Exploring the Contradictions* (1987) demonstrates the variety of uses to which the concept can be put. Andrew Dobson's *Justice and the Environment: Conceptions of Environmental Sustainability and Social Justice* (1998) is a theoretical exploration of the links between sustainable development and justice. William Lafferty and James Meadowcroft (eds), *Implementing Sustainable Development: Strategies and Initiatives in High Consumption Societies* (2000) is a good survey of national policies in industrialized countries. Paul Wapner, in 'World Summit on Sustainable Development: Toward a Post-Jo'burg Environmentalism', *Global Environmental Politics*, 3 (2003), 1–10, contains some sobering thoughts. Tim Luke's 'Sustainable Development as a Power/Knowledge System: The Problem of Governmentality', in Fischer and Black (eds), *Greening Environmental Policy*, is an uncompromising critique of the concept. Wilfred A. Beckerman's *A Poverty of Reason: Sustainable Development and Economic Growth* (2002) is equally severe in its critique from a market liberalism direction.

18   From One Earth to One World

An Overview by the World Commission on Environment and Development

In the middle of the twentieth century, we saw our planet from space for the first time. Historians may eventually find that this vision had a greater impact on thought than did the Copernican revolution of the sixteenth century, which upset the human self-image by revealing that the Earth is not the centre of the universe. From space, we see a small and fragile ball dominated not by human activity and edifice but by a pattern of clouds, oceans, greenery, and soils. Humanity's inability to fit its doings into that pattern is changing planetary systems, fundamentally. Many such changes are accompanied by life-threatening hazards. This new reality, from which there is no escape, must be recognized—and managed.

Fortunately, this new reality coincides with more positive developments new to this century. We can move information and goods faster around the globe than ever before; we can produce more food and more goods with less investment of resources; our technology and science gives us at least the potential to look deeper into and better understand natural systems. From space, we can see and study the Earth as an organism whose health depends on the health of all its parts. We have the power to reconcile human affairs with natural laws and to thrive in the process. In this our cultural and spiritual heritages can reinforce our economic interests and survival imperatives.

This Commission believes that people can build a future that is more prosperous, more just, and more secure. Our report, *Our Common Future*, is not a prediction of ever-increasing environmental decay, poverty, and hardship in an ever more polluted world among ever-decreasing resources. We see instead the possibility for a new era of economic growth, one that must be based on policies that sustain and expand the environmental resource base. And we believe such growth to be absolutely essential to relieve the great poverty that is deepening in much of the developing world.

But the Commission's hope for the future is conditional on decisive political action now to begin managing environmental resources to ensure both sustainable human progress and human survival. We are not forecasting a future; we are serving a notice—an urgent notice based on the latest and best scientific evidence—that the time has come to take the decisions needed to secure the resources to sustain this and coming generations. We do not offer a detailed blueprint for action, but instead a pathway by which the peoples of the world may enlarge their spheres of co-operation.

I. The Global Challenge

SUCCESSES AND FAILURES

Those looking for success and signs of hope can find many: Infant mortality is falling; human life expectancy is increasing; the proportion of the world's adults who can read and write is climbing; the proportion of children starting school is rising; and global food production increases faster than the population grows.

But the same processes that have produced these gains have given rise to trends that the planet and its people cannot long bear. These have traditionally been divided into failures of 'development' and failures in the management of our human environment. On the development side, in terms of absolute numbers there are more hungry people in the world than ever before, and their numbers are increasing. So are the numbers who cannot read or write, the numbers without safe water or safe and sound homes, and the numbers short of woodfuel with which to cook and warm themselves. The gap between rich and poor nations is widening—not shrinking—and there is little prospect, given present trends and institutional arrangements, that this process will be reversed.

There are also environmental trends that threaten to radically alter the planet, that threaten the lives of many species upon it, including the human species. Each year another 6 million hectares of productive dryland turns into worthless desert. Over three decades, this would amount to an area roughly as large as Saudi Arabia. More than 11 million hectares of forests are destroyed yearly, and this, over three decades, would equal an area about the size of India. Much of this forest is converted to low-grade farmland unable to support the farmers who settle it. In Europe, acid precipitation kills forests and lakes and damages the artistic and architectural heritage of nations; it may have acidified vast tracts of soil beyond reasonable hope of repair. The burning of fossil fuels puts into the atmosphere carbon dioxide, which is causing gradual global warming. This 'greenhouse effect' may by early next century have increased average global temperatures enough to shift agricultural production areas, raise sea levels to flood coastal cities, and disrupt national economies. Other industrial gases threaten to deplete the planet's protective ozone shield to such an extent that the number of human and animal cancers would rise sharply and the oceans' food chain would be disrupted. Industry and agriculture put toxic substances into the human food chain and into underground water tables beyond reach of cleansing.

There has been a growing realization in national governments and multilateral institutions that it is impossible to separate economic development issues from environment issues; many forms of development erode the environmental resource upon which they must be based, and environmental degradation can undermine economic development. Poverty is a major cause and effect of global environmental problems. It is therefore futile to attempt to deal with environmental problems without a broader perspective that encompasses the factors underlying world poverty and international inequality.

The World Commission on Environment and Development first met in October 1984, and published its report 900 days later, in April 1987. Over those few days:

- The drought-triggered, environment-development crisis in Africa peaked, putting 35 million people at risk, killing perhaps a million.
- A leak from a pesticides factory in Bhopal, India, killed more than 2,000 people and blinded and injured over 200,000 more.
- Liquid gas tanks exploded in Mexico City, killing 1,000 and leaving thousands more homeless.
- The Chernobyl nuclear reactor explosion sent nuclear fallout across Europe, increasing the risks of future human cancers.
- Agricultural chemicals, solvents, and mercury flowed into the Rhine River during a warehouse fire in Switzerland, killing millions of fish and threatening drinking water in the Federal Republic of Germany and the Netherlands.
- An estimated 60 million people died of diarrhoeal diseases related to unsafe drinking water and malnutrition; most of the victims were children.

These concerns were behind the establishment in 1983 of the World Commission on Environment and Development by the UN General Assembly. The Commission is an independent body, linked to but outside the control of governments and the UN system. The Commission's mandate gave it three objectives: to re-examine the critical environment and development issues and to formulate realistic proposals for dealing with them; to propose new forms of international co-operation on these issues that will influence policies and events in the direction of needed changes; and to raise the levels of understanding and commitment to action of individuals, voluntary organizations, businesses, institutes, and governments.

Through our deliberations and the testimony of people at the public hearings we held on five continents, all the commissioners came to focus on one central theme: many present development trends leave increasing numbers of people poor and vulnerable, while at the same time degrading the environment. How can such development serve next century's world of twice as many people relying on the same environment? This realization broadened our view of development. We came to see it not in its restricted context of economic growth in developing countries. We came to see that a new development path was required, one that sustained human progress not just in a few places for a few years, but for the entire planet into the distant future. Thus 'sustainable development' becomes a goal not just for the 'developing' nations, but for industrial ones as well.

THE INTERLOCKING CRISES

Until recently, the planet was a large world in which human activities and their effects were neatly compartmentalized within nations, within sectors (energy, agriculture, trade), and within broad areas of concern (environmental, economic, social). These compartments have begun to dissolve. This applies in particular to the various global 'crises' that have seized public concern, particularly over the past decade. These are not separate crises: an environmental crisis, a development crisis, an energy crisis. They are all one.

The planet is passing through a period of dramatic growth and fundamental change. Our human world of 5 billion must make room in a finite environment for another human world. The population could stabilize at between 8 billion and 14 billion sometime next century, according to UN projections. More than 90 per cent of the increase will occur in the poorest countries, and 90 per cent of that growth in already bursting cities.

Economic activity has multiplied to create a $13 trillion world economy, and this could grow five- or tenfold in the coming half-century. Industrial production has grown more than fiftyfold over the past century, four-fifths of this growth since 1950. Such figures reflect and presage profound impacts upon the biosphere, as the world invests in houses, transport, farms, and industries. Much of the economic growth pulls raw material from forests, soils, seas, and waterways.

A mainspring of economic growth is new technology, and while this technology offers the potential for slowing the dangerously rapid consumption of finite resources, it also entails high risks, including new forms of pollution and the introduction to the planet of new variations of life forms that could change evolutionary pathways. Meanwhile, the industries most heavily reliant on environmental resources and most heavily polluting are growing most rapidly in the developing world, where there is both more urgency for growth and less capacity to minimize damaging side effects.

These related changes have locked the global economy and global ecology together in new ways. We have in the past been concerned about the impacts of economic growth upon the environment. We are now forced to concern ourselves with the impacts of ecological stress—degradation of soils, water regimes, atmosphere, and forests—upon our economic prospects. We have in the more recent past been forced to face up to a sharp increase in economic interdependence among nations. We are now forced to accustom ourselves to an accelerating ecological interdependence among nations. Ecology and economy are becoming ever more interwoven—locally, regionally, nationally, and globally—into a seamless net of causes and effects.

Impoverishing the local resource base can impoverish wider areas: Deforestation by highland farmers causes flooding on lowland farms; factory pollution robs local fishermen of their catch. Such grim local cycles now operate nationally and regionally. Dryland degradation sends environmental refugees in their millions across national borders. Deforestation in Latin America and Asia is causing more floods, and more destructive floods, in downhill, downstream nations. Acid precipitation and nuclear fallout have spread across the borders of Europe. Similar phenomena are emerging on a global scale, such as global warming and loss of ozone. Internationally traded hazardous chemicals entering foods are themselves internationally traded. In the next century, the environmental pressure causing population movements may increase sharply, while barriers to that movement may be even firmer than they are now.

Over the past few decades, life-threatening environmental concerns have surfaced in the developing world. Countrysides are coming under pressure from increasing numbers of farmers and the landless. Cities are filling with people, cars, and factories. Yet at the same time these developing countries must operate in a world in which the resources gap between most developing and industrial nations is widening, in which the industrial world dominates in the rule-making of some key international bodies, and in which the industrial world has already used much of the planet's ecological capital. This inequality is the planet's main 'environmental' problem; it is also its main 'development' problem.

International economic relationships pose a particular problem for environmental management in many developing countries. Agriculture, forestry, energy production, and mining generate at least half the gross national product of many developing countries and account for even larger shares of livelihoods and employment. Exports of natural resources remain a large factor in their economies, especially for the least developed. Most of these countries face enormous economic pressures, both international and domestic, to overexploit their environmental resource base.

The recent crisis in Africa best and most tragically illustrates the ways in which economics and ecology can interact destructively and trip into disaster. Triggered by drought, its real causes lie deeper. They are to be found in part in national policies that gave too little attention, too late, to the needs of smallholder agriculture and to the threats posed by rapidly rising populations. Their roots extend also to a global economic system that takes more out of a poor continent than it puts in. Debts that they cannot pay force African nations relying on commodity sales to overuse their fragile soils, thus turning good land to desert. Trade barriers in the wealthy nations—and in many developing ones—make it hard for Africans to sell their goods for reasonable returns, putting yet more pressure on ecological systems. Aid from donor nations has not only been inadequate in scale, but too often has reflected the priorities of the nations giving the aid, rather than the needs of the recipients. The production base of other developing world areas suffers similarly both from local failures and from the workings of international economic systems. As a consequence of the 'debt crisis' of Latin America, that region's natural resources are now being used not for development but to meet financial obligations to creditors abroad. This approach to the debt problem is short-sighted from several standpoints: economic, political, and environmental. It requires relatively poor countries simultaneously to accept growing poverty while exporting growing amounts of scarce resources.

A majority of developing countries now have lower per capita incomes than when the decade began. Rising poverty and unemployment have increased pressure on environmental resources as more people have been forced to rely more directly upon them. Many governments have cut back efforts to protect the environment and to bring ecological considerations into development planning.

The deepening and widening environmental crisis presents a threat to national security—and even survival—that may be greater than well-armed, ill-disposed neighbours and unfriendly alliances. Already in parts of Latin America, Asia, the Middle East, and Africa, environmental decline is becoming a source of political unrest and international tension. The recent destruction of much of Africa's dryland agricultural production was more severe than if an invading army had pursued a scorched-earth policy. Yet most of the affected governments still spend far more to protect their people from invading armies than from the invading desert.

Globally, military expenditures total about $1 trillion a year and continue to grow. In many countries, military spending consumes such a high proportion of gross national product that it itself does great damage to these societies' development efforts. Governments tend to base their approaches to 'security' on traditional definitions. This is most obvious in the attempts to achieve security through the development of potentially planet-destroying nuclear weapons systems. Studies suggest that the cold and dark nuclear winter following even a limited nuclear war could destroy plant and animal ecosystems and leave any human survivors occupying a devastated planet very different from the one they inherited.

The arms race—in all parts of the world—pre-empts resources that might be used more productively to diminish the security threats created by environmental conflict and the resentments that are fuelled by widespread poverty.

Many present efforts to guard and maintain human progress, to meet human needs, and to realize human ambitions are simply unsustainable—in both the rich and poor nations. They draw too heavily, too quickly, on already overdrawn environmental resource accounts to be affordable far into the future without bankrupting those accounts. They may show profits on the balance sheets of our generation, but our children will inherit the losses. We borrow environmental capital from future generations with no intention or prospect of repaying. They may damn us for our spendthrift ways, but they can never collect on our debt to them. We act as we do because we can get away with it: future generations do not vote; they have no political or financial power; they cannot challenge our decisions.

But the results of the present profligacy are rapidly closing the options for future generations. Most of today's decision makers will be dead before the planet feels the heavier effects of acid precipitation, global warming, ozone depletion, or widespread desertification and species loss. Most of the young voters of today will still be alive. In the Commission's hearings it was the young, those who have the most to lose, who were the harshest critics of the planet's present management.

SUSTAINABLE DEVELOPMENT

Humanity has the ability to make development sustainable—to ensure that it meets the needs of the present without compromising the ability of future generations to meet their own needs. The concept of sustainable development does imply limits—not absolute limits but limitations imposed by the present state of technology and social organization on environmental resources and by the ability of the biosphere to absorb the effects of human activities. But technology and social organization can be both managed and improved to make way for a new era of economic growth. The Commission believes that widespread poverty is no longer inevitable. Poverty is not only an evil in itself, but sustainable development requires meeting the basic needs of all and extending to all the opportunity to fulfil their aspirations for a better life. A world in which poverty is endemic will always be prone to ecological and other catastrophes.

Meeting essential needs requires not only a new era of economic growth for nations in which the majority are poor, but an assurance that those poor get their fair share of the resources required to sustain that growth. Such equity would be aided by political systems that secure

The Commission has sought ways in which global development can be put on a sustainable path into the twenty-first century. Some 5,000 days will elapse between the publication of our report and the first day of the twenty-first century. What environmental crises lie in store over those 5,000 days?

During the 1970s, twice as many people suffered each year from 'natural' disasters as during the 1960s. The disasters most directly associated with environment/development mismanagement—droughts and floods—affected the most people and increased most sharply in terms of numbers affected. Some 18.5 million people were affected by drought annually in the 1960s, 24.4 million in the 1970s. There were 5.2 million flood victims yearly in the 1960s, 15.4 million in the 1970s. Numbers of victims of cyclones and earthquakes also shot up as growing numbers of poor people built unsafe houses on dangerous ground.

The results are not in for the 1980s. But we have seen 35 million afflicted by drought in Africa alone and tens of millions affected by the better managed and thus less-publicized Indian drought. Floods have poured off the deforested Andes and Himalayas with increasing force. The 1980s seem destined to sweep this dire trend on into a crisis-filled 1990s.

effective citizen participation in decision making and by greater democracy in international decision making.

Sustainable global development requires that those who are more affluent adopt life-styles within the planet's ecological means—in their use of energy, for example. Further, rapidly growing populations can increase the pressure on resources and slow any rise in living standards; thus sustainable development can only be pursued if population size and growth are in harmony with the changing productive potential of the ecosystem.

Yet in the end, sustainable development is not a fixed state of harmony, but rather a process of change in which the exploitation of resources, the direction of investments, the orientation of technological development, and institutional change are made consistent with future as well as present needs. We do not pretend that the process is easy or straightforward. Painful choices have to be made. Thus, in the final analysis, sustainable development must rest on political will.

THE INSTITUTIONAL GAPS

The objective of sustainable development and the integrated nature of the global environment/development challenges pose problems for institutions, national and international, that were established on the basis of narrow preoccupations and compartmentalized concerns. Governments' general response to the speed and scale of global changes has been a reluctance to recognize sufficiently the need to change themselves. The challenges are both interdependent and integrated, requiring comprehensive approaches and popular participation.

Yet most of the institutions facing those challenges tend to be independent, fragmented, working to relatively narrow mandates with closed decision processes. Those responsible for managing natural resources and protecting the environment are institutionally separated from those responsible for managing the economy. The real world of interlocked economic and ecological systems will not change; the policies and institutions concerned must.

There is a growing need for effective international co-operation to manage ecological and economic interdependence. Yet at the same time, confidence in international organizations is diminishing and support for them dwindling.

The other great institutional flaw in coping with environment/development challenges is governments' failure to make the bodies whose policy actions degrade the environment responsible for ensuring that their policies prevent that degradation. Environmental concern arose from damage caused by the rapid economic growth following the Second World War. Governments, pressured by their citizens, saw a need to clean up the mess, and they established environmental ministries and agencies to do this. Many had great success—within the limits of their mandates—in improving air and water quality and enhancing other resources. But much of their work has of necessity been after-the-fact repair of damage; *re*forestation, *re*claiming desert lands, *re*building urban environments, *re*storing natural habitats, and *re*habilitating wild lands.

The existence of such agencies gave many governments and their citizens the false impression that these bodies were by themselves able to protect and enhance the environmental resource base. Yet many industrialized and most developing countries carry huge economic burdens from inherited problems such as air and water pollution, depletion of ground-water, and the proliferation of toxic chemicals and hazardous wastes. These have been joined by more recent problems—erosion, desertification, acidification, new chemicals, and new forms of waste—that are directly related to agricultural, industrial, energy, forestry, and transportation policies and practices.

The mandates of the central economic and sectoral ministries are also often too narrow, too concerned with quantities of production or growth. The mandates of ministries of industry include production targets, while the accompanying pollution is left to ministries of environment. Electricity boards produce power, while the acid pollution they also produce is left to other bodies to clean up. The present challenge is to give the central economic and sectoral ministries the responsibility for the quality of those parts of the human environment affected by their decisions, and to give the environmental agencies more power to cope with the effects of unsustainable development.

The same need for change holds for international agencies concerned with development lending, trade regulation, agricultural development, and so on. These have been slow to take the environmental effects of their work into account, although some are trying to do so.

The ability to anticipate and prevent environmental damage requires that the ecological dimensions of policy be considered at the same time as the economic, trade, energy, agricultural, and other dimensions. They should be considered on the same agendas and in the same national and international institutions.

This reorientation is one of the chief institutional challenges of the 1990s and beyond. Meeting it will require major institutional development and reform. Many countries that are too poor or small or that have limited managerial capacity will find it difficult to do this unaided. They will need financial and technical assistance and training. But the changes required involve all countries, large and small, rich and poor.

19 Sustainable Development: A New(ish) Idea for a New Century?

James Meadowcroft

It is an intriguing fact of late twentieth century life that just at the time when philosophers had proclaimed the final death of 'meta-narratives', the collapse of grand modernist dreams for re-moulding man and society and consciously shaping the human future—indeed, even the end of 'history' itself—international political leaders have come to identify themselves with an ambitious new project intended to act as the focus of human endeavour in the twenty-first century. This new project is 'sustainable development', and over the past decade international organizations, national governments, and local authorities have increasingly come to cite it as a fundamental objective of their activity.

In this article I would like to explore the character of this 'turn' towards sustainable development—particularly in relation to environmental policy-making in the industrialized countries.[1] The discussion will be organized in four parts. It will open with a conceptual and historical introduction to the notion of sustainable development. It will then move on to consider how the idea has been taken up practically by governments in developed states. The significance of the changes effected to date will form the focus for the third section. Finally some general observations will be offered about the (admittedly relatively brief) 'career' of sustainable development.

1. Sustainable Development: A Brief Introduction

Brought to international attention by the Report of the World Commission on Environment and Development (WCED) in 1987, sustainable development was formally endorsed by political leaders from more than a hundred and seventy countries at the Rio Earth Summit in 1992.[2] The WCED did not coin the expression 'sustainable development',[3] but it provided the term with a plausible content and a heady dose of legitimacy. Noting that a large proportion of the world's population still lived in poverty, that there were grave disparities in patterns of resource use between rich and poor countries, and that global ecosystems were already suffering acute stress, it called for an international consensus to re-orient economic activity in order to privilege the urgent developmental needs of the poor and to prevent irreversible damage to the global environment. For developing countries it proposed 'a new era of growth' to address poverty and under-development; for the more industrialized states it envisaged an intensive

From *Political Studies*, 48 (2000), 370–87.

effort to increase energy and materials efficiencies and to shift economic activity onto less environmentally-burdensome lines. What was required was that all countries commit themselves to making development 'sustainable'. In a now famous passage the Report explained that sustainable development was:

development that meets the needs of the present without compromising the ability of future generations to meet their own needs. It contains within it two key concepts: the concept of 'needs', in particular the essential needs of the world's poor, to which overriding priority should be given; and the idea of limitations imposed by the state of technology and social organization in the environment's ability to meet present and future needs.[4]

Although the Report was written 'by committee', and contains inconsistencies and contradictions typical of outputs of such a process, it was crafted carefully to accommodate various constituencies. The fundamental normative idea—that human societies will continue their quest for a better life, but that in doing so they should give priority to meeting the basic needs of the poor, while taking care not to 'foul the pond' for future generations—was intuitively appealing. Moreover, it appeared to offer a way out of the 'growth versus environment' polarity which typified environmental debate during the 1970s and early 1980s. It suggested that it was not a question of a choice *between* environmental protection and social advance, but rather a problem of selecting patterns of economic and social development compatible with sound environmental stewardship. The notion was one which could appeal to countries of both North and South—reflecting growing environmental awareness in the former, and the urgent development concerns of the latter.

Since memory of historical contexts is notoriously fickle, it is worth emphasizing that at the time the WCED was active there was grave concern about the debt crisis and economic stagnation in many poorer countries. The global consequences of environmental destruction were beginning to be widely perceived. Moreover East/West tension continued to preoccupy international decision makers. Sustainable development was therefore explicitly formulated as a '*bridging*' concept—as an idea that could draw together apparently distinct policy domains, and unite very different interests behind a common agenda. The title of the Report (*Our Common Future*) and those of its major sections ('Common Concerns', 'Common Challenges' and 'Common Endeavours') were meant in all seriousness—not as some later commentators have implied as a naive denial of opposed perspectives and interests; but rather as a deliberate attempt to transcend differences, construct shared understandings, and build a winning coalition for reform.

Key features of the approach championed by the WCED include the fact that it:

- focused on how to sustain a broad process of positive social change called 'development'. Such 'development' was understood as an advance in the material and moral circumstances of humanity—in a word, 'progress';
- employed the idea of 'meeting needs' to characterize the just aspirations of all peoples, but most particularly to emphasize the legitimate moral claims of (i) the world's poor and (ii) future generations. This priority on the needs of the poor, and the proviso that the ability of

future generations to meet their needs must not be compromised, help define the nature of those authentic forms of 'development' which were to be styled 'sustainable';

• invoked an idea of environmental limits as a potentially serious obstacle to continued social advance. The authors stressed that the environment's capacity to support human activity was not fixed in any simple way—different limits held for different resources, and improved technologies and social organization could enhance environmental carrying capacity. But they also affirmed that there were 'ultimate limits', and they argued that in some cases these environmental limits had already been breached by human activity.

It is important to note that because what is to be sustained in sustainable development is the *process* of improvement rather than any particular institution, practice or environment, an activity that is not itself sustainable could be a part—even an essential part—of an ongoing movement that was sustainable. Thus patterns of production, consumption, investment, or behaviour which could not be continued into the indefinite future can be components of a process of social development that might be so continued. In other words, because sustainable development focuses upon the maintenance of developmental momentum, it does not necessarily entail the preservation either of existing environmental systems or of prevailing social structures and practices. On the contrary, 'development' implies the potential transformation of both. Of course, without the preservation of much—in terms of planetary life support systems and environmental resources (but also in terms of valued social institutions and practices)—continued improvement would be unimaginable. But just what should be preserved and what should be altered is open to argument. Moreover, the boundaries of what can or must be preserved/changed will undoubtedly shift over time as the nature of society, configurations of natural systems, and their inter-relation evolve.

Following publication of the Brundtland Report sustainable development was relatively quickly taken up by national governments as well as by an array of international organizations. Definitions of sustainable development have proliferated, and 'sustainable' and 'sustainability' came to be coupled with a vast array of other terms.[5] Over time, the mainstream understanding of sustainable development has evolved somewhat: it has become common to stress the tri-une nature of the concept (that economic, social and environmental factors must be assessed together); the idea of 'participation' in environment and development decision-making has been increasingly emphasized; and the notion of 'the common but differentiated responsibilities' of countries of the North and the South has been more explicitly formulated.[6] On the practical side, the Earth Summit agreements (including the Rio Declaration on Environment and Development, the Climate Change Convention, the Biodiversity Convention, and Agenda 21) have been taken to represent an international 'consensus' around the sort of orientation required to make sustainable development a reality.[7] Yet despite this evolution, the basic understanding of sustainable development formulated in the Brundtland report has continued to anchor subsequent international discussion.

As one might expect, as an idea which was formulated deliberately to function as a new norm for global conduct,[8] sustainable development has been subject to a wealth of criticism. Many environmentalists have decried its 'anthropocentrism', deploring the fact that it unashamedly takes the promotion of human welfare as its central value. They argue that rather than worrying about sustaining development, we should be more concerned with sustaining the natural environment.[9] Moreover they complain that the term obscures the essential contradiction between environmental limits and the modern growth economy. On the other hand, 'developmental' critics have argued that sustainable development is little more than a crude attempt to impose a Northern environmental agenda on the South—forcing countries whose primary concern should be economic advance to adopt inappropriate environmental measures which are really intended to protect the economic hegemony of the industrialized states or to assuage the environmental consciences of rich consumers. Within the social sciences, energy has been deployed in definitional arguments, in teasing out logical inconsistencies of the idea, or in attempting to establish whether or not the term adds something to existing technical vocabularies.[10] Many commentators have decried the ambiguities associated with sustainable development. Some have suggested the term is so vacuous that it could be invoked to justify virtually any policy. Others have complained that there are no incontestable procedures for operationalizing sustainable development in terms of policy priorities. These last criticisms are misplaced. To be precise, they fail to understand that conceptual ambiguities and competing decontestations are the staple of political argument; nor do they appreciate that the WCED deliberately construed (or 'designed') sustainable development in open-textured terms. Sustainable development was not formulated as either a logical construct or an operational maxim—but rather as a potentially unifying political meta-objective, with a suggestive normative core. As this core has been passed down in the international process extending through UNCED to its follow ups (such as the United Nations Commission on Sustainable Development, and the 1997 General Assembly Special Session to Review the Implementation of Agenda 21) it has been understood to embody ideas about promoting human well-being, meeting the basic needs of the poor and protecting the welfare of future generations (intra- and inter-generational justice), preserving environmental resources and global life-support systems (respecting limits), integrating economics and environment in decision-making, and encouraging popular participation in development processes.

2. Government Engagement with Sustainable Development in the Industrialized Countries

More than a decade after the publication of the Brundtland Report the notion of sustainable development has now been accepted into governmental idiom in many developed countries. A recent study of the responses of ten governments in the industrial world to the coming of sustainable development found that, with the exception of the USA, all of the central governments examined regularly invoked the idea of 'sustainable development' to characterize policy orientations.[11] The term appears in prominent statements of government intent, in the publications of official agencies and advisory bodies, and in national plans and strategy documents. Increasingly it is enshrined in legislative enactments. In the UK, for example, sustainable development has been integrated into the guidance central authorities give for local land use planning; it is included in the official remit of the newly created Environment Agencies; and it lies at the core of a strategy process which is intended to systematize and assess achievement with regard to environmental objectives. In Sweden sustainable development has appeared in several important laws, it helps define the objectives of the new Environmental Code, and it has recently served as the focus for a major (£2 billion) spending programme by the Social Democrat administration.[12]

While central governments place varying degrees of emphasis on sustainable development, and highlight slightly different dimensions of the concept, they typically relate their understanding explicitly to the Brundtland Commission and to the UNCED process and its follow ups. The theme of protecting the global environment is all pervasive; so too is the idea of integrating environment and economy in decision-making at all levels of society: when sustainable development is invoked, this much is almost always implied.

Environment ministries and agencies have generally taken the lead in engaging with the idea, but departments concerned with natural resources, industry, agriculture and transport have increasingly become active. Foreign ministries and international development agencies have also been involved in the externally focused dimensions of sustainable development. Some governments have specified that all branches of the central administration must review their operations in light of the new paradigm. In Canada, for example, federal government departments are now required to produce sustainable development plans every four years; and these plans are periodically audited by the newly created Parliamentary Commissioner for the Environment and Sustainable Development.[13] Governments have also set up a wide range of advisory, consultative, educational, and research bodies intended to assist the generation of the policy response, to raise public awareness of the issue, and to draw major actors into dialogue over the implications of sustainable development. For example, in the UK there have been organizations such as the British Government Panel on Sustainable Development, the UK Roundtable on Sustainable Development, and Going for Green. Norway has set up a National Committee for International Environmental Issues, the Centre for Sustainable Production and Consumption (GRIP), and the Environmental Home Guard.

Much of what governments have done in the name of sustainable development constitutes a 're-packaging' of traditional pollution control and nature conservation activities. Measures to improve air quality, to strengthen flood defences, to encourage energy efficiency, or to protect endangered species are hardly new—but all now figure in governmental accounts of their action for sustainable development. This cannot simply be dismissed as a cynical public relations exercise. When presented as part of a larger social effort directed at sustainable development traditional environmental programmes acquire a new rationale. And clearly their continuation is a necessary—if not a sufficient—condition for pursuing sustainable development. But in addition to such efforts at 'reinterpretation', governmental engagement with sustainable development in industrialized countries has been accompanied by a series of new initiatives related to the management of domestic environmental burdens.

There has been reform to *structures and procedures* of governance, designed to integrate environmental problem-solving into the workings of the main branches of the public administration. It has been accepted—at least in principle—that environmental policy can not operate as a *post hoc* corrective to normal (that is non-environmental) decision processes; rather the environmental dimension should be factored-in from the outset. Thus responsibility for environmental performance cannot remain the exclusive concern of a specialized ministry of the environment, but must be shared across the administration—in much the same way that the budgetary implications of policy cannot be left to the finance ministry, but must inform decision-making throughout government. In Norway reforms to formalize the responsibilities of sectoral ministries for environmental performance were introduced in 1988.[14] In Sweden such cross governmental responsibility was promoted by the Environment Bills of 1987/88 and 1990/91. In the UK a system of 'green ministers' was established whereby a junior-minister in each major department had responsibility for monitoring environmental performance. In Norway and the UK high level committees were also established to co-ordinate environmental decision-making across government (in Norway, the State Secretaries Committee on Environmental Issues; and in the UK, the Cabinet Committee on the Environment). In many countries this 'sectoral integration' of environmental management functions has been linked to broader efforts to promote 'green' government—for example, by improving the environmental performance of public bodies with respect to energy budgets, recycling, waste disposal, and transport. Public procurement policies have also been identified as a key route to leverage environmental gains. Examples here include Japan's 'Action Plan for Greening Government Operation' and the Swedish 'Green Purchasing Initiative'.

Another important change has been the tendency to initiate more comprehensive *strategy and planning processes* focused on the environment and sustainable development. In 1992, for example, Australia issued a National Strategy for Ecologically Sustainable Development (NSESD) which had been prepared on the basis of substantial public inputs and which signalled a new phase of State/Commonwealth co-operation in the environmental field.[15] Japan published its first Environment Basic Plan in 1994 under the provisions of its new Environment Basic Law. The Netherlands has adopted the most comprehensive and systematic planning regime through the three (and a half) environmental policy plans that have been adopted since 1989.[16] A somewhat different approach has been taken in Norway where, rather than preparing a formal plan, the government has issued a series of authoritative statements to parliament to orient sustainable development policy and has integrated environmental issues into the state budget planning routines. The Swedish government has also issued periodic strategy statements, and a sustainable development plan prepared by the Swedish Environmental Protection Agency has dealt with issues under this organization's remit.

By the close of the decade a substantial majority of OECD countries had launched some form of national environment or sustainable development strategy process.[17] In comparison with earlier ventures in environmental policy-making these plans and strategies adopt a more comprehensive approach, attempting to propose management options for a significant proportion of environmental burdens within the national territory. They also have substantial integrative ambitions: the idea is to match biophysical and social inter-dependencies with analytical, regulatory, and remedial strategies based on cross-disciplinary, cross-sectoral and cross-jurisdictional action. They adopt a longer range approach—focusing directly on the next 4 or 5 years, but considering possible scenarios 20 or 30 years into the future. Furthermore, the idea of 'sustainable development' provides a key conceptual anchor for these plans and strategies, furnishing a context for the integration of environment and economic decision making and emphasizing a pre-occupation with the life support and amenity functions of the environment, and a concern with the needs of future generations. Yet despite a common form and substantive points of similarity, these exercises are in other respects quite different. Important dimensions of variation include the range of issues brought within the strategy framework, the legal and institutional basis of the process, the nature of the qualitative and quantitative goals, the 'one-shot' or iterative nature of the process, the forms of social participation involved in plan development, and the degree of ongoing political salience.[18] In addition to such national plans, governments have also developed an extensive array of sectoral or thematic strategies for managing environmental burdens, including specific plans related to climate change and biodiversity. Recent additions in the UK, for example, include Local Environment Agency Plans (LEAPs),[19] and integrated transport plans being drafted by local authorities.

Another trend associated with sustainable development has been the effort to employ more systematic mechanisms for *measuring environmental effects, and monitoring the impacts of policy*. Compared with the situation in the mid-eighties considerable progress has been made with respect to 'state of the environment' reporting, the inclusion of environmental impacts into satellite national accounts, and the design of indicators. Work at the OECD and UN system organizations has popularized the pressure/state/response approach to sustainable development indicators, and governments are now increasing their capacity to track environment and development trends. The formal adoption of sustainable development as a policy objective, its emphasis on combining environmental, economic and social assessment, as well as a general political climate favouring performance measures in the public service, have encouraged this move towards quantitative monitoring. The entry into force of the Climate Change and Biodiversity Conventions have strengthened this trend, particularly with respect to source and sink inventories for greenhouse gases, and registers of biodiversity. From the early 1990s the UK has, for example, gradually committed itself to an increasing range of environmental performance measures. The Labour government recently proposed a set of 'headline' sustainable development indicators which in draft form included items for economic growth, social investment, employment, health, education and training, housing quality, climate change, air pollution, transport, water quality, wildlife, land use, and waste.[20] Recently the German Environment Ministry proposed an 'Environment-Barometer for Germany' which includes indicators and targets for six crucial environmental policy areas related to sustainable development: air quality (SO_2, NO_x, NH_3 and VOC emissions—with a 70 per cent reduction target for the period 1990–2010); soil (the increase in the area covered by human settlement and traffic routes—with the aim of reducing this increase from 120 hectares per day in 1997 to 30 hectares per day in 2020); nature protection ('ecological priority areas'—with a target to preserve 10–15 per cent of the land unsettled in 1998 to form a biotope network by 2020); water (chemical quality class—with a target that by 2020 all water will meet specified standards); energy productivity (GNP per unit of primary energy consumption—to be doubled between 1990 and 2020); and raw materials (GNP per ton of materials—to be increased 2.5 times from 1993 to 2020).[21]

There has also been movement with respect to the *policy instruments* invoked to secure environmental gains. While it is undoubtedly true that the core of environmental governance has been—and remains—regulatory (based around fixing standards, issuing permits, and legal enforcement), the coming of sustainable development has been linked to more negotiated or co-operative approaches. This has been taken furthest in the Netherlands where an intricate network of 'covenants' between the authorities and economic 'target groups' commit the latter to realize specified environmental objectives within a fixed time frame.[22] Other countries have not followed the Netherlands in adopting so formal or comprehensive an approach to environmental agreements, but there has nevertheless been a broad proliferation of negotiative frameworks where public and private bodies interact to generate agreed approaches to sustainable development-related issues.[23] Another change has been an increased willingness to use taxes and charges to leverage environmental gains. Modest carbon charges have been imposed in a number of the smaller European countries including the Netherlands, Norway and Sweden. In the UK the Conservative government of the mid-1990s introduced a landfill tax and fuel price escalator, and the Labour government is now carrying forward ideas for urban road-use and parking fees. The new German government has also taken recent (hesitant) steps towards 'ecological tax reform'.[24]

These are some of the more prominent innovations which governments have presented as part of their 'turn' towards sustainable development, but there are other noteworthy elements including:

- programmes to improve energy and material efficiencies, to increase re-cycling and improve waste management—particularly those involving ideas for radically increasing factor productivity ('Factor 4' or 'Factor 10'),[25] implementing product life-cycle management (from design to disposal) or ecocycle approaches (as in the 1993 Swedish Ecocycle legislation);
- the encouragement of 'sustainable cities' and 'Local Agenda 21' initiatives, focused on economic and social regeneration and managing the environmental loadings of urban living;[26]
- a more systematic effort to develop institutions for international environmental governance;
- the 'greening' of international aid, by vetting development assistance programmes and projects; and
- the extension of activities and initiatives linked to the two major international conventions associated with sustainable development and the UNCED process—the Climate Change Convention and the Convention on Biodiversity.

3. Substance or Hyperbole?

In the proceeding section I have argued: first, that over the last decade the idea of sustainable development has to some significant degree been accepted into the politico-administrative vocabulary in many of the developed countries; and second, that sustainable development has been associated with a number of changes in the approach to environmental governance. Of course, causal links are hard to untangle here. It is difficult to prove that it is because governments began to talk of sustainable development that they then went on to adopt specific policies. What they are now describing as an orientation towards sustainable development is a complex mix of things that were already being done (but which have now been redescribed in terms of sustainable development), new things which they might have done anyway (but which can be conveniently brought under the new label), and other initiatives which are more directly related to the international discussion of sustainable development. Nevertheless, the practical result is that since the late 1980s the idea of sustainable development has been linked by central governments to a broad portfolio of policies and initiatives. The fact that jurisdictions where the language of sustainable development has *not* been taken up are also those where practical activities of the kind described above are weak or absent is also suggestive. The USA is a case in point here: for it is not just that the term sustainable development has failed to make a mark on the US scene, but also that principles and approaches which (in other countries) have been associated with sustainable development have not—at least in terms of national politics—won widespread acceptance.[27]

One way to approach an assessment of the significance of this turn towards sustainable development is to consider the extent to which the perspectives and policies presented by governments actually embody the elements of the concept as it has been elaborated through international discussion. Looking at what governments in the industrialized countries have done so far, it is possible to identify three major elements which capture how sustainable development has been understood: first, the integration of environment and economy in decision making; second, the expansion of societal participation in environmental management; and third, the internationalization of environmental policy making. Each of these elements is present in the idea of sustainable development as it has been elaborated through the UNCED process, and each has been consistently emphasized by national governments. With respect to *'integration'*, the merging of environmental concerns into the responsibilities of line ministries discussed above is significant. But here the term is used in a wider sense to denote the various ways in which the environmental dimension can be factored into societal decision-making at all levels. This includes integrated assessment and management of environmental burdens across media (air, water, land), the integration of environment into the concerns of public bodies at all levels (for example in land use planning), the widened deployment of environmental impact assessment, the development of eco-audits and eco-accounting, and other measures to encourage economic agents (producers and consumers) to consider environmental consequences. With respect to *'societal participation'*, sound environmental governance has been held to imply increasingly complex patterns of public and private co-operation. The idea of 'partnership' has been regularly invoked to capture the extension of dialogue and collaboration to manage the interaction of economic, social and environmental factors as society comes to terms with the implications of sustainable development. With respect to *'internationalization'* key developments include: government participation in an ever more dense array of international regimes and negotiating processes intended to manage global environmental burdens; development of regional environmental accords (including the NAFTA side agreement and the extension of European Union competence into the environmental field); the formulation by governments of more explicit environmental foreign policy goals; and the 'greening' of international development assistance.

The planning and strategy processes discussed in the previous section provide an illustration of how these three strands converge in practice. National plans and strategies have an obvious 'integrative' component. At the very least they have been drawn up on the basis of inter-ministerial consultation, and often they are sponsored by several ministries or by government as a whole. More broadly they facilitate the adjustment of political and economic actors to anticipated shifts in environmental pressures and policy orientations. The 'participative' strand is evident in the tendency for strategy processes to involve widening networks of social consultation—important to ensure their salience and acceptability. Finally, 'internationalization' is manifest in the extent to which objectives agreed in multi-lateral forums, and concern to fix national priorities for future rounds of cross national collaboration, are a prominent feature of such plans and strategies.

In contrast, other dimensions of sustainable development appear less obviously present in governmental responses in the industrialized world. Two elements stand out in particular: first, the rather weak engagement with the theme of *international equity*; and second, the muted effort to engage with the idea of transforming patterns of *consumption and production*. Although governments all refer to supporting economic progress in the developing world, only a few countries—such as the Netherlands and Sweden—have made public education around the 'solidarity' aspects of sustainable development a priority. Overall, international aid budgets fell throughout the 1990s, and the largest countries in particular—such as Germany, the UK, and Japan—have failed to meet the UN objective of allocating 0.7 per cent of GNP to international development assistance. Although governments have taken cautious steps to improve energy efficiencies and to encourage reductions in conventional pollutant loadings, they have hesitated to address broader issues of consumption and production.[28] From a sustainable development perspective both issues—international*ism* and consumption—are crucial. They relate to the particular responsibilities which rich countries are expected to assume—(a) to assist, not just the environmental clean up efforts, but also the legitimate developmental endeavours of the poor states, and (b) to reduce the overall burden, not just the rate of increase of the burden, they place on the global environment—so that room can be made for the increasing resource and sink requirements of a developing South.

Another way to approach the significance of governmental engagement with sustainable development is to consider the salience, scale and stability of the changes effected under the banner of this concept. How pertinent are the policies? How much has really altered? How lasting are the changes likely to be? Consider the four topics raised in the previous section. With respect to the integration of environmental concern across government, it is unclear how far the new structures and procedures have actually altered decision making in sectoral ministries. There is also the worry that cohesion of environmental policy *across* the sectors does not seems to have been secured. Moreover the role of the environment ministry in a government where everyone is (supposedly) concerned with environmental consequences remains unclear. The idea of an environmental 'super-ministry' riding-herd on other departments (as finance ministries sometimes do through their budget control functions) has not found favour. In some jurisdictions 'integration' has been almost entirely at the level of rhetoric—in Japan, for example, production oriented ministries and plans operate in parallel to organizations and plans centred on environmental sensitivity; and in the European Union the environment has remained marginal to key spending programmes such as the Common Agricultural Policy and the Structural Funds.[29] Elsewhere the integrative ideal has been more thoroughly pursued—in the Netherlands or Norway, for example. Yet generally, structures and procedures remain in flux. With respect to national planning and strategy processes a similar story can be told. Great variation exists among governments. Most initiatives remain relatively unstable. Canada, for example, tried a national Green Plan,[30] and a broad-based visioning exercise (the *'Projet de Société'*), before settling on the current departmental strategy regime. But the new system has yet to pass through a full cycle of planning/action/assessment, so judgements about its effectiveness or long term survival are premature. In Australia, a recent parliamentary review was sceptical about much of the governmental follow-up to the NSESD. Even in the Netherlands it is unclear whether NEPPs will remain a semi-permanent feature of Dutch politics, and debate continues about whether future plans should be merged with the land use planning system, or should incorporate other issues (such as international assistance). With respect to measurement, much of the work is exploratory, reliable runs of data have not yet accumulated, and specialized units remain vulnerable to periodic campaigns to reduce state expenditure. With respect to policy instruments, the jury is still out on the effectiveness of more inclusive and negotiated approaches. There is evidence that negotiations often result in stretched time frames and diluted environmental objectives; on the other hand, the Dutch covenants have succeeded in meeting many of their targets. Efforts to extend carbon taxes in Europe are frozen for now, and wider plans for 'ecological tax reform' have been slow to bear fruit. In short, a sceptic could claim that so far the salience, scale and stability of the reforms which have gone on under the banner of sustainable development are unimpressive.

Behind this discussion lurks an even broader question: to what extent are the policy responses elicited so far likely to lead to ultimate outcomes which are congruent with the long term objective of sustainable development? In other words, are the measures taken adequate to secure the stated objectives? To formulate a systematic strategy to address this question would take us well beyond scope of this essay. But the impressionistic evidence is not especially encouraging. If one considers the major sustainable development questions of climate change and biodiversity, the policy response so far has had a scarcely discernible impact on environmental loading across the OECD. Detailed mechanisms of the international climate change regime continue to be elaborated at successive Conferences Of the Parties, but most of the richest countries will fail to meet their original UNCED target of stabilizing emissions at 1990 levels by the year 2000. Those which do so will often have met the objective as a by-product of pursuing other (non climate related) ends.[31] It is not that policies implemented around climate change have failed to secure any emission reductions, but rather that efficiency gains have been swamped by emissions from increased economic activity (especially in the transport sector). As things stand, many countries will have serious difficulties achieving their Kyoto targets without heavy reliance on extra-territorial reductions secured under the Convention's 'flexibility mechanisms'. For its part, the Biodiversity Convention is not in good shape.[32] Despite progress in building up domestic competences on the issue in the industrialized countries, there is no discernible evidence 'on the ground' of any slowing in the pace of biodiversity loss globally, or in the developed world. Climate change has significant implications for biodiversity, but so too does the ever expanding space required by human activities. And in this regard the 'development' juggernaut continues to roll forward, even in the most environmentally conscious countries of the North.

4. Conclusion

The first part of this essay introduced the concept of sustainable development and described its entry into international political debate. The second considered how governments in industrially developed countries have engaged with sustainable development since it was popularized by the WCED in 1987. The third presented a tentative assessment of the character of this policy response. In conclusion I would like to offer some general reflections on the career of sustainable development to date. Clearly a comprehensive review of the impact of this idea would require examination of its reception by international bodies, by business and environmental groups in the developed countries, and by all levels of state and society in the developing world. Nevertheless, the more limited enquiry undertaken here can provide the basis for some observations.

The relatively rapid uptake of the idea of sustainable development by governments in the industrialized world is worth emphasizing once again. It is actually rather rare for a new normative concept to gain widespread cross-national acceptance—not just as a term of art deployed by international negotiators, or a specialist term accepted by a particular disciplinary or professional group—but as an idea that is absorbed into domestic political interchange across a variety of national polities. Yet sustainable development has achieved just such acceptance in little more than a decade. Remarkably, this is a notion which was explicitly formulated by an international body (but on the basis of ideas which were already rooted, or taking root, in certain national contexts and discursive communities), and which then proliferated 'downward' through transnational channels into national jurisdictions and sub-national politics.

Also of note is the sweeping nature of this ideational construct, which operates as a multidimensional bridging concept which links environment and development; local, national and international scales; present and future generations; efficiency and equity: government and societal actors; and so on. By combining notions of 'development' (which during the period after the Second World War became accepted as a central political objective for the poorer two thirds of the globe) and of the 'sustainable' (which during the 1970s became linked with environmental critiques of conventional social trajectories) the result has been a concept of broad sweep and ambition, which can be presented as a long term meta-objective of government.

Reasons for this relative 'success' include its rather open texture—which draws together key concerns about environment and development, while leaving ample room for different interests to contest their implications. Intimating both change and continuity, it urges the abandonment of inequitable and environmentally unsound practices while avoiding any suggestion of a direct assault on established centres of political and economic power. Strength is drawn from a core appeal to the notion of 'progress'—after all, it is the process of progressive social change called 'development' which is to be carried forward over time. Sustainable development therefore embodies an upbeat and positive message that contrasts with the perspectives of ecological (or developmental) doomsters.[33] Although the idea of progress has taken something of a beating during the twentieth century, and today intellectuals often like to snicker at the naive self-confidence of our Victorian fore-bearers, the idea of progress remains deeply embedded in our culture. The fact is, alternatives to progress are unpalatable. And sustainable development offers an image of progress suited to an increasingly inter-dependent world, where millions remain in poverty, and the rupture of ecological limits threatens future social advance. There is an underlying confidence in technological progress, but also a faith in the power of human reason to apprehend problems and to consciously remould social institutions and practices.[34] There is little doubt that the particular combination of concerns with equity and efficiency, growth and conservation, progress and stability, national responsibility and international co-operation displayed by sustainable development resonates strongly with the social democratic tradition. It is hardly coincidental that some of the more important figures involved in preparing the WCED report, as well as the countries which have taken up sustainable development with particular enthusiasm, are linked to social democracy. Yet sustainable development would not be the first normative idea to have had original affinities with one political tradition but later to have won acceptance across the ideological spectrum.

When considering the possible future of this concept—whether the discourse of sustainable development will (so to speak) turn out to be 'sustainable', or whether the idea will prove more ephemeral—it is worth keeping in mind that its resilience may be greater than many observers assume. Consider some of the charges levelled against the idea. One argument is that sustainable development needlessly complicates discussion of environmental issues by mixing together different sorts of problems—particularly by introducing issues of equity into the analysis of environmental burdens. Of course this appears to 'complicate' things—but the insight suggested by sustainable development is that equity issues *are already* entwined with the environmental problematic: that is to say, any approach to environmental management necessarily confronts distributional issues; and a refusal to engage with these simply results in an uncritical acceptance of received distributions of costs and benefits. A related charge is that sustainable development posits a simplistic relationship between poverty (or equity) and environmental sustainability, suggesting that poverty (or injustice) causes environmental destruction and that the elimination of poverty (or inequality or injustice) would therefore be good for the environment. There is no doubt that casual inter-linkages between poverty and environmental destruction are part of the sustainable development equation, but the main tenor of the Brundtland report was to link equity and the environment in another way. It argued that (a) there could be no valid moral foundation for refusing the peoples of the developing world the life chances offered to those in the rich countries; and (b) since human activities were already pressing on the frontiers of the environmentally sustainable; then (c) all countries should seek an alternative development trajectory which would bear more lightly on the planet; and (d) the rich countries had a particular responsibility to assist development in the South, while dramatically reducing their own environmental loadings. Parallel to this reasoning there was a similar chain of argument relating to the entitlements of future generations. In other words, equity was valued as an independent ideal (not primarily because of its 'functionality' for environmental sustainability); and considerations of equity, combined with observations about the environmental consequences of current economic activities, created imperatives for change.

Another line of criticism focuses on the human-centred character of 'sustainable development'—that sustaining the environment is *not* given centre stage. Several points can be made here. While human welfare is at the core of sustainable development, environmental concerns are clearly essential to its purview. First, and most obviously, the environment appears as a constraint on development decisions: environmental processes provide an essential foundation for human development, both in terms of broad planetary life-support systems, and the more specific environmental assets and amenities on which economic activity depends. Thus a substantial degree of environmental protection is required to keep development sustainable. Second, environmental issues are crucial to arguments about the character of authentic 'development'; specifically, with respect to determining the kinds of human/environment interaction that are most conductive to human well-being. A great range of preservationist measures can be justified as necessary to protect species, ecosystems and natural phenomena valued by humans and/or important for human welfare. Third, space can even be made to accommodate non-instrumental reasons for valuing nature: for it can be argued that authentic 'development' cannot be based on moral wrong, and so it must provide adequate recognition (where this is due) to the intrinsic value, and/or the rights, and/or the entitlement to ethical consideration of non-human natural entities. The Brundtland report was not so entirely anthropocentric as critics sometimes claim, and it makes explicit reference to ethical objections to the despoliation of nature. Of course the primary emphasis is on meeting human needs, and on sustainable use of the biosphere; but openings do exist to advance a less instrumental agenda within the discourse of sustainable development. Moreover, sustainable development does not have to be accepted as a hegemonic project, displacing all other ethical norms. It does not of itself provide an adequate environmental ethic, and for this we must look elsewhere. All this said, however, it should be appreciated that the human focus of sustainable development is one of the features that has permitted it to acquire the influence that it has had. Unsurprisingly, human beings remain mostly concerned with human ends. And to the extent that sustainable development has contributed to moderating environmental destruction it has been able to do so precisely because it reflects this pre-occupation.

Others have complained that sustainable development mistakenly assumes that all environment and development problems can be converted to win/win scenarios. In fact within the Brundtland report, and in the national and international discussions it sparked over the past decade, there is a clear recognition that hard choices and trade-offs must often be made. Other critics complain that sustainable development is not sufficiently radical in orientation for—at least on the dominant interpretation—it does not explicitly demand root and branch reform, the complete transformation of existing economic and political structures, a decisive shift in world views and a revolution in social practices. And yet sustainable development does call for fundamental structural reform to national and international systems so that the development process may be carried forward, so that poverty may be eliminated and breaches of the thresholds of physical sustainability avoided. Moreover sustainable development poses no *a priori* limits on the depth or breadth of the economic and political reforms that may be required to realize this objective. Not surprisingly governments have begun cautiously. But most already acknowledge that sustainable development will imply further profound changes to social practice. And in the longer term, policy failure and contradictions generated by partial solutions may lead to bouts of social learning and to the implementation of reforms that extend far beyond those initially envisaged by the political leaders of today.

Many of these lines of criticism actually reveal the potential resilience of sustainable development, and suggest why it continues to attract attention. Among its most important strengths are its focus on global issues, on linking economic and environmental decision making, on inter- and intra-generational equity, and on achieving structural reform while leaving it open to experience to establish the ultimate parameters of the required change. Such features help explain why sustainable development has been much more widely taken up than similar ideas such as those of 'eco-development', or 'ecological modernization'.

To date the changes governments have wrought in the name of sustainable development are in some senses remarkable and profound; but in others barely scratch the surface of the phenomena they purport to address. Sustainable development is, after all, just an idea and its future depends on what people actually do with it. If those who invoke it shy away from some of the more potent, but disconcerting, dimensions of the concept—especially those related to international equity and to the reduction of the environmental loading imposed by the North—the idea may yet be discredited with many constituencies. In particular, it is unclear whether developing countries will show continued acceptance of a concept which may be deemed to have failed to live up to its promise. One thing of which we can be sure, however, is that the sorts of environment and development issues which sustainable development was formulated to address are destined to be at the centre of international political argument in the coming century.

Notes

This article (especially the argument in sections 2 and 3) draws on insights gained during a three year collaborative study of governmental responses to sustainable development. The project 'Implementing sustainable development in high consumption societies: a comparative assessment of national strategies and initiatives' (COMPSUS) was co-ordinated by William Lafferty and James Meadowcroft. Other members of the team were Susan Baker, Christiane Beuermann, Gary Bryner, Katarina Eckerberg, Oluf Langhelle, Marie Louise van Muijen, Elim Papadakis, Glen Toner, Miranda Schreurs, and Stephen Young. The project was funded by ProSus (The Centre for Research and Documentation for a Sustainable Society. Oslo) and the UK Economic and Social Research Council (R000221956). The full findings of this project are to be presented in Lafferty and Meadowcroft (eds), *Implementing Sustainable Development* (Oxford: Oxford University Press, forthcoming). I would like to thank the members of the project team, and in particular William Lafferty, for helping clarify my perspective on issues discussed in this article. Any errors or inaccuracies are solely the responsibility of the author.

1. As the subsequent discussion will make clear, sustainable development is not just an 'environmental' concept, and it can be invoked as a normative meta-objective across the whole of government. It also has quite specific implications for international development policy, a point to which I will return in due course. Nevertheless, governments in the developed countries typically have argued that in light of their generally robust economies and established social welfare systems it is with respect to managing environmental burdens that the concept can be of most use. Some governments have made efforts to draw the idea of sustainable development into decision

making across a broad range of areas On occasion the expressions 'ecologically sustainable development' or 'environmentally sustainable development' are employed to make explicit the primary concern with environmental constraints.

2. World Commission on Environment and Development. *Our Common Future* (Oxford: Oxford University Press, 1987). 'Sustainable development' is cited in eleven of the 27 'principles' of the 'Rio Declaration on Environment and Development'. The full title of the action programme adopted at the United Nations Conference on Environment and Development (UNCED) in Rio was: 'Agenda 21: A Blueprint for Action for Global Sustainable Development into the 21st Century' (United Nations Conference on Environment and Development, *Agenda 21*, New York, United Nations, p. 13.)

3. References to 'sustainability' and the 'sustainable society' can be found in radical environmental literature from the 1970s. 'Sustainable development' was famously invoked in the *World Conservation Strategy* issued in 1980 by the International Union for the Conservation of Nature, the United Nations Environment Programme and the World Wildlife Fund. For a discussion see W. Adams, *Green Development* (London: Routledge, 1990).

4. WCED, *Our Common Future*, 43.

5. Early reviews of the literature on sustainable development can be found in D. Mitlin, 'Sustainable development: a guide to the literature', *Environment and Urbanization*, 4 (1992), 111–24; J. Pezzy, 'Sustainability: An Interdisciplinary Guide', *Environmental Values*, 1 (1992), 321–62; and S. Lele 'Sustainable development: A Critical Review', *World Development*, 19 (1991), 607–21. For a more analytical approach to understanding different approaches to sustainability, see A. Dobson, 'Environmental Sustainabilities: An Analysis and a Typology', *Environmental Politics*, 5 (1996), 401–28.

6. Arguably each of these ideas is already present within the Brundtland report, but subsequent international discussion centred on the UNCED process made their centrality to sustainable development more explicit.

7. For a discussion of the Earth Summit, see M. Grubb, M. Koch, K. Thompson, A. Munson, and F. Sullivan, *The Earth Summit Agreements: a Guide and Assessment* (London: Earthscan, 1993). For an overview of the UNCED process, consider D. Reid, *Sustainable Development an Introductory Guide* (London: Earthscan, 1995).

8. For sustainable development as an international norm, see W. Lafferty, 'The politics of sustainable development: global norms for national implementation', *Environmental Politics*, 5 (1996), 185–208.

9. See, for example, W. Sachs, 'Global Ecology and the Shadow of "Development"', in *Global Ecology: A New Arena of Political Conflict* (London: Zed, 1993), 3–21; and D. Richardson, 'The Politics of Sustainable Development', in S. Baker, M. Kousis, D. Richardson and S. Young (eds), *The Politics of Sustainable Development Theory, Policy and Practice within the European Union* (London: Routledge, 1997).

10. For an interesting exchange, consider W. Beckerman, 'Sustainable Development: Is It a Useful Concept?', *Environmental Values*, 3 (1994), 191–209; and M. Jacobs, 'Sustainable Development, Capital Substitution and Economic Humility: A Response to Beckerman', *Environmental Values*, 4 (1995), 57–68.

11. COMPSUS project For full details, see unnumbered note.

12. K. Eckerberg, working paper for COMPSUS project, 1999 One of the more important laws is: 'Targeting sustainable development: implementation of the UNCED decisions' (Prop 1993/94.111) See also: Ministry of the Environment, *The Environment Code* (Stockholm, 1998).

13. Government of Canada, *A Guide to Green Government* (Ottawa Minister of Supply and Services, 1995), and, G Toner, working paper for COMPSUS project, 1998.

14. M. Reitan, 'Norway A Case of "Splendid isolation"', in M. Andersen and D. Liefferink (eds), *European Environmental Policy the*

Pioneers (Manchester: Manchester University Press, 1997), and O. Langhelle, working paper for the COMPSUS project, 1998.

15. B. Dalal-Clayton, *Getting to Grips with Green Plans National Experience in Industrial Countries* (London Earthscan, 1996), and E. Papadakis, working paper for COMPSUS project, 1998.

16. These are the National Environmental Policy Plans: NEPP (1989), NEPP+ (1990), NEPP 2 (1993) and NEPP 3 (1998).

17. M. Janicke and H. Jorgens, 'National Environmental Policy Plans and Long-term Sustainable Development Strategies: Learning from International Experiences', *Environmental Politics*, 7 (1998), 27–54.

18. For discussion of dimensions of variation, see Janicke and Jorgens, 'National Environmental Policy Plans'; and J. Meadowcroft, 'The Politics of Sustainable Development Emergent Arenas and Challenges for Political Science', *International Political Science Review*, 20 (1999), 219–37.

19. For an example, see Environment Agency, *Local Environment Agency Plan Seven Vale. Consultation Draft* (Tewkesbury, Glos.: Environment Agency, 1999).

20. Department of the Environment, Transport and the Regions, *Sustainability Counts* (London. DETR, 1998).

21. Federal Ministry of the Environment, Nature Conservation and Nuclear Safety, *Sustainable Development in Germany, Draft Programme for Priority Areas in Environmental Policy Summary* (Bonn 1998). Note the contrast in emphasis with the UK approach, which has recently stressed drawing together the economic, social and environmental dimensions of sustainable development, while the German government chose to focus particular attention on the environmental themes.

22. For more on the Dutch covenants, see P. Glasbergen, 'Partnership as a Learning Process Environmental Covenants in the Netherlands', in P. Glasbergen (ed), *Co-operative Environmental Governance Public-Private Agreements as a Policy Strategy* (Dordrecht Kluwer, 1998).

23. For a discussion of the implications of such approaches, see J. Meadowcroft, Co-operative Management Regimes. Collaborative Problem-solving to Implement Sustainable Development', *International Negotiation*, 4 (1999), 1–30.

24. For a general discussion of eco-taxation see M. Andersen, *Governance by Green Taxation* (Manchester, Manchester University Press. 1994).

25. Factor productivity refers to the output per unit of resource input Factor 4 refers to getting 4 times more output per input (ie increasing materials and energy efficiency four fold). Factor 10 is a still more ambitious objective. See for example E. Weizsacker, A. Lovins and L. Lovins, *Factor Four Doubling Wealth, Halving Resourse Use, the New Report to the Club of Rome* (London Earthscan, 1997).

26. On Local Agenda 21, see H. Voisey, C. Beuermann, L. Sverdrup and T O'Riordan, 'The Political Significance of Local Agenda 21: The Early Stages of Some European Experience', *Local Environment*, 1 (1996), pp. 33–50: and W. Lafferty and K. Eckerberg (eds), *From Earth Summit to Local Forum Studies of Local Agenda 21 in Europe* (Oslo: ProSus, 1997).

27. G. Bryner, working paper for COMPSUS project, 1998.

28. Governments have shown little enthusiasm for programmes to alter consumption patterns. Some steps have been taken on eco-labelling, and consumer education—particularly in Germany, the Netherlands, Norway, and Sweden, Norway in particular has assumed a leadership role on the international level by supporting a work programme around 'sustainable production and consumption'. For results of a recent initiative financed by Norway, see N. Robins and S Roberts, *Consumption in a Sustainable World* (London: IIED, 1998).

29. S. Baker, 'The Evolution of European Environmental Policy: from Growth to Sustainable Development?', in Baker *et. al.*, *The Politics of Sustainable Development*.

284 **JAMES MEADOWCROFT**

30. On Canada's Green Plan, see G. Toner and B. Doern, 'Five Political and Policy Imperatives in Green Plan Formation: The Canadian Case'. *Environmental Politics*, 3 (1994), 395–420; and E. Darier, 'Environmental Governmentality: The Case of Canada's Green Plan', *Environmental Politics*, 5 (1996), 585–606.

31. For useful discussions of climate change, see T. O'Riordan and J Jager, *Politics of Climate Change: A European Perspective* (London: Routledge, 1996): and U. Collier and R. Lofstedt (eds), *Cases in Climate Change Policy* (London Earthscan, 1997).

32. D. McGraw, 'The Convention on Biological Diversity at the Cross-roads', paper presented to the workshop on 'Implementing policies of sustainable development: examining actor relationships and negotiating processes', 25–26 May 1998, Geneva.

33. J. Dryzek, *The Politics of the Earth* (Oxford: Oxford University Press, 1997).

34. For a further discussion of this point, see J. Meadowcroft, 'Planning for Sustainable Development' What can be Learnt from the Critics?', in M. Kenny and J. Meadowcroft (eds), *Planning Sustainability* (London: Routledge, 1999).

20 From Opposition to Orthodoxy: The Remaking of Sustainable Development

David Carruthers

Introduction

Sustainable development now stands as the dominant discourse on the environment-development problematic.[1] Because it promises to defuse long-standing tensions between environmental protection and economic growth, nearly everyone favors it, including individuals, firms, national and local governments, militaries, and the gamut of non-state actors. It has prompted so many business, government, academic, and nongovernmental publications and gatherings that it has been dubbed "the mantra that launched a thousand conferences."[2] Accompanied by liberal democracy and free markets, sustainable development is now a pillar of contemporary universalism, embraced from the industrialized north, to the less-developed south, to the post-communist east.

However, the sustainable development of today bears faint resemblance to its point of origin. The language of sustainability was once a discourse of resistance, fusing radical environmental consciousness with a critical rethinking of a failed development enterprise. It provoked challenging questions about scarcity and limits, affluence and poverty, global inequality, and the environmental viability of westernization. By today, sustainable development has been transformed, stripped of its critical content, and reconfigured for compatibility with the larger priorities of the post-Cold War era.

This paper tells the story of a counter-hegemonic discourse turned on its head to help legitimize a grand universal project of neoliberal globalization. It proceeds in three parts. The first takes us back to the origins of the sustainable development discourse, in a critical rethinking of development informed by the radical environmentalism of the 1970s. The second chronicles the transformation of the discourse and its rise to hegemony. The third section raises questions about the viability of the new sustainable development, and offers a concluding glimpse at a variety of alternatives that might hold out hope for a more authentically sustainable path.

From *Journal of Third World Studies*, 18: 2 (2001), 93–112.

The Old Sustainable Development: A Discourse of Resistance

From today's viewpoint, the conceptual origins of sustainable development are scarcely recognizable: an early-1970s environmental discourse about "the age of scarcity" and "the limits to growth."[3] Sustainability has earlier roots in the resource management concept of sustained yield.[4] As lunar spacecraft projected the first images of earth as a bounded sphere suspended in blackness, that concept became enmeshed with rising concern for the "carrying capacity" of finite ecological systems. Sustainability entered the environmental lexicon as part of an emerging reconceptualization of the relationship between human activities and nature's limits. Because fast-growing populations and economic processes (both capitalist and centrally planned) have in recent centuries proceeded on a *de facto* assumption of a boundless capacity for growth, the implications were ominous.

The new discourse of limits and scarcity, initially popularized by the Club of Rome and the Global 2000 reports, produced facile images of a "lifeboat earth" in great peril. Though often caricatured and dismissed as doom-saying, it fired the popular imagination, especially in the form of neo-Malthusian prognostications of explosive population growth, where the biological concept of carrying capacity was so tangibly apocalyptic.[5] It also pointed toward finite terrestrial "inputs" to a production-consumption pipeline, as well as earth's finite capacity to absorb the "outputs" of waste heat and pollution. Bolstered by the oil shocks of the 1970s, scarcity on the input end received the greatest initial attention. By the 1980s and 1990s, atmospheric pollution, acid rain, global warming, accumulating hazardous wastes, the depletion of the ozone layer, habitat destruction, and rising health threats refocused our attention increasingly on the output end; that is, on the biosphere's limited capacity to serve as a "waste sink" for the inevitable byproducts of all human production and consumption.

New thinking also prompted arcane academic analysis of the economic implications of thermodynamic processes, especially entropy, which was held up as theoretic evidence for the unsustainability of a political economy of infinite growth.[6] The renegade school of "steady-state" economists broke ranks with their peers, challenging the core beliefs of the discipline.[7] They preached not just an inherent tension, but an axiomatic incompatibility between environmental sustainability and the maximization of economic growth. Boundless growth was posited as a biophysical impossibility. Sustainability would ultimately require a "low throughput" economy.

Our principal concern here is with the impact of this revolution in environmental thinking on the relationship between the north and the south. How did the limits discourse play in the Third World, which comprises most of the planet's land and people? What did scarcity mean for the enterprise of development? I focus our attention on four answers: (1) duplication of the northern trajectory was no longer viable for the south, (2) distributional equity was now a matter of special salience, (3) broader disenchantment with the development enterprise was emerging at the same time, and (4) creative exploration was thus necessary to envision a development alternative.

First, in age of limits, the open-ended economic growth trajectory of the north would not be sustainable in the long run, not even ultimately for the rich countries. A political economy predicated on the assumption of infinite growth was, essentially, a dead end that the Third World would have to avoid. Consequently, an alternative, sustainable conception of development would have to be envisioned. For Herman Daly, the foremost spokesperson for the steady-state economy, qualitative development (or improvement) would have to become the global norm, rather than quantitative growth (or expansion). Sustainable development would have to be the opposite of sustained growth.[8]

Second, if there are limits on the planet's capacity to provide resources for production and to absorb waste heat and pollutants, then distributional justice would become the central global political issue. If there are biophysical limits to the total growth of the economic pie, then we cannot escape attending to the comparative size of the slices. In the north, this meant an uncomfortable recognition that northern affluence is the flip side of southern poverty. Northern "overdevelopment" and "overconsumption" demonstrated an unfair and lopsided distribution of global goods.[9] The northern path would not be viable for the south. The planet could not handle, ecologically, the universalization of a European or North American mass-consumption lifestyle. "We have seen that a few can live like this—but only if the rest do not."[10] Global sustainability would ultimately require facing up to the formidable political challenge of a significant redistribution of wealth and resource use.

Such pronouncements caused unease for southern officials. The over-whelming emphasis had for decades been on the maximization of economic growth and the explicit hope of thereby duplicating the irresistible, high-consumption northern lifestyle. From the southern perspective, if there is only so much net growth left for the planet to absorb, then the south should have priority.

Growth in GNP in poor countries means more food, clothing, shelter, basic education, and security, whereas for the rich country it means more electric toothbrushes, yet another brand of cigarettes, more tension and insecurity, and more force-feeding through advertising. . . . [The] upshot of these differences is that for the poor, growth in GNP is still a good thing, but for the rich it is probably a bad thing.[11]

Thirdly, and independently of rising environmental concern, the dogged pursuit of economic growth for its own sake was losing credibility in development circles anyway. For over two decades "development" had been treated as essentially synonymous with "economic growth"; the full range of state- or market-led development policies were oriented toward the maximization of economic growth at any cost.[12] Yet by the mid-1970s, it was inescapably clear throughout the Third World that decades of economic growth had produced only small pockets that vaguely resembled the broad-based development of the north. For the vast majority of southerners, economic growth—even dramatic, sustained, high levels of growth—had not produced significant material improvements in the quality of their lives. To the contrary, many millions more found themselves stranded on the immiserating fringes of modernizing societies. The development process itself had displaced them from traditional lands and ways of life, but without corresponding opportunities for absorption into the modern cash economy. Dispossession, marginalization, hyper-urbanization, and the explosion of precarious settlements and informal economies became symbols of a development enterprise that had gone tragically wrong, betraying its most fundamental promises.[13] In this climate of disenchantment and frustration, the modernization and growth strategies of the postwar era were placed on the defensive. Critical perspectives on underdevelopment found more solid footing, both north and south.[14] The most dramatic posited a polar world in which the wealth of the core countries accrued necessarily at the expense of the periphery, offering little hope for southerners to ever break free of the chains of neo-colonial subordination and dependence.[15]

Fourth, this critique of the development enterprise, when coupled with the emerging environmental perspective, began to inform a creative quest for a sustainable alternative. New formulations—grassroots development, pro-peasant development, eco-development, bottom-up development, people-centered development, and so forth—opened up myriad paths in the quest to conceive an alternative, ecologically-sustainable, socially-just development trajectory for the south.[16] While these sustainable development proposals varied, they shared certain general features. All were at some level modeled on humanity's best example of sustainability: low-impact hunter-gatherer and base agricultural societies. They shared a Gandhian emphasis on equity, basic needs, self-reliance, locality, and place—local control over the use of local resources. Likewise, there was a general preference for smallness in the scale of the enterprise, emphasizing community- and village-based designs. There was a natural affinity for "appropriate" or "intermediate" technologies, designed with local inputs and know-how, much cheaper than the capital-, import-, and energy-intensive technologies of the modern sector, but still offering dramatic improvements upon indigenous tools and techniques. Finally, they placed a high value on political decentralization and political openness, to enable popular participation, and to incorporate local knowledge and traditions of stewardship.

Interestingly, these radical critiques and creative efforts did resonate upward somewhat to the mainstream development institutions. The grim failures of growth-oriented strategies prompted a nominal policy reorientation on the part of most major development entities. The World Bank, the USAID (Agency for International Development), many United Nations agencies, and others were by that time expressing an official preference for "basic needs" strategies. They saw the lack of distributional equality as having widely undermined the growth-based model. The new official policy priorities of international and multilateral development agencies were, on the surface, based in sustainable grassroots development, both for urban popular classes and in pro-peasant and rural development initiatives.[17]

Efforts to envisage and support sustainable alternatives appeared in many corners of the Third World. The most prominent took the form of top-down, "integrated rural development" initiatives, which were later criticized for their failure to confront corrupt and inequitable power structures; the high-visibility cases fell far short of their stated goals.[18] Still, leaders in a smaller number of countries, from Tanzania to Nicaragua, from Papua New Guinea to Burkina Faso, carried out experimentation with appropriate technologies, sustainable designs, and grassroots development. Most exploration along these lines, then and now, remained the province of non-governmental organizations (NGOs). Especially prominent have been groups such as London's Intermediate Technology Development Group, San Francisco's Earth Island Institute, Oxfam, and London's International Institute for Environment and Development. However, NGO and grassroots initiatives remained comparatively marginal, certainly in official southern policy circles. Southern leaders were instead centrally occupied with the drive to reconfigure the rules of international trade and finance toward a fairer and more equitable "New International Economic Order."[19] That struggle came to an abrupt end in 1982, when the Third World debt crisis exploded on the scene, irrevocably altering the north-south relationship. By that time, the remaking of sustainable development was almost under way.

The New Sustainable Development: A Discourse of Hegemony

Given the relatively obscure origin of the concept as traced above, the question I pose here is the following: how in a very few years did a comparatively marginalized, genuinely radical idea, carried out in practice by idealists in a handful of creative pockets of grassroots experimentation in remote corners of the rural Third World, become utterly transformed in meaning, and rise to prominence as the near-universal ordering principle for environmental and development policy across most of the world?

The first step was taken in December 1983, when the Secretary-General of the United Nations selected Norwegian Prime Minister Gro Harlem Brundtland to head up a commission to study the problems of environment and development. The work of the Brundtland Commission (the WCED, or World Commission on Environment and Development) made a vital contribution to the evolution of environmental thinking. The WCED's report put the idea of sustainable development in the global spotlight. But this version of sustainable development had wriggled free of the constraints of its birth in a discourse of scarcity, limits, and the failures of development.

Humanity has the ability to make development sustainable—to ensure that it meets the needs of the present without compromising the ability of future generations to meet their own needs. The concept of sustainable development does imply limits—not absolute limits but limitations imposed by the present state of technology and social organization on environmental resources and by the ability of the biosphere to absorb the effects of human activities. But technological and social organization can be both managed and improved to make way for a new era of economic growth.[20]

The Brundtland report recast the debate on the environment-development nexus, giving unprecedented prominence to the principle of sustainability. Part of its impact lies in its timing, and in the changing character of environmental consciousness. The environmentalism of the 1970s had stressed local pollution and habitat issues and national regulatory policy. But by the late 1980s, popular awareness of the *global* dimensions of environmental problems had expanded dramatically. International connections were now tangible, the linkages highly popularized: Chernobyl's far reaching impact, northern hamburgers and tropical deforestation, skin cancer and the ozone hole, fossil fuels and the greenhouse effect, industrial pollutants and acid rain, pesticide exports and the "circle of poison," unregulated transnational corporations and toxic nightmares like Bhopal.

The Brundtland definition of sustainable development possessed a conceptual ambiguity that made it palatable to the widest possible audience. It was broad enough to capture the energy of this environmental reawakening and to resonate with the increasingly international nature of popular thinking about environmental problems. Its central concern for equity with present and future generations retained sufficient idealism to garnish the support of ecological purists and advocates for distributive justice. Yet its vague, contradictory stance on ecological limits and economic processes weakened that very threat, leaving just enough wiggle room so that pro-growth economists, business leaders, and governments could also comfortably embrace the concept.

Once launched, this de-fanged version of sustainable development was carried in a smooth trajectory right on into Rio de Janeiro, in June 1992, where it took a leading role under the brightest lights of the world stage, at the "Earth Summit," or UNCED (United Nations Conference on Environment and Development). By the end of the Rio summit, the new sustainable development had a written constitution: Agenda 21.[21] Endorsed by the official participants, this agreement is a comprehensive "action plan" that identifies environmental threats and defines the roles of various actors to realize common goals. We are most concerned here with its perspective on the relationship between sustainability and the global economy. Where Brundtland was vague, Agenda 21 boldly shed any vestige of the discourse of scarcity and limits. In order to achieve the broad support of national governments, the drafters recognized that economic growth would have to be recast from villain to hero. To dissolve the tension between open-ended growth and the limits of a finite biosphere, growth must be redeemed as the savior, essential to the global environmental solution. I focus here on three of the most important components of this complex conceptual achievement: poverty alleviation, free trade, and technological innovation, all presented as mutually enhancing.[22]

First, summit participants paid special attention to those categories of environmental degradation caused directly by poverty itself—the population, land, and resource pressures endemic in much of the Third World. The rural poor, driven by dire necessity, overcut, overfish, deplete, degrade, or are displaced to destructive urban settlements. If poverty is the environmental problem, then lifting people out of poverty is the solution. The best means to that end is the promotion of economic growth—the boundless expansion of the economic pie.

Second, participants had to confront the potentially conflictive relationship between trade and the environment. Consensus at Rio was built on the argument that environmental protection is a luxury that can best be afforded once relative affluence is attained. According to the prevailing Ricardian orthodoxy, free trade by comparative advantage maximizes benefits to all trading partners. Trade thus creates the wealth that enables later environmental repair. To promote poverty alleviation and general wellbeing, free trade should be the engine of renewed economic growth. Entrepreneurship and competitive markets should be supported domestically and internationally. Government restrictions on trade should be minimized to promote innovation and efficiency, and to maximize the free flow of goods and services. Care must be taken to ensure that only legitimate environmental and social concerns are protected by state action; protectionist impulses must not be permitted to disguise themselves in a green cloak.

Third, administrative and technological innovations would offer humanity's best hope for liberation from the constraints of a finite biosphere. That faith finds a deep resonance with the western legacy of control over nature, defended in environmental debates by "cornucopian" thinkers like economist Julian Simon.[23] The Brundtland report had provided the groundwork, by redefining limits not as absolutes, but as matters of technological capacity. By the 1990s, the age of scarcity seemed to have passed. Technological innovation had gotten us out of the tight corners of the 1970s, seemingly vindicating the cornucopian promise.[24] On the input side, new technologies and substitutions had relieved shortages; we now had oversupplies and falling prices. Innovations in recycling and pollution abatement promised progress on the output end for cleaning up polluted airsheds and watersheds. Sustainable development would thus rely on technological fixes, requiring continued innovation, public and private support for research and development of green technologies, and attentiveness to southward technology transfer.

Agenda 21 erased the line between "sustainable development" and "sustained economic growth." Once poised as polar opposites, these concepts were now practically synonymous. Liberated from the distasteful implications of scarcity and limits, sustainability had come full circle, back to an essential belief that open-ended growth will lift all boats. So reconstructed, the new sustainable development could fit neatly into place—an interlocking piece of the puzzle of a changing north-south relationship. The 1990s were a decade of triumphalism for the north, as it shook off old doubts about the virtues of growth and technology, and restored confidence in the universal applicability of the western path. Sustainable development could now stand alongside neoclassical capitalism and liberal democracy—the picture of hegemonic universalism.

This historical moment resulted from a confluence of events. First, the collapse of Soviet communism seemed to vindicate the superiority of neoclassical capitalism, delegitimizing the state's role in economic management. It placed the left on the defensive globally, including the environmental movement.[25] Simultaneously, the Asian "tigers" seemed to prove that the chains of dependency and subordination could be ruptured, redeeming ascent to the First World as a viable goal. More importantly, they engendered a myth of free-market success based on free trade, minimal government intervention, open economies, and export-led growth. Mythical lean tigers charged forward while bloated, statist "elephant" economies elsewhere in the developing world languished. Experts on East Asian political economy struggled to contain the damage from this grievous misrepresentation.[26] But their words of caution arrived too late to the corridors of global finance. Duplication of the mythical Asian miracle became the universal prescription for the debtors of the Third World, to be realized by strict neoliberal restructuring, enforced by northern creditors and institutions. As the debt crisis exploded, debtor nations found themselves with little latitude for policy choice. Faced with the pressing need for fresh capital to keep their economies afloat, most readily complied with the mandates of structural adjustment handed down by the creditor nations, the World Bank, and the International Monetary Fund.[27] Privatization, deregulation, "shock therapy" tariff reduction, capital mobility, and harsh fiscal austerity became the universal prescriptions for healing the debtors and salvaging westernization.

The new sustainable development thus arrived on the international scene at a propitious moment. Because neoliberalism is predicated on open-ended expansion and growth over equity, it cannot confront limits in nature. But the new sustainable development eliminated the conflict between neoliberal axioms and nature's limited resource and absorption capacities. It stepped easily into place as component of a universalizing project—a bundle of policies, myths, and faith, invoked to redeem a global duplication of the northern path to the high consumption lifestyle. With lean-state, free-market economies and democratic policies, the less-developed and post-communist worlds could again strive to duplicate the ascent to the First World.[28] Expanding markets and open economies provide for a new era of growth. Growing economies create resources and incentives to solve environmental problems. Economic liberalization bolsters political liberalization—a family of democratic partners in pursuit of peace and prosperity for all. The homogenization of the world has been saved.

Moreover, sustainable development has shed its Third World skin, and can now encompass all development processes—north, south, east, west; local, national, global; private, public, and non-profit. It is embraced by Third World and post-communist governments, frustrated by the failures of developmentalism, saddled with the environmental legacies of rapid industrialization, and desperate to save the dream of ascent to the First World. Because the new sustainability no longer threatens other priorities, First World governments are just as pleased as their southern counterparts to grant it a high institutional and policy profile. So too have supranational bodies, including the United Nations, the OECD, the World Bank, the European Union, and the North American Free Trade Area.[29] Because it emphasizes technology, private initiative, and enhanced market competition, business leaders have also responded, eager to shake off the image of rapaciousness and be refashioned as defenders of nature.[30] Finally, sustainable development is most concretely a reality in the transnational universe of NGOs, from the smallest local grassroots organizations in the shantytowns and villages of the Third World, through the middle terrain of supportive intermediary organizations, up to the gleaming offices of the wealthy international organizations of the north.[31]

It is little wonder that sustainable development today holds such broad appeal. How could it be otherwise? It is universally applicable. It dissolves the old conflict between growth and limits. It eliminates confrontation over who is entitled to the lion's share of remaining growth. It averts the question of northern overconsumption. It promises the compatibility of environmental preservation with the maximization of growth. It supports technological development and scientific progress. It offers equity for both present and future generations. And it plays a mutually supportive role with the other western universals—free markets and democratic politics.

Toward Authentic Sustainable Development

But what if the most basic premises of the new sustainable development are mistaken? The new wisdom holds that it is not only compatible with neoliberal restructuring, but the two are mutually enhancing. What if neoliberalism is in fact inimical to sustainability? Sustainable development, "the 'buzzword' of environmentalists, politicians, business leaders, and strategic planners alike—would appear to cloak an agenda that is just as destructive, just as undermining of peoples' rights and livelihoods as the development agenda of old."[32] Many observers have raised these concerns, fearing potentially tragic consequences for humans, nature, and our shared future.[33] While a decisive environmental critique of global neoliberalism lies beyond the scope of this essay, I seek to highlight here some of the most pressing areas of concern.

The first is equity. The sustainable development discourse recognizes both distributional and inter-generational equity in principle. Indeed, environmental equity with future generations is its centerpiece. But neoliberalism in practice, in the form currently promoted by structural adjustment policies of austerity and deregulation, and by the expansion of free trade regimes such as NAFTA and the WTO (World Trade Organization), fundamentally deepens socioeconomic inequality, both globally, and within countries. Dramatically rising socioeconomic polarization has been an indisputable feature of neoliberal reform, in virtually all contexts in which it has appeared. Sustainable development may assert distributive equity in word, but in practice it is wedded to policies which clearly undermine it.

Both distributive and inter-generational equity are threatened by a second concern: the fundamental ecological-economic problem of negative externalities. In uncorrected market exchanges, the selling prices of goods do not incorporate the full social and ecological costs of their production. In the absence of a serious global "ecological tax reform" or global standards for "true-cost pricing," the benefits of globalized production will accrue disproportionately to those players most effective at externalizing negative costs. From the devastation of chemical-, energy-, and water-intensive corporate agriculture (deforestation, erosion, pesticide poisoning, aquifer depletion, salination), to the poisoned neighborhoods surrounding export-processing zones, to the world's disappearing fisheries, the big winners in the globalizing economies of the neoliberal age are those most skilled at taking nature's inputs and absorptive capacities for free. This is the opposite of sustainability.

Increased capital mobility is a third major point of concern. In structural adjustment and in the negotiation of trade agreements, global neoliberalism has been predicated on the continued loosening of state restrictions on capital. Because most environmental policy is regulatory and because governments (local and national, north, south, east, and west) are pitted against one another in competition to attract and hold footloose capital investment, critics fear a deregulatory "race to the bottom." To offer investors the most attractive terms, the natural incentive is toward downward harmonization of environmental, labor, and public health standards. Anti-WTO protests in Seattle and elsewhere may have raised the profile of these issues, but in the predicted absence of an enforceable, global corporate code of conduct, neoliberal globalization will continue to impel producers to move the most humanly exploitive and ecologically destructive portions of the production process to desperate Third World and post-communist locales.

Inequity, externalization, and capital mobility work together to enable a great global act of self-deception. The rising abundance and falling cost of consumer goods in the north (and in the First-World enclaves of the south) directly reflect rising inequality. The fruits of middle-class buying power are being subsidized by the externalized ecological damage of hazardous, unregulated production in the Third World, and by the misery of workers in the "global assembly line." For producers, the payoff of a globalized system of production is that it masks the connection between benefits and costs; those who enjoy the former are delinked from the distant souls who pay the latter. Moving production offshore does more than reduce the burden of wages, infrastructure, taxes, or environmental and health compliance. By rewarding production methods that externalize negative costs in distant places, the world's affluent consumers are shielded, delinked from the ecological and human consequences of their consumption.

Finally, neoliberalism has not provided satisfactory answers to the hardest questions raised decades earlier. Is it genuinely ecologically viable to assume, on a bounded planet, the infinite expansion of economies, of populations, of GDP, of commerce, of international trade, of waste heat, of pollution? Of growth on all indicators, without end? We saw how the architects of the new sustainable development massaged the infinite-growth issue. But the challenges of its originators were answered more by omission than by evidence or by conceptual triumph. Since the gaps between rich and poor continue to widen dramatically, is not distributional justice even more pressing than it was in the age of scarcity? Given the rising and disproportionate ecological impact of the resource-consuming, highly-polluting northern lifestyle, can the planet physically support 4 or 5 billion more people walking as heavily on the earth as do a relative handful of North Americans today?[34] If the northern path is to be universalized, who will be left to pay the ecological costs? Can we really construct a global political economy in the shape of a pyramid, and then hold out as the goal for everyone to occupy its apex?[35]

The new sustainable development discourse sidesteps these questions, placing its faith in poverty alleviation, the expansion of trade, and technological innovation. Because neoliberalism has yielded such unsatisfying responses on poverty and trade, a lot rests on technological salvation. In the short run, such innovations have indisputably cheated the dire predictions of the limits-to-growth era. Still, some of this progress is illusionary—a function of delinked costs and benefits. Significant northern environmental purity, for example, has been purchased by a southward migration of negative ecological impacts in agriculture, mining, manufacturing, forestry, fisheries, and so on. It is also important to remember that the greatest achievements have been realized only on the input end of the productive process, allowing us to squeeze greater mileage out of diminishing resources. Technological innovations on the output end have not yet cheated the laws of thermodynamics. Few viable suggestions have appeared for the most vexing issues on the north-south agenda: water, oceans, air, greenhouse gases, climate change, the accumulation of toxic and radioactive wastes, the depletion of the ozone layer, species extinctions.

The new discourse has not satisfied the original spokespersons of the age of scarcity.[36] Brundtland-Rio wordsmithing notwithstanding, we have not dissipated the fundamental economic-ecological questions they first raised thirty years ago. Today's limits are not the simple, rigid, fixed caricature of an earlier era's simplistic doomsaying. But the premise of global neoliberalism is boundless growth. And boundless growth is still not likely to prove sustainable.

Today's sustainable development is premised on precisely the same economic injustices and biophysical impossibilities as the dominant discourse it once rose to oppose. It was originally born in popular struggle, a rallying cry to envision a more just future for the victims of a failed developmentalism. Its domain was the rural village and the urban ghetto of the dispossessed. It brought together activists and scholars, northerners and southerners, practitioners and thinkers, in a visionary search for diverse, local, ecological, just, and democratic alternatives to the ruinous verticalization and homogenization of the world.

The creative quest for a more sustainable, equitable, and participatory future did not stop just because the nomenclature changed meaning. The real struggle for sustainable development—the one actually practiced, on the ground, by millions of people, everywhere on the planet—has continued without pause. Far from the gleam of international diplomats, corporate boardrooms, powerful donor agencies, and supranational conferences, a "really existing" sustainable development survives and thrives exactly where it always has—at the grassroots, in the same fields and neighborhoods, and in the same hands and minds in which its original promise was born.

Indigenous and peasant ecological movements are active by the tens of thousands, from Africa, to Latin America, to Asia and the Pacific. The defense of biological diversity has been woven together with the defense of cultural diversity and the rescue of traditional ecological knowledge. Efforts to incorporate both new and inherited cultural experience, knowledge about resources, and values of smallness, stewardship, and place have been manifest in agroecology, aquaculture, agroforestry, seed banks, appropriate technology, and similar grassroots sustainability initiatives.[37]

Ecological feminism shares a similar sensitivity to the wisdom of the world's disenfranchised. Many Third World women work closely to the land, sustaining their households with the most basic human connection to nature. They harbor an intimate and sensitive relationship to local ecological systems, one often suppressed or violently denied by the masculine, western drive towards conquest and triumph over nature.[38] Carried by NGOs and grassroots groups into the field, feminist ecology bridges the gap between theory and practice.

Numerous threads of radical ecology have likewise been liberated from both northern and southern points of academic origin to inform alternative, ecologically sound social orders, policies, and practices. Not to brush over significant differences among them, social ecology, deep ecology, bioregionalism, postmodern localism, ecologism, and other proposals for radical decentralization share values of place, scale, nonviolence, solidarity with future generations, social justice, popular participation, and ecological balance.[39]

North America's environmental justice movement has unveiled profound racial and class inequities in exposure to environmental hazards, offering a powerful symbol of grassroots mobilization to blue-collar workers, Native Americans, farmworkers, and communities of color.[40] Now globally, the lens of environmental justice is helping to expose a world economy that strives to contain the negative costs of production in the communities of the politically and economic excluded. With its emphasis on equality, justice, and participation, it readily meshes with the popular struggles of Third World farmers, shantytown dwellers, factory workers, debtors, indigenous people, and others whose lives have been tapped to subsidize distant affluence. As a banner of resistance, it has yielded new cross-national strategies and coalitions, north and south.[41]

In the academic world, a renegade group of economists still struggles against disciplinary convention to construct a field of ecological economics, whose international association and publications strive toward practical applicability.[42] Like their steady-state forebears of a generation earlier, they challenge the sacred assumptions of their field. They strive to better comprehend and reconcile the relationship between natural and economic systems, in the areas of green accounting, national accounts, ecological tax reform, and other policy areas that might one day yield essential methods for making market exchanges more accurately reflect their true ecological costs.

Another group of mostly southern thinkers, writers, and activists has launched an intellectual "post-development" movement, building directly on decades of critical re-evaluation of developmentalism.[43] Unapologetic critics of development, they explicitly seek to write its epitaph. In creative and passionate prose and in real-world practice, they brazenly reject the development enterprise of the past five decades, denouncing it as illusion, failure, and epic tragedy. Appalled by the arrogance, violence, and presumptive universalism of the westernizing project, they stand firmly against the homogenizing juggernaut of neoliberal globalization. They are proud defenders of human diversity, celebrating and re-valuing the complex and varied fabric of life, practice, knowledge, and human experience.

We could extend or debate this list, but these diverse movements and struggles share certain key features. They provide continuity with the efforts of earlier generations, articulating the enduring values of genuine sustainability. They stand on conceptual and practical bridges linking the local with the global. They share a guarded stance toward co-optive, mainstream environment and development enterprises and organizations. The goal is often to create sustainability through actual practice, not through an explicitly political project. The quest for sustainable design frequently takes place not at the level of state policy, but in local pockets of creativity. That quest for autonomy often translates into isolation, and consequently, most of today's "really existing" sustainable development initiatives barely register a flicker on the radar screen of international attention.

However, to focus on the smallness of any given initiative is to miss the larger picture. Woven together, these movements present a rich tapestry of counter-hegemonic struggle. They are the most dynamic, vibrant, promising face of contemporary popular environmentalism. The discourse of sustainable development may have been usurped from its real-world practitioners. But the homogenizing globalization it now portends is being met from below with a countervailing force of "myriad small resistances"—local, diverse, sophisticated, and visionary.

Notes

1. Douglas Torgerson, 'The Uncertain Quest for Sustainability: Public Discourse and the Politics of Environmentalism," in Frank Fischer and Michael Black (eds.), *Greening Environmental Policy: The Politics of a Sustainable Future* (New York: St. Martin's, 1995); John Dryzek, *The Politics of the Earth* (New York: Oxford University Press, 1997).

2. Mark Dowie, *Losing Ground: American Environmentalism at the Close of the Twentieth Century* (Cambridge: MIT Press, 1995), 235.

3. Donella Meadows et al., *The Limits to Growth* (New York: New American Library, 1972); Herman Daly (ed.), *Toward a Steady-State Economy* (San Francisco: W. H. Freeman, 1973); Nicholas Georgescu-Roegen, "The Entropy Law and the Economic Problem," in

Daly, *Toward a Steady-State Economy*; William Ophuls, *Ecology and the Politics of Scarcity* (San Francisco: W. H. Freeman, 1977).

4. The maximum allowable harvest of a renewable resource that can be sustained indefinitely; e.g., game animals, forests, fisheries, kelp beds.

5. Paul Ehrlich, *The Population Bomb* (New York: Ballantine, 1968).

6. The first law of thermodynamics states that energy and matter can be neither created nor destroyed, only changed in form. The second, or entropy law, asserts that this process can proceed in only one direction, from a usable to a nonusable state. Production and consumption thus invariably return equal amounts of "high-entropy" waste heat and pollution to the environment. For the

economic implications, see Daly, *Toward a Steady-State Economy*; Ken Boulding, "The Economics of the Coming Spaceship Earth," in Daly, *Toward a Steady-State Economy*; Georgescu-Roegen, "The Entropy Law and the Economic Problem."

7. In a steady state economy, first conceived by J. S. Mill, production and consumption rates are equalized, as are births and deaths. See Daly, *Toward a Steady-State Economy*.

8. *Ibid.*; See also Herman Daly, *Beyond Growth: The Economics of Sustainable Development* (Boston: Beacon Press, 1996); Herman Daly and Kenneth Townsend (eds.), *Valuing the Earth: Economy, Ecology, Ethics* (Cambridge: MIT Press, 1993).

9. Ted Trainer, *Abandon Affluence!* (London: Zed Books, 1985); Alan Durning, *How Much is Enough?* (New York, Norton, 1992); The Ecologist, *Whose Common Future? Reclaiming the Commons* (Philadelphia: New Society, 1993); Tom Athanasiou, *Divided Planet: The Ecology of Rich and Poor* (New York: Little, Brown, and Company, 1996).

10. Ted Trainer, *Abandon Affluence!*, 248.

11. Daly, *Toward a Steady-State Economy*, 11–12.

12. Generally as measured by annual increases in GNP or GDP (Gross National or Domestic Product).

13. The betrayals of development have been chronicled by many scholars, including Vandana Shiva, *Staying Alive* (London: Zed Books, 1989); David Barkin, *Distorted Development* (Boulder CO: Westview, 1990); Wolfgang Sachs (ed.), *The Development Dictionary* (London, Zed Books, 1992); The Ecologist, *Whose Common Future?*; Arturo Escobar, *Encountering Development* (Princeton: Princeton University Press); Gilbert Rist, *The History of Development* (London: Zed Books).

14. Charles Wilber (ed.), *The Political Economy of Development and Underdevelopment* (New York: Random House, 1973); Ronald Chilcote and Mark Edelstein, *Latin America: The Struggle with Dependency and Beyond* (New York: Halstead, 1974).

15. Andre Gunder Frank, *Latin America: Underdevelopment or Revolution?* (New York:

Monthly Review Press); Samir Amin, *Unequal Development* (Hassocks: Harvester, 1969); Immanuel Wallerstein, *The Capitalist World Economy* (Cambridge: Cambridge University Press, 1979).

16. Ivan Illich, *Celebration of Awareness* (New York: Pantheon, 1969); E. F. Shumacher, *Small is Beautiful* (New York: Harper and Row, 1973); Richard Brown, "Appropriate Technology and the Grassroots: Toward a Development Strategy from the Bottom Up," *The Developing Economies*, 15: 3 (September 1977); Amritananda Das, *Foundations of Gandhian Economics* (Delhi: Center for the Study of Developing Societies, 1979); Irma Adelman, "Beyond Export-Led Growth," *World Development*, 12: 9 (1984); Bernhard Glaeser, *Ecodevelopment: Concepts, Projects, Strategies* (Oxford: Pergamon); David Korten and Rudi Kiauss (eds.), *People-Centered Development* (West Hartford CT: Kumarian Press, 1984).

17. Merilee Grindle, *Bureaucrats, Politicians, and Peasants in Mexico* (Berkeley: University of California, 1977); Escobar, *Encountering Development*.

18. *Ibid.*

19. Steven Krasner, *Structural Conflict: The Third World against Global Liberalism* (Berkeley: University of California, 1985).

20. WCED (World Commission on Environment and Development). *Our Common Future* (Oxford: Oxford University Press, 1987), 8.

21. Daniel Sitarz, *Agenda 21: The Earth Summit Strategy to Save our Planet* (Boulder, CO: Earthpress, 1993).

22. This discussion oversimplifies the dynamics at Rio and overstates the consensus. The summit was an immense, complex event, presenting a broad and conflictual array of government and popular concerns. For more thorough critiques of the resulting agreements, see David Korten, "Sustainable Development," *World Policy Journal*, 9: 1 (Winter 1991–2); Robin Broad and John Cavanagh, "Beyond the Myths of Rio: A New American Agenda for the Environment, *World Policy Journal*, 10: 1 (Spring 1993); Herman Daly, "Sustainable Growth: An

Impossibility Theorem," in Daly and Townsend, *Valuing the Earth*; The Ecologist, *Whose Common Future?*; Wolfgang Sachs, *Global Ecology: A New Arena of Political Conflict* (London: Zed Books, 1993).

23. Julian Simon, "Resources, Population, Environment: An Oversupply of False Bad News," *Science*, 208: 27 (June 1980); *The Ultimate Resource* (Princeton: Princeton University Press, 1981).

24. For an interesting discussion of Simon's victorious scarcity bet with neo-Malthusian Paul Ehrlich, see Athanasiou, *Divided Planet*.

25. The catastrophic environmental legacy of communism tarnished proposals for state-based correction of ecological market failures and demolished the argument that capitalism was the main environmental culprit. Less popular attention was paid to ethnonational and political factors undergirding the failure of the Soviet experiment, or to the excessively "growthmanic" character of communist development; see Kenneth Townsend, "Steady-State Economies and the Command Economy" in Daly and Townsend, *Valuing the Earth*: see also Athanasiou, *Divided Planet*.

26. With partial exceptions, development in the Asian NICs (newly-industrializing countries, Taiwan, Singapore, South Korea, Hong Kong) was characterized by deep and systematic state intervention, state investment in human capital, comparative equity in land and education, and strategic policy management, overseeing a cautious shift from import substitution to export promotion. See Colin Bradford, "East Asian 'Models': Myths and Lessons," in John Lewis and Valeriana Kallab (eds.), *Development Strategies Reconsidered* (New Brunswick: Transaction, 1986); Frederic Deyo (ed.), *The Political Economy of the New Asian Industrialism* (Ithaca: Cornell University Press, 1987); Robin Broad and John Cavanagh, "No More NICs," *World Policy Journal*, 10: 1 (Spring 1988); Walden Bello and Stephanie Rosenfeld, *Dragons in Distress* (San Francisco: Food First, 1990); David Gereffi and Donald Wyman (eds.), *Manufacturing Miracles* (Princeton: Princeton University Press, 1990): Stephen Haggard, *Pathways from the Periphery* (Ithaca: Cornell University Press, 1990); Robert Wade, *Governing the Market* (Princeton: Princeton University Press, 1990).

27. William Canak (ed.), *Lost Promises: Debt, Austerity, and Development in Latin America* (Boulder, Westview, 1989); Susan George, *The Debt Boomerang* (London: Pluto Press, 1992); Walden Bello, *Dark Victory: The United States, Global Poverty, and Structural Adjustment* (San Francisco: Food First, 1994); Jerry Mander and Edward Goldsmith (eds.), *The Case Against the Global Economy* (San Francisco: Sierra Club Books, 1996).

28. James Weaver, Michael Rock, and Kenneth Kusterer, *Achieving Broad-Based Sustainable Development* (West Hartford CT: Kumarian Press, 1996).

29. See OECD (Organization for Economic Cooperation and Development), *Sustainable Development: OECD Policy Approaches for the 21st Century* (Washington: OECD, 1997); Commission of the European Communities, *Toward Sustainability: A European Community Programme of Policy and Action in Relation to the Environment and Sustainable Development* (Luxembourg: Office for Official Publications of the European Communities, 1993); *Progress Report From the Commission* (Brussels, 10.01.1996 COM (95): 624-final. For critical analysis of the World Bank's sustainability initiatives see Bruce Rich, *Mortgaging the Earth* (Boston: Beacon, 1994); Jonathan Fox and David Brown (eds.), *The Struggle for Accountability* (Cambridge: MIT Press, 1998); Daly, *Beyond Growth*; Dryzek, *Politics of the Earth*.

30. Daniel Rubenstein, *Environmental Accounting for the Sustainable Corporation* (Westport CT: Quorom Books, 1994), Paul Shrivastava, *Greening Business* (Cincinnati: Thomas Executive Press, 1996); Steven Schmidheiny, *Changing Course: A Global Business Perspective on Development and the Environment* (Cambridge: MIT Press, 1992); Steven Schmidheiny and Federico Zorraqu'n,

Financing Change: The Financial Community, Eco-efficiency, and Sustainable Development (Cambridge: MIT Press, 1996); Theodore Panayotou, *Green Markets* (San Francisco: ICS Press, 1993).

31. While roughly 100 heads of state attended the Earth Summit, over 1400 NGOs were represented; Ken Conca, Michael Alberty, and Geoffrey Dabelko, *Green Planet Blues* (Boulder CO: Westview, 1995, p. 6). Many observers have argued that the rapid proliferation of such organizations demonstrates an emerging international civil society; see Ronnie Lipschutz, "Reconstructing World Politics: The Emergence of Global Civil Society," *Millennium*, 21: 3 (1992); Paul Wapner, *Environmental Activism and World Civic Politics* (Albany: SUNY Press, 1996); Julie Fisher, *The Road from Rio: Sustainable Development and the Nongovernmental Movement in the Third World* (Westport CT: Praeger, 1993).

32. The Ecologist, *Whose Common Future?*, vi.

33. Careful and sophisticated environmental critiques of neoliberalism abound, demonstrating a wide variety of perspectives. On the imperfections of the globally integrated economy see Herman Daly and John Cobb, *For the Common Good* (Boston: Beacon, 1989). Daly expands on the biophysical implications of expanding trade in *Beyond Growth*. Other important critiques include Barkin, *Distorted Development*; Angus Wright, *The Death of Ramón González* (Austin: University of Texas Press, 1990); David Korten, *When Corporations Rule the World* (West Hartford CT: Kumarian Press, 1995); Durning, *How Much is Enough?*; Robin Broad and John Cavanagh, "Beyond the Myths of Rio"; Bruce Campbell, *Moving in the Wrong Direction* (Ottawa: Canadian Centre for Policy Alternatives, 1993); The Ecologist, *Whose Common Future?*; Richard Hofrichter (ed.), *Toxic Struggles* (Philadelphia: New Society, 1993); Sachs, *Global Ecology*; Bello, *Dark Victory*; Jeremy Brecher and Tim Costello, *Global Village or Global Pillage?* (Boston: South End Press,

1994); Mander and Goldsmith, *The Case Against the Global Economy*; Athanasiou, *Divided Planet*; Majid Rahnema (ed.), *The Post-Development Reader* (London: Zed Books, 1997); Joshua Karliner, *The Corporate Planet* (San Francisco: Sierra Club Books, 1997).

34. For efforts to measure the relative ecological impact of northern and southern lifestyles, see Durning, *How Much is Enough?*; The Ecologist, *Whose Common Future?*; Escobar, *Encountering Development*; Athanasiou, *Divided Planet*.

35. C. Douglas Lummis, "Equality," in Sachs, *The Development Dictionary*.

36. See the responses of Donella Meadows, Dennis Meadows, and Jorgen Randers, *Beyond the Limits* (Post Mill VT: Chelsea Green, 1992); William Ophuls and A. Stephen Boyan, *Ecology and Politics of Scarcity Revisited* (San Francisco: W. H. Freeman, 1992); Daly and Townsend, *Valuing the Earth*; Daly, *Beyond Growth*.

37. Miguel Altieri, *Agroecology* (Boulder CO: Westview, 1987); Vandana Shiva, *The Violence of the Green Revolution* (Penang, Malaysia: Third World Network, 1991); Dharam Ghai and Jessica Vivian, *Grassroots Environmental Action: People's Participation in Sustainable Development* (New York: Routledge, 1992); Winona LaDuke, "A Society Based on Conquest Cannot be Sustained: Native Peoples and the Environmental Crisis," in Hofrichter, *Toxic Struggles*; Victor Toledo, "The Ecology of Indian Campesinos: A Development Alternative," *Akwekon*, XI: 2 (Summer 1994); David Barton Bray, "Peasant Organizations and the Permanent Reconstruction of Nature," *Journal of Environment and Development*, 4: 2 (Summer 1995); David Carruthers, "Indigenous Ecology and the Politics of Linkage in Mexican Social Movements," *Third World Quarterly*, 17: 5 (1996).

38. Shiva, *Staying Alive*; Vandana Shiva, *Close to Home: Women Reconnect Ecology, Health, and Development Worldwide* (Philadelphia: New Society, 1994); Rosi Braidotti et al., *Women, the Environment, and Sustainable*

Development (London: Zed Books, 1994); Valentine U. James (ed.), *Women and Sustainable Development in Africa* (Westport CT: Praeger, 1996); Rekha Mehra, "Involving Women in Sustainable Development," in Dennis Pirages (ed.), *Building Sustainable Societies* (Armonk NY: M. E. Sharpe, 1996); Carolyn Merchant, *Earthcare: Women and the Environment* (New York, Routledge, 1996).

39. On social ecology see Murray Bookchin, *The Ecology of Freedom* (San Francisco: Chesire Books, 1982); and *Remaking Society* (Boston: South End, 1990); Andrew Light (ed.), *Social Ecology after Bookchin* (New York: Guildford, 1998). On deep ecology see Bill Devall and George Sessions, *Deep Ecology* (Salt Lake City: Peregrine Books, 1985); Warwick Fox, *Toward a Transpersonal Ecology* (Boston: Shambala, 1990). On bioregionalism see Kirkpatrick Sale, *Dwellers in the Land: The Bioregional Vision* (San Francisco: Sierra Club Books, 1985). On postmodern localism see Gustavo Esteva and Madhu Suri Prakash, *Grassroots Postmodernism: Remaking the Soil of Cultures* (London: Zed Books, 1998). On ecologism see Hector Leis and Eduardo Viola, "Towards a Sustainable Future: The Role of Ecologism in the North-South Relationship," in Fischer and Black, *Greening Environmental Policy*. For other proposals for radical decentralization, see John Dryzek, *Rational Ecology* (New York: Basil Blackwell, 1987); Carolyn Merchant, *Radical Ecology* (London: Routledge, 1992); Bron Taylor: *Ecological Resistance Movements* (Albany: SUNY Press, 1995).

40. Robert Bullard (ed.), *Confronting Environmental Racism: Voices from the Grassroots* (Boston: South End Press, 1993);

Robert Bullard (ed.), *Unequal Protection: Environmental Justice and Communities of Color* (San Francisco: Sierra Club Books 1994); Hofrichter, *Toxic Struggles*; Bunyan Bryant, *Environmental Justice: Issues, Policies, Solutions* (Washington: Island Press, 1995); Laura Westra and Peter Wenz (eds.), *Facing Environmental Racism: Confronting Issues of Global Justice* (Lanham MD: Rowman and Littlefield, 1995); Daniel Faber (ed.), *The Struggle for Ecological Democracy: Environmental Justice Movements in the United States* (New York: Guildford, 1998).

41. Martin Khor, "Economics and Environmental Justice: Rethinking North-South Relations," in Hofrichter, *Toxic Struggles*; Chris Kiefer and Medea Benjamin, "Solidarity with the Third World: Building an International Environmental Justice Movement," in Hofrichter, *Toxic Struggles*; Esteva and Prakash, *Grassroots Postmodernism*.

42. Thomas Prugh et al., *Natural Capital and Human Economic Survival* (Solomons MD: ISEE Press, 1995); Robert Costanza, Olman Segura, and Juan Martinez-Alier (eds.), *Getting Down to Earth: Practical Applications of Ecological Economics* (Washington: Island Press, 1996); Daly, *Beyond Growth*.

43. Shiva, *Staying Alive*; Shiva, *Close to Home*; Sachs, *The Development Dictionary*; Sachs, *Global Ecology*; Escobar, *Encountering Development*; Richard Peet and Michael Watts (eds.), *Liberation Ecologies: Environment, Development, Social Movements* (New York: Routledge, 1996); Rahnema, *The Post-Development Reader*; Rist, *The History of Development*; Esteva and Prakash, *Grassroots Postmodernism*.

Section VII: Ecological Modernization

Ecological modernization shares sustainable development's interest in reconciling economic growth and environmental protection, but is much more explicit on how this might be done—at least in highly developed countries. The concept first saw the light of day in Germany in the early 1980s, and has since spread to several other European countries, which have now displaced the English-speaking countries as the leaders in environmental conservation. The essential idea is that a clean environment is actually good for business, for it connotes happy and healthy workers, profits for companies developing conservation technologies or selling green products, high-quality material inputs into production (for example, clean air and water) and efficiency in materials usage. Pollution, on the other hand, indicates wasteful use of materials. In addition, it is cheaper to tackle environmental problems before they get out of hand and require expensive remedial action. The extent to which such a reorientation of the economy will require a helping hand from government remains an open question.

The selection from John Barry describes the rise of ecological modernization in both theory and European practice. He points out that ecological modernization has both economic and political aspects, because it requires a particular kind of relationship between economic growth and pollution on the one hand, and a particular kind of government on the other. Barry also surveys criticisms, concluding that environmentalists should still have a problem with economic growth as such, regardless of the green veneer that ecological modernization provides.

The ecological modernization concept is not yet used outside Europe. However, the kind of green capitalism once advocated by former US Vice-President Al Gore is entirely consistent with the concept. Gore's program was not adopted in the United States, least of all by the administration in which he served. A similar spirit is found in the selection by Hawken, Lovins, and Lovins, whose *Natural Capitalism* would rest on better technology that yielded greater well-being while using less energy and resources, so polluting less. No political or economic restructuring would then be necessary. Ideas about cleaner and greener capitalism are also emerging in Japan, though again without explicit appeal to the European concept of ecological modernization.

Further Reading

Maarten Hajer in *The Politics of Environmental Discourse: Ecological Modernization and the Policy Process* (1995) provides a comprehensive analysis of the rise of ecological modernization in the Netherlands, and early resistance to it in the United Kingdom. Peter Christoff, in "Ecological Modernisation, Ecological Modernities," *Environmental Politics*, 5 (1996), nicely contrasts "weak" and "strong" versions of ecological modernization. Al Gore's thoughts on green capitalism appear in *Earth in the Balance* (1992). The technocratic agenda is further developed in L. Hunter Lovins, Ernst von Weizsäcker, and Amory B. Lovins, *Factor Four: Doubling Wealth, Halving Resource Use*

(1997). The prolific writings of Arthur P. J. Mol on ecological modernization include Mol and David Sonnenfeld, *Ecological Modernization Around the World* (2000; also published as a special issue of *Environmental Politics*, 9: 1 (2000)); Gert Spaargaren, Mol, and Frederick Buttel (eds), *Environment and Global Modernity* (2000). Another useful collection is Stephen Young (ed.), *The Emergence of Ecological Modernisation: Integrating the Environment and the Economy* (2000). Oluf Langhelle argues that ecological modernization is a poor substitute for sustainable development in 'Why Ecological Modernization and Sustainable Development Should not be Conflated', *Journal of Environmental Policy and Planning*, 2 (2000), 303–22.

21   Ecological Modernisation

John Barry

1 Introduction

Ecological modernisation, like sustainable development to which it is related (but with which it ought not to be conflated), means different things to different people. For some it represents an analysis of current and future environmental policy and politics (Weale 1992). For others, it denotes a new form of cultural politics, representing the greening of modernity (Hajer 1995), or a rounding out of Beck's (1992) theory of 'risk society' and reflexive modernisation, an essentially positive approach to dealing with environmental problems. For critics it is the objectionable and contradictory attempt to 'green capitalism' (Barry 1999a), or a de-radicalisation of sustainable development (Langhelle 2000). Over the last five years or so, ecological modernisation has come to occupy a central position in analyses of environmental politics and policy in the industrialised North, one that has been remarkably successful in moving from the German and Dutch contexts, within which it was developed, to environmental analyses of the wider industrialised world.

According to Young (2000: 2), 'ecological modernisation is about reconceptualising the relationship between the environment and the economy in the industrialised democracies', the implications of which can vary from minimalist interpretations, which imply the 'greening of business as usual' to more wide-ranging changes in state, economy and society (Christoff 1996, 2000).

The basic tenet of ecological modernisation is that the zero-sum character of environment–economic trade-offs is more apparent than real. Ecological modernisation challenges the idea that improvements in environmental quality or the protection of nature are necessarily inimical to economic welfare, the fundamental position which dominated the early response to the 'environmental crisis' in the 1960s and 1970s. In this earlier debate the green position was that a 'steady-state economy', in conjunction with zero-population growth, was the only economy–ecology relationship which could ensure long-term sustainability (Daly 1973, 1985; Olson and Landsberg 1975). In opposition to this idea, ecological modernisation suggests that economic competitiveness and growth are not incompatible with environmental protection. Indeed, on some versions of the ecological modernisation thesis, 'environmental protection [is] a . . . potential source for future growth' (Weale 1992: 76). Future economic prospects increasingly depend on achieving and maintaining high standards of environmental protection. Key

From E. Page and J. Proops (eds), *Environmental Thought* (Cheltenham: Edward Elgar Publishers, 2003), 191–213.

to this is separating economic growth from rising energy and material inputs (Dobson 1995; Jacobs 1996).

In general terms, then, ecological modernisation can be viewed as an account of how existing political and economic institutions have, through innovative changes, responded to public and environmental movement pressure for governments to 'do something' about environmental problems. Equally, ecological modernisation also relates to how industrial interests (specific sectors, such as energy or chemical, or specific corporations, such as BP) have responded to the increasing environmental regulatory regimes in the western world, and taken what opportunities there are in meeting or exceeding these environmental standards, while at the same time effecting cost savings and/or improving their competitive market position.

While the process of modernisation of the economy (capitalist industrialism) has caused environmental problems, the solution to them lies in the direction of more or better modernisation, not, as the early green movement and many radical environmental groups still hold, in radically altering or indeed rejecting modernisation. That is, what is required to cope with contemporary and future environmental problems is a suitably ecologically enlightened or rational evolution of modernisation; that is, 'ecological modernisation'. As Buttel (2000: 61) notes:

An ecological modernisation perspective hypothesises that while the most challenging environmental problems of this century and the next have (or will have) been caused by modernisation and industrialisation their solutions must necessarily lie in more—rather than less—modernisation and 'superindustrialisation'.

For Hajer (1995: 32), ecological modernisation is 'basically a modernist and technocratic approach to the environment that suggests that there is a techno-institutional fix for the present problems'.

The remainder of this chapter is structured as follows. Section 2 explores the origins of ecological modernisation theory, and Section 3 relates this notion to the new theory of the Environmental Kuznets Curve. The ecologically modernising state is examined in Section 4, with the case of the UK being considered in detail in Section 5. The role of the green movement in ecological modernisation is addressed in Section 6, and various critiques of the notion of ecological modernisation are explored in Section 7.

2 Origins of Ecological Modernisation Theory

Ecological modernisation for Weale is understood both as a legitimating ideology within certain liberal states' response to environmental problems, and as a new departure in environmental policy principles (Weale 1992: 79), while for others it has the status of a social theory (Mol 2000). As an approach to environmental policy analysis, ecological modernisation can be viewed as a descriptive-explanatory account, marking a new environmental policy discourse from within the existing institutions of the liberal state; a form of institutional learning. Its emergence and strength as an ideology lies mainly in its capacity to render the imperative for economic growth compatible with the imperative to protect environmental quality. The evolution of this perspective has been described by Potier (1990: 69):

By the mid-70s it had become clear that it is both environmentally and economically sound to anticipate the possible negative effects of an activity such as an industrial plant and to design it in such a way as to prevent pollution before it occurs.

At the same time, in the 1980s there developed a sizeable market for 'green' or 'environmentally friendly' products (Elkington and Burke, 1991). Finally there was greater public pressure for governments to tackle environmental problems (Young 1993: 53–6; Weale 1992: 167–70), as well as the legitimacy of government being increasingly tied up with providing environmental protection (Walker 1989: 38; Weale 1992: 1, 26). The congruence of these two factors, one from the demand-side and the other from the supply-side, represents the context within which ecological modernisation developed. To use economic terminology, one could say that ecological modernisation represents an 'equilibrium' policy position: a point at which meet the supply (of ecologically-friendly goods and services) and the demand (for those goods and greater levels of environmental quality). Thus it acts as an institutional (and ideological) compromise between dominant economic interests and imperatives, and specific ecological interests (non-radical and partial), and as Weale (1992: 89) suggests, a compromise between the economic imperative for capital accumulation, economic globalisation and political legitimacy and support.[1]

This is demonstrated by Weale's (1992: 75) analysis of it as a policy approach to pollution control, originating in a critical rejection of early 'command and control' policy approaches. Ecological modernisation as an ideology is largely constituted by government programmes and policy styles and traditions, particularly those of Germany (Weale 1992: 79–85), the Netherlands (Weale 1992: chap. 5), Sweden, and the European Union environmental programmes, particularly the *Fourth Environmental Action Programme* (Weale 1992: 76–7). Thus, one can say that the origins of ecological modernisation lie in the environmental discourse of policy elites.

Ecological modernisation theory is associated with the work of Huber in the 1980s, in which he stressed how technological developments would facilitate the emergence of an ecological stage in industrial development 'the dirty and ugly industrial caterpillar will transform into an ecological butterfly' (in Mol 1995: 37). Mol's view of ecological modernisation is as an empirical phenomenon: 'Ecological modernisation can thus be interpreted as the reflexive (institutional) reorganisation of industrial society in its attempt to overcome the ecological crisis' (Mol 1995: 394). Thus, there are descriptive and prescriptive uses and characters of ecological modernisation. That is, between:

- interpretations of ecological modernisation which see it as offering a valid analytical/explanatory account or framework for actual changes in environmental policy and interactions between the economy and ecology in western societies, and
- more prescriptive or normative/ideological accounts, which suggest ecological modernisation as the most appropriate sustainable model or pattern that such societies ought to follow (or that the green movement ought to champion).

This chapter, in focusing on ecological modernisation's descriptive and prescriptive aspects, identifies and interprets it as primarily a boundary setting organisational phenomenon, in which certain things, processes, actors, principles, etc., are 'organised in' and others are 'organised

Table 21.1 **An illustration of ecological modernisation**

	Leaders/inside	Laggards/outside
State	Denmark, Netherlands	Ireland, UK
Industry	Nokia, BP, Shell, Microsoft	Exxon, manufacturing-based SMEs
Environmental movement	Greenpeace, Sierra Club	Earth First!, direct action environmentalism, anti-globalisation
Political economy	Ecological modernisation, environmental Kuznets curve, environmental economics	Steady state economy, ecological economics
Environmental thinking	Ecological modernisation, Green social democracy/welfare	Deep ecology, ecosocialism, environmental justice

out'. In this way, ecological modernisation is interpreted as both marking what is 'possible', in terms of realising certain ecological goals, and serving as a standard (both normative with 'real world' examples) of what is also 'desirable', within the structures and comforts of contemporary western societies.

In all of the literature on the subject, it is clear that ecological modernisation operates by identifying certain institutional, political, economic, and ideological actors and processes, which are deemed both possible and desirable, from others which are (by corollary) deemed impossible/radical and undesirable.

If we focus on four factors (the state, industry, the environmental movement and environmental thinking), we can see how ecological modernisation distinguishes between what I have termed 'laggards' and 'leaders', or alternatively those 'inside' and those 'outside' the discursive and policy framework mapped and maintained by ecological modernisation, shown in Table 21.1.

3 Ecological Modernisation and the Environmental Kuznets Curve

The central claim of all interpretations of ecological modernisation converge on the notion that environmental protection is either a precondition for economic growth, or is compatible with it. In this way, ecological modernisation promises to overcome the long-standing opposition between economic growth (as conventionally understood, in terms of increases in formally paid employment in the cash economy, money income—both national and disposable personal income—increased trade and export of goods and services) and environmental protection (understood as improvements in air and water quality and decreasing levels of pollution), which was (and still is) a central constitutive feature of the green movement and political perspective.

In this way, the ecological modernisation thesis is similar in form, and is related to the Environmental Kuznets Curve (EKC) hypothesis. However, it is rather surprising that to date there has been hardly any work which looks at the EKC basis and evidence for the ecological modernisation thesis, as an empirically observable and verifiable phenomenon. The EKC hypothesis states that 'beyond a certain level of income some aspects of environmental quality improve further with economic growth' (Ekins 2000: 29). This is a view which is consistent with the overall claim of the ecological modernisation thesis, that stimulating conventional economic growth (although with different technological and other innovative means) ought to remain the main focus of state policy, which should aim to integrate the ecological preconditions/resources and negative externalities (via appropriately designed environmental policies) into economic policy (with a preference for market rather than state-based solutions).

A clear exposition of the EKC thesis is given by Panayotou, who concludes his econometric comparative study by pointing out that the EKC thesis:

... suggests that as the development process picks up, when a certain level of income per capita is reached, economic growth turns from an enemy of the environment into a friend ... If economic growth is good for the environment, then policies that stimulate growth such as trade liberalisation, economic restructuring and price reform ought to be good for the environment. This in turn would tend to suggest that the environment needs no particular attention, either in terms of domestic environmental policy or international pressure or assistance; resources can best be focused on achieving rapid economic growth to move quickly through the environmentally unfavourable stage of development to the environmentally favourable range of the Kuznets Curve. (Panayotou, 1993, p. 14)

While there are obvious connections between this identification of a very strong and positive relationship between economic growth, trade liberalisation, economic globalisation and improving environmental quality, and the ecological modernisation hypothesis, ecological modernisation would differ from this 'economistic *laissez faire*' view in that it would not contend that 'the environment needs no particular attention'. This is because one of its central, animating principles is that the state *does* (albeit gently and with a preference for market-based and voluntary measures) need to develop policies to deal with environmental problems, by integrating the environment into the (market-driven, growth-orientated and globalising) economy. A more nuanced (though still heavily pro-trade liberalisation) view on the EKC, which is more in keeping with the political and policy focus of ecological modernisation, is given by Cole (2000: 89), who points out that:

... although there is evidence that developed countries have 'grown out of' some pollution problems, it is important to stress that this is by no means an automatic process ... there is nothing inevitable about the relationship between per capita income and environmental quality, as encapsulated in the EKC fitted to historical data. Pollution levels have fallen only in response to investment and policy initiatives.

The central focus of ecological modernisation is thus the relationship between the economy and ecology, and the 'mainstreaming' of environmental considerations into state economic policy-making and corporate decision-making. Whether couched in terms of international competitiveness in the rapidly expanding environmental technology sector, or the cost savings of adopting less resource and energy intensive production processes, or the fact that introducing and implementing stringent environmental standards need not drastically reduce economic growth, income and employment, the basic message of ecological modernisation is that there is

no necessary opposition between economic growth as conventionally understood (GNP measures, trade, employment, etc.) and environmental protection and improvement, as indicated by
the EKC analysis.

4 The Ecologically Modernising State

As Weale (1992: 78) argues, ecological modernisation is, in many respects, a coping strategy
adopted by states in the face of demands for higher environmental protection, together with
the continuing demand for conventional economic growth. Ecological modernisation, particularly when placed within the context of a 'green welfarism' or green social democracy, may,
like the emergence of the welfare state before it, be construed as an attempt politically to regulate production (via setting emissions standards for example and the use of market instruments,
encouraging voluntary and self-regulation), in response to the socialisation of the (environmental) costs of production as a result of 'market failure'. For example, 'polluter-pays' legislation,
the precautionary principle, mandatory environmental impact assessments, etc., all of which
are central to ecological modernisation, can be regarded as ways in which the environmental
costs of production are either prevented or 'internalised' to some extent. In this way, ecological modernisation can be viewed as an ecological dimension to the modern state's 'crisis
management' function, and also marks an ecological dimension to the restructuring of the
state, within the context of a transformation of the state towards what some have termed the
'competition state'. That is, a state for which an over-riding and constitutive imperative is to
ensure or facilitate that economic activities located within the nation-state are successful; i.e.,
competitive within the global market (Cerny 1997: 259; Levi-Faur 1998; Hague and Harrop
2001: 255–62).

A central aspect of the state in ecological modernisation seems to be its 'enabling', coordinating and supporting role, in terms of encouraging technological innovation and greater
economic and ecologically efficient use of resources and energy. Through subsidies and research
and development assistance for renewable energy, or investment in fuel cell technology, to forms
of environmental regulation, setting emissions standards, environmental taxes and other regulatory mechanisms: 'Regulation can be used to drive the process of industrial innovation
with environmental and economic gains realised as a result' (Murphy and Gouldson 2000: 43).
Indeed, much of the 'modernisation' aspect of ecological modernisation rests on the central
emphasis on innovation, both technologically and in production processes and management
and distribution systems.[2] Smart production systems, 'doing more with less', applying novel
scientific breakthroughs (for example in renewable energy, biotechnology and information
and communication technology, such as nanotechnology) and developing and utilising 'clean'
technologies, are all hallmarks of the modern, dynamic, forward-looking, solutions-focused
character of ecological modernisation. While the state 'enables' and supports innovation, it is
left to the private sector to develop, test and market these new ecologically efficient innovations
and production methods.

Another feature of the ecologically modernising state, according to Mol (1995, 2000), is that it
shifts its environmental policy away from centralised to decentralised sites, adopts preventative

rather than curative or end-of-pipe solutions, from command and control policy styles to facilitating and enabling producer and consumers to make environmentally sound decisions. This emergence of an 'enabling', 'leaner' and more flexible state is sometimes referred to as 'political modernisation' by Janicke (1990) and others in the debate (Van Tatenhove et al. 2000), and is something very close to the 'third way' view of the role of the more limited, but focused state; an 'enabling' rather than a 'providing' state (Paterson and Barry 2003).

For some ecological modernisation theorists, ecological modernisation is 'a discursive strategy useful to governments seeking to manage ecological dissent and to relegitimise their social regulatory role' (Christoff 1996: 482). For example in the British case, discussed more below, the Prime Minister Tony Blair, in a number of key environmental speeches, has used ecological modernisation discourse in ways which not only portrayed the New Labour government as successful in grasping the nettle by being at the forefront of dealing with the environmental crisis (both nationally and globally), but also sought to criticise those parts of the UK environmental movement which were not 'on message' in terms of their acceptance of the ecological modernisation approach and project. In his speech, the green movement were thanked for putting environmental issues on the political agenda, but when it came to finding solutions to them, this is what he had to say:

We need to build a new coalition for the environment, a coalition that works with the grain of consumers, business and science, not against them. A coalition that harnesses consumer demand for a better environment, and encourages businesses to see the profit of the new green technologies. (Blair 2000)

Notable by its absence is the environmental movement.

As Young (2000: 13) points out, 'an important part of ecological modernisation was about adopting more inclusive approaches and marginalising the [environmental] radicals'.

While 'the environment' has been institutionalised within the political decision-making system, the ecological modernisation model does not mean that the state is the dominant or leading actor in the ecological modernisation of the economy. Rather, there is a marked preference for market-based solutions, with the role of government being the setting of environmental targets and leaving it to market actors to decide on how best to achieve them. Another perceived task for government is to offer financial and other support for 'ecologically efficient' forms of production (especially energy).

Here it is important to point out the views of prominent ecological modernisation theorists, such as Mol and especially Janicke (1990), on the limits to state action and state failure in general, and in particular in relation to the environment, which explains the preference within ecological modernisation for the use of market-based instruments, voluntary agreements and self-regulation by business (Neale 1997). This focus on the limits and limitations of political approaches to dealing with environmental problems (but which does not reject the state in favour of a 'free market environmentalist' approach), in which political approaches are defined as state ones, shows that the political economy which most closely maps on to ecological modernisation is 'environmental economics' (Pearce 1992). Environmental economics, in outlining a role for the state in conjunction with the market, to deal with environmental problems by internalising environmental externalities, and demonstrating the economic usefulness and value of environmental goods and services, articulates the same concerns with 'economising the environment' as ecological modernisation. The economisation of the environment is central to ecological modernisation, which for Murphy (2000: 3) means 'the introduction of economic concepts, mechanisms and principles into environmental policy'. This is a clear statement of the environmental economics political economy underpinning ecological modernisation, and helps explain the penchant within ecological modernisation for market based and entrepreneurial solutions, which turn collective ecological problems for society as a whole into selective economic opportunities for market actors (aided by the state). Environmental economics, unlike, say, ecological economics (Barry 1999b: 145–8) or green political economy (Barry 1999c: chap. 6; Dryzek 1996), is increasingly an accepted part of the state's bureaucratic/administrative response to environmental problems, and has become an embedded part of the discourse of environmental policy elites and policy-making. It is, therefore, unsurprising that ecological modernisation, as a description of changes in environmental policy styles and elites' decision-making, when developed or articulated as a prescriptive or political analytical account of environmental politics and policy in late-modern societies, should be so easily compatible with environmental economics.

The practical, policy-relevant and solutions-focused character of ecological modernisation, unlike radical green political alternatives, such as deep ecology or ecosocialism, make it immediately more attractive and possible to be used as an official or state approach to environmental governance. Equally attractive to electorally sensitive politicians and bureaucrats, is its 'positive-sum' promise/premise, in terms of economic growth *and* environmental quality/protection. As Hajer (1995: 64) points out:

Ecological modernisation is based on some credible and attractive story-lines: the regulation of the environmental problem appears as a positive-sum game; pollution is a matter of inefficiency, nature has a balance that should be respected; anticipation is better than cure.

The attractiveness of ecological modernisation, as a way to develop a policy response to environmental problems to governments, lies in the basic fact that ecological modernisation offers a relatively politically and electorally painless or 'win-win' policy choice. Susskind (2002) outlines this 'win-win' approach as a 'super-optimisation' approach to environment public policy. Taking the example of reducing water pollution he states that:

... a super-optimal policy with regard to reducing water pollution would not only reduce water pollution to the greatest extent possible but also do so in a way that spun off as much long-term investment in new technology as possible, created as many new jobs as possible for those who really needed them, and reduced pollution in other media at the same time. (Susskind 2002: 291)

A tall order indeed, but this positive 'win-win' scenario is at the heart of the promise of ecological modernisation, making it politically and electorally attractive to governments.

The political attractiveness of ecological modernisation has to do with certain key characteristics. Firstly, the fact that ecological modernisation does not require major structural changes in the economy, for example in its organisation or principles of ownership, is obviously a major advantage to dealing with environmental issues, as opposed to more radical alternatives. In terms of a distinction between the ends or outputs of the economy (goods and services) and the means (ecological, technological and economic), ecological modernisation is concerned mainly (but not exclusively) with finding more sustainable means (through technical innovation, new production methods) to more or less the same ends (continuing increases in material goods and services).

Secondly, and following on from this, ecological modernisation largely focuses on production rather than consumption—seeking new technologically innovative ways to 'make more with less' in terms of energy and materials. Thus, ecological modernisation is clearly a supply-side, as opposed to demand-side approach to environmental policy. That is, ecological modernisation does not engage with consumption issues of either challenging or regulating the demand for goods and services in the economy, nor with issues concerning the distribution of consumption within society. Ecological modernisation as a 'supply-side' policy, like all supply-side policies, attempts to circumvent, downplay or avoid issues of social or distributional in/justice and in/equality. It does this by obviating the need to engage in politically regulating overall demand, or adjusting the pattern of the distribution of consumption, by focusing policy and public attention on the supply, rather than the demand for or distribution of, economic goods and services.

5 Ecological Modernisation in Britain

An interesting case study in ecological modernisation is Britain and the New Labour government's attitude towards, and approach to, environmental problems and sustainable development. In this section I want to offer a critical overview of the putative ecological modernisation discourse of New Labour in general, and of Tony Blair in particular.

While, of course, publicly committed to 'sustainable development' and obliged by international treaties related to it, it is clear that the discourse of ecological modernisation is more amenable to the New Labour government's aims and self-understanding. The fact that it has the key concept of 'modernisation' in it, has obvious attractions for a government and Prime Minster for whom 'modernisation' is a central principle, if not *the* central principle. Though not always using the term, the New Labour government's environmental policy, and integration of the environment into other policy areas (technology, industrial policy, investment, transport, energy), fits with an ecological modernisation approach.

For example, in a speech made to the Confederation of British Industry and Green Alliance in October 2000, Tony Blair stated that:

The central theme of our approach is a more productive use of environmental resources. It is clear that if we are to continue to grow, and share the benefits of that growth, we must reduce the impact of growth on the environment. (Blair 2000)

This conjoining of continued economic growth with lowering environmental impact is clearly within an ecological modernisation discourse. The supply-side (highly technologically focused) emphasis of ecological modernisation is echoed in Blair's refusal to entertain any notion about government involvement in managing or regulating demand or consumption. For him:

... we should harness consumer demand, not stifle it. We should not be trying to reduce people's aspirations, but rather find innovative ways of satisfying those aspirations. As our societies become more prosperous, so people's demand for a better environment is growing. More and more people want to buy green. We should encourage that, and harness that green consumer power in our environmental policies. (Blair 2000)

That consumer demand is sovereign, and not to be challenged on environmental grounds (or any other), is one of the many links between New Labour's 'Third Way' and ecological modernisation. Equally, not only is consumer demand beyond political regulation or questioning, but the marketed commodities and services which constitute this demand are equally beyond negotiation. That is, once again in keeping with ecological modernisation, New Labour accepts the dominant view of economic growth in terms of marketed commodities and services. The fact that ecological modernisation goes 'with the grain' of the current capitalist organisation of the economy and established and aspirational consumption patterns, makes it perfectly suited to New Labour's needs. Similar comments to the ones made by the Prime Minister above can also be found in other institutions and aspects of the New Labour project, such as the Policy and Innovation Unit of the Cabinet Office. This Unit, set up after the first New Labour victory in 1997, is charged with formulating strategic ideas and blue-skies thinking on policy. In one project, on 'Resource Productivity and Renewable Energy', the ecological modernisation character is striking. The opening summary of this project states that:

Governments all over the world are seeking better ways to integrate economic growth and the need to meet environmental and social goals. Rising prosperity and higher rates of sustainable growth are key objectives. Greater resource productivity potentially offers a route to achieving faster growth sustainably—at the same time as reducing demands on the environment—by using fewer inputs of materials and energy for any given level of output. (Policy Innovation Unit 2001)

Michael Jacobs, in a Fabian Society pamphlet tellingly entitled *Environmental Modernisation*, has attempted both to 'promote' the discourse of ecological modernisation to New Labour as an ideologically appropriate 'Third Way' approach to the environment, and to use it to analyse New Labour's environmental performance. He offers a view of ecological modernisation in which, through technological improvements in resource efficiency, coupled with matching improvements in labour productivity (secured in part by New Labour education and labour policies), we can have our growing economic cake and non-negotiable 'economic aspirations', without this resulting in ecological problems. So, for example, Jacobs discusses how, in the context of general economic and industrial policy, the focus of Labour's strategy is to increase labour productivity. He suggests that the concept could be expanded or extended to increasing environmental productivity, referring to decreases in the ratio of natural resource throughput to GDP (Jacobs 1999: 30–1).

Jacobs' view is that a narrative needs to be found so that the environment can be integrated into the New Labour modernisation project, a central part of which requires that the environment be delinked from 'environmentalism' and (prominent sections of) the green movement. The attitude of New Labour and Blair to the environmental movement is revealing. Blair places the environmental movement, especially when it is regarded as standing in the way of progress or modernisation (protesting against road building, free trade or trials of genetically modified crops), as part of the 'forces of conservatism' allied against New Labour's modernisation project.

From the perspective of environmental modernisation, the crucial requirement here is to avoid the impression of being anti-car. There is no political mileage in this at all. Contrary to the claims of many environmentalists, cars have tremendous benefits, and people value them. . . . The issue is simply that in certain places, and at certain times, the number of cars on the road causes unacceptable congestion, and for this reason, in these places and times [city centres in daytime], car access will have to be constrained. (Jacobs 1999: 41)

The attempt to conceal conflict, to present politics as if it is a matter of finding the compromise, is a classic part of 'Third Way' rhetoric and, indeed, also fits with the 'win-win', 'positive-sum' logic of ecological modernisation.

6 Ecological Modernisation and The Green Movement

The emergence of ecological modernisation has presented the green movement with a series of strategic choices to be made, which can be simplified down to just two—acceptance (reluctant or enthusiastic) or rejection. In terms of the former, according to Toke (2001: 282) 'Environmental groups use the ecological modernisation vocabulary in order to seize the high ground of the dominant notion of "modernisation"', using ecological modernisation as a way to become an 'insider' voice, promoting environmental concerns within official state-corporate environmental governance. This strategic use by green groups and organisations of the discourse of ecological modernisation is evident in their seeking to gain access to state actors and the policy-making process, and to be seen to be 'inside' rather than 'outside' the environmental policy network.

There is also the incentive to use ecological modernisation as way of promoting a more positive and solutions-focused approach to environmental problems (through organisations such as *Forum for the Future*), to signal a shift from the confrontational, critical and radical-utopian approaches of earlier phases of, and groups within, the environmental movement. In many respects, this was related to the debate between *'fundi'* and *'realo'* elements which took place in most European green parties and movements, with the *realos* winning out eventually.[3] As Mol (2000: 49) puts it:

The self-perception of significant parts of the environmental movement from the early 1980s onwards was that their confrontational ideologies had resulted in only limited successes and were increasingly counter-productive in reaching their goals.

In terms of electoral support for green politics, it had become obvious that the 'doom and gloom' political rhetoric of impending 'eco-catastrophe' and its attendant radical solutions, had by the 1980s become increasingly unhelpful in mobilising support beyond the already con-verted. That the resolution of the ecological crisis does not imply the political rejection or wholesale transformation of existing state institutions, or the complete transformation of the economy and rejection of consumerism, is a politically powerful discourse in terms of generating and sustaining support for green politics. These observations may be taken to back Goodin's (1992: 119) statement that 'we can presumably live more or less in harmony with nature even in advanced industrial and post-industrial societies, without necessarily dropping out of those societies altogether', adding in a footnote: 'Indeed, the green political agenda would be even more pointless than its worst critic imagines were that not the case'. Ecological modernisation, from the perspective of parts of the environmental movement, thus provides a realistic/practical mechanism by which to secure environmental improvements, by playing a part in the ecological transformation of leading productive sectors of the modern capitalist economy. As Buttel (2000: 63–4) has noted:

... ecological modernisation has become attractive as a concept because it provides alternatives to the pessimistic connotations of frameworks such as the treadmill of production and the growth machine. Ecological modernisation expresses hope, and makes it more readily possible to identify and appreciate the significance of environmental success stories.

One could also explain the embracing of the discourse and rhetoric of ecological modernisation by sections of the environmental movement in Europe, in terms of its adoption of a more limited, realistic, partnership/stakeholder and solutions-orientated approach, in response to the changes in the underlying strategic 'political economy' of the state in the context of economic globalisation.

For Mol (2000: 49), the implication of ecological modernisation of the green movement is that:

In general, the state is no longer seen as the evident coalition partner of the environmental movement, if it ever was. In fact, in numerous cases the state is the enemy, as in instances of major infrastructural projects (highways, airports, location of industrial areas).

Mol points out that there are now strategic alliances and links between environmental organisations and business, which bypass the state. Again, the aim of such organisations as Forum for the Future, in 'positively engaging' with corporate actors in partnership relations to create solutions to environmental problems, would be an example of Mol's (2000: 49) point that: 'Environmental organisations are engaged in constant dynamic processes of coalition building with rapidly changing opponents and partners, with the aim of maximising and safeguarding environmental gains'. Mol's rather sweeping conclusion to this 'ecological modernisation' of the environmental movement is that:

... the role of the environmental movement will shift from that of a critical commentator outside societal developments to that of a critical—and still independent—participant in developments aimed at ecological transformation. (Mol 1995: 48)

Simply put, the ecological modernisation of the environmental movement will see it transform itself from a radical, outsider group or movement, to a co-opted, reformist one, committed to working with and within the existing structures of state-corporate environmental governance.

However, and not unsurprisingly, there are those who sharply disagree with Mol's 'integrationist/assimilationist' hypothesis, not least from within the green movement, where such strategic changes, guided by the ecological modernisation thesis, have resulted in serious divisions. A very public example of this, which illustrates the tensions that the ecological modernisation discourse, project and process cause for the green movement, can be seen in the debate between

Jonathan Porritt and George Monbiot in the September 2000 edition of *The Ecologist* magazine, entitled 'Does Working with Business Compromise the Environmentalist?'. Monbiot articulated a rejectionist view of the ecological modernisation thesis and a reassertion of the 'environment versus economy' divide (in the form of 'environmentalists versus business/corporations'), by stating that:

We must deal with corporations on our own terms or not at all. In the absence of draconian democratic controls or new market imperatives, they will remain the enemies of the environment. (Monbiot and Porritt 2000: 20–1)

Further, he accuses those within the environmental movement (and Porritt and his organisation Forum for the Future in particular), who choose this partnership approach to working with corporations and business to become more 'environmentally sustainable', of being naïve; he argues that it is impossible to transform corporations to be environmentally sustainable, and such an attitude simply lends them positive publicity to legitimate their continuing environmentally destructive practices.

Porritt's (Monbiot and Porritt 2000: 22) reply is basically that working with rather than against corporations is both a far more effective way to change them, and also to achieve tangible and positive environmental change. As he puts it, 'self-interest . . . works far more powerfully than vapid moralising when dealing with the company as a whole', and he goes on to state that:

The history of the environmental movement is indeed punctuated by the occasional 'dramatic' moment, but its real success lies in the unceasing, undramatic persuasion and pressure, leading to steady, incremental change amongst both politicians and business people. So fixated are you on a macho 'them and us' battleground that you deliberately ignore this rather more humble model of transformation. (Monbiot and Porritt 2000: 22–3)

From this it is clear why Tony Blair choose Porritt rather than Monbiot to chair the UK Sustainable Development Commission.

7 Critiques of Ecological Modernisation

At root, ecological modernisation works because the interests it balances are couched in the language of economic rationality. Environmental interests are considered only to the extent that these interests can be translated into the economic language of a cost-benefit calculation. In order for the environment to be protected, it must first be demonstrated to be a 'resource' or a form of 'natural capital', and preferably a resource or capital with some direct and immediate economic benefits. As pointed out above, the underlying political economy of ecological modernisation is neoclassical environmental economics. One of the main reasons for its political success and attractiveness as a state strategy to respond to environmental concerns, is that ecological modernisation 'economises the environment' rather than the much more radical implications of 'ecologising the economy'.

Ecological modernisation is to be distinguished from radical accounts of 'sustainable development' and 'green economics', which argue that the compatibility of environmental protection and economic imperatives is premised on the distinction between, and separation of, 'social development' and 'economic growth' (Eckersley 1992; World Commission on Environment and Development 1987). Ecological modernisation does not, for example, require alternative measurements of human welfare, or radically different understandings of 'progress' or development. Rather, dominant and conventional understandings of progress and development as economic growth (as measured by GNP), wealth and income, paid employment in the formal/money economy, increases in the consumption of commodities and services, etc., are accepted as the given (and therefore non-negotiable) ends or outputs of ecological modernisation, which seeks to achieve these ends with more ecologically friendly means. Neither does ecological modernisation take into account the global dimensions of the environmental crisis, nor the need for global political co-operation to deal with global environmental problems. On this issue, ecological modernisation is limited to being a domestic approach to domestic environmental problems. As Langhelle (2000: 22) notes:

Ecological modernisation seems unable to address the nature of these global environmental problems. . . . The implication of ecological modernisation as a paradigm for environmental policy is this environmental policies without any global anchoring.

Another weakness of ecological modernisation is its limited view of the 'environment', or the range of environmental issues, problems and protection it deals with. For example, unlike sustainable development, it is not concerned with biodiversity conservation, focusing as it does on water and air pollution, and minimising energy and material natural resources. In this way it reduces the environment to 'critical natural capital' in a manner similar to environmental economics, but with a crucial difference. Whereas 'critical natural capital' in environmental economics is defined as natural resources and processes which are essential for human life and welfare, in ecological modernisation, the resources that are critical are those essential to the process of economic growth and capital accumulation. Hence, ecological modernisation is narrowly selective in what parts of the 'environment' it is interested in. As Langhelle (2000: 22) notes, in contrasting ecological modernisation and sustainable development, 'conservation is an indispensable prerequisite for sustainable development in a way it is not for ecological modernisation'.

Ecological modernisation reconciles environmental and economic imperatives, perhaps because it shares with the ideology of 'sustainable development' an essentially ambiguous character, which reconciles erstwhile opposing interests; i.e., 'environmental' ones on the one hand, and 'industrial' ones on the other (Sachs 1995; Richardson 1997; Barry 1999a). While from an ideological green position this is a problem, from a practical political point of view it can be viewed as a positive advantage. Thus, ecological modernisation can be viewed as dealing with one aspect of social-environmental problems (between economy and ecology), from a state-centred 'administrative' perspective. It is not so much a comprehensive political theory, as a programme for environmental public policy.

The basic proposition of ecological modernisation is that economic growth is like Achille's Lance: the ecological harm it causes can be cured by technologically enhanced, greener, smarter economic growth. In not presenting any major structural challenges to the organisation, ownership and control of the economy, nor of the distribution of the fruits (and burdens) of economic growth, ecological modernisation is perfectly suited to reformist political programmes, such as that represented by New Labour in the UK. It is not hard to see the attraction of such 'win-win', 'positive-sum', 'solutions-focused' approaches to, and frameworks for, understanding the relationship between the modern industrial economy and its environmental preconditions, as well as the environmental concerns of citizens and the demands on the state. As a supply-side approach to the metabolism between economy and ecology, it promises more, or at least 'better', production and consumption, it does not unsettle or challenge consumer society, and nor does it deal with or recognise the issues of socio-economic injustice and environmental injustice in modern industrial societies.

One need not agree fully with Beck's (1992) assessment to see that his critique of state-centred responses to ecological problems does bring out some of the basic problems with ecological modernisation. According to him:

The dangers of such an eco-orientated state interventionism can be derived from the parallels to the welfare state: *scientific authoritarianism* and an *excessive bureaucracy*'. (Beck 1992: 230; emphasis in original)

Ecological modernisation remains concerned with finding means to determinate ends, and is unable to articulate the full range of normative issues relating to social-environmental affairs. When environmental problems become not just a matter of the most cost-effective legislative or market-based means by which they can be dealt with, environmental degradation may come to be seen not just as an economic externality requiring economic or scientific/technocratic answers, but also and primarily as normative issues requiring moral and political answers. That is, environmental problems are questions of 'right and wrong' and only subsequently matters of costs and benefits. At this point we may say that ecological modernisation has shaded into the political-normative process of collective ecological management. That is, a transformation has occurred within the political regulation of social-environmental interaction. The mark of this transformation is the politicisation (and not simply their bureaucratisation or 'marketisation') and moralisation of environmental problems. While collective ecological management is different in kind from ecological modernisation, this should not blind us to the areas of continuity between them. Within collective ecological management, this requires radicalising the institutional potentials of ecological modernisation, particularly in respect to the transformation of the nation-state, and the relationships between state, market and civil society. As Dryzek (1997: 144) puts it:

Ecological modernisation implies a partnership in which governments, businesses, moderate environmentalists, and scientists co-operate in the restructuring of the capitalist political economy.

Ingolfur Bluhdorn has recently advanced a very sophisticated assessment of ecological modernisation as a 'peace keeping strategy' within contemporary advanced societies. For him:

... ecological modernisation has not been forced on to contemporary society or purposefully installed in order to serve only the interests of some social sectors. Instead, it has emerged by means of evolution as a societal practice that is beneficial to all parties involved. ... Ecological modernisation is here to stay because it is a highly appropriate lubricant for the smooth transition to a politics which (re) distributes the opportunities of life according to the principles of wealth and power. (Bluhdorn 2000: 200)

Ecological modernisation is the appropriate political, economic and cultural mode for addressing ecological problems at this present stage of social development, since it does not challenge the underlying ownership relations and organisation of the capitalist economy (i.e., the mode of production), the organisation of the nation-state, nor consumer culture. It does not signal a radical, or even a major, change in society and therefore is perfectly suited to the prevailing limited opportunities available, desired or permitted by the prevailing and dominant political *Zeitgeist* in the west. As a form of supply-side environmental governance, ecological modernisation is simply too successful politically to be replaced; it allows us to have our cake and eat it, to be seen to 'do something' about the environment without any corresponding changes in how the state, the economy and our consumer-based societies are organised.

Given that the ecological modernisation thesis, of delinking economic growth from environmental damage, is one that can only be proved or disproved empirically (which explains the multiplicity of case studies in the ecological modernisation literature), there are 'doubts about the technocentric and overly optimistic nature of the core ecological modernisation ideas' (Murphy and Gouldson 2000: 43), and the empirical case that the type of ecological modernisation of the economy the theory prescribes actually results in major environmental improvements. For example, in relation to the EKC hypothesis upon which, it was suggested earlier, ecological modernisation rests for its empirical and prescriptive 'business as usual' character, Ekins (2000) has advanced a devastating critique of its empirical (and thus prescriptive) basis. Basing his analysis on detailed examination of the econometric studies and official data sources for the EKC thesis, he points out that:

These messages, based on official statistics of the richest countries' environmental quality seem almost completely to negate the EKC hypothesis. ... What the wider environmental assessments indicate is the complete lack of justification for conclusions that seek to use improvements that have occurred to argue there is as yet any correlation between income growth and improvements in environmental quality overall (Ekins 2000: 506–7).

More damagingly, recent work by Janicke, one of the main proponents of ecological modernisation, casts serious doubt on the delinking of economic growth and environmental protection. In a recent co-authored work we find this rather startling conclusion:

... active promotion of economic growth needs to be questioned ... ecologically-beneficial economic change tends to be neutralised by high growth. Growth rates themselves are an environmental problem. It is apparent that qualitative growth can in the long term only be limited growth, if ecologically negative growth effects are to be compensated by technological and structural change. ... The industrialised countries will not be able to afford the luxury of high growth rates for much longer. They will have to become accustomed to solving universal problems not by economic growth, but by political action, as in matters of distribution. (Janicke et al. 2000: 149)

This would seem to indicate that the supposed 'transcendence' of the environment versus growth debate has returned, giving a new lease of life to previous 'radical' green/environmental arguments for such anti-growth proposals as a steady state economy (Daly, 1973). Equally, and just as significantly, Janicke's view about the ending of high growth rates, and thus the breakdown of the ecological modernisation of the economy, and the shift from economic to political processes in dealing with the unsustainability between the economy and ecology, will focus environmental politics on issues of social and environmental in/justice and the related politics of distribution within western societies. The failure of ecological modernisation sustainably to integrate the economy and ecology may yet herald the re-emergence and re-legitimation of radical green alternatives to the capitalist growth economies of the West. The unrealistic and impractical may yet become both possible and necessary.

Notes

1. An example of the relationship between state legitimacy and environmental protection/regulation is given by Cole (2000), in the context of the fears of the pro-economic globalisation and trade liberalisation lobby in relation to 'green protectionism'; that is, the illegitimate use of environmental concerns to unnecessarily restrict global free trade. As he puts it:

   Since environmental regulation is a potential vote-winning issue, the concern of free traders is that governments will find it politically difficult to refuse to implement such protection and, as a result, the efficiency gains from world trade will be reduced.

   Furthermore, it is feared that nations may shield domestic markets from the competitive force of the world economy by using protectionism in the guise of environmental measures. (Cole 2000: 21)

2. 'Innovation is central to ecological modernisation of production because it is through innovation and change that environmental concerns can begin to be integrated into production' (Murphy 2001: 9).

3. As Buttel (2000: 59) notes: 'Ecological modernisation has thus been closely identified with the realist wing within the fundamentalist-realist divide within the German Green Party'.

References

Barry, J. (1999a), 'Marxism and Ecology', in A. Gamble, D. Marsh and T. Tant (eds), *Marxism and Social Science* (London: Macmillan).

Barry, J. (1999b), *Environment and Social Theory* (London: Routledge).

Barry, J. (1999c), *Rethinking Green Politics: Nature, Virtue, Progress* (London: Sage).

Beck, U. (1992), *Risk Society: Towards a New Modernity* (London: Sage).

Blair, T. (2000), 'Richer and Greener', Prime Minister's speech to the CBI/Green Alliance conference on the Environment, 24 October.

Bluhdorn, I. (2000), *Post-Ecologist Politics: Social Theory and the Abdication of the Ecologist Paradigm* (London: Routledge).

Buttel, F. (2000), 'Ecological Modernisation as Social Theory', *Geoforum*, **31**: 57–65.

Cerny, P. (1997), 'Paradoxes of the Competition State: The Dynamics of Political Globalisation', *Government and Opposition*, **36** (2): 251–74.

Christoff, P. (1996), 'Ecological Citizens and Ecologically Guided Democracy', in B. Doherty and M. de Geus (eds), *Democracy and Green Political Thought* (London: Routledge).

Christoff, P. (2000), 'Ecological Modernisation, Ecological Modernities', in S. Young (ed.), *The Emergence of Ecological Modernisation: Integrating the Environment and the Economy?* (London: Routledge).

Cole, M. (2000), *Trade Liberalisation, Economic Growth and the Environment* (Cheltenham: Edward Elgar).

Daly, H. (ed.) (1973), *Toward a Steady State Economy* (Freeman: San Francisco).

Daly, H. (1985), 'Economics and Sustainability: In Defense of a Steady-state Economy', in M. Tobias (ed.), *Deep Ecology* (San Diego: Avant).

Dobson, A. (1995), *Green Political Thought* (2nd edn) (London: Routledge).

Dryzek, J. (1996), 'Foundations for Environmental Political Economy: The Search for *homo ecologicus*', *New Political Economy*, **1** (1): 27–40.

Dryzek, J. (1997), *The Politics of the Earth*, Oxford: Oxford University Press.

Eckersley, R. (1992), *Environmentalism and Political Theory: An Ecocentric Approach* (London: University of London Press).

Ekins, P. (2000), *Economic Growth and Environmental Sustainability: The Prospects for Green Growth* (London: Routledge).

Elkington, J. and T. Burke (1991), *The Green Capitalists: How to Make Money and Protect the Environment* (London: Victor Gollancz).

Goodin, R. E. (1992), *Green Political Theory* (London: Polity Press).

Hague, R. and M. Harrop (2001), *Comparative Government and Politics: An Introduction* (5th edn) (Basingstoke: Palgrave).

Hajer, M. (1995), *The Politics of Environmental Discourse: Ecological Modernisation and the Policy Process* (Oxford: Oxford University Press).

Jacobs, M. (1996), *The Politics of the Real World* (London: Earthscan).

Jacobs, M. (1999), *Environmental Modernisation* (London: Fabian Society).

Janicke, M. (1990), *State Failure: The Impotence of Politics in Industrial Society* (Oxford: Polity Press).

Janicke, M., H. Mönch and M. Binder (2000), 'Structural Change and Environmental Policy', in S. Young (ed.), *The Emergence of Ecological Modernisation: Integrating the Environment and the Economy?* (London: Routledge).

Langhelle, O. (2000), 'Why Ecological Modernisation and Sustainable Development should not be Conflated', *Journal of Environmental Policy and Planning*, **2** (4): 303–22.

Levi-Faur, D. (1998), 'The Competition State as a Neomercantilist State: Understanding the Restructuring of National and Global Telecommunications', *Journal of Socio-Economics*, **27** (6): 665–85.

Mol, A. (1995), *The Refinement of Production: Ecological Modernisation Theory and the Dutch Chemical Industry* (Utrecht: Van Arkel).

Mol, A. (2000), 'The Environment Movement in an Era of Ecological Modernisation', *Geoforum*, **31**: 45–56.

Monbiot, G. and J. Porritt (2000), 'Does Working with Business Compromise the Environmentalist?', *The Ecologist*, **30** (6): 20–3.

Murphy, J. (2000), 'Editorial: Ecological Modernisation', *Geoforum*, **31**: 1–9.

Murphy, J. (2001), 'Ecological Modernisation: The Environment and the Transformation of Society', Oxford: OCEES Research Paper No. 20.

Murphy, J. and A. Gouldson (2000), 'Environmental Policy and Industrial Innovation: Integrating Environment and Economy Through Ecological Modernisation', *Geoforum*, **31**: 33–44.

Neale, A. (1997), 'Organising Environmental Self-regulation: Liberal Governmentality and the Pursuit of Ecological Modernisation in Europe', *Environmental Politics*, **6** (4): 1–25.

Olson, M. and H. Landsberg (eds) (1975), *The No-Growth Society* (London: Woburn).

Panayotou, T. (1993), 'Empirical Tests and Policy Analysis of Environmental Degradation at Different Stages of Economic Development', World Employment Programme Research Working Paper WEP 2–22/WP 238, Geneva: International Labour Office.

Paterson, M. and J. Barry (2003), 'The Ecology of the British State's Economic Strategy Under New Labour', in J. Barry and R. Eckersley (eds), *The Global Ecological Crisis and the Nation-State* (Boston: MIT Press).

Pearce, D. (1992), 'Green Economics', *Environmental Values*, **1** (1): 3–15.

Policy Innovation Unit (2001), 'Resource Productivity and Renewable Energy',

<http://www.cabinet-office.gov.uk/innovation/2001/resource/scope.shtml>.

Potier, M. (1990), 'Towards a Better Integration of Environmental, Economic and Other Governmental Policies', in N. Åkerman (ed.), *Maintaining a Satisfactory Environment: An Agenda for International Environmental Policy* (Boulder CO: Westview Press).

Richardson, D. (1997), 'The Politics of Sustainable Development', in S. Baker, M. Kousis, D. Richardson and S. Young (eds), *The Politics of Sustainable Development: Theory, Policy and Practice within the European Union* (London: Routledge).

Sachs, W. (1995), 'Global Ecology and the Shadow of Development', in G. Sessions (ed.), *Deep Ecology for the 21st Century* (Boston: Shambala).

Susskind, L. (2002), 'Super-optimisation: A New Approach to National Environmental Policymaking', in S. Nagel (ed.), *Handbook of Public Policy Evaluation* (London: Sage).

Toke, D. (2001), 'Ecological Modernisation: A Reformist Review', *New Political Economy*, **6** (2): 279–91.

Van Tatenhove, J., B. Arts and P. Leroy (2000), *Political Modernisation and the Environment: The Renewal of Environmental Policy Arrangements* (Dordrecht: Kluwer).

Walker, K. (1989), 'The State in Environmental Management: The Ecological Dimension', *Political Studies*, **37** (1): 25–38.

Weale, A. (1992), *The New Politics of Pollution* (Manchester: Manchester University Press).

World Commission on Environment and Development (1987), *Our Common Future* (Oxford: Oxford University Press).

Young, S. (1993), *The Politics of the Environment* (Manchester: Baseline).

Young, S. (ed.) (2000), *The Emergence of Ecological Modernisation: Integrating the Environment and the Economy?* (London: Routledge).

22 The Next Industrial Revolution

Paul Hawken, Amory Lovins, and L. Hunter Lovins

Imagine for a moment a world where cities have become peaceful and serene because cars and buses are whisper quiet, vehicles exhaust only water vapor, and parks and greenways have replaced unneeded urban freeways. OPEC has ceased to function because the price of oil has fallen to five dollars a barrel, but there are few buyers for it because cheaper and better ways now exist to get the services people once turned to oil to provide. Living standards for all people have dramatically improved, particularly for the poor and those in developing countries. Involuntary unemployment no longer exists, and income taxes have largely been eliminated. Houses, even low-income housing units, can pay part of their mortgage costs by the energy they *produce*; there are few if any active landfills; worldwide forest cover is increasing; dams are being dismantled; atmospheric CO_2 levels are decreasing for the first time in two hundred years; and effluent water leaving factories is cleaner than the water coming into them. Industrialized countries have reduced resource use by 80 percent while improving the quality of life. Among these technological changes, there are important social changes. The frayed social nets of Western countries have been repaired. With the explosion of family-wage jobs, welfare demand has fallen. A progressive and active union movement has taken the lead to work with business, environmentalists, and government to create "just transitions" for workers as society phases out coal, nuclear energy, and oil. In communities and towns, churches, corporations, and labor groups promote a new living-wage social contract as the least expensive way to ensure the growth and preservation of valuable social capital. Is this the vision of a utopia? In fact, the changes described here could come about in the decades to come as the result of economic and technological trends already in place.

This book is about these and many other possibilities.

It is about the possibilities that will arise from the birth of a new type of industrialism, one that differs in its philosophy, goals, and fundamental processes from the industrial system that is the standard today. In the next century, as human population doubles and the resources available per person drop by one-half to three-fourths, a remarkable transformation of industry and commerce can occur. Through this transformation, society will be able to create a vital economy that uses radically less material and energy. This economy can free up resources, reduce taxes on personal income, increase per-capita spending on social ills (while simultaneously reducing those ills), and begin to restore the damaged environment of the earth. These necessary changes done properly can promote economic efficiency, ecological conservation, and social equity.

From *Natural Capitalism* (Boston: Little, Brown and Co., 1999), 1–21).

The industrial revolution that gave rise to modern capitalism greatly expanded the possibilities for the material development of humankind. It continues to do so today, but at a severe price. Since the mid-eighteenth century, more of nature has been destroyed than in all prior history. While industrial systems have reached pinnacles of success, able to muster and accumulate human-made capital on vast levels, *natural capital*, on which civilization depends to create economic prosperity, is rapidly declining,[1] and the rate of loss is increasing proportionate to gains in material well-being. *Natural capital* includes all the familiar resources used by humankind: water, minerals, oil, trees, fish, soil, air, et cetera. But it also encompasses living systems, which include grasslands, savannas, wetlands, estuaries, oceans, coral reefs, riparian corridors, tundras, and rainforests. These are deteriorating worldwide at an unprecedented rate. Within these ecological communities are the fungi, ponds, mammals, humus, amphibians, bacteria, trees, flagellates, insects, songbirds, ferns, starfish, and flowers that make life possible and worth living on this planet.

As more people and businesses place greater strain on living systems, limits to prosperity are coming to be determined by natural capital rather than industrial prowess. This is not to say that the world is running out of commodities in the near future. The prices for most raw materials are at a twenty-eight-year low and are still falling. Supplies are cheap and appear to be abundant, due to a number of reasons: the collapse of the Asian economies, globalization of trade, cheaper transport costs, imbalances in market power that enable commodity traders and middlemen to squeeze producers, and in large measure the success of powerful new extractive technologies, whose correspondingly extensive damage to ecosystems is seldom given a monetary value. After richer ores are exhausted, skilled mining companies can now level and grind up whole mountains of poorer-quality ores to extract the metals desired. But while technology keeps ahead of depletion, providing what appear to be ever-cheaper metals, they only appear cheap, because the stripped rainforest and the mountain of toxic tailings spilling into rivers, the impoverished villages and eroded indigenous cultures—all the consequences they leave in their wake—are not factored into the cost of production.

It is not the supplies of oil or copper that are beginning to limit our development but life itself. Today, our continuing progress is restricted not by the number of fishing boats but by the decreasing numbers of fish; not by the power of pumps but by the depletion of aquifers; not by the number of chainsaws but by the disappearance of primary forests. While living systems are the source of such desired materials as wood, fish, or food, of utmost importance are the *services* that they offer,[2] services that are far more critical to human prosperity than are nonrenewable resources. A forest provides not only the resource of wood but also the services of water storage and flood management. A healthy environment automatically supplies not only clean air and water, rainfall, ocean productivity, fertile soil, and watershed resilience but also such less-appreciated functions as waste processing (both natural and industrial), buffering against the extremes of weather, and regeneration of the atmosphere.

Humankind has inherited a 3.8-billion-year store of natural capital. At present rates of use and degradation, there will be little left by the end of the next century. This is not only a matter of aesthetics and morality, it is of the utmost practical concern to society and all people. Despite reams of press about the state of the environment and rafts of laws attempting to prevent further loss, the stock of natural capital is plummeting and the vital life-giving services that flow from it are critical to our prosperity.

Natural capitalism recognizes the critical interdependency between the production and use of human-made capital and the maintenance and supply of natural capital. The traditional definition of capital is accumulated wealth in the form of investments, factories, and equipment. Actually, an economy needs four types of capital to function properly:

- human capital, in the form of labor and intelligence, culture, and organization
- financial capital, consisting of cash, investments, and monetary instruments
- manufactured capital, including infrastructure, machines, tools, and factories
- natural capital, made up of resources, living systems, and ecosystem services

The industrial system uses the first three forms of capital to transform natural capital into the stuff of our daily lives: cars, highways, cities, bridges, houses, food, medicine, hospitals, and schools.

The climate debate is a public issue in which the assets at risk are not specific resources, like oil, fish, or timber, but a life-supporting system. One of nature's most critical cycles is the continual exchange of carbon dioxide and oxygen among plants and animals. This "recycling service" is provided by nature free of charge. But today carbon dioxide is building up in the atmosphere, due in part to combustion of fossil fuels. In effect, the capacity of the natural system to recycle carbon dioxide has been exceeded, just as overfishing can exceed the capacity of a fishery to replenish stocks. But what is especially important to realize is that there is no known alternative to nature's carbon cycle service.

Besides climate, the changes in the biosphere are widespread. In the past half century, the world has a lost a fourth of its topsoil and a third of its forest cover. At present rates of destruction, we will lose 70 percent of the world's coral reefs in our lifetime, host to 25 percent of marine life.[3] In the past three decades, one-third of the planet's resources, its "natural wealth," has been consumed. We are losing freshwater ecosystems at the rate of 6 percent a year, marine ecosystems by 4 percent a year.[4] There is no longer any serious scientific dispute that the decline in every living system in the world is reaching such levels that an increasing number of them are starting to lose, often at a pace accelerated by the interactions of their decline, their assured ability to sustain the continuity of the life process. We have reached an extraordinary threshold.

Recognition of this shadow side of the success of industrial production has triggered the second of the two great intellectual shifts of the late twentieth century. The end of the Cold War and the fall of communism was the first such shift; the second, now quietly emerging, is the end of the war against life on earth, and the eventual ascendance of what we call natural capitalism.

Capitalism, as practiced, is a financially profitable, nonsustainable aberration in human development. What might be called "industrial capitalism" does not fully conform to its own accounting principles. It liquidates its capital and calls it income. It neglects to assign any value to the largest stocks of capital it employs—the natural resources and living systems, as well as the social and cultural systems that are the basis of human capital.

But this deficiency in business operations cannot be corrected simply by assigning monetary values to natural capital, for three reasons. First, many of the services we receive from living systems have no known substitutes at any price; for example, oxygen production by green plants. This was demonstrated memorably in 1991–93 when the scientists operating the $200 million Biosphere 2 experiment in Arizona discovered that it was unable to maintain life-supporting oxygen levels for the eight people living inside. Biosphere 1, a.k.a. Planet Earth, performs this task daily at no charge for 6 billion people.

Second, valuing natural capital is a difficult and imprecise exercise at best. Nonetheless, several recent assessments have estimated that biological services flowing directly into society from the stock of natural capital are worth at least $36 trillion annually.[5] That figure is close to the annual gross world product of approximately $39 trillion—a striking measure of the value of natural capital to the economy. If natural capital stocks were given a monetary value, assuming the assets yielded "interest" of $36 trillion annually, the world's natural capital would be valued at somewhere between $400 and $500 trillion—tens of thousands of dollars for every person on the planet. That is undoubtedly a conservative figure given the fact that anything we can't live without and can't replace at any price could be said to have an infinite value.

Additionally, just as technology cannot replace the planet's life-support systems, so, too, are machines unable to provide a substitute for human intelligence, knowledge, wisdom, organizational abilities, and culture. The World Bank's 1995 *Wealth Index* found the sum value of human capital to be three times greater than all the financial and manufactured capital reflected on global balance sheets.[6] This, too, appears to be a conservative estimate, since it counts only the market value of human employment, not uncompensated effort or cultural resources.

It is not the aim of this book to assess how to determine value for such unaccounted-for forms of capital. It is clear, however, that behaving as though they are valueless has brought us to the verge of disaster. But if it is in practice difficult to tabulate the value of natural and human capital on balance sheets, how can governments and conscientious business persons make decisions about the responsible use of earth's living systems?

Conventional Capitalism

Following Einstein's dictum that problems can't be solved within the mind-set that created them, the first step toward any comprehensive economic and ecological change is to understand the mental model that forms the basis of present economic thinking. The mind-set of the present capitalist system might be summarized as follows:

- Economic progress can best occur in free-market systems of production and distribution where reinvested profits make labor and capital increasingly productive.
- Competitive advantage is gained when bigger, more efficient plants manufacture more products for sale to expanding markets.
- Growth in total output (GDP) maximizes human well-being.
- Any resource shortages that do occur will elicit the development of substitutes.
- Concerns for a healthy environment are important but must be balanced against the requirements of economic growth, if a high standard of living is to be maintained.
- Free enterprise and market forces will allocate people and resources to their highest and best uses.

The origins of this worldview go back centuries, but it took the industrial revolution to establish it as the primary economic ideology. This sudden, almost violent, change in the means of production and distribution of goods, in sector after economic sector, introduced a new element that redefined the basic formula for the creation of material products: Machines powered by water, wood, charcoal, coal, oil, and eventually electricity accelerated or accomplished some or all of the work formerly performed by laborers. Human productive capabilities began to grow exponentially. What took two hundred workers in 1770 could be done by a single spinner in the British textile industry by 1812. With such astonishingly improved productivity, the labor force was able to manufacture a vastly larger volume of basic necessities like cloth at greatly reduced cost. This in turn rapidly raised standards of living and real wages, increasing demand for other products in other industries. Further technological breakthroughs proliferated, and as industry after industry became mechanized, leading to even lower prices and higher incomes, all of these factors fueled a self-sustaining and increasing demand for transportation, housing, education, clothing, and other goods, creating the foundation of modern commerce.[7]

The past two hundred years of massive growth in prosperity and manufactured capital have been accompanied by a prodigious body of economic theory analyzing it, all based on the fallacy that natural and human capital have little value as compared to final output. In the standard industrial model, the creation of value is portrayed as a linear sequence of extraction, production, and distribution: Raw materials are introduced. (Enter nature, stage left.) Labor uses technologies to transform these resources into products, which are sold to create profits. The wastes from production processes, and soon the products themselves, are somehow disposed of somewhere else. (Exit waste, stage right.) The "somewheres" in this scenario are not the concern of classical economics: Enough money can buy enough resources, so the theory goes, and enough "elsewheres" to dispose of them afterward.

This conventional view of value creation is not without its critics. Viewing the economic process as a disembodied, circular flow of value between production and consumption, argues economist Herman Daly, is like trying to understand an animal only in terms of its circulatory system, without taking into account the fact it also has a digestive tract that ties it firmly to its environment at both ends. But there is an even more fundamental critique to be applied here, and it is one based on simple logic. The evidence of our senses is sufficient to tell us that all economic activity—all that human beings are, all that they can ever accomplish—is embedded within the workings of a particular planet. That planet is not growing, so the somewheres and elsewheres are always with us. The increasing removal of resources, their transport and use, and their replacement with waste steadily erodes our stock of natural capital.

With nearly ten thousand new people arriving on earth every hour, a new and unfamiliar pattern of scarcity is now emerging. At the beginning of the industrial revolution, labor was overworked and relatively scarce (the population was about one-tenth of current totals), while global stocks of natural capital were abundant and unexploited. But today the situation has been reversed: After two centuries of rises in labor productivity, the liquidation of natural resources at their extraction cost rather than their replacement value, and the exploitation of living systems as if they were free, infinite, and in perpetual renewal, it is people who have become an abundant resource, while *nature* is becoming disturbingly scarce.

Applying the same economic logic that drove the industrial revolution to this newly emerging pattern of scarcity implies that, if there is to be prosperity in the future, society must make its use of *resources* vastly more productive—deriving four, ten, or even a hundred times as much benefit from each unit of energy, water, materials, or anything else borrowed from the planet and consumed. Achieving this degree of efficiency may not be as difficult as it might seem because from a materials and energy perspective, the economy is massively inefficient. In the United States, the materials used by the metabolism of industry amount to more than twenty times every citizen's weight per day—more than one million pounds per American per year. The global flow of matter, some 500 billion tons per year, most of it wasted, is largely invisible. Yet obtaining, moving, using, and disposing of it is steadily undermining the health of the planet, which is showing ever greater signs of stress, even of biological breakdown. Human beings already use over half the world's accessible surface freshwater, have transformed one-third to one-half of its land surface, fix more nitrogen than do all natural systems on land, and appropriate more than two-fifths of the planet's entire land-based primary biological productivity.[8] The doubling of these burdens with rising population will displace many of the millions of other species, undermining the very web of life.

The resulting ecological strains are also causing or exacerbating many forms of social distress and conflict. For example, grinding poverty, hunger, malnutrition, and rampant disease affect one-third of the world and are growing in absolute numbers; not surprisingly, crime, corruption, lawlessness, and anarchy are also on the rise (the fastest-growing industry in the world is security and private police protection); fleeing refugee populations have increased throughout the nineties to about a hundred million; over a billion people in the world who need to work cannot find jobs, or toil at such menial work that they cannot support themselves or their families;[9] meanwhile, the loss of forests, topsoil, fisheries, and freshwater is, in some cases, exacerbating regional and national conflicts.

What would our economy look like if it fully valued *all* forms of capital, including human and natural capital? What if our economy were organized not around the lifeless abstractions of neoclassical economics and accountancy but around the biological realities of nature? What if Generally Accepted Accounting Practice booked natural and human capital not as a free amenity in putative inexhaustible supply but as a finite and integrally valuable factor of production? What if, in the absence of a rigorous way to practice such accounting, companies started to act *as if* such principles were in force? This choice is possible and such an economy would offer a stunning new set of opportunities for all of society, amounting to no less than the *next industrial revolution*.

Capitalism as if Living Systems Mattered

Natural capitalism and the possibility of a new industrial system are based on a very different mind-set and set of values than conventional capitalism. Its fundamental assumptions include the following:

- The environment is not a minor factor of production but rather is "an envelope containing, provisioning, and sustaining the entire economy."[10]

- The limiting factor to future economic development is the availability and functionality of *natural capital*, in particular, life-supporting services that have no substitutes and currently have no market value.
- Misconceived or badly designed business systems, population growth, and wasteful patterns of consumption are the primary causes of the loss of natural capital, and all three must be addressed to achieve a sustainable economy.
- Future economic progress can best take place in democratic, market-based systems of production and distribution in which *all* forms of capital are fully valued, including human, manufactured, financial, and natural capital.
- One of the keys to the most beneficial employment of people, money, and the environment is radical increases in resource productivity.
- Human welfare is best served by improving the quality and flow of desired services delivered, rather than by merely increasing the total dollar flow.
- Economic and environmental sustainability depends on redressing global inequities of income and material well-being.
- The best long-term environment for commerce is provided by true democratic systems of governance that are based on the needs of people rather than business.

This book introduces four central strategies of natural capitalism that are a means to enable countries, companies, and communities to operate by behaving as if all forms of capital were valued. Ensuring a perpetual annuity of valuable social and natural processes to serve a growing population is not just a prudent investment but a critical need in the coming decades. Doing so can avert scarcity, perpetuate abundance, and provide a solid basis for social development; it is the basis of responsible stewardship and prosperity for the next century and beyond.

1. **Radical Resource Productivity.** Radically increased resource productivity is the cornerstone of natural capitalism because using resources more effectively has three significant benefits: It slows resource depletion at one end of the value chain, lowers pollution at the other end, and provides a basis to increase worldwide employment with meaningful jobs. The result can be lower costs for business and society, which no longer has to pay for the chief causes of ecosystem and social disruption. Nearly all environmental and social harm is an artifact of the uneconomically wasteful use of human and natural resources, but radical resource productivity strategies can nearly halt the degradation of the biosphere, make it more profitable to employ people, and thus safeguard against the loss of vital living systems and social cohesion.

2. **Biomimicry.** Reducing the wasteful throughput of materials—indeed, eliminating the very idea of waste—can be accomplished by redesigning industrial systems on biological lines that change the nature of industrial processes and materials, enabling the constant reuse of materials in continuous closed cycles, and often the elimination of toxicity.

3. **Service and Flow Economy.** This calls for a fundamental change in the relationship between producer and consumer, a shift from an economy of goods and purchases to one of *service* and *flow*. In essence, an economy that is based on a flow of economic services can better protect the ecosystem services upon which it depends. This will entail a new perception of

value, a shift from the acquisition of goods as a measure of affluence to an economy where the continuous receipt of quality, utility, and performance promotes well-being. This concept offers incentives to put into practice the first two innovations of natural capitalism by restructuring the economy to focus on relationships that better meet customers' changing value needs and to reward automatically both resource productivity and closed-loop cycles of materials use.

4. **Investing in Natural Capital.** This works toward reversing world-wide planetary destruction through reinvestments in sustaining, restoring, and expanding stocks of natural capital, so that the biosphere can produce more abundant ecosystem services and natural resources.

All four changes are interrelated and interdependent; all four generate numerous benefits and opportunities in markets, finance, materials, distribution, and employment. Together, they can reduce environmental harm, create economic growth, and increase meaningful employment.

Resource Productivity

Imagine giving a speech to Parliament in 1750 predicting that within seventy years human productivity would rise to the point that one person could do the work of two hundred. The speaker would have been branded as daft or worse. Imagine a similar scene today. Experts are testifying in Congress, predicting that we will increase the productivity of our resources in the next seventy years by a factor of four, ten, even one hundred. Just as it was impossible 250 years ago to conceive of an individual's doing two hundred times more work, it is equally difficult for us today to imagine a kilowatt-hour or board foot being ten or a hundred times more productive than it is now.

Although the movement toward radical resource productivity has been under way for decades, its clarion call came in the fall of 1994, when a group of sixteen scientists, economists, government officials, and business people convened and, sponsored by Friedrich Schmidt-Bleek of the Wuppertal Institute for Climate, Environment, and Energy in Germany, published the "Carnoules Declaration." Participants had come from Europe, the United States, Japan, England, Canada, and India to the French village of Carnoules to discuss their belief that human activities were at risk from the ecological and social impact of materials and energy use. The Factor Ten Club, as the group came to call itself, called for a leap in resource productivity to reverse the growing damage. The declaration began with these prophetic words: "Within one generation, nations can achieve a ten-fold increase in the efficiency with which they use energy, natural resources and other materials."[11]

In the years since, Factor Ten (a 90 percent reduction in energy and materials intensity) and Factor Four (a 75 percent reduction) have entered the vocabulary of government officials, planners, academics, and business people throughout the world.[12] The governments of Austria, the Netherlands, and Norway have publicly committed to pursuing Factor Four efficiencies. The same approach has been endorsed by the European Union as the new paradigm for sustainable development. Austria, Sweden, and OECD environment ministers have urged the adoption of Factor Ten goals, as have the World Business Council for Sustainable Development and the United Nations Environment Program (UNEP).[13] The concept is not only common parlance for most environmental ministers in the world, but such leading corporations as Dow Europe and Mitsubishi Electric see it as a powerful strategy to gain a competitive advantage. Among all major industrial nations, the United States probably has the least familiarity with and understanding of these ideas.

At its simplest, increasing resource productivity means obtaining the same amount of utility or work from a product or process while using less material and energy. In manufacturing, transportation, forestry, construction, energy, and other industrial sectors, mounting empirical evidence suggests that radical improvements in resource productivity are both practical and cost-effective, even in the most modern industries. Companies and designers are developing ways to make natural resources—energy, metals, water, and forests—work five, ten, even one hundred times harder than they do today. These efficiencies transcend the marginal gains in performance that industry constantly seeks as part of its evolution. Instead, *revolutionary* leaps in design and technology will alter industry itself as demonstrated in the following chapters. Investments in the productivity revolution are not only repaid over time by the saved resources but in many cases can *reduce* initial capital investments.

When engineers speak of "efficiency," they refer to the amount of output a process provides per unit of input. Higher efficiency thus means doing more with less, measuring both factors in physical terms. When economists refer to efficiency, however, their definition differs in two ways. First, they usually measure a process or outcome in terms of expenditure of money—how the market value of what was produced compares to the market cost of the labor and other inputs used to create it. Second, "economic efficiency" typically refers to how fully and perfectly market mechanisms are being harnessed to minimize the monetary total factor cost of production. Of course it's important to harness economically efficient market mechanisms, and we share economists' devotion to that goal. But to avoid confusion, when we suggest using market tools to achieve "resource productivity" and "resource efficiency," we use those terms in the engineering sense.

Resource productivity doesn't just save resources and money; it can also improve the quality of life. Listen to the din of daily existence—the city and freeway traffic, the airplanes, the garbage trucks outside urban windows—and consider this: The waste and the noise are signs of inefficiency, and they represent money being thrown away. They will disappear as surely as did manure from the nineteenth-century streets of London and New York. Inevitably, industry will redesign everything it makes and does, in order to participate in the coming productivity revolution. We will be able to see better with resource-efficient lighting systems, produce higher-quality goods in efficient factories, travel more safely and comfortably in efficient vehicles, feel more comfortable (and do substantially more and better work)[14] in efficient buildings, and be better nourished by efficiently grown food. An air-conditioning system that uses 90 percent less energy or a building so efficient that it needs no air-conditioning at all may not fascinate the average citizen, but the fact that they are quiet and produce greater comfort while reducing energy costs should appeal even to technophobes. That such options save money should interest everyone.

As subsequent chapters will show, the unexpectedly large improvements to be gained by resource productivity offer an entirely new terrain for business invention, growth, and development. Its advantages can also dispel the long-held belief that core business values and environmental responsibility are incompatible or at odds. In fact, the massive inefficiencies that are causing environmental degradation almost always cost more than the measures that would reverse them.

But even as Factor Ten goals are driving reductions in materials and energy flows, some governments are continuing to create and administer laws, policies, taxes, and subsidies that have quite the opposite effect. Hundreds of billions of dollars of taxpayers' money are annually diverted to promote inefficient and unproductive material and energy use. These include subsidies to mining, oil, coal, fishing, and forest industries as well as agricultural practices that degrade soil fertility and use wasteful amounts of water and chemicals. Many of these subsidies are vestigial, some dating as far back as the eighteenth century, when European powers provided entrepreneurs with incentives to find and exploit colonial resources. Taxes extracted from labor subsidize patterns of resource use that in turn displace workers, an ironic situation that is becoming increasingly apparent and unacceptable, particularly in Europe, where there is chronically high unemployment. Already, tax reforms aimed at increasing employment by shifting taxes away from people to the use of resources have started to be instituted in the Netherlands, Germany, Britain, Sweden, and Denmark, and are being seriously proposed across Europe.

In less developed countries, people need realistic and achievable means to better their lives. The world's growing population cannot attain a Western standard of living by following traditional industrial paths to development, for the resources required are too vast, too expensive, and too damaging to local and global systems. Instead, radical improvements in resource productivity expand their possibilities for growth, and can help to ameliorate the polarization of wealth between rich and poor segments of the globe. When the world's nations met in Brazil at the Earth Summit in 1992 to discuss the environment and human development, some treaties and proposals proved to be highly divisive because it appeared that they put a lid on the ability of nonindustrialized countries to pursue development. Natural capitalism provides a practical agenda for development wherein the actions of both developed and developing nations are mutually supportive.

Biomimicry

To appreciate the potential of radical resource productivity, it is helpful to recognize that the present industrial system is, practically speaking, a couch potato: It eats too much junk food and gets insufficient exercise. In its late maturity, industrial society runs on life-support systems that require enormous heat and pressure, are petrochemically dependent and materials-intensive, and require large flows of toxic and hazardous chemicals. These industrial "empty calories" end up as pollution, acid rain, and greenhouse gases, harming environmental, social, and financial systems. Even though all the reengineering and downsizing trends of the past decade were supposed to sweep away corporate inefficiency, the U.S. economy remains astoundingly inefficient: It has been estimated that only 6 percent of its vast flows of materials actually end up in products.[15] Overall, the ratio of waste to the *durable* products that constitute material wealth may be closer to one hundred to one. The whole economy is less than 10 percent—probably only a few percent—as energy-efficient as the laws of physics permit.[16]

This waste is currently rewarded by deliberate distortions in the marketplace, in the form of policies like subsidies to industries that extract raw materials from the earth and damage the biosphere. As long as that damage goes unaccounted for, as long as virgin resource prices are maintained at artificially low levels, it makes sense to continue to use virgin materials rather than reuse resources discarded from previous products. As long as it is assumed that there are "free goods" in the world—pure water, clean air, hydrocarbon combustion, virgin forests, veins of minerals—large-scale, energy- and materials-intensive manufacturing methods will dominate, and labor will be increasingly marginalized.[17] In contrast, if the subsidies distorting resource prices were removed or reversed, it would be advantageous to employ more people and use fewer virgin materials.

Even without the removal of subsidies, the economics of resource productivity are already encouraging industry to reinvent itself to be more in accord with biological systems. Growing competitive pressures to save resources are opening up exciting frontiers for chemists, physicists, process engineers, biologists, and industrial designers. They are reexamining the energy, materials, and manufacturing systems required to provide the specific qualities (strength, warmth, structure, protection, function, speed, tension, motion, skin) required by products and end users and are turning away from mechanical systems requiring heavy metals, combustion, and petroleum to seek solutions that use minimal inputs, lower temperatures, and enzymatic reactions. Business is switching to imitating biological and ecosystem processes replicating natural methods of production and engineering to manufacture chemicals, materials, and compounds, and soon maybe even microprocessors. Some of the most exciting developments have resulted from emulating nature's life-temperature, low-pressure, solar-powered assembly techniques, whose products rival anything human-made. Science writer Janine Benyus points out that spiders make silk, strong as Kevlar but much tougher, from digested crickets and flies, without needing boiling sulfuric acid and high-temperature extruders. The abalone generates an inner shell twice as tough as our best ceramics, and diatoms make glass, both processes employing seawater with no furnaces. Trees turn sunlight, water, and air into cellulose, a sugar stiffer and stronger than nylon, and bind it into wood, a natural composite with a higher bending strength and stiffness than concrete or steel. We may never grow as skillful as spiders, abalone, diatoms, or trees, but smart designers are apprenticing themselves to nature to learn the benign chemistry of its processes.

Pharmaceutical companies are becoming microbial ranchers managing herds of enzymes. Biological farming manages soil ecosystems in order to increase the amount of biota and life per acre by keen knowledge of food chains, species interactions, and nutrient flows, minimizing crop losses and maximizing yields by fostering diversity. Meta-industrial engineers are creating "zero-emission" industrial parks whose tenants will constitute an industrial ecosystem in which one company will feed upon the nontoxic and useful wastes of another. Architects and builders are creating structures that process their own wastewater, capture light, create energy, and provide habitat for wildlife and wealth for the community, all the while improving worker productivity, morale, and health.[18] High-temperature, centralized power plants are starting to be replaced by smaller-scale, renewable power generation. In chemistry, we can look forward to the end of the witches' brew of dangerous substances invented this century, from DDT, PCB, CFCs, and Thalidomide to Diddrin and xeno-estrogens. The eighty thousand different chemicals now manufactured end up everywhere, as Donella Meadows remarks, from our "stratosphere to our sperm." They were created to accomplish functions that can now be carried out far more efficiently with biodegradable and naturally occurring compounds.

Service and Flow

Beginning in the mid-1980s, Swiss industry analyst Walter Stahel and German chemist Michael Braungart independently proposed a new industrial model that is now gradually taking shape. Rather than an economy in which *goods* are made and sold, these visionaries imagined a *service economy* wherein consumers obtain *services* by leasing or renting goods rather than buying them outright. (Their plan should not be confused with the conventional definition of a service economy, in which burger-flippers outnumber steelworkers.) Manufacturers cease thinking of themselves as sellers of products and become, instead, deliverers of service, provided by long-lasting, upgradeable durables. Their goal is selling results rather than equipment, performance and satisfaction rather than motors, fans, plastics, or condensers.

The system can be demonstrated by a familiar example. Instead of purchasing a washing machine, consumers could pay a monthly fee to obtain the *service* of having their clothes cleaned. The washer would have a counter on it, just like an office photocopier, and would be maintained by the manufacturer on a regular basis, much the way mainframe computers are. If the machine ceased to provide its specific service, the manufacturer would be responsible for replacing or repairing it at no charge to the customer, because the washing machine would remain the property of the manufacturer. The concept could likewise be applied to computers, cars, VCRs, refrigerators, and almost every other durable that people now buy, use up, and ultimately throw away. Because products would be returned to the manufacturer for continuous repair, reuse, and remanufacturing, Stahel called the process "cradle-to-cradle."[19]

Many companies are adopting Stahel's principles. Agfa Gaevert pioneered the leasing of copier services, which spread to the entire industry.[20] The Carrier Corporation, a division of United Technologies, is creating a program to sell coolth (the opposite of warmth) to companies while retaining ownership of the air-conditioning equipment. The Interface Corporation is beginning to lease the warmth, beauty, and comfort of its floor-covering services rather than selling carpets.

Braungart's model of a *service economy* focuses on the nature of material cycles. In this perspective, if a given product lasts a long time but its waste materials cannot be reincorporated into new manufacturing or biological cycles, then the producer must accept responsibility for the waste with all its attendant problems of toxicity, resource over-use, worker safety, and environmental damage. Braungart views the world as a series of metabolisms in which the creations of human beings, like the creations of nature, become "food" for interdependent systems, returning to either an industrial or a biological cycle after their useful life is completed. To some, especially frugal Scots and New Englanders, this might not sound a novel concept at all. Ralph Waldo Emerson once wrote, "Nothing in nature is exhausted in its first use. When a thing has served an end to the uttermost, it is wholly new for an ulterior service."[21] In simpler times, such proverbial wisdom had highly practical applications. Today, the complexity of modern materials makes this almost impossible. Thus, Braungart proposed an Intelligent Product System whereby those products that do not degrade back into natural nutrient cycles be designed so that they can be deconstructed and completely reincorporated into *technical nutrient* cycles of industry.[22]

Another way to conceive of this method is to imagine an industrial system that has no provision for landfills, outfalls, or smokestacks. If a company knew that nothing that came into its factory could be thrown away, and that everything it produced would eventually return, how would it design its components and products? The question is more than a theoretical construct, because the earth works under precisely these strictures.

In a *service economy*, the product is a means, not an end. The manufacturer's leasing and ultimate recovery of the product means that the product remains an asset. The minimization of materials use, the maximization of product durability, and enhanced ease of maintenance not only improve the customer's experience and value but also protect the manufacturer's investment and hence its bottom line. *Both* producer and customer have an incentive for continuously improving resource productivity, which in turn further protects ecosystems. Under this shared incentive, both parties form a relationship that continuously anticipates and meets the customer's evolving value needs—and meanwhile rewards both parties for reducing the burdens on the planet.

The service paradigm has other benefits as well: It increases employment, because when products are designed to be reincorporated into manufacturing cycles, waste declines, and demand for labor increases. In manufacturing, about one-fourth of the labor force is engaged in the fabrication of basic raw materials such as steel, glass, cement, silicon, and resins, while three-quarters are in the production phase. The reverse is true for energy inputs: Three times as much energy is used to extract virgin or primary materials as is used to manufacture products from those materials. Substituting reused or more durable manufactured goods for primary materials therefore uses less energy but provides more jobs.[23]

An economy based on a service-and-flow model could also help stabilize the business cycle, because customers would be purchasing flows of services, which they need continuously, rather than durable equipment that's affordable only in good years. Service providers would have an incentive to keep their assets productive for as long as possible, rather than prematurely scrapping them in order to sell replacements. Over- and undercapacity would largely disappear, as business would no longer have to be concerned about delivery or backlogs if it is contracting from a service provider. Gone would be end-of-year rebates to move excess automobile inventory, built for customers who never ordered them because managerial production quotas were increased in order to amortize expensive capital equipment that was never needed in the first place. As it stands now, durables manufacturers have a love-hate relationship with durability. But when they become service providers, their long- and short-term incentives become perfectly attuned to what customers want, the environment deserves, labor needs, and the economy can support.[24]

Investing in Natural Capital

When a manufacturer realizes that a supplier of key components is overextended and running behind on deliveries, it takes immediate action lest its own production lines come to a halt.

Living systems are a supplier of key components for the life of the planet, and they are now falling behind on their orders. Until recently, business could ignore such shortages because they didn't affect production and didn't increase costs. That situation may be changing, however, as rising weather-related claims come to burden insurance companies and world agriculture. (In 1998, violent weather caused upward of $90 billion worth of damage worldwide, a figure that represented more weather-related losses than were accounted for through the entire decade of the 1980s. The losses were greatly compounded by deforestation and climate change, factors that increase the frequency and severity of disasters. In human terms, 300 million people were permanently or temporarily displaced from their homes; this figure includes the dislocations caused by Hurricane Mitch, the deadliest Atlantic storm in two centuries.)[25] If the flow of services from industrial systems is to be sustained or increased in the future for a growing population, the vital flow of life-supporting services from living systems will have to be maintained and increased. For this to be possible will require investments in natural capital.

As both globalization and Balkanization proceed, and as the per-capita availability of water, arable land, and fish continue to decline (as they have done since 1980), the world faces the danger of being torn apart by regional conflicts instigated at least in part by resource shortages or imbalances and associated income polarization.[26] Whether it involves oil[27] or water,[28] cobalt or fish, access to resources is playing an ever more prominent role in generating conflict. In addition, many social instabilities and refugee populations—twelve million refugees now wander the world—are created or worsened by ecological destruction, from Haiti to Somalia to Jordan. On April 9, 1996, Secretary of State Warren Christopher gave perhaps the first speech by an American cabinet officer that linked global security with the environment. His words may become prophetic for future foreign policy decisions: "... [E]nvironmental forces transcend borders and oceans to threaten directly the health, prosperity and jobs of American citizens. . . . [A]ddressing natural resource issues is frequently critical to achieving political and economic stability, and to pursuing our strategic goals around the world."

Societies need to adopt shared goals that enhance social welfare but that are not the prerogatives of specific value or belief systems. Natural capitalism is one such objective. It is neither conservative nor liberal in its ideology, but appeals to both constituencies. Since it is a means, and not an end, it doesn't advocate a particular social outcome but rather makes possible many different ends. Therefore, whatever the various visions different parties or factions espouse, society can work toward resource productivity now, without waiting to resolve disputes about policy.

The chapters that follow describe an array of opportunities and possibilities that are real, practical, measured, and documented. Engineers have already designed hydrogen-fuel-cell-powered cars to be plug-in electric generators that may become the power plants of the future. Buildings already exist that make oxygen, solar power, and drinking water and can help pay the mortgage while their tenants work inside them. Deprintable and reprintable papers and inks, together with other innovative ways to use fiber, could enable the world's supply of lumber and pulp to be grown in an area about the size of Iowa. Weeds can yield potent pharmaceuticals; cellulose-based plastics have been shown to be strong, reusable, and compostable; and luxurious carpets can be made from landfilled scrap. Roofs and windows, even roads, can do double duty as solar-electric collectors, and efficient car-free cities are being designed so that men and women no longer spend their days driving to obtain the goods and services of daily life. These are among the thousands of innovations that are resulting from natural capitalism.

This book is both an overview of the remarkable technologies that are already in practice and a call to action. Many of the techniques and methods described here can be used by individuals and small businesses. Other approaches are more suitable for corporations, even whole industrial sectors; still others better suit local or central governments. Collectively, these techniques offer a powerful menu of new ways to make resource productivity the foundation of a lasting and prosperous economy—from Main Street to Wall Street, from your house to the White House, and from the village to the globe.

Although there is an overwhelming emphasis in this book on what we do with our machines, manufacturing processes, and materials, its purpose is to support the human community and all life-support systems. There is a large body of literature that addresses the nature of specific living systems, from coral reefs to estuarine systems to worldwide topsoil formation. Our focus is to bring about those changes in the human side of the economy that can help preserve and reconstitute these systems, to try and show for now and all time to come that there is no true separation between how we support life economically and ecologically.

Notes

1. Marine Conservation Biology Institute 1998, U.S. National Academy of Sciences and British Royal Society 1992.
2. Daily 1997.
3. Coral Reef Alliance 1998.
4. Worldwide Fund for Nature (Europe) 1998.
5. Costanza et al. 1997, using 1994 dollars in which the value was at least $33 trillion.
6. Details are in World Bank 1995 at 57–66, and 1997.
7. Deane & Cole 1969.
8. Vitousek et al. 1986, 1997.
9. International Labor Organization 1994.
10. Daly 1997.
11. Schmidt-Bleek et al. 1997.
12. Present at the Club in September 1996 were: Jacqueline Aloise de Larderel, Director, UNEP-IE, Paris; Willy Bierter, Director, Institut für Produktdauer-Forschung, Giebenach, Switzerland; Wouter van Dieren, President, Institute for Environment and Systems Analysis, Amsterdam; Hugh Faulkner, formerly Executive Director, Business Council for Sustainable Development; Claude Fussler, Vice President/Environment, Dow Europe; Mike Goto, Director, Institute of Ecotoxicology, Gakushuin University, Tokyo; Leo Jansen, Director, Dutch Sustainable Technology Programme; Ashok Khosla, President, Development Alternatives, New Delhi; Franz Lehner, President, Institute for Labor and Technology, Gelsenkirchen, Germany; Jim MacNeill, MacNeill & Associates, formerly Secretary General, Brundtland Commission, Ottawa, Canada; Wolfgang Sachs, Chairperson, Greenpeace Germany; Ken Saskai, Osaka University; Friedrich Schmidt-Bleek, Vice-President, Wuppertal Institute; Walter Stahel, Director, Institute de la Durabilité, Geneva; Paul Weaver, Director, Centre for EcoEfficiency and Enterprise, University of Portsmouth; Ernst Ulrich von Weizsäcker, President, Wuppertal Institute; Jan-Olaf Willums, Director, World Business Council for Sustainable Development, Geneva; Heinz Wohlmeyer, President, Austrian Association for Agroscientific Research; Ryoichi Yamamoto, President of MRS-Japan, Institute of Industry Science, University of Tokyo.
13. Gardner & Sampat 1998 at 26 provides a useful summary of many such initiatives.
14. Romm & Browning 1994.

15. Ayres 1989.
16. American Institute of Physics 1975, adjusted for progress and new insights since then.
17. Stahel & Reday-Mulvey 1981.
18. Friend 1996.
19. Stahel also coined the term "extended product responsibility" (EPR), which is cradle-to-cradle from the manufacturer's point of view. EPR is now becoming a mandated or voluntary standard in many European industries.
20. Stahel & Børlin 1987.
21. Emerson 1994 at 26.
22. As far as we know, the term "technical nutrient" was first used by Michael Braungart in a conversation with William A. McDonough.
23. Stahel 1981.
24. Womack & Jones 1996; Womack, personal communication, 28 February 1999.
25. *San Francisco Chronicle* 1998.
26. Kaplan 1994, 1997.
27. Yergin 1991.
28. Gleick 1998.

References

American Institute of Physics (1975), "Efficient Use of Energy, American Physical Society Studies on the Technical Aspects of the More Efficient Use of Energy." Conference Proceedings No. 25, AIP, New York, NY.

Ayres, R. U. (1989), *Technology and Environment* (Washington, DC: National Academy of Sciences).

Coral Reef Alliance (1998), "Reefs in Danger: Threats to Coral Reefs Around the World," October 22.

Costanza, R., d'Arge, R., de Groot, R., Farber, S., Grasso, M., Hannon, B., Limburg, K., Naeem, S., O'Neill, R. V., and Paruelo, J. (1997), "The Value of the World's Ecosystem Services and Natural Capital," *Nature*, 387 (May 15): 253–60.

Daily, G. C. (1997) (ed.), *Nature's Services: Societal Dependence on Natural Ecosystems* (Washington, DC: Island Press).

Daly, H. E. (1997), "Uneconomic Growth: From Empty-World to Full-World Economics," Rice University, DeLange-Woodlands Conference on Sustainable Development: Managing the Transition, Houston, TX,

Deane, P., and Cole, W. A. (1969), *British Economic Growth, 1688–1959*, 2nd edn. (Cambridge: Cambridge University Press).

Emerson, R. W. (1994), *Nature and Other Writings* (Boston, MA: Shambhala), 9–10.

Environmental Building News (1995), "What's New in Construction Waste Management," *EBN*, 4(6): 14 (28 Birge St., Suite 30,

Brattleboro, VT 05301, 802/257-7300, fax -7304; <ebn@ebuild.com, www.ebuild.com>).

Friend, G. (1996), "Ecomimesis: Copying Ecosystems for Fun and Profit," *The New Bottom Line*, Feb. 4, <gfriend@igc.apc.org>.

Gardner, G., and Sampat, P. (1998), "Mind Over Matter: Recasting the Role of Materials in Our Lives," Worldwatch Paper 144, Worldwatch Institute, Washington, DC, December.

Gleick, P. H. (1998), *The World's Water 1998–1999: The Biennial Report on Freshwater Resources* (Washington, DC: Island Press; updated at <www.worldwater.org>).

International Labor Organization (1994), *The World Employment Situation, Trends and Prospects*, press release, ILO, Washington, DC, and Geneva, Switzerland, March 6.

Kaplan, R. (1997), "The Future of Democracy," *Atlantic Monthly* (December).

____ (1994), "The Coming Anarchy," *Atlantic Monthly* (February).

Marine Conservation Biology Institute (1998), "Troubled Waters: A Call for Action," MCBI, Redmond, WA, January, <www.mcbi.org>.

Romm, J. J., and Browning, W. D. (1994), "Greening the Building and the Bottom Line: Increasing Productivity Through Energy-Efficient Design," Rocky Mountain Institute Publication #D94–27.

San Francisco Chronicle (1998), "Natural Disasters Around World Cost Record $89 Billion in 1998," November 28.

Schmidt-Bleek, F., et al. (1997), "Statement to Government and Business Leaders,"

Wuppertal Institute, Wuppertal, Germany.

Stahel, W. R., and Børlin, M. (1987), *Strategie économique de la durabilité*, Société de Banque Suisse, Geneva, Switzerland.

——, and Reday-Mulvey, G. (1981), *Jobs for Tomorrow, the Potential for Substituting Manpower for Energy* (New York: Vantage Press).

Vitousek, P., et al. (1986), "Human Appropriation of the Products of Photosynthesis," *BioScience*, 34 (May): 368–73.

——, Mooney, H. A., Lubchenco, J., and Melillo, J. M. (1997), "Human Domination of Earth's Ecosystems," *Science*, 277 (July): 494–9.

Womack, J. P., and Jones, D. T. (1996), *Lean Thinking: Banish Waste and Create Wealth in Your Corporation* (New York: Simon and Schuster), summarized in "Beyond Toyota: How to Root Out Waste and Pursue Perfection," *Harv. Bus. Rev.* (Sept./Oct.): 140–58, Reprint 96511.

World Bank (1995), *Monitoring Environmental Progress: A Report on Work in Progress, Environmentally Sustainable Development* (Washington, DC: World Bank).

—— (1997), *Expanding the Measure of Wealth: Indicators of Environmentally Sustainable Development*, Environmentally Sustainable Development Studies and Monographs Series No. 17 (Washington, DC: World Bank).

Worldwide Fund for Nature Europe (1998), "A Third of World's Natural Resources Consumed Since 1970: Report," Agence France-Presse, October.

Yergin, D. (1991), *The Prize: The Epic Quest for Oil, Money, and Power* (London: Simon and Schuster).

PART FOUR

GREEN SOCIAL CRITIQUES

We turn now to a number of radical ecologies, their analyses of the sources of and solutions to ecological problems, and their accounts of the relationship between social practices and ecological problems. These critiques consider the way we think about nature, and the institutionalization of that thought in social, cultural, and economic practices. Such practices turn out to dominate not only nature, but also the poor and working classes, women, indigenous peoples, people of colour, and the global south. For these schools of ecological thought, neither piecemeal reform nor economic tinkering is enough to deal with the dire problems we face. The ecological crisis is related to a number of other social problems, and it will take both radical rethinking and radical restructuring of political procedures and institutions—domestically and internationally—to address our current predicament. The schools of thought represented in the following sections, however, differ on the extent to which we should emphasize political structure, social consciousness, and identity.

Section VIII: Deep Ecology, Bioregionalism, and Ecocentrism

Of the eco-philosophies that inform the more radical part of the spectrum of ecological politics, the most popular, or at least well-known, is deep ecology. The Norwegian philosopher Arne Naess founded this school of ecological thought in 1973, with the publication of his classic differentiation between mainstream environmentalism—shallow ecology—and his ideal of a deeper, more long-range notion of ecology. For deep ecology, the environmental crisis is, at its centre, a crisis of consciousness. The way we *think* about nature and our relations with it is, pure and simple, wrong. A change in the way we understand and relate to nature is the top priority for addressing the environmental crisis. Deep ecologists seek a major reduction in human arrogance when it comes to dealing with the natural world.

Some deep ecologists focus on two 'ultimate norms' articulated by Naess, two key ways to think more deeply about nature. The first is a recognition of the necessity of the self-realization of one's potential—for both humans and the rest of the natural world. Everyone and everything, in this view, should develop and live without interference, as all life has a value and a potential in and for itself, and not just for others. Secondly, deep ecology calls for 'biocentric equality', or what others have called variously 'biocentrism' or 'ecocentrism'. This notion elevates the self-realization to a *right*, such that all creatures, and the earth itself, have a right to be and to develop to their full potential. Does this mean that humans are *equal* to worms? For deep ecologists, this may not necessarily be the case *legally*, but we should be considered equal in the sense that we are both members of a larger biotic community.

Naess's founding essay is essentially a list of seven normative tenets of deep ecology—what he calls a 'value priority system' that has been 'inspired' by knowledge of ecological systems. While the focus is on values, Naess does attempt to explore what a deep ecological *politics* would look like, with a cursory mention of class egalitarianism, local autonomy, and decentralization. While Naess is a philosopher, a number of environmental activists have used notions of deep ecology to define and defend radical political action in defence of nature. To follow up on this more political theme, we have included two essays which translate the philosophy of deep ecology into political action and relations. The selection by Dave Foreman, one of the founders of the radical environmental group Earth First!, articulates the type of politics he believes deep ecology requires. Foreman argues that a biocentric worldview necessitates putting the Earth and its wildlands before human welfare in any political decision-making, emphasizes a change in personal lifestyles, and defends the sabotage of projects which threaten the wild. Jim Dodge offers a less flashy, but just as radical, implementation of the ideals of radical ecology in his discussion of the theory and practice

342 SECTION VIII: DEEP ECOLOGY, BIOREGIONALISM, ECOCENTRISM

of bioregionalism. Bioregionalism is the philosophy and practice of living in place. Dodge distills bioregional practice down into two key elements: resistance and renewal. Resistance is to any practice that continues the destruction of natural systems; renewal is achieved through political participation at the local level.

Finally, Robyn Eckersley takes a more recent look at ecocentric theory. Eckersley examines the grounds on which ecocentrism would extend moral and political inclusion to nature, explores many of the critiques of ecocentrism, and discusses the constructive, democratic, and pluralistic potential of the discourse. Eckersley covers this ethical ground in a clearly political way, and so builds a bridge between the insights of ecocentrism and the more social and political concerns of Section IX.

Further Reading

Deep ecology and bioregionalism have many definers and defenders. The canon of deep ecology includes Bill Devall and George Sessions, *Deep Ecology: Living as if Nature Mattered* (1985), Naess's own *Ecology, Community, and Lifestyle* (1989), and Warwick Fox's *Toward a Transpersonal Ecology* (1990). Three classics of bioregionalism are Kirkpatrick Sale's *Dwellers in the Land: The Bioregional Vision* (1985), and the edited volumes *Thinking Like a Mountain: Toward a Council of All Beings* (1988), and *Home! Reinhabiting North America: A Bioregional Reader* (1992). *Bioregionalism* (1998), edited by Michael McGinnis, brings together bioregional theory and practice in one volume. Robyn Eckersley's ecocentrism is developed at length in her *Environmentalism and Political Theory* (1992).

Deep ecology in practice, embodied in Earth First! and other groups, is explored in *The Earth First Reader: Ten Years of Radical Environmentalism* (1991), edited by Dave Foreman and John Davis; and Rik Scarce, *Eco-Warriors: Understanding the Radical Environmental Movement* (1990). For a view of Earth First! actions in Britain, see Derek Wall, *Earth First! and the Anti-Roads Movement: Radical Environmentalism and Comparative Social Movements* (1999). Both deep ecological action and bioregional understanding have been defined and inspired by literary works. See, for example, Ed Abbey's classic *The Monkey Wrench Gang* (1976), and Gary Snyder's *Turtle Island* (1974).

Deep ecology, however, has its share of both sympathizers and critics from within environmental theory. A good set appears in Katz, Light, and Rothenberg's edited volume *Beneath the Surface: Critical Essays on the Philosophy of Deep Ecology* (2000). Some of the links and contrasts between deep ecology and ecofeminism are explored in various essays in Irene Diamond and Gloria Orenstein (eds), *Reweaving the World: The Emergence of Ecofeminism* (1990). (Much) more critically, Murray Bookchin has argued the limitations of a political philosophy based on bio- or ecocentrism. Bookchin's concerns are mostly with the anti-left and misanthropic writings of Earth First!ers like Dave Foreman and Christopher Manes. See his essay 'Social Ecology Versus Deep Ecology', in *Socialist Review*, 18: 3: 9–29 (1988). Bookchin and Foreman did 'make-up' after this heated conflict; their illuminating debate is in Bookchin and Foreman, *Defending the Earth* (1991). Tim Luke's *Ecocritique* (1997) is a curmudgeonly attack on a wide variety of both moderate and radical, shallow and deep ecologies. Luc Ferry's *The New Ecological Order* (1995) is ostensibly a critique of deep ecology, but Ferry's real target is any radical environmentalism with a tinge of ecocentrism, which he links to totalitarianism. Much more sympathetic, and comprehensive in its coverage of a range of environmentalisms, is Peter Hay, *Main Currents in Western Environmental Thought* (2002).

23 The Shallow and the Deep, Long-Range Ecology Movement: A Summary

Arne Naess

Ecologically responsible policies are concerned only in part with pollution and resource deple-tion. There are deeper concerns which touch upon principles of diversity, complexity, autonomy, decentralization, symbiosis, egalitarianism, and classlessness.

The emergence of ecologists from their former relative obscurity marks a turning-point in our scientific communities. But their message is twisted and misused. A shallow, but presently rather powerful movement, and a deep, but less influential movement, compete for our attention. I shall make an effort to characterize the two.

1. The Shallow Ecology Movement

Fight against pollution and resource depletion. Central objective: the health and affluence of people in the developed countries.

2. The Deep Ecology Movement

(1) Rejection of the man-in-environment image in favour of the relational, total-field image. Organ-isms as knots in the biospherical net or field of intrinsic relations. An intrinsic relation between two things *A* and *B* is such that the relation belongs to the definitions or basic constitutions of *A* and *B*, so that without the relation, *A* and *B* are no longer the same things. The total-field model dissolves not only the man-in-environment concept, but every compact thing-in-milieu concept—except when talking at a superficial or preliminary level of communication.

(2) Biospherical egalitarianism—in principle. The 'in principle' clause is inserted because any realistic praxis necessitates some killing, exploitation, and suppression. The ecological field-worker acquires a deep-seated respect, or even veneration, for ways and forms of life. He reaches an understanding from within, a kind of understanding that others reserve for fellow men and

Reprinted from Arne Naess, 'The Shallow and the Deep, Long-Range Ecology Movement: A Summary', *Inquiry* 16 (1983), 95–100, by permission of Scandinavian University Press, Oslo, Norway.

for a narrow section of ways and forms of life. To the ecological field-worker, *the equal right to live and blossom* is an intuitively clear and obvious value axiom. Its restriction to humans is an anthropocentrism with detrimental effects upon the life quality of humans themselves. This quality depends in part upon the deep pleasure and satisfaction we receive from close partnership with other forms of life. The attempt to ignore our dependence and to establish a master—slave role has contributed to the alienation of man from himself.

Ecological egalitarianism implies the reinterpretation of the future-research variable, 'level of crowding', so that *general* mammalian crowding and loss of life-equality is taken seriously, not only human crowding. (Research on the high requirements of free space of certain mammals has, incidentally, suggested that theorists of human urbanism have largely underestimated human life-space requirements. Behavioural crowding symptoms (neuroses, aggressiveness, loss of traditions . . .) are largely the same among mammals.)

(3) Principles of diversity and of symbiosis. Diversity enhances the potentialities of survival, the chances of new modes of life, the richness of forms. And the so-called struggle of life, and survival of the fittest, should be interpreted in the sense of ability to coexist and cooperate in complex relationships, rather than ability to kill, exploit, and suppress. 'Live and let live' is a more powerful ecological principle than 'Either you or me'.

The latter tends to reduce the multiplicity of kinds of forms of life, and also to create destruction within the communities of the same species. Ecologically inspired attitudes therefore favour diversity of human ways of life, of cultures, of occupations, of economies. They support the fight against economic and cultural, as much as military, invasion, and domination, and they are opposed to the annihilation of seals and whales as much as to that of human tribes or cultures.

(4) Anti-class posture. Diversity of human ways of life is in part due to (intended or unintended) exploitation and suppression on the part of certain groups. The exploiter lives differently from the exploited, but both are adversely affected in their potentialities of self-realization. The principle of diversity does not cover differences due merely to certain attitudes or behaviours forcibly blocked or restrained. The principles of ecological egalitarianism and of symbiosis support the same anti-class posture. The ecological attitude favours the extension of all three principles to any group conflicts, including those of today between developing and developed nations. The three principles also favour extreme caution towards any overall plans for the future, except those consistent with wide and widening classless diversity.

(5) Fight against pollution and resource depletion. In this fight ecologists have found powerful supporters, but sometimes to the detriment of their total stand. This happens when attention is focused on pollution and resource depletion rather than on the other points, or when projects are implemented which reduce pollution but increase evils of the other kinds. Thus, if prices of life necessities increase because of the installation of anti-pollution devices, class differences increase too. An ethics of responsibility implies that ecologists do not serve the shallow, but the deep ecological movement. That is, not only point (5), but all seven points must be considered together.

Ecologists are irreplaceable informants in any society, whatever their political colour. If well organized, they have the power to reject jobs in which they submit themselves to institutions or to planners with limited ecological perspectives. As it is now, ecologists sometimes serve masters who deliberately ignore the wider perspectives.

(6) Complexity, not complication. The theory of ecosystems contains an important distinction between what is complicated without any Gestalt or unifying principles—we may think of finding our way through a chaotic city—and what is complex. A multiplicity of more or less lawful, interacting factors may operate together to form a unity, a system. We make a shoe or use a map or integrate a variety of activities into a workaday pattern. Organisms, ways of life, and interactions in the biosphere in general, exhibit complexity of such an astoundingly high level as to colour the general outlook of ecologists. Such complexity makes thinking in terms of vast systems inevitable. It also makes for a keen, steady perception of the profound *human ignorance* of biospherical relationships and therefore of the effect of disturbances.

Applied to humans, the complexity-not-complication principle favours division of labour, *not fragmentation of labour*. It favours integrated actions in which the whole person is active, not mere reactions. It favours complex economies, an integrated variety of means of living. (Combinations of industrial and agricultural activity, of intellectual and manual work, of specialized and non-specialized occupations, of urban and non-urban activity, of work in city and recreation in nature with recreation in city and work in nature ...)

It favours soft technique and 'soft future-research', less prognosis, more clarification of possibilities. More sensitivity towards continuity and live traditions, and—most important-ly—towards our state of ignorance.

The implementation of ecologically responsible policies requires in this century an exponential growth of technical skill and invention—but in new directions, directions which today are not consistently and liberally supported by the research policy organs of our nation-states.

(7) Local autonomy and decentralization. The vulnerability of a form of life is roughly proportional to the weight of influences from afar, from outside the local region in which that form has obtained an ecological equilibrium. This lends support to our efforts to strengthen local self-government and material and mental self-sufficiency. But these efforts presuppose an impetus towards decentralization. Pollution problems, including those of thermal pollution and recirculation of materials, also lead us in this direction, because increased local autonomy, if we are able to keep other factors constant, reduces energy consumption. (Compare an approximately self-sufficient locality with one requiring the importation of foodstuff, materials for house construction, fuel, and skilled labour from other continents. The former may use only 5 per cent of the energy used by the latter.) Local autonomy is strengthened by a reduction in the number of links in the hierarchical chains of decision (For example a chain consisting of local board, municipal council, highest sub-national decision-maker, a state-wide institution in a state federation, a federal national government institution, a coalition of nations, and of institutions, e.g. EEC top levels, and a global institution, can be reduced to one made up of local board,

nation-wide institution, and global institution.) Even if a decision follows majority rules at each step, many local interests may be dropped along the line, if it is too long.

Summing up, then, it should, first of all, be borne in mind that the norms and tendencies of the Deep Ecology movement are not derived from ecology by logic or induction. Ecological knowledge and the lifestyle of the ecological field-worker have *suggested, inspired, and fortified* the perspectives of the Deep Ecology movement. Many of the formulations in the above seven-point survey are rather vague generalizations, only tenable if made more precise in certain directions. But all over the world the inspiration from ecology has shown remarkable convergencies. The survey does not pretend to be more than one of the possible condensed codifications of these convergencies.

Secondly, it should be fully appreciated that the significant tenets of the Deep Ecology movement are clearly and forcefully *normative*. They express a value priority system only in part based on results (or lack of results, cf. point (6)) of scientific research. Today, ecologists try to influence policy-making bodies largely through threats, through predictions concerning pollutants and resource depletion, knowing that policy-makers accept at least certain minimum *norms* concerning health and just distribution. But it is clear that there is a vast number of people in all countries, and even a considerable number of people in power, who accept as valid the wider norms and values characteristic of the Deep Ecology movement. There are political potentials in this movement which should not be overlooked and which have little to do with pollution and resource depletion. In plotting possible futures, the norms should be freely used and elaborated.

Thirdly, insofar as ecology movements deserve our attention, they are *ecophilosophical* rather then ecological. Ecology is a *limited* science which makes *use* of scientific methods. Philosophy is the most general forum of debate on fundamentals, descriptive as well as prescriptive, and political philosophy is one of its subsections. By an *ecosophy* I mean a philosophy of ecological harmony or equilibrium. A philosophy as a kind of *sofia* wisdom, is openly normative, it contains *both* norms, rules, postulates, value priority announcements, *and* hypotheses concerning the state of affairs in our universe. Wisdom is policy wisdom, prescription, not only scientific description and prediction.

The details of an ecosophy will show many variations due to significant differences concerning not only 'facts' of pollution, resources, population, etc., but also value priorities. Today, however, the seven points listed provide one unified framework for ecosophical systems.

In general system theory, systems are mostly conceived in terms of causally or functionally interacting or interrelated items. An ecosophy, however, is more like a system of the kind constructed by Aristotle or Spinoza. It is expressed verbally as a set of sentences with a variety of functions, descriptive and prescriptive. The basic relation is that between subsets of premises and subsets of conclusions, that is, the relation of derivability. The relevant notions of derivability may be classed according to rigour, with logical and mathematical deductions topping the list, but also according to how much is implicitly taken for granted. An exposition of an ecosophy must necessarily be only moderately precise considering the vast scope of relevant ecological and normative (social, political, ethical) material. At the moment, ecosophy might profitably use models of systems, rough approximations of global systematizations. It is the global character, not preciseness in detail, which distinguishes an ecosophy. It articulates and integrates the efforts of an ideal ecological team, a team comprising not only scientists from an extreme variety of disciplines, but also students of politics and active policy-makers.

Under the name of *ecologism*, various deviations from the deep movement have been championed—primarily with a one-sided stress on pollution and resource depletion, but also with a neglect of the great differences between under- and over-developed countries in favour of a vague global approach. The global approach is essential, but regional differences must largely determine policies in the coming years.

Selected Literature

Commoner, B., *The Closing Circle: Nature, Man, and Technology* (New York: Alfred A. Knopf, 1971).

Ehrlich, P. R., and Ehrlich, A. H., *Population, Resources, Environment: Issues in Human Ecology*, 2nd edn. (San Francisco: W. H. Freeman & Co., 1972).

Ellul, J., *The Technological Society*, English edn. (New York: Alfred A. Knopf, 1964).

Glacken, C. J., *Traces on the Rhodian Shore: Nature and Culture in Western Thought* (Berkeley: University of California Press, 1967).

Kato, H., 'The Effects of Crowding', Quality of Life Conference, Oberhausen, April 1972.

McHarg, Ian L., *Design with Nature* (New York: Doubleday & Co., 1969; paperback 1971).

Meynaud, J., *Technocracy*, English edn. (Chicago: Free Press of Glencoe, 1969).

Mishan, E. J., *Technology and Growth: The Price We Pay* (New York: Frederick A. Praeger, 1970).

Odum, E. P., *Fundamentals of Ecology*, 3rd edn. (Philadelphia: W. E. Saunders Co., 1971).

Shepard, Paul, *Man in the Landscape* (New York: A. A. Knopf).

24 Putting the Earth First

Dave Foreman

These are the times that try men's souls; the summer soldier and the sunshine patriot will, in this crisis, shrink from the service of his country, but he that stands it now, deserves the love and thanks of man and woman.

(Thomas Paine)

In July 1987, seven years after the campfire gathering that spawned Earth First!, I rose among the Ponderosa Pines and scattered shafts of sunlight on the North Rim of the Grand Canyon and mounted a stage festooned with Earth First! banners and American flags. Before me sat several hundred people: hippies in tie-dyed shirts and Birkenstocks, rednecks for wilderness in cowboy boots and hats, middle-class hikers in waffle stompers, graybeards, and children. The diversity was impressive. The energy was overpowering. Never in my wildest dreams had I imagined the Earth First! movement would attract so many. Never had I hoped that we would have begun to pack such a punch. We were attracting national attention; we were changing the parameters of the debate about ecological issues; we had become a legend in conservation lore.

Yet, after seven years, I was concerned we were losing some of our clarity of purpose, and blurring our focus. In launching Earth First!, I had said, "Let our actions set the finer points of our philosophy." But now I was concerned that the *what* of our actions might be overwhelming the *why*. For some of those newly attracted to Earth First!, action seemed to be its own justification. I felt a need to return to wilderness fundamentalism, to articulate what I thought were the principles that defined the Earth First! movement, that gave it a specific identity. The response to the principles I offered that day was so overwhelmingly positive that I elaborated on them in the *Earth First! Journal* later that fall. Here they are.

A placing of Earth first in all decisions, even ahead of human welfare if necessary. Our movement is called "Earth First!" not "People First!" Sometimes what appears to be in the short-term interest of human beings as a whole, a select group of human beings, or individual human beings is detrimental to the short-term or long-term health of the biosphere (and to the actual long-term welfare of human beings). Earth First! does not argue that native diversity should be preserved if it can be done without negatively impacting the material "standard of living" of a group of human beings. We simply state that native diversity should be preserved, that natural diversity building for three and a half billion years should be left unfettered. Human beings must adjust to the planet; it is supreme arrogance to expect the planet and all it contains to adjust to the demands of humans. In everything human society does, the primary consideration should be for the long-term health and biological diversity of Earth. After that, we can consider the welfare of humans. We should be kind, compassionate, and caring with other people, but Earth comes first.

A refusal to use human beings as the measure by which to value others. An individual human life has no more intrinsic value than does an individual Grizzly Bear life. Human suffering resulting from drought and famine in Ethiopia is tragic, yes, but the destruction there of other creatures and habitat is even more tragic. This leads quickly into the next point:

An enthusiastic embracing of the philosophy of Deep Ecology or biocentrism. This philosophy states simply and essentially that all living creatures and communities possess intrinsic value, inherent worth. Natural things live for their own sake, which is another way of saying they have value. Other beings (both animal and plant) and even so-called "inanimate" objects such as rivers and mountains are not placed here for the convenience of human beings. Our biocentric worldview denies the modern concept of "resources." The dominant philosophy of our time (which contains Judeo-Christianity, Islam, capitalism, Marxism, scientism, and secular humanism) is anthropocentrism. It places human beings at the center of the universe, separates them from nature, and endows them with unique value. EF!ers are in direct opposition to that philosophy. Ours is an ecological perspective that views Earth as a community and recognizes such apparent enemies as "disease" (e.g. malaria) and "pests" (e.g. mosquitoes) not as manifestations of evil to be overcome but rather as vital and necessary components of a complex and vibrant biosphere.

A realization that wilderness is the real world. The preservation of wilderness is the fundamental issue. Wilderness does not merely mean backpacking parks or scenery. It is the natural world, the arena for evolution, the caldron from which humans emerged, the home of the others with whom we share this planet. Wilderness is the real world; our cities, our computers, our airplanes, our global business civilization all are but artificial and transient phenomena. It is important to remember that only a tiny portion of the history of the human species has occurred outside of wilderness. The preservation of wildness and native diversity is *the* most important issue. Issues directly affecting only humans pale in comparison. Of course, ecology teaches us that all things are connected, and in this regard all other matters become subsets of wilderness preservation—the prevention of nuclear war, for example—but the most important campaigns being waged today are those directly on behalf of wilderness.

A recognition that there are far too many human beings on Earth. There are too many of us everywhere—in the United States, in Nigeria; in cities, in rural areas; with digging hoes, with tractors. Although there is obviously an unconscionable maldistribution of wealth and the basic necessities of life among humans, this fact should not be used—as some leftists are wont to do—to argue that overpopulation is not the problem. It *is* a large part of the problem; there are far too many of us *already*—and our numbers continue to grow astronomically. Even if inequitable distribution could be solved, six billion human beings converting the natural world to material goods and human food would devastate natural diversity.

This basic recognition of the overpopulation problem does not mean that we should ignore the economic and social causes of overpopulation, and shouldn't criticize the accumulation of wealth in fewer and fewer hands, the maldistribution of "resources," and the venality of multinational corporations and Third World juntas alike, but simply that we must understand that Great Blue Whales, Jaguars, Black Rhinoceroses, and rain forests are not compatible with an exploding human population.[1]

A deep questioning of, and even an antipathy to, "progress" and "technology." In looking at human history, we can see that we have lost more in our "rise" to civilization than we have gained. We can see that life in a hunter-gatherer society was on the whole healthier, happier, and more secure than our lives today as peasants, industrial workers, or business executives. For every material "achievement" of progress, there are a dozen losses of things of profound and ineffable value. We can accept the pejoratives of "Luddite" and "Neanderthal" with pride. (This does not mean that we must immediately eschew all the facets of technological civilization. We are *of* it, and use it; this does not mean that we can't critique it.)

A refusal to accept rationality as the only way of thinking. There is room for great diversity within Earth First! on matters spiritual, and nowhere is tolerance for diversity more necessary. But we can all recognize that linear, rational, logical left brain thinking represents only part of our brain and consciousness. Rationality is a fine and useful tool, but it is just that—a tool, one way of analyzing matters. Equally valid, perhaps more so, is intuitive, instinctive awareness. We can become more cognizant of ultimate truths by sitting quietly in the wild than by studying in a library. Reading books, engaging in logical discourse, and compiling facts and figures are necessary in the modern context, but they are not the only ways to comprehend the world and our lives. Often our gut instincts enable us to act more effectively in a crisis than does careful rational analysis. An example would be a patient bleeding to death in a hospital emergency room—you can't wait for all the tests to be completed. Your gut says, "Act!" So it is with Earth First!'s actions in Earth's current emergency.

A lack of desire to gain credibility or "legitimacy" with the gang of thugs running human civilization. It is basic human nature to want to be accepted by the social milieu in which you find yourself. It hurts to be dismissed by the arbiters of opinion as "nuts," "terrorists," "wackos," or "extremists." But we are not crazy; we happen to be sane humans in an insane human society in a sane natural world. We do not have "credibility" with Senator Mark Hatfield or with Maxxam chairman Charles Hurwitz—but they do not have credibility with us! (We do have their attention, however.) They are madmen destroying the pure and beautiful. Why should we "reason" with them? We do not share the same worldview or values. There is, however, a dangerous pitfall here that some alternative groups fall into. That is that we gain little by being consciously offensive, by trying to alienate others. We can be strong and unyielding without being obnoxious.

The American system is very effective at co-opting and moderating dissidents by giving them attention and then encouraging them to be "reasonable" so their ideas will be taken seriously. Putting a critic on the evening news, on the front page of the newspaper, in a national magazine—all of these are methods the establishment uses to entice one to share their world-view and to enter the negotiating room to compromise. The actions of Earth First!—both the bold and the comic—have gained attention. If they are to have results, we must resist the siren's offer of credibility, legitimacy, and a share in the decision-making. We are thwarting the system, not reforming it. While we are therefore not concerned with political credibility, it must be remembered that the arguments and actions of Earth First! are based on the understandings of ecology. It is vitally important that we have biological credibility.

An effort to go beyond the tired, worn-out dogmas of left, right, and middle-of-the-road. These doctrines, whether blaming capitalism, communism, or the devil for all the problems in the world, merely represent internecine squabbles between different factions of humanism. Yes, multinational corporations commit great evil (the Soviet Union is essentially a state-run multinational corporation); there is a great injustice in the world; the rich are getting richer and the poor poorer—but all problems cannot be simplistically laid at the feet of evil capitalists in the United States, Europe, and Japan. Earth First! is not left or right; we are not even in front. Earth First! should not be in the political struggle between humanist sects at all. We're in a wholly different game.

An unwillingness to set any ethnic, class, or political group of humans on a pedestal and make them immune from questioning. It's easy, of course, to recognize that white males from North America and Europe (as well as Japanese males) hold a disproportionate share of responsibility for the mess we're in; that upper- and middle-class consumers from the First World take an excessive portion of the world's "resources" and therefore cause greater per capita destruction than do other peoples. But it does not follow that everyone else is blameless.

The Earth First! movement has great affinity with aboriginal groups throughout the world. They are clearly in the most direct and respectful relationship with the natural world. Earth First! should back such tribes in the common struggle whenever possible without compromising our ideals. For example, we are supportive of the Dine (Navajo) of Big Mountain against relocation, but this does not mean we overlook the severe overgrazing by domestic sheep on the Navajo Reservation. We may be supportive of subsistence life-styles by natives in Alaska, but we should not be silent about clearcutting old-growth forest in southeast Alaska by native corporations, or about the Eskimo Doyon Corporation's push for oil exploration and development in the Arctic National Wildlife Refuge. It is racist either to condemn or to pardon someone based on their ethnic background.

Similarly, we are inconsistent when we castigate Charles Hurwitz for destroying the last wilderness redwood forest, yet feel sympathy for the loggers working for him. Industrial workers, by and large, share the blame for the destruction of the natural world. They may be yoked by the big-money boys, but they are generally willing servants who share the worldview of their bosses that Earth is a smorgasbord of resources for the taking. Sometimes, in fact, it is the sturdy yeoman from the bumpkin proletariat who holds the most violent and destructive attitudes toward the natural world (and toward those who would defend it).[2] Workers are victims of an unjust economic system, but that does not absolve them of what they do. This is not to deny that some woods workers oppose the destruction of ancient forests, that some may even be Earth First!ers, but merely that it is inappropriate to overlook abuse of the natural world simply because of the rung the perpetrators occupy on the economic ladder.

Some argue that workers are merely struggling to feed their families and are not delighting in destroying the natural world. They say that unless you deal with the needs of loggers to make a living, you can't save the forest. They also claim that loggers are manipulated by their bosses to express anti-wilderness viewpoints. I find this argument to be patronizing to loggers and other workers. When I read comments from timber fellers expressing hatred toward pristine forests and toward conservationists, it is obvious that they willingly buy into the worldview of the lumber barons. San Francisco's *Image Magazine* reports on a letter to the editor written by one logger: "Working people trying to feed their families have little time to be out in the woods acting like children and making things hard for other working people. . . . Anyone out there have a recipe for spotted owl? Food stamps won't go far, I'm afraid. And since they're always being shoved down my throat, I thought I'd like mine fried."[3] Bumper stickers proclaiming "Kill an owl. Save a logger." are rife in the Northwest. I at least respect the logger who glories in felling a giant tree and who hunts Spotted Owls enough to grant him the mental ability to have his own opinions instead of pretending he is a stupid oaf, manipulated by his bosses and unable to think for himself.

Of course the big timber companies do manipulate their workers with scare tactics about mill closings and wilderness lockups, but many loggers (or cat-skinners, oilfield workers, miners, and the like) simply hate the wild and delight in "civilizing" it. Even educating workers about ecological principles will not necessarily change the attitudes of many; there are basic differences of opinion and values. Conservationists should try to find common ground with loggers and other workers whenever possible, but the sooner we get rid of Marxist views about the noble proletariat, the better.

A willingness to let our actions set the finer point of our philosophy and a recognition that we must act. It is possible to debate endlessly the finer points of dogma, to feel that every nuance of something must be explored before one can act. Too often, political movements become mere debating societies where the participants engage in philosophical masturbation and never get down to the vital business at hand. Others argue that you have no right to argue for environmental preservation until you are living a pure, non-impacting life-style. We will never figure it all out, we will never be able to plan any campaign in complete detail, none of us will ever entirely transcend a polluting life-style—but we can act. We can act with courage, with determination, with love for things wild and free. We can't be perfect, but we can *act*. We are warriors. Earth First! is a warrior society. We have a job to do.

An acknowledgment that we must change our personal life-styles to make them more harmonious with natural diversity. We must eschew surplusage. Although to varying degrees we are all captives of our economic system and cannot break entirely free, we must practice what we preach to the best of our ability. Arne Naess, the Norwegian philosopher and originator of the term "Deep Ecology," points out that we are not able to achieve a true "Deep Ecology" life-style, but it is the responsibility of each of us to move in that direction. Most of us still need to make a living that involves some level of participation in "the system." Even for activists, there are trade-offs—flying in a jetliner to help hang a banner on the World Bank in Washington, DC, in order to bring international attention to the plight of tropical rain forests; using a computer to write a book printed on tree pulp that will catalyze people to take action; driving a pickup truck down a forest road to gain access to a proposed timber sale for preventive maintenance. We need to be aware of these trade-offs, and to do our utmost to limit our impact.

A commitment to maintaining a sense of humor, and a joy in living. Most radicals are a dour, holier-than-thou, humorless lot. Earth First!ers strive to be different. We aren't rebelling against the system because we're losing in it. We're fighting for beauty, for life, for joy. We kick up our heels in delight in the wilderness, we smile at a flower and a hummingbird. We laugh. We laugh at our opponents—and, more important, we laugh at ourselves.

An awareness that we are animals. Human beings are primates, mammals, vertebrates. EF!ers recognize their animalness; we reject the New Age eco-la-la that says we must transcend our base animal nature and take charge of our evolution in order to become higher, moral beings. We believe we must return to being animal, to glorying in our sweat, hormones, tears, and blood. We struggle against the modern compulsion to become dull, passionless androids. We do not live sanitary, logical lives; we smell, taste, see, hear, and feel Earth; we live with gusto. We *are* Animal.

An acceptance of monkeywrenching as a legitimate tool for the preservation of natural diversity. Not all Earth First!ers monkeywrench, perhaps not even the majority, but we generally accept the idea and practice of monkeywrenching. Look at an EF! T-shirt. The monkeywrench on it is a symbol of resistance, an heir of the *sabot*—the wooden shoe dropped in the gears to stop the machine, from whence comes the word *sabotage*. The mystique and lore of "night work" pervades our tribe, and with it a general acceptance that strategic monkeywrenching is a legitimate tool for defense of the wild.

And finally: Earth First! is a warrior society. In addition to our absolute commitment to and love for this living planet, we are characterized by our willingness to defend Earth's abundance and diversity of life, even if that defense requires sacrifices of comfort, freedom, safety, or, ultimately, our lives. A warrior recognizes that her life is not the most important thing in her life. A warrior recognizes that there is a greater reality outside her life that must be defended. For us in Earth First!, that reality is Earth, the evolutionary process, the millions of other species with which we share this bright sphere in the void of space.

Not everyone can afford to make the commitment of being a warrior. There are many other roles that can—and must—be played in defense of Earth. One may not constantly be able to carry the burden of being a warrior; it may be only a brief period in one's life. There are risks and pitfalls in being a warrior. There may not be applause, there may not be honors and awards from human society. But there is no finer applause for the warrior of the Earth than the call of the loon at dusk or the sigh of wind in the pines.

Later that evening as I looked out over the darkening Grand Canyon, I knew that whatever hardships the future might bring, there was nothing better and more important for me to do than to take an intransigent stand in defense of life, to not compromise, to continue to be a warrior for the Earth. To be a warrior for the Earth regardless of the consequences.

Notes

1. Two excellent books on the population issue that are also sensitive to social and economic issues are William R. Catton, Jr.'s *Overshoot: The Ecological Basis of Revolutionary Change* (Urbana, Ill. and Chicago: University of Illinois Press, 1982), and *The Population Explosion*, by Paul and Anne Ehrlich (New York: Simon and Schuster, 1990). No one concerned with the preservation of biological diversity should be without these.

2. A case in point involves the Spotted Owl, a threatened species dependent on ancient forests. These little owls are easily attracted by playing tapes of their call. Loggers in the Northwest are going into old-growth forests with tape recorders and shotguns to exterminate Spotted Owls. They feel that if they do so, they will eliminate a major reason to stop the logging of these pristine forests.

3. Jane Kay, "Tree Wars," *San Francisco Examiner Image Magazine* (17 December 1989).

25 Living By Life: Some Bioregional Theory and Practice

Jim Dodge

I want to make it clear from the outset that I'm not all that sure what bioregionalism is. To my understanding, bioregionalism is an idea still in loose and amorphous formulation, and presently is more hopeful declaration than actual practice. In fact, "idea" may be too generous: bioregionalism is more properly a notion, which is variously defined as a general idea, a belief, an opinion, an intuition, an inclination, an urge. Furthermore, as I think will prove apparent, bioregionalism is hardly a new notion; it has been the animating cultural principle through 99 percent of human history, and is at least as old as consciousness. Thus, no doubt, the urge.

My purpose here is not really to define bioregionalism—that will take care of itself in the course of things—but to mention some of the elements that I see composing the notion, and some possibilities for practice. I speak with no special privilege on the matter other than my longstanding and fairly studious regard for the subject, a regard enriched by my teachers and numerous bioregional friends. My only true qualification is that I'm fool enough to try.

"Bioregionalism" is from the Greek *bios* (life) and the French *region* (region), itself from the Latin *regia* (territory), and earlier, *regere* (to rule or govern). Etymologically, then, bioregionalism means life territory, place of life, or perhaps by reckless extension, government by life. If you can't imagine that government by life would be at least 40 billion times better than government by the Reagan administration, or Mobil Oil, or any other distant powerful monolith, then your heart is probably no bigger than a prune pit and you won't have much sympathy for what follows.

A central element of bioregionalism—and one that distinguishes it from similar politics of place—is the importance given to natural systems, both as the source of physical nutrition and as the body of metaphors from which our spirits draw sustenance. A natural system is a community of interdependent life, a mutual biological integration on the order of an ecosystem, for example. What constitutes this community is uncertain beyond the obvious—that it includes all interacting life forms, from the tiniest fleck of algae to human beings, as well as their biological processes. To this bare minimum, already impenetrably complex, bioregionalism adds the influences of cultural behavior, such as subsistence techniques and ceremonies. Many people further insist—sensibly, I think—that this community/ecosystem must also include the planetary processes and the larger figures of regulation: solar income, magnetism, gravity, and so

From *CoEvolution Quarterly*, 32 (1981), 6–12. Reprinted with permission.

forth. Bioregionalism is simply biological realism; in natural systems we find the physical truth of our being, the real obvious stuff like the need for oxygen as well as the more subtle need for moonlight, and perhaps other truths beyond those. Not surprisingly, then, bioregionalism holds that the health of natural systems is directly connected to our own physical/psychic health as individuals and as a species, and for that reason natural systems and their informing integrations deserve, if not utter veneration, at least our clearest attention and deepest respect. No matter how great our laws, technologies, or armies, we can't make the sun rise every morning nor the rain dance on the goldenback ferns.

To understand natural systems is to begin an understanding of the self, its common and particular essences—literal self-interest in its barest terms. "As above, so below," according to the old-tradition alchemists; natural systems as models of consciousness. When we destroy a river, we increase our thirst, ruin the beauty of free-flowing water, forsake the meat and spirit of the salmon, and lose a little bit of our souls.

Unfortunately, human society has also developed technologies that make it possible to lose big chunks all at once. If we make just one serious mistake with nuclear energy, for instance, our grandchildren may be born with bones like overcooked spaghetti, or torn apart by mutant rats. Global nuclear war is suicide: the "losers" die instantly; the "winners" inherit slow radiation death and twisted chromosomes. By any sensible measure of self-interest, by any regard for life, nuclear war is abhorrent, unthinkable, and loathsomely stupid, and yet the United States and other nations spend billions to provide that possibility. It is the same mentality that pooh-poohs the growing concentration of poisons in the biosphere. It's like the farmer who was showing off his prize mule to a stranger one day when the mule suddenly fell over sideways and died. The farmer looked at the body in bewildered disbelief: "Damn," he said, "I've had this mule for 27 years and it's the first time he's ever done this." To which the stranger, being a biological realist, undoubtedly replied, "No shit."

While I find an amazing depth of agreement among bioregionalists on what constitutes *bios*, and on what general responsibilities attend our place in the skein of things, there is some disagreement—friendly but passionate—on what actually constitutes a distinct biological region (as opposed to arbitrary entities, like states and counties, where boundaries are established without the dimmest ecological perception, and therefore make for cultural incoherence and piecemeal environmental management). Since the very gut of bioregional thought is the integrity of natural systems and culture, with the function of culture being the mediation of the self and the ecosystem, one might think "bioregion" would be fairly tightly defined. But I think it must be kept in mind that, to paraphrase Poe and Jack Spicer, we're dealing with the grand concord of what does not stoop to definition. There are, however, a number of ideas floating around regarding the biological criteria for a region. I'll mention some of them below, limiting the example to Northern California.

One criterion for determining a biological region is biotic shift, a percentage change in plant/animal species composition from one place to another—that is, if 15 to 25 percent of the species where I live are different from those where you live, we occupy different biological regions. We probably also experience different climates and walk on different soils, since those differences are reflected in species composition. Nearly everyone I've talked with agrees that biotic shift is a fairly slick and accurate way to make bioregional distinctions; the argument is over the percentage, which invariably seems arbitrary. Since the change in biotic composition is usually gradual, the biotic shift criterion permits vague and permeable boundaries between regions, which I personally favor. The idea, after all, is not to replace one set of lines with another, but simply to recognize inherent biological integrities for the purpose of sensible planning and management.

Another way to biologically consider regions is by watershed. This method is generally straightforward, since drainages are clearly apparent on topographical maps. Watershed is usually taken to mean river drainage, so if you live on Cottonwood Creek you are part of the Sacramento River drainage. The problem with watersheds as bioregional criteria is that if you live in San Francisco you are also part of the Sacramento (and San Joaquin) River drainage, and that's a long way from Cottonwood Creek. Since any long drainage presents similar problems, most people who advance the watershed criterion make intradrainage distinctions (in the case of the Sacramento: headwaters, Central Valley, west slope Sierra, east slope Coast Range, and delta/bay). The west slope of the Coast Range, with its short-running rivers and strong Pacific influence, is often considered as a whole biological area, at least from the Gualala River to the Mattole River or, depending on who you're talking to, from the Russian River to the Eel River, though they aren't strictly west slope Coast Range rivers. The Klamath, Smith, and Trinity drainages are often considered a single drainage system, with the arguable inclusion of the Chetco and the Rogue.

A similar method of bioregional distinction is based upon land form. Roughly, Northern California breaks down into the Sierra, the Coast Range, the Central Valley, the Klamath Range, the southern part of the Cascade Range, and the Modoc Plateau. Considering the relationship between topography and water, it is not surprising that land form distinctions closely follow watersheds.

A different criterion for making bioregional distinctions is, awkwardly put, cultural/phenomenological: you are where you perceive you are; your turf is what you think it is, individually and collectively. Although the human sense of territory is deeply evolved and cultural/perceptual behavior certainly influences the sense of place, this view seems to me a bit anthropocentric. And though it is difficult *not* to view things in terms of human experience and values, it does seem wise to remember that human perception is notoriously prey to distortion and the strange delights of perversity. Our species hasn't done too well lately working essentially from this view; because we're ecological dominants doesn't necessarily mean we're ecological determinants. (In fairness, I should note that many friends think I'm unduly cranky on this subject.)

One of the more provocative ideas to delineate bioregions is in terms of "spirit places" or psyche-tuning power-presences, such as Mount Shasta and the Pacific Ocean. By this criterion, a bioregion is defined by the predominate physical influence where you live. You have to live in its presence long enough to truly feel its force within you and that it's not mere descriptive geography.

Also provocative is the notion that bioregion is a vertical phenomenon having more to do with elevation than horizontal deployment—thus a distinction between hill people and flatlanders, which in Northern California also tends to mean country and city. A person living at 2,000 feet in the Coast Range would have more in cultural common with a Sierra dweller at a similar altitude than with someone at sea level 20 miles away.

To briefly recapitulate, the criteria most often advanced for making bioregional distinctions are biotic shift, watershed, land form, cultural/phenomenological, spirit presences, and elevation. Taken together, as I think they should be, they give us a strong sense of where we're at and the life that enmeshes our own. Nobody I know is pushing for a quick definition anyway. Bioregionalism, whatever it is, occupies that point in development (more properly, renewal) where definition is unnecessary and perhaps dangerous. Better now to let definitions emerge from practice than impose them dogmatically from the git-go.

A second element of bioregionalism is anarchy. I hesitate using that fine word because it's been so distorted by reactionary shitheads to scare people that its connotative associations have become bloody chaos and fiends amok, rather than political decentralization, self-determination, and a commitment to social equity. Anarchy doesn't mean out of control; it means out of *their* control. Anarchy is based upon a sense of interdependent self-reliance, the conviction that we as a community, or a tight, small-scale federation of communities, can mind our own business, and can make decisions regarding our individual and communal lives and gladly accept the responsibilities and consequences of those decisions. Further, by consolidating decision-making at a local, face-to-face level without having to constantly push information through insane bureaucratic hierarchies, we can act more quickly in relation to natural systems and, since we live there, hopefully with more knowledge and care.

The United States is simply too large and complex to be responsibly governed by a decision-making body of perhaps 1,000 people representing 220,000,000 Americans and a large chunk of the biosphere, especially when those 1,000 decision makers can only survive by compromise and generally are forced to front for heavy economic interests (media campaigns for national office are expensive). A government where one person represents the interests of 220,000 others is absurd, considering that not all the people voted for the winning representative (or even voted) and especially considering that most of those 220,000 people are capable of representing themselves. I think people do much better, express their deeper qualities, when their actions matter. Obviously one way to make government more meaningful and responsible is to involve people directly day by day, in the processes of decision, which only seems possible if we reduce the scale of government. A bioregion seems about the right size: say close to a small state, or along the lines of the Swiss canton system or American Indian tribes.

If nothing else, bioregional government—which theoretically would express the biological and cultural realities of people-in-place—would promote the diversity of biosocial experimentation; and in diversity is stability. The present system of national government seems about to collapse on the weight of its own emptiness. Our economy is dissolving like wet sugar. Violence is epidemic. The quality of our workmanship—always the hallmark of a proud people—has deteriorated so badly that we're ashamed to classify our products as durable goods. Our minds have been homogenized by television, which keeps our egos in perpetual infancy while substituting them for a sense of the self. Our information comes from progressively fewer sources, none of them notably reliable. We spend more time posturing than we do getting it on. In short, American culture has become increasingly gutless and barren in our lifetimes, and the political system little more than a cover for an economics that ravages the planet and its people for the financial gain of very few. It seems almost a social obligation to explore alternatives. Our much-heralded standard of living hasn't done much for the quality of our daily lives; the glut of commodities, endlessly hurled at us out of the vast commodity spectacle, is just more shit on the windshield.

I don't want to imply that bioregionalism is the latest sectarian addition to the American Left, which historically has been more concerned with doctrinal purity and shafting each other than with effective practice. It's not a question of working within the system or outside the system, but simply of working, *somewhere*, to pull if off. And as I mentioned at the beginning, I'm not so sure bioregionalism even has a doctrine to be pure about—it's more a sense of direction (uphill, it seems) than the usual leftist highway to Utopia . . . or Ecotopia for that matter.

Just for the record, and to give some credence to the diversity of thought informing bioregionalism, I want to note some of the spirits I see at work in the early formulation of the notion: pantheists, Wobs, Reformed Marxists (that is, those who see the sun as the means of production), Diggers, libterrerans, Kropotkinites (mutual aid and coevolution), animists, alchemists (especially the old school), lefty Buddhists, Situationists (consummate analysts of the commodity spectacle), syndicalists, Provos, born-again Taoists, general outlaws, and others drawn to the decentralist banner by raw empathy.

A third element composing the bioregional notion is spirit. Since I can't claim any spiritual wisdom, and must admit to being virtually ignorant on the subject, I'm reluctant to offer more than the most tentative perceptions. What I think most bioregionalists hold in spiritual common is a profound regard for life—all life, not just white Americans, or humankind entire, but frogs, roses, mayflies, coyotes, lichens: all of it: the gopher snake and the gopher. For instance, we don't want to save the whales for the sweetsie-poo, lily-romantic reasons attributed to us by those who profit from their slaughter; we don't want them saved merely because they are magnificent creatures, so awesome that when you see one close from an open boat your heart roars; we want to save them for the most selfish of reasons; without them we are diminished.

In the bioregional spirit view we're all one creation, and it may seem almost simple-minded to add that there is a connection—even a necessary unity—between the natural world and the human mind (which may be just a fancy way of saying there is a connection between life and existence). Different people and groups have their own paths and practices and may describe this connection differently—profound, amusing, ineluctable, mysterious—but they all acknowledge the importance of the connection. The connection is archaic, primitive, and so obvious that it hasn't received much attention since the rise of Christian dominion and fossil-fuel industrialism. If it is a quality of archaic thought to dispute the culturally enforced dichotomy between the spiritual and the practical, I decidedly prefer the archaic view. What could possibly be of more *practical* concern than our spiritual well-being as individuals, as a species, and as members of a larger community of life? The Moral Majority certainly isn't going to take us in that direction; they're interested in business as usual, as their golden boy, James Watt, has demonstrated. We need fewer sermons and more prayers.

This sense of bioregional spirit isn't fixed to a single religious form or practice. Generally it isn't Christian-based or noticeably monotheistic, though such views aren't excluded. I think the main influences are the primitive animist/Great Spirit tradition, various Eastern and esoteric religious practices, and plain ol' paying attention. I may be stretching the accord, but I also see a shared awareness that the map is not the journey, and for that reason it is best to be alert and to respond to the opportunities presented rather than waste away wishing life would offer some worthy spiritual challenge (which it does, constantly, anyway). Call it whatever seems appropriate—enlightenment, fulfillment, spiritual maturity, happiness, self-realization—it has to be earned, and to be earned it has to be lived, and that means bringing it into our daily lives and working on it. Instant gratifications are not the deepest gratifications, I suspect, though Lord knows they certainly have their charms. The emphasis is definitely on the practice, not the doctrine, and especially on practicing what you preach; there is a general recognition that there are many paths, and that they are a further manifestation of crucial natural diversity. I might also note for serious backsliders that the play is as serious as the work, and there is a great willingness to celebrate; nobody is interested in a spirit whose holiness is constantly announced with sour piety and narrow self-righteousness.

Combining the three elements gives a loose idea of what I take to be bioregionalism: a decentralized, self-determined mode of social organization; a culture predictated upon biological integrities and acting in respectful accord; and a society which honors and abets the spiritual development of its members. Or so the theory goes. However, it's not mere theory, for there have been many cultures founded essentially upon those principles; for example, it has been the dominant cultural mode of inhabitation on this continent. The point is not to go back, but to take the best forward. Renewal, not some misty retreat into what was.

Theories, ideas, notions—they have their generative and reclamative values, and certainly a loveliness, but without the palpable intelligence of practice they remain hovering in the nether regions of nifty entertainments or degrade into more flamboyant fads and diversions like literary movements and hula-hoops. Practice is what puts the heart to work. If theory establishes the game, practice is the gamble, and the first rule of all gambling games has it like this: you can play bad and win; you can play good and lose; but if you play good over the long haul you're gonna come out alright.

Bioregional practice (or applied strategy) can take as many forms as the imagination and nerves, but for purpose of example I've hacked it into two broad categories; resistance and renewal. Resistance involves a struggle between the bioregional forces (who represent intelligence, excellence, and care) and the forces of heartlessness (who represent a greed so lifeless and forsaken it can't even pass as ignorance). In a way, I think it really is that simple, that there is, always, a choice about how we will live our lives, that there is a state of constant opportunity for both spiritual succor and carnal delight, and that the way we choose to live is the deepest expression of who we truly are. If we consistently choose against the richest possibilities of life, against kindness, against beauty, against love and sweet regard, then we aren't much. Our only claim to dignity is trying our best to do what we think is right, to put some heart in it, some soul, flower and root. We're going to fall on our asses a lot, founder on our pettiness and covetousness and sloth, but at least there is the effort, and that's surely better than being just another quivering piece of the national cultural jello. Or so it seems to me.

However, the primary focus of resistance is not the homogeneous American supraculture— that can be resisted for the most part simply by refusing to participate while at the same time trying to live our lives the way we think we should (knowing we'll get no encouragement what-soever from the colonial overstructure). Rather, the focus of resistance is against the continuing destruction of natural systems. We can survive the ruthless homogeneity of national culture because there are many holes we can slip through, but we cannot survive if the natural systems that sustain us are destroyed. That has to be stopped if we want to continue living on this planet. That's not "environmentalism"; it's ecology with a vengeance. Personally, I think we should develop a Sophoclean appreciation for the laws of nature, and submit. Only within the fractional time frame of fossil-fuel industrialization have we begun to seriously insult the environment and impudently violate the conditions of life. We've done a great deal of damage in a very short time, and only because of the amazing flexibility of natural systems have we gotten away with it so far. But I don't think we'll destroy the planet; she will destroy us first, which is perhaps only to say we'll destroy ourselves. The most crucial point of resistance is choosing not to.

And then we must try to prevent others from doing it for us all, since by allowing monopoly-capital centralized government (which, like monotheism, is not so much putting all your eggs in one basket as dropping your one egg in a blender), we have given them the power to make such remote-control decisions. The way to prevent it is five-fold: by being a model for an alternative; by knowing more than they do; by being politically astute; by protecting what we value; and by any means necessary. (I think it's important to note that there is nearly complete agreement that nonviolence is the best means available, and that the use of violence is always a sad admission of desperation. Besides, they have all the money, guns, and lawyers. People advocating violent means are probably not very interested in living much longer.)

I think political smarts are best applied in the local community and county. Most crucial land use decisions, for instance, are made at the county level by boards of supervisors. The representative-to-constituent ratio is obviously much better in a county than in a country, and therefore informed and spirited constituents have a far greater influence on decisions and policies. Work to elect sympathetic representatives. Put some money where your heart is. Go to your share of the generally boring meetings and hearings. Challenge faulty information (thus the importance of knowing more than they do). Create alternatives. Stand your ground.

Buying land is also a strong political move; "ownership" is the best protection against gross environmental abuse, just as living on the land is the best defence against mass-media gelatin culture, assuming the quality of information influences the quality of thought. Owning land also affords increased political leverage within the present system. Besides, bioregionalism without a tangible land base would be like love without sex; the circuits of association wouldn't be complete. (Of course, it isn't necessary to own land to either appreciate it or resist its destruction, and I hope nobody infers that bioregionalism is for land aristocracy.)

The growth and strength of the "environmental movement" in the past decade has encouraged awareness about the destruction of natural systems and the consequences of such callous disregard. This is all to the good, and we should continue to stay in their faces on critical issues. But it's going to be continual crisis ecology unless we come up with a persuasive economic alternative; otherwise, most people will go on choosing progress over maturity, for progress is deeply equated with payroll, and money, to most people, means life. It's that cold. It's also basically true, and many friends share my chagrin that it took us so long to grasp that truism.

It now seems painfully obvious that the economic system must be transformed if we hope to protect natural systems from destruction in the name of Mammon. Economics seems to baffle everyone, especially me. I have no prescriptions to offer, except to note that it doesn't have to be one economic system, and that any economics should include a fair measure of value. What's needed is an economy that takes into true account the cost of biospheric destruction and at the same time feeds the family. People must be convinced that it's in their best economic interest to maintain healthy biological systems. The best place to meet this challenge is where you live—that is, personally and within the community.

It's probably also fairly plain that changing the economic system will involve changing our conception of what constitutes a fulfilled life and cracking the cultural mania for mindless consumption and its attendant waste. To realize what is alive within us, the who of who we are, we have to know what we truly need, and what is enough. As Marshall Sahlins has pointed out, affluence can be attained either through increasing production or reducing needs. Since increased production usually means ravaged natural systems, the best strategy seems the reduction of needs, and hopefully the consequent recognition that enough is plenty. A truly affluent society is one of material sufficiency and spiritual riches.

While we're keeping up this resistance in our daily lives—and I think it is in the quality of daily life rather than momentary thrills that the heart is proven—we can begin repairing the natural systems that have been damaged. Logged and mined watersheds need to be repaired. Streams have to be cleared. Trees planted. Checkdams built to stop gully erosion. Long-term management strategies developed. Tough campaigns waged to secure funding for the work. There's a strong effort in this direction happening in Northern California now, much of it through worker co-ops and citizens' groups, with increasingly cooperative help from local and state agencies. This work has really just begun, and the field is wide open. So far it seems to satisfy the two feelings that prompted it: the sense that we have a responsibility to renew what we've wasted and the need to practice "right livelihood," or work that provides a living while promoting the spirit.

Natural system renewal (or rehabilitation, or enhancement, or whatever other names it goes by) could well be our first environmental art. It requires a thorough knowledge of how natural systems work, delicate perceptions of specific sites, the development of appropriate techniques, and hard physical work of the kind that puts you to bed after dinner. What finer work than healing the Earth, where the rewards are both in the doing and the results? It deserves our participation and support. For the irrefutable fact of the matter is that if we want to explore the bioregional possibility, we've got to work, got to get dirty—either by sitting on our asses at environmental hearings or by busting them planting trees in the rain. Sniveling don't make it.

The chances of bioregionalism succeeding, like the chances of survival itself, are beside the point. If one person, or a few, or a community of people, live more fulfilling lives from bioregional practice, then it's successful. This country has a twisted idea of success: it is almost always a quantitative judgment—salary, wins, the number of rooms in the house, the amount of people you command. Since bioregionalism by temperament is qualitative, the basis of judgment should be shifted accordingly. What they call a subculture, we call friends.

Most of the people I talk with feel we have a fighting chance to stop environmental destruction within 50 years and to turn the culture around within 800 to 1,000 years. "Fighting chance" translates as long odds but good company, and bioregionalism is obviously directed at people whose hearts put a little gamble in their blood. Since we won't live to see the results of this hoped-for transformation, we might as well live to start it right, with the finest expressions of spirit and style we can muster, keeping in mind that there's only a functional difference between the flower and the root, that essentially they are part of the same abiding faith.

The Sun still rises every morning. Dig in.

26 Ecocentric Discourses: Problems and Future Prospects for Nature Advocacy

Robyn Eckersley

Introduction

Since the theme of this conference is ecological discourse, I propose to explore and take stock of the troubled evolution of certain discourses in western environmental philosophy that seek to defend biological diversity.[1] Variously referred to as ecocentric or biocentric, these discourses have been in the forefront of mounting a critique of anthropocentrism or human chauvinism, philosophically defending the intrinsic value of nature and politically defending the setting aside of large tracts of habitat along with other policy changes to ensure the flourishing of nonhuman species.[2] Although there is considerable variety among the philosophical and ethical discourses that can be broadly described as ecocentric, they all share the conviction that the western philosophical tradition has elevated and celebrated humanity at the expense of nonhuman nature and that this has helped to sanction the domination of nature. The quest has been to find a new moral vocabulary that includes nonhuman species in the circle of moral considerability, that acknowledges ecological interdependence, and that seeks new policies and laws that provide more concerted protection for nonhuman species and ecosystems.

However, notwithstanding over two decades of development, ecocentric discourses remain controversial and they have generated a range of critical responses from philosophers and cultural critics, some of whom are sceptical of, and others sympathetic to, the ecocentric project. Some of these sceptical counter-discourses have sought to reinstate humanism as the foundation of environmental ethics. Others have accused ecocentric theorists of being misanthropic or fascist.[3] More sympathetic critics have taken issue with the idea of intrinsic value as an objective property of nonhuman life forms. Yet subjectivist accounts of intrinsic value have been deemed unsatisfactory by many nonanthropocentric theorists for denying nonhuman agency and reducing nonhuman species to mere passive recipients of human valuation.[4] In the wake of these critiques and divisions, many believe it is necessary to abandon, transcend, or at least destabilize what now seem fraught and old-fashioned distinctions between intrinsic and instrumental value, anthropocentrism and ecocentrism, culture and nature.[5] Indeed, it appears that

From Robyn Eckersley, 'Ecocentric Discourses: Problems and Prospects for Nature Advocacy', Tamkang Review Vol XXXIV, No. 3–4, Spring-Summer (2004), 155–86.

the God-like task of assessing precisely which bits of nature ought to be designated intrinsically valuable has itself emerged as an arrogant and foolhardy exercise.

More generally, ecofeminists, environmental justice advocates, postcolonialists, and post-structuralists have drawn attention to the role of class, gender, power, and language in the social construction of nature—moves that have seen, for example, the deconstruction of the concept of wilderness as an expression of western, patriarchal, neo-romantic, and/or middle-class longings.[6] More recently, environmental pragmatists have criticized certain nonanthropocentric theories (most notably, those of J. Baird Callicott, Laura Westra, and Holmes Rolston III)[7] for being monistic, dogmatic, and therefore incapable of dealing with environmental pluralism.[8] For pragmatists, environmental problems ought to be solved democratically by the people affected, not by armchair environmental philosophers who expect policy makers simply to apply their environmental ethical theories in a formulaic fashion. From this pragmatist perspective, what we urgently need is not *applied* philosophy but rather *practical* philosophy—the coming together of a community of inquirers to discuss and resolve practical environmental problems, drawing on local cultural resources.[9]

Much of the first wave of green political theorists (myself included) had strenuously defended the critique of anthropocentrism and sought to emphasize this as a distinctive and new feature of political thought vis-à-vis so-called 'mainstream' political theories.[10] However, a number of 'second wave' green political theorists are now inclined to reject the anthropocentric/ecocentric distinction as unhelpful and have sought instead to emphasize the humanist credentials of green politics and redirect attention towards questions of human ecological stewardship, ecological virtue, and what might be the legitimate use (or illegitimate abuse) of natural resources and ecosystems.[11] This second wave of green political theory has also sought to engage more directly with debates in mainstream political theory, focusing on fruitful points of convergence among environmental and social concerns, and particularly democratic theory.[12]

In all, the mounting and multifaceted critique of the nonanthropocentric project and the increasing interest among environmental pragmatists and green political theorists generally in questions of democratic theory and practice have served to sideline nonanthropocentric philosophical discourses as merely one set of discourses among many. More pointedly, these critiques suggest that nonanthropocentric discourses are not especially helpful to consensus building in a multicultural world.

In this paper, I reflect on the future viability of the nonanthropocentric project of 'liberating nature' by exploring what might be rescued in the wake of the various epistemological, ethical, and political critiques of past efforts to bring nonhuman species into Kant's 'kingdom of ends'. I do not seek to provide a systematic overview of the debate between various nonanthropocentric theorists and their more numerous critics. Rather my concern is to draw selectively on some of these debates in order to explore the *methods* that have been enlisted by nonanthropocentric theorists (and their critics) to argue their case. More importantly, my strategy is to suggest that we focus on 'nature advocacy' as a *democratic* task, and to link it (structurally and historically) with the social and environmental justice movements. If one accepts that environmental conflicts should be resolved by democratic means (and here one must side with environmental pluralists rather than monists), then focusing on the democratic task of nature advocacy, and taking stock of the procedures, protocols, rhetorical devices, and analogical methods of persuasion that have been enlisted by leading environmental philosophers and activists, would seem to be a fruitful line of inquiry. Such a focus not only redirects attention to the role of advocacy in a democracy (a focus that restores the democratic credentials of ecocentric discourses which now seem so impugned), but also sensitizes nature advocates to the possibilities and limitations of some of the arguments that have thus far been deployed.

In modern times, it generally goes without saying that we humans already belong to Kant's 'kingdom of ends', that we all possess 'inherent dignity' and (for liberals and more radical emancipatory theorists) the right to self-determination or self-realization. The task for nonanthropocentric theorists has typically been how to open the moral door to nonhuman species *by analogy with the human case*. I shall argue that herein lies a conundrum: that the attempt to use the human case as a reference point invariably leads to invidious comparison between the human and the nonhuman in ways that demean nonhumans (and sometimes humans as well). However, I shall also argue that ultimately this is a problem that cannot be entirely avoided if we humans are to communicate with each other in ways that seek to enlist and extend reasonably established moral norms in order to stretch conventional moral horizons. Philosophers who have taken 'the linguistic turn' have also emphasized the role of metaphor in moral progress, and the rhetorical nature of social reality.[13] Efforts to persuade others typically requires beginning from some common or familiar understanding and then reasoning from the common and familiar to the less common and less familiar. In what follows, I explore the pitfalls and critical possibilities associated with this method of argument and suggest that critical political ecology provides a less problematic basis for navigating these issues than traditional liberal moral or political philosophy.[14] Although both are traceable to the Enlightenment quest for autonomy, liberalism has become complacent while critical theory has continued to question the protocols of political dialogue and political representation and the boundaries of the moral and political community in space and time.

Back to the Beginning

Many of the early philosophical discourses concerned to 'liberate' all or some parts of nonhuman nature took the following form. While recognizing that nonhuman species are important resources for sustaining human livelihoods, the idea that nonhuman species should be considered valuable *only* as resources was rejected as one-dimensional, degrading of both human and nonhuman nature, and likely to sanction the accelerated extinction rates for redundant, 'useless', or inconvenient species. If species had no use or benefit to humankind, or if technological substitutes could be found for the services provided by a particular species of plant or animal, then it would be 'no great mischief' if that species were to vanish from the earth.[15] Resources, after all, are mere 'indices of utility to industrial society'.[16]

For all its problems, the intuitive appeal of the notion of intrinsic value in nonhuman species was one way of saying that nonhuman species, like human species, matter—that they are worthy, they have their own forms of agency, and they are valuable above and beyond their use value to humans. Enlisting the notion of intrinsic value (or 'inherent value') was also a means by which to expose and challenge 'the arrogance of humanism'[17] or human chauvinism—the idea that humans are the crown of creation, the culmination of evolution, the only morally considerable beings entitled to a permanent place in the sun, as if the sole purpose of the rest of nature was to serve humanity.

For some nonanthropocentric theorists, if the welfare of nonhuman species was to be taken seriously and the destruction of their habitat considered a grave matter that should be non-negotiable (or at least much less negotiable than it currently is), then it also seemed necessary to defend an objectivist theory of intrinsic value that transcended the preferences and aesthetic tastes of humans.[18] After all, if human rights claims—based on the inherent dignity of the person—could trump competing arguments based on social utility, then so should the moral rights of nonhuman species trump utilitarian arguments for development. This was merely a case of rounding out the (liberal) revolution.

While the logic of the early argumentative strategy seemed straightforward enough, the task of articulating a theory of intrinsic value and defending an alternative biocentric or ecocentric philosophy has been anything but straightforward. Indeed, J. Baird Callicott described this problem as the 'central and most recalcitrant problem for environmental ethics'.[19] For example, environmental philosophers divided over what the relevant properties of intrinsic value should be—was it sentience, aliveness, 'the subject of a life', autopoiesis? If environmental ethics was to have policy relevance, these matters had to be resolved in a practical, parsimonious, and persuasive way. And the choice was not insignificant: it would determine how much of nonhuman nature would be included in the circle of moral and legal protection, and—more importantly—what character that protection would take.

Many of the early efforts to extend moral considerability to nonhuman species attempted to build up a larger, transhuman moral order through the extension of widely accepted, basic principles that underpin distinctly human emancipatory movements, most notably Kantian and utilitarian moral philosophy. In this sense, nonanthropocentric environmental ethics remained profoundly indebted to anthropocentric ethics, as Anthony Weston has astutely observed.[20] Nonetheless, for Weston, 'the project of going beyond anthropocentrism still looks wild, incautious, intellectually overexcited'.[21] He attributes this to the fact that this radical environmental philosophical project is still in its 'orginatory phase'—a phase of uncertainty and experimentation, with no secure foothold in dominant cultural understandings in the west. Indeed, Weston concedes that a great deal of exploration and metaphor is required in the early stages of the development of new values.[22] Yet he goes on to note, perceptively, that the success of these explorations depends to a large extent 'in the way they open up the possibility of new connections, not in the way they settle or "close" any questions'.[23] Weston's observations provide a good entry point for exploring both the discursive possibilities and the problems associated with drawing analogies between the human and the nonhuman.

Some of the most influential of the early efforts to extend moral considerability to nonhuman species involved the radical extension of *individualist* liberal moral philosophy to the environment. This form of moral extensionism—which finds its classical expression in Peter Singer's book *Animal Liberation* and Christopher Stone's legal essay 'Should Trees Have Standing?'—has since become part of the standard repertoire of those wishing to impugn human chauvinism.[24]

The argument runs as follows. An animal or 'natural entity' need not be a fully competent moral *agent* (equipped with Kantian powers of moral reasoning) in order to be recognized as a worthy moral *subject*, that is, as a being that is entitled to moral consideration. This is because, in the human domain, there are plenty of examples of individuals who do not possess any or full moral agency but who nonetheless deserve our respect and attentive care (infants, intellectually handicapped persons, the senile). We recognize these persons as morally considerable because they are ends-in-themselves and/or because they are beings capable of suffering or otherwise being harmed, even though they cannot necessarily return recognition in the way that fully competent moral agents can. However, once we accept that morally incompetent humans are nonetheless morally considerable, then this argument maintains that there is no good reason for not accepting nonhuman others as morally considerable on the grounds that they too are ends-in-themselves or otherwise capable of suffering or being harmed. According to this line of argument, our failure to extend moral considerability to nonhuman species is symptomatic of speciesism or human chauvinism—an unwarranted prejudice against nonhuman others *just because they are not human.*

Now this strategy of progressive moral extensionism has been employed to defend quite different moral frameworks. Singer has used this form of reasoning to argue that not just humans but all *sentient* creatures (i.e., those with the capacity to suffer) ought to be treated as morally considerable in the sense of having their particular 'interests' considered in the policy process. Whereas Singer's argument draws upon *moral* analogies and anomalies, Stone's argument rests upon *legal* analogies and anomalies. According to Stone, given that the Anglo-American legal system grants various sorts of rights to nonhuman entities (churches, corporations, ships, municipalities), there is no good reason for not extending legal rights to natural entities as well, such as mountains and rivers, to be enforced by human legal guardians when they can be shown to be harmed. While Stone's discussion mainly focuses on legal devices for protecting wild nature, an incipient ecocentric moral argument is nonetheless discernible in his discussion. For Stone, then, the creative and rhetorical possibilities in the rights discourse are far from exhausted.

Second Thoughts

John Rodman was the first to warn of the dangers associated with the attempt to build up a larger, transhuman moral order through the extension of basic moral principles that underpin distinctly human emancipatory movements. As early as 1975, in his lengthy review of Singer's and Stone's work, he singled out for attention what he called The Method of Argument from Human Analogy and Anomaly.[25] Now the point of Rodman's critique was to show that, while Stone's and Singer's argumentative strategy is appealing, it unwittingly conveys a double message. On the one hand, it invites us to travel beyond the familiar by recognizing the moral status of some or all members of the nonhuman world—essentially because there is no good reason not to, and to avoid inconsistency in our moral reasoning and behaviour. On the other hand, Rodman argues that this same process of morally elevating nonhuman others by analogy with *anomalous* human cases is degrading and patronizing since it relegates nonhuman others 'to the status of inferior human beings, species anomalies . . . moral half-breeds having rights without obligations'.[26]

In the case of Singer's argument for animal liberation, Rodman suggests that what we have is 'not a revolution in ethics but something analogous to the Reform Bill of 1832, when the British aristocracy extended selected rights to the upper middle classes'.[27] While Rodman accepts that we should not ignore suffering, he insists that it ought not to be the pivotal criteria in framing our moral relations with nonhuman (or indeed human) others. It is, after all, conceivable that humans may, through selective breeding and genetic engineering, produce domesticated animals that are no longer capable of suffering, thereby robbing animal liberationists of their grounds of objection to factory farming, vivisection, and other cruel practices. By Rodman's lights, the real force of Singer's critique of factory farming stems not merely from the suffering it causes, but from an objection to our treatment of living organisms as machines, because, as he puts it 'we react indignantly to the spectacle of external mechanical conditions being imposed upon natural entities that have their own internal structures, needs, and potentialities'.[28] For Rodman, what is missing from these early attempts to argue for the moral considerability of nonhumans is any effort to regard such beings as 'having their own existence, their own character and potentialities, their own forms of excellence, their own integrity, their own grandeur'.[29]

Rodman is careful to enlist a vocabulary that is not so obviously modelled on the human case, but can nonetheless encompass humans. Thus, humans, birds, bees, trees, and micro-organisms all still have something in common, but these commonalities are formulated at a highly abstract level that tries to avoid reasoning *from* the human case by finding points of connection across all living beings. Yet to suggest that all beings have their own 'character', 'needs', and 'potentiality' can still be seen as betraying an underlying (liberal?) commitment to autonomy.[30]

Nonetheless, Rodman's early critique has been echoed with increasing sophistication by a growing line of critical political ecologists (which includes postcolonialists and ecofeminists) who are sympathetic with the ecocentric project but sensitive to the problem of invidious comparison. Writing ten years later, for example, Neil Evernden argued that it is a fatal flaw for environmentalists to try to squeeze some of their moral constituency (say apes and some other mammals) into the human prototype, reckoning that saving some is better than saving none.[31] Conforming to the requirements and modes of rationality of the dominant culture has rarely served the interests of diverse minority cultures. Identifying only with those nonhuman others who are like us (e.g., mammals) is even less likely to permit the flourishing of diverse nonhuman species.

Given that there are limits in the human capacity for *sympathetic* identification with non-human species that bear no resemblance to ourselves, we need to question whether this kind of identification is an appropriate basis upon which to ground respect for nonhuman others. Indeed, the whole point of the contemporary debate about respecting difference (whether cultural or biological) is that 'the other' does not have to be 'like us' before we accord it any recognition and respect.[32] If, as Todorov asks in exploring the relationship between self and other, loving the other means projecting ourselves or our own ideals onto the other, then does the other really need our love?[33] Indigenous peoples certainly did not need the 'love' of Christian missionaries. Bears and lions do not need the love of circus audiences and many wild creatures could probably do without the love of ecotourists.

More recently, Val Plumwood has shown how we must remain sensitive to the many ways in which the dualisms of self/other and human/nonhuman 'create a web of incorporations and exclusions'.[34] Webs of inclusion and exclusion typically operate by the more powerful group excluding those who lack something that is possessed and deemed by the more powerful group to be the measure of worth (such as reason, civilization, moral agency, or language). According to Plumwood, this 'master consciousness' recognizes the other 'only to the extent that it is assimilated to the self, or incorporated into the self and its system of desires and needs: only as colonised by the self. The master consciousness cannot tolerate unassimilated otherness'.[35] Plumwood's notion of 'unassimilated otherness' attempts to break more decisively with any human analogies. Nonetheless, her argument is still indebted to, and builds upon, postliberal emancipatory thought—most notably ecofeminism and postcolonialism.

One of the most difficult problems with any project of 'moral extensionism' is that there are numerous and obvious points at which the analogy with humans, with human autonomy, and with human emancipatory struggles breaks down. For example, nonhuman species are not, so far as we know, rational moral agents capable of citizenship. They cannot return moral recognition, at least not in the way that humans can return recognition. They cannot organize or mobilize politically and, with the possible exception of certain mammals, they cannot communicate with us with the degree of precision to enable humans to understand and formulate their needs, interests, and strivings with any confidence and certainty.

Despite these obvious differences, it is extremely difficult and probably impossible to avoid all resort to human reference points and human analogies if *human* advocates for the concerted protection of biological diversity are to communicate with, and enlist the understanding and support of, other *humans*. Indeed, it is precisely the communicative power of analogies that explains why many of the pioneering critics of human speciesism and anthropocentrism (such as Singer, Regan, and the Routleys) began with the human case, employing (after Rodman) the 'progressive extension model of ethics'.[36] The point, after all, is to *persuade* other humans to reinterpret how we should collectively understand, and interact with, the rest of nature. One way of understanding the troubled history of this debate, then, is as a history of not entirely successful experiments with different vocabularies and analogies that are intended to *open up* new ways of thinking about, imagining, inhabiting, and interacting with the rest of nature.

I believe these experiments ought to continue. And at the current juncture, critical political ecology—which encompasses ecofeminist and postcolonial thought—provides a more promising basis from which to explore both continuities and differences between humans and other species, between human autonomy and nonhuman agency, and what 'solidarity' and 'nondomination' might mean between humans and other humans, and between humans and nonhuman species.

Whereas deep ecologists, such as Arne Naess and Warwick Fox, had sought to cultivate human solidarity with nonhuman nature by 'inviting' us to expand our identification with the world around us, to consider the rest of nature part as of our expanded self,[37] ecofeminists, postcolonialists, and difference theorists have placed more emphasis on the need to acknowledge difference rather than sameness or unity. The deep ecology idea that we can spontaneously act to defend nonhuman interests that are harmed or compromised, as if they are our own interests (being part of our larger self), is an idea that is—for many ecofeminists—based on a fusion or rejection of difference. As Val Plumwood has argued:

Although we may (as relational selves) assume the overarching interests of the other's general wellbeing and react to that as bound up with our own, it is crucial to our being able to defend that well-being that we retain a clear sense of the other as distinct beings with different, perhaps entirely different, interests from ours.[38]

She goes to argue that acknowledging such difference is also necessary if we are to avoid the colonizing dynamic that seeks to assimilate the other into the colonizer's own version of self. Yet at the same time, in western traditions in particular, we also need to acknowledge continuities and commonalities with the rest of nature in order to undermine the idea that the 'truly human' is somehow outside nature, the body and the biological world.[39]

In much traditional western ethics, philosophy, and political theory, it has been common to begin by asking 'what does it mean to be human?' and to identify those features that distinguish humans from the rest of nature, such as sophisticated tool-making, moral reasoning, language, spirituality (usually Judaeo-Christian), and 'civilization'. From these features were built ethical and political ideas that promoted whatever traits were selected as 'human-defining'. However, beginning in this way often meant that, if we are to be fully human, we must *promote* these uniquely human characteristics and thereby widen the existential gulf between humans and the rest of nature. To the extent to which we enlist these traits as the basis for progressive moral extensionism, then it becomes the basis of oppression for those humans who lack such characteristics (women, non-Europeans, other species).

Framing the problem in terms of exclusionary dualisms (of self/other and human/nonhuman) provides a different way of highlighting the common logic between various forms of oppression and intolerance of difference, whether patriarchy, imperialism, racism, *or* human chauvinism. Whether such intolerance is directed towards human or nonhuman others, there seems to be no non-question begging standpoint from which to justify the claim that the traits of those with the power to define and assert their superiority are more valuable than the traits of those who lack such power.[40] While there are countless ways in which we might distinguish humans from nonhumans species, there are also countless ways in which particular nonhuman species may be distinguished from both humans and other nonhuman species. To insist that only uniquely human traits should serve as the criteria of moral considerability is nothing if not self-serving.

Following Plumwood, the challenge, then, is to recognize continuity, interdependence and some commonality to avoid hyper-separation between humans and the rest of nature, on the one hand, while also acknowledging the many areas of incommensurability, on the other. However, in the west at least, in view of the degree of hyper-separation I would suggest that the best place to start is the broadest level of commonality (say the biological and ecological embeddedness of all life-forms, the common need for sustenance and security). From this basic commonality, and bearing in mind interdependence, we can then move to recognize the differences that need to be taken into account to enable, as far as possible, *mutual* flourishing.

From Liberalism to Critical Political Ecology

Despite the increased sensitivity to invidious comparison by the new generation of more critical theorists, they still remain ecocentric in the sense that they still pursue the idea of respect for nonhuman others. And although the argument is now couched in terms of a broader—and less human-centred notion of autonomy or nondomination—it still has roots in the Enlightenment ideals of autonomy and critique. Looking back, perhaps the first wave of ecocentric political theorists (myself included) had conflated what is *distinctive* about green political thought with what is the more *fundamental or animating idea*, from which new and different applications emerge. What is groundbreaking and distinctive about ecocentric political thought is not the principle of autonomy/nondomination per se, but rather the *radical extension* of this familiar idea to a new domain—nonhuman nature. This radical extension necessarily depends for its success on acceptance of the more basic principle of autonomy that emerged and has been fashioned and refashioned in the context of ongoing human emancipatory political and ideological struggles in a range of different social and political domains. During this process, the principle of autonomy has been subjected to a range of immanent critiques that have enabled it to outgrow its somewhat cramped, liberal origins. For example, classical liberals such as John Locke understood autonomy as something that was possessed by atomistic individuals as a 'natural right'. Individuals were posited as socially and ecologically detached, an understanding that reduced both human and the nonhuman others to a set of constraints against which, or as instrumental means through which, individual self-realization is achieved. However, for broadly critical political ecologists, autonomy is a relational concept, something that is constituted by, and dependent upon, social structures and social meanings. Social and ecological communities are not constraints on individual autonomy but rather preconditions for human and nonhuman agency and flourishing. In this sense, critical political ecologists have sought to adjust autonomy to a world of more complex and intense economic, technological and ecological interdependence while also seeking to continue and extend the emancipatory project to human and nonhuman others.

If we take the metaphor of the tree, we might think of critical theory as the root and trunk, and critical political ecology as one of the more recent branches in this ongoing political development. Such a metaphor directs attention to the historical continuity between different social emancipatory struggles (represented by other branches of the tree) and the radical ecology movement's quest for the 'liberation of nature'. The metaphor also helps us to appreciate the distinctive lines of development in these respective struggles, which cannot be collapsed into each other despite their common root, and which also have the potential to 'grow apart' *or* intertwine in complementary ways over time.

Characterizing the underlying animating principle of critical political ecology in these more generic (and more familiar) terms not only connects it with the normative orientation and method of immanent critique of this broader tradition of critical theory. It also connects it more directly with practical human emancipatory struggles (while acknowledging the potential conflicts that may arise from 'historical branching'). Such a characterization has obvious political/strategic advantages. In particular, recognizing the continuity in the struggle to emancipate both human and nonhuman nature provides the best reply to those critics who continue to misrepresent ecocentric approaches as only concerned to rescue nature *at the expense of* humanity, as if ecocentrics were indifferent or even hostile to human flourishing. The anthropocentric/ecocentric and instrumental/intrinsic value distinctions were never intended to drive a wedge between human and nonhuman interests. Quite the contrary—the concern has always been to reconcile or mutually accommodate these interests within a more encompassing framework. Yet it has been widely interpreted by critics as creating such a wedge, conveying the misleading impression of a necessary conflict and a zero sum game between the interests and needs of the human and nonhuman worlds.

The anthropocentric/ecocentric dichotomy has also proved troublesome in the way it has been taken to convey the (misleading) impression that the primary culprit for the ecological crisis is an arrogant, blanket humanity pitted against a defenceless nonhuman nature. Such a framing (whether advanced mischievously or innocently) is clearly problematic in obscuring the fact that not all humans are equally responsible for, or equally troubled or affected by, environmental destruction. Indeed, a central insight of critical political ecology (particularly ecofeminism) is that the domination of nature is a complex phenomenon that has been managed and mediated by privileged social classes and impersonal social and economic systems that have systematically brought benefits to some humans at the expense of others. The result is that certain privileged social classes, social groups, and nations have achieved what Mary Mellor has called a 'parasitical transcendence' from human and nonhuman communities.[41] In effect, a minority of the human race has been able to deny ecological and social responsibility and transcend biological embodiment and ecological limits (i.e., achieve greater physical resources, more time, and more space) *only at the expense of others*, that is, by exploiting, excluding, marginalizing, and depriving human *and* nonhuman others. Val Plumwood has encapsulated this problem in the idea of 'remoteness'. That is, privileged social classes have been able to remain remote (spatially, temporarily, epistemologically, and technologically) from most of the ecological consequences of their decisions in ways that perpetuates ecological irrationality and environmental injustice.[42]

Critical political ecology, and the environmental justice movement generally, have been in the vanguard of pointing to the historical and ideological connections between the domination of nonhuman nature and the domination of subaltern social groups—most notably women, workers, and indigenous peoples. While a closer inspection of critical political ecology clearly reveals that the anthropocentric/ecocentric distinction and the critique upon which it rests need not function in the blunt way in which critics have suggested, a reframing of the fundamental principle of critical political ecology as 'respect for differently situated others', reinterpreted in a ecological context, might also assist in foreclosing such misreadings.

Ultimately, critical political ecology seeks to locate and incorporate the demand for social and environmental justice (understood here in a distributive sense to include a fair distribution of the benefits and risks of social cooperation and the minimization of those risks in relation to an expanded moral community) in the broader context of the demand for dialogic or communicative justice (understood as a fair/free communicative context in which wealth and risk production and distribution decisions takes place in ways that are reflectively acceptable by 'differently situated others' or their representatives in the case of nonhuman species and future generations). Expressed in these terms, critical political ecology is not merely compatible with democracy—it seeks the radicalization of democracy. As we shall see, this also provides the best reply to the environmental pragmatists' anti-foundationalist critique of ecocentrism.

The Anti-Foundationalist Turn

Alongside the deepened sensitivity about the problem of invidious comparison is a general tendency to shy away from the difficult (and sometimes faintly comical) attempt to draw a clear line between morally considerable beings and morally inconsiderable ones—a task that had preoccupied objectivist nonanthropocentric applied ethicists. Whereas modernists such as Peter Singer once boldly drew the line between a shrimp and an oyster (the former were sentient and possessed interests that mattered, the latter were not sentient and therefore did not need to be considered in the moral calculus unless they were useful to sentient creatures), most critical and postmodern theorists have declined to embark upon such an exercise. Instead, they have preferred to employ looser metaphors and a vocabulary that accepts shadings and gradations in moral valuation, along with different cultural orientations and practices that are appropriate to different environments (e.g., why shouldn't Eskimos be allowed to eat whale meat?). Indeed, environmental monism, objectivist intrinsic value theories, and abstract and universalist environmental philosophies have all been seriously challenged by the general anti-foundationalist movement in the social sciences and humanities, which has underscored the partial and situated nature of human knowledge and cultural understanding.

It is noteworthy that among those few critical post-structuralists who are still concerned to speak about nonhuman nature other than as passive, meaningless, and valueless material, awaiting inscription and valuation by human subjects, the use of analogies and metaphors has been unavoidable. For example, Jim Cheney has suggested that if we are to acknowledge the agency of nature, then we must think of it as a 'conversational partner'.[43] Postmodern feminists such as Donna Harraway have sought to emphasize the agency of nonhuman nature by drawing on native American wisdom; nature may be understood as Coyote, or trickster, because it confounds our attempts to pin it down in terms of any neat set of dualisms, such as nature/culture. Similarly, her notion of humans as 'cyborgs' seeks to destabilize the dualisms of natural/unnatural and animal/machine.[44]

This search for a 'non-dualist' vocabulary from which to rethink cultural-ecological relations and develop a 'multicultural ecology'[45] has been a necessary and important one, but the relativization of environmental values that has necessarily accompanied this new direction of enquiry has also fundamentally changed the task of environmental philosophy. Whereas the early nonanthropocentric philosophers were strong advocates for the preservation of nature, aligned themselves with the wilderness and species preservation movement, and trenchantly attacked capitalist development, consumerism, and mass tourism, anti-foundationalist environmental philosophers have been primarily concerned to deconstruct meanings and dethrone what might be called conventional nonanthropocentric theory. The political motivations and implications of these critiques have not always been clearly discernible and they have attracted strong rejoinders from more conventional theorists (so-called 'naive realists') who have sought to reassert their scientific, philosophical, and political project of saving nature, particularly Big Wilderness.[46]

Among those anti-foundationalists who remain concerned about environmental problems, the focus has shifted from substantive policy intervention to questions of philosophical method and democratic process. Environmental pragmatists, in particular, have argued that environmental problems must be solved by means of inclusive democratic deliberation that is practically focused, and respectful of the plurality of environmental values in particular communities. For Andrew Light and Eric Katz, environmental pragmatism primarily offers a method of enquiry based on the American pragmatist tradition, rather than a substantive environmental philosophy.[47] Since environmental problem solving should be undertaken by the affected stakeholders, the role of the environmental philosopher is simply one of defending and assisting with the search for the optimal communicative conditions in which deliberation, creative conflict resolution, adaptive management, and social learning can take place. In this process, pragmatists argue that deep-seated cultural, philosophical, and religious differences can be held in check or deftly side-stepped by pragmatic necessity, without resort to arguments about intrinsic values. As Ben Minteer has pointed out, the American pragmatist John Dewey had rejected the idea that any entity should be considered an end-in-itself, since such a notion tended to insulate the entity as independent and somehow above cultural criticism, and preclude the need for democratic deliberation. Dewey thus introduces a situational, pluralist ethic that judges all arguments and moral claims to the degree to which they can assist in solving the problem at hand. This also directs attention to the real world of practice and policy making.[48]

Although pragmatism, as a method of environmental enquiry, has many advantages, particularly in deeply conflictual situations, it has three significant limitations from the point of view of critical political ecology.[49] The first is that its single-minded, narrow focus on practical problem solving and conflict resolution runs the risk of facilitating decisions that are too accommodating of the existing constellation of social forces that drive environmental degradation. In short, it is insufficiently *critical* from the point of view of oppressed or marginal social groups (not to mention nonhuman species).

The second problem is that it is too instrumentalist in the way it seeks to foreclose noninstrumental dialogue or deep religious, philosophical, or cultural engagement about fundamental differences, or noninstrumental encounters with the nonhuman world. Instead it narrows attention to how a particular community of stakeholders should *use* nature, based only on practical experience and experimentation. In this respect, democratic engagement is understood in purely functional terms.[50] Yet for critical theorists, particularly descendants of the Frankfurt School, keeping the dialogue alive for its own sake is ultimately more important than solving practical problems, especially if mutual understanding is to be enhanced. After all, it is difficult simultaneously to listen and be genuinely open to the other while also engaging in instrumental calculations of one's environmental claims in relation to others. Ironically, such openness to others is likely to be increased the more the pressure to make practical decisions is reduced.

Finally, although deliberation is more conducive to the protection of environmental public goods than bargaining or the mere aggregation of preferences, there is nothing especially environmental about this method of enquiry. Although purportedly anti-foundational, it ultimately comes to rest on liberal humanist moral foundations, based on respect for individuals. In this sense, critical political ecologists could argue that environmental pragmatism is not pluralist enough in that its moral foundations and methods do not provide any systematic inclusion of the interests of nonhuman others. At best, it permits nonhuman nature advocacy in those circumstances where self-appointed advocates happen to be present among the community of stakeholders. Even in theses circumstances, self-appointed nature advocates must be able to convince others that protecting the environment is more *instrumentally* valuable than using it. In this sense, environmental pragmatism may be seen as restricting the further pluralization of values and the widening of the terms of political contestation.

While environmental pragmatisim has good democratic credentials (particularly vis-à-vis the particular non-anthropocentric monistic theories it has criticized), at best these credentials seem to work at the level of environmental mediation and conflict reconciliation, not environmental *advocacy*. This applies especially in relation to advocacy on behalf of parties or interests who cannot represent themselves (nonhuman species or future generations) but sometimes also to marginalized and oppressed social groups who are excluded from, but may be affected by, policy decisions.

Of course, *both* mediation and advocacy are vital to a healthy democracy. However, they play different roles and often operate at different stages of political opinion and will formation. The role of the nature advocate or environmental justice advocate is less about conflict resolution and much more about shifting horizons and changing social structures. It is also about criticizing the existing constellation of social forces and political values that cause harm, or otherwise exclude or marginalize, the constituency they seek to represent. The advocate's role in this context is necessarily that of a relentless critic of the status quo, one who seeks to argue a case and, where necessary, contest received wisdom. The point is not to accommodate existing values and practices but rather to challenge, inspire, cajole, and persuade others to think and act differently. Whereas pragmatists are interested in practical environmental problem solving and conflict resolution, advocates sometimes deliberately generate conflict by disrupting conventional understandings and practices, including democratic protocols, in order to challenge those social forces that are seen to stand in the way of, in this case, the protection of nonhuman species. The democratic tasks of advocacy and mediation are quite different, then, and often in tension. Sometimes this tension can be productively managed, sometimes not, but it cannot, and ought not, be eliminated if a democracy is to permit social transformation (rather than merely incremental change).

Conclusion: Reinvigorating Nature Advocacy

For those supportive of both ecocentrism *and* democracy, most of the effort in recent years has gone into exploring what a green or ecological democracy might mean in theory and practice. The key concerns have been how we might refashion democratic institutions in ways that give nonhuman others (and future generations) some kind of proxy political representation, some kind of opportunity to have their interests considered in the policy and legislative process in more systematic ways. This entails searching for appropriate procedural rules and new forms of political participation and representation.

But such a democracy requires not just institutions but also creative and substantive *argument*, as well rhetoric, storytelling, theatre, satire, and other political performances, that will actually persuade and move others of the importance and appropriateness of respecting and protecting nonhuman nature. Green democratic procedures do not themselves guarantee particular outcomes, win arguments, or move audiences—they merely enable greener dialogue. Surprisingly, this argumentative dimension of the challenge has been given much less attention by environmental philosophers and green political theorists preoccupied with democratic innovation.[51] Yet, as Michael Bruner and Max Oelschlaeger remind us, those who succeed in defining the terms of the debate also determine, in large measure, the outcome.[52] Anti-environmentalists have been especially skilled at framing environmental problems in terms of slogans and overdrawn oppositions (such as 'people versus pandas', 'jobs versus the environment') in ways that generate resentment towards environmental concerns among lay publics. Bruner and Oelschlaeger suggest that this demands a *critical rhetoric* from nature advocates (one that exposes the constrained terms of debate and the role of power), a *persuasive rhetoric* that evokes the sentiments, and an *architectonic rhetoric* that offers new ecological narratives that open up new ways of approaching ecological problems.[53]

In this paper I have sketched some of the ways these arguments have been formulated, and drawn out some of the problems and possibilities. In many ways, the task today is much more perilous than it was twenty years ago, given the global dimensions of so many ecological problems, and the need for nature advocates to communicate across class, gender, and cultural boundaries in the transnational public sphere. Indeed, in view of the critiques traversed above, the challenges now facing the nature advocate in our global community could be seen as positively intimidating and may be framed as follows: how to find and develop a mode of argument that encapsulates the idea of respect for nonhuman nature for its own sake; that does not privilege self-serving human attributes over non-human ones; that does not see nature as some passive substance to be acted on or valued by humans but rather recognizes some form of agency in nature; that goes beyond a mere instrumental valuation of nature's services; that is not narrowly confined to particular cultures (e.g., western) and linguistic (e.g., English) communities, but can speak across, and appeal to, a wide variety of human cultures (and languages); that is not misanthropic and can recognize the needs of human communities to sustain their livelihoods from ecosystems.

While most cultures and societies recognize human dependence on nature, not all cultures necessarily embrace human emancipatory politics, let alone the idea of 'emancipating nonhuman nature'. It is therefore always easier to fall back on the vocabulary of prudence rather than morality precisely because this language is more likely to reach across more cultures than arguments to do with nonanthropocentrism and intrinsic values. And these less controversial arguments can sometimes achieve the same outcome, as Bryan Norton has long maintained in his so-called 'convergence hypothesis'.[54]

However, anthropocentric, instrumental arguments do not *always* lead to the same outcome and it is for this reason that nature advocates cannot afford to surrender to the easier argumentative route if they are to remain nature advocates. It is under these circumstances that the demands of ecological justice appear to conflict with environmental pragmatism. But the response to this problem is not to forsake democracy for environmental justice, but rather to *radicalize* democracy in order to achieve environmental justice.

For all the problems associated with moral extensionism, it nonetheless remains useful because of its communicative power, so I will end with the analogy of human rights. In another context, Simon Chesterman points out: 'It is a curious irony of human rights in late modernity that even as the political commitment to them has grown, philosophical commitment has waned.'[55] Human rights have outgrown their liberal origins and are now supported by a plurality of philosophical, religious, and cultural perspectives. So if a cross-cultural consensus in support of human rights can grow in the absence of a single philosophical foundation, then it seems to me reasonable to anticipate and foster a cross-cultural consensus in support of something like the 'moral standing' of nonhuman species. But whether this will eventuate will partly depend on the persuasive power of nature advocates.

Notes

1. Thanks to Peter Christoff for helpful feedback on this paper.

2. I include under the broad rubric of ecocentric or biocentric discourses nonanthropocentric intrinsic value theory, deep ecology, transpersonal ecology, Leopold's land ethic, ecofeminism and critical post-structural investigations of the nature/culture divide.

3. An example of the former is Tony Lynch and David Wells, 'Non-anthropocentrism? A Killing Objection', *Environmental Values*, 7: 2 (1998), 158–63. An example of the latter is Murray Bookchin's *Re-enchanting Humanity: A Defense of the Human Spirit Against Antihumanism, Misanthropy, Mysticism and Primitivism* (New York: Cassell, 1995).

4. See, for example, Bryan Norton, 'Democracy and Environmentalism: Foundations and Justifications in Environmental Policy', in Ben A. Minteer and Bob Pepperman Taylor (eds), *Democracy and the Claims of Nature: Critical Perspectives for a New Century* (Lanham: Rowman and Littlefield, 2002), 11–32. For an ecocentric critique of subjectivist approaches, see J. Baird Callicott, 'Rolston on Intrinsic Value: A Deconstruction', *Environmental Ethics*, 14: 2 (1992), 129–43.

5. Some have rejected the instrumental/intrinsic value distinction as a dead-end, such as Anthony Weston in 'Beyond Intrinsic Value: Pragmatism in Environmental Ethics', in Andrew Light and Eric Katz (eds), *Environmental Pragmatism* (London:

Routledge, 1996), 285–306. Others have replaced intrinsic values with a continuum of instrumental to noninstrumental values, noting that we must be open to a variety of in-between positions, such as Lori Gruen in 'Refocusing Environmental Ethics: From Intrinsic Value to Endorsable Valuations', *Philosophy and Geography*, 5: 2 (2002), 153–64. Others have sought to widen the scope of instrumental value, such as Bryan Norton in 'Epistemology and Environmental Values', *The Monist*, 75 (1992), 208–26, or have rejected the anthropocentric/ecocentric distinction as unhelpful, such as John Barry in *Rethinking Green Politics* (London: Sage Publications, 1999).

6. See, for example, Jane Bennett and William Chaloupka (eds), *In the Nature of Things: Language, Politics, and the Environment* (Minneapolis: University of Minnesota Press, 1993) and William Cronon, 'The Trouble with Wilderness; or, Getting Back to the Wrong Nature', in William Cronon (ed.), *Uncommon Ground: Toward Reinventing Nature* (New York: Norton, 1995).

7. See, for example, J. Baird Callicott, 'The Conceptual Foundations of the Land Ethic', in J. Baird Callicott (ed.), *A Companion to a Sand County Almanac: Interpretive and Critical Essays* (Madison: University of Wisconsin Press, 1987); Laura Westra, *Living in Integrity: A Global Ethic to Restore a Fragmented Earth* (Lanham, MD: Rowman and Littlefield, 1998); and Holmes Rolston III,

Environmental Ethics: Duties to and Values in the Natural World (Philadelphia: Temple University Press, 1987) and *Philosophy Gone Wild: Essays in Environmental Ethics* (Buffalo, NY: Prometheus Books, 1986).

8. See, for example, Bryan Norton, 'Why I am Not a Nonanthropocentrist: Callicott and the Failure of Monistic Inherentism', *Environmental Ethics*, 17 (1995), 341–58; Andrew Light and Eric Katz (eds), *Environmental Pragmatism* (London: Routledge, 1996); and the essays by Norton, Minteer and Bowersox in Ben A. Minteer and Bob Pepperman Taylor (eds), *Democracy and the Claims of Nature: Critical Perspectives for a New Century* (Lanham: Rowman and Littlefield, 2002).

9. Bryan Norton, 'Integration or Reduction: Two Approaches to Environmental Values', in Andrew Light and Eric Katz (eds), *Environmental Pragmatism* (London: Routledge, 1996), 105–38, at p. 108.

10. See, in particular, Andrew Dobson, *Green Political Thought* (London: HarperCollins, 1990, and subsequent editions); Robyn Eckersley, *Environmentalism and Political Theory: Toward an Ecocentric Approach* (Albany, NY: SUNY Press, 1992) and Andrew McLaughlin, *Regarding Nature: Industrialism and Deep Ecology* (Albany, NY: SUNY Press, 1993).

11. Indeed, Tim Hayward has recently argued that this distinction now functions as an obstacle to dialogue, in *Political Theory and Ecological Values* (New York: St Martin's Press, 1998), 5–6, while John Barry maintains that it is 'a false and damaging dichotomy' (*Rethinking Green Politics*, p. 13).

12. In addition to the work of Tim Hayward and John Barry, see also Kate Soper, *What is Nature?* (Oxford: Blackwell, 1995); Douglas Torgerson, *The Promise of Green Politics: Environmentalism and the Public Sphere* (Durham: Duke University Press, 1999); and David Schlosberg, *Environmental Justice and the New Pluralism: The Challenge of Difference for Environmentalism* (Oxford: Oxford University Press, 1999). On democracy and the environment, see William M. Lafferty and James Meadowcroft (eds), *Democracy and the Environment: Problems and Prospects* (Cheltenham, UK: Edward Elgar, 1996); Brian Doherty and Marius de Geus (eds), *Democracy and Green Political Thought: Sustainability, Rights and Citizenship* (London: Routledge, 1996); and Robyn Eckersley, *The Green State: Rethinking Democracy and Sovereignty* (Cambridge, MA: MIT Press, 2004).

13. Richard Rorty, *Objectivity, Relativism, and Truth: Philosophical Papers* (Cambridge: Cambridge University Press, 1991).

14. Critical political ecology may be understood as a distinctive green branch of critical theory that draws on the classical Frankfurt School insights into the links between the domination of human and nonhuman nature, while also building on more recent, kindred developments in radical environmental philosophy and politics (including ecofeminism, postcolonialism, and the environmental justice movement).

15. With apologies to Alistair McCleod's novel by the same.

16. Neil Evernden, 'The Environmentalist's Dilemma', in the *Paradox of Environmentalism* (Downsview, Ontario: Faculty of Environmental Studies, York University, 1984), 10.

17. See David Ehrenfeld, *The Arrogance of Humanism* (New York: Oxford University Press, 1981).

18. Tom Regan, 'The Nature and Possibility of an Environmental Ethic', *Environmental Ethics*, 3: 1 (1981), 19–34.

19. J. Baird Callicott, 'Intrinsic Value, Quantum Theory and Environmental Ethics', *Environmental Ethics* 7: 3 (1985), 257–75, at p. 257 (abstract).

20. Weston, 'Before Environmental Ethics', in Andrew Light and Eric Katz (eds), *Environmental Pragmatism* (London: Routledge, 1996), 139–60, at p. 139.

21. Ibid. 143.

22. Ibid. 147.

23. Ibid. 150.

24. Peter Singer, *Animal Liberation: A New Ethics for Our Treatment of Animals* (New York:

The New Review, 1975) and Christopher Stone, *Should Trees Have Standing?: Toward Legal Rights for Natural Objects* (Los Altos, CA: Kaufman, 1974).

25. John Rodman, 'The Liberation of Nature?', *Inquiry*, 20 (1977), 83–145, at p. 87.
26. Ibid. 94.
27. Ibid. 91.
28. Ibid. 100.
29. Ibid. 94.
30. This is consistent with Rodman's interest in the work of liberals such as J. S. Mill and T. H. Green.
31. Evernden, 'The Environmentalist's Dilemma', 10.
32. Brian Luke, 'Solidarity Across Diversity: A Pluralistic Raprochement of Environmentalism and Animal Liberation', in Roger S. Gottlieb (ed.), *The Ecological Community: Environmental Challenges for Philosophy, Politics, and Morality* (New York: Routledge, 1997), 333–58.
33. Tzvetan Todorov, *The Conquest of America: The Question of the Other*, trans. Richard Howard (New York: Harper and Row, 1984), 168.
34. Val Plumwood, *Feminism and the Mastery of Nature* (London: Routledge 1993), 143.
35. Ibid. 52.
36. Rodman, 'The Liberation of Nature?', 97.
37. Arne Naess, 'The Shallow and the Deep, Long-Range Ecology Movement. A Summary', *Inquiry*, 16 (1973), 95–100; 'Self-Realization: An Ecological Approach to Being in the World', *The Trumpeter*, 4 (1987), 35–42; and Warwick Fox, *Toward a Transpersonal Ecology: Developing New Foundations for Environmental Ethics* (Boston: Shambhala, 1990).
38. Val Plumwood, 'Deep Ecology, Deep Pockets and Deep Problems: A Feminist, Ecosocialist Analaysis', in Eric Katz, Andrew Light, and David Rothenberg (eds.), *Beneath the Surface: Critical Essays in the Philosophy of Deep Ecology* (Cambridge, MA: The MIT Press, 2000), 59–84, at p. 63.
39. Ibid. 64.
40. James P. Sterba, 'Reconciling Anthropocentric and Nonanthropocentric

Environmental Ethics', *Environmental Values*, 3: 3 (1994), 229–44, at p. 230.
41. Mary Mellor, *Feminism and Ecology* (New York: New York University Press, 1997).
42. Val Plumwood, *Environmental Culture: The Ecological Crisis of Reason* (London: Routledge, 2002), esp. pp. 72–80.
43. Jim Cheney. 'Postmodern Environmental Ethics: Ethics as Bioregional Narrative', *Environmental Ethics*, 11 (1989), 117–34; Christopher J. Preston, 'Conversing with Nature in a Postmodern Epistemological Framework', *Environmental Ethics*, 22: 3 (2000), 227–40. Modernists such as John S. Dryzek have also enlisted the idea of nature as a communicative partner. See John S. Dryzek, 'Green Reason: Communicative Ethics for the Biosphere', *Environmental Ethics*, 12 (1990), 195–210.
44. Donna Harraway, 'Situated Knowledges: The Science Question in Feminism and the Privilege of Partial Perspective', *Feminist Studies*, 14: 3 (1988), 575–99, and *Simians, Cyborgs and Women* (New York: Routledge, 1991).
45. See Adrian Ivakhiv, 'Toward a Multicultural Ecology', *Organization and Environment*, 15: 4 (2002), 389–409.
46. For example, Michael Soule and Gary Lease (eds), *Reinventing Nature? Responses to Postmodern Deconstruction* (Washington DC: Island Press, 1995).
47. Andrew Light and Eric Katz (eds), *Environmental Pragmatism* (London: Routledge, 1996). Note, however, that some pragmatists, such as Bryan Norton, have defended environmental pragmatism as a substantive philosophy in the sense that they maintain it is consistent with principles of sustainability. Norton, 'Integration or Reduction', 122–3.
48. Ben Minteer, 'Intrinsic Value for Pragmatists?' *Environmental Ethics*, 23: 1 (2001), 57–75.
49. A more developed critique can be found in Robyn Eckersley, 'Environmental Pragmatism, Ecocentrism, and Deliberative Democracy: Between Problem-Solving and

Fundamental Critique', in Ben A. Minteer and Bob Pepperman Taylor (eds), *Democracy and the Claims of Nature: Critical Perspectives for a New Century* (Lanham: Rowman and Littlefield, 2002), 49–69.

50. This is not to argue that pragmatists deny non-instrumental human valuations of nature; only that they steer enquiry and policy making towards practical problem solving regarding the *use* of nature.

51. Two exceptions are Michael Bruner and Max Oelschlaeger, 'Rhetoric, Environmentalism, and Environmental Ethics', *Environmental Ethics*, 16: 4 (1994), 377–96, and Torgerson, *The Promise of Green Politics*.

52. Bruner and Oelschlaeger, 'Rhetoric, Environmentalism, and Environmental Ethics', 391.

53. Ibid. 395

54. Bryan Norton, *Toward Unity Among Environmentalists* (New York: Oxford University Press, 1991).

55. Simon Chesterman, 'Human Rights as Subjectivity: The Age of Rights and the Politics of Culture', *Millennium*, 27: 1 (1998), 97–118, at p. 97.

Section IX: Social and Socialist Ecology

As demonstrated by the readings in the previous section, deep ecology and bioregionalism focus on forging a new relationship between humans and their environment, and denounce human arrogance towards nature. Social and socialist ecologists agree with the need to radicalize ecology and our understanding of nature. However, their central concern is with the social, cultural, and economic sources of ecological problems. It is not enough to deal with our understanding of, and feelings about, the natural world; we must analyse what it is in contemporary capitalist and industrial societies that has brought environmental crisis. Only with a thorough social and economic critique can we really understand *why* we abuse nature in the way that we do, and, so, develop ways of relating to nature—and each other—in less dominating and destructive ways.

Murray Bookchin is the intellectual founder of social ecology. His writings about human society's effects on the natural world span four decades, beginning with *Our Synthetic Environment* in 1962. For Bookchin, the central ecological problem is not our lack of reverence or respect for nature. Rather, it is that we justify as 'natural' the whole range of social and economic inequalities, hierarchies, and dominating relationships that damage human societies as well as ecological ones. Bookchin argues that if you understand nature as a nasty, brutish, and competitive world, then the only possible structure of human society is one that attempts to dominate and tame nature. Domination becomes the necessary way of life, and we create hierarchies—with humans above nature, men above women, owners above labour, and some races and ethnicities above others. Social ecology traces both ecological and social problems—pollution, destruction of ecosystems, poverty, inequality—to the concept of domination that we have read in nature.

To counter this entrenched domination, Bookchin follows a long line of anarchist thinkers and naturalists, starting with Peter Kropotkin, who argue that nature is not the blind, cruel, stingy, competitive, hostile environment that we are often taught. Rather, nature is a participatory realm of interactive life forms: creative, cooperative, symbiotic, and productive. If nature is a realm of freedom, participation, and mutual aid, human society can be the same. Bookchin believes that with a radicalized sense of the way nature really works, the human potential for cooperation can be tapped and released. Once we see that hierarchy and domination in human society is institutional, rather than biological, we can work more symbiotically both amongst ourselves and with the rest of the natural world. The selection from Bookchin here first differentiates social ecology from what he sees as the less critical and more misanthropic deep ecology; he then goes on to describe his vision of a more cooperative co-development of human and natural societies.

Ynestra King, having worked for years with Bookchin at the Institute for Social Ecology in Vermont, approaches ecofeminism from the perspective of social ecology. Her argument, as for many ecofeminists, is that there is a relationship between the despoliation of nature and the domination of women. The central reason for women's oppression is their association with nature. In this selection, King addresses the basic question of whether this women/nature association is potentially emancipatory, or whether it provides a rationale for further and continued domination. Some ecofeminists celebrate women's supposed connection with nature, and see it as a source of female freedom outside the destructive world of men. Other feminists, suspicious of the notion of ecofeminism, insist on being liberated from the association with nature, which they see as an imprisoning female ghetto. King argues for a move beyond this dualism, insisting that human culture is itself an inherent part of nature.

We have selected Joel Kovel to represent eco-Marxism and socialist ecology. Kovel is the recently appointed editor of the eco-socialist journal *Capitalism, Nature, Socialism* (replacing James O'Connor, who is one of the founders and theoretical anchors of the field). Socialist ecology focuses on how capitalism destroys the conditions of production—both land, which it uses up, despoils, or poisons, and labour, which it weakens with production-induced illnesses. As capitalism refuses to take the costs of this destruction into account, its practices lead to an ecological crisis. Much of the ecosocialist literature is focused on the critique of capital and its effects; the chapter of Kovel's book *The Enemy of Nature*, reproduced here, focuses on reconstructive ideas. Kovel outlines key elements of an ecosocialist society, as well as a description of a path to get there. He argues for 'ensembles' of ecosocialist practice, which would develop both the social relationships and the driving forces eventually to replace capitalism.

Further Reading

In social ecology, the required reading is Bookchin, Bookchin, and more Bookchin. His works include *Toward an Ecological Society* (1980), *The Ecology of Freedom* (1982), *The Modern Crisis* (1986), *The Philosophy of Social Ecology* (1990), and *Remaking Society* (1990). Broadly sympathetic is Brian Tokar's *The Green Alternative* (1987) and various essays in a book edited by John Clark that honours Bookchin, *Renewing the Earth* (1990). But Bookchin is not the only source of social ecology; many of his past colleagues and collaborators contributed to a volume edited by Andrew Light that looks forward to *Social Ecology After Bookchin* (1998). For more on a social (and socialist) ecology-oriented ecofeminism, see *The Death of Nature* (1980) and *Ecological Revolutions* (1989) by Carolyn Merchant, *Ecofeminism* (1993), edited by Maria Mies and Vandana Shiva, Val Plumwood's *Feminism and the Mastery of Nature* (1993) and *Environmental Culture: The Ecological Crisis of Reason* (2002), and Ariel Salleh's *Ecofeminism as Politics: Nature, Marx, and the Postmodern* (1998).

Along more socialist or eco-Marxist lines, the journal *Capitalism, Nature, Socialism* is a constant source. Classics of eco-socialism include Hugh Stretton's *Capitalism, Socialism, and the Environment* (1976), Allan Schnaiberg's *The Environment* (1980), Andre Gorz's *Ecology as Politics* (1980). More recent work includes David Harvey's *Justice, Nature, and the Geography of Difference* (1996), James O'Conner's *Natural Causes: Essays in Ecological Marxism* (1997) and John Bellamy Foster's *Marx's Ecology: Materialism and Nature* (2000) and *Ecology Against Capitalism* (2002).

27 Society and Ecology

Murray Bookchin

The problems which many people face today in "defining" themselves, in knowing "who they are"—problems that feed a vast psychotherapy industry—are by no means personal ones. These problems exist not only for private individuals; they exist for modern society as a whole. Socially, we live in desperate uncertainty about how people relate to each other. We suffer not only as individuals from alienation and confusion over our identities and goals; our entire society, conceived as a single entity, seems unclear about its own nature and sense of direction. If earlier societies tried to foster a belief in the virtues of cooperation and care, thereby giving an ethical meaning to social life, modern society fosters a belief in the virtues of competition and egotism, thereby divesting human association of all meaning—except, perhaps, as an instrument for gain and mindless consumption.

We tend to believe that men and women of earlier times were guided by firm beliefs and hopes—values that defined them as human beings and gave purpose to their social lives. We speak of the Middle Ages as an "Age of Faith" or the Enlightenment as an "Age of Reason." Even the pre-World War II era and the years that followed it seem like an alluring time of innocence and hope, despite the Great Depression and the terrible conflicts that stained it. As an elderly character in a recent, rather sophisticated, espionage movie put it: what he missed about his younger years during World War II were their "clarity"—a sense of purpose and idealism that guided his behaviour.

That "clarity," today, is gone. It has been replaced by ambiguity. The certainty that technology and science would improve the human condition is mocked by the proliferation of nuclear weapons, by massive hunger in the Third World, and by poverty in the First World. The fervent belief that liberty would triumph over tyranny is belied by the growing centralization of states everywhere and by the disempowerment of people by bureaucracies, police forces, and sophisticated surveillance techniques—in our "democracies" no less than in visibly authoritarian countries. The hope that we would form "one world," a vast community of disparate ethnic groups that would share their resources to improve life everywhere, has been shattered by a rising tide of nationalism, racism, and an unfeeling parochialism that fosters indifference to the plight of millions.

We believe that our values are worse than those held by people of only two or three generations ago. The present generation seems more self-centred, privatized, and mean-spirited by

From Murray Bookchin, *Remaking Society: Pathways to a Green Future* (Boston: South End Press, 1990), 19–39. Reprinted with permission.

comparison with earlier ones. It lacks the support systems provided by the extended family, community, and a commitment to mutual aid. The encounter of the individual with society seems to occur through cold bureaucratic agencies rather than warm, caring people.

This lack of social identity and meaning is all the more stark in the face of the mounting problems that confront us. War is a chronic condition of our time; economic uncertainty, an allpervasive presence; human solidarity, a vaporous myth. Not least of the problems we encounter are nightmares of an ecological apocalypse—a catastrophic breakdown of the systems that maintain the stability of the planet. We live under the constant threat that the world of life will be irrevocably undermined by a society gone mad in its need to grow—replacing the organic by the inorganic, soil by concrete, forest by barren earth, and the diversity of life-forms by simplified ecosystems; in short, a turning back of the evolutionary clock to an earlier, more inorganic, mineralized world that was incapable of supporting complex life-forms of any kind, including the human species.

Ambiguity about our fate, meaning, and purpose thus raises a rather startling question: is society itself a curse, a blight on life generally? Are we any better for this new phenomenon called "civilization" that seems to be on the point of destroying the natural world produced over millions of years of organic evolution?

An entire literature has emerged which has gained the attention of millions of readers: a literature that fosters a new pessimism toward civilization as such. This literature pits technology against a presumably "virginal" organic nature; cities against countryside; countryside against "wilderness"; science against a "reverence" for life; reason against the "innocence" of intuition; and, indeed, humanity against the entire biosphere.

We show signs of losing faith in all our uniquely human abilities—our ability to live in peace with each other, our ability to care for our fellow beings and other life-forms. This pessimism is fed daily by sociobiologists who locate our failings in our genes, by antihumanists who deplore our "antinatural" sensibilities, and by "biocentrists" who downgrade our rational qualities with notions that we are no different in our "intrinsic worth" than ants. In short, we are witnessing a widespread assault against the ability of reason, science, and technology to improve the world for ourselves and life generally.

The historic theme that civilization must inevitably be pitted against nature, indeed, that it is corruptive of human nature, has re-surfaced in our midst from the days that reach back to Rousseau—this, precisely at a time when our need for a truly human and ecological civilization has never been greater if we are to rescue our planet and ourselves. Civilization, with its hallmarks of reason and technics, is viewed increasingly as a new blight. Even more basically, society as a phenomenon in its own right is being questioned so much so that its role as integral to the formation of humanity is seen as something harmfully "unnatural" and inherently destructive.

Humanity, in effect, is being defamed by human beings themselves, ironically, as an accursed form of life that all but destroys the world of life and threatens its integrity. To the confusion that we have about our own muddled time and our personal identities, we now have the added confusion that the human condition is seen as a form of chaos produced by our proclivity for wanton destruction and our ability to exercise this proclivity all the more effectively because we possess reason, science, and technology.

Admittedly, few antihumanists, "biocentrists," and misanthropes, who theorize about the human condition, are prepared to follow the logic of their premises to such an absurd point. What is vitally important about this medley of moods and unfinished ideas is that the various forms, institutions, and relationships that make up what we should call "society" are largely ignored. Instead, just as we use vague words like "humanity" or zoological terms like *homo sapiens* that conceal vast differences, often bitter antagonisms, that exist between privileged whites and people of colour, men and women, rich and poor, oppressor and oppressed; so do we, by the same token, use vague words like "society" or "civilization" that conceal vast differences between free, nonhierarchical, class, and stateless societies on the one hand, and others that are, in varying degrees, hierarchical, class-ridden, statist, and authoritarian. Zoology, in effect, replaces socially oriented ecology. Sweeping "natural laws" based on population swings among animals replace conflicting economic and social interests among people.

Simply to pit "society" against "nature," "humanity" against the "biosphere," and "reason," "technology," and "science" against less developed, often primitive forms of human interaction with the natural world, prevents us from examining the highly complex differences and divisions within society so necessary to define our problems and their solutions.

Ancient Egypt, for example, had a significantly different attitude toward nature than ancient Babylonia. Egypt assumed a reverential attitude toward a host of essentially animistic nature deities, many of which were physically part human and part animal, while Babylonians created a pantheon of very human political deities. But Egypt was no less hierarchical than Babylonia in its treatment of people and was equally, if not more, oppressive in its view of human individuality. Certain hunting peoples may have been as destructive of wildlife, despite their strong animistic beliefs, as urban cultures which staked out an over-arching claim to reason. When these many differences are simply swallowed up together with a vast variety of social forms by a word called "society," we do severe violence to thought and even simple intelligence. Society *per se* becomes something "unnatural." "Reason," "technology," and "science" become things that are "destructive" without any regard to the social factors that condition their use. Human attempts to alter the environment are seen as threats—as though our "species" can do little or nothing to improve the planet for life generally.

Of course, we are not any less animals than other mammals, but we are more than herds that browse on the African plains. The way in which we are more—namely, the *kinds* of societies that we form and how we are divided against each other into hierarchies and classes—profoundly affects our behaviour and our effects on the natural world.

Finally, by so radically separating humanity and society from nature or naïvely reducing them to mere zoological entities, we can no longer see how human nature is *derived* from nonhuman nature and social evolution from natural evolution. Humanity becomes estranged or alienated not only from itself in our "age of alienation," but from the natural world in which it has always been rooted as a complex and thinking life-form.

Accordingly, we are fed a steady diet of reproaches by liberal and misanthropic environmentalists alike about how "we" as a species are responsible for the breakdown of the environment. One does not have to go to enclaves of mystics and gurus in San Francisco to find this species-centred, asocial view of ecological problems and their sources. New York City will do just as well.

I shall not easily forget an "environmental" presentation staged by the New York Museum of Natural History in the 1970s in which the public was exposed to a long series of exhibits, each depicting examples of pollution and ecological disruption. The exhibit which closed the presentation carried a startling sign, "The Most Dangerous Animal on Earth," and it consisted simply of a huge mirror which reflected back the human viewer who stood before it. I clearly recall a black child standing before the mirror while a white school teacher tried to explain the message which this arrogant exhibit tried to convey. There were no exhibits of corporate boards or directors planning to deforest a mountainside or government officials acting in collusion with them. The exhibit primarily conveyed one, basically misanthropic, message: people *as such*, not a rapacious society and its wealthy beneficiaries, are responsible for environmental dislocations—the poor no less than the personally wealthy, people of colour no less than privileged whites, women no less than men, the oppressed no less than the oppressor. A mythical human "species" had replaced classes; individuals had replaced hierarchies; personal tastes (many of which are shaped by a predatory media) had replaced social relationships; and the disempowered who live meagre, isolated lives had replaced giant corporations, self-serving bureaucracies, and the violent paraphernalia of the State.

The Relationship of Society to Nature

Leaving aside such outrageous "environmental" exhibitions that mirror privileged and under-privileged people in the same frame, it seems appropriate at this point to raise a highly relevant need: the need to bring society back into the ecological picture. More than ever, strong emphases must be placed on the fact that nearly *all ecological problems are social problems*, not simply or primarily the result of religious, spiritual, or political ideologies. That these ideologies may foster an anti-ecological outlook in people of all strata hardly requires emphasis. But rather than simply take ideologies at their face value, it is crucial for us to ask from whence these ideologies develop.

Quite frequently, economic needs may compel people to act against their best impulses, even strongly felt natural values. Lumberjacks who are employed to clear-cut a magnificent forest normally have no "hatred" of trees. They have little or no choice but to cut trees just as stockyard workers have little or no choice but to slaughter domestic animals. Every community or occupation has its fair share of destructive and sadistic individuals, to be sure, including misanthropic environmentalists who would like to see humanity exterminated. But among the vast majority of people, this kind of work, including such onerous tasks as mining, are not freely chosen occupations. They stem from need and, above all, they are the product of social arrangements over which ordinary people have no control.

To understand present-day problems—ecological as well as economic and political—we must examine their social causes and remedy them through social methods. "Deep," "spiritual," anti-humanist, and misanthropic ecologies gravely mislead us when they refocus our attention on social symptoms rather than social causes. If our obligation is to look at changes in social relationships in order to understand our most significant ecological changes, these ecologies steer us away from society to "spiritual," "cultural," or vaguely defined "traditional" sources.

The Bible did not create European antinaturalism; it served to justify an antinaturalism that already existed on the continent from pagan times, despite the animistic traits of pre-Christian religions. Christianity's antinaturalistic influence became especially marked with the emergence of capitalism. Society must not only be brought into the ecological picture to understand why people tend to choose competing sensibilities—some, strongly naturalistic; others, strongly antinaturalistic—but we must probe more deeply into society itself. We must search out the *relationship of society to nature*, the *reasons* why it can destroy the natural world, and, alternatively, the reasons why it has and still can *enhance, foster*, and *richly contribute* to natural evolution.

Insofar as we can speak of "society" in any abstract and general sense—and let us remember that every society is highly unique and different from others in the long perspective of history—we are obliged to examine what we can best call "socialization," not merely "society." Society is a given arrangement of relationships which we often take for granted and view in a very fixed way. To many people today, it would seem that a market society based on trade and competition has existed "forever," although we may be vaguely mindful that there were pre-market societies based on gifts and cooperation. Socialization, on the other hand, is a *process*, just as individual living is a process. Historically, the *process* of socializing people can be viewed as a sort of social infancy that involves a painful rearing of humanity to social maturity.

When we begin to consider socialization from an in-depth viewpoint, what strikes us is that society itself in its most primal form stems very much *from* nature. Every social evolution, in fact, is virtually an extension of natural evolution into a distinctly human realm. As the Roman orator and philosopher, Cicero, declared some two thousand years ago: "by the use of our hands, we bring into being within the realm of Nature, a second nature for ourselves." Cicero's observation, to be sure, is very incomplete: the primeval, presumably untouched "realm of Nature" or "first nature," as it has been called, is reworked in whole or part into "second nature" not only by the "use of our hands." Thought, language, and complex, very important biological changes also play a crucial and, at times, a decisive role in developing a "second nature" within "first nature."

I use the term "reworking" advisedly to focus on the fact that "second nature" is not simply a phenomenon that develops outside of "first nature"—hence the special value that should be attached to Cicero's use of the expression "*within* the realm of Nature". To emphasize that "second nature" or, more precisely, society (to use this word in its broadest possible sense) emerges from *within* primeval "first nature' is to re-establish the fact that social life always has a naturalistic dimension, however much society is pitted against nature in our thinking. *Social* ecology clearly expresses the fact that society is not a sudden "eruption" in the world. Social life does not necessarily face nature as a combatant in an unrelenting war. The emergence of society is a *natural* fact that has its origins in the biology of human socialization.

The human socialization process from which society emerges—be it in the form of families, bands, tribes, or more complex types of human intercourse—has its source in parental relationships, particularly mother and child bonding. The biological mother, to be sure, can be replaced in this process by many surrogates, including fathers, relatives, or, for that matter, all members of a community. It is when *social* parents and *social* siblings—that is, the human community that surrounds the young—begin to participate in a system of care, that is ordinarily undertaken by biological parents, that society begins to truly come into its own.

Society thereupon advances beyond a mere reproductive group toward institutionalized human relationships, and from a relatively formless animal community into a clearly structured social *order*. But at the very inception of society, it seems more than likely that human beings were socialized into "second nature" by means of deeply ingrained blood ties, specifically maternal ties. We shall see that in time the structures or institutions that mark the advance of humanity from a mere animal community into an authentic society began to undergo far-reaching changes and these changes become issues of paramount importance in social ecology. For better or worse, societies develop around status groups, hierarchies, classes, and state formations. But reproduction and family care remain the abiding biological bases for every form of social life as well as the originating factor in the socialization of the young and the formation of a society. As Robert Briffault observed in the early half of this century, the "one known factor which establishes a profound distinction between the constitution of the most rudimentary human group and all other animal groups [is the] association of mothers and offspring which is the sole form of true social solidarity among animals. Throughout the class of mammals, there is a continuous increase in the duration of that association, which is the consequence of the prolongation of the period of infantile dependence,"[1] a prolongation which Briffault correlates with increases in the period of fetal gestation and advances in intelligence.

The biological dimension that Briffault adds to what we call society and socialization cannot be stressed too strongly. It is a decisive presence, not only in the origins of society over ages of animal evolution, but in the daily recreation of society in our everyday lives. The appearance of a newly born infant and the highly extended care it receives for many years reminds us that it is not only a human being that is being reproduced, but society itself. By comparison with the young of other species, children develop slowly and over a long period of time. Living in close association with parents, siblings, kin groups, and an ever-widening community of people, they retain a plasticity of mind that makes for creative individuals and ever-formative social groups. Although nonhuman animals may approximate human forms of association in many ways, they do not create a "second nature" that embodies a cultural tradition, nor do they possess a complex language, elaborate conceptual powers, or an impressive capacity to restructure their environment purposefully according to their own needs.

A chimpanzee, for example, remains an infant for only three years and a juvenile for seven. By the age of ten, it is a full-grown adult. Children, by contrast, are regarded as infants for approximately six years and juveniles for fourteen. A chimpanzee, in short, grows mentally and physically in about half the time required by a human being, and its capacity to learn or, at least to think, is already fixed by comparison with a human being, whose mental abilities may expand for decades. By the same token, chimpanzee associations are often idiosyncratic and fairly limited. Human associations, on the other hand, are basically stable, highly institutionalized, and they are marked by a degree of solidarity, indeed, by a degree of creativity that has no equal in nonhuman species as far as we know.

This prolonged degree of human mental plasticity, dependency, and social creativity yields two results that are of decisive importance. First, early human association must have fostered a strong predisposition for *interdependence* among members of a group—not the "rugged individualism" we associate with independence. The overwhelming mass of anthropological evidence suggests that participation, mutual aid, solidarity, and empathy were the social virtues early human groups emphasized within their communities. The idea that people are dependent upon each other for the good life, indeed, for survival, followed from the prolonged dependence of the young upon adults. Independence, not to mention competition, would have seemed utterly alien, if not bizarre, to a creature reared over many years in a largely dependent condition. Care for others would have been seen as the perfectly natural outcome of a highly acculturated being that was, in turn, clearly in need of extended care. Our modern version of individualism, more precisely, of egotism, would have cut across the grain of early solidarity and mutual aid—traits, I may add, without which such a physically fragile animal like a human being could hardly have survived as an adult, much less as a child.

Second, human interdependence must have assumed a highly structured form. There is no evidence that human beings normally relate to each other through the fairly loose systems of bonding we find among our closest primate cousins. That human social bonds can be dissolved or de-institutionalized in periods of radical change or cultural breakdown is too obvious to argue here. But during relatively stable conditions, human society was never the "horde" that anthropologists of the last century presupposed as a basis for rudimentary social life. On the contrary, the evidence we have at hand points to the fact that all humans, perhaps even our distant hominid ancestors, lived in some kind of structured family groups, and, later, in bands, tribes, villages, and other forms. In short, they bonded together (as they still do), not only emotionally and morally, but also structurally in contrived, clearly definable, and fairly permanent institutions.

Nonhuman animals may form loose communities and even take collective protective postures to defend their young from predators. But such communities can hardly be called structured, except in a broad, often ephemeral, sense. Humans, by contrast, create highly formal communities that tend to become increasingly structured over the course of time. In effect, they form not only communities, but a new phenomenon called *societies*.

If we fail to distinguish animal communities from human societies, we risk the danger of ignoring the unique features that distinguish human social life from animal communities—notably, the ability of society to *change* for better or worse and the factors that produce these changes. By reducing a complex society to a mere community, we can easily ignore how societies differed from each other over the course of history. We can also fail to understand how they elaborated simple differences in status into firmly established hierarchies, or hierarchies into economic classes. Indeed, we risk the possibility of totally misunderstanding the very meaning of terms like "hierarchy" as highly organized systems of command and obedience—these, as distinguished from personal, individual, and often short-lived differences in status that may, in all too many cases, involve no acts of compulsion. We tend, in effect, to confuse the strictly institutional creations of human will, purpose, conflicting interests, and traditions, with community life in its most fixed forms, as though we were dealing with inherent, seemingly unalterable, features of society rather than fabricated structures that can be modified, improved, worsened—or simply abandoned. The trick of every ruling elite from the beginnings of history to modern times has been to identify its own socially created hierarchical systems of domination with community life *as such*, with the result being that human-made institutions acquire divine or biological sanction.

A given society and its institutions thus tend to become reified into permanent and unchangeable entities that acquire a mysterious life of their own apart from nature—namely, the products of a seemingly fixed "human nature" that is the result of genetic programming at the very inception of social life. Alternatively, a given society and its institutions may be dissolved into nature as merely another form of animal community with its "alpha males," "guardians," "leaders," and "horde"-like forms of existence. When annoying issues like war and social conflict are raised, they are ascribed to the activity of "genes" that presumably give rise to war and even "greed."

In either case, be it the notion of an abstract society that exists apart from nature or an equally abstract natural community that is indistinguishable from nature, a dualism appears that sharply separates society *from* nature, or a crude reductionism appears that dissolves society *into* nature. These apparently contrasting, but closely related, notions are all the more seductive because they are so simplistic. Although they are often presented by their more sophisticated supporters in a fairly nuanced form, such notions are easily reduced to bumper-sticker slogans that are frozen into hard, popular dogmas.

Social Ecology

The approach to society and nature advanced by social ecology may seem more intellectually demanding, but it avoids the simplicities of dualism and the crudities of reductionism. Social ecology tries to show how nature slowly *phases* into society without ignoring the differences between society and nature on the one hand, as well as the extent to which they merge with each other on the other. The everyday socialization of the young by the family is no less rooted in biology than the everyday care of the old by the medical establishment is rooted in the hard facts of society. By the same token, we never cease to be mammals who still have primal natural urges, but we institutionalize these urges and their satisfaction in a wide variety of social forms. Hence, the social and the natural continually permeate each other in the most ordinary activities of daily life without losing their identity in a shared process of interaction, indeed, of interactivity.

Obvious as this may seem at first in such day-to-day problems as caretaking, social ecology raises questions that have far-reaching importance for the different ways society and nature have interacted over time and the problems these interactions have produced. How did a divisive, indeed, seemingly combative, relationship between humanity and nature emerge? What were the institutional forms and ideologies that rendered this conflict possible? Given the growth of human needs and technology, was such a conflict really unavoidable? And can it be overcome in a future, ecologically oriented society?

How does a rational, ecologically oriented society fit into the processes of natural evolution? Even more broadly, is there any reason to believe that the human mind—itself a product of natural evolution as well as culture—represents a decisive highpoint in natural development, notably, in the long development of subjectivity from the sensitivity and self-maintenance of the simplest life-forms to the remarkable intellectuality and self-consciousness of the most complex?

In asking these highly provocative questions, I am not trying to justify a strutting arrogance toward nonhuman life-forms. Clearly, we must bring humanity's uniqueness as a species, marked by rich conceptual, social, imaginative, and constructive attributes, into synchronicity with nature's fecundity, diversity, and creativity. I have argued that this synchronicity will not be achieved by opposing nature to society, nonhuman to human life-forms, natural fecundity to technology, or a natural subjectivity to the human mind. Indeed, an important result that emerges from a discussion of the interrelationship of nature to society is the fact that human intellectuality, although distinct, also has a far-reaching natural basis. Our brains and nervous systems did not suddenly spring into existence without a long antecedent natural history. That which we most prize as integral to our humanity—our extraordinary capacity to think on complex conceptual levels—can be traced back to the nerve network of primitive invertebrates, the ganglia of a mollusk, the spinal cord of a fish, the brain of an amphibian, and the cerebral cortex of a primate.

Here, too, in the most intimate of our human attributes, we are no less products of natural evolution than we are of social evolution. As human beings we incorporate within ourselves aeons of organic differentiation and elaboration. Like all complex life-forms, we are not only part of natural evolution; we are also its heirs and the products of natural fecundity.

In trying to show how society slowly grows out of nature, however, social ecology is also obliged to show how society, too, undergoes differentiation and elaboration. In doing so, social ecology must examine those junctures in social evolution where splits occurred which slowly brought society into opposition to the natural world, and explain how this opposition emerged from its inception in prehistoric times to our own era. Indeed, if the human species is a life-form that can consciously and richly enhance the natural world, rather than simply damage it, it is important for social ecology to reveal the factors that have rendered many human beings into parasites on the world of life rather than active partners in organic evolution. This project must be undertaken not in a haphazard way, but with a serious attempt to render natural and social development coherent in terms of each other, and relevant to our times and the construction of an ecological society.

Perhaps one of social ecology's most important contributions to the current ecological discussion is the view that the basic problems which pit society against nature emerge from *within* social development itself—not *between* society and nature. That is to say, the divisions between society and nature have their deepest roots in divisions within the social realm, namely, deep-seated conflicts between human and human that are often obscured by our broad use of the word "humanity."

This crucial view cuts across the grain of nearly all current ecological thinking and even social theorizing. One of the most fixed notions that present-day ecological thinking shares with liberalism, Marxism, and conservatism is the historic belief that the "domination of nature" requires the domination of human by human. This is most obvious in social theory. Nearly all of our contemporary social ideologies have placed the notion of human domination at the centre of their theorizing. It remains one of the most widely accepted notions, from classical times to the present, that human freedom from the "domination of man by nature" entails the domination of human by human as the earliest means of production and the use of human beings as instruments for harnessing the natural world. Hence, in order to harness the natural world, it has been argued for ages, it is necessary to harness human beings as well, in the form of slaves, serfs, and workers.

That this instrumental notion pervades the ideology of nearly all ruling elites and has provided both liberal and conservative movements with a justification for their accommodation to the status quo, requires little, if any, elaboration. The myth of a "stingy" nature has always been used to justify the "stinginess" of exploiters in their harsh treatment of the exploited—and it has provided the excuse for the political opportunism of liberal, as well as conservative, causes. To "work within the system" has always implied an acceptance of domination as a way of "organizing" social life and, in the best of cases, a way of freeing humans from their presumed domination by nature.

What is perhaps less known, however, is that Marx, too, justified the emergence of class society and the State as stepping stones toward the domination of nature and, presumably, the liberation of humanity. It was on the strength of this historical vision that Marx formulated his materialist conception of history and his belief in the need for class society as a stepping stone in the historic road to communism.

Ironically, much that now passes for antihumantistic, mystical ecology involves exactly the same kind of thinking—but in an inverted form. Like their instrumental opponents, these ecologists, too, assume that humanity is dominated by nature, be it in the form of "natural laws" or an ineffable "earth wisdom" that must guide human behaviour. But while their instrumental opponents argue the need to achieve nature's "surrender" to a "conquering" active-aggressive humanity, antihumanist and mystical ecologists argue the case for achieving humanity's passive-receptive "surrender" to an "all-conquering" nature. However much the two views may differ in their verbiage and pieties, *domination* remains the underlying notion of both: a natural world conceived as a taskmaster—either to be controlled or obeyed.

Social ecology springs this trap dramatically by re-examining the entire concept of domination, be it in nature and society or in the form of "natural law" and "social law." What we normally call domination in nature is a human projection of highly organized systems of *social* command and obedience onto highly idiosyncratic, individual, and asymmetrical forms of often mildly coercive behaviour in animal communities. Put simply, animals do not "dominate" each other in the same way that a human elite dominates, and often exploits, an oppressed social group. Nor do they "rule" through institutional forms of systematic violence as social elites do. Among apes, for example, there is little or no coercion, but only erratic forms of dominant behaviour. Gibbons and orangutans are notable for their peaceable behaviour toward members of their own kind. Gorillas are often equally pacific, although one can single out "high status," mature, and physically strong males among "lower status," younger and physically weaker ones. The "alpha males" celebrated among chimpanzees do not occupy very fixed "status" positions within what are fairly fluid groups. Any "status" that they do achieve may be due to very diverse causes.

One can merrily skip from one animal species to another, to be sure, falling back on very different, asymmetrical reasons for searching out "high" versus "low status" individuals. The procedure becomes rather silly, however, when words like "status" are used so flexibly that they are allowed to include mere differences in group behaviour and functions, rather than coercive actions.

The same is true for the word "hierarchy." Both in its origins and its strict meaning, this term is highly social, not zoological. A Greek term, initially used to denote different levels of deities and, later, of clergy (characteristically, Hierapolis was an ancient Phrygian city in Asia Minor that was a centre for mother goddess worship), the word has been mindlessly expanded to encompass everything from beehive relationships to the erosive effects of running water in which a stream is seen to wear down and "dominate" its bedrock. Caring female elephants are called "matriarchs" and attentive male apes who exhibit a great deal of courage in defense of their community, while acquiring very few "privileges," are often designated as "patriarchs." The absence of an organized system of rule—so common in hierarchical human communities and subject to radical institutional changes, including popular revolutions—is largely ignored.

Again, the different functions that the presumed animal hierarchies are said to perform, that is, the asymmetrical causes that place one individual in an "alpha status" and others in a lesser one, is understated where it is noted at all. One might, with much the same aplomb, place all tall sequoias in a "superior" status over smaller ones, or, more annoyingly, regard them as an "elite" in a mixed forest "hierarchy" over "submissive" oaks, which, to complicate matters, are more advanced on the evolutionary scale. The tendency to mechanically project social categories onto the natural world is as preposterous as an attempt to project biological concepts onto geology. Minerals do not "reproduce" the way life-forms do. Stalagmites and stalactites in caves certainly do increase in size over time. But in no sense do they grow in a manner that even remotely corresponds to growth in living beings. To take superficial resemblances, often achieved in alien ways, and group them into shared identities, is like speaking of the "metabolism" of rocks and the "morality" of genes.

This raises the issue of repeated attempts to read ethical, as well as social, traits into a natural world that is only *potentially* ethical insofar as it forms a basis for an objective social ethics. Yes, coercion does exist in nature; so does pain and suffering. However, *cruelty* does not. Animal intention and will are too limited to produce an ethics of good and evil or kindness and cruelty. Evidence of inferential and conceptual thought is very limited among animals, except for primates, cetaceans, elephants, and possibly a few other mammals. Even among the most intelligent animals, the limits to thought are immense in comparison with the extraordinary capacities of socialized human beings. Admittedly, we are substantially less than human today in view of our still unknown potential to be creative, caring, and rational. Our prevailing society serves to inhibit, rather than realize, our human potential. We still lack the imagination to know how much our finest human traits could expand with an ethical, ecological, and rational dispensation of human affairs.

By contrast, the known nonhuman world seems to have reached visibly fixed limits in its capacity to survive environmental changes. If mere *adaptation* to environmental changes is seen as the criterion for evolutionary success (as many biologists believe), then insects would have to be placed on a higher plane of development than any mammalian life-form. However, they would be no more capable of making so lofty an intellectual evaluation of themselves than a "queen bee" would be even remotely aware of her "regal" status—a status, I may add, that only humans (who have suffered the social domination of stupid, inept, and cruel kings and queens) would be able to impute to a largely mindless insect.

None of these remarks are meant to metaphysically oppose nature to society or society to nature. On the contrary, they are meant to argue that what unites society with nature in a graded evolutionary continuum is the remarkable extent to which human beings, living in a rational, ecologically oriented society, could *embody* the *creativity* of nature—this, as distinguished from a purely *adaptive* criterion of evolutionary success. The great achievements of human thought, art, science, and technology serve not only to monumentalize culture, *they serve also to monumentalize natural evolution itself.* They provide heroic evidence that the human species is a warm-blooded, excitingly versatile, and keenly intelligent life-form—not a cold-blooded, genetically programmed, and mindless insect—that expresses *nature's* greatest powers of creativity.

Life-forms that create and consciously alter their environment, hopefully in ways that make it more rational and ecological, represent a vast and indefinite extension of nature into fascinating, perhaps unbounded, lines of evolution which no branch of insects could ever achieve—notably, the evolution of a fully *self-conscious* nature. If this be humanism—more precisely, ecological humanism—the current crop of antihumanists and misanthropes are welcome to make the most of it.

Nature, in turn, is not a scenic view we admire through a picture window—a view that is frozen into a landscape or a static panorama. Such "landscape" images of nature may be spiritually elevating but they are ecologically deceptive. Fixed in time and place, this imagery makes it easy for us to forget that nature is not a static vision of the natural world but the long, indeed cumulative, *history* of natural development. This history involves the evolution of the inorganic, as well as the organic, realms of phenomena. Wherever we stand in an open field, forest, or on a mountain top, our feet rest on ages of development, be they geological strata, fossils of long-extinct life-forms, the decaying remains of the newly dead, or the quiet stirring of newly emerging life. Nature is not a "person," a "caring Mother," or, in the crude materialist language of the last century, "matter and motion." Nor is it a mere "process" that involves repetitive cycles like seasonal changes and the building-up and breaking-down process of metabolic activity—some "process philosophies" to the contrary notwithstanding. Rather, natural history is a *cumulative* evolution toward ever more varied, differentiated, and complex forms and relationships.

This *evolutionary* development of increasingly variegated entities, most notably, of life-forms, is also an evolutionary development which contains exciting, latent possibilities. With variety, differentiation, and complexity, nature, in the course of its own unfolding, opens new directions for still further development along alternative lines of natural evolution. To the degree that animals become complex, self-aware, and increasingly intelligent, they begin to make those elementary choices that influence their own evolution. They are less and less the passive objects of "natural selection" and more and more the active subjects of their own development.

A brown hare that mutates into a white one and sees a snow-covered terrain in which to camouflage itself is *acting* on behalf of its own survival, not simply "adapting" in order to survive. It is not merely being "selected" by its environment; it is selecting its own environment and making a *choice* that expresses a small measure of subjectivity and judgement.

The greater the variety of habitats that emerge in the evolutionary process, the more a given life-form, particularly a neurologically complex one, is likely to play an active and judgemental role in preserving itself. To the extent that natural evolution follows this path of neurological development, it gives rise to life-forms that exercise an ever-wider latitude of choice and a nascent form of freedom in developing themselves.

Given this conception of nature as the cumulative history of more differentiated levels of material organization (especially of life-forms) and of increasing subjectivity, social ecology establishes a basis for a meaningful understanding of humanity and society's place in natural evolution. Natural history is not a "catch-as-catch-can" phenomenon. It is marked by tendency, by direction, and, as far as human beings are concerned, by conscious purpose. Human beings and the social worlds they create can open a remarkably expansive horizon for development of the natural world—a horizon marked by consciousness, reflection, and an unprecedented freedom of choice and capacity for conscious creativity. The factors that reduce many life-forms to largely adaptive roles in changing environments are replaced by a capacity for consciously adapting environments *to* existing and new life-forms.

Adaptation, in effect, increasingly gives way to creativity and the seemingly ruthless action of "natural law" to greater freedom. What earlier generations called "blind nature" to denote nature's lack of any moral direction, turns into "free nature," a nature that slowly finds a voice and the means to relieve the needless tribulations of life for all species in a highly conscious humanity and an ecological society. The "Noah Principle" of preserving every existing life-form simply for its own sake—a principle advanced by the antihumanist, David Ehrenfeld—has little meaning without the presupposition, at the very least, of the existence of a "Noah"—that is, a conscious life-form called humanity that might well rescue life-forms that nature itself would extinguish in ice ages, land desiccation, or cosmic collisions with asteroids.[2] Grizzly bears, wolves, pumas, and the like, are not safer from extinction because they are exclusively in the "caring" hands of a putative "Mother Nature." If there is any truth to the theory that the great Mesozoic reptiles were extinguished by climatic changes that presumably followed the collision of an asteroid with the earth, the survival of existing mammals might well be just as precarious in the face of an equally meaningless natural catastrophe unless there is a conscious, ecologically oriented life-form that has the technological means to rescue them.

The issue, then, is not whether social evolution stands opposed to natural evolution. The issue is *how* social evolution can be situated *in* natural evolution and *why* it has been thrown—needlessly, as I will argue—against natural evolution to the detriment of life as a whole. The capacity to be rational and free does not assure us that this capacity will be realized. If social evolution is seen as the potentiality for expanding the horizon of natural evolution along unprecedented creative lines, and human beings are seen as the potentiality for nature to become self-conscious and free, the issue we face is *why* these potentialities have been warped and *how* they can be realized.

It is part of social ecology's commitment to natural evolution that these potentialities are indeed real and that they can be fulfilled. This commitment stands flatly at odds with a "scenic" image of nature as a static view to awe mountain men or a romantic view for conjuring up mystical images of a personified deity that is so much in vogue today. The splits between natural and social evolution, nonhuman and human life, an intractable "stingy" nature and a grasping, devouring humanity, have all been specious and misleading when they are seen as inevitabilities. No less specious and misleading have been reductionist attempts to absorb social into natural evolution, to collapse culture into nature in an orgy of irrationalism, theism, and mysticism, to equate the human with mere animality, or to impose a contrived "natural law" on an obedient human society.

Whatever has turned human beings into "aliens" in nature are social changes that have made many human beings "aliens" in their own social world: the domination of the young by the old, of women by men, and of men by men. Today, as for many centuries in the past, there are still oppressive human beings who literally own society and others who are owned by it. Until society can be reclaimed by an undivided humanity that will use its collective wisdom, cultural achievements, technological innovations, scientific knowledge, and innate creativity for its own benefit and for that of the natural world, all ecological problems will have their roots in social problems.

Notes

1. Robert Briffault, "The Evolution of the Human Species," in V. F. Calverton (ed.), *The Making of Man* (New York: Modern Library, 1931), 765–6.

2. David Ehrenfeld, *The Arrogance of Humanism* (New York: Oxford University Press, 1978), 207.

28 Toward an Ecological Feminism and a Feminist Ecology

Ynestra King

[Woman] became the embodiment of the biological function, the image of nature, the subjugation of which constituted that civilization's title to fame. For millennia men dreamed of acquiring absolute mastery over nature, of converting the cosmos into one immense hunting ground. It was to this that the idea of man was geared in a male-dominated society. This was the significance of reason, his proudest boast.

(Horkheimer and Adorno 1972: 248)

All human beings are natural beings. That may seem like an obvious statement, yet we live in a culture which is founded on repudiation and domination of nature. This has a special significance for women because, in patriarchal thought, women are believed to be closer to nature than men. That gives women a particular stake in ending the domination of nature—in healing the alienation between human and nonhuman nature. That is the ultimate goal of the ecology movement, but the ecology movement is not necessarily feminist. For the most part, ecologists, with their concern for nonhuman nature, have yet to understand that they have a particular stake in ending the domination of women because a central reason for woman's oppression is her association with the despised nature they are so concerned about. The hatred of women and the hatred of nature are intimately connected and mutually reinforcing. Starting with this premise, this chapter explores why feminism and ecology need each other and suggests the very beginnings of a theory of ecological feminism—ecofeminism.

What is ecology? Ecological science concerns itself with the interrelationships of all forms of life. It aims to harmonize nature, human and nonhuman. It is an integrative science in an age of fragmentation and specialization of knowledge. It is also a critical science, which grounds and necessitates a critique of our existing society. It is a reconstructive science in that it suggests directions for reconstructing human society in harmony with the natural environment.

Ecologists are asking the pressing questions of how we might survive on the planet and develop systems of food and energy production, architecture, and ways of life which will allow human beings to fulfill our material needs and live in harmony with nonhuman nature. This work has led to a social critique by biologists and an exploration of biology and ecology by social thinkers. The perspective that self-consciously attempts to integrate both biological and social

From *Machina Ex Dea: Feminist Perspectives on Technology* (New York: Pergamon Press, 1983), 118–28. Reprinted by permission of the author.

aspects of the relationship between human beings and their environment is known as "social ecology." This perspective, developed primarily by Murray Bookchin (1982), has embodied the anarchist critique which links domination and hierarchy in human society to the despoliation of nonhuman nature.[1] While this analysis is useful, social ecology without feminism is incomplete.

Feminism grounds this critique of domination by identifying the prototype of other forms of domination, that of man over woman. Potentially, feminism creates a concrete global community of interests among particularly life-oriented peoples of the world: women. Feminist analysis supplies theory, program, and process without which the radical potential of social ecology remains blunted. The theory and movement known as ecofeminism pushes social ecology to understand the necessary connections between ecology and feminism so that social ecology can reach its own avowed goal of creating a free and ecological way of life.

What are these connections? Social ecology challenges the dualistic belief that nature and culture are separate and opposed. Ecofeminism finds misogyny at the root of that opposition. Ecofeminist principles are based on the following beliefs:

1. The building of Western industrial civilization in opposition to nature interacts dialectically with and reinforces the subjugation of women because women are believed to be closer to nature in this culture against nature.

2. Life on earth is an interconnected web, not a hierarchy. There is not a natural hierarchy, but a multitiered human hierarchy projected onto nature and then used to justify social domination. Therefore ecofeminist movement politics and culture must show the connections between all forms of domination, including the domination of nonhuman nature, and be itself antihierarchical.

3. A healthy, balanced ecosystem, including human and nonhuman inhabitants, must maintain diversity. Ecologically, environmental simplification is as significant a problem as environmental pollution. Biological simplification, i.e. wiping out of whole species, corresponds to reducing human diversity into faceless workers, or to the homogenization of taste and culture through mass consumer markets. Social life and natural life are literally simplified to the inorganic for the convenience of market society. Therefore, we need a decentralized global movement founded on common interests but celebrating diversity and opposing all forms of domination and violence. Potentially, ecofeminism is such a movement.

4. The survival of the species necessitates a renewed understanding of our relationship to nature, of our own bodily nature and nonhuman nature around us; it necessitates a challenging of the nature—culture dualism and a corresponding radical restructuring of human society according to feminist and ecological principles.

When we speak of transformation we speak more accurately out of the vision of a process which will leave neither surfaces nor depths unchanged, which enters society at the most essential level of the subjugation of women and nature by men. (Rich 1979: 248)

The ecology movement, in theory and practice, attempts to speak for nature, the "other" which has no voice and is not conceived of subjectively in our civilization. Feminism represents the refusal of the original "other" in patriarchal human society to remain silent or to be the "other" any longer. Its challenge of social domination extends beyond sex to social domination of all kinds because the domination of sex, race, class, and nature are mutually reinforcing. Women are the "others" in human society who have been silent in public, and who now speak through the feminist movement.

Women, Nature, and Culture: The Ecofeminist Position

In the process of building Western industrial civilization, nature became something to be dominated, overcome, made to serve the needs of men. She was stripped of her magical powers and properties as these beliefs were relegated to the trashbin of superstition. Nature was reduced to "natural resources" to be exploited by human beings to fulfill human needs and purposes which were defined in opposition to nature (see Merchant 1980).[2] A dualistic Christianity had become ascendant with the earlier demise of old Goddess religions, paganism, and animistic belief systems (Reuther 1975). With the disenchantment of nature came the conditions for unchecked scientific exploration and technological exploitation (Merchant 1980). We bear the consequences today of beliefs in unlimited control over nature and in science's ability to solve any problem, as nuclear power plants are built without provisions for waste disposal, or satellites sent into space without provision for retrieval.

In this way, nature became "other," something essentially different from the dominant to be objectified and thus subordinated. Women, who are identified with nature, have been similarly objectified and subordinated in patriarchal society. Women and nature, in this sense, are the original "others." Simone de Beauvoir (1968) has clarified this connection. For de Beauvoir, "transcendence" is the work of culture, it is the work of men. It is the process of overcoming immanence, a process of culture-building which is opposed to nature and which is based on the increasing domination of nature. It is enterprise. Immanence, symbolized by woman, is that which calls man back, that which reminds man of what he wants to forget. It is his own links to nature that he must forget and overcome to achieve manhood and transcendence:

Man seeks in woman the Other as Nature and as his fellow being. But we know what ambivalent feelings Nature inspires in man. He exploits her, but she crushes him, he is born of her and dies in her; she is the source of his being and the realm that he subjugates to his will; Nature is a vein of gross material in which the soul is imprisoned, and she is the supreme reality; she is contingence and Idea, the finite and the whole; she is what opposes the Spirit, and the Spirit itself. Now ally, now enemy, she appears as the dark chaos from whence life wells up, as this life itself, and as the over-yonder toward which life tends. Woman sums up Nature as Mother, Wife, and Idea; these forms now mingle and now conflict, and each of them wears a double visage. (de Beauvoir 1968: 144)

For de Beauvoir, patriarchal civilization is almost the denial of men's mortality—of which women and nature are incessant reminders. Women's powers of procreation are distinguished from the powers of creation, the accomplishments through the vehicle of culture by which men achieve immortality. And yet, this transcendence over women and nature can never be total. Hence, the ambivalence, the lack of self without other, the dependence of the self on the other both materially and emotionally. Thus develops a love—hate fetishization of women's bodies, which finds its ultimate manifestation in the sadomasochistic, pornographic displays of women as objects to be subdued, humiliated, and raped—the visual enactment of these fears and desires.[3]

An important contribution of de Beauvoir's work is to show that men seek to dominate women and nature for reasons which are not simply economic. They do so as well for psychological reasons which involve a denial of a part of themselves, as do other male culture-making activities. The process begins with beating the tenderness and empathy out of small boys and directing their natural human curiosity and joy in affecting the world around them into arrogant attitudes and destructive paths.

For men raised in woman-hating cultures, the fact that they are born of women and dependent upon nonhuman nature for existence is frightening. The process of objectification, of the making of women and nature into "others" to be appropriated and dominated, is based on a profound forgetting by men. They forget that they are born of women, dependent on women in their early helpless years, and dependent on nonhuman nature all their lives, which allows first for objectification and then for domination. "The loss of memory is a transcendental condition for science. All objectification is a forgetting" (Horkheimer and Adorno 1972: 230).

But the denied part of men is never fully obliterated. The memory remains in the knowledge of mortality and the fear of women's power. A basic fragility of gender identity therefore exists that surfaces when received truths about women and men are challenged and the sexes depart from the "natural" roles. Opposition to the not-very-radical US Equal Rights Amendment can be partially explained on these grounds. More threatening are homosexuality and the gay liberation movement because they name a more radical truth—that sexual orientation is not indelible, nor is it naturally heterosexual. Lesbianism, particularly, which suggests that women, who possess this bottled up, repudiated primordial power, can be self-sufficient, reminds men that they may not be needed. Men are forced into remembering their own need for women to enable them to support and mediate the construction of their private reality and their public civilization. Again, there is the need to repress memory and suppress women.

The recognition of the connections between woman and nature or of women's bridge-like position poses three possible directions for feminism. One direction is the integration of women into the world of culture and production by severing the woman/nature connection. Writes anthropologist Sherry Ortner, "Ultimately both men and women can and must be equally involved in projects of creativity and transcendence. Only then will women be seen as aligned with culture, in culture's ongoing dialectic with nature" (1974: 87). This position does not necessarily question nature/culture dualism itself, and it is the position taken by most socialist-feminists (see King 1981) and by de Beauvoir and Ortner despite their insights into the connections between women and nature. They seek the severance of the woman/nature connection as a condition of women's liberation. Other feminists have built on the woman/nature connection by reinforcing this connection: woman and nature, the spiritual and intuitive versus men and the culture of patriarchal rationality.[4] This position also does not necessarily question nature/culture dualism itself or recognize that women's ecological sensitivity and life orientation is a socialized perspective which could be socialized right out of us depending on our day-to-day lives. There is no reason to believe that women placed in positions of patri-archal power will act any differently from men or that we can bring about feminist revolution without a conscious understanding of history and a challenge to economic and political power structures.

Ecofeminism suggests a third direction: that feminism recognize that although the nature/culture opposition is a product of culture, we can, nonetheless, *consciously choose* not to sever the woman nature connections by joining male culture. Rather, we can use it as a vantage point for creating a different kind of culture and politics that would integrate intuitive/spiritual and ration-al forms of knowledge, embracing both science and magic insofar as they enable us to transform the nature/culture distinction itself and to envision and create a free, ecological society.

Ecofeminism and The Intersections of Feminism and Ecology

The implications of a culture based on the devaluation of life-giving (both biological and social) and the celebration of life-taking are profound for ecology and for women. This fact about our culture links the theories and the politics of the ecology and the feminist movements. Adrienne Rich has written,

We have been perceived for too many centuries as pure Nature, exploited and raped like the earth and solar system; small wonder if we now long to become Culture; pure spirit, mind. Yet it is precisely this culture and its political institutions which have split us off from itself. In so doing it has also split itself off from life, becoming the death culture of quantification, abstraction, and the will to power which has reached its most refined destructiveness in this century. It is culture and politics of abstraction which women are talking of changing, of bringing into accountability in human terms. (1976: 285)

The way to ground a feminist critique of "this culture and politics of abstraction" is with a self-conscious ecological perspective that we apply to all theories and strategies, in the way that we are learning to apply race and class factors to every phase of feminist analysis.

Similarly, ecology requires a feminist perspective. Without a thorough feminist analysis of social domination that reveals the interconnected roots of misogyny and a hatred of nature, ecology remains an abstraction: it is incomplete. If male ecological scientists and social ecologists fail to deal with misogyny, the deepest manifestation of nature-hating in their own lives, they are not living the ecological lives or creating the ecological society they claim.

The goals of harmonizing humanity and nonhuman nature, at both the experiential and theoretical levels, cannot be attained without the radical vision and understanding available from feminism. The ecofeminist perspective thus affects our technology. Including everything from the digging stick to nuclear bombs, technology signifies the tools that human beings use to interact with nature. The twin concerns of ecofeminism with human liberation and with our relationship to nonhuman nature open the way to developing a set of technological ethics required for decision making about technology.

Ecofeminism also contributes an understanding of the connections between the domination of persons and the domination of nonhuman nature. Ecological science tells us that there is no hierarchy in nature itself, but rather a hierarchy in human society. Building on this unmasking of the ideology of natural hierarchy of persons, ecofeminism uses its ecological perspective to develop the position that there is no hierarchy in nature: among persons, between persons and the rest of the natural world, or among the many forms of nonhuman nature. We live on the earth with millions of species, only one of which is the human species. Yet, the human species, in its patriarchal form, is the only species which holds a conscious belief that it is entitled to dominion over the other species, and the planet. Paradoxically, the human species is utterly dependent on nonhuman nature. We could not live without the rest of nature: it could live without us.

Ecofeminism draws on another basic principle of ecological science, unity in diversity, and develops it politically. Diversity in nature is necessary, and enriching. One of the major effects of industrial technology—capitalist or socialist—is environmental simplification. Many species are being simply wiped out, never to be seen on the earth again. In human society, commodity capitalism is intentionally simplifying human community and culture so that the same products can be marketed anywhere to anyone. The prospect is for all of us to be alike, with identical needs and desires, around the globe: Coca Cola in China, blue jeans in Russia, and American rock music virtually everywhere. Few peoples of the earth have not had their lives touched and changed to some degree by the technology of industrialization. Ecofeminism as a social movement resists this social simplification through supporting the rich diversity of women the world over, and finding a oneness in that diversity. Politically, ecofeminism opposes the ways that differences can separate women from each other through the oppressions of class, privilege, sexuality, race, and nationality.

The special message of ecofeminism is that, when women suffer through both social domination and the domination of nature, most of life on this planet suffers and is threatened as well. For the brutalization and oppression of women is connected with the hatred of nature and with other forms of domination, and with threatened ecological catastrophe. It is significant that feminism and ecology as social movements have emerged now, as nature's revolt against domination plays itself out in human history and nonhuman nature at the same time. As we face slow environmental poisoning and the resulting environmental simplification, or the possible unleashing of our nuclear arsenals, we can hope that the prospect of the extinction of life on the planet will provide a universal impetus to social change. Ecofeminism supports utopian visions of harmonious, diverse, decentralized communities, using only those technologies based on ecological principles, as the only practical solution for the continuation of life on earth.

Visions and politics are joined as an ecofeminist culture and politic begin to emerge. Central to this development is ecofeminist praxis: taking direct action to effect changes that are immediate and personal as well as long term and structural. Direct actions include learning holistic health and alternate ecological technologies, living in communities which explore old and new forms of spirituality that celebrate all life as diverse expressions of nature, considering the ecological consequences of our lifestyles and personal habits, and participating in creative public forms of resistance. This sometimes involves engaging in nonviolent civil disobedience to physically stop the machines which are arrayed against life.

Toward An Ecofeminist Praxis: Feminist Antimilitarism

Theory never converts simply or easily into practice; in fact, theory often lags behind practice, attempting to articulate the understanding behind things people are already doing. Praxis is the unity of thought and action, or theory and practice. Many of the women who founded the feminist antimilitarist movement in Europe and the United States share the ecofeminist perspective I have articulated. I believe that the movement as I will briefly describe it here grows out of such an understanding. For the last three years, I have been personally involved in the feminist antimilitarist movement, so the following is a firsthand account of this example of ecofeminist praxis.

The connections between violence against women, a militarized culture, and the development and deployment of nuclear weapons have long been evident to pacifist feminists (Deming 1974). Ecofeminists like myself, whose concerns with all of life stem from an understanding of the connections between misogyny and the destruction of nature, began to see militarism and the death-courting weapons industry as the most immediate threat to continued life on the planet, while the ecological effects of other modern technologies pose a more long-term threat. In this manner, militarism has become a central issue for most ecofeminists. Along with this development, many of us accepted the analysis of violence made by pacifist feminists and, therefore, began to see nonviolent direct action and resistance as the basis of our political practice.

The ecofeminist analysis of militarism is concerned with the militarization of culture and the economic priorities reflected by our enormous "defense" budgets and dwindling social services budgets. Together, these pose threats to our freedom and threaten our lives, even if there is no war and none of the nuclear weapons are ever used. We have tried to make clear the particular ways that women suffer from war-making—as spoils to victorious armies, as refugees, as disabled and older women and single mothers who are dependent on dwindling social services. We connect the fear of nuclear annihilation with women's fear of male violence in our everyday lives. The level of weaponry as well as the militaristic economic priorities are products of patriarchal culture that speaks violence at every level. For ecofeminists, military technology reflects a pervasive cultural political situation. It is connected with rape, genocide, and imperialism; with starvation and homelessness; the poisoning of the environment; and the fearful lives of the world's peoples—especially those of women. Military and state power hierarchies join and reinforce each other through military technology.

Particularly as shaped by ecofeminism, the feminist antimilitarist movement in the United States and Europe is a movement against a monstrously destructive technology and set of power relationships embodied in militarism.

Actions have been organized at the Pentagon in the United States and at military installations in Europe. The Women's Pentagon Action was conceived at an ecofeminist conference I initiated and organized with several other women in spring 1980.[5] It has taken place at the Pentagon twice so far, on November 16 and 17, 1980, and November 15 and 16, 1981. It included about 2,000 women the first year, and more than twice that the second. We took care to make the actions reflect all our politics. Intentionally, there were no speakers, no leaders; the action sought to emphasize the connections between the military issue and other ecofeminist issues. The action was planned in four stages, reflecting the depth and range of the emotions felt and the interconnection of issues, and culminating in direct resistance. A Unity Statement, describing the group's origins and concerns was drafted collectively. In the first stage, "mourning," we walked among the graves at Arlington National Cemetery and placed tombstones symbolically for all the victims of war and other forms of violence against women, beginning with a market for "the unknown woman." The second stage was "rage," a venting of our anger. Next, the group circled the Pentagon, reaching all the way around, and singing for the stage of "empowerment." The final stage, "defiance," included a civil disobedience action in which women blocked entrances and were arrested in an act of nonviolent direct resistance. The choice to commit civil disobedience was made individually, without pressure from the group.[6]

The themes of the Women's Pentagon Action have carried over into other actions our group has participated in, including those organized by others. At the June 12–14, 1982, disarmament demonstrations in New York City, the group's march contingent proclaimed the theme: "A feminist world is a nuclear free zone," the slogan hanging beneath a huge globe held aloft. Other banners told of visions for a feminist future and members wore bibs that read "War is manmade," "Stop the violence in our lives," and "Disarm the patriarchy." There have been similar actions, drawing inspiration from the original Women's Pentagon Actions elsewhere in the United States and in Europe. In California, the Bohemian Club—a male-only playground for corporate, government, and military elite—was the site of a demonstration by women who surrounded the club in protest (Starhawk 1982: 168). In England, on December 12, 1982, 30,000 women surrounded a US military installation, weaving into the fence baby clothes, scarves, and other objects which meant something to them. At one point, spontaneously, the word "FREEDOM" rose from the lips of the women and was heard round and round the base. Three thousand women nonviolently blocked the entrances to the base on December 13 (see Fisher 1983).

The politics being created by these actions draw on women's culture: embodying what is best in women's life-oriented socialization, building on women's differences, organizing antihierarchically in small groups in visually and emotionally imaginative ways, and seeking an integration of issues. There actions exemplify ecofeminism. While technocratic experts (including feminists) argue the merits and demerits of weapons systems, ecofeminism approaches the disarmament issue on an intimate and moral level. Ecofeminism holds that a personalized, decentralized, life-affirming culture and politics of direct action are crucially needed to stop the arms race and transform the world's priorities. Because such weaponary does not exist apart from a contempt for women and all of life, the issue of disarmament and threat of nuclear war is a feminist issue. It is the ultimate human issue and the ultimate ecological issue. And so ecology, feminism, and liberation for all of nature, including ourselves, are joined.

Notes

1. I am indebted to Bookchin for my own theoretical understanding of social ecology which is basic to this chapter.

2. Merchant interprets the Scientific Revolution as the death of nature, and argues that it had a particularly detrimental effect on women.

3. See Susan Griffin (1981) for a full development of the relationship between nature-hating, woman-hating, and pornography.
4. Many such feminists call themselves ecofeminists. Some of them cite Susan Griffin's *Woman and Nature* (1978) as the source of their understanding of the deep connections between women and nature, and their politics. *Woman and Nature* is an inspirational poetic work with political implications. It explores the terrain of our deepest naturalness, but I do not read it as a delineation of a set of politics. To use Griffin's work in this way is to make it into something it was not intended to be. In personal conversation and in her more politically explicit works such as *Pornography and Silence* (1981), Griffin is antidualistic, struggling to bridge the false oppositions of nature and culture, passion and reason. Both science and poetry are deeply intuitive processes. Another work often cited by ecofeminists is Mary Daly's *Gyn/ecology* (1978). Daly, a theologian/philosopher, is also an inspirational thinker, but she is a genuinely dualistic thinker, reversing the "truths" of patriarchal theology. While I have learned a great deal from Daly, my perspective differs from hers in that I believe that any truly ecological politics including ecological feminism must be ultimately antidualistic.
5. "Women and Life on Earth: Ecofeminism in the 80s," Amherst, Mass., March 21–23, 1980. Each of my sister founders of Women and Life on Earth contributed to the theory of ecofeminism I have articulated here, and gave me faith in the political potential of an ecofeminist movement. All of them would probably disagree with parts of this chapter. Nonetheless, I thank Christine Di Stefano, Deborah Gaventa, Anna Gyorgy, Amy Hines, Sue Hoffman, Carol Iverson, Grace Paley, Christina Rawley, Nancy Jack Todd, and Celeste Wesson.
6. See Ynestra King (1983) for my personal account and evaluation of the action.

References

Bookchin, Murray (1982), *The Ecology of Freedom: The Emergence and Dissolution of Hierarchy* (Palo Alto, Calif.: Cheshire Books).

Daly, Mary (1978), *Gyn/ecology: The Metaethics of Radical Feminism* (Boston: Beacon Press).

de Beauvoir, Simone (1968), *The Second Sex* (New York: Modern Library, Random House).

Deming, Barbara (1974), *We Cannot Live Without our Lives* (New York: Grossman).

Fisher, Berenice (1983), "Woman Ignite English Movement," *Womanews* (February).

Griffin, Susan (1978), *Woman and Nature: The Roaring Inside Her* (New York: Harper & Row).

—— (1981), *Pornography and Silence: Culture's Revenge against Nature* (New York: Harper & Row).

Horkheimer, Max, and Adorno, Theodor W. (1972), *Dialectic of Enlightenment* (New York: Seabury Press).

King, Ynestra (1981), "Feminism and the Revolt of Nature," *Heresies*, 13 (Fall), 12–16.

—— (1983), "All is Connectedness: Scenes from the Women's Pentagon Action USA," in Lynne Johnes (ed.), *Keeping the Peace: A Women's Peace Handbook* (London: The Women's Press).

Merchant, Carolyn (1980), *The Death of Nature: Women, Ecology, and the Scientific Revolution* (New York: Harper & Row).

Ortner, Sherry B. (1974), "Is Female to Male as Nature is to Culture?", in Michelle Zimbalist Rosaldo and Louise Lamphere (eds), *Women, Culture and Society* (Stanford, Calif.: Stanford University Press), 67–87.

Reuther, Rosemary (1975), *New Woman/New Earth: Sexist Ideologies and Human Liberation* (New York: Seabury Press).

Rich, Adrienne (1976), *Of Woman Born* (New York: W. W. Norton).

—— (1979), *On Lies, Secrets, and Silence: Selected Prose* (New York: W. W. Norton).

Starhawk (1982), *Dreaming the Dark: Magic, Sex and Politics* (Boston: Beacon Press).

29 Ecosocialism

Joel Kovel

....

If we imagine that decrees are all that is needed to get away from competition, we shall never get away from it. And if we go so far as to propose to abolish competition while retaining wages, we shall be proposing nonsense by royal decree. But nations do not proceed by royal decree. Before framing such ordinances, they must at least have changed from top to bottom the conditions of their industrial and political existence, and consequently their whole manner of being.

(Marx, *The Poverty of Philosophy*[1])

Revolutions become feasible when a people decides that their present social arrangements are intolerable, when they believe that they can achieve a better alternative, and when the balance of forces between them and that of the system is tipped in their favour. None of these conditions is close to being met at present for the ecosocialist revolution, which would seem to make the exercise upon which we are about to embark academic. But the present is one thing, and the future another. If the argument that capital is incorrigibly ecodestructive and expansive proves to be true, then it is only a question of time before the issues raised here achieve explosive urgency. And considering what is at stake and how rapidly events can change under such circumstances, it is most definitely high time to take up the question of ecosocialism as a living process—to consider what its vision of society may be and what kind of path there may be towards its achievement.

The present chapter is the most practical and yet also the most speculative of this work. Beaten down by the great defeats of Utopian and socialist ideals, few today even bother to think about the kinds of society that could replace the present with one of ecological rationality, and most of that speculation is within a green paradigm limited by an insufficient appreciation of the regime of capital and of the depths needed for real change. Instead, Greens tend to imagine an orderly extension of community, accompanied by the use of instruments that have been specifically created to keep the present system going, such as parliamentary elections and various tax policies. Such measures make transformative sense, however, only if seen as prefigurations of something more radical—something by definition not immediately on the horizon. It will be our job here to begin the process of drawing in this not-yet-seen. The only certainty is that the result will at most be a rough and schematic model of what actually might emerge.

However uncertain the end point, the first two steps on the path are clearly laid out, and are within the reach of every conscientious person. These are that people ruthlessly criticize the capitalist system 'from top to bottom', and that they include in this a consistent attack on the

From Kovel, *The Enemy of Nature* (London: Zed Books, 2002), 222–44.

widespread belief that there can be no alternative to it. If one believes that capital is not only basically unjust but radically unsustainable as well, the prime obligation is to spread the news, just as one should feel obliged to tell the inhabitants of a structurally unsound house doomed to collapse of what awaits them unless they take drastic measures. To continue the analogy, for the critique to matter it needs to be combined with an attack on the false idea that we are, so to speak, trapped in this house, with no hope of fixing it or getting out.

The belief that there can be no alternative to capital is ubiquitous—and no wonder, given how wonderfully convenient the idea is to the ruling ideology.[2] That, however, does not keep it from being nonsense, and a failure of vision and political will. Whether or not the vision of ecosocialism offered here has merit, the notion that there is no other way of organizing an advanced society other than capital does not follow. Nothing lasts for ever, and what is humanly made can theoretically be unmade. Of course it could be the case that the job of changing it is too hard and capital is as far as humanity can go, in which instance we must simply accept our fate stoically and try to palliate the results. But we don't know this and *cannot* know this. There is no proving it one way or the other, and only inertia, fear of change or opportunism can explain the belief in so shabby an idea as that there can be no alternative to capital for organizing society.

Logic alone neither persuades nor gives hope; something more solid and material is required, a combination of the dawning insight of just how incapable capital is of resolving the crisis, along with some spark that breaks through the crust of inert despair and cynicism by means of which we have adapted to the system. At some point—it has to happen if capital is the efficient cause—the realization will dawn that all the sound ideas for, say, regulating the chemical industries, or preserving forest ecosystems, or doing something serious about species-extinctions, or global warming, or whatever point of ecosystemic disintegration is of concern, are not going to be realized by appealing to local changes in themselves, or the Democratic Party, or the Environmental Protection Agency, or the courts, or the foundations, or ecophilosophies, or changes in consciousness—for the overriding reason that we are living under a regime that controls the state and the economy, and will have to be overcome at its root if we are to save the future.

Relentless criticism can delegitimate the system and release people into struggle. And as struggle develops, victories that are no more than incremental by their own terms—stopping a meeting of the IMF, the hopes stirred forth by a campaign such as Ralph Nader's in 2000—can have a symbolic effect far greater than their external result, and constitute points of rupture with capital. This rupture is not a set of facts added to our knowledge of the world, but a change in our relation to the world. Its effects are dynamic, not incremental, and like all genuine insights it changes the balance of forces and can propagate very swiftly. Thus the release from inertia can trigger a rapid cascade of changes, so that it could be said that the forces pressing towards radical change need not be linear and incremental, but can be exponential in character. In this way, conscientious and radical criticism of the given, even in advance of having blueprints for an alternative, can be a material force, because it can seize the mind of the masses of people. There is no greater responsibility for intellectuals.

In what follows, there will be neither blueprints nor omniscience, although I will be laying out certain hypothetical situations as a way of framing ideas. The overall task can be stated simply enough: if an ecological mode of production is the goal, what sort of practical steps can be defined to get us there? What might an ecosocialist society look like? How are the grand but abstract terms of basic change to be expressed as functions of lived life? And how can the path towards an ecosocialism that is not sharply defined incorporate the goal towards which it moves?

Ecological Ensembles and The Modelling of Ecosocialist Development

If ecological politics is to be prefigurative and interstitial, then it must begin with what is at hand, and according to its potential for realizing integral ecosystems. Let us call any such unit an ecological ensemble. It consists of a human ecosystem viewed from the standpoint of its potential for ecological production. What we look for is the growth and interconnection of ecological ensembles, from islands within the capitalist sea, to a kind of archipelago that further coheres, finally, into a continent of ecosocialism.

The notion of ecological ensembles is deliberately cast widely, thus any of the following would qualify:

- an organic farm
- an affinity group engaging in direct action against the World Bank
- a small community credit union
- a performed cultural work, engaging an audience
- an intentional community
- a political party
- a classroom, or a child within it
- the Du Pont corporation
- a neighbourhood in Manhattan—or Manhattan itself, or New York State, or the USA.

At its end, this list seems to become a *reductio ad absurdum*. It is preposterous, many would say, to think of Du Pont, or the USA, in the same breath as an organic farm in terms of their potential for ecosocialism. And what does a child have in common with any of these? One might as well put the World Bank on the list along with the affinity group stopping traffic in an effort to bring the Bank to heel.

Well, yes, one might as well, since the World Bank, too, is an ecosystem, insofar as the human world is that sub-set of nature whose ecosystemic being is given through production, and since all production contains some moment pressing toward universality. In this respect a child, more particularly a child in relation to its human and sensuous world, is certainly an ecosystem, as is any organized portion of the human world. It follows that even the bleakest capitalist enterprise has some ecosocialist potential. However, the judgement of bleakness applied to such an enterprise means, in effect, that its development has left the path of ecosystemic wholeness for the alternative and cancerous from of capitalist accumulation. As this is the case for DuPont and the World Bank, we may say that they are ecological ensembles with a very low internal ecosocialist potential, confined, say, to a pledge taken by the former to cut its greenhouse gas emissions, or in the case of the Bank, by the conscientious impulses of some staff members, all of which are hemmed in and tamed by the powerful force field of capital that they exist to serve, and therefore become mainly used for greenwashing and public relations. Nor will this potential develop spontaneously; it will develop only after very strenuous and protracted action taken against these institutions. Action of the sort is provided by the affinity group, by reason of which we would say that this kind of ecological ensemble has a high ecosocialist potential; indeed, that it is not just active, but *activating*—although it must be added that this potential exists at present as a loosely configured set of points scattered relatively harmlessly over the political landscape.

The general model of ecosocialist development is to foster the activating potentials of ensembles in order to catalyse the emergence of others so as to draw together those points into ever more dynamic bodies. The praxis by which this takes place is *dialectical*, that is, it comprises the active bringing and holding together of negations, as when the affinity group confronts the World Bank, or when a person confronts a painful truth. Negation in political confrontation defines what it means to struggle, and it has multiple aspects: the group offers itself as a counter-institution, more internally democratic and with enhanced ecocentric potentials; it offers direct critique of the Bank and seeks to educate others in the same, thereby bringing a painful truth to bear; and finally, it seeks to shut down the Bank, at least for a while, by blocking access to its meeting. The development of a human ecosystem depends greatly on the degree of recognition it appropriates, in this case the degree of understanding the affinity group holds of the Bank (and the police, politicians, media, and so on, who support the bank); and also of the fidelity, internal coherence, and so forth, of the group—in short, its capacity to stay together in dialectical activity throughout the period of confrontation. And the longer and more sustained the confrontation, the more developed the dialectic, the more mobilized the holding together (this being the insertion point of ecofeminist values into ecosocialist practice), and the more integral the ecosystem so produced.

The model can be applied to ensembles engaged in economic activity, such as the credit union, where the coefficient of use-value over exchange-value, uv/xv, can be expanded. Community enterprises of this sort objectively tend to keep capital local and away from being leached into the great pool of ecodestruction; at the same time, they subjectively tend to detach people from capital's force field and induce ever-widening degrees of ecological production.[3] Two broad types of function differentiate themselves from this matrix, and, remaining differentiated, continually stay in contact: those having to do with the production, proper, of ecological use-values, as, for example, in the growing of food according to organic principles; and those having to do with the activation, or transforming of labour itself, the maker of all use-values as it engages nature. It may be said of activating groups such as the affinity group that their production becomes one of ecosocialist possibilities. This is seen prefiguratively in their theoretical production, which starts from the present level and achieves a fuller and more radical understanding from the struggle itself. Needless to say, this distinction must not be regarded too rigidly, for in fact the process described is equally possible within groups, and indeed, within individuals. As struggle develops, activation is spread across the whole social field, and gradually comes to define a new set of orienting principles that will coalesce into a 'party-like' formation. In this way there arises, interwoven in combinations presently impossible to predict, growing islands of relatively ecological production, along with the emergence, along other dimensions, of a guiding political spirit embodied in nascent organizations, whose work enables the bringing of productive ensembles together and strengthening their resolve. All of this is presumed to be played out against the backdrop of a gathering realization that capital is the efficient cause of the ecological crisis.

The next step to be imagined in this development is the emergence of more formal organizations, taking the shape of micro-communities serving the combined functions of *resistance* to capital, *production* of an ecological/socialist alternative to it, and mutual interconnection of their semi-autonomous sites through the vision of a common goal. To weave one possibility, the affinity group at some point 'settles in', constructing its ties now along more formally productive lines and drawing their lives more closely together around this. We can think of these along the lines of the Bruderhof discussed in the previous chapter, with an anti-capitalist intention formed out of the combined withdrawal of value from exchange and its replacement with transformed use-value production. As we saw with that religious commune, a powerful spiritual movement is necessary to neutralize capital's force field and provide the protective umbrella to permit ecosystemic development. It is akin to the greenhouse that allows young plants to grow during the winter, allowing certain radiation in, and holding it in so that the young shoots may be protected from the cold. There is no reason why this cannot be Christian, although it would have to be a post-patriarchal Christianity in order to realize the goals of ecological production. By the same reasoning, there is no need that it be Christian at all, or religious, either, so long as it is post-patriarchal and post-capitalist, and spiritually attuned to the logic of ecological production. Spiritualities arise prior to their religious construction. They are formed from the striving of human being beyond the given, and there is ample resource within those forms of being that negate the domination of nature to give content to an emergent ecological spirituality—including, it should be emphatically added, from within the socialist tradition itself, which had a glorious spirituality when it had genuine claims on the Utopian imagination.[4] Nor need this spirituality be proclaimed as such. In a time saturated with New Age huckstering, that spirituality is best which does not announce itself, and truest to the extent that ego is transcended in a greater cause.[5]

Such a development will undoubtedly be highly uneven. Certain areas—for example, organic agriculture or permaculture—are favoured in terms of being able to produce ecologically realized use-values; thus for them, the numerator of the coefficient uv/xv can be increased relatively independently, raising the potential to break loose of capital. Other areas—for example, the emergent anti-globalization movements—are relatively more able to diminish the denominator, exchange-value, through political practice, thus achieving the same general effect. Clearly, however, the processes in either case can go only so far before becoming snared by the force field—the organic farmer by the brutal intrusion of market forces, which impose debt, competition and the need to exploit labour; the affinity group member, who is most typically a student, by the need to make a living, with all its attendant compromises, as well as by the powerful forces of state repression.

Practices that in the same motion enhance use-values and diminish exchange-values are the ideal in terms of ecosocialist potential. Needless to say, the student radical can then go on to law school and study to become a defender of the people and earth; just so, the organic farmer can find him/herself 'naturally' positioned to adopt Green political values and to organize accordingly—and in all such cases the possibility exists for unified ecosocialist practice to emerge collectively as this happens. But there are also types of activity yet closer to the ideal, where both aspects of the uv/xv coefficient can change directly in relation to each other—for example, education. As current educational policy in the US grinds down the living child into an interchangeable part for the great capitalist machine, the possibility of resistance immediately arises for teachers of conscience. By organizing against the system and criticizing its educational policy, one necessarily protests the regime of exchange inasmuch as education under capitalism moves toward standardization, quantification and the treatment of children as passive containers to be shaped into docile workers and consumers. But it also requires reshaping one's practice as an educator, toward a model that, whatever its particular shape, regards the child as an active, self-determining being who lives through mutual recognition. In this way the teaching process becomes the production of ecosystemic use-values even as its political arm attacks the rule of exchange-value. Note, too, that this can occur in advance of an explicit assault on capital, being located rather at the point of capital's penetration into life-worlds.[6]

A highly salient example applies to the alternative media community, situated at the Archimedean point of capitalist legitimation and control. Here prefigurations of the new society in the form of the 'Indymedia' centres have recently arisen, as collectives of radical media activists in the cities visited by anti-globalization protests. Initially set up to document the protests in ways denied by corporate media, the independent centres tended to stay on after the waves of street protests receded. Their way having been prepared by a generation of media activists, the centres manifest a flexible and open structure, a democratic rendering of the use-values of new technologies such as the Internet, and a continual involvement in wider struggle. They grow and gather into national and international collectives, forming nodes on a growing web unified by an increasingly anti-capitalist vision. The same force that binds together the movement for democratic media also keeps it ecosystemic, that is democratically communitarian, and to that degree unwilling to compromise with the powers that be. In this way the spontaneously developing collective evolves into a *community of resistance*, one defined by praxis rather than place, and, in contrast to the plan of traditional Green theory, cosmopolitan to the core.[7]

It is essential to not get carried away by these successes. Media workers occupy one end of the spectrum of labour favourably configured for the spinning off of ecosocialist possibilities. However, the emancipation of labour requires that the entire international division of labour be overcome, and this is a problem the difficulty of which can scarcely be overestimated. Capital's domination of labour is predicated on separating workers from the means of production, and also from each other. This is the foundation of its triumph, and has become sedimented into the labour movement itself, which, being dependent upon jobs within existing capitalist workplaces, often shares with capital a resistance to environmental protection, or is divided nationally or regionally, North and South having many separate agendas. But the problem is equivalently that of existing environmentalism, with its single-issue focus on protecting natural habitats without concern for labour. The entire impasse cries out for the synthesis of an ecological production in which there is no contradiction between labour and nature, and creative work for all. But that is the goal, and a long way off; our job in the here and now is to develop prefigurative ensembles for it. The best candidates would be autonomous zones of production within which ecocentric potentials can be developed. At present, these appear drastically Utopian and out of reach for most industries. For auto workers, say, to build productive communities, as radical media workers are doing, is a fantasy under present conditions. Not only does it encounter the crippling blows suffered by the labour movements over generations, it must also face the globalized productive system in which motor vehicles today are virtually made everywhere, with labour so divided that nobody outside the inner circles of the corporation can even track its path.

In sum, the current potential of organized labour to reclaim its use value is low, and the international division of labour may be the most backward point of prefiguration. Yet even here, significant openings exist to bring along ecosystemic development. Three can be noted, two of them tendencies, the third a necessary possibility.

First, we might remind ourselves again of the Bruderhof, who survive rather well in a heavily industrialized market thanks to their communistic mode of social organization, which blunts the effects of capital's force field. Such a model can be duplicated widely through a limited portion of the industrial system. No, it will not presently include the making of automobiles, passenger planes, missiles, telecommunication networks, and so on. But this leaves a considerable amount of industrial production open to the incursions of developing ecological ensembles, so long as these are protected from the force field through a heightened anti-capitalist intentionality. That is what has been missing by and large from the much-touted green business movement, which accordingly has succumbed time and again to the nefarious effects of the market. There is nothing wrong with 'green enterprise', therefore, so long as it does not sink into 'green capitalism', with its accompaniment of exploiting labour, competition for market share, and so forth.

This tells us little about the great mass of proletarians whose labour holds up the capitalist world. However, even here there have been significant stirrings, as the class struggle has become internationalized in the face of globalization, and even begun to take on an ecological consciousness. In the first six months of 2000, huge strikes, some of general proportions, broke out across the globe: Nigeria, South Africa, South Korea, India, Uruguay and Argentina, to cite only the most massive. What makes this significant in terms of our argument is that the strikes represent points of rebellion against *globalized* capital, mainly as administered by the IMF, though carried out by national bourgeoisies.[8] This introduces a universalizing moment into labour politics, drawing the eyes of labour to wider horizons—within each nation (in India, for example, the strikers, 20 million strong, included farmers and factory workers), between nations, and, critically, toward an ecological inclusion of nature. When the instrument of capital is less the individual firm attempting to maximize value-extraction and cut costs than the boundary-dissolving instruments of globalization, then grounds for a genuinely globalized resistance are also in place. For the IMF, World Bank and WTO put their pressure on whole nations, and a nation in this context comprises territory along with the society upon it. It is globalization's destiny to break boundaries, but this means also that global capital's regime cannot legitimate itself as did the classical nation-state, leaving the realm of nature open for recovery by oppositional forces. When the forests as well as the hospitals and trade unions are subjected to capital's onslaught, resistance begins to encompass nature as well as labour.

In fact, labour's most cherished values are already immanently ecocentric. When working people sing 'Solidarity forever', they express humanity's deepest wishes for wholeness. The notion of a 'union' itself prefigures solidarity, as a process of coming together, a joining of working people into a larger entity. Solidarity is as much a subjective experience as it is an objective connection. Subjectively, solidarity corresponds to a partial dissolving of the harsh separateness imposed by egoic being, replacing it by joining into a collectivity appropriating a previously suppressed power, and achieving historical agency. If, under capital, all that is solid melts into air, with the self-organization of labour, what been alienated achieves effective solidity, that is, ecosystemic integrity. The mutual receptivity it engages is one of the most intense and ennobling experiences that human beings can undergo.

Whether this can be extended depends on a third development not yet on the horizon, but necessary if ecosocialism is to move forward. We have spoken of the activating potentials aroused in ecological ensembles. At first, these are scattered and, given the present intellectual climate, remote from an anti-capitalist orientation, much less the further development into a demand for socialism. As these develop into communities of resistance, their activating potentials can come together into the germ of a consciously 'Ecosocialist Party', an organization that takes it upon itself, from country to country, and transnationally as well, consciously to organize the struggle.

The Ecosocialist Party and Its Victory

Two models of party-building dominated the last century: the parliamentary parties of the bourgeois democracies and the 'vanguard' Leninist party of the Bolshevik tradition. Neither model can suit the ecosocialist project, which cannot be voted into power, and dies immediately if internal democracy is not made integral to its growth, as proved the case with Leninism. Leninist parties succeeded in installing first-epoch socialism chiefly because they were configured to the largely pre-capitalist societies in which the revolutions succeeded. Those capitalisms vanquished by first-epoch socialism were either imperial offshoots of metropolitan capital, or backward regimes grafted on to a largely precapitalist society. They encompassed neither the internal penetration nor the external global reach of capital's present order, both of which radically change the revolutionary project.

Modern capitalism legitimates itself by invoking 'democratic values'. This is spurious, as we have seen, but, however unfulfilled, it is a real promise that rests upon a definite foundation. By fragmenting life-worlds and traditional hierarchies, capital sets humanity loose into an unfree freedom of formal liberty and stunted development. The uneasy balance is kept going in capitalist institutions, which bind it for purpose of accumulation. To go beyond capital, one begins, then, with the betrayed promise of freedom and builds from there. It follows that the means of transformation have to be as free as the ends. That is why vanguardism, where the party is separate from as well as ahead of the people, is a non-starter in today's climate. Only a freely evolving praxis of participation can mobilize the imagination and bring together the innumerable points at which anti-capitalist struggle originates. And only a 'party-like' formation that postulates a goal common to all struggles without constraining them from above can organize this into 'solidarity solidified' and press toward power. Thus the party is formed from its own dialectic; it is a 'holding together' both objectively and subjectively—the former being the provision of material conditions, the latter being the attunement to intersubjective and relational nuance, all subsumed into the practical notion that dialectic is a matter of artfulness and subtlety.

Though open to individuals, the ecosocialist party should be grounded in communities of resistance. Delegation from such communities will supply the cadre of party activists as such, and the assembly that is its strategic and deliberative body. The party is to be internally funded through contributions by members, structured in such a way that no alienating force can take financial control. The delegates and such administrative bodies as may arise within this structure are to rotate on a regular basis and to be subject to recall. Further, the deliberations of the assembly, indeed all the activities of the party except certain tactical questions (for example, the details of a direct action), are to be open and transparent. Let the world see clearly what the party stands for—if this is worthwhile, it will only draw in more participants; if not, one needs to find out sooner rather than later.

The various green parties that have arisen across the world (as of this writing, in some 80 countries) are an important movement in this direction. Experience has shown, however, that by defining themselves as a progressive populism within the framework of bourgeois democracy, greens are solidifying as a kind of intermediate formation that stops considerably short of what is needed for transformation.[9] Green activists continue to make valuable contributions, but their parties lack a prefigurative vision surpassing the given society. As a result, green parties tend to lapse into narrow reformism and anarchic bickering. And when they have achieved some state power, as in Europe, greens have proven loyal to capital, giving it a shield of ecological responsibility.

One sign of the limits of green politics as currently practised has been a severe inability to reach out to communities of non-European origin. Frequently chastised for their lily-white make-up, greens regularly inveigh against the problem and resolve to do better. Yet little changes. The reason cuts to the core of the green dilemma: the parochial values intrinsic to their localism. Unless the notion of community is advanced in a universalizing way, it loses transformative power and, despite good intentions, drifts towards ethnocentricity. Therefore the greens' inertia on questions such as immigration and prison reform, and their general inability to appeal with more than token gestures to blacks and Latinos, are no oversight. These are manifestations of an inability to see beyond capital itself that all too often renders green politics, to choose an unfashionable but vivid term, petty-bourgeois.

With anti-capitalism the point of reference, one sees the whole of society, as well as its concrete workings. The ecological crisis and imperial expansion now appear as distinct and deeply connected manifestations of the same dynamic—invasive, cancerous growth tearing up nature and humanity. Today's buzzword, 'globalization', is imperialism's currently prime manifestation. But the history of empire is a narrative of the creation of peoples and the races themselves, including the subalterns who inhabit the South. From this perspective, a politics against and beyond capital needs to be as firmly rooted in overcoming racism as in ecological mending. The two themes intersect directly in the 'environmental justice' movement, grounded in the defence against capitalist penetration and pollution by communities of colour, and often led by women.[10]

Ecosocialism will be international or it will be nothing. And when its history is written, a starting point will be noted as 1 January 1994—the day that NAFTA went into effect and the EZLN (Zapatista Army for National Liberation) launched a revolution of the oppressed in Chiapas, Mexico. The Zapatistas provide perhaps the first model of a revolutionary movement on a bioregional scale. Despite constant harassment by an army vastly superior in firepower, the Zapatistas retain a kind of ecosystemic integrity. They form a society within a state and without a state, productively united in resistance. What Marx said of the Paris Commune, that it lived the idea of the 'dictatorship of the proletariat', could be said, therefore, of the Zapatista path, with the wider lesson that there can be no single way valid for all peoples, but rather a multiplicity of ways defined by concrete societies, joined in common opposition to global capital.[11]

Another variant, more defined and less embattled, is the town of Gaviotas in the Colombian highlands. Here, beginning in 1971, one of the harshest environments on earth has been transformed by creative labour using ecologically rational technology. On what was once a blighted and arid plain, the soil toxic with naturally occurring aluminium, today stands a reforestation project larger than all the rest of Colombia's projects combined, some 6 million trees, a source of resin and musical instruments. These and other commodities are produced outside capitalist circuits, and without a capitalist state—in other words, with enhanced use-values and reduced exchange-value—an island of non-capitalist and ecological production that could become part of an archipelago of anti-capitalist and ecological production.[12]

If, that is, oppositional forces became strong enough, and took the shape, broadly conceived, of an international people's ecosocialist party or effective coalition of similarly constructed bodies. Then one day there could be a furtherance of the pressure on instruments of global capital that began with the great agitations of 1999–2000. James O'Connor has recently imagined something of this sort:

if you think about it, poverty can be abolished in a few months, assuming the political will and the economic and ecological resources. First step, make poverty abolition the basic goal of international politics. Second step, allocate some billions of dollars of World Bank, IMF, regional development bank, and other monies to the task at hand. Third step, employ these monies, not for human capital or any other kind of capital, but to use local biomass for building homes, schools, and the rest; paying (well) public health and medical technicians, teachers of the 'pedagogy of the oppressed' variety, psychologists of the Fanon-type, planners of the Kerala[13] or Gaviota variety, and organizers of the type presently engaged in the anti-globalist movement (including NGO people of course) . . . Then, choose investment projects, not in terms of [Environmental Impact Reports] that seek to minimize damage to local or regional ecologies but rather to maximize ecological values, community values, cultural values, public health values, and so on: a simple reversal of existing capitalist values and investment criteria. Not 'safe food' but 'nourishing food.' Not 'adequate housing' but 'excellent housing.' Not 'mass transport' but 'public transit of different types that are a pleasure to utilize.' Obviously, not 'chemical-laced' agriculture but 'pesticide-free agronomy.' Not 'food monopolies' but 'farm-to-market global distribution.' The tragedy is that so many people know 'what is to be done,' based on tens of thousands of local and regional experiments and practices, from the allocation of water to the production and allocation of steel (in the U.S. during WWII, for example), yet we can do little to make a world in which use value subordinates exchange value (and concrete labor subordinates abstract labor) given the present-day monopoly of power by capital, capital markets, the capitalist state, and capitalist international agencies. Just suppose the IMF, WB, et al., were reduced to the status of the IHO, ILO, and other branches of the 'international peoples' state,' while the latter's power was expanded to the level of the present-day WB and IMF. That would be something, wouldn't it? The problem of course is not a technical one, a practical problem, but a political problem, the problem of capitalist power, in and outside the markets, and no movement can challenge capitalist power with success without adopting its own political aims and socio-economic alternatives.[14]

Yes, it would be something. And because a movement of the sort will be ecosocialist and not populist, it will be infused with a spirit that agitates for these changes yet regards them prefiguratively and does not settle for them. This is the reason we postulate a goal far off the present map: because it offers the hope, vision and energy to transform the present.

If such events as O'Connor envisions were to come to pass, they would not yet be ecosocialism, but they would form a kind of self-generative and non-linear dialectic that can rapidly accelerate the motion toward ecosocialism. After all, it is the 'tens of thousands of local and regional experiments and practices' who would have had to join with communities of activation to make this possible, and whose power would be accordingly magnified by it. And being magnified, the Zapatistas, and the Gaviotistas, and the Indymedia centres that connect them, and the politicized collectives of farmers from around the world, and the teacher's associations, and the ecologically radicalized fractions of the labour movement, and the little Bruderhof-like manufacturing collectives making ecologically sane products with the aid of local credit unions, and all the ten thousand locally originating but universally striving community formations—all would come together in solidarity to make such an event, and, in its aftermath, to press for further transformation.

There is no point in predicting a scenario according to which this will expand, beyond the condition that it occur in the context of capital's incapability of regulating the ecological crisis. At some time within this span, the communities arising from the process may be imagined to grow to a point of relative autonomy such that they can begin providing material support for activists, with bases of operation and—in the case of those considerable number of communities producing food, wool, hemp, solar technology, and so on—the actual means of subsistence for people engaged in revolutionary struggle. It must also be presumed—a large but feasible order—that these people will have developed the spiritual and psychological strength enabling them to go forward. For there should be no mistake: the struggle for ecosocialism is no technical or voluntaristic process, but a radical transforming of self as well as world to link up in ever-widening and deepening solidarity. Here is where post-patriarchal values will come forward, radicalizing human being itself for the struggle.

Now the movement of events is self-sustaining, rapid and dramatic. Communities of place and of praxis increasingly coalesce to form miniature societies, and these enter into relations with others both inside and outside the national boundary. Capital may be expected to respond with heightened efforts at repression. A heroic phase begins, with much sacrifice. The awesome might of the capital system now encounters a set of factors it has never dealt with before:

- The forces against it are both numerous and dispersed.
- They operate with changed needs, and on the basis of a kind of production capable of sustaining itself with small inputs and labour-intensive technologies; and they have secure bases

and 'safe houses' in the intentional communities of resistance, now extending across national boundaries.

- Their many allies in the interstices of the mainstream society are capable of forming support groups and 'underground railroads'.
- As with all successful forms of revolutionary protest, the oppositional forces are capable of shutting down normal production through strikes, boycotts, and mass actions.
- The forces of capital have lost confidence, and are further undermined by support for the revolution within the alternative parties and their various niches in the state. This extends to armies and police. When the first of these lays down their arms and joins the revolution, the turning point is reached.
- The behaviour of the revolutionaries is spiritually superior, and the examples they set are given credibility and persuasiveness by the brute facts of the crisis and the gathering realization that what is at stake here is not so much the redistribution of wealth as the sustenance of life itself.

Thus it could be that in an increasingly hectic period, millions of people take to the streets, and join together in global solidarity—with each other, with the communities of resistance, and with their comrades in other nations—bringing normal social activity to a halt, petitioning the state and refusing to take 'no' for an answer, and driving capital into ever smaller pens. With defections mounting and the irreducible fact all around that the people demand a new beginning in order to save the planetary ecology, the state apparatus passes into new hands, the expropriators are expropriated, and the 500-year regime of capital falls.

A Usufructuary of The Earth

From the standpoint of a higher economic form of society, private ownership of the globe by single individuals will appear quite as absurd as private ownership of one man by another. Even a whole society, a nation, or even all simultaneously existing societies taken together, are not the owners of the globe. They are only its possessors, its usufructuaries, and, like *boni patres familias*, they must hand it down to succeeding generations in an improved condition.[15]

Thus wrote Karl Marx, in the third volume of *Capital*. The notion of usufruct is an ancient one, with roots going back to the Code of Hammurabi, although the word itself arises in Roman law, where it applied to ambiguities between masters and slaves with respect to property. It appears again in Islamic law, and in the legal arrangements of the Aztecs and the Napoleonic Code—indeed, wherever the notion of property reveals its inherent contradictions. Interestingly, the Latin word condenses the two meanings of *use*—as in use-value, and *enjoyment*—as in the gratification expressed in freely associated labour. As commonly understood today, a usufructuary relationship is where one uses, enjoys—and through that, improves—another's property, as, for instance, community groups would use, enjoy and improve an abandoned city lot by collectively building a garden there.

Because we are human to the degree that we creatively engage nature, the self is defined through its extensions into the material world. We become who we are by *appropriating* nature, transforming and incorporating it, and it is within this frame that the notion of property logically arises. Therefore a person with no possessions whatsoever is no individual at all, as s/he has no particular grounding in nature. It follows that in an ecologically realized society everyone will have rights of ownership—a place of one's own, decorated according to taste, personal possessions, such as books, clothing, objects of beauty, likewise—and, of special significance, rights of use and ownership over those means of production necessary to express the creativity of human nature. This latter most definitely includes the body—whence the reproductive rights of women are logically secured, along with the rights of free sexual expression.

The notion of property becomes self-contradictory because each individual person emerges in a tissue of social relations, and, in Donne's words, is never an island. Each self is therefore a part of all other selves, and property is inexorably tied into a dialectic with others. This may be imagined as a set of nested circles. At the centre is the self, and here ownership exists in relatively absolute terms, beginning with the body, intrinsically the property of each person. As the circles extend, issues of sharing arise from early childhood on, each potentially resolvable according to the principle that the full self is enhanced more by giving than by taking. For a realized being is generous. The more lightly material possessions weigh upon the self, the more fully can one give, and the richer one becomes. It is the work of socialism to make this potentiality actual.

The domain of use-value will be the site of contestation. To restore use-value means to take things concretely and sensuously, as befits an authentic relation of ownership—but by the same gesture, lightly, since things are enjoyed for themselves and not as buttresses for a shaky ego. Under capital, as Marx famously saw, what is produced is fetishized by the shroud of exchange-value—made remote and magical. In the fetishized world, nothing is ever really owned, since everything can be exchanged, taken away and abstracted. This stimulates the thirst for possessions that rages under capitalist rule. The unappeasable craving for things—and money to get things—is the necessary underpinning of accumulation and the subjective dynamic of the ecological crisis. The circuits of capitalist society are defined by *having*—and excluding others from having—until we arrive at a society of gated communities inhabited by lonely egos, each split from all and the atomized selves split from nature.[16] They can only be resolved in a society that permits this hunger to wither, and this requires the release of labour from the bondage imposed by exchange value.

Ecosocialist society will be defined by *being*, achieved by giving oneself to others and restoring a receptive relation to nature. Ecosystemic integrity is to be restored across all the nested circles of human participation—the family, the community, the nation, the international community, or, with a leap across the humanity/nature membrane, the planet, and, beyond it, the universe. For capital, property rights of the individual ego are sacrosanct, and become solidified into class structures, whence they succeed in dispossessing masses of people from their inherent ownership of the means to produce creatively. This is only the legal aspect of a regime of fetishized relations. Within ecosocialism, the bounds of the individual ego are surpassed as use-value overcomes exchange-value and opens a way for the realization of intrinsic value. In the new society, the right of an individual freely to appropriate the means of self-expression is paramount. Society is structured to give this primacy by differentiating ownership between individual and collectivity. Although each person—and each family as the extension of personhood into reproduction—has an inalienable right to good housing, the ownership as such of the housing and the land upon which it stands is collective, and granted by the collectivity. In this way, there arise distinct limits on the amount of property individuals can control, both from the standpoint of domestic usage as well as that of the control over productive resources. No person is to be allowed to arrogate such resources, therefore, as would permit the alienation of means of production from another. There will be no such arrangement as now obtains, where well over a billion absolutely landless people, along with several billion more who must sell themselves on the market because they are effectively without control over more than the slenderest threads of property, confront a tiny fraction who own virtually all the wealth-producing world. Extending further out along the nested circles, we find that those things essential for social production are to be shared by all and not owned by the few.

The extension proceeds, as Marx realizes, to the planetary level, and devolves downward from there to govern the particular laws of ecosocialist society. Taken all in all, the earth we inhabit should be regarded not as our collective property but as a wondrous matrix from which we emerge and to which we return. Perhaps it will be easier to dislodge the ruling class from their cancerous ownership if we remind ourselves that this is not done to transfer ownership to 'the people' or some surrogate. Indeed, ownership of the planet is a pathetic illusion. It is plain *hubris* to think that the earth, or nature, can be owned—and stupid to boot, as though one can own that which gives us *being*, and whose becoming we express. The notion of standing over and against the earth in order to own it is central to the domination of nature. A usufructuary is all we can claim with regard to the earth. But this demands that our species proves its worth by using, enjoying and improving the globe that is our home. From that reigning principle can be derived those individual regulations that are to subserve the metabolism between humanity and nature called ecosocialism. No class ownership of the means of production stands at one pole, absolute ownership of one's self as the other—for the self is the earth emerging into consciousness at this one point of individuality; while the institutions of ecosocialist society exist to set going the ways of using, enjoying and improving our common firmament.

The society that emerges from the storm of the revolution will at first be only marginally capable of fulfilling this project. Its highest priority is to set things going in a truly ecosocialist direction and its first goal is to secure the 'free association of producers'. Each term here needs to be respected. The association is *free* because in it people self-determine; hence society must make means of production accessible to all. It is a free *association* because life is collective; therefore the relevant political unit is a collectivity drawn together by mutual productive activity. And it is of *producers*, which is to be taken in the human-natural sense and not economistically. This means that the whole making of the human world is to be taken into account rather than just that which contributes or controls exchange-value. Since a core goal of ecosocialism is the diminution of exchange-value's domain, it valorizes forms of productive activity to the degree that these foster ecosystemic integrity, whether this be the raising of beautiful children, the growing of organic gardens, the playing of excellent string quartets, the cleaning of streets, the making of composting toilets, or the invention of new technologies for turning solar energy into fuel cells.

To secure the association, we need ways of preventing the emergence of alienating agencies. Private ownership of means of production has been shown to be the chief of these under capital, but the Soviets showed that the state can just as well fill this role. And since the gain of state power by the revolution is essential for redirecting society, so must the revolution give high priority to building ways of preventing the state from turning into a monster over society. A key principle is the internal development of true democracy, the absence of which crippled all previous socialisms. That is why alternative party-building in the pre-revolutionary period is important—not to win state power in the here and now, which is out of the question, but to democratize the state insofar as possible, and to train people in the ways of self-governance so that when the revolution is made they will be in a position to sustain democratic development. Another essential principle is the enfranchisement of productive communities, enabling power to flow from the producers—or, since everyone produces and has multiple productive affiliations, from those collectivities that best express their free association and the enhancement of ecosystemic integrity.

As the revolution begins its work, we find that society comprises four fractions. First are those who have engaged in revolutionary practice, either as political agents and/or as members of communities of resistance. Second are those who did not participate actively yet whose productive activity is directly compatible with ecological production—the housewives, nurses, schoolteachers, librarians, technicians, independent farmers, and so on, along with the very old, the very young, the ill, and those on welfare or otherwise marginalized (including many of those in prison). Third are those whose pre-revolutionary practice was given over to capital—the bourgeoisie proper, along with those legions involved in work worthless from an ecosocialist standpoint—the PR men, the car salesmen, the ad executives, the supermodels, the cast of 'Survivor' and like shows, loan sharks, security guards, wealth psychologists, and so on. Finally, we find arrayed between the second and third categories the workers whose activity added surplus value to capitalist commodities, as industrial proletarians, field hands, truckdrivers, and so forth. Many of these latter worked in polluting, ecologically destructive settings; others in industries that have little or no place in an ecologically rational society, for example weapons factories or those making diet sodas. All will have to be provided for and retrained if society is to be rebuilt.

Clearly, it will be no easy matter to reallocate productive activity among so vast an assemblage. The following broad principles may be useful:

- An interim assembly of delegates from the revolutionary communities of resistance constitutes itself as an agency to handle the redistribution of social roles and assets, to make sure that all are provided for out of common stocks, and to exert such force as is necessary to reorganize society. The assembly will convene in widespread locations and send delegations to regional, state, national and international bodies. Each level will have an executive council with rotating leadership, recallable by votes from the level below.
- Productive communities (and now they may be authentically called 'cooperatives'), whether of place or praxis, form the political as well as economic unit of society. The priority of those groups who made the revolution will be to organize others and create paths for the rapid assimilation of other workers to the network of productive communities. This includes all able-bodied people, the ex-perpetrators of capital as well, who—with a few

egregiously criminal exceptions—will be allowed to participate in building an ecosocialist world.

- People may join whatever unit they wish (although standards will have to be set, as for health-care providers), and can have associate membership in others—for example, a doctor who is also a father can join his local health service community and have associate membership in the child-rearing community, the community theatre, and so on. The interim assembly will have to devise incentives to make sure that vital functions are maintained. In the initial stages, before ecosocialist values have been fully internalized, these would include differential remuneration, perhaps a factor of three separating the least from most paid.
- In each locality, one such community would directly administer the area of jurisdiction. For example, town government would be considered a collective whose product is the provision of ecologically sound governance—and also an assembly elected by all the inhabitants of that area. Each area, therefore, may have several assemblies—one for administration, another for wider spheres of governance.
- Each productive community participates fully as soon as it demonstrates its fidelity to ecosocialist principles. And as it joins, it plays a political role in its local assembly, sending delegates and votes to the next level.
- Two vitally important functions will devolve on to the more central assemblies. The first will be to monitor the degree that communities under its jurisdiction are contributing to ecosystemic integrity, and to give a kind of weight to communities according to their contribution. This supervisory body potentially has considerable power, limited, however, by the fact that it serves at the behest of the productive communities themselves.
- The second function pertains to the general coordination of social activities, the provision of society-wide services like rail systems, the allocation of resources, the reinvestment of the social product, and the harmonization of relations between regions at all levels, including the international. There is no avoiding a state-like function, which must be eventually transferred from the interim assembly and handled at the level of the society as a whole through appropriate and democratically responsive committees. The key to its success—and to that of the system as a whole—lies in the degree to which democracy has become a living presence in society.

Notes

1. Marx 1963: 107. I became acquainted with this passage through Mészáros 1996.
2. 'There is no alternative', is often acronymously called 'TINA', is a phrase ascribed to Margaret Thatcher, and useful for rhetorical purposes. I will eschew it/her here, because of the misogynistic implication.
3. See Gunn and Gunn 1991 and Meeker-Lowry 1988 for discussion of how to build local economies in an anti-capitalist direction.

Gare 2000 advocates the building of such institutions as a major prefigurative step toward ecosocialism.

4. The British socialists' use of Blake's anthem from *Milton*, 'And did those feet in ancient time/Walk upon England's mountains green?' ending with the immortal words, 'I will not cease from mental fight,/Nor shall my sword sleep in my hand,/ Till we have built Jerusalem,/ In England's green and

pleasant land' (Blake 1977: 514), is the best example, especially for how readily it translates into the terms of ecosocialism.
5. Meister Eckhart has a splendid saying, 'Let us pray to God to be rid of "God"', which applies perfectly here. For a general discussion, see Kovel 1998.
6. All 'progressive' education, in my view, follows this model, famously laid out by Paulo Freire (Freire 1970).
7. By August 2000, there were 28 such centres, in places ranging from Los Angeles to the Congo. For the many aspects of the alternative media movement, see Halleck 2001.
8. Moody 2000. For example, the IMF forced the Nigerian government to deregulate and end its $2 billion subsidy of fuel prices, the resultant rise of which precipitated a general strike. In Korea, the strikes were in opposition to draconian working hours imposed by the IMF as a condition for bailing the country out of the financial crisis of 1998. In South Africa, 4 million workers protested IMF-imposed austerity from the mid-1990s.

In India, 20 million walked out, in a strike aimed, in the words of one of its leaders, 'against the surrender of the country's economic autonomy before the World Trade Organization and the International Monetary Fund'. Similar patterns were seen in Uruguay and Argentina, as new presidents took office scurrying to impose IMF austerity. See also Moody 1997.
9. Rensenbrink 1999 exemplifies this tendency. For a detailed account of green politics in the USA from an ecofeminist perspective, see Gaard 1998.
10. Faber 1998.
11. Marx 1978.
12. Weisman 1998.
13. A state in southern India with a long record of communist administrations and remarkable ecological development, including the empowerment of women. See Parayil 2000.
14. O'Connor 2001.
15. Marx 1967: 776.
16. Prefigured by Marx in the 1844 manuscripts. Marx 1978.

References

Blake, W. (1977), "The Sick Rose", from "Songs of Experience," and *Milton*, in Alicial Ostriker (ed.), *The Complete Poems* (Harmondsworth: Penguin).

Faber, D. (1998) (ed.), *The Struggle for Ecological Democracy* (New York: Guilford).

Freire, P. (1970), *Pedagogy of the Oppressed* (New York: Continuum).

Gaard, G. (1998), *Ecological Politics* (Philadelphia: Temple University Press).

Gare, A. (2000), "Creating an Ecological Socialist Future," *Capitalism, Nature, Socialism*, 11 (2): 23–40.

Gunn, C. and Gunn, H. (1991), *Reclaiming Capital* (Ithaca, NY: Cornell University Press).

Halleck, D. (2001), *Hand-Held Visions* (New York: Fordham University Press).

Kovel, J. (1998), *History and Spirit*, 2nd edn. (Warner, NH: Essential Books).

Marx, K. (1963) [1847], *The Poverty of Philosophy* (New York: International Publishers).

Marx, K. (1967) [1894], *Capital, Vol. 3*, ed. Frederick Engels (New York: International Publishers).

Marx, K. (1978) [1844], *Economic and Philosophic Manuscripts of 1844*. In R. Tucker (ed.), *The Marx-Engels Reader* (New York: W. W. Norton, 1978), 66–125.

Marx, K. and Engels, F. (1978) [1871], *The Civil War in France*. In R. Tucker (ed.), *The Marx-Engels Reader* (New York: W. W. Norton, 1978), 618–52.

Meeker-Lowery, S. (1988), *Economics as if the Earth Really Mattered* (Philadelphia: New Society Publishers).

Mészáros, I. (1996), *Beyond Capital* (New York: Monthly Review Press).

Moody, K. (1997), *Workers in a Lean World* (London: Verso).

Moody, K. (2000), "Global Labor Stands up to Global Capital," *Labor Notes*, July: 8.

O'Connor, J. (2001), "House Organ," *Capitalism, Nature, Socialism*, 13 (1): 1.

Parayil, G. (2000) (ed.), *Kerala: The Development Experience* (London: Zed Books).

Rensenbrink, J. (1999), *Against All Odds* (Raymond, ME: Leopold Press).

Tucker, R. (1978) (ed.), *The Marx-Engels Reader* (New York: W. W. Norton).

Weisman, A. (1998), *Gaviotas* (White River Junction, VT: Chelsea Green).

Section X: Environmental Justice

The basic claim, and organizing principle, of the North American environmental justice movement is that the poor, people of colour, and indigenous peoples are disproportionately at risk from environmental hazards. The movement asserts an inequity in the siting of toxic waste sites, hazardous materials landfills, incinerators, municipal landfills, and polluting industry. It has addressed issues as diverse as occupational illnesses borne by the poor and people of colour (such as those linked to dioxin, pesticide, or solvent exposure) and the displacement and poisoning of indigenous populations faced with uranium mining or hydro-electric dams.

While there is substantial diversity in the movement (which some might argue is actually a number of distinct, yet related, movements), its political focus is generally centred on distributive justice, cultural recognition, and procedural equity. Community groups argue for more equity (and overall reduction) in exposure to environmental risks and hazards, but they also often demand recognition of their unique cultural positions and participation in the development of environmental policy. In this, the movement challenges both mainstream environmental organizing and reformist efforts on the part of government. Large mainstream environmental groups are seen as too distant, paternalistic, and unrepresentative; and governmental reforms are often criticized for not only failing to address questions of the distribution of hazards, but also for not involving communities in the policy process. In response to the political shortcomings of these organizing strategies, the environmental justice movement has eschewed traditional, centralized organizations and has instead relied on the networking of local groups in regions or around particular issues. These networks not only lobby government agencies, but often take their case, and their collective power, directly to targeted industries, corporations, and/or communities.

Our first selection is a statement of the 'Principles of Environmental Justice' adopted at the First National People of Color Environmental Leadership Summit in October 1991 in Washington, DC. This statement identifies the environmental problems targeted by the movement and the politics needed to address them. The selection by Robert Bullard, one of the leading academic observers of the movement, lays out elements of what he calls the 'environmental justice framework' and discusses key issues for the movement. Finally, the piece by Celene Krauss examines the politicization of women in the environmental justice movement. From their common experience and perspective as mothers, and their particular cultural identities, Krauss argues that women in the movement have become keenly aware of the gender, class, and ethnic dimensions of environmental inequities. Along the way, they have learned much about the biases of the political process and the limitations of mainstream environmental organizing.

Further Reading

The first, and classic, book on environmental justice is Robert Bullard's *Dumping in Dixie: Race, Class, and Environmental Quality* (3rd edition, 2000). There are a number of good anthologies on environmental justice, including two by Bullard himself: *Confronting Environmental Racism: Voices from the Grassroots* (1993) and *Unequal Protection: Environmental Justice and Communities of Color* (1994). Bunyan Bryant has also edited two volumes: *Race and the Incidence of Environmental Hazards* (1992), which focuses on the analysis of racial inequities in environmental risk, and *Environmental Justice: Issues, Policies, and Solutions* (1995), which develops policy suggestions. David Camacho's *Environmental Injustices, Political Struggles* (1998) also examines policy issues. Daniel Faber (ed.), *The Struggle for Ecological Democracy: Environmental Justice Movements in the United States* (1998), is another excellent general collection. A recent collection examines the interface of environmental justice and sustainability: Julian Ageyman, Robert Bullard, and Bob Evans (eds), *Just Sustainabilities* (2003).

A fine analysis of the development of environmental justice is offered by Luke Cole and Sheila Foster in *From the Ground Up: Environmental Racism and the Rise of the Environmental Justice Movement* (2000). For an examination of the environmental justice movement as an example of a new form of pluralist politics, see David Schlosberg, *Environmental Justice and the New Pluralism: The Challenge of Difference for Environmentalism* (1999). Nicholas Low and Brendan Gleeson, in *Justice, Society, and Nature* (1999), blend theory and practice, distribution and ecocentrism, domestic and international concerns. An excellent source of environmental justice information online, along with links to various issues and groups, can be found through Clark Atlanta University's Environmental Justice Resource Center, headed by Robert Bullard (<http://www.ejrc.cau.edu/>).

30 Principles of Environmental Justice

First National People of Color Environmental Leadership Summit

Preamble

We the people of color, gathered together at this multi-national People of Color Environmental Leadership Summit, to begin to build a national and international movement of all peoples of color to fight the destruction and taking of our lands and communities, do hereby re-establish our spiritual interdependence to the sacredness of our Mother Earth; to respect and celebrate each of our culture's languages and beliefs about the natural world and our roles in healing ourselves; to insure environmental justice; to promote economic alternatives which would contribute to the development of environmentally safe livelihoods; and, to secure our political, economic and cultural liberation that has been denied for over 500 years of colonization and oppression, resulting in the poisoning of our communities and land and the genocide of our peoples, do affirm and adopt these Principles of Environmental Justice:

1. **Environmental justice** affirms the sacredness of Mother Earth, ecological unity and the interdependence of all species, and the right to be free from ecological destruction.

2. **Environmental justice** demands that public policy be based on mutual respect and justice for all peoples, free from any form of discrimination or bias.

3. **Environmental justice** mandates the right to ethical, balanced and responsible uses of land and renewable resources in the interest of a sustainable planet for humans and other living things.

4. **Environmental justice** calls for universal protection from nuclear testing, extraction, production and disposal of toxic/hazardous wastes and poisons and nuclear testing that threaten the fundamental right to clean air, land, water, and food.

5. **Environmental justice** affirms the fundamental right to political, economic, cultural and environmental self-determination of all peoples.

6. **Environmental justice** demands the cessation of the production of all toxins, hazardous wastes, and radioactive materials, and that all past and current producers be held strictly accountable to the people for detoxification and the containment at the point of production.

From 'Principles of Environmental Justice'. Adopted at the First National People of Color Environmental Leadership Summit, Washington DC, October 1991.

7. **Environmental justice** demands the right to participate as equal partners at every level of decision-making including needs assessment, planning, implementation, enforcement and evaluation.

8. **Environmental justice** affirms the right of all workers to a safe and healthy work environment, without being forced to choose between an unsafe livelihood and unemployment. It also affirms the right of those who work at home to be free from environmental hazards.

9. **Environmental justice** protects the right of victims of environmental injustice to receive full compensation and reparations for damages as well as quality health care.

10. **Environmental justice** considers governmental acts of environmental injustice a violation of international law, the Universal Declaration on Human Rights, and the United Nations Convention on Genocide.

11. **Environmental justice** must recognize a special legal and natural relationship of Native Peoples to the US government through treaties, agreements, compacts, and covenants affirming sovereignty and self-determination.

12. **Environmental justice** affirms the need for urban and rural ecological policies to clean up and rebuild our cities and rural areas in balance with nature, honoring the cultural integrity of all our communities, and providing fair access for all to the full range of resources.

13. **Environmental justice** calls for the strict enforcement of principles of informed consent, and a halt to the testing of experimental reproductive and medical procedures and vaccinations on people of color.

14. **Environmental justice** opposes the destructive operations of multi-national corporations.

15. **Environmental justice** opposes military occupation, repression and exploitation of lands, peoples and cultures, and other life forms.

16. **Environmental justice** calls for the education of present and future generations which emphasizes social and environmental issues, based on our experience and an appreciation of our diverse cultural perspectives.

17. **Environmental justice** requires that we, as individuals, make personal and consumer choices to consume as little of Mother Earth's resources and to produce as little waste as possible; and make the conscious decision to challenge and reprioritize our lifestyles to insure the health of the natural world for present and future generations.

Adopted October 7, 1991, Washington, DC.

31 Environmental Justice in the 21st Century

Robert D. Bullard

Hardly a day passes without the media discovering some community or neighborhood fighting a landfill, incinerator, chemical plant, or some other polluting industry. This was not always the case. Just three decades ago, the concept of environmental justice had not registered on the radar screens of environmental, civil rights, or social justice groups.[1] Nevertheless, it should not be forgotten that Dr. Martin Luther King, Jr. went to Memphis in 1968 on an environmental and economic justice mission for the striking black garbage workers. The strikers were demanding equal pay and better work conditions. Of course, Dr. King was assassinated before he could complete his mission.

Another landmark garbage dispute took place a decade later in Houston, when African American homeowners in 1979 began a bitter fight to keep a sanitary landfill out of their suburban middle-income neighborhood.[2] Residents formed the Northeast Community Action Group or NECAG. NECAG and their attorney, Linda McKeever Bullard, filed a class action lawsuit to block the facility from being built. The 1979 lawsuit, *Bean v. Southwestern Waste Management, Inc.*, was the first of its kind to challenge the siting of a waste facility under civil rights law.

The landmark Houston case occurred three years before the environmental justice movement was catapulted into the national limelight in the rural and mostly African American Warren County, North Carolina. The environmental justice movement has come a long way since its humble beginning in Warren County, North Carolina where a PCB landfill ignited protests and over 500 arrests. The Warren County protests provided the impetus for an U.S. General Accounting Office study, *Siting of Hazardous Waste Landfills and Their Correlation with Racial and Economic Status of Surrounding Communities*.[3] That study revealed that three out of four of the off-site, commercial hazardous waste landfills in Region 4 (which comprises eight states in the South) happen to be located in predominantly African-American communities, although African-Americans made up only 20% of the region's population. More important, the protesters put "environmental racism" on the map. Fifteen years later, the state of North Carolina is required to spend over $25 million to clean up and detoxify the Warren County PCB landfill.

The Warren County protests also led the Commission for Racial Justice to produce *Toxic Waste and Race*,[4] the first national study to correlate waste facility sites and demographic characteristics. Race was found to be the most potent variable in predicting where these facilities were located—more powerful than poverty, land values, and home ownership. In 1990, *Dumping*

Online at <www.ejrc.cau.edu/ejinthe21century.htm>.

in Dixie: Race, Class, and Environmental Quality chronicled the convergence of two social movements—social justice and environmental movements—into the environmental justice movement. This book highlighted African-Americans environmental activism in the South, the same region that gave birth to the modern civil rights movement. What started out as local and often isolated community-based struggles against toxics and facility siting blossomed into a multi-issue, multi-ethnic, and multi-regional movement.

The 1991 First National People of Color Environmental Leadership Summit was probably the most important single event in the movement's history. The Summit broadened the environmental justice movement beyond its early anti-toxics focus to include issues of public health, worker safety, land use, transportation, housing, resource allocation, and community empowerment.[5] The meeting also demonstrated that it is possible to build a multi-racial grassroots movement around environmental and economic justice.[6]

Held in Washington, DC, the four-day Summit was attended by over 650 grassroots and national leaders from around the world. Delegates came from all fifty states including Alaska and Hawaii, Puerto Rico, Chile, Mexico, and as far away as the Marshall Islands. People attended the Summit to share their action strategies, redefine the environmental movement, and develop common plans for addressing environmental problems affecting people of color in the United States and around the world.

On September 27, 1991, Summit delegates adopted 17 "Principles of Environmental Justice." These principles were developed as a guide for organizing, networking, and relating to government and nongovernmental organizations (NGOs). By June 1992, Spanish and Portuguese translations of the Principles were being used and circulated by NGOs and environmental justice groups at the Earth Summit in Rio de Janeiro.

In response to growing public concern and mounting scientific evidence, President Clinton on February 11, 1994 (the second day of the national health symposium) issued Executive Order 12898, "Federal Actions to Address Environmental Justice in Minority Populations and Low-Income Populations." This Order attempts to address environmental injustice within existing federal laws and regulations.

Executive Order 12898 reinforces the 35-year old Civil Rights Act of 1964, Title VI, which prohibits discriminatory practices in programs receiving federal funds. The Order also focuses the spotlight back on the National Environmental Policy Act (NEPA), a twenty-five-year-old law that set policy goals for the protection, maintenance, and enhancement of the environment. NEPA's goal is to ensure for all Americans a safe, healthful, productive, and aesthetically and culturally pleasing environment. NEPA requires federal agencies to prepare a detailed statement on the environmental effects of proposed federal actions that significantly effect the quality of human health.

The Executive Order calls for improved methodologies for assessing and mitigating impacts, health effect from multiple and cumulative exposure, collection of data on low-income and minority populations who may be disproportionately at risk, and impacts on subsistence fishers and wildlife consumers. It also encourages participation of the impacted populations in the various phases of assessing impacts—including scoping, data gathering, alternatives, analysis, mitigation, and monitoring.

The Executive Order focuses on "subsistence" fishers and wildlife consumers. Everybody does not buy fish at the supermarket. There are many people who are subsistence fishers, who fish for protein, who basically subsidize their budgets, and their diets by fishing from rivers, streams, and lakes that happen to be polluted. These subpopulations may be underprotected when basic assumptions are made using the dominant risk paradigm.

Many grassroots activists are convinced that waiting for the government to act has endangered the health and welfare of their communities. Unlike the federal EPA, communities of color did not first discover environmental inequities in 1990. The federal EPA only took action on environmental justice concerns in 1990 after extensive prodding from grassroots environmental justice activists, educators, and academics.[7]

People of color have known about and have been living with inequitable environmental quality for decades—most without the protection of the federal, state, and local governmental agencies.[8] Environmental justice advocates continue to challenge the current environmental protection apparatus and offer their own framework for addressing environmental inequities, disparate impact, and unequal protection.

An Environmental Justice Framework

The question of environmental justice is not anchored in a debate about whether or not decision makers should tinker with risk management. The framework seeks to prevent environmental threats before they occur.[9] The environmental justice framework incorporates other social movements that seek to eliminate harmful practices (discrimination harms the victim), in housing, land use, industrial planning, health care, and sanitation services. The impact of redlining, economic disinvestment, infrastructure decline, deteriorating housing, lead poisoning, industrial pollution, poverty, and unemployment are not unrelated problems if one lives in an urban ghetto or barrio, rural hamlet, or reservation.

The environmental justice framework attempts to uncover the underlying assumptions that may contribute to and produce unequal protection. This framework brings to the surface the ethical and political questions of "who gets what, why, and how much." Some general characteristics of the framework include:

(1) *The environmental justice framework incorporates the principle of the "right" of all individuals to be protected from environmental degradation.* The precedents for this framework are the Civil Rights Act of 1964, Fair Housing Act of 1968 and as amended in 1988, and Voting Rights Act of 1965.

(2) *The environmental justice framework adopts a public health model of prevention (elimination of the threat before harm occurs) as the preferred strategy.* Impacted communities should not have to wait until causation or conclusive "proof" is established before preventive action is taken. For example, the framework offers a solution to the lead problem by shifting the primary focus from treatment (after children have been poisoned) to prevention (elimination of the threat via abating lead in houses).

Overwhelming scientific evidence exists on the ill-effects of lead on the human body. However, very little action has been taken to rid the nation of childhood lead poisoning in urban areas.

Former Health and Human Secretary Louis Sullivan tagged the "number one environmental health threat to children."[10]

The Natural Resources Defense Council, NAACP Legal Defense and Educational Fund, ACLU, and Legal Aid Society of Alameda County joined forces in 1991 and won an out-of-court settlement worth $15–20 million for a blood-lead testing program in California. The *Matthews v. Coye* lawsuit involved the State of California not living up to the federally-mandated testing of some 557,000 poor children for lead who receive Medicaid. This historic agreement triggered similar actions in other states that failed to live up to federally-mandated screening.[11]

Lead screening is an important element in this problem. However, screening is not the solution. Prevention is the solution. Surely, if termite inspections can be mandated to protect individual home investment, a lead-free home can be mandated to protect public health. Ultimately, the lead abatement debate, public health (who is affected) vs. property rights (who pays for cleanup), is a value conflict that will not be resolved by the scientific community.

(3) *The environmental justice framework shifts the burden of proof to polluters/dischargers who do harm, discriminate, or who do not give equal protection to racial and ethnic minorities, and other "protected" classes.* Under the current system, individuals who challenge polluters must "prove" that they have been harmed, discriminated against, or disproportionately impacted. Few impacted communities have the resources to hire lawyers, expert witnesses, and doctors needed to sustain such a challenge.

The environmental justice framework would require the parties that are applying for operating permits (landfills, incinerators, smelters, refineries, chemical plants, etc.) to "prove" that their operations are not harmful to human health, will not disproportionately impact racial and ethnic minorities and other protected groups, and are nondiscriminatory.

(4) *The environmental justice framework would allow disparate impact and statistical weight, as opposed to "intent," to infer discrimination.* Proving intentional or purposeful discrimination in a court of law is next to impossible, as demonstrated in *Bean v. Southwestern Waste*. It took nearly a decade after *Bean v. Southwestern Waste* for environmental discrimination to resurface in the courts.

(5) *The environmental justice framework redresses disproportionate impact through "targeted" action and resources.* This strategy would target resources where environmental and health problems are greatest (as determined by some ranking scheme but not limited to risk assessment). Reliance solely on "objective" science disguises the exploitative way the polluting industries have operated in some communities and condones a passive acceptance of the status quo. Human values are involved in determining which geographic areas are worth public investments. In the 1992, EPA report *Securing Our Legacy*, the agency describes geographic initiatives as "protecting what we love."[12]

The strategy emphasizes "pollution prevention, multimedia enforcement, research into causes and cures of environmental stress, stopping habitat loss, education, and constituency building."[13] Geographic initiatives are underway in the Chesapeake Bay, Great Lakes, Gulf of Mexico programs, and the U.S.–Mexican Border program. Environmental justice targeting would channel resources to "hot spots," communities that are overburdened with more than their "fair" share of environmental and health problems.

The dominant environmental protection paradigm reinforces instead of challenges the stratification of people (race, ethnicity, status, power, etc.), place (central cities, suburbs, rural areas, unincorporated areas, Native American reservations, etc.), and work (i.e., office workers are afforded greater protection than farm workers). The dominant paradigm exists to manage, regulate, and distribute risks. As a result, the current system has (1) institutionalized unequal enforcement, (2) traded human health for profit, (3) placed the burden of proof on the "victims" and not the polluting industry, (4) legitimated human exposure to harmful chemicals, pesticides, and hazardous substances, (5) promoted "risky" technologies such as incinerators, (6) exploited the vulnerability of economically and politically disenfranchised communities, (7) subsidized ecological destruction, (8) created an industry around risk assessment, (9) delayed cleanup actions, and (10) failed to develop pollution prevention as the overarching and dominant strategy.[14]

The mission of the federal EPA was never designed to address environmental policies and practices that result in unfair, unjust, and inequitable outcomes. EPA and other government officials are not likely to ask the questions that go to the heart of environmental injustice: What groups are most affected? Why are they affected? Who did it? What can be done to remedy the problem? How can the problem be prevented? Vulnerable communities, populations, and individuals often fall between the regulatory cracks.

Impetus for a Paradigm Shift

The environmental justice movement has changed the way scientists, researchers, policy makers, and educators go about their daily work. This "bottom-up" movement has redefined environment to include where people live, work, play, go to school, as well as how these things interact with the physical and natural world. The impetus for changing the dominant environmental protection paradigm did not come from within regulatory agencies, the polluting industry, academia, or the "industry" that has been built around risk management. The environmental justice movement is led by a loose alliance of grassroots and national environmental and civil rights leaders who question the foundation of the current environmental protection paradigm.

Despite significant improvements in environmental protection over the past several decades, millions of Americans continue to live, work, play, and go to school in unsafe and unhealthy physical environments.[15] During its 30-year history, the U.S. EPA has not always recognized that many of our government and industry practices (whether intended or unintended) have adverse impact on poor people and people of color. Growing grassroots community resistance emerged in response to practices, policies, and conditions that residents judged to be unjust, unfair, and illegal. Discrimination is a fact of life in America. Racial discrimination is also illegal.

The EPA is mandated to enforce the nation's environmental laws and regulations equally across the board. It is also required to protect all Americans—not just individuals or groups who can afford lawyers, lobbyists, and experts. Environmental protection is a right, not a privilege reserved for a few who can "vote with their feet" and escape or fend off environmental stressors that address environmental inequities.

Equity may mean different things to different people. Equity is distilled into three broad categories: procedural, geographic, and social equity.

Procedural equity refers to the "fairness" question: the extent that governing rules, regulations, evaluation criteria, and enforcement are applied uniformly across the board and in a nondiscriminatory way. Unequal protection might result from nonscientific and undemocratic decisions, exclusionary practices, public hearings held in remote locations and at inconvenient times, and use of English-only material as the language to communicate and conduct hearings for non-English speaking publics.

Geographic equity refers to location and spatial configuration of communities and their proximity to environmental hazards, noxious facilities, and locally unwanted land uses (LULUs) such as landfills, incinerators, sewer treatment plants, lead smelters, refineries, and other noxious facilities. For example, unequal protection may result from land-use decisions that determine the location of residential amenities and disamenities. Unincorporated, poor, and communities of color often suffer a "triple" vulnerability of noxious facility siting.

Social equity assesses the role of sociological factors (race, ethnicity, class, culture, life styles, political power, etc.) on environmental decision making. Poor people and people of color often work in the most dangerous jobs, live in the most polluted neighborhoods, and their children are exposed to all kinds of environmental toxins on the playgrounds and in their homes.

The nation's environmental laws, regulations, and policies are not applied uniformly—resulting in some individuals, neighborhoods, and communities being exposed to elevated health risks. A 1992 study by staff writers from the *National Law Journal* uncovered glaring inequities in the way the federal EPA enforces its laws. The authors write: There is a racial divide in the way the U.S. government cleans up toxic waste sites and punishes polluters. White communities see faster action, better results and stiffer penalties than communities where blacks, Hispanics and other minorities live. This unequal protection often occurs whether the community is wealthy or poor.[16]

These findings suggest that unequal protection is placing communities of color at special risk.

The National *Law Journal* study supplements the findings of earlier studies and reinforces what many grassroots leaders have been saying all along: not only are people of color differentially impacted by industrial pollution, they can expect different treatment from the government. Environmental decision-making operates at the juncture of science, economics, politics, special interests, and ethics. The current environmental model places communities of color at special risk.

The Impact of Racial Apartheid

Apartheid-type housing, development, and environmental policies limit mobility, reduce neighborhood options, diminish job opportunities, and decrease choices for millions of Americans.[17] The infrastructure conditions in urban areas are a result of a host of factors including the distribution of wealth, patterns of racial and economic discrimination, redlining, housing and real estate practices, location decisions of industry, and differential enforcement of land use and environmental regulations. Apartheid-type housing and development policies have resulted in limited mobility, reduced neighborhood options, decreased environmental choices, and diminished job opportunities for African Americans.

Race still plays a significant part in distributing public "benefits" and public "burdens" associated with economic growth. The roots of discrimination are deep and have been difficult to eliminate. Housing discrimination contributes to the physical decay of inner-city neighborhoods and denies a substantial segment of the African American community a basic form of wealth accumulation and investment through home ownership.[18] The number of African American homeowners would probably be higher in the absence of discrimination by lending institutions.[19] Only about 59 percent of the nation's middle-class African Americans own their homes, compared with 74 percent of whites.

Eight out of every ten African Americans live in neighborhoods where they are in the majority. Residential segregation decreases for most racial and ethnic groups with additional education, income, and occupational status. However, this scenario does not hold true for African Americans. African Americans, no matter what their educational or occupational achievement or income level, are exposed to higher crime rates, less effective educational systems, high mortality risks, more dilapidated surroundings, and greater environmental threats because of their race. For example, in the heavily populated South Coast air basin of the Los Angeles area, it is estimated that over 71 percent of African Americans and 50 percent of Latinos reside in areas with the most polluted air, while only 34 percent of whites live in highly polluted areas.[20]

It has been difficult for millions of Americans in segregated neighborhoods to say "not in my backyard" (NIMBY) if they do not have a backyard.[21] Nationally, only about 44 percent of African Americans own their homes compared to over two-thirds of the nation as a whole. Homeowners are the strongest advocates of the NIMBY positions taken against locally unwanted land uses or LULUs such as the construction of garbage dumps, landfills, incinerators, sewer treatment plants, recycling centers, prisons, drug treatment units, and public housing projects. Generally, white communities have greater access than people of color communities when it comes to influencing land use and environmental decision making.

The ability of an individual to escape a health-threatening physical environment is usually related to affluence. However, racial barriers complicate this process for many Americans.[22] The imbalance between residential amenities and land uses assigned to central cities and suburbs cannot be explained by class factors alone. People of color and whites do not have the same opportunities to "vote with their feet" and escape undesirable physical environments.

Institutional racism continues to influence housing and mobility options available to African Americans of all income levels—and is a major factor that influences quality of neighborhoods they have available to them. The "web of discrimination" in the housing market is a result of action and inaction of local and federal government officials, financial institutions, insurance companies, real estate marketing firms, and zoning boards. More stringent enforcement mechanisms and penalties are needed to combat all forms of discrimination.

Uneven development between central cities and suburbs combined with the systematic avoidance of inner-city areas by many businesses have heightened social and economic inequalities. For the past two decades, manufacturing plants have been fleeing central cities and taking their jobs with them. Many have moved offshore to Third World countries where labor is cheap and environmental regulations are lax or nonexistent.

Industry flight from central cities has left behind a deteriorating urban infrastructure, poverty, and pollution. What kind of replacement industry can these communities attract? Economically depressed communities do not have a lot of choices available to them. Some workers have become so desperate that they see even a low-paying hazardous job as better than no job at all. These workers are forced to choose between unemployment and a job that may result in risks to their health, their family's health, and the health of their community. This practice amounts to "economic blackmail." Economic conditions in many people of color communities make them especially vulnerable to this practice.

Some polluting industries have been eager to exploit this vulnerability. Some have even used the assistance of elected officials in obtaining special tax breaks and government operating permits. Clearly, economic development and environmental policies flow from forces of production and are often dominated and subsidized by state actors. Numerous examples abound where state actors have targeted cities and regions for infrastructure improvements and amenities such as water irrigation systems, ship channels, road and bridge projects, and mass transit systems. On the other hand, state actors have done a miserable job in protecting central city residents from the ravages of industrial pollution and nonresidential activities valued as having a negative impact on quality of life.[23]

Racial and ethnic inequality is perpetuated and reinforced by local governments in conjunction with urban-based corporations. Race continues to be a potent variable in explaining urban land use, streets and highway configuration, commercial and industrial development, and industrial facility siting. Moreover, the question of "who gets what, where, and why" often pits one community against another.[24]

Zoning and Land Use

Some residential areas and their inhabitants are at a greater risk than the larger society from unregulated growth, ineffective regulation of industrial toxins, and public policy decisions authorizing industrial facilities that favor those with political and economic clout.[25] African Americans and other communities of color are often victims of land-use decision making that mirrors the power arrangements of the dominant society. Historically, exclusionary zoning (and rezoning) has been a subtle form of using government authority and power to foster and perpetuate discriminatory practices.

Zoning is probably the most widely applied mechanism to regulate urban land use in the United States. Zoning laws broadly define land for residential, commercial, or industrial uses, and may impose narrower land-use restrictions (e.g., minimum and maximum lot size, number of dwellings per acre, square feet and height of buildings, etc.). Zoning ordinances, deed restrictions, and other land-use mechanisms have been widely used as a "NIMBY" (not in my backyard) tool, operating through exclusionary practices. Thus, exclusionary zoning has been used to zone against something rather than for something. With or without zoning, deed restrictions or other devices, various groups are unequally able to protect their environmental interests. More often than not, people of color communities get shortchanged in the neighborhood protection game.

In Houston, Texas, a city that does not have zoning, NIMBY was replaced with the policy of "PIBBY" (place in blacks, back yard).[26] The city government and private industry targeted landfills, incinerators, and garbage dumps for Houston's black neighborhoods for more than five decades. These practices lowered residents' property values, accelerated physical deterioration, and increased disinvestment in the communities. Moreover, the discriminatory siting of landfills and incinerators stigmatized the neighborhoods as "dumping grounds" for a host of other unwanted facilities, including salvage yards, recycling operations, and automobile "chop shops."[27]

The Commission for Racial Justice's landmark *Toxic Wastes and Race* study found race to be the single most important factor (i.e., more important than income, home ownership rate, and property values) in the location of abandoned toxic waste sites.[28] The study also found that (1) three out of five African Americans live in communities with abandoned toxic waste sites; (2) sixty percent (15 million) African Americans live in communities with one or more abandoned toxic waste sites; (3) three of the five largest commercial hazardous waste landfills are located in predominately African American or Latino communities and accounts for 40 percent of the nation's total estimated landfill capacity; and (4) African Americans are heavily overrepresented in the population of cities with the largest number of abandoned toxic waste sites, which include Memphis, St. Louis, Houston, Cleveland, Chicago, and Atlanta.

Waste facility siting imbalances that were uncovered by the U.S. General Accounting Office (GAO) in 1983 have not disappeared.[29] The GAO discovered three out of four of the offsite commercial hazardous waste landfills in Region IV (Alabama, Florida, Georgia, Kentucky, Mississippi, North Carolina, South Carolina, and Tennessee) were located in predominately African American communities. African Americans still made up about one-fifth of the population in EPA Region IV. In 2000, 100 percent of the offsite commercial hazardous wastes landfills in the region is dumped in two mostly African Americans communities.

Environmental Racism

Many of the differences in environmental quality between black and white communities result from institutional racism. Institutional racism influences local land use, enforcement of environmental regulations, industrial facility siting, and where people of color live, work, and play. The roots of institutional racism are deep and have been difficult to eliminate. Discrimination is a manifestation of institutional racism and causes life to be very different for whites and blacks. Historically, racism has been and continues to be a major part of the American sociopolitical system, and as a result, people of color find themselves at a disadvantage in contemporary society.

Environmental racism is real. It is just as real as the racism found in the housing industry, educational institutions, employment arena, and judicial system. What is environmental racism and how does one recognize it? *Environmental racism refers to any policy, practice, or directive that differentially affects or disadvantages (whether intended or unintended) individuals, groups, or communities based on race or color.* Environmental racism combines with public policies and industry practices to provide benefits for whites while shifting costs to people of color.[30]

Environmental racism is reinforced by government, legal, economic, political, and military institutions.

Environmental decision making and policies often mirror the power arrangements of the dominant society and its institutions. Environmental racism disadvantages people of color while providing advantages or privileges for whites. A form of illegal "exaction" forces people of color to pay costs of environmental benefits for the public at large. The question of who pays and who benefits from the current environmental and industrial policies is central to this analysis of environmental racism and other systems of domination and exploitation.

Racism influences the likelihood of exposure to environmental and health risks as well as accessibility to health care.[31] Many of the nation's environmental policies distribute the costs in a regressive pattern while providing disproportionate benefits for whites and individuals who fall at the upper end of the education and income scale. Numerous studies, dating back to the seventies, reveal that people of color have borne greater health and environmental risk burdens than the society at large.[32]

Elevated public health risks are found in some populations even when social class is held constant. For example, race has been found to be independent of class in the distribution of air pollution,[33] contaminated fish consumption,[34] location of municipal landfills and incinerators,[35] toxic waste dumps,[36] cleanup of superfund sites,[37] and lead poisoning in children.[38]

Lead poisoning is a classic example of an environmental health problem that disproportionately impacts children of color at every class level. Lead affects between 3 to 4 million children in the United States—most of whom are African American and Latinos who live in urban areas. Among children 5 years old and younger, the percentage of African American children who have excessive levels of lead in their blood far exceeds the percentage of whites at all income levels.

In 1988, the federal Agency for Toxic Substances Disease Registry (ATSDR) found that for families earning less than $6,000, 68 percent of African American children had lead poisoning, compared with 36 percent for white children. In families with income exceeding $15,000, more than 38 percent of African American children suffer from lead poisoning compared with 12 percent of whites. The average blood lead level has dropped for all children with the phasing out of leaded gasoline. Today, the average blood lead level for all children in the U.S. is under 6 ug/dl.[39] However, these efforts have not had the same positive benefits on all populations. There is still work to be done to address the remaining problem. The lead problem is not randomly distributed across the nation. The most vulnerable populations are low-income African American and Hispanic American children who live in older urban housing.[40]

Figures reported in the July 1994 *Journal of the American Medical Association* on the Third National Health and Nutrition Examination Survey (NHANES III) revealed that 1.7 million children (8.9 percent of children aged 1 to 5) are lead poisoned, defined as blood lead levels equal to or above 10 ug/dl.[41] Lead-based paint (chips and dust) is the most common source of lead exposure for children. Children may also be exposed through soil and dust contamination built up from vehicle exhaust, lead concentration in soils in urban areas, lead dust brought into the home on parents work clothes, lead used in ceramics and pottery, folk medicines, and lead in plumbing.

The Right to Breathe Clean Air

Urban air pollution problems have been with us for some time now. Before the federal government stepped in, issues related to air pollution were handled primarily by states and local governments. Because states and local governments did such a poor job, the federal government set out to establish national clean air standards. Congress enacted the Clean Air Act (CAA) in 1970 and mandated the U.S. Environmental Protection Agency (EPA) to carry out this law. Subsequent amendments (1977 and 1990) were made to the CAA that form the current federal program. The CAA was a response to states unwillingness to protect air quality. Many states used their lax enforcement of environmental laws as lures for business and economic development.[42]

Central cities and suburbs do not operate on a level playing field. They often compete for scarce resources. One need not be a rocket scientist to predict the outcome between affluent suburbs and their less affluent central city competitors.[43] Freeways are the lifeline for suburban commuters, while millions of central-city residents are dependent on public transportation as their primary mode of travel. But recent cuts in mass transit subsidies and fare hikes have reduced access to essential social services and economic activities. Nevertheless, road construction programs are booming—even in areas choked with automobiles and air pollution.[44]

The air quality impacts of transportation are especially significant to people of color who are more likely than whites to live in urban areas with reduced air quality. National Argonne Laboratory researchers discovered that 437 of the 3,109 counties and independent cities failed to meet at least one of the EPA ambient air quality standards.[45] Specifically, 57 percent of whites, 65 percent of African Americans, and 80 percent of Hispanics live in 437 counties with substandard air quality. Nationwide, 33 percent of whites, 50 percent of African Americans, and 60 percent of Hispanics live in the 136 counties in which two or more air pollutants exceed standards. Similar patterns were found for the 29 counties designated as nonattainment areas for three or more pollutants. Again, 12 percent of whites, 20 percent of African Americans, and 31 percent of Hispanics resided in the worse nonattainment areas.

Asthma is an emerging epidemic in the United States. The annual age-adjusted death rate from asthma increased by 40% between 1982 through 1991, from 1.34 to 1.88 per 100,000 population,[46] with the highest rates being consistently reported among blacks aged 15–24 years of age during the period 1980–1993.[47] Poverty and minority status are important risk factors for asthma mortality.

Children are at special risk from ozone.[48] Children also represent a considerable share of the asthma burden. It is the most common chronic disease of childhood. Asthma affects almost 5 million children under 18 years. Although the overall annual age-adjusted hospital discharge rate for asthma among children under 15 years old decreased slightly from 184 to 179 per 100,000 between 1982 and 1992, the decrease was slower compared to other childhood diseases,[49] resulting in a 70% increase in the proportion of hospital admissions related to asthma during the 1980s. Inner city children have the highest rates for asthma prevalence, hospitalization, and mortality.[50] In the United States, asthma is the fourth leading cause of disability among children aged less than 18 years.[51]

The public health community has insufficient information to explain the magnitude of some of the air pollution-related health problems. However, they do know that persons suffering from asthma are particularly sensitive to the effects of carbon monoxide, sulfur dioxides, particulate matter, ozone, and nitrogen oxides. Ground-level ozone may exacerbate health problems such as asthma, nasal congestions, throat irritation, respiratory tract inflammation, reduced resistance to infection, changes in cell function, loss of lung elasticity, chest pains, lung scarring, formation of lesions within the lungs, and premature aging of lung tissues.[52]

Nationally, African Americans and Latino Americans have significantly higher prevalence of asthma than the general population. A 1996 report from the federal Centers for Disease Control shows hospitalization and deaths rates from asthma increasing for persons twenty-five years or less.[53] The greatest increases occurred among African Americans. African Americans are two to six times more likely than whites to die from asthma.[54] Similarly, the hospitalization rate for African Americans is 3 to 4 times the rate for whites.

A 1994 CDC-sponsored study showed that pediatric emergency department visits at Atlanta Grady Memorial Hospital increased by one-third following peak ozone levels. The study also found that asthma rate among African American children is 26 percent higher than the asthma rate among whites.[55] Since children with asthma in Atlanta may not have visited the emergency department for their care, the true prevalence of asthma in the community is likely to be higher.

Exploitation of Land, Environment, and People

Environmental decision-making and local land-use planning operate at the juncture of science, economics, politics, and special interests that place communities of color at special risk.[56] This is especially true in America's Deep South. The Deep South has always been thought of as a backward land based on its social, economic, political, and environmental policies. By default, the region became a "sacrifice zone," a sump for the rest of the nation's toxic waste.[57] A colonial mentality exists in the South where local government and big business take advantage of people who are politically and economically powerless. Many of these attitudes emerged from the region's marriage to slavery and the plantation system—a brutal system that exploited humans and the land.[58] The Deep South is stuck with this unique legacy—the legacy of slavery, Jim Crow, and white resistance to equal justice for all. This legacy has also affected race relations and the region's ecology. Southerners, black and white, have less education, lower incomes, higher infant mortality, and lower life expectancy than Americans elsewhere. It should be no surprise that the environmental quality that Southerners enjoy is markedly different from that of other regions of the country.

The South is characterized by "look-the-other-way environmental policies and giveaway tax breaks."[59] It is our nation's Third World where "political bosses encourage outsiders to buy the region's human and natural resources at bargain prices."[60] Lax enforcement of environmental regulations have left the region's air, water, and land the most industry-befouled in the United States.

Toxic waste discharge and industrial pollution are correlated with poorer economic conditions. Louisiana typifies this pattern. Nearly three-fourths of Louisiana's population—more than 3 million people—get their drinking water from underground aquifers. Dozens of the aquifers are threatened by contamination from polluting industries.[61] The Lower Mississippi River Industrial Corridor has over 125 companies that manufacture a range of products including fertilizers, gasoline, paints, and plastics. This corridor has been dubbed "Cancer Alley" by environmentalists and local residents.[62] Ascension Parish typifies what many people refer to as a toxic "sacrifice zone." In two parish towns of Geismer and St. Gabriel, 18 petrochemical plants are crammed into a nine-and-a-half-square-mile area. Petrochemical plants discharge millions of pounds of pollutants annually into the water and air.

Louisiana citizens subsidize this corporate welfare with their health and the environment.

Tax breaks given to polluting industries have created a few jobs a high cost. Nowhere is the polluter-welfare scenario more prevalent than in Louisiana. The state is a leader in doling out corporate welfare to polluters. A 1998 *Time Magazine* article reported that in the 1990s, Louisiana wiped off the books $3.1 billion in property taxes to polluting companies.[63] The state's top five worse polluters received $111 million dollars over the past decade.

Global Dumping Grounds

There is a direct correlation between exploitation of land and exploitation of people. It should not be a surprise to anyone to discover that Native Americans have to contend with some of the worst pollution in the United States.[64] Native American nations have become prime targets for waste trading.[65] More than three dozen Indian reservations have been targeted for landfills, incinerators, and other waste facilities.[66] The vast majority of these waste proposals were defeated by grassroots groups on the reservations. However, "radioactive colonialism" is alive and well.[67] The legacy of institutional racism has left many sovereign Indian nations without an economic infrastructure to address poverty, unemployment, inadequate education and health care, and a host of other social problems. In 1999, Eastern Navajo reservation residents have filed suit against the Nuclear Regulatory Commission to block uranium mining in Church Rock and Crown Point communities.

Hazardous waste generation and international movement of hazardous waste pose some important health, environmental, legal, and ethical dilemmas. It is unlikely that many of the global hazardous waste proposals can be effectuated without first addressing the social, economic, and political context in which hazardous wastes are produced (industrial processes), controlled (regulations, notification and consent documentation), and managed (minimization, treatment, storage, recycled, transboundary shipment, pollution prevention, etc.). The "unwritten" policy of targeting Third World nations for waste trade received international media attention in 1991. Lawrence Summers, at the time he was chief economist of the World Bank, shocked the world and touched off an international scandal when his confidential memorandum on waste trade was leaked. Summers writes: " 'Dirty' Industries: Just between you and me, shouldn't the World Bank be encouraging MORE migration of the dirty industries to the LDCs?"[68]

Consumption and production patterns, especially in nations with wasteful "throw-away" life styles as the United States, and the interests of transnational corporations create and maintain unequal and unjust waste burdens within and between affluent and poor communities, states, and regions of the world. Shipping hazardous wastes from rich communities to poor communities is not a solution to the growing global waste problem. Not only is it immoral, but it should be illegal. Moreover, making hazardous waste transactions legal does not address the ethical issues imbedded in such transactions.[69] The practice is a manifestation of power arrangements and a larger stratification system where some people and some places are assigned greater value than others.

In the real world, all people, communities, and nations are not created equal. Some populations and interests are more equal than others. Unequal interests and power arrangements have allowed poisons of the rich to be offered as short term remedies for poverty of the poor. This scenario plays out domestically (as in the United States where low-income and people of color communities are disproportionately impacted by waste facilities and "dirty" industries) and internationally (where hazardous wastes move from OECD states flow to non-OECD states).

The conditions surrounding the more than 1,900 maquiladoras, assembly plants operated by American, Japanese, and other foreign countries, located along the 2,000-mile U.S.-Mexico border may further exacerbate the waste trade.[70] The industrial plants use cheap Mexican labor to assemble imported components and raw material and then ship finished products back to the United States. Nearly a half million Mexican workers are employed in the maquiladoras.

A 1983 agreement between the United States and Mexico required American companies in Mexico to return waste products to the United States. Plants were required to notify the federal EPA when returning wastes. Results from a 1986 survey of 772 maquiladoras revealed that only 20 of the plants informed the U.S. EPA that they were returning waste to the United States, even though 86 percent of the plants used toxic chemicals in their manufacturing process. Much of the wastes end up being illegally dumped in sewers, ditches, and the desert. All along the Lower Rio Grande River Valley maquiladoras dump their toxic wastes into the river, from which 95 percent of the region's residents get their drinking water.[71]

The disregard for the environment and public safety has placed border residents' health at risk. In the border cities of Brownsville, Texas and Matamoras, Mexico, the rate of anencephaly—babies born without brains—is four times the national average. Affected families have filed lawsuits against 88 of the area's 100 maquiladoras for exposing the community to xylene, a cleaning solvent that can cause brain hemorrhages, and lung and kidney damage.

Contaminated well and drinking water looms as major health threats. Air pollution in the colonias has contributed to a raging asthma and respiratory epidemic. The Mexican environmental regulatory agency is understaffed and ill-equipped to adequately enforce its environmental laws.[72] Only time will tell if the North American Free Trade Agreement (NAFTA) will "fix" or exacerbate the public health, economic, and the environmental problems along the U.S.–Mexico border.

Setting the Record Straight

The environmental protection apparatus is broken and needs to be fixed. The environmental justice movement has set out clear goals of eliminating unequal enforcement of environmental, civil rights, and public health laws. Environmental justice leaders have made a difference in the lives of people and the physical environment. They have assisted public decision makers in identifying "at risk" populations, toxic "hot spots," research gaps, and action models to correct existing imbalances and prevent future threats. However, impacted communities are not waiting for the government or industry to get their acts together. Grassroots groups have taken the offensive to ensure that government and industry do the right thing.

Communities have begun to organize their own networks and force their inclusion into the mainstream of public decision making. They have also developed communication channels among environmental justice leaders, grassroots groups, professional associations (i.e., legal, public health, education, etc.), scientific groups, and public policy makers to assist them in identifying "at risk" populations, toxic "hot spots," research gaps, and work to correct imbalances.

In response to growing public concern and mounting scientific evidence, President Clinton Executive Order 12898. The Executive Order is not a new law. It only reinforces what has been the law of the land for over three decades. Environmental justice advocates are calling for vigorous enforcement of civil rights laws and environmental laws.

The number of environmental justice complaints is expected to escalate against industry, government, and institutions that receive federal funds. Citizens have a right to challenge discrimination including environmental discrimination. It is a smokescreen for anyone to link Title VI or other civil rights enforcement to economic disinvestment in low-income and people of color communities. There is absolutely no empirical evidence to support the contention environmental justice hurts brownfields redevelopment efforts.

The EPA has awarded over 200 Brownfield grants. In 1998, the agency had received some five dozen Title VI complaints. It is worth noting that not a single Title VI complaint involves a brownfields site. On the other hand, two decades of solid empirical evidence documents the impact of racial redlining on African American and other communities of color. Racial redlining by banks, savings and loans, insurance companies, grocery chains, and even pizza delivery companies thwarts economic vitality in black communities—not enforcement of civil rights laws. Racial redlining was such a real problem that Congress passed the Community Reinvestment Act in 1977.

States have had three decades to implement Title VI of the Civil Rights Act of 1964. Most states have chosen to ignore the law. States need to do a better job assuring nondiscrimination in the application and implementation of permitting decisions, enforcement, and investment decisions. Environmental justice also means sharing in the benefits. Governments must live up to their mandate of protecting all people and the environment. Anything less is unacceptable. The solution to environmental injustice lies in the realm of equal protection of all individuals, groups, and communities. No community, rich or poor, urban or suburban, black or white, should be allowed to become a "sacrifice zone" or the dumping ground.

Hazardous wastes and "dirty" industries have followed the "path of least resistance." Poor people and poor communities are given a false choice of "no jobs and no development" versus "risky low-paying jobs and pollution." Industries and governments (including the military) have often exploited the economic vulnerability of poor communities, poor states, poor regions, and poor nations for their "risky" operations. The environmental justice movement challenges toxic colonialism, environmental racism, and the international toxics trade at home and abroad.

Notes

1. Robert D. Bullard, *Dumping in Dixie: Race, Class and Environmental Quality* (Boulder, CO: Westview Press, 1994).
2. Robert D. Bullard, "Solid Waste Sites and the Black Houston Community," *Sociological Inquiry*, 53 (spring 1983), 273–88.
3. U.S. General Accounting Office, *Siting of Hazardous Waste Landfills and Their Correlation with Racial and Economic Status of Surrounding Communities* (Washington, DC: Government Printing Office, 1983).
4. Commission for Racial Justice, *Toxic Wastes and Race in the United States* (New York: United Church of Christ, 1987).
5. Charles Lee, *Proceedings: The First National People of Color Environmental Leadership Summit* (New York: United Church of Christ Commission for Racial Justice, 1992).
6. See Dana Alston, "Transforming a Movement: People of Color Unite at Summit against Environmental Racism," *Sojourner*, 21 (1992), 30–1.
7. William K. Reilly, "Environmental Equity: EPA's Position," *EPA Journal*, 18 (March/April 1992), 18–19.
8. See R. D. Bullard and B. H. Wright, "The Politics of Pollution: Implications for the Black Community," *Phylon*, 47 (March 1986), 71–8.
9. Robert D. Bullard, "Race and Environmental Justice in the United States," *Yale Journal of International Law*, 18 (winter, 1993), 319–35; Robert D. Bullard, "The Threat of Environmental Racism." *Natural Resources & Environment*, 7 (winter, 1993), 23–6, 55–6.
10. Louis Sullivan, "Remarks at the First Annual Conference on Childhood Lead Poisoning," in Alliance to End Childhood Lead Poisoning, *Preventing Child Lead Poisoning: Final Report* (Washington, DC: Alliance to End Childhood Lead Poisoning, October, 1991), A-2.
11. See Bill Lann Lee, "Environmental Litigation on Behalf of Poor, Minority Children,

Matthews v. Coye: A Case Study." Paper presented at the Annual Meeting of the American Association for the Advancement of Science, Chicago (February 9, 1992).
12. Ibid. 32.
13. Ibid.
14. Robert D. Bullard, "The Environmental Justice Framework: A Strategy for Addressing Unequal Protection." Paper presented at Resources for the Future Conference on Risk Management, Annapolis, MD (November 1992).
15. Paul Mohai and Bunyan Bryant, "Race, Poverty, and the Environment," *EPA Journal*, 18 (March/April 1992), 1–8; R. D. Bullard, "In Our Backyards," *EPA Journal*, 18 (March/April 1993), 11–12; D. R. Wernette and L. A. Nieves, "Breathing Polluted Air," *EPA Journal*, 18 (March/April 1992), 16–17; Patrick C. West, "Health Concerns for Fish-Eating Tribes?" *EPA Journal*, 18 (March/April 1992), 15–16.
16. Marianne Lavelle and Marcia Coyle, "Unequal Protection," *National Law Journal* (September 21, 1992), S1–S2.
17. Robert D. Bullard (ed.), *Confronting Environmental Racism: Voices from the Grassroots* (Boston: South End Press, 1993), ch. 1; Robert D. Bullard, "Waste and Racism: A Stacked Deck?" *Forum for Applied Research and Public Policy*, 8 (spring, 1993), 29–35; Robert D. Bullard (ed.), *In Search of the New South: The Black Urban Experience in the 1970s and 1980s* (Tuscaloosa, AL: University of Alabama Press, 1991).
18. Florence Wagman Roisman, "The Lessons of American Apartheid: The Necessity and Means of Promoting Residential Racial Integration," *Iowa Law Review*, 81 (December 1995), 479–525.
19. Joe R. Feagin, "A House is Not a Home: White Racism and U.S. Housing Practices," in R. D. Bullard, J. E. Grigsby, and Charles Lee (eds), *Residential Apartheid: The*

American Legacy (Los Angeles: UCLA Center for Afro-American Studies Publication, 1994), 17–48.

20. Eric Mann, *L.A.'s Lethal Air: New Strategies for Policy, Organizing, and Action* (Los Angeles: Labor/Community Strategy Center, 1991), 31.

21. Jim Motavalli, "Toxic Targets: Polluters that Dump on Communities of Color are Finally Being Brought to Justice," *E Magazine*, 4 (July/August 1997), 29–41.

22. Joe Bandy, "Reterritorializing Borders: Transnational Environmental Justice Movement on the U.S.–Mexico Border," *Race, Gender, and Class*, 5 (1997), 80–103.

23. See Bunyan Bryant and Paul Mohai, *Race and the Incidence of Environmental Hazards* (Boulder, CO: Westview Press, 1992); Bunyan Bryant (ed.), *Environmental Justice* (Washington, DC: Island Press, 1995), 8–34.

24. R. Pinderhughes, "Who Decides What Constitute a Pollution Problem?" *Race, Gender, and Class*, 5 (1997), 130–52.

25. Diane Takvorian, "Toxics and Neighborhoods Don't Mix," *Land Use Forum: A Journal of Law, Policy and Practice*, 2 (winter 1993), 28–31; R. D. Bullard, "Examining the Evidence of Environmental Racism," *Land Use Forum: A Journal of Law, Policy, and Practice*, 2 (winter 1993), 6–11.

26. For an in-depth examination of the Houston case study, see R. D. Bullard, *Invisible Houston: The Black Experience in Boom and Bust* (College Station, TX: Texas A&M University Press, 1987), 60–75.

27. Ruth Rosen, "Who Gets Polluted: The Movement for Environmental Justice," *Dissent* (spring, 1994), 223–30; R. D. Bullard, "Environmental Justice: It's More than Waste Facility Siting," *Social Science Quarterly*, 77 (September 1996), 493–9.

28. Commission for Racial Justice, *Toxic Wastes and Race in the United States*, xiii–xiv.

29. See U.S. General Accounting Office, *Siting of Hazardous Waste Landfills and Their Correlation with Racial and Economic Status of Surrounding Communities* (Washington, DC: U.S. General Accounting Office, 1983), 1.

30. See Robert D. Bullard (ed.), *Confronting Environmental Racism: Voices from the Grassroots* (Boston: South End, 1993); Robert D. Bullard, "The Threat of Environmental Racism," *Natural Resources & Environment*, 7 (winter, 1993), 23–6; Bunyan Bryant and Paul Mohai (eds), *Race and the Incidence of Environmental Hazards* (Boulder, CO: Westview Press, 1992); Regina Austin and Michael Schill, "Black, Brown, Poor and Poisoned: Minority Grassroots Environmentalism and the Quest for Eco-Justice," *The Kansas Journal of Law and Public Policy*, 1 (1991), 69–82; Kelly C. Colquette and Elizabeth A. Henry Robertson, "Environmental Racism: The Causes, Consequences, and Commendations," *Tulane Environmental Law Journal*, 5 (1991), 153–207; Rachel D. Godsil, "Remedying Environmental Racism," *Michigan Law Review*, 90 (1991), 394–427.

31. See Bullard and Feagin, "Racism and the City," 55–76; Robert D. Bullard, "Dismantling Environmental Racism in the USA," *Local Environment*, 4 (1999), 5–19.

32. See W. J. Kruvant, "People, Energy, and Pollution," in D. K. Newman and Dawn Day (eds), *The American Energy Consumer* (Cambridge, MA: Ballinger, 1975), 125–67; Robert D. Bullard, "Solid Waste Sites and the Black Houston Community." *Sociological Inquiry*, 53 (spring, 1983), 273–88; United Church of Christ Commission for Racial Justice, *Toxic Wastes and Race in the United States* (New York: Commission for Racial Justice, 1987); Dick Russell, "Environmental Racism." *The Amicus Journal*, 11 (spring, 1989), 22–32; Eric Mann, *L.A.'s Lethal Air: New Strategies for Policy, Organizing, and Action* (Los Angeles: Labor/Community Strategy Center, 1991); D. R. Wernette and L. A. Nieves, "Breathing Polluted Air: Minorities are Disproportionately Exposed," *EPA Journal*, 18 (March/April 1992), 16–17; Bryant and Mohai, *Race and the Incidence of Environmental Hazards*; Benjamin Goldman and Laura J. Fitton, *Toxic Wastes and Race Revisited* (Washington, DC: Center for Policy

Alternatives, NAACP, and United Church of Christ, 1994).

33. See Myrick A Freedman, "The Distribution of Environmental Quality," in Allen V. Kneese and Blair T. Bower (eds), *Environmental Quality Analysis* (Baltimore: Johns Hopkins University Press for Resources for the Future, 1971); Michel Gelobter, "The Distribution of Air Pollution by Income and Race." Paper presented at the Second Symposium on Social Science in Resource Management, Urbana, Illinois (June 1988); Gianessi et al., "The Distributional Effects of Uniform Air Pollution Policy in the U.S.," *Quarterly Journal of Economics* (May 1979), 281–301.

34. Patrick C. West, J. Mark Fly, and Robert Marans, "Minority Anglers and Toxic Fish Consumption: Evidence from a State-Wide Survey in Michigan," In Bryant and Mohai, *Race and the Incidence of Environmental Hazards*, 100–13;

35. Robert D. Bullard, "Solid Waste Sites and the Black Houston Community," *Sociological Inquiry*, 53 (spring, 1983), 273–88; Robert D. Bullard, *Invisible Houston: The Black Experience in Boom and Bust* (College Station, TX: Texas A&M University Press, 1987), ch. 6; Robert D. Bullard, "Environmental Racism and Land Use, "*Land Use Forum: A Journal of Law, Policy & Practice*, 2 (spring, 1993), 6–11.

36. United Church of Christ Commission for Racial Justice, *Toxic Wastes and Race*; Paul Mohai and Bunyan Bryant, "Environmental Racism: Reviewing the Evidence," in Bryant and Mohai, *Race and the Incidence of Environmental Hazards*; Paul Stretesky and Michael J. Hogan, "Environmental Justice: An Analysis of Superfund Sites in Florida," *Social Problems*, 45 (May 1998), 268–87.

37. Marianne Lavelle and Marcia Coyle, "Unequal Protection: The Racial Divide in Environmental Law," *National Law Journal* (September 21, 1992).

38. Agency for Toxic Substances Disease Registry, *The Nature and Extent of Lead Poisoning in Children in the United States: A Report to Congress* (Atlanta: U.S. Department of Health and Human Resources, 1988), 1–12.

39. J. Schwartz and R. Levine, "Lead: An Example of the Job Ahead," *EPA Journal*, 18 (March/April 1992), 32–44.

40. Centers for Disease Control and Prevention, "Update: Blood Lead Levels—United States, 1991–1994," *Mortality and Morbidity Weekly Report*, 46: 7 (February 21, 1997), 141–6.

41. James L. Pirkle, D. J. Brody, E. W. Gunter, R. A. Kramer, D. C. Paschal, K. M. Glegal, and T. D. Matte, "The Decline in Blood Lead Levels in the United States: The National Health and Nutrition Examination Survey (NHANES III)," *Journal of the American Medical Association*, 272 (1994), 284–91.

42. Arnold W. Reitze, Jr., "A Century of Air Pollution Control Law: What Worked; What Failed; What Might Work," *Environmental Law*, 21 (1991), 1549.

43. For an in-depth discussion of transportation investments and social equity issues see R. D. Bullard and G. S. Johnson (eds), *Just Transportation: Dismantling Race and Class Barriers to Mobility* (Gabriola Island, BC: New Society Publishers, 1997).

44. Sid Davis, "Race and the Politics of Transportation in Atlanta," in Bullard and Johnson, *Just Transportation*, 84–96; Environmental Justice Resource Center, *Sprawl Atlanta: Social Equity Dimensions of Uneven Growth and Development*. A Report prepared for the Turner Foundation, Atlanta: Clark Atlanta University (January 1999).

45. D. R. Wernette and L. A. Nieves, "Breathing Polluted Air: Minorities are Disproportionately Exposed," *EPA Journal*, 18 (March 1992), 16–17.

46. CDC, "Asthma—United States, 1982–1992," *MMWR*, 43 (1995), 952–5.

47. CDC, "Asthma Mortality and Hospitalization Among Children and Young Adults—United States, 1980–1993," *MMWR*, 45 (1996), 350–3.

48. Anna E. Pribitkin, "The Need for Revision of Ozone Standards: Why Has the EPA Failed to Respond?" *Temple Environmental Law & Technology Journal*, 13 (1994), 104.

49. CDC/NCHS, *Health United States 1994*. DHHS Pub.No.(PHS) 95–1232; Tables 83, 84, 86, 87.

50. CDC, "Asthma—United States, 1982–1992."

51. CDC, "Disabilities Among Children Aged Less Than or Equal to 17 years—United States, 1991–1992," *MMWR*, 44 (1995), 609–13.

52. U.S. EPA, "Review of National Ambient Air Quality Standards for Ozone, Assessment of Scientific and Technical Information," OAQPS Staff Paper (Research Triangle Park, NC: EPA, 1996); Haluk Ozkaynk, John D. Spengler, Marie O'Neil, Jianping Xue, Hui Zhou, Kathy Gilbert, and Sonja Ramstrom, "Ambient Ozone Exposure and Emergency Hospital Admissions and Emergency Room Visits for Respiratory Problems in Thirteen U.S. Cities," in American Lung Association, *Breathless: Air Pollution and Hospital Admissions/Emergency Room Visits in 13 Cities* (Washington, DC: American Lung Association, 1996); American Lung Association, *Out of Breath: Populations-at-Risk to Alternative Ozone Levels* (Washington, DC: American Lung Association, 1995).

53. CDC, "Asthma Mortality and Hospitalization Among Children and Young Adults—United States, 1980–1993."

54. CDC, "Asthma: United States, 1980–1990," *MMWR*, 39 (1992), 733–5.

55. Mary C. White, Ruth Etzel, Wallace D. Wilcox, and Christine Lloyd, "Exacerbations of Childhood Asthma and Ozone Pollution in Atlanta," *Environmental Research*, 65 (1994), 56.

56. See R. D. Bullard, "The Legacy of Apartheid and Environmental Racism," *St. John's Journal of Legal Commentary*, 9 (Spring, 1994), 445–74.

57. Donald Schueler, "Southern Exposure," *Sierra*, 77 (November/December 1992), 45.

58. Robert D. Bullard, "Ecological Inequities and the New South: Black Communities under Siege," *Journal of Ethnic Studies*, 17 (winter 1990), 101–15; Donald L. Barlett and James B. Steele, "Paying a Price for Polluters," *Time* (November 23, 1998), 72–80.

59. Schueler, "Southern Exposure," 46.

60. Ibid. 46–7.

61. James O'Byrne and Mark Schleifstein, "Drinking Water in Danger," *The Times Picayune* (February 19, 1991), A5.

62. Conger Beasley, "Of Poverty and Pollution: Keeping Watch in Cancer Alley," 39–45.

63. Barlett and Steele, "Paying a Price for Polluters," 77.

64. See Conger Beasley, "Of Pollution and Poverty: Deadly Threat on Native Lands," *Buzzworm*. 2: 5 (1990), 39–45; Robert Tomsho, "Dumping Grounds: Indian Tribes Contend with Some of the Worst of America's Pollution," *The Wall Street Journal* (November 29, 1990); Jane Kay, "Indian Lands Targeted for Waste Disposal Sites," *San Francisco Examiner* (April 10, 1991); Valerie Taliman, "Stuck Holding the Nation's Nuclear Waste," *Race, Poverty & Environment Newsletter* (fall 1992), 6–9.

65. See Bradley Angel, *The Toxic Threat to Indian Lands: A Greenpeace Report* (San Francisco: Greenpeace, 1992); Al Geddicks, *The New Resource Wars: Native and Environmental Struggles Against Multinational Corporations* (Boston: South End Press, 1993).

66. Jane Kay, "Indian Lands Targeted for Waste Disposal Sites."

67. Ward Churchill and Winona LaDuke, "Native America: The Political Economy of Radioactive Colonialism," *Insurgent Sociologist*, 13: 1 (1983), 61–3.

68. Greenpeace, "The Logic Behind Hazardous Waste Export", *Greenpeace Waste Trade Update* (First Quarter 1992), 1–2.

69. Dana Alston and Nicole Brown, "Global Threats to People of Color," in R. D. Bullard (ed.), *Confronting Environmental Racism: Voices from the Grassroots* (Boston: Southend Press, 1993), 179–94.

70. Roberto Sanchez, "Health and Environmental Risks of the Maquiladora in Mexicali," *Natural Resources Journal*, 30: 1 (1990), 163–86.

71. Beatriz Johnston Hernandez, "Dirty Growth," *The New Internationalist* (August 1993).

72. T. Barry and B. Simms, *The Challenge of Cross Border Environmentalism: The U.S.–Mexico Case* (Albuquerque, NM: The Inter-Hemispheric Education Resource Center, 1994).

32 Women of Color on the Front Line

Celene Krauss

Toxic waste disposal is a central focus of women's grass-roots environmental activism.[1] Toxic waste facilities are predominantly sited in working-class and low-income communities and communities of color, reflecting the disproportionate burden placed on these communities by a political economy of growth that distributes the costs of economic growth unequally.[2] Spurred by the threat that toxic wastes pose to family health and community survival, female grass-roots activists have assumed the leadership of community environmental struggles. As part of a larger movement for environmental justice, they constitute a diverse constituency, including working-class housewives and secretaries, rural African American farmers, urban residents, Mexican American farm workers, and Native Americans.

These activists attempt to differentiate themselves from what they see as the white, male, middle-class leadership of many national environmental organizations. Unlike the more abstract, issue-oriented focus of national groups, women's focus is on environmental issues that grow out of their concrete, immediate experiences.[3] Female blue-collar activists often share a loosely defined ideology of environmental justice and a critique of dominant social institutions and mainstream environmental organizations, which they believe do not address the broader issues of inequality underlying environmental hazards. At the same time, these activists exhibit significant diversity in their conceptualization of toxic waste issues, reflecting different experiences of class, race, and ethnicity.

This chapter looks at the ways in which different working-class women formulate ideologies of resistance around toxic waste issues and the process by which they arrive at a concept of environmental justice. Through an analysis of interviews, newsletters, and conference presentations, I show the voices of white, African American, and Native American female activists and the resources that inform and support their protests. What emerges in an environmental discourse that is mediated by subjective experiences and interpretations and rooted in the political truths women construct out of their identities as housewives, mothers, and members of communities and racial and ethnic groups.

The Subjective Dimension of Grass-Roots Activism

Grass-roots protest activities have often been trivialized, ignored, and viewed as self-interested actions that are particularistic and parochial, failing to go beyond a single-issue focus. This view

From Robert D. Bullard (ed.), *Unequal Protection: Environmental Justice and Communities of Color* (San Francisco: Sierra Club Books, 1994), 256–71. Reprinted with permission.

of community grass-roots protests is held by most policymakers as well as by many analysts of movements for progressive social change.[4]

In contrast, the voices of blue-collar women engaged in protests regarding toxic waste issues tell us that single-issue protests are about more than the single issue. They reveal a larger world of power and resistance, which in some measure ends up challenging the social relations of power. This challenge becomes visible when we shift the analysis of environmental activism to the experiences of working-class women and the subjective meanings they create around toxic waste issues.

In traditional sociological analysis, this subjective dimension of protest has often been ignored or viewed as private and individualistic. Feminist theory, however, helps us to see its importance. For feminists, the critical reflection on the everyday world of experience is an important subjective dimension of social change.[5] Feminists show us that experience is not merely a personal, individualistic concept. It is social. People's experiences reflect where they fit in the social hierarchy. Thus, blue-collar women of differing backgrounds interpret their experiences of toxic waste problems within the context of their particular cultural histories, starting from different assumptions and arriving at concepts of environmental justice that reflect broader experiences of class and race.

Feminist theorists also challenge a dominant ideology that separates the "public" world of policy and power from the "private" and personal world of everyday experience. By definition, this ideology relegates the lives and concerns of women relating to home and family to the private, nonpolitical arena, leading to invisibility of their grass-roots protests about issues such as toxic wastes.[6] As Ann Bookman has noted in her important study of working-class women's community struggles, women's political activism in general, and working-class political life at the community level in particular, remain "peripheral to the historical record . . . where there is a tendency to privilege male political activity and labor activism."[7] The women's movement took as its central task the reconceptualization of the political itself, critiquing this dominant ideology and constructing a new definition of the political, located in the everyday world of ordinary women rather than in the world of public policy. Feminists provide a perspective for making visible the importance of particular, single-issue protests regarding toxic wastes by showing how ordinary women subjectively link the particulars of their private lives with a broader analysis of power in the public sphere.

Social historians such as George Rudé have pointed out that it is often difficult to understand the experience and ideologies of resistance because ordinary working people appropriate and reshape traditional beliefs embedded within working-class culture, such as family and community.[8] This point is also relevant for understanding the environmental protests of working-class women. Their protests are framed in terms of the traditions of motherhood and family; as a result, they often appear parochial or even conservative. As we shall see, however, for working-class women, these traditions become the levers that set in motion a political process, shaping the language and oppositional meanings that emerge and providing resources for social change.

Shifting the analysis of toxic waste issues to the subjective experience of ordinary women makes visible a complex relationship between everyday life and the larger structures of public power. It reveals the potential for human agency that is hidden in a more traditional sociological approach and provides us with a means of seeing "the sources of power which subordinated groups have created."[9]

The analysis presented in this chapter is based on the oral and written voices of women involved in toxic waste protests. Interviews were conducted at environmental conferences such as the First National People of Color Environmental Leadership Summit, Washington, DC, 1991, and the World Women's Congress for a Healthy Planet, Miami, Florida, 1991, and by telephone. Additional sources include conference presentations, pamphlets, books, and other written materials that have emerged from this movement. This research is part of an ongoing comparative study that will examine the ways in which experiences of race, class, and ethnicity mediate women's environmental activism. Future research includes an analysis of the environmental activism of Mexican American women in addition to that of the women discussed here.

Toxic Waste Protests and The Resource of Motherhood

Blue-collar women do not use the language of the bureaucrat to talk about environmental issues. They do not spout data or marshal statistics in support of their positions. In fact, interviews with these women rarely generate a lot of discussion about the environmental problem per se. But in telling their stories about their protest against a landfill or incinerator, they ultimately tell larger stories about their discovery or analysis of oppression. Theirs is a political, not a technical, analysis.

Working-class women of diverse racial and ethnic backgrounds identify the toxic waste movement as a women's movement, composed primarily of mothers. Says one woman who fought against an incinerator in Arizona and subsequently worked on other anti-incinerator campaigns throughout the state, "Women are the backbone of the grass-roots groups; they are the ones who stick with it, the ones who won't back off." By and large, it is women, in their traditional role as mothers, who make the link between toxic wastes and their children's ill health. They discover the hazards of toxic contamination: multiple miscarriages, birth defects, cancer deaths, and so on. This is not surprising, as the gender-based division of labor in a capitalist society gives working-class women the responsibility for the health of their children.

These women define their environmental protests as part of the work that mothers do. Cora Tucker, an African American activist who fought against uranium mining in Virginia and who now organizes nationally, says:

It's not that I don't think that women are smarter, [she laughs] but I think that we are with the kids all day long. . . . If Johnny gets a cough and Mary gets a cough, we try to discover the problem.

Another activist from California sums up this view: "If we don't oppose an incinerator, we're not doing our work as mothers."

For these women, family serves as a spur to action, contradicting popular notions of family as conservative and parochial. Family has a very different meaning for these women than it does for the middle-class nuclear family. Theirs is a less privatized, extended family that is open, permeable, and attached to community. This more extended family creates the networks and resources that enable working-class communities to survive materially given few economic resources.[10] The destruction of working-class neighborhoods by economic growth deprives blue-collar communities of the basic resources of survival; hence the resistance engendered by toxic waste issues. Working-class women's struggles over toxic waste issues are, at root, issues about survival. Ideologies of motherhood, traditionally relegated to the private sphere, become political resources that working-class women use to initiate and justify their resistance. In the process of protest, working-class women come to reject the dominant ideology, which separates the public and private arenas.

Working-class women's extended network of family and community serves as the vehicle for spreading information and concern about toxic waste issues. Extended networks of kinship and friendship become political resources of opposition. For example, in one community in Detroit, women discovered patterns of health problems while attending Tupperware parties. Frequently, a mother may read about a hazard in a newspaper, make a tentative connection between her own child's ill health and the pollutant, and start telephoning friends and family, developing an informal health survey. Such a discovery process is rooted in what Sarah Ruddick has called the everyday practice of mothering.[11] Through their informal networks, they compare notes and experiences and develop an oppositional knowledge used to resist the dominant knowledge of experts and the decisions of government and corporate officials.

These women separate themselves from "mainstream" environmental organizations, which are seen as dominated by white, middle-class men and concerned with remote issues. Says one woman from Rahway, New Jersey: "The mainstream groups deal with safe issues. They want to stop incinerators to save the eagle, or they protect trees for the owl. But we say, what about the people?"

Another activist implicitly criticizes the mainstream environmental groups when she says of the grass-roots Citizens' Clearinghouse for Hazardous Wastes:

Rather than oceans and lakes, they're concerned about kids dying. Once you've had someone in your family who has been attacked by the environment—I mean who has had cancer or some other disease—you get a keen sense of what's going on.

It is the traditional, "private" women's concerns about home, children, and family that provide the initial impetus for blue-collar women's involvement in issues of toxic waste. The political analyses they develop break down the public-private distinction of dominant ideology and frame a particular toxic waste issue within broader contexts of power relationships.

The Role of Race, Ethnicity, and Class

Interviews with white, African American, and Native American women show that the starting places for and subsequent development of their analyses of toxic waste protests are mediated by issues of class, race, and ethnicity.

White working-class women come from a culture in which traditional women's roles center on the private arena of family. They often marry young; although they may work out of financial necessity, the primary roles from which they derive meaning and satisfaction are those of mothering and taking care of family. They are revered and supported for fulfilling the ideology of a patriarchal family.[12] And these families often reflect a strong belief in the existing political system. The narratives of white working-class women involved in toxic waste issues are filled with the process by which they discover the injustice of their government, their own insecurity about entering the public sphere of politics, and the constraints of the patriarchal family, which ironically prevent them from becoming fully active in the defense of their family, especially in their protest. Their narratives are marked by a strong initial faith in "their" government, as well as a remarkable transformation as they become disillusioned with the system. They discover "that they never knew what they were capable of doing in defense of their children."

For white working-class women, whose views on public issues are generally expressed only within family or among friends, entering a more public arena to confront toxic waste issues is often extremely stressful. "Even when I went to the PTA," says one activist, "I rarely spoke. I was so nervous." Says another: "My views have always been strong, but I expressed them only in the family. They were not for the public." A strong belief in the existing political system is characteristic of these women's initial response to toxic waste issues. Lois Gibbs, whose involvement in toxic waste issues started at Love Canal, tells us, "I believed if I had a problem I just had to go to the right person in government and he would take care of it."

Initially, white working-class women believe that all they have to do is give the government the facts and their problem will be taken care of. They become progressively disenchanted with what they view as the violation of their rights and the injustice of a system that allows their children and family to die. In the process, they develop a perspective of environmental justice rooted in issues of class, the attempt to make democracy real, and a critique of the corporate state. Says one activist who fought the siting of an incinerator in Sumter County, Alabama: "We need to stop letting economic development be the true God and religion of this country. We have to prevent big money from influencing our government."

A recurring theme in the narratives of these women is the transformation of their beliefs about government and power. Their politicization is rooted in the deep sense of violation, betrayal, and hurt they feel when they find that their government will not protect their families. Lois Gibbs sums up this feeling well:

I grew up in a blue-collar community. We were very into democracy. There is something about discovering that democracy isn't democracy as we know it. When you lose faith in your government, it's like finding out your mother was fooling around on your father. I was very upset. It almost broke my heart because I really believed in the system. I still believe in the system, only now I believe that democracy is of the people and by the people, the people have to move it, it ain't gonna move by itself.

Echoes of this disillusionment are heard from white blue-collar women throughout the country. One activist relates:

We decided to tell our elected officials about the problems of incineration because we didn't think they knew. Surely if they knew that there was a toxic waste dump in our county they would stop it. I was politically naive. I was real surprised because I live in an area that's like the Bible Belt of the South. Now I think the God of the United States is really economic development, and that has got to change.

Ultimately, these women become aware of the inequities of power as it is shaped by issues of class and gender. Highly traditional values of democracy and motherhood remain central to their lives. But in the process of politicization through their work on toxic waste issues, these values become transformed into resources of opposition that enable women to enter the public arena and challenge its legitimacy. They justify their resistance as a way to make democracy real and to protect their children.

White blue-collar women's stories are stories of transformations: transformations into more self-confident and assertive women; into political activists who challenge the existing system and feel powerful in that challenge; into wives and mothers who establish new relationships with their spouses (or get divorced) and new, empowering relationships with their children as they provide role models of women capable of fighting for what they believe in.

African American working-class women begin their involvement in toxic waste protests from a different place. They bring to their protests a political awareness that is grounded in race and that shares none of the white blue-collar women's initial trust in democratic institutions. These women view government with mistrust, having been victims of racist policies throughout their lives. Individual toxic waste issues are immediately framed within a broader political context and viewed as environmental racism. Says an African American activist from Rahway, New Jersey:

When they sited the incinerator for Rahway, I wasn't surprised. All you have to do is look around my community to know that we are a dumping ground for all kinds of urban industrial projects that no one else wants. I knew this was about environmental racism the moment that they proposed the incinerator.

An African American woman who fought the siting of a landfill on the South Side of Chicago reiterates this view: "My community is an all-black community isolated from everyone. They don't care what happens to us." She describes her community as a "toxic doughnut":

We have seven landfills. We have a sewer treatment plant. We have the Ford Motor Company. We have a paint factory. We have numerous chemical companies and steel mills. The river is just a few blocks away from us and is carrying water so highly contaminated that they say it would take seventy-five years or more before they can clean it up.

This activist sees her involvement in toxic waste issues as a challenge to traditional stereotypes of African American women. She says, "I'm here to tell the story that all people in the projects are not lazy and dumb!"

Some of these women share experiences of personal empowerment through their involvement in toxic waste issues. Says one African American activist:

Twenty years ago I couldn't do this because I was so shy. . . . I had to really know you to talk with you. Now I talk. Sometimes I think I talk too much. I waited until my fifties to go to jail. But it was well worth it. I never went to no university or college, but I'm going in there and making speeches.

However, this is not a major theme in the narratives of female African American activists, as it is in those of white blue-collar women. African American women's private work as mothers has traditionally extended to a more public role in the local community as protectors of the race. As a decade of African American feminist history has shown, African American women have historically played a central role in community activism and in dealing with issues of race and economic injustice.[13] They receive tremendous status and recognition from their community. Many women participating in toxic waste protests have come out of a history of civil rights activism, and their environmental protests, especially in the South, develop through community organizations born during the civil rights movement.[14] And while the visible leaders are often male, the base of the organizing has been led by African American women, who, as Cheryl Townsend Gilkes has written, have often been called "race women," responsible for the "racial uplift" of their communities.[15]

African American women perceive that traditional environmental groups only peripherally relate to their concerns. As Cora Tucker relates:

This white woman from an environmental group asked me to come down to save a park. She said that they had been trying to get black folks involved and that they won't come. I said, "Honey, it's not that they aren't concerned, but when their babies are dying in their arms they don't give a damn about a park." I said, "They want to save their babies. If you can help them save their babies, then in turn they can help you save your park." And she said, "But this is a real immediate problem." And I said, "Well, these people's kids dying is immediate."

Tucker says that white environmental groups often call her or the head of the NAACP at the last minute to participate in an environmental rally because they want to "include" African Americans. But they exclude African Americans from the process of defining the issues in the first place. What African American communities are doing is changing the agenda.

Because the concrete experience of African Americans' lives is the experience and analysis of racism, social issues are interpreted and struggled with within this context. Cora Tucker's story of attending a town board meeting shows that the issue she deals with is not merely the environment but also the disempowerment she experiences as an African American woman. At the meeting, white women were addressed as Mrs. So-and-So by the all-white, male board. When Ms. Tucker stood up, however, she was addressed as "Cora":

One morning I got up and I got pissed off and I said, "What did you call me?" He said, "Cora," and I said, "The name is Mrs. Tucker." And I had the floor until he said. "Mrs. Tucker." He waited five minutes before he said "Mrs. Tucker." And I held the floor. I said, "I'm not gonna let you call me Cora!" And when he said, "Yes, Mrs. Tucker," I said, "Mr. Chairman, I don't call you by your first name and I don't want you to call me by mine. My name is Mrs. Tucker. And when you want me, you call me Mrs. Tucker." It's not that—I mean it's not like you gotta call me Mrs. Tucker, but it was the respect.

In discussing this small act of resistance as an African American woman, Cora Tucker is showing how environmental issues may be about corporate and state power, but they are also about race. For female African American activists, environmental issues are seen as reflecting environmental racism and linked to other social justice issues, such as jobs, housing, and crime. They are viewed as part of a broader picture of social inequity based on race. Hence, the solution articulated in a vision of environmental justice is a civil rights vision—rooted in the everyday experience of racism. Environmental justice comes to mean the need to resolve the broad social inequities of race.

The narratives of Native American women are also filled with the theme of environmental racism. However, their analysis is laced with different images. It is a genocidal analysis rooted in the Native American cultural identification, the experience of colonialism, and the imminent endangerment of their culture. A Native American woman from North Dakota, who opposed a landfill, says:

Ever since the white man came here, they keep pushing us back, taking our lands, pushing us onto reservations. We are down to 3 percent now, and I see this as just another way for them to take our lands, to completely annihilate our races. We see that as racism.

Like that of the African American women, these women's involvement in toxic waste protests is grounded from the start in race and shares none of the white blue-collar women's initial belief in the state. A Native American woman from southern California who opposed a landfill on the Rosebud Reservation in South Dakota tells us:

Government did pretty much what we expected them to do. They supported the dump. People here fear the government. They control so many aspects of our life. When I became involved in opposing the garbage landfill, my people told me to be careful. They said they annihilate people like me.

Another woman involved in the protest in South Dakota describes a government official's derision of the tribe's resistance to the siting of a landfill:

If we wanted to live the life of Mother Earth, we should get a tepee and live on the Great Plains and hunt buffalo.

Native American women come from a culture in which women have had more empowered and public roles than is the case in white working-class culture. Within the Native American community, women are revered as nurturers. From childhood, boys and girls learn that men depend on women for their survival. Women also play a central role in the decision-making process within the tribe. Tribal council membership is often equally divided between men and women; many women are tribal leaders and medicine women. Native American religions embody a respect for women as well as an ecological ethic based on values such as reciprocity and sustainable development: Native Americans pray to Mother Earth, as opposed to the dominant culture's belief in a white, male, Anglicized representation of divinity.[16]

In describing the ways in which their culture integrates notions of environmentalism and womanhood, one woman from New Mexico says:

We deal with the whole of life and community; we're not separated, we're born into it—you are it. Our connection as women is to the Mother Earth, from the time of our consciousness. We're not environmentalists. We're born into the struggle of protecting and preserving our communities. We don't separate ourselves. Our lifeblood automatically makes us responsible; we are born with it. Our teaching comes from a spiritual base. This is foreign to our culture. There isn't even a word for dioxin in Navajo.

In recent years, Native American lands have become common sites for commercial garbage dumping. Garbage and waste companies have exploited the poverty and lack of jobs in Native American communities and the fact that Native American lands, as sovereign nation territories, are often exempt from local environmental regulations. In discussing their opposition to dumping, Native American women ground their narratives in values about land that are inherent in the Native American community. They see these projects as violating tribal sovereignty and the deep meaning of land, the last resource they have. The issue, says a Native American woman from California, is

protection of the land for future generations, not really as a mother, but for the health of the people, for survival. Our tribe bases its sovereignty on our land base, and if we lose our land base, then we will be a lost people. We can't afford to take this trash and jeopardize our tribe.

If you don't take care of the land, then the land isn't going to take care of you. Because everything we have around us involves Mother Earth. If we don't take care of the land, what's going to happen to us?

In the process of protest, these women tell us, they are forced to articulate more clearly their cultural values, which become resources of resistance in helping the tribe organize against a landfill. While many tribal members may not articulate an "environmental" critique, they well understand the meaning of land and their religion of Mother Earth, on which their society is built.

Conclusion

The narratives of white, African American, and Native American women involved in toxic waste protests reveal the ways in which their subjective, particular experiences lead them to analyses of toxic waste issues that extend beyond the particularistic issue to wider worlds of power. Traditional beliefs about home, family, and community provide the impetus for women's involvement in these issues and become a rich source of empowerment as women reshape traditional language and meanings into an ideology of resistance. These stories challenge traditional views of toxic waste protests as parochial, self-interested, and failing to go beyond a single-issue focus. They show that single-issue protests are ultimately about far more and reveal the experiences of daily life and resources that different groups use to resist. Through environmental protests, these women challenge, in some measure, the social relations of race, class, and gender.

These women's protests have different beginning places, and their analyses of environmental justice are mediated by issues of class and race. For white blue-collar women, the critique of the corporate state and the realization of a more genuine democracy are central to a vision of environmental justice. The definition of environmental justice that they develop becomes rooted in the issue of class. For women of color, it is the link between race and environment, rather than between class and environment, that characterizes definitions of environmental justice. African American women's narratives strongly link environmental justice to other social justice concerns, such as jobs, housing, and crime. Environmental justice comes to mean the need to resolve the broad social inequities of race. For Native American women, environmental justice is bound up with the sovereignty of the indigenous peoples.

In these women's stories, their responses to particular toxic waste issues are inextricably tied to the injustice they feel as mothers, as working-class women, as African Americans, and as Native Americans. They do not talk about their protests in terms of single issues. Thus, their political activism has implications far beyond the visible, particularistic concern of a toxic waste dump site or the siting of a hazardous waste incinerator.

Notes

1. This chapter is a revised version of an article written by Celene Krauss, "Women and Toxic Waste Protests," *Qualitative Sociology*, 16: 3 (1993), 247–62. For additional reading on women and toxic waste protests, see e.g. Lawrence C. Hamilton, "Concern about Toxic Wastes: Three Demographic Predictors," *Sociological Perspectives*, 28 (1985), 463–86; Celene Krauss, "Blue-Collar Women and Toxic Waste Protests," in Richard Hofrichter (ed.), *Toxic Struggles* (Philadelphia: New Society, 1993); Mary Pardo, "Mexican American Women Grassroots Community Activists: 'Mothers of East Los Angeles,'" *Frontier*, 11 (1990), 1–7; Cynthia Hamilton, "Women, Home, and Community," *Woman of Power*, 20 (1991), 42–5; Sherry Cable, "Women's Social Movement Involvement: The Role of Structural Availability in Recruitment and Participation Processes," *Sociological Quarterly*, 33 (1992).

2. Writings on the relationship of race, class, and inequities in the siting of environmental facilities include Allan Schnaiberg, *The Environment: From Surplus to Scarcity* (New York: Oxford University Press, 1980); Robert D. Bullard, *Dumping in Dixie: Race, Class, and Environmental Quality* (Boulder, Colo: Westview Press, 1990); Robert D. Bullard and Beverly H. Wright, "Dumping Grounds in a Sunbelt City," *Urban Resources*, 2 (1985), 37–9; United Church of Christ Commission for Racial Justice, *Toxic Wastes and Race in the United States: A National Study of the Racial and Socioeconomic Characteristics of Communities with Hazardous Waste Sites* (New York: United Church of Christ Commission for Racial Justice, 1987); Phil Brown and Edwin J. Mikkelsen, *No Safe Place: Toxic Waste, Leukemia, and Community Action* (Berkeley: University of California Press, 1990); Bunyan Bryant and Paul Mohai (eds), *Race and Incidence of Environmental Hazards* (Boulder, Colo: Westview Press, 1992).

3. The relationship between environmental grass-roots activism and concrete experience is developed in Krauss, "Blue-Collar Women and Toxic Waste Protests"; Celene Krauss, "Community Struggles and the Shaping of Democratic Consciousness," *Sociological Forum*, 4 (1989), 227–38; Vandana Shiva *Staying Alive: Women, Ecology and Development* (London: Zed, 1989); Dorceta Taylor, "Can the Environmental Movement Attract and Maintain the Support of Minorities?," in Bunyan Bryant and Paul Mohai (eds), *Proceedings of the Michigan Conference on Race and the Incidence of Environmental Hazards* (Ann Arbor: University of Michigan, School of Natural Resources, 1990), 28–59.

4. For a complex analysis of single-issue community protests, see Joseph M. Kling and Prudence S. Posner (eds), *Dilemmas of Activism: Class, Community, and the Politics of Local Mobilization* (Philadelphia: Temple University Press, 1990). Also see Robert Bellah, "Populism and Individualism," *Social Polity*, Fall 1985.

5. For illustrations of feminist theories and methodologies that develop this perspective, read Patricia Hill Collins, *Black Feminist Thought: Knowledge, Consciousness, and the Politics of Empowerment* (Boston: Unwin Hyman, 1990); Nancy Hartsock, *Money, Sex and Power* (Boston: Northeastern University Press, 1984); Dorothy Smith, *The Everyday World as Problematic: A Feminist Sociology* (Boston: Northeastern University Press, 1987).

6. For an analysis of the private-public split in feminist political theory, see Susan Okin, *Women in Western Political Thought* (Princeton: Princeton University Press, 1979); Jean Bethke Elshtain, *Public Man, Private Woman* (Princeton: Princeton University Press, 1981); Martha A. Ackelsberg, "Communities, Resistance, and Women's Activism: Some Implications for a Democratic Polity," in Ann Bookman and Sandra Morgen (eds), *Women and the Politics of Empowerment* (Philadelphia: Temple University Press, 1988), 53–76.

7. Sandra Morgen, " 'It's the Whole Power of the City Against Us!': The Development of Political Consciousness in a Women's Health Care Coalition," in Bookman and Morgen (eds), *Women and the Politics of Empowerment*, 97.

8. See George Rudé, *Ideology and Popular Protest* (New York: Pantheon, 1980). Others include Herbert Gutman, *Work, Culture and Society in Industrializing America* (New York: Vintage, 1977); Sheila Rowbotham, *Women, Resistance and Revolution* (New York: Vintage, 1974); E. P. Thompson, *The Making of the English Working Class* (New York: Vintage, 1966).

9. Sheila Rowbotham, *Women's Consciousness, Man's World* (New York: Penguin, 1973).

10. The relationship of extended families, friendship networks, and the community activism of working-class women is explored by numerous writers. See e.g. Terry Haywoode, "Working Class Feminism: Creating a Politics of Community, Connection, and Concern," Ph.D. diss. (The Graduate School and University Center of the City University of New York, 1990). For the importance of this relationship in African American communities, read Nancy Naples, "Activist Mothering: Cross-Generational Continuity in the Community Work of Women from Low-Income Urban Neighborhoods," *Gender and Society*, May 1992; Patricia Hill Collins, *Black Feminist Thought: Knowledge, Consciousness, and the Politics of Empowerment* (Boston: Unwin Hyman, 1990); Karen Sacks, "Generations of Working-Class Families," in Karen Sacks (ed.), *My Troubles are Going to Have Trouble with Me: Everyday Trials and Triumphs of Women Workers* (New Brunswick, NJ: Rutgers University Press, 1984) 15–38; Carol Stack, *All Our Kin: Strategies for Survival in a Black Community* (New York: Harper Colophon, 1974). Family networks also play an important role in Native American communities. See e.g. Rayna Greene, "American Indian Women: Diverse leadership for Social Change," in Lisa Albrect and Rose Brewer (eds), *Bridges of Power: Women's Multicultural Alliances* (Philadelphia: New Society, 1990).

11. See Sara Ruddick, *Maternal Thinking: Towards a Politics of Peace* (New York: Ballantine, 1989).

12. Terry Haywoode, "Working Class Feminism: Creating a Politics of Community, Connection, and Concern," paper presented at the annual meeting of the American Sociological Association, Pittsburgh, Pennsylvania, August 1992; Ida Susser, *Norman Street: Poverty and Politics in an Urban neighborhood* (New York: Oxford University Press, 1982).

13. Paula Giddings, *When and Where I Enter: The Impact of Black Women on Race and Sex in America* (New York: Morrow, 1984). Also, in *Black Feminist Thought*, Patricia Hill Collins develops the history of African American women as "othermothers" in her discussion of community activism.

14. Bullard, *Dumping in Dixie*.

15. Cheryl Townsend Gilkes, "Building in Many Places: Multiple Commitments and Ideologies in Black Women's Community Work," in Bookman and Morgen (eds), *Women and the Politics of Empowerment*.

16. See Teresa Amott and Julie Mathaei, *Race, Gender & Work: A Multicultural Economic History of Women in the United States* (Boston: South End Press, 1991); Rayna Greene, "American Indian Women: Diverse Leadership for Social Change"; Annette M. Jaimes and Theresa Halsey, "American Indian Women at the Center of Indigenous Resistance in North America," in Annette M. Jaimes (ed.), *The State of Native America* (Boston: South End Press, 1992).

Section XI: Southern and Indigenous Perspectives

Environmental justice has pushed states and environmental movements in the North, in particular the USA, to reconsider just what 'environment' means, and what parts of the population are interested in 'environmental' issues. As with environmental justice in the North, the focus on the lived, everyday environment is central to corresponding movements in the global South. Against the image of a concern for nature as a post-materialist luxury that only arises when one is comfortable, secure, and fed, environmentalism is seen as a pressing concern for the poor too. Southern and indigenous activists frequently have to fight against the misconception that the poor are uninterested in nature, or in environmental issues.

Ramachandra Guha addresses the central question of the 'Environmentalism of the Poor'. He argues that while poor individuals and southern nations may not be as obviously active in the preservation of species or defence of a northern conception of wilderness, they are dedicated to addressing environmental destruction, which directly affects their ways of life and prospects for survival. Guha contrasts 'full-stomach' and 'empty-stomach' environmentalism. The point is that environmentalism is not simply post-materialist; those with material needs in the South simply focus on issues of everyday life, rather than the 'big outside' of northern wilderness aficionados. This does not mean that the poor are not interested in ecosystems; southern environmentalism often needs to battle industries and interests that harm the natural systems that support poor communities.

Vandana Shiva picks up on this point, and asks us to focus on the impacts of globalization and environmental manipulation on the lives of ordinary people in the South. Shiva discusses the impacts of economic modernization and 'development' on communities. Her argument is that local knowledge and practices are devalued in this process, and the local environment suffers from a singular, capital-driven idea of globalization. The move to monocultures based in the industrialization of agriculture is a direct threat to existing 'polycultures' based in traditional local knowledges. Shiva is critical of the whole idea of development as an attempt to impose alien western imperatives on the Third World that is disempowering to indigenous societies, to women, and, ultimately, to nature.

Winona Laduke also addresses this relationship between the threat to indigenous ways of life and to nature itself. LaDuke celebrates the grassroots and land-based efforts of "native environmentalism." The selection here, from her book *All Our Relations*, discusses how human practices need to be changed in order to match and respect the natural world and natural laws. But these principles also need to be embedded in a legal framework, which Laduke believes could be guided by indigenous insights. From the Iroquois teaching of understanding the impact of our actions on the seventh generation from now, Laduke argues the importance of codifying the right of future generations to environmental security.

Like the other authors in this section, Fabienne Bayet, an Aboriginal author and activist from Australia, stresses the importance of the indigenous connection to the land. Bayet, however, notes the twofold discrimination suffered by Aboriginal people. First, their relationship with the land was so devalued during colonization that Australia was declared *terra nullius*, or unoccupied, unimproved wasteland. When, finally, environmental values came to be recognized, and land was set aside as 'wilderness' in national parks and nature preserves, native peoples were again excluded. Bayet notes the dehumanization so caused, and insists that all of Australia, including so-called wilderness, is an Aboriginal artefact. Rather than stereotyping native peoples as either 'noble savages' or 'arch-conservationists', environmental movements need to understand the diverse realities of Aboriginal lives on the land.

Further Reading

Ramachandra Guha and Vandana Shiva have dedicated themselves to bringing the realities and lessons of the South to northern environmentalists (and academics). Guha and Martinez-Alier's *Varieties of Environmentalism* (1997) is an introduction to contrasts between environmentalisms of the North and South. Oxford University Press has released three of Guha's works in one volume, *The Ramachandra Guha Omibus* (2004). Juan Martinez-Alier offers his own perspective in *Environmentalism of the Poor: A Study of Ecological Conflicts and Valuation* (2003). Vandana Shiva's publications are numerous, and include *Biopiracy: The Plunder of Knowledge and Nature* (1997), *Stolen Harvest: The Hijacking of the Global Food Supply* (1999), and *Water Wars: Pollution, Profits, and Privatization* (2002).

Publications addressing indigenous environmentalism are also numerous. LaDuke's writings are collected in *The Winona LaDuke Reader* (2002). For overviews, see Jace Weaver (ed.), *Defending Mother Earth* (1996), Ward Churchill's *Struggle for the Land* (2002), and, for a particularly comprehensive and global picture, Bruce E. Johansen's *Indigenous Peoples and Environmental Issues: An Encyclopedia* (2003). Web resources include The Indigenous Environmental Network, <www.ienearth.org>, and the Center for Indigenous Environmental Resources, <www.cier.ca>.

33 The Environmentalism of the Poor[1]

Ramachandra Guha

The environmentalists in any area seemed very easy to identify. They were, quite simply, members of the local aristocracy ... The environmental vision is an aristocratic one ... It can only be sustained by people who have never had to worry about security.

(US Journalist William Tucker, 1977)

The first lesson is that the main source of environmental destruction in the world is the demand for natural resources generated by the consumption of the rich (whether they are rich nations or rich individuals and groups within nations) ... The second lesson is that it is the poor who are affected the most by environmental destruction.

(Indian Journalist Anil Agarwal, 1986)

The Origins of Conflict

When India played South Africa in a cricket international in Calcutta, the great Indian cricketer, Sunil Gavaskar, was asked by a fellow television commentator to predict the likely winner. 'I tried to look into my crystal ball,', answered Gavaskar 'but it is clouded up by the Calcutta smog.' He might well have added: 'To clear it I then dipped my crystal ball in the river Hooghly [which flows alongside the city's cricket stadium], but it came up even dirtier than before.'

The quality of air and water in Calcutta is representative of conditions in all Indian cities; small wonder that foreign visitors come equipped with masks and bottles of Perrier. Less visible to the tourist, and to urban Indians themselves, is the continuing environmental degradation in the countryside. Over 100 million hectares, or one-third of India's land area, has been classed as unproductive wasteland. Much of this was once forest and land ground; the rest, farmland destroyed by erosion and salinisation. The uncontrolled exploitation of groundwater has led to an alarming drop in the water table, in some areas by more than five metres. There is an acute shortage of safe water for drinking and domestic use. As the ecologist Jayanta Bandyopadhyay has remarked, water rather than oil will be the liquid whose availability (or lack of it) will have a determining influence on India's economic future.[2]

The bare physical facts of the deterioration of India's environment are by now well established.[3] But more serious still are its human consequences, the chronic shortages of natural resources in the daily life of most Indians. Peasant women have to trudge further and further for fuelwood

From Ramachandra Guha and Juan Martinez-Alier (eds), *Varieties of Environmentalism* (London: Earthscan, 1997), 3–21.

for their hearth. Their menfolk, meanwhile, are digging deeper and deeper for a trickle of water to irrigate their fields. Forms of livelihood crucially dependent on the bounty of nature, such as fishing, sheep-rearing or basket-weaving, are being abandoned all over India. Those who once subsisted on these occupations are joining the band of 'ecological refugees', flocking to the cities in search of employment. The urban population itself complains of shortages of water, power, construction material and (for industrial units) of raw material.

Such shortages flow directly from the abuse of the environment in contemporary India, the too rapid exhaustion of the resource base without a thought to its replenishment. Shortages lead, in turn, to sharp conflicts between competing groups of resource users. These conflicts often pit poor against poor, as when neighbouring villages fight over a single patch of forest and its produce, or when slum dwellers come to blows over the trickle of water that reaches them, one hour each day from a solitary municipal tap. Occasionally they pit rich against rich, as when the wealthy farmers of the adjoining states of Karnataka and Tamil Nadu quarrel over the water of the river Kaveri. However, the most dramatic environmental conflicts set rich against poor. This, for instance, is the case with the Sardar Sarovar dam on the Narmada river in central India. The benefits from this project will flow primarily to already pampered and prosperous areas of the state of Gujarat, while the costs will be disproportionately borne by poorer peasants and tribal communities in the upstream states of Madhya Pradesh and Maharashtra. These latter groups, who are to be displaced by the dam, are being organised by the Narmada Bachao Andolan (Save the Narmada Movement), which is indisputably the most significant environmental initiative in India today.

The 'Indian environmental movement' is an umbrella term that covers a multitude of these local conflicts, initiatives and struggles. The movement's origins can be dated to the Chipko movement, which started in the Garhwal Himalaya in April 1973. Between 1973 and 1980, over a dozen instances were recorded where, through an innovative technique of protest, illiterate peasants—men, women and children—threatened to hug forest trees rather than allow them to be logged for export. Notably, the peasants were not interested in saving the trees *per se*, but in using their produce for agricultural and household requirements. In later years, however, the movement turned its attention to broader ecological concerns, such as the collective protection and management of forests, and the diffusion of renewable energy technologies.[4]

The Chipko movement was the forerunner of and in some cases the direct inspiration for a series of popular movements in defence of community rights to natural resources. Sometimes these struggles revolved around forests; in other instances, around the control and use of pasture, and mineral or fish resources. Most of these conflicts have pitted rich against poor: logging companies against hill villagers, dam builders against forest tribal communities, multinational corporations deploying trawlers against traditional fisherfolk in small boats. Here one party (e.g. loggers or trawlers) seeks to step up the pace of resource exploitation to service an expanding commercial—industrial economy, a process which often involves the partial or total dispossession of those communities who earlier had control over the resource in question, and whose own patterns of utilisation were (and are) less destructive of the environment.

More often than not, the agents of resource-intensification are given preferential treatment by the state, through the grant of generous long leases over mineral or fish stocks, for example, or the provision of raw material at an enormously subsidised price. With the injustice so compounded, local communities at the receiving end of this process have no recourse except direct action, resisting both the state and outside exploiters through a variety of protest techniques. These struggles might perhaps be seen as the manifestation of a new kind of class conflict. Where 'traditional' class conflicts were fought in the cultivated field or in the factory, these new struggles are waged over gifts of nature such as forests and water, gifts that are coveted by all but increasingly monopolised by a few.

There is, then, an unmistakable material context to the upsurge of environmental conflict in India; the shortages of, threats to and struggles over natural resources. No one could even suggest, with regard to India, what two distinguished scholars claimed some years ago with regard to American environmentalism, namely that it had exaggerated or imagined the risk posed by ecological degradation.[5] All the same, the environmentalism of the poor is neither universal nor pre-given—there are many parts of India (and the South more generally) where the destruction of the environment has generated little or no popular response. To understand where, how and in what manner environmental conflict articulates itself requires the kind of location-specific work, bounded in time and space, that social scientists have thus far reserved for studies of worker and peasant struggles.

This chapter focuses on an environmental conflict that was played out between 1984 and 1991 in the southern Indian state of Karnataka. This conflict is perhaps not as well known outside India as the Chipko or Narmada movements. But its unfolding powerfully illustrates the same, countrywide processes of resource deprivation and local resistance.

Claiming The Commons in Karnataka

On 14 November 1984, the government of Karnataka entered into an agreement with Harihar Polyfibres, a rayon-producing unit located in the north of the state; the company forms part of the great Indian industrial conglomerate owned by the Birla family. By this agreement a new company was formed, called the Karnataka Pulpwoods Limited (KPL), in which the government had a holding of 51 per cent and Harihar Polyfibres held 49 per cent. KPL was charged with growing eucalyptus and other fast-growing species of trees for the use by Harihar Polyfibres. For this purpose, the state had identified 30,000 hectares of common land, spread over four districts in the northern part of Karnataka. This land was nominally owned by the state (following precedents set under British colonial rule, when the state had arbitrarily asserted its rights of ownership over non-cultivated land all over India), but the grass, trees and shrubs standing on it were extensively used in surrounding villages for fuel, fodder and other materials.[6]

The land was granted by the state to KPL on a long lease of 40 years, and for a ridiculously low annual rent of one rupee per acre. As much as 87.5 per cent of the produce was to go directly to Harihar Polyfibres; the private sector company also had the option of buying the remaining 12.5 per cent. All in all, this was an extraordinarily advantageous arrangement for the Birla-owned firm. The government of Karnataka was even willing to stand guarantee for the loans that were to finance KPL's operations: loans to be obtained from several nationalised banks, one of which was, ironically, the National Bank of Agriculture and Rural Development.

For years before the formation of KPL the wood-based industry, faced with chronic short-ages of raw material, had been clamouring for captive plantations. Forests were being depleted all over India; in fact, this deforestation had itself been caused primarily by over-exploitation of trees to meet industrial demand. Although the state had granted them handsome subsid-ies in the provision of timber from government forests, paper, rayon and plywood compa-nies were keen to acquire firmer control over their sources of supply. Indian law prohibited large-scale ownership of land by private companies: in the circumstances, joint-sector com-panies (i.e., units jointly owned by the state and private capital) provided the most feasible option. Indeed, no sooner had KPL been formed then industrialists in other parts of India began pressing state governments to start similar units with their participation and for their benefit.

But, of course, paper and rayon factories were not alone in complaining about shortages of woody biomass. A decade earlier, the Chipko movement had highlighted the difficulties faced by villagers in gaining access to the produce of the forests. In the wake of Chipko had arisen a wide-ranging debate on forest policy, with scholars and activists arguing that state forest policies had consistently discriminated against the rights of peasants, tribals and pastoralists, while unduly favouring the urban—industrial sector.[7]

There was little question that, as a result of these policies, shortages of fuel and fodder had become pervasive throughout rural India. In Karnataka itself, one study estimated that while the annual demand for fuelwood in the state was 12.4 million tonnes (mt), the annual production was 10.4 mt—a shortfall of 16 per cent. In the case of fodder, the corresponding figures were 35.7 and 23 mt, respectively—a deficit of as much as 33 per cent.[8]

The fodder crisis in turn illustrated the crucial importance of species choice in programmes of reforestation. From the early 1960s, the government's Forest Department had enthusiastically promoted the plantation of eucalyptus on state-owned land. In many parts of India, rich, diverse natural forests were felled to make way for single-species plantations of this tree of Australian origin. As in the Thai district of Pakham (discussed in the Introduction), this choice was clearly dictated by industry, for eucalyptus is a quick growing species sought after by both paper and rayon mills. But it is totally unsuitable as fodder—indeed, one reason eucalyptus was planted by the Forest Department was that it is not browsed by cattle and goats, thus making regeneration that much easier to achieve. Environmentalists deplored this preference for eucalyptus, which was known to have negative effects on soil fertility, water retention and on biological diversity generally. Eucalyptus was, moreover, a 'plant which socially speaking has all the characteristics of a weed', in that it benefited industry at the expense of the rural poor, themselves hard hit by biomass shortages. These critics advocated the plantation and protection instead of multi-purpose, indigenous tree species more suited for meeting village requirements of fuel, fodder, fruit and fibre.[9]

In the context of this wider, all-India debate, the formation of KPL seemed a clearly partisan move in favour of industry, as the lands it took over constituted a vital, and often irreplaceable, source of biomass for small peasants, herdsmen and wood-working artisans. Within months of its establishment, the new company became the object of severe criticism. In December 1984, the state's pre-eminent writer and man of letters, Dr Kota Shivram Karanth, wrote an essay in the most popular Kannada daily, calling on the people of Karnataka to totally oppose 'this friendship between Birlas and the government and the resulting joint-sector company'.

The opposition to KPL grew after 15 July 1986, the date on which the state actually transferred the first instalment of land (3,590 hectares) to KPL. Even as the company was preparing the ground for planting eucalyptus, petitions and representations were flying thick and fast between the villages of north Karnataka (where the land was located) and the state capital of Bangalore, 250 miles to the south. The Chief Minister of Karnataka, Ramkrishna Hegde, was deluged with letters from individuals and organisations protesting against the formation of KPL; one letter, given wide prominence, was signed by a former Chief Minister, a former Chief Justice and a former Minister, respectively. Meanwhile, protest meetings were organised at several villages in the region. The matter was also raised in the state legislature.[10]

In the forefront of the movement against KPL was the Samaj Parivartan Samudaya (Association for Social Change, SPS), a voluntary organisation working in the Dharwad district of Karnataka. The SPS had in fact cut its teeth in a previous campaign against Harihar Polyfibres. It had organised a movement against the pollution of the Tungabhadra river by the rayon factory, whose untreated effluents were killing fish and undermining the health and livelihood of villagers living downstream. On 2 October 1984 (Mahatma Gandhi's birth anniversary), SPS held a large demonstration outside the production unit of Harihar Polyfibres; then in December 1985, it filed a public interest litigation in the High Court of Karnataka against the State Pollution Control Board for its failure to check the pollution of the Tungabhadra by the Birla factory.[11]

Before that petition could come up for hearing, SPS filed a public interest writ against Karnataka Pulpwoods Limited, this time in the Supreme Court of India in New Delhi. SPS was motivated to do so by a similar writ in the state High Court, filed by a youth organisation working among the farmers in the Sagar *taluka* (county) of the adjoining Shimoga district. Here, in a significant judgement, Justice Bopanna issued a stay order instructing the Deputy Commissioner of Shimoga to ensure that common land was not arbitrarily transferred to KPL, and that villagers be allowed access to fodder, fuel and other usufruct from the disputed land.[12]

Submitted in early 1987, the Supreme Court petition was primarily the handiwork of SPS. The petitioners spoke on behalf of the 500,000 villagers living in the region of KPL's operations, the people most directly affected by the action of the state in handing over common land to one company. The transferred land, said the petition, 'is the only available land vested in the village community since time immemorial and is entirely meant for meeting their basic needs like fodder, fuel, small timber, etc. Neither agriculture could be carried out, nor the minimum needs of life, such as leaves, firewood and cattle fodder could be sustained without the use of the said lands.'

In this context, the petition continued, the arbitrary and unilateral action of the state amounted to the passing of 'control of material resources from the hands of common people to capitalists'. This was a 'stark abuse of power', violating not just the general canons of social justice but also two provisions of the Indian Constitution itself: the right to fair procedure guaranteed by Article 14, and the right to life and liberty (in this case, of the village community) vested under Article 21 of the Constitution. Finally, the petitioners contended that the planting of monocultures of

Eucalyptus, as envisaged by KPL, would have a 'disastrous effect on the ecological balance of the region'.[13]

The arguments of equity and ecological stability aside, this petition is notable for its insistence that the lands in contention were common rather than state property, 'vested in the village community since time immemorial'. Here the claims of time and tradition were counterposed to the legal status quo, through which the state both claimed and enforced rights of ownership. In this respect the petition was perfectly in line with popular protests in defence of forest rights, which since colonial times have held the Forest Department to be an agent of usurpation, taking over by superior physical force land which by right belonged to the community.[14]

On 24 March 1987, the Supreme Court responded to the petition by issuing a stay order, thus preventing the government of Karnataka from transferring any more land to KPL. Encouraged by this preliminary victory, SPS now turned to popular mobilisation in the villages. In May, it held a training camp in non-violence at Kusnur, a village in Dharwad district, where 400 hectares of land had already been transferred to KPL. A parallel organisation of villagers, the Guddanadu Abhivruddi Samiti (Hill Areas Development Committee) was initiated to work alongside SPS. The two groups held a series of preparatory meetings in Kusnur and other villages nearby for a protest scheduled for 14 November 1987, to coincide with the third anniversary of the formation of KPL.

On 14 November, about 2,000 people converged at Kusnur. Men, women and children took an oath of non-violence in a school yard, and then proceeded for a novel protest, termed the Kithiko-Hachiko (Pluck-and-Plant) satyagraha. Led by drummers, waving banners and shouting slogans, the protesters moved on to the disputed area. Here they first uprooted 100 saplings of Eucalyptus before planting in their place tree species useful locally for fruit and for fodder. Before dispersing, the villagers took a pledge to water and tend the saplings they had planted.[15]

The next major development in the KPL case was the partial vacation, on 26 April 1988, by the Supreme Court of the stay it had granted a year previously. Now it allowed the transfer of a further 3,000 hectares to KPL (such interim and ad hoc grants of land were also allowed in 1989 and 1990).[16] The court seeming to have let them down, SPS prepared once more for direct action. They commenced training camps in the villages, planned to culminate in a fresh Pluck-and-Plant satyagraha. Meanwhile, journalists sympathetic to their movement intensified the press campaign against KPL.[17]

The mounting adverse publicity, and the prospect of renewed popular protest, forced the government of Karnataka to seek a compromise. On 3 June 1988, the Chief Secretary of the state government (its highest ranking official) convened a meeting attended by representatives of SPS, KPL and the Forest Department. He suggested the setting up of a one-man commission, comprising the distinguished ecologist Madhav Gadgil, to enquire into the conflicting claims (and demands) of the villagers and KPL. Until the commission submitted its report, KPL was asked to suspend its operations in Dharwad district, and SPS to withdraw its proposed monsoon satyagraha.

The setting up of committees and commissions is of course a classic delaying tactic, in India resorted to by colonial and democratic governments alike, to defuse and contain popular protest.

In this case, the government had no intention of formally appointing the Madhav Gadgil Commission, for the ecologist was known to be a critic of the industrial bias of state forest policy,[18] and likely to report adversely on KPL. Thus the commission was never set up; in response, SPS started organising another Pluck-and-Plant *satyagraha* for 8 August 1988. This time, however, the protesters were arrested and removed before they could reach KPL's eucalyptus plot.

In later years, non-violent direct action continued to be a vital plank of SPS's strategy. In an attempt to link more closely the issues of industrial pollution and the alienation of common land, it organised in August 1989, in the towns of Hangal and Ranibennur, public bonfires of rayon cloth made by Harihar Polyfibres. The burning of mill-made cloth recalled the bonfires of Manchester textiles during India's freedom movement. Whereas that campaign stood for national self-reliance or *swadeshi*, this one affirmed *village* self-reliance by rejecting cloth made of artificial fibre. The following year, 1990, SPS reverted to its own patented method of protest. On Indian independence day (15th August), it invited the respected Chipko leader Chandi Prasad Bhatt to lead a Pluck-and-Plant *satyagraha* in the Nagvand village of the Hirekerrur taluka of Dharwad.[19]

While these protests kept the issue alive at the grassroots, SPS continued to make use of the wider political and legal system to its advantage. Through friendly contacts in the state administration, it obtained copies of four orders issued in 1987 by the Chief Conservator of Forests (General), an official known to be particularly close to the Birlas. By these orders he had transferred a further 14,000 hectares of forest land to KPL, an area far in excess of what the Supreme Court had allowed. On the basis of these 'leaked' documents, SPS filed a further Contempt and Perjury petition in October 1988.

Meanwhile, the SPS persuaded public sector banks to delay the release of funds to KPL, pending the final hearing and settlement of the case in the Supreme Court. It had also effectively lobbied the government of India in New Delhi to clarify its own position on KPL-style schemes. In February 1988, an official of the Union Ministry of Environment and Forests, making a deposition in the Supreme Court, stated unambiguously that the raising of industrial plantations by joint-sector companies required the prior permission of the government of India. Later the same year, a new National Forest Policy was announced, which explicitly prohibited monocultural plantations on grounds of ecological stability. In June 1989 the Secretary of the Ministry of Environment and Forests wrote to the government of Karnataka expressing his disquiet about the KPL project.

Within Karnataka, resolutions asking the government to cancel the KPL agreement were passed by local representative bodies, including several *Mandal Panchayats*, local councils each representing a group of villages, as well as the *Zilla Parishad* (district council) of Dharwad. This was followed by a letter to the Chief Minister, signed by 54 members of the state legislature and sent on 11 July 1990, asking him to close down KPL so as 'to reserve village common land for the common use of villagers'. With public opinion and the central government arrayed against it, and possibly anticipating an adverse final judgement in the Supreme Court, the government of Karnataka decided to wind up KPL. The company's closure was formally announced at a board meeting on 27 September 1990, but by then KPL had already ceased operations. In its report for the previous financial year (April 1989 to March 1990) the company complained that 'during the year the plantation activity has practically come to a standstill, excepting raising 449 hectares of plantations'—a tiny fraction of the 30,000 hectares of common land it had once hoped to capture for its exclusive use.

A Vocabulary of Protest

The struggle against KPL had as its mass base, so to speak, the peasants, pastoralists, and fisherfolk directly affected by environmental abuse. Yet key leadership roles were assumed by activists who, although they came from the region, were not themselves directly engaged in production. Of the SPS activists involved more or less full-time in the movement, one had been a labour organiser, a second a social worker and progressive farmer, a third a biology PhD and former college lecturer, and a fourth an engineer who had returned to India after working for years in the United States. Crucial support was also provided by intellectuals more distant from the action. These included the greatest living Kannada writer, Dr Shivram Karanth, a figure of high moral authority and for this reason the first petitioner in the Supreme Court case against KPL. A co-petitioner was the Centre for Science and Environment, a respected Delhi-based research and advocacy group whose influence in the media and in the government was shrewdly drawn on by the activists from Karnataka.

This unity, of communities at the receiving end of ecological degradation and of social activists with the experience and education to negotiate the politics of protest, has been characteristic of environmental struggles in India. In other respects, too, the SPS-led struggle was quite typical. For underlying the KPL controversy were a series of oppositions that frame most such conflicts in India: rich versus poor, urban versus rural, nature for profit versus nature for subsistence, the state versus the people. However the KPL case was atypical in one telling respect, for environmental movements of the poor only rarely end in emphatic victory.

To put it in more explicitly ecological terms, these conflicts pit 'ecosystem people'—that is, those communities which depend very heavily on the natural resources of their own locality—against 'omnivores', individuals and groups with the social power to capture, transform and use natural resources from a much wider catchment area; sometimes, indeed, the whole world. The first category of ecosystem people includes the bulk of India's rural population: small peasants, landless labourers, tribals, pastoralists, and artisans. The category of omnivores comprises industrialists, professionals, politicians, and government officials—all of whom are based in the towns and cities—as well as a small but significant fraction of the rural élite, the prosperous farmers in tracts of heavily irrigated, chemically fertilised Green Revolution agriculture. The history of development in independent India can then be interpreted as being, in essence, a process of resource capture by the omnivores at the expense of ecosystem people. This has in turn created a third major ecological class: that of 'ecological refugees', peasants-turned-slum dwellers, who eke out a living in the cities on the leavings of omnivore prosperity.[20]

In this framework, the 'environmentalism of the poor' might be understood as the resistance offered by ecosystem people to the process of resource capture by omnivores: as embodied in movements against large dams by tribal communities to be displaced by them, or struggles by peasants against the diversion of forest and grazing land to industry. In recent years, the most important such struggle has been the Narmada Bachao Andolan (NBA), the movement representing the ecosystem people who face imminent displacement by a huge dam on the Narmada river in central India. The movement has been led by the forty-year-old Medha Patkar, a woman of courage and character once described by a journalist as an 'ecological Joan of Arc'.

A detailed analysis of the origins and development of the Narmada conflict cannot be provided here,[21] but there is one aspect of the movement that is of particular relevance to this book; namely, its flexible and wide-ranging vocabulary of protest.

The term 'vocabulary of protest' is offered as an alternative to Charles Tilly's well-known concept of the 'repertoire of contention'. Tilly and his associates have done pioneering work on the study of dissent and direct action. Their work has focused on the techniques most characteristic of different societies, social groups or historical periods. Tilly's own understanding of direct action tends to be a narrowly instrumental one, with participants drawing on, from a broader repertoire of contention, those techniques which most effectively defend or advance their economic and political interests.[22] But in fact techniques of direct action have at the same time an utilitarian and an expressive dimension. In adopting a particular strategy, social protesters are both trying to defend their interests *and* passing judgement on the prevailing social arrangements. The latter, so to say, ideological dimension of social protest needs to be inferred even when it is not formally articulated—the fact that protesting peasants do not distribute a printed manifesto does not mean that they do not have developed notions of right and wrong. In field or factory, ghetto or grazing ground, struggles over resources, even when they have tangible material origins, have always also been struggles over meaning. Thus my preference for the term 'vocabulary of protest'—for 'vocabulary' more than 'repertoire', and 'protest' more than 'contention'—helps to clarify the notion that most forms of direct action, even if unaccompanied by a written manifesto, are both statements of purpose and of belief. In the act of doing, protesters are saying something too. Thus the Kithiko-Hachiko *satyagraha* was not simply an affirmation of peasant claims over disputed property: as a strategy of protest, its aim was not merely to insist, 'This land is ours', but also, and equally significantly, to ask, 'What are trees for?'

To return to the Narmada Bachao Andolan. Like the anti-KPL struggle, the Narmada movement has operated simultaneously on several flanks: a strong media campaign, court petitions, and the lobbying of key players such as the World Bank, which was to fund a part of the dam project. Most effectively, though, it has deployed a dazzlingly varied vocabulary of protest, in defence of the rights of the peasants and tribal communities which were to be displaced by the dam.

These strategies of direct action might be classified under four broad headings. First, there is the collective *show of strength*, as embodied in demonstrations (Hindi: *pradarshan*) organised in towns and cities. Mobilising as many people as they can, protesters march through the town, shouting slogans, singing songs, winding their way to a public meeting that marks the procession's culmination. The aim here is to assert a presence in the city, which is the locus of local, provincial or national power. The demonstrators carry a message that is at once threatening and imploring: in effect, telling the rulers (and city people in general), 'do not forget us, the dispossessed in the countryside. We can make trouble, but not if you hand out justice'.

Second, there is the *disruption of economic life* through more militant acts of protest. One such tactic is the *hartal* or *bandh* (shut-down strike), wherein shops are forced to down shutters and buses to pull off the roads, bringing normal life to a standstill. A variation of this is the *rasta roko* (road blockade), through which traffic on an important highway is blocked by squatting protesters, sometimes for days on end. These techniques are rather more coercive than persuasive, spotlighting the economic costs to the state (or to other sections of the public) if they do not yield to the dissenters.

Whereas the *hartal* or *rasta roko* aim at disrupting economic activity across a wide area, a third type of action is more sharply focused on an individual target. For instance, the *dharna* or sit-down strike is used to stop work at a specific dam site or mine. Sometimes the target is a figure of authority rather than a site of production; thus protesting peasants might *gherao* (surround) a high public official, allowing him to move only after he has heard their grievances and promised to act upon them.

The fourth generic strategy of direct action aims at putting moral pressure on the state as a whole, not merely on one of its functionaries. Pre-eminent here is the *bhook hartal*, the indefinite hunger strike undertaken by the charismatic leader of a popular movement. This technique was once used successfully by Sunderlal Bahuguna of the Chipko movement; in recent years, it has been resorted to on several occasions by Medha Patkar, the remarkable leader of the Narmada Bachao Andolan. In the *bhook hartal*, the courage and self-sacrifice of the individual leader is directly counterposed to the claims to legitimacy of the state. The fast is usually carried out in a public place, and closely reported in the media. As the days drag on, and the leader's health perilously declines, the state is forced into a gesture of submission—if only the constitution of a fresh committee to review the case in contention.

The *bhook hartal* is most often the preserve of a single, heroic, exemplary figure. A sister technique, also aimed at *shaming the state*, is more of a collective undertaking. This is the *jail bharo andolan* (literally, 'movement to fill the jails'), in which protesters peacefully and deliberately court arrest by violating the law, hoping the government would lose face by putting behind bars large numbers of its own citizens. The law most often breached is Section 144 of the Criminal Procedure Code, invoked, in anticipation of social tension, to prohibit gatherings of more than five people.

The *pradarshan, hartal, rasta roko, dharna, gherao, bhook hartal* and *jail bharo andolan* are some of the techniques which make up the environmental movement's vocabulary of protest. This is a vocabulary shared across the spectrum of protesting groups, but new situations constantly call for new innovations. In the 1970s, peasants in Garhwal developed the idiosyncratic but truly effective Chipko technique; in the 1980s, the SPS in Dharwad, opposing eucalyptus plantations, thought up the Kithiko-Hachiko *satyagraha*; and now, in the 1990s, the Narmada Bachao Andolan has threatened a *jal samadhi* (water burial), saying its cadres would refuse to move from the villages scheduled for submergence even after the dam's sluice gates are closed and the waters start rising.

The techniques of direct action itemised above have, of course, deep and honourable origins. They were first forged, in India's long struggle for freedom from British rule, by Mohandas

Karamchand 'Mahatma' Gandhi. In developing and refining this vocabulary of protest, Gandhi drew on Western theories of civil disobedience as well as traditions of peasant resistance within India itself.[23]

In fact, Mahatma Gandhi provides the environmental movement with both a vocabulary of protest and an ideological critique of development in independent India. The invocation of Gandhi is thus conducted through what might be called a rhetoric of betrayal. For the sharpening of environmental conflict has vividly brought to light the failed hopes of India's freedom struggle. That movement commanded a mass base among the peasantry, assiduously developed by Gandhi himself, and freedom promised a new deal for rural India. And yet, after 1947 the political élite has worked to ensure that the benefits of planned economic development have flown primarily to the urban—industrial complex.

The KPL case illustrates this paradox as well as any other. On one side were the peasants and pastoralists of north Karnataka; on the other, an insensitive state government in league with the second largest business conglomerate in the country. As one protester expressed it in Kusnur: 'Our forefathers who fought to get rid of the foreign yoke thought that our country would become a land of milk and honey once the British were driven out. But now we see our rulers joining hands with the monopolists to take away basic resources like land, water and forests from the (village) people who have traditionally used 'them for their livelihood.' In much the same vein, a Chipko activist once told the present writer: 'After independence, we thought our forests would be used to build local industries and generate local employment, and our water resources to light our lamps and run our flour mills.' But to his dismay, the Himalayan forests continued to service the paper and turpentine factories of the plains, and the rivers were dammed to supply drinking water to Delhi and electricity to the national grid which feeds into industries and urban agglomerations all over India. While private industry has thus gained privileged access to natural resources, the burden of environmental degradation has fallen heavily on the rural poor. To invoke a slogan made famous by the Narmada Bachao Andolan, this has been a process of 'destructive development'—destructive both of rural society and of the natural fabric within which it rests. In a bitter commentary on this process, the common people of Dharwad district have come to refer to the noxious air outside Harihar Polyfibres as 'Birla Perfume', to the water of the Tungabhadra river as 'Birla Teertha' (holy water of the Birlas), and to the eucalyptus as 'Birla Kalpataru' (the Birla wonder tree).[24]

The environmental movement's return to Gandhi is then also a return to his vision for free India: a vision of a 'village-centred economic order' that has been so completely disregarded in practice. Perhaps it is more accurate to see this as a rhetoric of betrayal *and* of affirmation, as symbolised in the dates most often chosen to launch (or end) programmes of direct action. These dates are 2 October, Gandhi's birth anniversary; 15 August, Indian Independence Day; and most poignantly, 8 August, on which day in 1942 Gandhi's last great anti-colonial campaign was launched, the Quit India movement—in invoking this environmentalists are asking the state and the capitalists, the rulers of today, to 'quit' their control over forests and water.

Two Kinds of Environmentalism

In the preceding sections of this chapter, the KPL controversy has been used to outline the origins, trajectory and rhetoric of the environmental movement in India. In conclusion, let us broaden the discussion by briefly contrasting the 'environmentalism of the poor' with the more closely studied phenomenon of First World environmentalism. This analysis derives, for the most part, from my own research on the United States and India, two countries, ecologically and culturally diverse, but at very different 'stages' of economic development. These are the countries and environmental movements I know best, and yet, because of their size and importance, they might be taken as representative, more generally, of the North and the South.[25]

I begin with the origins of the environmental impulse in the two contexts. Environmental movements in the North have, I think, been convincingly related to the emergence of a post-materialist or post-industrial society. The creation of a mass consumer society has not only enlarged opportunities for leisure but also provided the means to put this time off work to the most diverse uses. Nature is made accessible through the car, now no longer a monopoly of the élite but an artefact in almost everyone's possession. It is the car which, more than anything else, opens up a new world, of the wild, that is refreshingly different from the worlds of the city and the factory. In a curious paradox, this 'most modern creation of industry' becomes the vehicle of anti-industrial impulses, taking one to distant adventures, to 'homey little towns, enchanting fairy tale forests, far from stale routine, functional ugliness or the dictates of the clock'.[26] Here lies the source of popular support for the protection of wilderness in the United States—namely, that nature is no longer restricted to the privileged few, but available to all.

In India, still dominantly a nation of villages, environmentalism has emerged at a relatively early stage in the industrial process. Nature-based conflicts, it must be pointed out once again, are at the root of the environmental movement in countries such as India. These conflicts have their root in a lopsided, iniquitous and environmentally destructive process of development in independent India. They are played out against a backdrop of visible ecological degradation, the drying up of springs, the decimation of forests, the erosion of the land. The sheer immediacy of resource shortages means that direct action has been, from the beginning, a vital component of environmental action. Techniques of direct action often rely on traditional networks of organisation, the village and the tribe, and traditional forms of protest, the *dharna* and the *bhook hartal*.

Northern environmentalism, in contrast, relies rather more heavily on the 'social movement organisation'—such as the Sierra Club or the Friends of the Earth—with its own cadre, leadership and properly audited sources of funds. This organisation then draws on the methods of redressal available in what are, after all, more complete democracies—methods such as the court case, the lobbying of legislators and ministers, the exposure on television or in the newspaper. But the experience of recent years somewhat qualifies this contrast between militant protest in the one sphere and lobbying and litigation in the other. Indian environmentalists (as with the KPL case) are turning increasingly to the courts as a supplement to popular protest, while in America, radicals disaffected by the gentle, incremental lobbying of mainstream groups have taken to direct action—the spiking of trees, for example—to protect threatened wilderness.

In both the North and the South, however, environmentalism has been, in good measure, a response to the failure of politicians to mobilize effectively on the issue of, as the case may be, the destruction of the wilderness or the dispossession of peasants by a large dam. In India, for instance, the environmental movement has drawn on the struggles of marginal populations—hill peasants, tribal communities, fishermen, people displaced by construction of dams—neglected by the existing political parties. And as a 'new social movement', environmentalism in the North emerged, in the first instance, outside the party process. Some environmentalists considered themselves as neither left nor right, representing a constituency that was anti-class or, more accurately, post-class.[27] However, over time the environmental constituency became part of the democratic process, sometimes through the formation of Green parties that fight, and even occasionally win, elections.

Origins and political styles notwithstanding, the two varieties of environmentalism perhaps differ most markedly in their ideologies. The environmentalism of the poor originates as a clash over productive resources: a third kind of class conflict, so to speak, but one with deep ecological implications. Red on the outside, but green on the inside. In Southern movements, issues of ecology are often interlinked with questions of human rights, ethnicity and distributive justice. These struggles, of peasants, tribals and so on, are in a sense deeply conservative (in the best sense of the word), refusing to exchange a world they know, and are in partial control over, for an uncertain and insecure future. They are a defence of the locality and the local community against the nation. At the same time, the sharper edge to environmental conflict, and its close connections to subsistence and survival, have also prompted a thoroughgoing critique of consumerism and of uncontrolled economic development.

In contrast, the wilderness movement in the North originates outside the production process. It is in this respect more of a single-issue movement, calling for a change in attitudes (towards the natural world) rather than a change in systems of production or distribution. Especially in the United States, environmentalism has, by and large, run parallel to the consumer society without questioning its socio-ecological basis, its enormous dependence on the lands, peoples and resources of other parts of the globe.[28] It is absorbed not so much with relations within human society, as with relations between humans and other species. Here the claims of national sovereignty are challenged not from the vantage point of the locality, but from the perspective of the biosphere as a whole. This is a movement whose self-perception is that of a vanguard, moving from an 'ethical present' where we are concerned only with nation, region and race to an 'ethical future' where our moral development moves from a concern with plants and animals to ecosystems and the planet itself.[29]

In the preceding paragraphs, I have sketched a broad-brush comparison between two movements, in two different parts of the world, each carrying the prefix 'environmental'. One must, of course, qualify this picture by acknowledging the diversity of ideologies and of forms of action within each of these two trends. In the United States, anti-pollution struggles form a tradition of environmental action which has a different focus from the 'wilderness crusade'. Such, for instance, is the movement for environmental justice in the United States, the struggles of low-class, often black communities against the incinerators and toxic waste dumps that, by accident and frequently by design, come to be sited near them (and away from affluent neighbourhoods).

One American commentator, Ruth Rosen, has nicely captured the contrast between the environmental justice movement and the wilderness lovers. 'At best', she writes, 'the large, mainstream environmental groups focus on the health of the planet—the wilderness, forests and oceans that cannot protect themselves. In contrast, the movement for environmental justice, led by the poor, is not concerned with overabundance, but with the environmental hazards and social and economic inequalities that ravage their communities.'[30]

Likewise, the Northern wilderness crusade has its representatives in the Third World, who spearhead the constitution of vast areas as national parks and sanctuaries, strictly protected from 'human interference'. Southern lovers of the wilderness come typically from patrician backgrounds, and have shown little regard for the fate of the human communities who, after parkland is designated as 'protected', are abruptly displaced without compensation from territory that they have lived on for generations and come to regard as their own.[31]

These caveats notwithstanding, there remains, on the whole, a clear distinction, in terms of origins and forms of articulation, between how environmental action characteristically expresses itself in the North and in the South. Take these two episodes of protest, one from California, the other from central India, the last illustrations of this chapter.

In May 1979, a young American environmentalist, Mark Dubois, chained himself to a boulder in the Stanislaus river in California. The canyon where he lay formed part of the reservoir of the New Melones dam, whose construction Dubois and his organisation, Friends of the River, had long but unsuccessfully opposed. In October 1978, the Army Corps of Engineers had completed the dam, and the following April it closed the floodgates. The level of the reservoir started to rise, and it appeared as if the campaign to 'Save the Stanislaus' had failed. But then, in an act of rare heroism, Mark Dubois went into the waters and chained himself to a rock. He chose a hidden spot, and only one friend knew of the location.[32]

Fourteen years later, an uncannily similar strategy of protest was threatened against another dam, on another river and on another continent. In August 1993, with the onset of the Indian monsoon, the vast reservoir of the Sardar Sarovar dam on the Narmada river began filling up to capacity. It now seemed that the decade-long Narmada Bachao Andolan had irrevocably lost its fight. But the leader of the movement, Medha Patkar, decided to drown herself in the waters. Patkar announced her decision to walk into the river on 6 August, with a group of colleagues, but at a place and time not to be disclosed. Fearing detention by the police, Patkar disappeared into the countryside weeks before the appointed date.

I dare say Medha Patkar had not heard of Mark Dubois, but the parallels in their chosen forms of protest are striking indeed. Both formed part of ongoing, popular movements against large dams. It was only when the movement seemed to have failed that Patkar and Dubois decided to throw the last card in their pack, offering their lives to stop the dam. Notably, in both cases the political system was alert (or open) enough not to allow the environmentalists to make this supreme sacrifice. In Stanislaus, the Corps of Engineers stopped filling the reservoir, and sent search parties by air and on land to find and rescue Dubois. In the Narmada valley, Patkar and her band were found and prevailed upon to withdraw their *samarpan dal* (martyrs squad), in return for which the Government of India promised a fresh, independent review of the Sardar Sarovar project.

While the strategies of direct action might have been superficially similar, their underlying motivations were not. Mark Dubois and his colleagues were striving, above all, to save the Stanislaus canyon as one of the last remaining examples of the unspoilt Californian wilderness. As Dubois wrote to the Colonel of the Corps of Engineers prior to entering the river: 'All the life of this canyon, its wealth of archaeological and historical roots to our past, and its unique geological grandeur are enough reasons to protect this canyon *just for itself*. But in addition, all the spiritual values with which this canyon has filled tens of thousands of folks should prohibit us from committing the unconscionable act of wiping this place off the face of the earth'.[33]

In contrast, Patkar and her colleagues hoped not only to save the Narmada river itself, but also (and more crucially) the tens of thousands of peasants to be displaced by the dam being built on the river. When completed the Sardar Sarovar project will submerge a total of 245 villages, with an estimated total population of 66,675 people, most of whom are tribals and poor peasants.[34] True, the dam will also inundate old-growth forests and historic sites, but it will most emphatically of all destroy the living culture of the human communities who live by the Narmada river. It is thus that the struggle of Patkar and her associates becomes—as they put it in a message written on the 42nd anniversary of Mahatma Gandhi's martydom—a move 'towards our ultimate goal of [a] socially just and ecologically sustainable model of development'.[35]

The Stanislaus/Narmada or Dubois/Patkar comparison illustrates a more fundamental difference between two varieties of environmentalism. The action of Mark Dubois, heroic though it undoubtedly was, was quite in line with the dominant thrust of the environmental movement in the North towards the protection of pristine, unspoilt nature: a reservoir of biological diversity and enormous aesthetic appeal which serves as an ideal (if temporary) haven from the urban workaday world. In protecting the wild, it asserts, we are both acknowledging an ethical responsibility towards other species and enriching the spiritual side of our own existence. In contrast, the action of Medha Patkar was consistent with the dominant thrust of the environmental movement in India, which strongly highlights the questions of production and distribution within human society. It is impossible to say, with regard to India, what Jurgen Habermas has claimed of the European green movement: namely, that it is sparked not 'by problems of distribution, but by concern for the grammar of forms of life'.[36] 'No Humanity without Nature!', the epitaph of the Northern environmentalist, is here answered by the equally compelling slogan 'No Nature without Social Justice!'[37]

Notes

1. This chapter is based on a paper first presented at a conference on 'Dissent and Direct Action in the Late Twentieth Century', organised by the Harry and Frank Guggenheim Foundation at Otavalo, Ecuador, in June 1994.
2. J. Bandyopadhyay, 'Political Economy of Drought and Water Scarcity', *Economic and Political Weekly*, 12 December 1987.
3. Most authoritatively, perhaps, in the first two Citizens Reports on the Indian environment, brought out by New Delhi's Centre for Science and Environment in 1982 and 1985.
4. The development of the Chipko movement is discussed in Ramachandra Guha, *The Unquiet Woods: Ecological Change and Peasant Resistance in the Himalaya* (New Delhi:

478   **RAMACHANDRA GUHA**

Oxford University Press and Berkeley:
University of California Press, 1989).

5. See Mary Douglas and Aaron Wildavsky, *Risk and Culture: An Essay on the Selection of Technical and Environmental Dangers* (Berkeley: University of California Press, 1982).

6. Aside from specific sources cited later, this discussion of the KPL case also draws on numerous unpublished and locally printed documents, as well as my own fieldwork and interviews in the region.

7. See, among other works, Anon, *Undeclared Civil War: A Critique of the Forest Policy* (New Delhi: Peoples Union for Democratic Rights, 1982); Walter Fernandes and Sharad Kulkarni (eds), *Towards a New Forest Policy* (New Delhi: Indian Social Institute, 1983); Ramachandra Guha, 'Forestry in British and Post–British India: A Historical Analysis', *Economic and Political Weekly*, in two parts, 29 October and 5–12 November 1983.

8. Madhav Gadgil and Madhulika Sinha, 'The Biomass Budget of Karnataka', in Cecil J. Saldanha (ed.), *The State of Karnataka's Environment* (Bangalore: Centre for Taxonomic Studies, 1985).

9. See Anil Agarwal and Sunita Narain (eds), *The State of India's Environment: A Citizens' Report 1984–85* (New Delhi: Centre for Science and Environment, 1985); J. Bandyopadhyay and Vandana Shiva, *Ecological Audit of Eucalyptus Cultivation* (Dehradun: Natraj Publishers, 1984).

10. *Jagruta Vani* (quarterly newsletter of the Samaj Parivartan Samudaya, Dharwad), volume 2, number 4, December 1986.

11. Writ Petition number 19483 in the High Court of Karnataka, Bangalore (SPS and others versus Karnataka State Pollution Control Board and others). On the anti-pollution movement, see also S.R. Hiremath, 'How to Fight a Corporate Giant', in Anil Agarwal, Darryl D'Monte and Ujjwala Samarth (eds), *The Fight for Survival* (New Delhi: Centre for Science and Environment, 1987).

12. Sadanand Kanvalli, *Quest for Justice* (Dharwad: SPS and others, 1990), 7.

13. Writ Petition (Civil) number 35 of 1987 in the Supreme Court of India, New Delhi (Dr K. Shivram Karanth, SPS et al. versus the State of Karnataka, KPL et al.)

14. Cf Ramachandra Guha and Madhav Gadgil, 'State Forestry and Social Conflict in British India', *Past and Present*, 123 (May 1989).

15. Ajit Bhattacharjea, 'Satyagraha in Kusnur', in two parts, *Deccan Herald* (Bangalore), 19 and 20 November 1987. Coined by Mahatma Gandhi, the term 'satyagraha' (literally, 'truth-force') is used generically in India to denote any form of non-violent direct action.

16. S. R. Hiremath, 'The Karnataka Pulpwoods Limited Case', paper presented at the training workshop on Environment, People and the Law, Centre for Science and Environment, New Delhi, 12–15 October 1992.

17. Ajit Bhattacharjea, 'KPL Strikes Back' and 'Kusnur: Significant Success', in *Deccan Herald*, issues of 5 May and 15 June 1988 respectively.

18. See, for instance, Madhav Gadgil, S. Narendra Prasad and Rauf Ali, 'Forest Policy and Forest Management in India: A Critical Review', *Social Action*, 27: 1 (1983).

19. *The Hindu* (Bangalore), 20 August 1990.

20. For a fuller definition and application of these categories, see Madhav Gadgil and Ramachandra Guha, *Ecology and Equity: the Use and Abuse of Nature in Contemporary India* (London: Routledge, 1995).

21. The interested reader is referred to, among other works, Bradford Morse et al. *The Sardar Sarovar Project: The Report of the Independent Review* (Washington: The World Bank, 1993); Amita Baviskar, *In the Belly of the River: Adivasi Battles over Nature in the Narmada Valley* (New Delhi: Oxford University, 1995); Gadgil and Guha, *Ecology and Equity*, ch. 3.

22. Tilly's works include *From Mobilization to Revolution* (Reading, MA: Addison–Wesley, 1978) and *The Contentious French* (Cambridge, MA: Harvard University Press, 1986). Cf. also the Tilly-inspired two-part special section entitled 'Historical Perspectives on Social Movements', *Social Science History*, 17: 2 and 3 (summer and fall, 1993).

23. In contemporary India these 'Gandhian' techniques are by no means the sole preserve of the environmental movement. They are used in all sorts of social struggles: by farmers wanting higher fertiliser subsidies, hospital workers wanting greater security of tenure, or ethnic minorities fighting for a separate province.

24. Kanvalli, *Quest for Justice*, 1.

25. Important studies of American environmentalism include, to select from a vast and ever proliferating literature, W. R. Burch, Jr, *Daydreams and Nightmares: A Sociological Essay on the American Environment* (New York: Harper & Row, 1971); Donald Fleming, 'Roots of the New Conservation Movement', in Fleming and Bernard Bailyn (eds), *Perspectives in American History, Volume VI* (Cambridge, MA: Charles Warren Center for Studies in American History, 1972); Linda Graber, *Wilderness as Sacred Space* (Washington, DC: Association of American Geographers, 1976); Roderick Nash, *Wilderness and the American Mind*, 3rd edn. (New Haven, CT: Yale University Press, 1983); Alfred Runte, *National Parks: The American Experience* (Lincoln: University of Nebraska Press, 1984); Stephen Fox, *The American Conservation Movement: John Muir and His Legacy* (Madison: University of Wisconsin Press, 1985); Samuel P. Hays, *Beauty, Health and Permanence: Environmental Politics in the United States, 1955–1985* (New York: Cambridge University Press, 1987); and, most recently, Philip Shabecoff, *A Fierce Green Fire: The American Environmental Movement* (New York: Hill & Wang, 1993). We cite some only influential books, without taking notice of a huge outcrop of journal and magazine articles. There is nothing like this profusion of work with regard to the environmental movement in India. Useful overviews are provided in Anil Agarwal, 'Human–Nature Interactions in a Third World Country', *The Environmentalist*, 6: 3 (1987) and in Bina Agarwal, 'The Gender and Environment Debate: Lessons from India', *Feminist Studies*, 18: 1 (1992). Other relevant writings include Guha, *The Unquiet Woods*; Vandana Shiva, with J. Bandyopadhyay, P. Hegde, B. V. Krishnamurthy, J. Kurien, G. Narendranath, V. Ramprasad and S. T. S. Reddy, *Ecology and the Politics of Survival* (New Delhi: Sage, 1991); Madhav Gadgil and Ramachandra Guha, 'Ecological Conflicts and the Environmental Movement in India', *Development and Change*, 25: 1 (1994); Baviskar, *In the Belly of the River* (New Delhi: Oxford University Press, 1995).

26. Wolfgang Sachs, *For Love of the Automobile: Looking Back into the History of our Desires* (Berkeley: University of California Press, 1992), 150–1.

27. A point first made by the British sociologist Stephen Cotgrove in his book *Catastrophe or Cornucopia?* (Chichester: Wiley, 1982).

28. This silence is more fully explored in Ramachandra Guha and Juan Martinez-Alier (eds), *Varieties of Environmentalism* (London: Earthipan, 1997), ch. 5.

29. Cf. Roderick Nash, *The Rights of Nature: A History of Environmental Ethics* (Madison: University of Wisconsin Press, 1989).

30. Ruth Rosen, 'Who Gets Polluted: The Movement for Environmental Justice', *Dissent* (New York; spring 1994), 229. Cf also Andrew Szasz, *Ecopopulism: Toxic Waste and the Movement for Environmental Justice* (Minneapolis: University of Minnesota Press, 1994); Bunyan Bryant (ed.), *Environmental Justice: Issues, Policies and Solutions* (Washington D.C.: Island Press, 1995).

31. Cf Patrick C. West and Steven R. Brechin (eds), *Resident Peoples and National Parks: Social Dilemmas and Strategies in International Conservation* (Tucson: The University of Arizona Press, 1991).

32. Tim Palmer, *Stanislaus: The Struggle for a River* (Berkeley: University of California Press, 1982), ch. 8.

33. Mark Dubois to Colonel Donald O'Shei, reproduced in ibid. 163–4 (author's italics).

34. Anon., *The Narmada Valley Project: A Critique* (New Delhi: Kalpavriksh, 1988).

35. Circular letter from Medha Patkar and others, dated 30 January 1990.

36. Habermas, 'New Social Movements', *Telos*, 49 (1981). Habermas further observes: 'This new

type of (environmental) conflict is an expression of the "silent revolution" in values and attitudes that R. Inglehart has ascertained for entire populations.' This endorsement of the post-materialist thesis seemingly denies (as does Inglehart) the very material roots of environmental conflict in industrialised societies.

37. Smitu Kothari and Pramod Parajuli, 'No Nature without Social Justice: A Plea for Ecological and Cultural Pluralism in India', in Wolfgang Sachs (ed.), *Global Ecology: A New Arena of Political Conflict* (London: Zed Books, 1993).

34 Poverty and Globalization

Vandana Shiva

Recently, I was visiting Bhatinda in Punjab because of an epidemic of farmers' suicides. Punjab used to be the most prosperous agricultural region in India. Today every farmer is in debt and despair. Vast stretches of land have become water-logged desert. And as an old farmer pointed out, even the trees have stopped bearing fruit because heavy use of pesticides have killed the pollinators—the bees and butterflies.

And Punjab is not alone in experiencing this ecological and social disaster. Last year I was in Warangal, Andhra Pradesh where farmers have also been committing suicide. Farmers who traditionally grew pulses and millets and paddy have been lured by seed companies to buy hybrid cotton seeds referred to by the seed merchants as 'white gold', which were supposed to make them millionaires. Instead, they became paupers.

Their native seeds have been displaced with new hybrids which cannot be saved and need to be purchased every year at high cost. Hybrids are also very vulnerable to pest attacks. Spending on pesticides in Warangal has shot up 2000 per cent from $2.5 million in the 1980s to $50 million in 1997. Now farmers are consuming the same pesticides as a way of killing themselves so that they can escape permanently from unpayable debt.

The corporations are now trying to introduce genetically engineered seed which will further increase costs and ecological risks. That is why farmers like Malla Reddy of the Andhra Pradesh Farmers' Union had uprooted Monsanto's genetically engineered Bollgard cotton in Warangal.

On March 27, 25-year-old Betavati Ratan took his life because he could not pay back debts for drilling a deep tube well on his two-acre farm. The wells are now dry, as are the wells in Gujarat and Rajasthan where more than 50 million people face a water famine.

The drought is not a 'natural disaster'. It is 'man-made'. It is the result of mining of scarce ground water in arid regions to grow thirsty cash crops for exports instead of water prudent food crops for local needs.

It is experiences such as these which tell me that we are so wrong to be smug about the new global economy. I will argue in this lecture that it is time to stop and think about the impact of globalization on the lives of ordinary people. This is vital to achieve sustainability.

Seattle and the World Trade Organization protests [in 1999] have forced everyone to think again. Throughout this lecture series people have referred to different aspects of sustainable

BBC Reith Lecture 2000; online at
<http://news.bbc.co.uk/hi/english/static/events/reith_2000/lecture5.htm>.

development taking globalization for granted. For me it is now time radically to re-evaluate what we are doing. For what we are doing in the name of globalization to the poor is brutal and unforgivable. This is specially evident in India as we witness the unfolding disasters of globalization, especially in food and agriculture.

Who feeds the world? My answer is very different to that given by most people.

It is women and small farmers working with biodiversity who are the primary food providers in the Third World, and, contrary to the dominant assumption, their biodiversity-based small farms are more productive than industrial monocultures.

The rich diversity and sustainable systems of food production are being destroyed in the name of increasing food production. However, with the destruction of diversity, rich sources of nutrition disappear. When measured in terms of nutrition per acre, and from the perspective of biodiversity, the so-called 'high yields' of industrial agriculture or industrial fisheries do not imply more production of food and nutrition.

Yields usually refers to production per unit area of a single crop. Output refers to the total production of diverse crops and products. Planting only one crop in the entire field as a mono-culture will of course increase its individual yield. Planting multiple crops in a mixture will have low yields of individual crops, but will have high total output of food. Yields have been defined in such a way as to make the food production on small farms by small farmers disap-pear. This hides the production by millions of women farmers in the Third World—farmers like those in my native Himalaya who fought against logging in the Chipko movement, who in their terraced fields even today grow Jhangora (barnyard millet), Marsha (Amaranth), Tur (Pigeon Pea), Urad (Black gram), Gahat (horse gram), Soya Bean (Glycine Max), Bhat (Glycine Soya)—endless diversity in their fields. From the biodiversity perspective, biodiversity-based productivity is higher than monoculture productivity. I call this blindness to the high product-ivity of diversity a 'Monoculture of the Mind', which creates monocultures in our fields and in our world.

The Mayan peasants in the Chiapas are characterized as unproductive because they pro-duce only 2 tons of corn per acre. However, the overall food output is 20 tons per acre when the diversity of their beans and squashes, their vegetables, and their fruit trees are taken into account.

In Java, small farmers cultivate 607 species in their home gardens. In sub-Saharan Africa, women cultivate 120 different plants. A single home garden in Thailand has 230 species, and African home gardens have more than 60 species of trees.

Rural families in the Congo eat leaves from more than 50 species of their farm trees.

A study in eastern Nigeria found that home gardens occupying only 2 per cent of a household's farmland accounted for half of the farm's total output. In Indonesia 20 per cent of household income and 40 per cent of domestic food supplies come from the home gardens managed by women.

Research done by FAO has shown that small biodiverse farms can produce thousands of times more food than large, industrial monocultures.

And diversity, in addition to giving more food, is the best strategy for preventing drought and desertification.

What the world needs to feed a growing population sustainably is biodiversity intensification, not the chemical intensification or the intensification of genetic engineering. While women and small peasants feed the world through biodiversity, we are repeatedly told that without genetic engineering and globalization of agriculture the world will starve. In spite of all empirical evidence showing that genetic engineering does not produce more food and in fact often leads to a yield decline, it is constantly promoted as the only alternative available for feeding the hungry.

That is why I ask, who feeds the world?

This deliberate blindness to diversity, the blindness to nature's production, production by women, and production by Third World farmers, allows destruction and appropriation to be projected as creation.

Take the case of the much flouted 'golden rice' or genetically engineered vitamin A rice as a cure for blindness. It is assumed that without genetic engineering we cannot remove vitamin A deficiency. However, nature gives us abundant and diverse sources of vitamin A. If rice was not polished, rice itself would provide vitamin A. If herbicides were not sprayed on our wheat fields, we would have bathua, amaranth, mustard leaves as delicious and nutritious greens that provide vitamin A.

Women in Bengal use more than 150 plants as greens—Hinche sak (Enhydra fluctuans), Palang sak (Spinacea oleracea), Tak palang (Rumex vesicarious), Lal Sak (Amaranthus gangeticus)—to name but a few.

But the myth of creation presents biotechnologists as the creators of vitamin A, negating nature's diverse gifts and women's knowledge of how to use this diversity to feed their children and families.

The most efficient means of rendering the destruction of nature, local economies, and small autonomous producers is by rendering their production invisible.

Women who produce for their families and communities are treated as 'non-productive' and 'economically' inactive. The devaluation of women's work, and of work done in sustainable economies, is the natural outcome of a system constructed by capitalist patriarchy. This is how globalization destroys local economies and destruction itself is counted as growth.

And women themselves are devalued. Because many women in the rural and indigenous communities work cooperatively with nature's processes, their work is often contradictory to the dominant market-driven 'development' and trade policies. And because work that satisfies needs and ensures sustenance is devalued in general, there is less nurturing of life and life-support systems.

The devaluation and invisibility of sustainable, regenerative production is most glaring in the area of food. While patriarchal division of labour has assigned women the role of feeding their families and communities, patriarchal economics and patriarchal views of science and technology magically make women's work in providing food disappear. 'Feeding the World' becomes disassociated from the women who actually do it and is projected as dependent on global agribusiness and biotechnology corporations.

However, industrialization and genetic engineering of food and globalization of trade in agriculture are recipes for creating hunger, not for feeding the poor.

Everywhere, food production is becoming a negative economy, with farmers spending more to buy costly inputs for industrial production than the price they receive for their produce. The consequence is rising debts and epidemics of suicides in both poor and rich countries.

Economic globalization is leading to a concentration of the seed industry, increased use of pesticides, and, finally, increased debt. Capital-intensive, corporate-controlled agriculture is being spread into regions where peasants are poor but, until now, have been self-sufficient in food. In the regions where industrial agriculture has been introduced through globalization, higher costs are making it virtually impossible for small farmers to survive.

The globalization of non-sustainable industrial agriculture is literally evaporating the incomes of Third World farmers through a combination of devaluation of currencies, increase in costs of production and a collapse in commodity prices.

Farmers everywhere are being paid a fraction of what they received for the same commodity a decade ago. The Canadian National Farmers Union put it like this in a report to the senate this year:

While the farmers growing cereal grains—wheat, oats, corn—earn negative returns and are pushed close to bankruptcy, the companies that make breakfast cereals reap huge profits. In 1998, cereal companies Kellogg's, Quaker Oats, and General Mills enjoyed return on equity rates of 56%, 165% and 222% respectively. While a bushel of corn sold for less than $4, a bushel of corn flakes sold for $133. . . . Maybe farmers are making too little because others are taking too much.

And a World Bank report has admitted that 'behind the polarisation of domestic consumer prices and world prices is the presence of large trading companies in international commodity markets'.

While farmers earn less, consumers pay more. In India, food prices have doubled between 1999 and 2000. The consumption of food grains in rural areas has dropped by 12%. Increased economic growth through global commerce is based on pseudo surpluses. More food is being traded while the poor are consuming less. When growth increases poverty, when real production becomes a negative economy, and speculators are defined as 'wealth creators', something has gone wrong with the concepts and categories of wealth and wealth creation. Pushing the real production by nature and people into a negative economy implies that production of real goods and services is declining, creating deeper poverty for the millions who are not part of the dot.com route to instant wealth creation.

Women—as I have said—are the primary food producers and food processors in the world. However, their work in production and processing is now becoming invisible.

Recently, the McKinsey corporation said: 'American food giants recognize that Indian agro-business has lots of room to grow, especially in food processing. India processes a minuscule 1 per cent of the food it grows compared with 70 per cent for the U.S.'.

It is not that we Indians eat our food raw. Global consultants fail to see the 99% food processing done by women at household level, or by the small cottage industry, because it is not controlled by global agribusiness. In all, 99% of India's agroprocessing has been intentionally kept at the small level. Now, under the pressure of globalization, things are changing. Pseudo hygiene laws are being used to shut down local economies and small-scale processing.

In August 1998, small-scale local processing of edible oil was banned in India through a 'packaging order' which made the sale of open oil illegal and required all oil to be packaged in plastic or aluminium. This shut down tiny "ghanis" or cold pressed mills. It destroyed the market for our diverse oilseeds—mustard, linseed, sesame, groundnut, coconut.

And the take-over of the edible oil industry has affected 10 million livelihoods. The take-over of flour or "atta" by packaged branded flour will cost 100 million livelihoods. And these millions are being pushed into new poverty.

The forced use of packaging will increase the environmental burden of millions of tonnes of waste.

The globalization of the food system is destroying the diversity of local food cultures and local food economies. A global monoculture is being forced on people by defining everything that is fresh, local, and handmade as a health hazard. Human hands are being defined as the worst contaminants, and work for human hands is being outlawed, to be replaced by machines and chemicals bought from global corporations. These are not recipes for feeding the world, but for stealing livelihoods from the poor to create markets for the powerful.

People are being perceived as parasites, to be exterminated for the 'health' of the global economy.

In the process, new health and ecological hazards are being forced on Third World people through dumping of genetically engineered foods and other hazardous products.

Recently, because of a WTO ruling, India has been forced to remove restrictions on all imports.

Among the unrestricted imports are carcasses and animal waste parts that create a threat to our culture and introduce public health hazards such as Mad Cow Disease.

The US Center for Disease Prevention in Atlanta has calculated that nearly 81 million cases of food borne illnesses occur in the USA every year. Deaths from food poisoning have gone up more than four times due to deregulation. Most of these infections are caused by factory farmed meat. The USA slaughters 93 million pigs, 37 million cattle, 2 million calves, 6 million horses, goats and sheep, and 8 billion chickens and turkeys each year.

Now the giant meat industry of US wants to dump contaminated meat produced through violent and cruel methods on Indian consumers.

The waste of the rich is being dumped on the poor. The wealth of the poor is being violently appropriated through new and clever means like patents on biodiversity and indigenous knowledge.

Patents and intellectual property rights are supposed to be granted for novel inventions. But patents are being claimed for rice varieties such as the basmati for which my valley—where I was born—is famous, or pesticides derived from the Neem which our mothers and grandmothers have been using.

Rice Tec, a US-based company, has been granted Patent no. 5,663,484 for basmati rice lines and grains.

Basmati, neem, pepper, bitter gourd, turmeric—every aspect of the innovation embodied in our indigenous food and medicinal systems is now being pirated and patented. The knowledge of the poor is being converted into the property of global corporations, creating a situation where the poor will have to pay for the seeds and medicines they have evolved and have used to meet their own needs for nutrition and health care.

Such false claims to creation are now the global norm, with the Trade Related Intellectual Property Rights Agreement of the World Trade Organization forcing countries to introduce regimes that allow patenting of life forms and indigenous knowledge.

Instead of recognizing that commercial interests build on nature and on the contribution of other cultures, global law has enshrined the patriarchal myth of creation to create new property rights to life forms just as colonialism used the myth of discovery as the basis of the take-over of the land of others as colonies.

Humans do not create life when they manipulate it. Rice Tec's claim that it has made 'an instant invention of a novel rice line', or Roslin Institute's claim that Ian Wilmut 'created' Dolly denies the creativity of nature, the self-organizational capacity of life forms, and the prior innovations of Third World communities.

Patents and intellectual property rights are supposed to prevent piracy. Instead they are becoming the instruments of pirating the common traditional knowledge from the poor of the Third World and making it the exclusive "property" of western scientists and corporations.

When patents are granted for seeds and plants, as in the case of basmati, theft is defined as creation, and saving and sharing seed is defined as theft of intellectual property. Corporations which have broad patents on crops such as cotton, soya bean, mustard are suing farmers for seed saving and hiring detective agencies to find out if farmers have saved seed or shared it with neighbours.

The recent announcement that Monsanto is giving away the rice genome for free is misleading, because Monsanto has never made a commitment that it will never patent rice varieties or any other crop varieties.

Sharing and exchange, the basis of our humanity and of our ecological survival has been redefined as a crime. This makes us all poor.

Nature has given us abundance; women's indigenous knowledge of biodiversity, agriculture, and nutrition has built on that abundance to create more from less, to create growth through sharing.

The poor are pushed into deeper poverty by making them pay for what was theirs. Even the rich are poorer, because their profits are based on the theft and on the use of coercion and violence. This is not wealth creation but plunder.

Sustainability requires the protection of all species and all people and the recognition that diverse species and diverse people play an essential role in maintaining ecological processes. Pollinators are critical to fertilization and generation of plants. Biodiversity in fields provides vegetables, fodder, medicine, and protection to the soil from water and wind erosion.

As humans travel further down the road to non-sustainability, they become intolerant of other species and blind to their vital role in our survival.

In 1992, when Indian farmers destroyed Cargill's seed plant in Bellary, Karnataka, to protest against seed failure, the Cargill Chief Executive stated: 'We bring Indian farmers smart technologies which prevent bees from usurping the pollen.' When I was participating in the United Nations Biosafety Negotiations, Monsanto circulated literature to defend its herbicide resistant

Roundup ready crops on grounds that they prevent 'weeds from stealing the sunshine'. But what Monsanto calls weeds are the green fields that provide vitamin A rice and prevent blindness in children and anaemia in women.

A worldview that defines pollination as 'theft by bees' and claims biodiversity 'steals' sunshine is a worldview which itself aims at stealing nature's harvest by replacing open, pollinated varieties with hybrids and sterile seeds, and destroying biodiverse flora with herbicides such as Roundup. The threat posed to the Monarch butterfly by genetically engineered crops is just one example of the ecological poverty created by the new biotechnologies. As butterflies and bees disappear, production is undermined. As biodiversity disappears, with it go sources of nutrition and food.

When giant corporations view small peasants and bees as thieves, and through trade rules and new technologies seek the right to exterminate them, humanity has reached a dangerous threshold. The imperative to stamp out the smallest insect, the smallest plant, the smallest peasant comes from a deep fear—the fear of everything that is alive and free. And this deep insecurity and fear is unleashing the violence against all people and all species.

The global free trade economy has become a threat to sustainability and the very survival of the poor and other species is at stake not just as a side effect or as an exception but in a systemic way through a restructuring of our worldview at the most fundamental level. Sustainability, sharing, and survival are being economically outlawed in the name of market competitiveness and market efficiency.

I want to argue here tonight that we need to urgently bring the planet and people back into the picture.

The world can be fed only by feeding all beings that make the world.

In giving food to other beings and species, we maintain conditions for our own food security. In feeding earthworms, we feed ourselves. In feeding cows, we feed the soil, and in providing food for the soil, we provide food for humans. This worldview of abundance is based on sharing and on a deep awareness of humans as members of the earth family. This awareness that in impoverishing other beings we impoverish ourselves, and in nourishing other beings we nourish ourselves, is the real basis of sustainability.

The sustainability challenge for the new millennium is whether global economic man can move out of the worldview based on fear and scarcity, monocultures and monopolies, appropriation and dispossession and shift to a view based on abundance and sharing, diversity and decentralization, and respect and dignity for all beings.

Sustainability demands that we move out of the economic trap that is leaving no space for other species and other people. Economic globalization has become a war against nature and the poor. But the rules of globalization are not god-given. They can be changed. They must be changed. We must bring this war to an end.

Since Seattle, a frequently used phrase has been the need for a rule-based system. Globalization is the rule of commerce and it has elevated Wall Street to be the only source of value. As a result, things that should have high worth—nature, culture, the future—are being devalued and destroyed. The rules of globalization are undermining the rules of justice and sustainability, of compassion and sharing. We have to move from market totalitarianism to an earth democracy.

We can survive as a species only if we live by the rules of the biosphere. The biosphere has enough for everyone's needs if the global economy respects the limits set by sustainability and justice.

As Gandhi had reminded us: 'The earth has enough for everyone's needs, but not for some people's greed.'

35 All Our Relations

Winona LaDuke

Introduction

The last 150 years have seen a great holocaust. There have been more species lost in the past 150 years than since the Ice Age. During the same time, Indigenous peoples have been disappearing from the face of the earth. Over 2,000 nations of Indigenous peoples have gone extinct in the western hemisphere, and one nation disappears from the Amazon rainforest every year.

There is a direct relationship between the loss of cultural diversity and the loss of biodiversity. Wherever Indigenous peoples still remain, there is also a corresponding enclave of biodiversity. Trickles of rivers still running in the Northwest are home to the salmon still being sung back by Native people. The last few Florida panthers remain in the presence of traditional Seminoles, hidden away in the great cypress swamps of the Everglades. Some of the largest patches of remaining prairie grasses sway on reservation lands. One half of all reservation lands in the United States is still forested, much of it old-growth. Remnant pristine forest ecosystems, from the northern boreal forests to the Everglades, largely overlap with Native territories.

In the Northwest, virtually every river is home to a people, each as distinct as a species of salmon. The Tillamook, Siletz, Yaquina, Alsea, Siuslaw, Umpqua, Hanis, Miluk, Colville, Tututni, Shasta, Costa, and Chetco are all peoples living at the mouths of salmon rivers. One hundred and seven stocks of salmon have already become extinct in the Pacific Northwest, and 89 are endangered. "Salmon were put here by the Creator, and it is our responsibility to harvest and protect the salmon so that the cycle of life continues," explains Pierson Mitchell of the Columbia River Intertribal Fishing Commission.[1] "Whenever we have a funeral, we mourn our loved one, yes, but we are also reminded of the loss of our salmon and other traditional foods," laments Bill Yallup Sr., the Yakama tribal chairman.[2]

The stories of the fish and the people are not so different. Environmental destruction threatens the existence of both. The Tygh band of the Lower Deschutes River in Oregon includes a scant five families, struggling to maintain their traditional way of life and relationship to the salmon. "I wanted to dance the salmon, know the salmon, say goodbye to the salmon," says Susana Santos, a Tygh artist, fisherwoman, and community organizer. "Now I am looking at the completion of destruction, from the Exxon Valdez to . . . those dams. . . . Seventeen fish came down the river last year. None this year. The people are the salmon, and the salmon are the people. How do you quantify that?"[3]

From Winona LaDuke, *All Our Relations* (Cambridge, MA: South End Press, 1999), 1–6 and 197–200.

Native American teachings describe the relations all around—animals, fish, trees, and rocks—as our brothers, sisters, uncles, and grandpas. Our relations to each other, our prayers whispered across generations to our relatives, are what bind our cultures together. The protection, teachings, and gifts of our relatives have for generations preserved our families. These relations are honored in ceremony, song, story, and life that keep relations close—to buffalo, sturgeon, salmon, turtles, bears, wolves, and panthers. These are our older relatives—the ones who came before and taught us how to live. Their obliteration by dams, guns, and bounties is an immense loss to Native families and cultures. Their absence may mean that a people sing to a barren river, a caged bear, or buffalo far away. It is the struggle to preserve that which remains and the struggle to recover that characterizes much of Native environmentalism. It is these relationships that industrialism seeks to disrupt. Native communities will resist with great determination.

Salmon was presented to me and my family through our religion as our brother. The same with the deer. And our sisters are the roots and berries. And you would treat them as such. Their life to you is just as valuable as another person's would be. (Margaret Saluskin, Yakama)[4]

THE TOXIC INVASION OF NATIVE AMERICA

There are over 700 Native nations on the North American continent. Today, in the United States, Native America covers 4 percent of the land, with over 500 federally recognized tribes. Over 1,200 Native American reserves dot Canada. The Inuit homeland, Nunavut, formerly one-half of the Northwest Territories, is an area of land and water, including Baffin Island, five times the size of Texas, or the size of the entire Indian subcontinent. Eighty-five percent of the population is Native.

While Native peoples have been massacred and fought, cheated, and robbed of their historical lands, today their lands are subject to some of the most invasive industrial interventions imaginable. According to the World-watch Institute, 317 reservations in the United States are threatened by environmental hazards, ranging from toxic wastes to clearcuts.

Reservations have been targeted as sites for 16 proposed nuclear waste dumps. Over 100 proposals have been floated in recent years to dump toxic waste in Indian communities.[5] Seventy-seven sacred sites have been disturbed or desecrated through resource extraction and development activities.[6] The federal government is proposing to use Yucca Mountain, sacred to the Shoshone, as a dumpsite for the nation's high-level nuclear waste. Over the last 45 years, there have been 1,000 atomic explosions on Western Shoshone land in Nevada, making the Western Shoshone the most bombed nation on earth.

Over 1,000 slag piles and tailings from abandoned uranium mines sit on Diné land, leaking radioactivity into the air and water. Nearby is the largest coal strip mine in the world, and some groups of Diné teenagers have a cancer rate 17 times the national average. According to Tom Goldtooth, executive director of the Indigenous Environmental Network,

Most Indigenous governments are over 22 years behind the states in environmental infrastructure development. The EPA has consistently failed to fund tribes on an equitable basis compared with the states. The EPA has a statutory responsibility to allocate financial resources that will provide an equitable allocation between tribal governments and states.[7]

THE DESCENDANTS OF LITTLE THUNDER

In our communities, Native environmentalists sing centuries-old songs to renew life, to give thanks for the strawberries, to call home fish, and to thank Mother Earth for her blessings. We are the descendants of Little Thunder, who witnessed the massacre that cleared out the Great Plains to make way for the cowboys, cattle, and industrial farms. We have seen the great trees felled, the wolves taken for bounty, and the fish stacked rotting like cordwood. Those memories compel us, and the return of the descendants of these predators provoke us to stand again, stronger, and hopefully with more allies. We are the ones who stand up to the land eaters, the tree eaters, the destroyers and culture eaters.

We live off the beaten track, out of the mainstream in small villages, on a vast expanse of prairie, on dry desert lands, or in the forests. We often drive old cars, live in old houses and mobile homes. There are usually small children and relatives around, the kids careening underfoot. We seldom carry briefcases, and we rarely wear suits. You are more likely to find us meeting in a local community center, outside camping, or in someone's house than at a convention center or at a $1,000-per-plate fundraiser.

We organize in small groups, close to 200 of them in North America, with names like Native Americans for a Clean Environment, Diné CARE (Citizens Against Ruining Our Environment), Anishinaabe Niijii, and the Gwichin Steering Committee. We are underfunded at best, and more often not funded at all, working out of our homes with a few families or five to ten volunteers. We coalesce in national or continental organizations such as Indigenous Environmental Network, a network of 200-plus members, which through a diverse agenda of providing technical and political support to grassroots groups seeking to protect their land, preserve biodiversity, and sustain communities, seeks ultimately to secure environmental justice. Other such groups include the Southwest Network for Environmental and Economic Justice, Honor the Earth, Indigenous Women's Network, Seventh Generation Fund, and others. In addition are the regional organizations and those based on a shared ecosystem or cultural practice, such as the California Indian Basket-weavers Association, Great Lakes Basketmakers, or Council of Elders.

Despite our meager resources, we are winning many hard-fought victories on the local level. We have faced down huge waste dumps and multinational mining, lumber, and oil companies. And throughout the Native nations, people continue to fight to protect Mother Earth for future generations. Some of the victories described in this book include a moratorium on mining in the sacred hills of Northern Cheyenne, Blackfeet, and Crow territory; an international campaign that stopped the building of mega-dams in northern Canada; the restoration of thousands of acres of White Earth land in Minnesota; and the rebuilding of a nation in Hawai'i.

Grassroots and land-based struggles characterize most of Native environmentalism. We are nations of people with distinct land areas, and our leadership and direction emerge from the land up. Our commitment and tenacity spring from our deep connection to the land. This relationship to land and water is continuously reaffirmed through prayer, deed, and our way of being—*minobimaatisiiwin*, the "good life." It is perhaps best remembered in phrases like: *This is where my grandmother's and children's umbilical cords are buried. ... That is where the great giant lay down to sleep. . . . These are the four sacred Mountains between which the Creator instructed us to live. . . . That is the last place our people stopped in our migration here to this village.*

WHITE EARTH

I live on an Anishinaabeg reservation called White Earth in northern Minnesota, where I work on land, culture, and environmental issues locally through an organization called the White Earth Land Recovery Project and nationally through a Native foundation called Honor the Earth. We, the Anishinaabeg, are a forest culture. Our creation stories, culture, and way of life are entirely based on the forest, source of our medicinal plants and food, forest animals, and birch-bark baskets.

Virtually my entire reservation was clearcut at the turn of the century. In 1874, Anishinaabe leader Wabunoquod said, "I cried and prayed that our trees would not be taken from us, for they are as much ours as is this reservation."[8] Our trees provided the foundation for major lumber companies, including Weyerhauser, and their destruction continued for ten decades.

In 1889 and 1890 Minnesota led the country in lumber production, and the state's northwest region was the leading source of timber. Two decades later, 90 percent of White Earth land was controlled by non-Indians, and our people were riddled with diseases. Many became refugees in nearby cities. Today, three-fourths of all tribal members live off the reservation. Ninety percent of our land is still controlled by non-Indians.

There is a direct link in our community between the loss of biodiversity—the loss of animal and plant life—and the loss of the material and cultural wealth of the White Earth people. But we have resisted and are restoring. Today, we are in litigation against logging expansion, and the White Earth Land Recovery Project works to restore the forests, recover the land, and restore our traditional forest culture. Our experience of survival and resistance is shared with many others. But it is not only about Native people.

In the final analysis, the survival of Native America is fundamentally about the collective survival of all human beings. The question of who gets to determine the destiny of the land, and of the people who live on it—those with the money or those who pray on the land—is a question that is alive throughout society. The question is posed eloquently by Lil'wat grandmother Loretta Pascal:

This is my reason for standing up. To protect all around us, to continue our way of life, our culture. I ask them, "Where did you get your right to destroy these forests? How does your right supercede my rights?" These are our forests, these are our ancestors.[9]

These are the questions posed in the chapters ahead. Through the voices and actions featured here, there are some answers as well. Along with the best of my prayers is a recognition of the depth of spirit and commitment to all our relations, and the work to protect and recover them. As Columbia River Tribes activist Ted Strong tells us,

If this nation has a long way to go before all of our people are truly created equally without regard to race, religion, or national origin, it has even farther to go before achieving anything that remotely resembles equal treatment for other creatures who called this land home before humans ever set foot upon it. . . . While the species themselves—fish, fowl, game, and the habitat they live in—have given us unparalleled wealth, they live crippled in their ability to persist and in conditions of captive squalor. . . . This enslavement and impoverishment of nature is no more tolerable or sensible than enslavement and impoverishment of other human beings. . . . Perhaps it is because we are the messengers that not only our sovereignty as [Native] governments but our right to identify with a deity and a history, our right to hold to a set of natural laws as practiced for thousands of years is under assault. Now more than ever, tribal people must hold onto their timeless and priceless customs and practices.[10]

"The ceremony will continue," Strong says. "This is a testament to the faith of the Indian people. No matter how badly the salmon have been mistreated, no matter how serious the decline. It has only made Native people deeper in their resolve. It has doubled their commitment. It has rekindled the hope that today is beginning to grow in many young people."[11]

The Seventh Generation

Somewhere between the teachings of western science and those of the Native community there is some agreement on the state of the world. Ecosystems are collapsing, species are going extinct, the polar icecaps are melting, and nuclear bombings and accidents have contaminated the land.

According to Harvard biologist Edward O. Wilson, 50,000 species are lost every year. Three-quarters of the world's species of birds are declining, and one-quarter of all mammalian species are endangered. Tropical rainforests, freshwater lakes, and coral reefs are at immediate risk, and global warming and climate change will accelerate the rate of biological decline dramatically.[12]

The writing is on the wall, in bold letters. There is no easy answer, and even scientists themselves seem to recognize the necessity of finding new strategies and understandings. In an unusual gathering in late 1998, for instance, NASA scientists met with Indigenous elders to discuss global warming and to hear the elders' suggestions on possible solutions. The response the scientists received may have been only part of what they had hoped for. As one observer summarized, the elders pretty much responded, "You did it, you fix it."[13]

In the final analysis, we humans can *say* whatever we would like—rationalize, revise statistical observations, extend deadlines, and make accommodations for a perceived "common good." But "natural law," as Yakama fisherman and former director of the Columbia Intertribal Fishing Commission Ted Strong explains, "is a hard and strict taskmaster."[14] Dump dioxin into the river, and you will inevitably eat or drink it. Assent to acceptable levels of radioactive emissions, and sooner or later, those sensitive cells in the human body will likely respond.

The challenge at the cusp of the millennium is to transform human laws to match natural laws, not vice versa. And to correspondingly transform wasteful production and voracious consumption. America and industrial society must move from a society based on conquest to one steeped in the practice of survival.

In order to do that, we must close the circle. The linear nature of industrial production itself, in which labor and technology turn natural wealth into consumer products and wastes, must be transformed into a cyclical system. In the best scenario, natural resources must be reused or not used at all, and waste production cut to a mere trickle. Those who watch carefully—*onaanaagadawaa-bandanaawaa*—know that this will require a technological, cultural, and legal transformation.

Many Indigenous teachings consider the present a time of change. Anishinaabeg teachings recognize this time of change for the people of the Seventh Fire as both a reality and an opportunity. According to these prophecies, Anishinaabeg people retrace their steps to find what was left by the trail. There are two separate roads from which to choose, for both the Anishinaabeg and those called the "light-skinned people."

Anishinaabeg elder Eddie Benton Benai, from the Lac Courte Orielles reservation in Wisconsin, is a teacher of the Anishinaabeg Midewiwin society. He discusses the two roads as

the road to technology and the other road to Spiritualism. They [elders] feel that the road of technology represents a continuation of headlong rush to technological development. This is the road . . . that has led to modern society, to a damaged and seared earth . . . . The [other] road represents the slower path that Traditional Native people have traveled and are now seeking again. The Earth is not scorched on this trail. The grass is still growing there.[15]

A similar teaching of the Six Nations Iroquois Confederacy recognizes the importance of future generations. "In each deliberation, we must consider the impact on the seventh generation from now," they say; that is, undertake conservative thinking, and use careful deliberation. Such consideration would have preempted thousands of decisions made by the U.S. government.

RETHINKING THE CONSTITUTION

Walt Bresette, an Anishinaabe man from the Red Cliff reservation in northern Wisconsin, passed to the next world in early 1999. His passing was a huge loss to the Native environmental movement. But his groundbreaking work on re-envisioning the Constitution and Native treaty rights for the benefit of all people and the earth continues. Bresette was part of the Seventh Generation movement, a movement that calls for a radical amendment to the U.S. Constitution.

The preamble to the U.S. Constitution declares its intent to be to "secure the blessings of liberty, to ourselves, and our posterity." In reality, U.S. laws have been transformed by corporate interests to cater to elite interests in society. While the U.S. Constitution makes no mention of corporations, according to anti-corporate analysts Richard Grossman and Frank Adams, "the history of Constitutional law is, as former Supreme Court Justice Felix Frankfurter said, 'the history of the impact of the modern corporation on the American scene.'" Over the course of two centuries of court decisions, corporate contracts and their rates of return have been redefined as property that should be protected under the Constitution. In this way the "common good" has been redefined as "maximum corporate production and profit."[16]

Appointed judges have handed down decision after decision increasing the privileges of corporations. Corporations have been granted the power of "eminent domain" and the right to inflict "private injury and personal damage" when pursuing "progressive improvements." Most significantly, in 1886, the Supreme Court treated private corporations as "natural person[s]" protected by the Constitution and "sheltered by the Bill of Rights and the Fourteenth Amendment."[17]

Consequently, American public policy and the legal system have largely come to reflect short-term views despite the intergenerational perspective foundational to the U.S. Constitution. At the 1995 United Nations Conference on the Status of Women in Beijing, Corrine Kumar from the Asian Women's Human Rights Campaign spoke of the legal challenges in the national and international arena of this era. "The violence of the times," she explained, "has outstripped the law."[18] We have little understanding of or protection from the combined and cumulative impact of industrialism's complicated chemical soup on our bodies, ecosystems, or future generations. Public policy is lagging far behind our ability to destroy ourselves.

The rights of the people to use and enjoy air, water, and sunlight are essential to life, liberty, and the pursuit of happiness. These basic human rights have been impaired by those who discharge toxic substances into the air, water, and land. Contaminating the commons must be recognized as a fundamental wrong in our system of laws, just as defacing private property is wrong. On that basis, the Seventh Generation Amendment to the Constitution of the United States declares,

The right of citizens of the U.S. to enjoy and use air, water, sunlight, and other renewable resources determined by the Congress to be common property shall not be impaired, nor shall such use impair their availability for use by the future generations.[19]

Bresette's other work included transforming court decisions on treaty rights into tools to transform northern Wisconsin into a sustainable, protected region. The Supreme Court's 1983 *Voigt* decision affirmed Anishinaabeg hunting, fishing, and gathering rights in ceded land in northern Wisconsin and was initially greeted with widespread outrage by non-Indians. Since then, the broader community has come to accept these rights, and Bresette and others want to expand them in ways that would benefit Indians and non-Indians alike. "A close reading of the court ruling suggests that these harvesting rights actually set extremely high environmental standards, certainly the highest in any region of the state," Bresette argued. In other words, the *Voigt* decision can be interpreted to mean not only that Indians have the right to fish and hunt in the ceded territory, but also the right to be able to "eat those fish and deer." That means that the state "should be prohibited from allowing damage to the fish by loose environmental regulation."[20]

We must follow Bresette's example and charge ourselves with curbing the rights of corporations and special interests, transforming the legal institutions of the United States back toward the preservation of the commons, and preserving everyone's rights, not just those of the economically privileged. On a community level, we must support local self-reliance and the recovery of Indigenous systems of knowledge, jurisdiction, practice, and governance.

Native people in our own reservation communities must dialogue about change, the path ahead, the options, and how we will make a better future for our children. As the conveners of the Indigenous Environmental Statement of Principles note,

Our traditional laws lead us to understand that economic development cannot subsist on a deteriorating resource base. The environment cannot be maintained and protected when "growth" does not account for the cost of environmental and cultural destruction.[21]

The choice between the technological and the spiritual will be based on both collective and individual decisions, both simple and complex. For just as life itself is a complex web of relationships and organisms, so is the fabric of a community and a culture that chooses its future. Either way, according to Indigenous worldviews, there is no easy fix, no technological miracle.

The challenge of transformation requires the diligence and patient work evidenced by many of the people discussed in this book. And from the Everglades to the subarctic, their voices for change are increasing in volume.

There is, in many Indigenous teachings, a great optimism for the potential to make positive change. Change *will* come. As always, it is just a matter of who determines what that change will be.

Notes

1. Pierson Mitchell in *Wana Chinook Tymoo*, a publication of the Columbia River Intertribal Fishing Commission (winter, 1999), 12–13.
2. Bill Yallup Sr. in *Wana Chinook Tymoo*.
3. Interview with Susana Santos, October 1996.
4. Interview with Margaret Saluskin, June 1994.
5. Seventh Generation Fund, "1995 Funding Proposal for Environment Program," Arcata, CA. See also Council of Energy Resource Tribes, "Inventory of Hazardous Waste Generators and Sites on Selected Indian Reservations," Denver, CO, July 1985.
6. Interview with Chris Peters, Seventh Generation Fund, May 4, 1994.
7. Akwesasne Task Force on the Environment, "Superfund Clean Up of Akwesasne: Case Study in Environmental Injustice," *International Journal of Contemporary Sociology* (October 1997), 4.
8. Wabunoquod, quoted in Robert H. Keller, "An Economic History of Indian Treaties of the Great Lakes Region," *American Indian Journal* (1976), 14.
9. Interview with Loretta Pascal, June 22, 1995.
10. Ted Strong, in *Wana Chinook Tymoo*.
11. Ted Strong, Panel Presentation, Lewis and Clark University, October 22, 1998.
12. Lester R. Brown, Christopher Flavin, and Hilary French, *State of the World 1997: A Worldwatch Institute Report on Progress Toward a Sustainable Society* (New York: W.W. Norton and Co., 1997), 13.
13. Interview with Bob Gough, November 15, 1999.
14. Ted Strong, Panel Presentation, Lewis and Clark University, October 23, 1998.
15. Eddie Benton Benai, "Seven Fires," cited in Terrance Nelson (ed.), *Okiijida: The Warrior Society* (Okiijida, Letellier, Manitoba, Canada: ROGCO, 1998), 4.
16. Richard Grossman and Frank Adams, in Jerry Mander and Edward Goldsmith (eds), *The Case Against the Global Economy, and For a Turn Toward the Local* (San Francisco: Sierra Club Books, 1996), 376.
17. Ibid. 384.
18. Corrine Kumar, United Nations Conference on the Status of Women, Beijing, China, September 7, 1995.
19. Walt Bresette et al., "Seventh Generation Amendment," Anishinaabe Niijii flyer, Bayfield, WI, March 1996.
20. Interview with Walt Bresette, July 9, 1997.
21. "Indigenous Environmental Statement of Principles," Albuquerque, NM, Native Law Institute (1995), 28.

36 Overturning the Doctrine: Indigenous People and Wilderness—Being Aboriginal in the Environmental Movement

Fabienne Bayet

I am Aboriginal, my mother is Aboriginal, as is my mother's mother. I also consider myself as an environmentalist, conservationist, greenie, whatever. I care about this planet, this landscape we live in. So, am I black or green? Black on the outside and green on the inside, or the other way around? Perhaps there is no clear definition, I am both green and black, swirling colours which combine to make my identity, me. Not a pretty sight.

Seriously, as part of this identity, and in the face of many other greenies, I cannot remove humans from the landscape. Aboriginal people are an integral part of the Australian landscape. We are the land, the land is us. As one Aboriginal woman put it recently at a rally against the Hindmarsh Island Bridge, in South Australia, 'I am the Coorong, I am Goolwa.' How then do I deal with a common green ideology often advocated, and used as a major selling concept, by some wilderness groups. 'Wilderness', in this perspective, denotes land which is wild, unihabited, or inhabited only by wild animals. Such conceptions of wilderness and conservation are yet another form of paternalism and dispossession if they continue to conceptually remove Aboriginal people from the Australian landscape.

How then do I also deal with an issue that has rocked Aboriginal and non-Aboriginal relations for the past eighteen months—Native Title and the overturning of the doctrine of *terra nullius*? In essence, one of my issues is about the overturning of the doctrine of *terra nullius* through native title and whether this influences concepts of wilderness within the green movement. This then links back to my belief that human beings cannot really be removed from the landscape, regardless of whether it's sustainable or not.

Aboriginal Perceptions of Native Title

Despite constant stereotyping as 'miserable nomads' or 'noble savages', Aboriginal and Torres Strait Islander people lived very complex, diverse lifestyles throughout the continent and its

From *Social Alternatives*, 19: 4 (July 1994), 1–19.

islands before European invasion, although the ways communities acquired food and resources for living differed according to which ecological area they lived in. All Aboriginal and Torres Strait Islander people held spiritual beliefs relating to why they existed and why their world was like it was. Aboriginal people traditionally have a strong physical and spiritual bond with the Australian landscape through the Dreaming. This is the time of creation when the mystical and powerful ancestors of the Aboriginal people moved over the featureless earth and sea, and formed the environmental features found today.

The descendants of these people have the responsibility of caring for the sacred site and preserving sacred objects by ceremonies that in turn ensure the well-being of the land and the plants and animals upon which their livelihood depends. These [responsibilities], together with the sacred sites and associated sacred objects, constitute, in Aboriginal terms, inalienable title to the land.[1]

Non-Aboriginal, Common-Law Definition

In the High Court's *Mabo v. Queensland* judgement, the majority held that, under the introduced English common law of 1788 and thereafter, Australia was not legally—or in fact—a vacant territory, but was occupied and possessed by indigenous communities with traditions and customs of their own.[2]

The term 'native title' conveniently describes the interests and rights of indigenous inhabitants in land, whether communal, group, or individual, possessed under the traditional laws and the 'traditional' customs acknowledged and observed by the indigenous inhabitants.[3]

The High Court has ruled that native title exists where Aboriginal people have a continuing connection with land which goes back to their ancestors who occupied the land in 1788 (when Europeans came to Australia.)

Legislation defines the expression 'native title' or 'native title rights and interest' as: 'the communal, group or individual rights and interests of Aboriginal or Torres Strait Islanders in relation to land or waters.'[4]

The rights and interests of such a group are to be possessed under the traditional laws acknowledged, and the traditional customs observed, by the Aboriginal or Torres Strait Islanders.

The Aboriginal peoples or Torres Strait Islanders, by those laws and customs, must have a connection with the land or waters; and such rights and interests are to be recognized by the common [non-Aboriginal] law of Australia.

The Dreaming

To understand the cultural differences, and to understand the key conceptual basis of such terms as *terra nullius*, native title, and wilderness, one must examine the history and culture deriving from and influencing the Aboriginal and the environmental movements.

The Dreaming lays down the laws concerning the accessing of resources from the environment. The environment relates directly to social organization, kinship and social obligations, sacred law, offences against property and persons, marriage, and an individual's relationship with the land.

Aboriginal land and the meaning behind it passes on information about the environment to each generation, depending on where each person was conceived, when she/he quickened within the womb, and the totemic associations of the father and mother. On this basis certain resources could be gained in different areas by accessing kinship rights. Conversely, restriction and taboos would apply to other persons in other areas. As a result of these checks and balances, sanctuaries occurred throughout the environment where certain species could be reproduced without threat of destruction. Aboriginal people perceive the Australian landscape as their cultural domain. It was their traditional duty to be custodians of the land.

The main difference between Aboriginal and non-Aboriginal cultures lies in attitudes to the land and the changes made to the environment through the accessing of resources.

THE SEPARATION OF PEOPLE FROM LAND

Another dimension of the division between culture and the environment held by western society relates to the Eurocentric work ethic and the human domination over land.

The Eurocentric work ethic held by the settlers dictated that the 'land must be toiled with your own sweat' and the environment possessed, changed and exploited to its fullest extent. 'To the settlers . . . natural Australia was an uncouth waste. They were programmed to change, improve, dominate, exploit.'[5]

In this process the original inhabitants were dispossessed of their land and cultural roots. The western land ethic dictated that 'progress' and development were the ultimate justifications for the dispossession of the original custodians.

The Aboriginal population was perceived as consisting of savages who did not exploit the land to its potential (according to European agricultural expectations), thus Aboriginal people were considered to have no right of property ownership. The entire continent was perceived to be empty of meaningful human occupation, bringing about the term *terra nullius*: unoccupied wasteland.

Non-Aboriginal society has exploited the land beyond sustainability. This has led to an environmental awakening. The notion of valuing wilderness for its own sake motivates the environmental movement.

Those areas that were deemed to be economically non-viable for development, and some which were aesthetically pleasing according to non-Aboriginal perspectives, have been put aside, deemed to be beyond human society and culture.

Wilderness has been idealized as a way to counteract the undesirable element of non-Aboriginal civilization. This has been linked to the idea that civilization, urbanization, and technology have made the human species weak in its 'unnatural' state. Wilderness has been perceived as restoring humans to strength, an avenue to 'recharge the batteries'. As a result there has been a movement towards forming reserves and national parks, in order to protect the land from human interference, urbanization, and development.

INDIGENOUS PEOPLES VERSES WILDERNESS

The concept of wilderness as nature, without any trace of human interaction, dehumanizes the indigenous peoples living within that landscape.

To indigenous peoples the land is no abstract wilderness. The whole of Australia is an Aboriginal artefact. The whole of the continent has been affected by Aboriginal people living out their Dreaming obligations.

For outsiders, Aboriginal people were seen to be so much in tune with nature that they were treated as part of the wilderness, almost like animals. Those concerned about the destruction of the environment have often promoted Aboriginal people as super-conservationists. Although this is an acknowledgement that Aboriginal people have sustained the Australian landscape for thousands of years, it stresses the relationship of the noble savage with an idealized 'garden of Eden', once again distorting the reality of the landscape we live in. In effect, the doctrine of *terra nullius* lives on under the conceptual banner of wilderness: a land without human interaction or impact.

This perception of Aboriginal people denied them an independent dimension from 'wilderness' and made them, in effect, invisible and mute as a society. The potential for self-determination was denied until the stark realities of environmental degradation forced environmentalists and others to look at Aboriginal land and resource management in a new light.

Even so, when National Parks were created in order to preserve the wilderness, as written into Australian legislation, Aboriginal people were no longer able to access resources since wilderness was legally defined as land devoid of any human interaction. Consequently, Aboriginal people now perceive National Parks and wilderness legislation as the second wave of dispossession, which denies their customary inherited right to use land for hunting, gathering, building, rituals, and birthing rites. The concession that allows traditional hunting practices in some national parks is simply another form of colonial thinking. This is regarded by Aboriginal people as an unfair and unrealistic imposition forced upon them by the western, dominant society.

Land ownership, access, and use is considered priority number one for Aboriginal people. Without land there is no base for the structure of Aboriginal culture. Aboriginal people, however, are no longer predominantly hunters and gatherers due to the dispossession and decimation of their societies. Aboriginal people are looking to alternatives for land management, which will meet their traditional obligations, as well as the constraints of contemporary economic survival. Aboriginal communities see no option but to compete within the Australian economy (often on a non-sustainable basis). The Central Land Council writes:

Our land is our life. We look at it in a different way to non-Aboriginal people. For us, land isn't simply a resource to be exploited. It provides us with food and materials for life, but it also provides our identity and it must be looked after, both physically and spiritually. If we abuse our land, or allow someone else to abuse it, we too suffer. [However] the many resource development projects and commercial enterprises now operating on Aboriginal land show that respecting our land rights can be compatible with national economic development. .... economic activity on Aboriginal land contributes significantly to the Australian economy through a number of avenues.[6]

This is an indication of the cultural clash between Aboriginal interests and the conservation perspective.

Some environmentalists fear that allowing Aboriginal communities to claim National Parks and to hunt in them would threaten the ecological diversity of the area and the survival of endangered species. As reported in Habitat:

'No longer will they be National Parks but Government-sanctioned killing fields of our once protected ecology', a long-time member of the Daintree Wilderness Action Group claimed. 'Almost 100 years of protection ripped up, shot up, burnt up, stuffed.'[7]

This is one area where the environmental and Aboriginal movements start parting company. The major difference between the Aboriginal (black) and environmental (green) movements is that each group has an ideology constructed from differing cultural backgrounds. The environmental movement's wilderness perspective is seen by Aboriginal people as a continuation of paternalism and colonialism. Thus, Toyne and Johnston comment on:

a new wave of dispossession—the denial of Aboriginal peoples' rights to land in the name of nature conservation. The creation of national parks, wilderness areas or wild life sanctuaries could be every bit as threatening and destructive to Aboriginal people as were the pastoral stations or the farms of past generations.[8]

It is not surprising therefore, that Aboriginal people remain ambivalent about green issues, since in their purest form green values deny black rights.

In most states, conservation areas and National Parks have been created without the involvement or consent of Aboriginal people. When the Winychanam people sought to purchase a cattle station in their country on Cape York, the 1976 Bjelke-Petersen National Party declared the property and land around the area as the Archer River National Park. The Winychanam felt they had been denied the chance for economic self-determination and saw the creation of the Park as the government's implementation of its racist policies.

Another example of this perceived 'green dispossession' is the World Heritage nomination of north Queensland's Wet Tropic Rainforests in 1987. This brought opposition from the local Yarrabah Aboriginal community as they had hoped to create a saw-milling operation from their local lease.

The West Australian Liberal Government of 1977 declared a large area of the Martu's expansive country, in the Gibson Desert, as the Ruddal River National Park in reaction to criticism that Western Australia did not have enough conservation areas. The Martu people are outraged, not just because of the physical disruption to their lives from mining, but because of further limitations placed on them by the creation of a National Park. The Martu people were not consulted in its planning. They do not want a National Park imposed on their land, especially as they cannot receive federal funding for infrastructure because they don't have title to land.[9]

Despite such examples of Aboriginal dispossession through conservation, the green movement and Aboriginal communities are coming together for the benefit of the land. The majority of the green movement is trying to acknowledge Aboriginal ownership of land, their cultural power and their relationships with the land, and their skills in land management.

Successful alliances are beginning to form. For example, the Uluru-Kata Tjuta and Kakadu National Parks are located on Aboriginal land which has been leased to the Australian National

Parks and Wildlife Service. Local traditional landowners form a majority on the Park's Boards of Management and are employed as rangers and cultural interpreters. Their knowledge of the country is a vital ingredient in successful environmental management.

Aboriginal people are also using wilderness arguments to protect the Cape York area from the proposed Space Station development.[10]

Increasingly, and successfully, Aboriginal people are becoming more involved in National Park and conservation management as rangers, through representation on park boards of management, and, most importantly, through ownership. However, as yet, Aboriginal ownership proposals for National Parks in South Australia, Western Australia, and Tasmania have not yet been made, although it is something that should and will occur in the future, if social and ecological justice is to remain on the social agenda.

In part, these moves represent a recognition on behalf of conservationists that Aboriginal people possess traditional land management skills which will be of great benefit in managing national parks and conservation areas. It seems that non-Aboriginal environmentalists are putting Aboriginal people back into the landscape; Aboriginal people consider that they never left it.

Native Title and Wilderness

Many environmentalists, while supporting Aboriginal lobby groups against non-sustainable industries in the Native Title debate, are now wondering how the overturning of *terra nullius* will affect areas particularly considered reserves from human interaction and impacts. One concept which is particularly emotive, is that of wilderness. The concepts of wilderness could be perceived as conceptually outside the Native Title legislation and Aboriginal land ownership.

What some environmentalists may fail to realize is that Aboriginal people still have to participate in the policy of assimilation by following Eurocentric legal processes in order to justify their claim, regardless of whether the land in question is 'wilderness' or not. Aboriginal people still have to participate in perpetuating the dominant stereotype of 'traditional cultural practices' and 'communal ownership' if they are to retain any remnants of ownership.

Once again Aboriginal people are still expected to be 'civilized' while retaining static stereotypes imposed on them since invasion. The conservation movement will have to address Native Title and the dispossessing doctrine of wilderness if they are to find common ground between cultural self-determination and ecological sustainability.

IS ECOTOURISM THE ANSWER?

A potential avenue currently being pursued by both black and green movements is the new rise of ecotourism. However, ecotourism, whether on a sustainable or non-sustainable basis, raises a number of issues for indigenous peoples and environmental interest groups, relating to the blending of the concepts nature and culture.

It could be argued that non-Aboriginal environmentalists are once again putting the onus on the victim of the invasion, through the conceptualization of ecotourism. Aboriginal people remain on the lowest socio-economic rung of Australia's society. The pressures on them to succeed in building a new industry is extraordinary. However, Aboriginal people need to seek alternatives away from non-sustainable development. Many questions need to be debated amongst environmentalists, ecotourism operators, and indigenous peoples. Some of these include:

- Is ecotourism sustainable on a cultural basis?
- Is ecotourism yet another form of pressure on Aboriginal society and communities—this time on those least affected by the invasion and urbanisation of Australia?
- Will ecotourism quite simply be perpetuating the stereotype of the non-urban Aboriginal?
- Will ecotourism quite simply be perpetuating the stereotype of the wandering noble savage, the hunter-gatherer, remnant of the stone age, or is ecotourism an appropriate avenue of reconciliation?
- Will ecotourism open avenues through which non-Aboriginal people can explore and understand Aboriginal people, eventually venturing into relating with urban Aboriginals?
- Will ecotourism be yet another barrier between urban Aboriginals being ignored for the sake of the 'traditional' Aboriginal stereotype that will sell?

Conclusion

While acknowledging that there are major differences between Aboriginal and non-Aboriginal approaches to land management and conservation, it must be emphasized that there is no single overarching 'Aboriginal viewpoint', any more than there is any single 'green ideology'. Indeed, it would be true to say that within the Aboriginal context of Native Title and self-determination, there is a wide variety of approaches to development, use of resources, land management, and sustainability. By the same token, there are many shades of green, from 'dark' greenies who will not countenance any human involvement within the landscape, up to the pragmatic 'lighter greenies' who can identify the realities of economic needs.

The environmental movement must stop stereotyping Aboriginal people as noble savages or arch-conservationists and must recognize the rights of Aboriginal people to choose self-determination on a contemporary, realistic basis. Brown writes:

Only if we negotiate management of significant areas with indigenous communities will we able to protect both the ecological and cultural values of the land. Management plans which are imposed as pre-conditions on Aboriginal ownership will never operate effectively.[11]

Nevertheless development cannot continue as though there are no environmental limits. Cultural survival relates very much to ecologically sustainable land management, as it is no use retaining culture now if people cannot sustain themselves on the land for generations to come. In this sense Aboriginal communities should not use the argument of cultural survival, through economics, to initiate or continue non-sustainable land management. By the same token, if conservation groups are going to insist on the dispossession of Aboriginal communities through Wilderness legislation then they must make more of an effort to find alternative means of accessing resources for Aboriginal communities, and may have to back up their argument by providing financial support. Conservationists cannot expect to be received well if they continue to impose environmental responsibility on Aboriginal communities. This could be perceived as a continuation of the 'noble savage' myth. In the same way, non-Aboriginal people have to confront and overcome their inherited view of Aboriginal people, and allow themselves to seek an equality in joint land access and management.

Through the environmental movement the Australian community is beginning to recognize that the relationship to the environment must be re-evaluated, and, as the Native Title debate has demonstrated, an integral part in that evaluation lies in the fact that Australia was, and is, Aboriginal land.

As Albert Mullet writes:

It's taken 200 years for whites to ask black people to share their knowledge. Two hundred years? Why has it taken so long to ask about and show respect for 40,000 years of wisdom, culture and experience?[12]

Notes

1. Mildred Kirk, *A Change of Ownership: Aboriginal Land Rights* (Queensland, Australia: Jacaranda Press, 1986).
2. Aboriginal and Torres Strait Islander Commission, The Mabo Judgement, Canberra, 1993.
3. Richard Bartlett, et al., *The Mabo Decision* (Melbourne, Australia: Butterworths, 1993).
4. Native Title Act, Legislation, AGPS, 1993.
5. Derek Whitelock *Conquest to Conservation* (South Australia, Australia: Wakefield Press, 1985).
6. Central and Northern Land Councils, *Our land. Our life* (Alice Springs, Northern Territory, Australia, 1991).
7. M. Horstman, 'Cape York Peninsula: Forging a Black-Green alliance', in *Habitat Australia: Caring for Country. Aboriginal Perspectives on Conservation*, The Australian Conservation Foundation, Victoria, 19: 3 (June 1991), 19–22.
8. P. Toyne and R. Johnston, 'Reconciliation, or the New Dispossession', in *Habitat Australia; Caring for Country. Aboriginal Perspectives on Conservation*, The Australian Conservation Foundation, Victoria, 19: 3 (June 1991), 8–10.
9. Ibid.
10. M. Horstman, 'Cape York Peninsula: Forging a Black–Green Alliance', in *Habitat Australia: Caring for Country. Aboriginal Perspectives on Conservation*, The Australian Conservation Foundation, Victoria, 19: 3 (June 1991), 19–22.
11. A. J. Brown, *Keeping the Land Alive: Aboriginal People and Wilderness Protection in Australia* (Sydney, Australia: The Environmental Defender's Office Ltd/The Wilderness Society, 1993).
12. Ibid.

PART FIVE

SOCIETY, THE STATE, AND THE ENVIRONMENT

How might green critiques of the sort canvassed in Part Four be put into political practice? In Part Five we look at the prospects for different sorts of political change, and how they might be brought about through the efforts of environmental movements and the institutionalization of ecological democracy. These sections look forward to a green politics that moves beyond the conventional forms presently entrenched in the liberal democratic states, to new kinds of democratic practices in civil society, states, and global politics.

Section XII: The Green Movement

Environmental politics often comes to life in social movements. These movements involve a diverse array of individuals, groups, and coalitions organizing in order to bring about changes in environmental policies and practices. While numerous political and economic reforms have been achieved at local, national, and international levels, it is arguable that these would not be possible without the pressure of the environmental movement, which is the focus of this section.

Our first three selections emphasize the importance of political activity outside conventional political structures—we are, after all, discussing *movements*, which are, by definition, partly outside traditional political parties and processes. Douglas Torgerson discusses three necessary dimensions of radical politics that begin with, but eventually transcend, the 'movement' image. The most familiar is an orientation towards reform and policy change. Less familiar is the constitutive dimension that includes the expansion of discourse, more creative forms of action, and various alterations of political life. This is the transformative aspect of green politics, seen in more critical environmental theories and movements. Still less familiar is the performative dimension, outside the instrumental and functional, yet an influence on both. Here, Torgerson stresses the intrinsic value of action, found in enjoyment of unconventional politics itself.

Paul Wapner also addresses the public sphere of movement politics, and claims that continued action in civil society can often get things done without state assistance—or even in the face of state recalcitrance. Wapner argues that environmental non-governmental organizations (NGOs) and what he calls 'transnational environmental activist organizations' (TEAGs) occupy a space outside traditional politics. The organizations he writes about are not simply interest groups that have formed to influence the state, as they work both with and, importantly, against states. In addition, environmental groups in 'world civic politics' focus on influencing the ecological sensibility of citizens and directly pressuring corporations to change environmentally destructive practices.

David Schlosberg's essay focuses on the innovative political structure of the environmental justice movement, the development of networks. Rather than a traditional movement organization, which is often vertically organized and directed from the top, the environmental justice movement exemplifies a horizontal, networked, and rhizomatic structure. Schlosberg examines the internal forms and processes of network politics, from beginnings in the recognition of difference and pre-existing social networks, to the development of interlinked political organizations. Networks are also contrasted with the traditional forms of mainstream organizations in terms of political strategy and lasting impacts.

Environmentalists have long debated whether or not to shun the state in favour of oppositional politics. This question becomes more pertinent in states with multi-party systems, and the tension was illustrated by the long-running split between the *Fundi* and *Realo* factions of the German

Greens (resolved in favour of the *Realos*). The basic question is whether the green movement should emphasize movement-building, cultural transformation, and oppositional politics, or participation in (and so compromise with) the existing political process. Thomas Poguntke offers an overview of a straightforward question: what have environmental movements achieved when they have entered the state as green parties? True to the themes in this section, however, Poguntke looks at success both in terms of policy outcome in the state and continued relations with the social movement outside.

Further Reading

For further development of their themes, see Torgerson's *The Promise of Green Politics: Environmentalism and the Public Sphere* (1999), Wapner's *Environmental Activism and World Civic Politics* (1996), and Schlosberg's *Environmental Politics and the New Pluralism* (1999). The focus on the importance of civil society for environmental movements is also examined at the national level by Dryzek, Downes, Hunold, and Schlosberg's *Green States and Social Movements* (2003), and at the international level by Ronnie Lipschutz in *Global Civil Society and Global Environmental Governance* (1995). Brian Doherty's *Ideas and Actions in the Green Movement* (2002) also addresses many of the issues raised in this section.

Recent edited volumes on environmental movements are numerous and include Chris Rootes (ed.), *Environmental Movements: Local, National, and Global* (1999), Chris Rootes (ed.), *Environmental Protest in Western Europe* (2004), and Bron Taylor (ed.), *Ecological Resistance Movements* (1995). The more general literature on new social movements is also instructive (because the Greens constitute one of the most important such movements). Good sources include Mario Diani and Doug McAdam, *Social Movements and Networks* (2003), Jeff Goodwin and James Jasper, *The Social Movements Reader* (2003), and Alberto Melucci, *Nomads of the Present: Social Movements and Individual Needs in Contemporary Society* (1989).

37 Farewell to the Green Movement? Political Action and the Green Public Sphere

Douglas Torgerson

Green politics poses a challenge to the instrumentalism of the industrial world, throwing into question the hierarchical and often technocratic tendencies of modern governance while promising a new kind of politics (Torgerson 1999a). At the same time, green politics is guided by a strong sense of purpose, arising from pressing concerns about how to prevent the rampant destruction of nature and the self-destruction of humanity. The big questions in green political thought centre on ends and means: what are appropriate green goals and how can they be achieved? In a reformist vein, we find commitment to promote the ecologically rational functioning of economy and society; among radicals, we find dedication to a project of social transformation. In both of these contexts, however, there is an ironic paradox. Although challenging instrumentalism, green politics itself takes on a distinctly instrumentalist cast.

Some might argue that the more instrumental the focus, the better (e.g., Goodin 1992). None the less, there are also tendencies that ascribe value to democratic citizenship and political action. A rethinking of political action is, indeed, already present in green politics. Yet, the significance of this so far remains unclear because green political thought has yet to address adequately a key question—the meaning of politics.

This essay addresses that question with reference to the work of Hannah Arendt, the political theorist who has been described as offering 'the most radical rethinking of political action' in the twentieth century (Villa 1996: 4).[1] Drawing on her concept of politics and, more broadly, on her threefold conceptualisation of the active life, we here fashion a model of politics that includes three dimensions: functional, constitutive, and performative. What Arendt's idea of politics prizes is the intrinsic value of political debate. The essay examines green politics in a way that both follows and departs from Arendt, looking for the significance of debate not only in performative politics, but in functional and constitutive politics as well.

We shall see that the green *movement* is a metaphor that is overdone and needs to be mixed with the that of the *green public sphere* if the potential value of debate in the three dimensions is to be realised. At the same time, the very constitution of a green public sphere calls for all three dimensions of green politics to be involved. The point is not to displace the notion of movement

From *Environmental Politics*, 11: 1 (2000), 133–45.

altogether, but to relax the inhibitions that this governing metaphor exerts on the theory and practice of green politics.

I. Rethinking Political Action: A Three-Dimensional Approach

What stands out in Arendt's thought is a conception of politics that is radically non-instrumental, that prizes politics for its own sake as something intrinsically valuable. Arendt contends that politics is an art, but not in the usual sense. She is intent to distinguish her idea of politics not just from scientist fantasies, but from any notion that would subordinate politics to instrumentality. It is thus that she insists that the political art is not just any kind of art. It is not an art—such as painting, sculpture, or architecture—that results in a finished product. Politics is, rather, a performing art.

She thus advances a performative, theatrical image of politics; the value is not in a lasting result, but in the performance itself, as it is in drama and music. She especially focuses here on Machiavelli's concept of *virtù* and provides a unique translation: not simply political skill or prowess, but *virtuosity*. Departing radically from conventional thinking, Arendt thus invites us to view the value of politics as something intrinsic to political action itself, not as something extrinsic and thus dependent on outcomes (1968: 137, 153; 1958: 206–7). She speaks of 'the actual content of political life' as 'the joy and gratification that arise out of being in company with our peers, out of acting together and appearing in public, out of inserting ourselves into the world by word and deed . . . ' (1968: 263).

Arendt advances her non-instrumental understanding of politics in the context of a threefold conception of the 'active life' (1958). She labels the three forms 'labour', 'work', and 'action'. Of these she singles out action and celebrates it in a context of a pervasive instrumentalism that threatens to destroy it. Labour and work are both instrumental, but with an important difference. Labour is a matter of economic activity; here human beings effect their necessary interchange with nature, their 'metabolism' with nature (as Arendt repeats a formulation of Marx). Work is a matter of constructing artifacts that last, endure over time; in the most general sense, human civilisation constitutes such as end. Unlike labour and work, both directed toward extrinsic ends, the purpose of action is intrinsic. Especially recognisable as speech, action is conduct that is meaningful and inventive; through it, human beings come to reveal themselves and recognise one another: 'This revelatory quality of speech and action', Arendt explains, 'comes to the fore where people are *with* others and neither for nor against them—that is, in sheer human togetherness' (1958: 176).

Arendt's celebration of the intrinsic value of politics has perplexed many because it seems to take the politics out of politics. Indeed, her conception is one-sided. Viewing her idea as a mere aesthetic indulgence, some simply reject it out of hand. Others are attracted to her accent on participation, but still want politics to prove its worth with results. They read Arendt with a view to showing that she cannot—and does not—consistently maintain a non-instrumental view of politics. This approach, however, loses sight of what is really distinctive about her position. Accentuating rather than diminishing the one-sided character of her conception offers us an exaggeration that draws attention to what is missed by more familiar and reasonable conceptions.

Arendt's tripartite conceptualisation of the active life—labour, work, and action—itself suggests a way of retaining the distinctiveness of her conception while giving more common notions their due. By drawing on her scheme, we can formulate a three-dimensional model of politics that both includes and distinguishes the functional, the constitutive, and the performative (Torgerson 1999*a*: chs 1, 7).

This tripartite scheme allows us to include the instrumental features of politics without excluding what Arendt singles out and prizes. The instrumental side is to be found in *functional politics* (corresponding to the category of labour) and in *constitutive politics* (corresponding to the category of work). Functional politics deals with the operations of a socio-economic system, especially in its interchange with non-human nature. Constitutive politics deals with constructing or changing a civilisation as a cultural artifice, from the shape of its institutions to the identities of its inhabitants and the character of their discourse. By contrast with the instrumental side of politics, we can recognise a non-instrumental *performative politics* (corresponding to the category of action).[2]

To conceptualise politics in these three dimensions departs from Arendt, but also draws on an implicit tendency in her work. Conceptualised in strictly performative terms, politics would exclude both functional and constitutive dimensions. However, Arendt's performative politics clearly presupposes functional and constitutive outcomes. In functional terms, there clearly must be some provision for human needs. In constitutive terms, performance depends on a human artifice, a cultural space of institutions and identities that allows for political action. But are these instrumental dimensions part of politics?

Arendt may herself open the door to saying yes when she speaks of the 'essence' of politics as being 'debate' (1968: 241). Of course, what she prizes is not the outcome of debate—or its consequences—but debate as performance. She emphatically does not say that the essence of politics is something like policy formation or the interplay of power relationships. But it still remains possible—without dismissing her non-instrumental, performative sense of politics—to consider the idea of politics-as-debate in connection with more conventional ways of understanding politics. Debate clearly is central to performative politics, but how might debate be important as well to both functional and constitutive politics?

In her insistence that politics possesses intrinsic value Arendt displayed a certain commonality with the social movements of the 1960s. For these movements, including the nascent green movement, revived 'a positive concept of politics' promoting 'the practice of citizenship' (George Kateb, quoted in Kariel 1989: 91). Even though other goals were certainly more central to these movements, they did not advocate democracy just in the sense of procedures—as liberal democratic theory might conceive it—but also in the sense of political action valuable for its own sake.

Green politics shares with other social movements an image of political action that poses an at least implicit challenge to modern governance in its authoritarian and oligarchical aspects. To rethink the meaning of politics is thus not to impose something, but to identify in explicit terms something already present in green politics that is capable of further development.

The feminist slogan 'the personal is political' represents an especially important rethinking of politics. Open to various interpretations, the phrase suggests at least these key points: (1) that political actors are shaped through their personal lives and inescapably give expression to the personal in public life; (2) that power pervades the domain of the personal, especially through the legacy of patriarchal family relationships; and (3) that matters previously excluded from political attention as being merely personal are thus entirely legitimate public issues.

If the idea is carried just a little further, however, we arrive at the conclusion that 'politics is everywhere' (Seidel 1985: 45). Then, however, the notion of politics tends to be reduced to power relations: since power is everywhere, the reasoning goes, so too is politics. What is left out of this conceptualisation is space for a politics that is not strictly instrumental. Framed in instrumental terms, challenges to objectionable features of modern governance have no alternative to offer except a realignment of power (cf. Fraser 1989: ch. 1).

Is there a way out of an instrumental framework? In recalling the public sphere of bourgeois society in earlier centuries, Jürgen Habermas (1989, 1992) appears to offer an escape route. This public sphere was, despite its many inequities, at least guided by a principle of communication that called for freedom and equality. What is required by the principle, in other words, is a kind of communicative practice that cannot be reduced to force or manipulation. Although never completely achieved in practice, this basic principle has to be assumed by the participants and can be invoked as a standard to criticise practical shortcomings (Benhabib 1990). For Habermas, the principle thus points to the possibility of a public sphere in modern society where the path of social development can be discussed and assessed. The principle means that everyone concerned would be called upon to seek not control, but an understanding based on listening with respect. Much the same idea has been repeated by others, though with significant revisions, and numerous challenges to the liberal democratic model of government draw attention to the communicative potential of the public sphere or, perhaps, a plurality of public spheres.[3] Democratisation, on this view, must put an end to citizen quiescence, to the sway of mass media propaganda, and to faith in technocratic rationalism.

What Habermas and others sympathetic to this view generally share, however, is a conception that remains fastened to instrumentality (Habermas 1992: 446–52). For the goal ultimately is one of giving authoritative direction to social development. The instrumentalism of this conception of the public sphere perhaps becomes evident only by contrast with the celebration, as we have seen in Arendt, of political action in the public realm. An Arendtian qualification to the idea of the public sphere is needed, indeed, in adequately conceptualising a green public sphere.

II. What's in a Metaphor? The Green Public Sphere

Anxiety can be detected in many central questions of the green movement. Who is genuinely green, who is not? Who should be included in the movement, and who should be expelled? What does it really mean to be green? When does light green become indistinguishable from grey? These questions arise from the apparent strategic imperative to build a green movement that, unified and coherent, is prepared to face its challenges with clear direction and unflinching purpose.

This anxious concern about unity and coherence, however, overlooks something obvious. A reframing of discourse may, as John Dryzek has suggested, be 'the enduring legacy' of environmentalism (1996b: 121). What has emerged is a 'language of environment' that creates the possibility of new forms of contention and argument, a new world of debate. This world establishes the terms of what is debatable, of what can be argued and how. This is an 'arguable world', in other words, a context 'where things are discovered, conflicts are fought, people agree and differ afresh' (Myerson and Rydin 1996: 32). It is thus that a green public sphere is emerging, throwing into question the industrialist presuppositions that prevail in public discourse.

Environmentalism promotes a way of speaking about the environment that before was not possible or even imaginable. The new discourse makes it possible to recognise, define, and meaningfully discuss environmental problems. Whatever else it may do, the green movement constructs this green discourse and promotes a forum for it—a green public sphere—that challenges a previously comfortable industrialism.

The green movement is widely acknowledged to be diverse, and—despite anxious concerns about achieving unity and coherence—diversity is sometimes seen as one of its virtues. Various green strategies none the less typically have one thing in common: the very metaphor of social *movement*. In an interesting case of reasoning by analogy, indeed, Werner Hülsberg explicitly makes a strategic argument on the basis of this metaphor (1988: 209):

> Now every movement, as the name suggests, has to do with 'movement': it has to remain in motion, otherwise it comes to an end. There are, however, objective and subjective limits to this 'movement' which have to do with the general stage of awareness and development of class conflict. There are limits to the expansion of a social movement which, if the movement fails to break through them, bring about a decline and a search for new forms.

Another author asks why a movement falters and 'what might get it moving again' (Gaard 1998: 11). Still another calls for an approach that will 'generate real forward motion' (Szaz 1994: 164).

These metaphorical gestures allude to the larger image of the movement of history. The image can, indeed, be traced to the idealist Hegelian view of the process of world history as being a dialectical movement of mind. More significant, however, is the reaction of Marxian historical materialism against the notion of history as a logical 'movement of pure reason' (Marx and Engels 1969: 41). For, as Marx himself put it, he was promoting instead 'a practical movement, a *revolution*' (n.d.: 103). As the idea of social movement developed through the late nineteenth and early twentieth centuries, the image would emerge of 'a huge wave of humanity' stretching 'to the distant horizon' (Werner Sombart, quoted in Wilkinson (1971: 21)).

The metaphor of movement reinforces green concerns about what it means to be green. We need to ask about the genuine identity of the movement because we must avoid tendencies that threaten to get the movement off course. Amid demands for the movement to have a definite direction, indeed, the instrumental character of the metaphor becomes evident. A clear identity and a concerted direction are seen as essential to a coherent green strategy (e.g., Bahro 1986; Bookchin 1990; Carter 1993; Hawkins 1988; cf. Dobson 1995).

What makes these concerns so pressing? Is some Great Leader going to emerge to mandate a uniform direction for the movement? Much strategic thinking seems to labour under some such notion. However, if one *accepts* the green movement as broad and diverse—inescapably uneven and fragmented, partially cooperative and partially conflictual—the metaphor of movement becomes easier to question. The point is not to abandon the metaphor entirely, but to mix it with another, that of the green public sphere.[4]

A consistency between means and ends is often regarded as a key feature of coherent green theory and practice (Eckersley 1988: 59). The effect of the metaphor of movement, however, is to accentuate the separation: the means must cover a great distance to reach their destination. Precisely because green ends often seem so doubtful of achievement, there may be something necessary and inescapable about the metaphor of a green movement. None the less, another metaphor is also possible, one that involves activity emerging within a place. The green public sphere shows us not the path of a movement, but the space of a discourse.

This metaphor suggests not the need for theoretical and practical coherence so that a unified *we* can get on with its journey, but focuses attention rather on a *we* that partially exists—one that has a capacity for shared meaning, but also depends on disagreement as well as agreement to nourish its discourse and the human relationships that constitute it. As a space for discussion, the green public sphere is governed by no single direction, but displays an interest in a plurality of opinions, however inconvenient and troubling they might be. Of course, the green public sphere cannot be something that is altogether boundless: even meaningful disagreements require certain limits and coherence. With the green public sphere, nonetheless, the distinct inclination is toward inclusion.

Must we say farewell to the green movement in order to escape the totalising logic of instrumentalism? This might seem to be the implication here, but we do not need to say goodbye to anything except an uncritical acceptance of the presuppositions of that metaphor. We begin to do this as soon as we recognise the metaphorical character of the phrase rather than remaining stuck in a literal framework. Then it becomes possible for our thinking to be oriented to a green public sphere as well as a green movement. Mixing metaphors in this way relaxes the grip of instrumentalism without necessarily denying goals.

Even though the green movement does, of course, have a long way to go, the precious communicative space of the emerging green public sphere may not travel well. The *we* of the green public sphere is not an instrument of strategy but the shared space of a common world. In this context, the point is not for everyone to agree on everything but for the meaningful disagreement of debate to be both allowed and encouraged.

III. Three Dimensions of Green Politics

By focusing on three *dimensions* of green politics, we do not portray a political space of discrete elements but draw attention to interconnections and indicate ways in which the different dimensions relate to one another. Functional green politics shows a face of reform, an inclination to work within established systems in order to make them more ecologically rational. In a green context, constitutive politics usually presents a radical face, a concern with qualitative change, ultimately the transformation of existing socio-economic systems, cultures, and human identities. So far, of course, this is familiar territory. Something novel happens, though, when we consider the significance of performative green politics. Here the normal categories of reformism or radicalism no longer apply.

Green performative politics is interested in the intrinsic value of politics-as-debate. Significantly, however, this very interest presents a challenge to conventional approaches oriented to reform or radical change; for these have not made debate central and, indeed, have often sought to put an end to debate. Putting an end to debate has actually been central to the modern tendency of politics to be eclipsed by rationalistic schemes, through either the technocratic management of mass society or—what amounts to its mirror image—the comprehensive transformation of society by a social movement under the aegis of a coherent linking of theory and practice. The boldly different focus that performative politics places on debate leads us to ask what role debate might play in both functional and constitutive contexts. As we shall see, this question challenges both functional and constitutive green politics: an enhanced role for debate raises the prospect, indeed, of a particular kind of radical reformism—an incremental radicalism.

(I) FUNCTIONAL GREEN POLITICS

With its reform orientation, functional green politics promotes public policy changes aimed at making advanced industrial society more ecologically rational. The primary focus is thus on finding ways to influence the outcomes of established policy processes by employing a variety of environmental policy tools. Functional green politics also displays a constitutive inclination when it appeals to notions like sustainable development and ecological modernisation, but in a way that is sharply rejected by radical greens who maintain that reform measures—even when dressed up in new slogans—can do no more than reinforce an industrialism that is environmentally destructive at its core.

Functional green politics, indeed, unavoidably engages with the largely technocratic orientation of established policy professionalism, which typically displays a commitment to maintain the orderly functioning of advanced industrial society. Even policy professionalism, however, has come to display counter-tendencies. A clear tension is evident between those committed to the conventional technocratic orientation and those promoting an approach that is clearly discursive and thus open to participation by non-expert citizens. The key to this dissenting professionalism, in a word, is debate—the promotion of a policy dialogue that challenges the monological character of technocratic rationalism (e.g., Fischer 1992; Torgerson 1996, 1997, 1999a: ch. 4; Williams and Matheny 1995).

Although primarily attuned to functional politics—and thus a reform framework—dissenting professionalism also anticipates the constitutive prospect of the discursive redesign of policy processes. In a green framework, this tendency is reinforced by interventions that, although they directly address specific policy problems, also promote larger changes by influencing agenda setting, problem definition, and the epistemological criteria that determine what counts as relevant and legitimate policy knowledge.[5]

(II) CONSTITUTIVE GREEN POLITICS

Green radicalism departs from functional politics with a constitutive project of social transformation. The lack of any coherent and clearly plausible programme for radical change, however, invites rather desperate scenarios of crisis and catastrophe that, in one way or another, mimic rather clichéd Marxist scenarios (though without the working class as hero). The pattern is repeated even when the hope for change itself dissipates: 'the very best thing for the planet', one radical green has thus declared, 'might be a massive world-wide economic depression': 'Amid the terrible hardships this would create for countless people, at least the machinery would stop for a while, and the Earth could take a breather' (Plant 1991: 3).

None the less, disillusionment with old approaches to theory and practice has fostered a decentred approach to radical change designed to avoid the problems of traditional Marxism. This approach, which has influenced green strategic thinking, depends on no central agent of change, but on a complementary interplay of social movements that, though diverse, all tend in their own ways to oppose oppression and promote democracy.

With its reliance on a range of diverse social forces, this decentred approach contains both liberal democratic and radically utopian elements. These elements, though at odds, both enter into a contingent and unstable equilibrium: 'a fundamental nodal point', as Laclau and Mouffe (1985: 155) put it, 'in the construction of the political'. The key to the approach is 'a plurality of social logics' constituted in 'a plurality of spaces' (190), the 'proliferation of radically new and different political spaces' (1985: 181). At the same time, the project calls for 'the construction of a new "common sense" which changes the identities of the different groups' so that the differing discursive practices converge in a complementary manner (1985: 183). This serves to institutionalise openness, constructing a 'space' of 'contradictory tension' that invites plurality (1985: 189). Here there is a diversity rather than unity of discourse: 'Discursive *discontinuity* becomes primary and constitutive'. There is 'a polyphony of voices, each of which constructs its own irreducible discursive identity' (1985: 191).

Even with the accent on openness, there remains a principle of exclusion in the approach. There is a spirit of determined refusal, of uncompromising resistance to established institutions and the prevailing configuration of power (Laclau and Mouffe 69–70, 168–9; Carroll 1992). An appearance of strategic coherence depends on this opposition. Social movements are viewed in regard to how they might fit with the larger project of transforming society. Whatever fails to fit clearly with this project is prone to be seen as a prop for the *status quo*. Because reformist tendencies within a movement tend to be rejected as being in complicity with oppressive forces, however, the accent on diversity and inclusiveness risks being overwhelmed by the need to clearly identify an enemy that will help to maintain a coherent oppositional identity. What is thrown into question at this point is precisely what proponents of transformative politics themselves often warn against: exclusionary thinking that imagines a privileged theoretical position able to guide the process of social change.

Committed to a basic affirmation or negation of the established order, both reform and radical orientations tend toward exaggerated totalisations. Radical reformism, however, occupies a middle ground, focused neither on narrow political manoeuvering nor on a grand and sweeping transformation. The focus, rather, is on finding and using vulnerable points in the established order in a way that does not pose an immediate challenge but enhances the potential to alter the functioning of the system in the direction of radical change.

Those who promote change typically face a 'mobilization of bias' (Schattscheinder 1975) that excludes dramatic changes in agenda setting, problem definition, and epistemology that could alter established policy dynamics (Torgerson 1996; 1997; 1999a: ch. 4). These exclusions often appear to be inescapable imperatives, written in the nature of things. As circumstances change, however, these very imperatives can become mutually incompatible, thus tending to undermine the system. We find this same idea, indeed, both in the Marxian concept of contradiction and in systems theory focused on problems of adaptability in dynamic, open systems (cf. March 1989). Enhancing the adaptability of a system, however, can create unintended consequences.

Bachrach and Baratz's (1970) model of the policy process pictures inputs and throughputs producing policy outcomes that loop back to increase or decrease the stability of established power relationships, thus setting the stage for altered dynamics in subsequent developments. In light of this model, adjustments that seem minor can become part of a wider pattern of outcomes that contain both unexpected and unintended elements. There is thus an ambivalent potential in efforts to enhance system adaptability. Challenging the apparent imperatives of a system certainly will bring various defence mechanisms into play. But there is no predicting whether these will prove successful. Not only are there limits to human knowledge, in this regard, but also a potential for the imperatives of the system to turn against one another.

Although shaped by its institutionalisation in the established order of functional politics, environmental policy also remains in part an accomplishment of more radical green tendencies that are critical of this world. Radical critics are right to underscore the propensity for this world to blunt the radical thrust of potential changes. It is wrong, however, to suggest that changes are thus necessarily constrained. Outcomes depend on a larger context of power dynamics, in which green radicalism plays a part. No one can predict or control what will happen in this context.

Even though radical reformism enters a gap created by the implausibility of comprehensive strategies for social transformation, the approach itself often seems inclined toward its own comprehensiveness, to exhibit a faith in a stable strategic orientation capable of providing reliable, overall direction for the path of change. Here the strategy could, in principle, be clearly formulated and used as a common map so that further disagreement and debate would be unnecessary, indeed detrimental. However, a kind of radical reformism can also be conceived in terms of a decentred orientation, in which differences would guarantee continuing debate. The tension and ambivalence evident in the green movement would thus not need to be eliminated but could be part of an *incremental radicalism* (Torgerson 1994; 1999a: ch. 7). Here functional and constitutive politics would intertwine, even though differences and strenuous oppositions between radicals and reformers would remain.

A decentred incremental radicalism is not actually a strategy in any conventional sense. We cannot exactly say what is to be done. Thinking in these terms none the less serves to expose false guarantees of a unified theory and practice, to unsettle fixed positions, and to undermine the assurance of true believers. All this may well pose a problem for the green movement, as it is conventionally conceived, but it would seem to be salutary for the prospects of debate in the green public sphere.

(III) PERFORMATIVE GREEN POLITICS

Green politics readily makes sense if we think of reforms in a functional mode as addressing ecological irrationalities of industrialism. Similarly, green politics makes sense if we think of efforts in a constitutive mode to transform society, perhaps along the lines of an ecological utopia. Green politics, that is, at least *makes sense* in these connections, whether or not we actually agree with the goals or the means to achieve them. It all makes sense because it fits with presuppositions of instrumentalism. However, would green politics make sense without a purpose outside itself? Does it make sense to think of an intrinsically valuable green performative politics? The very idea seems like a contradiction in terms that denies the real importance of green politics. If we were to value green politics for its own sake, would we not simply be rendering it impotent for important green purposes while allowing another human institution an unwarranted privilege?

If we recall Arendt, we can find at least one reason for championing the intrinsic value of politics: concern that modernity so neglects this value that the possibility of politics itself is undermined. For Arendt, the instrumentalisation of politics renders it fragile by depriving it of real purpose. Would there be any rationale for functional or constitutive politics once their ends had been attained? Could we not replace functional politics with technocratic management? Would the coherent direction of a coordinated social movement not serve the ends of constitutive politics? Would there be any need for debate?

Valuing political action for its own sake at least defends against modernity's antipolitical tendencies. Doing so enhances prospects for active democratic life while weighing against authoritarian or totalitarian prospects. To say this, however, is of course ultimately just to make another instrumentalist move: we value politics not really for its own stake but for the desirable effects of doing so. So we still face the question of what, after all, is the intrinsic value of politics?

For Arendt, this value is to be found in the virtuosity of political action, especially in debate. Arendt's account of the content of this value changes over the course of her work. In the context of the social movements of the 1960s, she affirmed the discovery of the times that political action was 'fun' (1972: 203). In affirming such an apparently frivolous value, Arendt seems to depart from her earlier celebrations of glory (1958), public happiness (1965), or joy (1968). What remains constant, none the less, is the idea there is value in action. In performative politics, the accent is placed on theatricality, as can be seen in political moments when instrumentalism is attenuated, displaced by a joy of performance.

Are there any tendencies within green politics that recognise value intrinsic to politics? Is the green movement not necessarily a crusade to achieve pressing goals? Often, indeed, visions of tragic heroism tempt green politics. While attracted to tragic scenarios, green politics also at times expresses an inclination, celebrating the comic, to turn the world upside down and crown the fool (Torgerson 1999a: ch. 5). The often comic gestures of groups like Greenpeace, indeed, are not merely stunts and antics, but a kind of language. From the start, green politics has invoked the idiom of the carnivalesque to expose the seriousness of officialdom as a mask that hides the irrationality of its rationality.

In the early years of environmentalism, Joseph W. Meeker's *The Comedy of Survival* (1974) threw into question the often tragic aura of the movement, proclaiming the flexibility and vitality of the comic while suggesting that tragic heroism was itself part of the problem: the human quest to dominate nature contains the tragic presumption that humanity is somehow privileged in the nature of things. More recently, Meeker has come out with a revised edition (1997) that conveys more directly the key message of the book: a challenge to the work ethic on behalf of a 'play ethic'. He distinguishes (17–18, 10) between 'finite' and 'infinite' games. 'Finite games', 'characterized by . . . clear goals', are common in numerous settings, including 'politics as usual'. For Meeker, 'play . . . is that spontaneous behavior whose only purpose is to please its participants and keep them playing. When goals or objectives appear . . . play disappears'. In an infinite game, however, there is no goal except an intrinsic one, 'infinite play'. Meeker calls this 'a manifestation of the comic way' and advances a key political insight: 'During play, all players are equal': 'There are no playful tyrants', he maintains, 'and no tyrannical players'.

If a game is pressed into the service of extrinsic ends, its playful quality will diminish and it will cease to be fun. It may be, though, that political debate is a kind of language game that cannot simply be made an instrument for external service. For the debating game to be played well, it needs to be played, in part at least, for its own sake.

For an intrinsically valuable politics to flourish, it needs to find its own metaphors, to enact debate on its own terms. George Lakoff and Mark Johnson may help to suggest the nature of non-instrumental politics, indeed, with a striking contrast between two metaphors for argument (1980: 5):

> Imagine a culture where an argument is viewed as a dance, the participants are seen as performers, and the goal is to perform in a balanced and aesthetically pleasing way. In such a culture, people would view arguments differently, carry them out differently, and talk about them differently. But we would probably not view them as arguing at all: they would simply be doing something different . . . Perhaps the most neutral way of describing this difference . . . would be to say that we have a discourse form in terms of battle and they have one structured in terms of dance.

Such an imaginative move seems to be needed if we are to really understand Arendt's meaning when she calls politics a performing art. We begin to see what it might mean for political debate to take on the aspect of an infinite game where the players are, above all, committed to keeping the game going. Clearly this cannot be the whole of green politics—or any kind of politics—but it is a needed dimension of the green public sphere.

IV. Constituting the Green Public Sphere

To speak of a green public sphere is to suggest a metaphor capable of helping to refocus and enhance existing tendencies in both theory and practice. Constituting the green public sphere is not a project altogether alien to green politics, but is a tendency that is already implicit, often obscured by the metaphor of movement. The project would mean involving green politics in functional, constitutive, and performative modes, all being needed dimensions of the green public sphere.

The inclination to promote a green public sphere is especially obscured when the metaphor of movement is part of an effort to promote a comprehensive radical strategy of social transformation. Plotting such a strategy tends to mean adopting a no-nonsense attitude and establishing clear criteria to use in identifying and excommunicating enemies internal to the movement.

A comprehensive radical strategy would be centred in constitutive politics and would neglect—even dismiss—functional politics and incremental changes with the potential to enhance the green public sphere. Such changes would not pertain so much to environmental policy, as usually understood, as to a larger domain of policy contexts. Communications policy, access to information, and provisions for citizen participation would be key points of reference. So too would social and economic policies—as in basic income proposals for example—designed to reduce the fears and insecurities that undermine the ability of citizens to focus concern on environmental problems (Offe 1992; Offe et al. 1996; cf. Johnson 1973).

The performative dimension of politics needs to become a distinct focus of attention if it is to be understood, valued and promoted. As Arendt herself recognises, however, action as performance cannot stand alone: 'a definite space had to be secured and a structure built', she says in reference to ancient Greece, 'where all subsequent actions could take place, that space being the public realm of the *polis* . . . ' (1958: 194–5). Performative politics thus depends on constitutive politics, the creation of a 'space of appearance' (1958: 199) as a condition for action. If politics is valued only in instrumental terms, however, the outlook for constituting a space for political action becomes tenuous. What Arendt especially fears is the tendency of social movements to cut off discussion, ending debate and—along with it—the possibility of political action. The problem is intensified because any kind of constitutive politics has something arbitrary, even violent, about it: there is no avoiding exclusions. In the absence of impartiality, though, what becomes important is a partiality for political action. This means a constitutive politics that is oriented by a principle that affirms politics for its own sake (1965: 214–15).

The green public sphere is not some clearly defined institution. It has emerged from changing patterns of interconnection among places where green discourse is practiced. The language of environment is, of course, all too frequently spoken as a foreign tongue. We find it spoken fairly fluently if we look to such places as green political parties, some academic venues, grassroots groups, and environmental organisations. When it is allowed, it tends to be spoken awkwardly in business corporations and state agencies. The green idiom none the less exerts an influence—both functional and constitutive—on agenda setting, problem definition, and epistemological criteria in the policy process.

By advancing green discourse, green politics helps to constitute the green public sphere. But the emergence of this discourse has depended significantly on green political activities that have proceeded under the metaphorical banner of a progressive social movement, conceived in distinctly instrumentalist terms. The prospect of promoting a green public sphere thus sets in sharp relief the question of means and ends. This prospect emerges in a context of power where the nascent green public sphere is vulnerable to attack. Neither its promotion nor its very survival can be taken for granted: both require strategic practices. Faced with this problem, the green movement is often beset with internal strife, and many greens find themselves inclined to excommunicate elements that, failing to fit with a coherent programme, endanger progress along the clear path of the movement.

Any social movement clearly needs to have some kind of communication, but this does not necessarily have to be debate. Strategic considerations in a social movement, indeed, can seriously undermine the potential for an open exchange of opinions. However, if such an exchange of opinions is valued—for whatever reason—a movement will tend to understand and constitute itself as a public sphere.

No matter how open, flexible, and inclusive it might be, the green public sphere cannot avoid boundaries. In contrast to the green movement, however, the green public sphere has a necessary commitment to debate; its inclination is not simply tolerance, but a cultivation and provocation of disagreements that will stimulate an exchange and development of differing opinions. This means that the boundaries of the green public sphere are inclined to be contested, permeable, and indeterminate. The green public sphere, moreover, is conducive to a performative politics that celebrates the intrinsic value of debate. It is possible to imagine the green movement surviving without much debate, but ending debate would destroy the green public sphere. Although it cannot be entirely open, the green public sphere cannot exclude the openness that debate demands.

Notes

1. The focus of this discussion is strictly on Arendt's view of politics. For attempts to assess the possibly green character of her thinking, see Whiteside (1994, 1998), Macauley (1996).

2. Performative politics is here conceived *not* as an 'alternative' form of politics (cf. Meyer 2000), but as a dimension of political action that instrumentalist fixations typically obscure. Any political action is at least potentially multidimensional in its significance for human values, both in terms of the multiplicity of its outcomes and in terms of its intrinsic characteristics: with regard, that is, to both product and process. Singling out the process value of politics—to the exclusion of its product value—surely ends in an awkwardly one-sided concept, as Pitkin (1981) has stressed in an important critique of Arendt. However, such a critique also risks obscuring what Arendt's exaggeration reveals. Hence it is important to delineate an unambiguously multidimensional concept of politics that explicitly preserves the performative along with the functional and constitutive dimensions. Although there should be no ambiguity about the multidimensional character of this concept, the concept itself necessarily remains

ambivalent in the sense that it does not presuppose any fixed relationship among these three dimensions of political action. The significance of any dimension depends on context, both in describing political action and in prescribing tactics, strategies, and goals. The key point here is not to ignore the potential significance of the performative in describing or prescribing green political action.

3. See Young (1990: chs 4, 6), Fraser (1992). A key question is one of genre as it pertains to the scope and limits of argumentation (Torgerson 1999a: esp. ch. 8).

4. Another worthwhile metaphor to mix in is that of a 'network', which can grow and expand but cannot move forward (Schlosberg, 1999; Torgerson, 1999a: ch. 7).

5. Toxic waste provides an apt example of the interplay of agenda setting, problem definition, and epistemology in the policy process (Torgerson 1997; 1999a: ch. 4). Although largely a reform discourse, sustainable development displays a radical potential in certain contexts (Torgerson 1999a: ch. 3). There is a similar potential with ecological modernisation (Hajer 1995; Christoff 1996; Torgerson 1999a: chs 4, 7).

References

Arendt, Hannah (1958), *The Human Condition* (Chicago, IL: University of Chicago Press).
—— (1965), *On Revolution* (New York: Viking Press).
—— (1968), *Between Past and Future: Eight Exercises in Political Thought* (New York: Viking Press).
—— (1972), *Crises of the Republic* (New York: Harcourt, Brace, Jovanovich).

Bachrach, Peter and Morton S. Baratz (1970), *Power and Poverty: Theory and Practice* (New York: Oxford University Press).

Bahro, Rudolph (1986), *Building the Green Movement*, trans. Mary Tyler (London: GMP Publishers).

Benhabib, Seyla (1990), 'Communicative Ethics and Contemporary Controversies in Practical Philosophy', in Seyla Benhabib and Fred Dallmayr (eds), *The Communicative Ethics Controversy* (Cambridge, MA: The MIT Press), 33–69.

Bookchin, Murray (1990), *Remaking Society: Pathways to a Green Future* (Boston, MA: South End Press).

Calhoun, Craig (ed.) (1992), *Habermas and the Public Sphere* (Cambridge, MA: The MIT Press).

Carroll, William K. (ed.) (1992), *Organizing Dissent: Contemporary Social Movements in Theory and Practice* (Toronto: Garamond Press).

Carter, Alan (1993), 'Towards a Green Political Theory', in Andrew Dobson and Paul Lucardie (eds), *The Politics of Nature: Explorations in Green Political Theory* (London: Routledge), 39–62.

Christoff, Peter (1996), 'Ecological Modernisation, Ecological Modernities', *Environmental Politics*, 5(3): 476–500.

Dobson, Andrew (1995), *Green Political Thought* (London: 2nd edn, Routledge).

Dryzek, John. S. (1994). 'Ecology and Discursive Democracy: Beyond Liberal Capitalism and the Administrative State', in Martin O'Connor (ed.), *Is Capitalism Sustainable? Political Economy and the Politics of Ecology* (New York: Guildford Press), 176–97.

——— (1996a), *Democracy in Capitalist Times: Ideals, Limits, and Struggles* (Oxford: Oxford University Press).

——— (1996b), 'Strategies of Ecological Democratization', in William M. Lafferty and James Meadowcroft (eds), *Democracy and the Environment* (Cheltenham, UK: Edward Elgar), 108–24.

——— (2000). *Deliberative Democracy and Beyond: Liberals, Critics, Contestations* (Oxford: Oxford University Press).

Eckersley, Robyn (1988), 'Green Politics: A Practice in Search of a Theory?' *Alternatives: Perspectives on Society, Technology and Environment*, 15(4): 52–61.

Fischer, Frank (1992), 'Participatory Expertise: Toward the Democratization of Policy Science', in William N. Dunn and Rita M. Kelly (eds), *Advances in Policy Studies since 1950* (New Brunswick, NJ: Transaction Publishers), 351–76.

Fraser, Nancy (1989), *Unruly Practices: Power, Discourse, and Gender in Contemporary Social Theory* (Minneapolis, MN: University of Minnesota Press).

——— (1992), 'Rethinking the Public Sphere: A Contribution to the Critique of Actually Existing Democracy', in Craig Calhoun (ed.), *Habermas and the Public Sphere* (Cambridge, MA: The MIT Press), 109–42.

Gaard, Greta (1998), *Ecological Politics: Ecofeminists and the Greens*, Philadelphia, PA: Temple University Press.

Goodin, Robert E. (1992), *Green Political Theory* (Cambridge: Polity Press).

Habermas, Jürgen (1989), *The Structural Transformation of the Public Sphere: An Inquiry into a Category of Bourgeois Society*, trans. Thomas Burger (Cambridge, MA: MIT Press).

——— (1992), 'Further Reflections on the Public Sphere', in Craig Calhoun (ed.), *Habermas and the Public Sphere* (Cambridge, MA: The MIT Press), 421–61.

Hajer, Maarten A. (1995), *The Politics of Environmental Discourse: Ecological Modernization and the Policy Process* (Oxford: Oxford University Press).

Hawkins, Howard (1988), 'The Potential of the Green Movement', *New Politics*, 5: 85–105.

Hülsberg, Werner (1988), *The German Greens: A Social and Political Profile*, trans. Gus Fagan (London: Verso).

Johnson, Warren A. (1973), 'The Guaranteed Income as an Environmental Measure', in Herman E. Daly (ed.), *Toward a Steady-State Economy* (San Francisco, CA: W.H. Freeman), 175–89.

Kariel, Henry S. (1989), *The Desperate Politics of Postmodernism* (Amherst, MA: University of Massachusetts Press).

Laclau, Ernesto and Chantel Mouffe (1985), *Hegemony and Socialist Strategy: Towards a Radical Democratic Politics* (London: Verso).

Lakoff, George and Mark Johnson (1980), *Metaphors We Live By* (Chicago, IL: University of Chicago Press).

Macauley, David (1996), 'Hannah Arendt and the Politics of Place: From Earth Alienation to *Oikos*', in David Macauley (ed.), *Minding Nature: The Philosophers of Ecology* (New York: Guilford Press), 102–33.

March, James G. (1989), 'The Technology of Foolishness', in James G. March, *Decisions and Organizations* (Oxford: Basil Blackwell), 253–65.

Marx, Karl (n.d.), *The Poverty of Philosophy* (Moscow: Foreign Languages Publishing House).

―― and Frederick Engels (1969), *The German Ideology* (Part 1) in Karl Marx and Frederick Engels, *Selected Works*, vol. 1 (Moscow: Progress Publishers).

Meeker, Joseph W. (1974), *The Comedy of Survival: Studies in Literary Ecology* (New York: Charles Scribners' Sons).

―― (1997), *The Comedy of Survival: Literary Ecology and a Play Ethic*, 3rd edn (Tucson, AZ: University of Arizona Press).

Meyer, John M. (2000), Review of Douglas Torgerson, *The Promise of Green Politics: Environmentalism and the Public Sphere*, *American Political Science Review*, 94(1): 181–2.

Myerson, George and Yvonne Rydin (1996), *The Language of Environment: A New Rhetoric* (London: UCL Press).

Offe, Claus (1992), 'A Non-Productivist Design for Social Policies', in Philippe Van Parijs (ed.), *Arguing for Basic Income: Ethical Foundations for a Radical Reform* (London: Verso), 61–78.

―― et al. (1996), 'A Basic Income Guaranteed by the State: A Need of the Moment in Social Policy', in Claus Offe, *Modernity and the State* (Cambridge, MA: The MIT Press), 201–21.

Pitkin, Hanna (1981), 'Justice: On Relating Public and Private', *Political Theory*, 9(3): 327–52.

Plant, Christopher (1991), 'Green Business in a Gray World—Can it Be Done?' in Christopher Plant and Judith Plant (eds), *Green Business: Hope or Hoax? Toward an Authentic Strategy for Restoring the Earth* (Philadelphia, PA: New Society Publishers), 1–8.

Schattscheinder, E. E. (1975), *The Semisovereign People* (Hinsdale, IL: The Dryden Press).

Schlosberg, David (1999), *Environmental Justice and the New Pluralism: The Challenge of Difference for Environmentalism* (Oxford: Oxford University Press).

Seidel, Gill (1985), 'Political Discourse Analysis', in Teun A, van Dijk (ed.), *Handbook of Discourse Analysis*, vol. 4 (London: Academic Press), 43–60.

Szaz, Andrew (1994), *EcoPopulism: Toxic Waste and the Movement for Environmental Justice* (Minneapolis, MN: University of Minnesota Press).

Torgerson, Douglas (1994), 'Strategy and Ideology in Environmentalism: A Decentered Approach to Sustainability', *Industrial and Environmental Crisis Quarterly*, 8(4): 295–331.

―― (1996), 'Power and Insight in Policy Discourse: Postpositivism and Problem Definition', in Laurent Dobuzinskis, Michael Howlett, and David Laycock (eds.), *Policy Studies in Canada: The State of the Art*, Toronto: University of Toronto Press, pp. 266–89.

―― (1997), 'Policy Professionalism and the Voices of Dissent: The Case of Environmentalism', *Polity*, 29(3): 345–75.

―― (1999a), *The Promise of Green Politics: Environmentalism and the Public Sphere* (Durham, NC: Duke University Press).

―― (1999b), 'Three Dimensions of Politics: Thinking with and against Arendt', a paper presented in the Methodologies Graduate Program Speakers Series, 'Re-Thinking the Political', Trent University, Peterborough, Ontario, 28 Jan.

Villa, Dana R. (1996), *Arendt and Heidegger: The Fate of the Political* (Princeton, NJ: Princeton University Press).

Whiteside, Kerry H. (1994), 'Hannah Arendt and Ecological Politics', *Environmental Ethics*, 16(4): 339–58.

―― (1998), 'Worldliness and Respect for Nature: An Ecological Application of Hannah Arendt's Conception of Culture', *Environmental Values*, 7(1): 25–40.

Wilkinson, Paul (1971), *Social Movement* (New York: Praeger Publishers).

Williams, Bruce A. and Albert R. Matheny (1995), *Democracy, Dialogue, and Environmental Disputes: The Contested Languages of Social Regulation* (New Haven, CT: Yale University Press).

Young, Iris Marion (1990), *Justice and the Politics of Difference* (Princeton, NJ: Princeton University Press).

38 Politics Beyond the State: Environmental Activism and World Civic Politics

Paul Wapner

Interest in transnational activist groups such as Greenpeace, European Nuclear Disarmament (END), and Amnesty International has been surging. Much of this new attention on the part of students of international relations is directed at showing that transnational activists make a difference in world affairs, that they shape conditions which influence how their particular cause is addressed. Recent scholarship demonstrates, for example, that Amnesty International and Human Rights Watch have changed state human rights practices in particular countries.[1] Other studies have shown that environmental groups have influenced negotiations over environmental protection of the oceans, the ozone layer, and Antarctica and that they have helped enforce national compliance with international mandates.[2] Still others have shown that peace groups helped shape nuclear policy regarding deployments in Europe during the cold war and influenced Soviet perceptions in a way that allowed for eventual superpower accommodation.[3] This work is important, especially insofar as it establishes the increasing influence of transnational nongovernmental organization (NGOs) on states. Nonetheless, for all its insight, it misses a different but related dimension of activist work—the attempt by activists to shape public affairs by working within and across societies themselves.

Recent studies neglect the societal dimension of activists' efforts in part because they subscribe to a narrow understanding of politics. They see politics as a practice associated solely with government and thus understand activist efforts exclusively in terms of their influence upon government. Seen from this perspective, transnational activists are solely global pressure groups seeking to change states' policies or create conditions in the international system that enhance or diminish interstate cooperation. Other efforts directed toward societies at large are ignored or devalued because they are not considered to be genuinely political in character.

Such a narrow view of politics in turn limits research because it suggests that the conception and meaning of transnational activist groups is fixed and that scholarship therefore need only measure activist influence on states. This article asserts, by contrast, that the meaning of activist groups in a global context is not settled and will remain problematic as long as the strictly societal dimension of their work is left out of the analysis. Activist efforts within and across societies are a proper object of study and only by including them in transnational activist research can one render an accurate understanding of transnational activist groups and, by extension, of world politics.

This article focuses on activist society-oriented activities and demonstrates that activist organizations are not simply transnational pressure groups, but rather are political actors in their own right. The main argument is that the best way to think about transnational activist societal efforts is through the concept of "world civic politics." When activists work to change conditions without directly pressuring states, their activities take place in the civil dimension of world collective life or what is sometimes called global civil society.[4] Civil society is that arena of social engagement which exists above the individual yet below the state.[5] It is a complex network of economic, social, and cultural practices based on friendship, family, the market, and voluntary affiliation.[6] Although the concept arose in the analysis of domestic societies, it is beginning to make sense on a global level. The interpenetration of markets, the intermeshing of symbolic meaning systems, and the proliferation of transnational collective endeavors signal the formation of a thin, but nevertheless present, public sphere where private individuals and groups interact for common purposes. Global civil society as such is that slice of associational life which exists above the individual and below the state, but also across national boundaries. When transnational activists direct their efforts beyond the state, they are politicizing global civil society.

Like its domestic counterpart, global civil society consists of structures that define and shape public affairs. For example, market forces shape the way vast numbers of people in various countries act with reference to issues of public concern. Additionally, voluntary associations affiliated with trade, cultural expression, religion, science, and production have widespread influence. In targeting these processes and institutions, activists use the realms of transnational social, cultural, and economic life to influence world public affairs.

One can appreciate the idea of world civic politics by drawing an analogy between activist efforts at the domestic and international levels. According to Melucci, Habermas, Offe, and others, the host of contemporary domestic peace, human rights, women's, and human potential movements in the developed world both lobby their respective governments and work through their societies to effect change. In this latter regard, movements identify and manipulate non-state levers of power, institutions, and modes of action to alter the dynamics of domestic collective life.[7] The French antinuclear movement, the German Green Party in its early years, and the feminist movement in the United Kingdom represent significant attempts to politicize various arenas and thereby bring about change.[8] Likewise, present-day grassroots organizations—from new populism in the United States to Christian-based communities in Latin America and alternative development organizations in India—are both targeting their governments and nurturing modes of political expression outside state control.[9] Finally, the early years of Solidarity in Poland and Charter 77 in Czechoslovakia illustrate the multifaceted character of activist politics. Recognizing the limits of influencing their respective states, Solidarity and Charter 77 created and utilized horizontal societal associations involving churches, savings associations, literary ventures, and so forth to bring about widespread change. As with the other organizations, this does not mean that they ignored the state but rather that they made a strategic decision to explore the political potential of unofficial realms of collective action.[10] In each instance groups target government officials when it seems likely to be efficacious. If this approach fails or proves too dangerous, however, they seek other means of affecting widespread conditions and practices.[11] Analytically, these other means are found in civil society.

Moved up a political notch, this form of politics helps explain the efforts of transnational activist groups. Amnesty International, Friends of the Earth, Oxfam, and Greenpeace target governments and try to change state behavior to further their aims. When this route fails or proves less efficacious, they work through transnational economic, social, and cultural networks to achieve their ends. The emphasis on world civic politics stresses that while these latter efforts may not translate easily into state action, they should not be viewed as simply matters of cultural or social interest. Rather, they involve identifying and manipulating instruments of power for shaping collective life. Unfortunately, the conventional wisdom has taken them to be politically irrelevant.

In the following I analyze the character of world civic politics by focusing on one relatively new sector of this activity, transnational environmental activist groups (TEAGs). As environmental dangers have become part of the public consciousness and a matter of scholarly concern in recent years, much attention has been directed toward the transboundary and global dimensions of environmental degradation. Ozone depletion, global warming, and species extinction, for instance, have consequences that cross state boundaries and in the extreme threaten to change the organic infrastructure of life on earth. Responding in part to increased knowledge about these problems, transnational activist groups have emerged whose members are dedicated to "saving the planet." World Wildlife Fund, Friends of the Earth, Greenpeace, Conservation International, and Earth Island Institute are voluntary associations organized across state boundaries that work toward environmental protection at the global level. TEAGs have grown tremendously since the 1970s, with the budgets of the largest organizations greater than the amount spent by most countries on environmental issues and equal to, if not double, the annual expenditure of the United Nations Environment Program (UNEP).[12] Furthermore, membership in these groups has grown throughout the 1980s and 1990s to a point where millions of people are currently members of TEAGs.[13] This article demonstrates that, while TEAGs direct much effort toward state policies, their political activity does not stop there but extends into global civil society. In the following, I describe and analyze this type of activity and, in doing so, make explicit the dynamics and significance of world civic politics.

This article is divided into five sections. The first places my argument within theoretical literature of international relations to highlight where my thesis is similar to and yet different from earlier efforts to underscore the role of nongovernmental organizations. The second is an empirical presentation of the way TEAGs specifically practice world civic politics. It describes how they foster an ecological sensibility and explicates the significance of this form of politics. The third section outlines how environmental groups pressure corporations and explores the political dimension of this strategy. The fourth section describes how TEAGs empower local communities and considers the ramifications for world politics. In each of these instances activists operate outside the province of state-to-state interaction yet engage in genuine political activity. The final section evaluates the concept of world civic politics from a theoretical perspective.

Two caveats are in order before proceeding. First, although I refer to transnational environmental activist groups in general, the focus here is on so-called northern organizations. These are groups that originated in advanced industrial societies and, although they have offices throughout both the developed and the developing worlds, maintain their central headquarters in the North. An implicit assumption is that an understanding of northern organizations will shed light upon transnational activist groups in general; this premise, however, may turn out to be false.[14] Second, I do not mean to suggest that transnational environmental organizations have a monopoly on ecological wisdom, are the harbingers of an ecologically sound future, or are beyond criticism. Like all other political actors, activists have their own problems. One must question, for example, their use and at times misuse of scientific evidence; their accountability (they are not elected officials); and the complex and often antagonistic relations among different transnational groups. I do not address these aspects of activist groups in detail here, although in a number of places I refer to particular instances when they become relevant. This is not to overlook the problems associated with transnational activist groups so much as to maintain a focus on the type of politics they employ to further their goals. In other words, one need not necessarily support the work of transnational environmental groups to understand how they operate in the international arena.

Beyond the Transnationalist Debate

Throughout the 1960s and early 1970s NGOs were the objects of tremendous scholarly attention. At the time the statecentric model of world politics was undergoing one of its many attacks and NGOs were enlisted in the assault. Many scholars argued that since nonstate actors were growing in number and power, students of world politics would be better served by paying attention to these as well as, if not instead of, nation-states. For example, a substantial number of multinational corporations (MNCs) had assets in excess of the gross national product (GNP) of certain states and had projects in numerous countries,[15] leading many scholars to argue that MNCs were curtailing state action and represented an independent variable for explaining world events.[16] Likewise, advances in communications technology opened the way for nonstate actors such as revolutionary groups, the Catholic church, and political parties to play a greater role in world politics. Innovations in overseas travel, international wire services, computer networks, and telecommunications were enabling these actors to influence the ideas, values, and political persuasions of people around the globe. Scholars argued that they were having a significant impact on questions of peace, international morality, and the salience of political issues.[17] In short, the surge in transnational activity suggested that the state might not be the most important variable for explaining world events.[18]

The debate over the relative importance of the state in world affairs had an impact in the field insofar as it convinced realists—those who most explicitly privileged the state in the 1960s and 1970s—that NGOs matter.[19] To be sure, this took some effort. Defenders of the strictly state-centric model argued, for example, that the proliferation of NGOs was a function of hegemonic stability and thus derivative of interstate behavior.[20] Others challenged the contention that transnationalism was increasing interdependence between states and hence restricting states' ability to control events, and argued instead that the amount of interdependence had actually been on the decrease.[21] Furthermore, many claimed that despite the rise in the number of nonstate actors, NGOs were not a factor in the most consequential world events at the time and that, indeed, compared with nation-states, nonstate actors were of only marginal political importance.[22] Notwithstanding these arguments, by the 1980s NGOs had made their presence felt and scholars began to take them seriously as a legitimate object of study.

The debate about NGOs, while important, suffered premature closure, because scholars ultimately saw NGO significance in terms of state power. That is, NGOs assumed prominence in subsequent studies only to the extent that they affected state policies; their influence on world affairs apart from this role was neglected.[23] One of the reasons for this is that the debate itself was framed in a way that could have had only this result. Scholars saw the controversy as a "unit of analysis" problem. They argued over which variable was the proper object of research in world politics. In order to understand world affairs, should one study, for instance, MNCs, the state, revolutionary groups, or transnational political parties? With the problem formulated in this way, transnationalists were associated with a "sovereignty at bay" model of world politics, which claimed that NGOs were eclipsing states as the key independent actors in world affairs.[24] Unfortunately, this set up the debate as an either/or proposition: either the state was the primary mover and shaker of world affairs or it was not. As a result, critics had only to demonstrate the superior causal agency of the state to dismiss or greatly deflate the transnationalist challenge—which is exactly what occurred.[25]

More recently, a resurgence of interest in NGOs has led to efforts to conceptualize them outside the unit-of-analysis problem. Most of this work is part of a broader set of concerns loosely associated with the so-called third debate, the argument over the proper paradigm for studying international relations. The origins of the third debate lie in the questioning of the statecentric model of the 1970s and 1980s, but it has since expanded to include epistemological, ontological, and axiological concerns.[26] Interest in NGOs has emerged under the rubric of the third debate insofar as scholars have advanced a number of propositions regarding how, why, and to what extent NGOs matter in world affairs based on sophisticated understandings of power, knowledge, and agency. Notable here is Rosenau's notion of sovereignty-free actors and the influence of microprocesses on macrophenomena,[27] Walker's insights concerning the critical component of social movements,[28] and Falk's understanding of the antistatist logic of activist groups.[29] My work takes these propositions as a point of departure but seeks to situate them within a broader frame of reference. In my view the analytic significance of these and similar efforts can be advanced by encompassing them within a larger investigation into the nature of world politics.

Throughout the earlier transnationalist debate, scholars never questioned the essential quality of world political activity. Having lost part of the argument, after being forced to acknowledge the centrality of the state, they failed to ask what constitutes relevant political behavior, what power is, and which dimensions of collective life are most significant for bringing about changes in human practices. Students of international relations fell back on the traditional notion that genuine political activity is the interaction of nation-states, that power consists in the means available to states, and that the state system is *the* arena for affecting human behavior throughout the world. Thus, NGOs became important, but only because they influenced state behavior. They did not affect world affairs in their own right.[30] Current research can fall into this same trap if not understood to be part of a more fundamental type of examination.[31]

   This article studies NGOs with a particular focus on the meaning of world politics. It eschews an understanding in which the multifarious activities of actors gain relevance only insofar as they affect states, and concentrates instead on identifying NGO activity that orders, directs, and manages widespread behavior throughout the world. One can get a sense of this through a study of transnational environmental activist groups. In doing so, however, one must focus on the political action per se of these organizations and trace its world significance and interpret its meaning independent of the argument about relative causal weight. That is, one must be more interested in understanding the nature of certain types of political action than in ranking different agents that engage in politics. By doing so, scholars will be able to recognize that NGOs are significant in world affairs not only because they influence states but also because they affect the behavior of larger collectivities throughout the world. They do so by manipulating governing structures of global civil society.

Disseminating an Ecological Sensibility

Few images capture the environmental age as well as the sight of Greenpeace activists positioning themselves between harpoons and whales in an effort to stop the slaughter of endangered sea mammals. Since 1972, with the formal organization of Greenpeace into a transnational environmental activist group, Greenpeace has emblazoned a host of such images onto the minds of people around the world. Greenpeace activists have climbed aboard whaling ships, parachuted from the top of smokestacks, plugged up industrial discharge pipes, and floated a hot air balloon into a nuclear test site. These direct actions are media stunts, exciting images orchestrated to convey a critical perspective toward environmental issues. Numerous other organizations, including the Sea Shepherds Conservation Society, Earth-First! and Rainforest Action Network, engage in similar efforts. The dramatic aspect attracts journalists and television crews to specific actions and makes it possible for the groups themselves to distribute their own media presentations. Greenpeace, for example, has its own media facilities; within hours it can provide photographs to newspapers and circulate scripted video news spots to television stations in eighty-eight countries.[32] The overall intent is to use international mass communications to expose antiecological practices and thereby inspire audiences to change their views and behavior vis-à-vis the environment.[33]

   Direct action is based on two strategies. The first is simply to bring what are often hidden instances of environmental abuse to the attention of a wide audience: harpooners kill whales on the high seas; researchers abuse Antarctica; significant species extinction takes place in the heart of the rain forest; and nuclear weapons are tested in the most deserted areas of the planet. Through television, radio, newspapers, and magazines transnational activist groups bring these hidden spots of the globe into people's everyday lives, thus enabling vast numbers of people to "bear witness" to environmental abuse.[34] Second, TEAGs engage in dangerous and dramatic actions that underline how serious they consider certain environmental threats to be. That activists take personal risks to draw attention to environmental issues highlights their indignation and the degree of their commitment to protecting the planet. Taken together, these two strategies aim to change the way vast numbers of people see the world—by dislodging traditional understandings of environmental degradation and substituting new interpretive frames. This was put particularly well by Robert Hunter, a founding member of Greenpeace, who participated in the group's early antiwhaling expeditions. For Hunter, the purpose of the effort was to overturn fundamental images about whaling: where the predominant view was of brave men battling vicious and numerous monsters of the deep, Greenpeace documented something different. As Hunter put it:

Soon, images would be going out into hundred of millions of minds around the world, a completely new set of basic images about whaling. Instead of small boats and giant whales, giant boats and small whales; instead of courage killing whales, courage saving whales; David had become Goliath, Goliath was now David; if the mythology of Moby Dick and Captain Ahab had dominated human consciousness about Leviathan for over a century, a whole new age was in the making.[35]

Raising awareness through media stunts is not primarily about changing governmental policies, although this may of course happen as state officials bear witness or are pressured by constituents to codify into law shifts in public opinion or widespread sentiment. But this is only one dimension of TEAG direct action efforts. The new age envisioned by Hunter is more than passing environmental legislation or adopting new environmental policies. Additionally, it involves convincing all actors—from governments to corporations, private organizations, and ordinary citizens—to make decisions and act in deference to environmental awareness. Smitten with such ideas, governments will, activists hope, take measures to protect the environment. When the ideas have more resonance outside government, they will shift the standards of good conduct and persuade people to act differently even though governments are not requiring them to do so. In short, TEAGs work to disseminate an ecological sensibility to shift the governing ideas that animate societies, whether institutionalized within government or not, and count on this to reverberate throughout various institutions and collectivities.

The challenge for students of international relations is to apprehend the effects of these efforts and their political significance. As already mentioned, scholars have traditionally focused on state policy and used this as the criterion for endowing NGOs with political significance. Such a focus, however, misses the broader changes initiated by NGOs beyond state behavior. To get at this dimension of change requires a more sociological orientation toward world affairs.[36] One such orientation is a so-called fluid approach.

The fluid approach has been used in the study of domestic social movements but can be adopted to analyze TEAGs.[37] It gauges the significance of activist groups by attending to cultural expressions that signal cognitive, affective, and evaluative shifts in societies. Observers are attuned to the quickening of actions and to changes in meaning and perceive that something new is happening in a wide variety of places. When analyzing the peace movement, for instance, a fluid approach recognizes that activists aim not only to convince governments to cease making war but also to create more peaceful societies. This entails propagating expressions of nonviolence, processes of conflict resolution, and, according to some, practices that are more cooperative than competitive. A fluid approach looks throughout society and interprets shifts in such expressions as a measure of the success of the peace movement.[38] Similarly, a fluid approach acknowledges that feminist groups aim at more than simply enacting legislation to protect women against gender discrimination. Additionally, they work to change patriarchal practices and degrading representations of women throughout society. Thus, as Joseph Gusfield notes, the successes of the feminist movement can be seen "where the housewife finds a new label for discontents, secretaries decide not to serve coffee and husbands are warier about using past habits of dominance."[39] A fluid approach, in other words, interprets activist efforts by noticing and analyzing, in the words of Herbert Blumer, a "cultural drift," "societal mood," or "public orientation" felt and expressed by people in diverse ways.[40] It focuses on changes in lifestyle, art, consumer habits, fashion, and so forth and sees these, as well as shifts in laws and policies, as consequences of activist efforts.

Applied to the international arena, a fluid approach enables one to appreciate, however imperfectly, changes initiated by transnational activists that occur independently of state policies. With regard to TEAGs, it allows one to observe how an environmental sensibility infiltrates deliberations at the individual, organizational, corporate, governmental, and interstate levels to shape world collective life.

Consider the following. In 1970 one in ten Canadians said the environment was worthy of being on the national agenda; twenty years later one in three felt not only that it should be on the agenda but that it was the most pressing issue facing Canada.[41] In 1981, 45 percent of those polled in a US survey said that protecting the environment was so important that "requirements and standards cannot be too high and continuing environmental improvements must be made regardless of cost"; in 1990, 74 percent supported the statement.[42] This general trend is supported around the world. In a recent Gallup poll majorities in twenty countries gave priority to safeguarding the environment even at the cost of slowing economic growth; additionally, 71 percent of the people in sixteen countries, including India, Mexico, South Korea, and Brazil, said they were willing to pay higher prices for products if it would help to protect the environment.[43]

These figures suggest a significant shift in awareness and concern about the environment over the past two decades. It is also worth noting that people have translated this sentiment into changes in behavior. In the 1960s the US Navy and Air Force used whales for target practice. Twenty-five years later an international effort costing $5 million was mounted to save three whales trapped in the ice in Alaska.[44] Two decades ago corporations produced products with little regard for their environmental impact. Today it is incumbent upon corporations to reduce negative environmental impact at the production, packaging, and distribution phases of industry.[45] When multilateral development banks and other aid institutions were established after the Second World War, environmental impact assessments were unheard of; today they are commonplace.[46] Finally, twenty years ago recycling as a concept barely existed. Today recycling is mandatory in many municipalities around the world, and in some areas voluntary recycling is a profit-making industry. (Between 1960 and 1990 the amount of municipal solid waste recovered by recycling in the United States more than quintupled.)[47] In each of these instances people are voluntarily modifying their behavior in part because of the messages publicized by activists. If one looked solely at state behavior to account for this change, one would miss a tremendous amount of significant world political action.

A final, if controversial, example of the dissemination of an ecological sensibility is the now greatly reduced practice of killing harp seal pups in northern Canada. Throughout the 1960s the annual Canadian seal hunt took place without attracting much public attention or concern. In the late 1960s and throughout the 1970s and 1980s the International Fund for Animals, Greenpeace, the Sea Shepherds Conservation Society, and a host of smaller preservation groups saw this—in hindsight inaccurately, according to many—as a threat to the continued existence of harp seals in Canada. They brought the practice to the attention of the world, using, among other means, direct action. As a result, people around the globe, but especially in Europe, changed their buying habits and stopped purchasing products made out of the pelts. As a consequence, the market for such merchandise all but dried up with the price per skin plummeting.[48] Then, in 1983, the European Economic Community (EEC) actually banned the importation of seal pelts.[49] It is significant that the EEC did so only after consumer demand had already dropped dramatically.[50] Governmental policy, that is, may have simply been an afterthought and ultimately unnecessary. People acted in response to the messages propagated by activist groups.[51]

When Greenpeace and other TEAGs undertake direct action or follow other strategies to promote an ecological sensibility, these are the types of changes they are seeking. At times, governments respond with policy measures and changed behavior with respect to environmental issues. The failure of governments to respond, however, does not necessarily mean that the efforts of activists have been in vain. Rather, they influence understandings of good conduct throughout societies at large. They help set the boundaries of what is considered acceptable behavior.[52]

When people change their buying habits, voluntarily recycle garbage, boycott certain products, and work to preserve species, it is not necessarily because governments are breathing down their necks. Rather, they are acting out of a belief that the environmental problems involved are severe, and they wish to contribute to alleviating them. They are being "stung," as it were, by an ecological sensibility. This sting is a type of governance. It represents a mechanism of authority that can shape widespread human behavior.

Multinational Corporate Politics

In 1991 the multinational McDonald's Corporation decided to stop producing its traditional clamshell hamburger box and switch to paper packaging in an attempt to cut back on the use of disposable foam and plastic. In 1990 Uniroyal Chemical Company, the sole manufacturer of the apple-ripening agent Alar, ceased to produce and market the chemical both in the United States and abroad. Alar, the trade name for daminozide, was used on most kinds of red apples and, according to some, found to cause cancer in laboratory animals. Finally, in 1990 Starkist and Chicken of the Sea, the two largest tuna companies, announced that they would cease purchasing tuna caught by setting nets on dolphins or by any use of drift nets; a year later Bumble Bee Tuna followed suit. Such action has contributed to protecting dolphin populations around the world.

In each of these instances environmental activist groups—both domestic and trans-national—played an important role in convincing corporations to alter their practices. To be sure, each case raises controversial issues concerning the ecological wisdom of activist pressures, but it also nevertheless demonstrates the effects of TEAG efforts. In the case of McDonald's, the corporation decided to abandon its foam and plastic containers in response to prodding by a host of environmental groups. These organizations, which included the Citizens Clearinghouse for Hazardous Waste, Earth Action Network, and Kids against Pollution, organized a "send-back" campaign in which people mailed McDonald's packaging to the national headquarters. Additionally, Earth Action Network actually broke windows and scattered supplies at a McDonald's restaurant in San Francisco to protest the company's environmental policies. The Environmental Defense Fund (EDF) played a mediating role by organizing a six-month, joint task force to study ways to reduce solid waste in McDonald's eleven thousand restaurants worldwide. The task force provided McDonald's with feasible responses to activist demands.[53] What is clear from most reports on the change is that officials at McDonalds did not believe it necessarily made ecological or economic sense to stop using clamshell packaging but that they bent to activist pressure.[54]

Uniroyal Chemical Company ceased producing Alar after groups such as Ralph Nader's Public Interest Research Group (PIRG) and the Natural Resources Defense Council (NRDC) organized a massive public outcry about the use of the product on apples in the USA and abroad. In 1989 NRDC produced a study that found that Alar created cancer risks 240 times greater than those declared safe by the US Environmental Protection Agency (EPA).[55] This was publicized on CBS's *60 Minutes* and led to critical stories in numerous newspapers and magazines. Moreover, activists pressured supermarket chains to stop selling apples grown with Alar and pressured schools to stop serving Alar-sprayed apples. The effects were dramatic. The demand for apples in general shrank significantly because of the scare, lowering prices well below the break-even level.[56] This led to a loss of $135 million for Washington State apple growers alone.[57] Effects such as these and continued pressure by activist groups convinced Uniroyal to cease production of the substance not only in the USA but overseas as well. Like McDonalds, Uniroyal changed its practices not for economic reasons nor to increase business nor because it genuinely felt Alar was harmful. Rather, it capitulated to activist pressure. In fact, there is evidence from nonindustry sources suggesting that Alar did not pose the level of threat publicized by activists.[58]

Finally, in the case of dolphin-free tuna, Earth Island Institute (EII) and other organizations launched an international campaign in 1985 to stop all drift-net and purse seine fishing by tuna fleets. For unknown reasons, tuna in the Eastern Tropical Pacific Ocean swim under schools of dolphins. For years tuna fleets have set their nets on dolphins or entangled dolphins in drift nets as a way to catch tuna. While some fleets still use these strategies, the three largest tuna companies have ceased doing so. TEAGs were at the heart of this change. Activists waged a boycott against all canned tuna, demonstrated at stockholders' meetings, and rallied on the docks of the Tuna Boat Association in San Diego. Furthermore, EII assisted in the production of the film *Where Have All the Dolphins Gone?* which was shown throughout the United States and abroad; it promoted the idea of "dolphin-safe" tuna labels to market environmentally sensitive brands; and it enlisted Heinz, the parent company of Starkist, to take an active role in stopping the slaughter of dolphins by all tuna companies. Its efforts, along with those of Greenpeace, Friends of the Earth, and others, were crucial to promoting dolphin-safe tuna fishing.[59] One result of these efforts is that dolphin kills associated with tuna fishing in 1993 numbered fewer than 5,000. This represents one-third the mortality rate of 1992, when 15,470 dolphins died in nets, and less than one-twentieth of the number in 1989, when over 100,000 dolphins died at the hands of tuna fleets.[60] These numbers represent the effects of activist efforts. Although governments did eventually adopt domestic dolphin conservation policies and negotiated partial international standards to reduce dolphin kills, the first such actions came into force only in late 1992 with the United Nations moratorium on drift nets. Moreover, the first significant actions against purse seine fishing, which more directly affects dolphins, came in June 1994 with the United States International Dolphin Conservation Act.[61] As with the Canadian seal pup hunt, government action in the case of tuna fisheries largely codified changes that were already taking place.

In each instance, activist groups did not direct their efforts at governments. They did not target politicians; nor did they organize constituent pressuring. Rather, they focused on corporations themselves. Through protest, research, exposés, orchestrating public outcry, and organizing joint consultations, activists won corporate promises to bring their practices in line with environmental concerns. The levers of power in these instances were found in the economic realm of collective life rather than in the strictly governmental realm. Activists understand that the economic realm, while not the center of traditional notions of politics, nevertheless furnishes channels for effecting widespread changes in behavior; they recognize that the economic realm is a form of governance and can be manipulated to alter collective practices.

Perhaps the best example of how activist groups, especially transnational ones, enlist the economic dimensions of governance into their enterprises is the effort to establish environmental oversight of corporations. In September 1989 a coalition of environmental, investor, and church interests, known as the Coalition for Environmentally Responsible Economies (CERES), met in New York City to introduce a ten-point environmental code of conduct for corporations. One month later CERES, along with the Green Alliance, launched a similar effort in the United Kingdom. The aim was to establish criteria for auditing the environmental performance of large domestic and multinational industries. The code called on companies to, among other things, minimize the release of pollutants, conserve nonrenewable resources through efficient use and planning, utilize environmentally safe and sustainable energy sources, and consider demonstrated environmental commitment as a factor in appointing members to the board of directors. Fourteen environmental organizations, including TEAGs such as Friends of the Earth and the International Alliance for Sustainable Agriculture, publicize the CERES Principles (formerly known as the Valdez Principles, inspired by the Exxon *Valdez* oil spill) and enlist corporations to pledge compliance. What is significant from an international perspective is that signatories include at least one Fortune 500 company and a number of multinational corporations. Sun Company, General Motors, Polaroid, and a host of other multinational corporations have pledged compliance or are at least seriously considering doing so. Because these companies operate in numerous countries, their actions have transnational effects.

The CERES Principles are valuable for a number of reasons. In the case of pension funds, the code is being used to build shareholder pressure on companies to improve their environmental performance. Investors can use it as a guide to determine which companies practice socially responsible investment. Environmentalists use the code as a measuring device to praise or criticize corporate behavior. Finally, the Principles are used to alert college graduates on the job market about corporate compliance with the code and thus attempt to make environmental issues a factor in one's choice of a career. Taken together, these measures force some degree of corporate accountability by establishing mechanisms of governance to shape corporate behavior. To be sure, they have not turned businesses into champions of environmentalism, nor are they as effectual as mechanisms available to governments. At work, however, is activist discovery and manipulation of economic means of power.[62]

Via the CERES Principles and other forms of pressure, activists thus influence corporate behavior.[63] McDonald's, Uniroyal, and others have not been changing their behavior because governments are breathing down their necks. Rather, they are voluntarily adopting different ways of producing and distributing products. This is not to say that their actions are more environmentally sound than before they responded to activists or that their attempt to minimize environmental dangers is sincerely motivated. As mentioned, environmental activist groups do not have a monopoly on ecological wisdom, nor is corporate "greening" necessarily well intentioned.[64] Nonetheless, the multinational corporate politics of transnational groups are having an effect on the way industries do business. And to the degree that these enterprises are involved in issues of widespread public concern that cross state boundaries, activist pressure must be understood as a form of world politics.

Empowering Local Communities

For decades TEAGs have worked to conserve wildlife in the developing world. Typically, this has involved people in the First World working in the Third World to restore and guard the environment. First World TEAGs—ones headquartered in the North—believed that Third World people could not appreciate the value of wildlife or were simply too strapped by economic pressures to conserve nature. Consequently, environmental organizations developed, financed, and operated programs in the field with little local participation or input.

While such efforts saved a number of species from extinction and set in motion greater concern for Third World environmental protection, on the whole they were unsuccessful at actually preserving species and their habitats from degradation and destruction.[65] A key reason for this was that they attended more to the needs of plants and especially animals than to those of the nearby human communities. Many of the earth's most diverse and biologically rich areas are found in parts of the world where the poorest peoples draw their livelihood from the land. As demographic and economic constraints grow tighter, these people exploit otherwise renewable resources in an attempt merely to survive.[66] Ecological sustainability in these regions, then, must involve improving the quality of life of the rural poor through projects that integrate the management of natural resources with grassroots economic development.

Often after having supported numerous failed projects, a number of TEAGs have come to subscribe to this understanding and undertake appropriate actions. World Wildlife Fund (WWF) or World Wide Fund for Nature, as it is known outside English-speaking countries, is an example of such an organization. WWF is a conservation group dedicated to protecting endangered wildlife and wildlands worldwide. It originated in 1961 as a small organization in Switzerland, making grants to finance conservation efforts in various countries. Over the past thirty years it has grown into a full-scale global environmental organization with offices in over twenty countries. Within the past decade, WWF has established a wildlands and human needs program, a method of conservation to be applied to all WWF projects linking human economic well-being with environmental protection. It structures a game management system in Zambia, for example, which involves local residents in antipoaching and conservation efforts, and the channeling of revenues from tourism and safaris back into the neighboring communities that surround the preserves.[67] It informs a WWF-initiated Kilum Mountain project in the Cameroon that is developing nurseries for reforestation, reintroducing indigenous crops, and disseminating information about the long-term effects of environmentally harmful practices.[68] Finally, it is operative in a project in St Lucia, where WWF has lent technical assistance to set up sanitary communal waste disposal sites, improved marketing of fish to reduce overfishing, and protected mangroves from being used for fuel by planting fast-growing fuel-wood trees.[69] WWF is not alone in these efforts. The New Forests Project, the Association for Research and Environmental Aid (AREA), the Ladakh Project, and others undertake similar actions.

In these kinds of efforts, TEAGs are not trying to galvanize public pressure aimed at changing governmental policy or directly lobbying state officials; indeed, their activity takes place far from the halls of congresses, parliaments, and executive offices. Rather, TEAGs work with ordinary people in diverse regions of the world to try to enhance local capability to carry out sustainable development projects. The guiding logic is that local people must be enlisted in protecting their own environments and that their efforts will then reverberate through wider circles of social interaction to affect broader aspects of world environmental affairs.[70]

Independent of the content of specific projects, the efforts of TEAGs almost always bring local people together.[71] They organize people into new forms of social interaction, and this makes for a more tightly woven web of associational life. To the degree that this is attentive to ecological issues, it partially fashions communities into ecologically sensitive social agents. This enables them more effectively to resist outside forces that press them to exploit their environments, and it helps them assume a more powerful role in determining affairs when interacting with outside institutions and processes. To paraphrase Michael Bratton, hands-on eco-development projects stimulate and release popular energies in support of community goals.[72] This strengthens a community's ability to determine its own affairs and influence events outside its immediate domain.

The dynamics of environmental destruction often do not originate at the local or state level. Poor people who wreck their environments are generally driven to do so by multiple external pressures. Embedded within regional, national, and ultimately global markets, living under political regimes riven by rivalries and controlled by leadership that is not popularly based, penetrated by MNCs, and often at the mercy of multilateral development banks, local people respond to the consumptive practices and development strategies of those living in distant cities or countries.[73] Once empowered, however, communities can respond to these pressures more successfully. For example, since 1985 tens of thousands of peasants, landless laborers, and tribal people have demonstrated against a series of dams in the Narmada Valley that critics believe will cause severe environmental and social damage. The Sardar Sarovar projects are intended to produce hydroelectric energy for the states of Gujarat, Madhya Pradesh, and Maharashtra and have been supported by the governments of these states, the Indian government, and until recently the World Bank. Resistance started locally, but since 1985 it has spread with the formation by local and transnational groups of an activist network that operates both inside India and abroad to thwart the project. While the final outcome has yet to be determined, local communities have already redefined the debate about the environmental efficacy of large dam projects, as well as those having to do with displacement and rehabitation. As a result, the Indian government, the World Bank, and other aid agencies now find themselves profoundly hesitant about future dam projects; indeed, in 1993 the Indian government withdrew its request for World Bank funding to support the Sardar Sarovar project.[74] Finally, local communities have served notice, through their insistence that they will drown before they let themselves be displaced, that they are better organized to resist other large-scale, external environmental and developmental designs.[75]

Local empowerment affects wider arenas of social life in a positive, less reactive fashion when communities reach out to actors in other regions, countries, and continents. Indeed, the solidification of connections between TEAGs and local communities itself elicits responses from regional, national, and international institutions and actors. This connection is initially facilitated when TEAGs that have offices in the developed world transfer money and resources to Third World communities. In 1989, for example, northern NGOs distributed $6.4 billion to developing countries, which is roughly 12 percent of all public and private development aid.[76] Much of this aid went to local NGOs and helped to empower local communities.[77]

This pattern is part of a broader shift in funding from First World governments. As local NGOs become better able to chart the economic and environmental destinies of local communities, First World donors look to them for expertise and capability. For instance, in 1975 donor governments channeled $100 million through local NGOs; in 1985 the figure had risen to $1.1 billion.[78] This represents a shift on the part of Official Development Assistance (ODA) countries. In 1975 they donated only 0.7 percent of their funding through Third World NGOs; in 1985 the figure rose to 3.6 percent.[79] This pattern is further accentuated when First World governments turn to transnational NGOs in the North for similar expertise. According to a 1989 OECD report, by the early 1980s virtually all First World countries adopted a system of co-financing projects implemented by their national NGOs. "Official contributions to NGOs' activities over the decades have been on an upward trend, amounting to $2.2 billion in 1987 and representing 5 percent of total ODA," according to the report.[80] While much of this was funneled through voluntary relief organizations such as Catholic Relief Services, overall there has been an upgrading in the status of NGOs concerned with development and environmental issues.[81]

Increased aid to local NGOs has obvious effects on local capability. It enhances the ability of communities to take a more active and effectual role in their economic and environmental destinies. The effects are not limited, however, to a more robust civil society. Many of the activities and certainly the funding directly challenge or at least intersect with state policies; thus, governments are concerned about who controls any foreign resources that come into the country. When funds go to NGOs, state activity can be frustrated. This is most clear in places like Kenya and Malaysia, where environmental NGOs are part of broader opposition groups. In these instances outside aid to local groups may be perceived as foreign intervention trying to diminish state power. At a lesser degree of challenge, outside support may simply minimize the control government exercises over its territory. Empowering local communities diminishes state authority by reinforcing local loyalties at the expense of national identity. At a minimum, this threatens government attempts at nation building. Put most broadly, TEAGs pose a challenge to state sovereignty and more generally redefine the realm of the state itself. Thus, while TEAGs may see themselves working outside the domain of the state and focusing on civil society per se, their actions in fact have a broader impact and interfere with state politics.

Nevertheless, it would be misleading to think about TEAGs as traditional interest groups. Rather, with their hands-on development/environmental efforts TEAGs attempt to work independent of governmental activity at the level of communities themselves. That their activities end up involving them in the political universe of the state is indicative of the porous boundary between local communities and the state or, more broadly, between the state and civil society. It does not mean that activist efforts in civil society gain political relevance only when they intersect state activities.[82]

The grassroots efforts of transnational environmental activists aim to engage people at the level at which they feel the most immediate effects—their own local environmental and economic conditions. At this level, TEAGs try to use activism itself, rooted in the actual experience of ordinary people, as a form of governance. It can alter the way people interact with each other and their environment, literally to change the way they live their lives. To the degree that such efforts have ramifications for wider arenas of social interaction—including states and other actors—they have world political significance.

World Civic Politics

The predominant way to think about NGOs in world affairs is as transnational interest groups. They are politically relevant insofar as they affect state policies and interstate behavior. In this article I have argued that TEAGs, a particular type of NGO, have political relevance beyond this. They work to shape the way vast numbers of people throughout the world act toward the environment using modes of governance that are part of global civil society.

Greenpeace, Sea Shepherds Conservation Society, and Earth First!, for example, work to disseminate an ecological sensibility. It is a sensibility not restricted to governments nor exclusively within their domain of control. Rather, it circulates throughout all areas of collective life. To the degree this sensibility sways people, it acts as a form of governance. It defines the boundaries of good conduct and thus animates how a host of actors—from governments to voluntary associations and ordinary citizens—think about and act in reference to the environment.

A similar dynamic is at work when TEAGs pressure multinational corporations. These business enterprises interact with states, to be sure, and state governments can restrict their activities to a significant degree. They are not monopolized by states, however, and thus their realm of operation is considerably beyond state control. Due to the reach of multinational corporations into environmental processes, encouraging them to become "green" is another instance of using the governing capacities outside formal government to shape widespread activities.

Finally, when TEAGs empower local communities, they are likewise not focused primarily on states. Rather, by working to improve people's day-to-day economic lives in ecologically sustainable ways, they bypass state apparatuses and activate governance that operates at the community level. As numerous communities procure sustainable development practices, the efforts of TEAGs take effect. Moreover, as changed practices at this level translate up through processes and mechanisms that are regional, national, and global in scope, the efforts by TEAGs influence the activities of larger collectivities, which in turn shape the character of public life.

I suggested that the best way to think about these activities is through the category of "world civic politics." When TEAGs work through transnational networks associated with cultural, social, and economic life, they are enlisting forms of governance that are civil as opposed to official or state constituted in character. Civil, in this regard, refers to the quality of interaction that takes place above the individual and below the state yet across national boundaries. The concept of world civic politics clarifies how the forms of governance in global civil society are distinct from the instrumentalities of state rule.

At the most foundational level, states govern through legal means that are supported by the threat or use of force. To be sure, all states enjoy a minimum of loyalty from their citizens and administrate through a variety of nonlegal and noncoercive means. Ultimately, however, the authority to govern per se rests on the claim to a monopoly over legitimate coercive power. By contrast, civic power has no legally sanctioned status and cannot be enforced through the legitimate use of violence. It rests on persuasion and more constitutive employment of power in which people change their practices because they have come to understand the world in a way that promotes certain actions over others or because they operate in an environment that induces them to do so. Put differently, civic power is the forging of voluntary and customary practices into mechanisms that govern public affairs. When TEAGs disseminate an ecological sensibility, pressure corporations, or empower local communities, they are exercising civic power across national boundaries. They are turning formerly nonpolitical practices into instruments of governance; they are, that is, politicizing global civil society.

The distinction between state and civic power rests on the more fundamental differentiation between the state and civil society as spheres of collective life. According to Hegel, the thinker most associated with contrasting the two, civil society is a sphere or "moment" of political order in which individuals engage in free association. Although it is an arena of particular needs, private interests, and divisiveness, it is also one in which citizens can come together to realize joint aims.[83] As it is more generally understood, civil society is the arena beyond the individual.[84] It is there that people engage in spontaneous, customary, and nonlegalistic forms of association with the intention of pursuing "great aims in common," as Tocqueville put it.[85] The state, on the other hand, is a complex network of governmental institutions—including the military, the bureaucracy, and executive offices—that together constitute a legal or constitutional order. This order is undergirded by formal, official authority and aims to administer and control a given territory.[86]

While distinct analytically, civil society is never wholly autonomous or completely separate from the activities of states. As Gramsci and others have argued, state rule often permeates civil society to consolidate power. In these instances, the state and civil society are practically indistinguishable as schools, councils, universities, churches, and even activist groups are regulated, monitored, or run by the state itself.[87] At other times, societies are less saturated by the presence of the state and a robust civil society enjoys a significant degree of independence. But even here, it is inaccurate to assume a sharp distinction. The boundaries of the state are always ill defined and essentially amorphous, overlapping with civil society itself.[88] Because the boundaries between the state and civil society are elusive, porous, and mobile, when actions take place in one realm—although they have a distinct quality of efficacy about them—they have consequences for the other.

The same is true at the global level, and the notion of world civic politics is not meant to obscure this. While global civil society is analytically a distinct sphere of activity, it is shaped by, and in turn shapes, the state system. States' actions greatly influence the content and significance of economic, social, and cultural practices throughout the world and vice versa. While not emphasized above, when TEAGs disseminate an ecological sensibility, pressure corporations, or work to empower local communities, their efforts are neither immune from nor wholly independent of state activity. In each instance, activist efforts intersect with the domain of the state even if this is not the initial intention.[89] What is absolutely essential to recognize, however, is that it is not the entanglements and overlaps with states and the state system that make efforts in global civil society "political." Transnational activism does not simply become politically relevant when it intersects with state behavior. Rather, its political character consists in the ability to use diverse mechanisms of governance to alter and shape widespread behavior. That these networks happen to imbricate the domain of states reveals more about the contours and texture of the playing field within which activists and others operate than about the character of politics itself.

At stake in this analysis, then, is the concept of world politics. Implicit is the understanding that politics in its most general sense concerns the interface of power and what Cicero called *res publico*, the public domain.[90] It is the employment of means to order, direct, and manage human behavior in matters of common concern and involvement. Generically, at least, this activity has nothing to do with government or the state. Government, on the one hand, is an institution that coordinates and shapes public life, by virtue of its authority to make decisions binding on the whole community. The state, on the other hand, is a particular modality of government that emerged in the modern period and came to be associated with political rule itself.[91] Possessing as it does military, administrative, legislative, and juridical bodies, the state has become the most able mechanism to reach into and affect the lives of vast numbers of people. Notwithstanding the extensive governing capability of government and the state, however, neither exhausts the realm of the political. Other actors govern public affairs; other actors shape, direct, and order widespread practices regarding issues of public involvement.[92] The concept of world civic politics aims to clarify conceptually the political character of governing efforts not associated with the state. It specifies the quality of governance activists employ and distinguishes it from the instrumentalities of state rule.

A final note on the conceptual boundaries of world civic politics: a focus on the civil dimension of world collective life is not meant to obscure the central importance of interstate relations in world affairs. States are the main actors in the international system and will remain so for the indefinite future. In this regard, the concept of world civic politics is not meant to replace or subsume interstate relations. Rather, it is offered as a way of augmenting scholarly understanding. It must be considered alongside state-centered analyses. For this reason, it is still worthwhile measuring and interpreting the lobbying efforts of TEAGs and refining scholarly comprehension of NGO influence on states. Nonetheless, a sensitivity to world civic politics makes clear that this cannot be done to the exclusion of the more general societal efforts employed by TEAGs and NGOs—a failure to take note of the world civic efforts of nonstate actors leaves one with only a partial picture of world affairs and thus presents an incomplete understanding of world politics itself.

Notes

The author wishes to thank the John D. and Catherine T. MacArthur Foundation and the School of International Service at the American University for generous financial support for this project. The author also wishes to thank Daniel Deudney, Richard Falk, Nicholas Onuf, Leslie Thiele, and Michael Walzer for helpful comments on earlier drafts.

1. See e.g. David Forsythe, *Human Rights and World Politics*, 2nd edn. (Lincoln: University of Nebraska Press, 1989); Kathryn Sikkink, "Human Rights Issue-Networks in Latin America," *International Organization*, 47 (Summer 1993); Robert Goldman, "International Humanitarian Law: Americas Watch's Experience in Monitoring Internal Armed Conflict," *American University Journal of International Law and Policy*, 9 (Fall 1993).

2. See e.g. Kevin Stairs and Peter Taylor, "Non-Governmental Organizations and the Legal Protection of the Oceans: A Case Study," and Barbara Bramble and Gareth Porter, "Non-Governmental Organizations and the Making of US International Environmental Policy," both in Andrew Hurrell and Benedict Kingsbury (eds.), *The International Politics of the Environment* (Oxford: Clarendon Press, 1992); Lee Kimble, "The Role of Non-Governmental Organizations in Antarctic Affairs," in Christopher Joyner and Sudhir Chopra (eds), *The Antarctica*

Legal Regime (Dordrecht, Netherlands: Martinus Nijhoff, 1988); Gareth Porter and Janet Brown, *Global Environmental Politics* (Boulder, Colo.: Westview Press, 1991); P. J. Sands, "The Role of Non-Governmental Organizations in Enforcing International Environmental Law," in W. E. Butler (ed.), *Control over Compliance with International Law* (Dordrecht, Netherlands: Martinus Nijhoff, 1991).

3. See e.g. Thomas Rochon, *Mobilizing for Peace: The Antinuclear Movements in Western Europe* (Princeton: Princeton University Press, 1988); David Cortright, *Peace Works: The Citizen's Role in Ending the Cold War* (Boulder, Colo.: Westview Press, 1993).

4. On the concept of "global civil society," see Richard Falk, *Explorations at the Edge of Time* (Philadelphia: Temple University Press, 1992); and Ronnie Lipschultz, "Restructuring World Politics: The Emergence of Global Civil Society," *Millennium*, 21 (Winter 1992).

5. There is no single, static definition of civil society. The term has a long and continually evolving, if not contestable, conceptual history. For an appreciation of the historical roots of the term and its usage in various contexts, see Jean Cohen and Andrew Arato, *Civil Society and Political Theory* (Cambridge, Mass.: MIT Press, 1992); John Keane,

"Despotism and Democracy: The Origins and Development of the Distinction between Civil Society and the State, 1750–1850," in Keane (ed.), *Civil Society and the State: New European Perspectives* (London: Verso, 1988).

6. I follow a Hegelian understanding of civil society, which includes the economy within its domain. Later formulations, most notably those offered by Gramsci and Parsons, introduce a three-part model that differentiates civil society from both the state and the economy. See Talcott Parsons, *The System of Modern Societies* (Englewood Cliffs, NJ: Prentice-Hall, 1971); Antonio Gramsci, *Prison Notebooks* (New York: International Publishers, 1971). For an extensive argument to exclude the economy from civil society, see Cohen and Arato (n. 5).

7. Alberto Melucci, "The Symbolic Challenge of Contemporary Movements," *Social Research*, 52 (Winter 1985); Jurgen Habermas, "Introduction," in Habermas (ed.), *Observations of "The Spiritual Situation of the Age,"* trans. Andrew Buchwalter (Cambridge, Mass.: MIT Press, 1985); idem, "Social Movements," *Telos*, no. 49 (Fall 1981); Claus Offe, "Challenging the Boundaries of Institutional Politics: Social Movements since the 1960s," in Charles Maier (ed.), *Changing Boundaries of the Political* (Cambridge: Cambridge University Press, 1987). See generally Russell Dalton and Manfred Kuechler (eds), *Challenging the Political Order: New Social and Political Movements in Western Democracies* (New York: Oxford University Press, 1990).

8. Alain Touraine, *Anti-Nuclear Protest* (Cambridge: Cambridge University Press, 1983); Fritjof Capra and Charlene Spretnak, *Green Politics* (London: Hutchinson, 1984); Joyce Gelb, "Feminism and Political Action," in Dalton and Kuechler (n. 7).

9. Harry Boyte, "The Pragmatic Ends of Popular Politics," in Craig Calhoun (ed.), *Habermas and the Public Sphere* (Cambridge, Mass.: MIT Press, 1992); Richard Shaull, *Heralds of a New Reformation: The Poor of South and North America* (New York: Orbis Books, 1984); Anil Agarwal, "Ecological Destruction and the Emerging Patterns of Poverty and People's Protests in Rural India," *Social Action*, 35 (January–March 1985). See generally Alan During, "Action at the Grassroots: Fighting Poverty and Environmental Decline," *Worldwatch Paper 88* (Washington, DC: Worldwatch Institute, 1989).

10. In these cases, groups could not politicize existing civil societies but actually had to create them. See Adam Michnik, *Letters from Prison and Other Essays*, trans. Maya Latynski (Berkeley: University of California Press, 1985); Václav Haval, *Open Letters: Selected Writings, 1965–1990*, ed. Paul Wilson (New York: Alfred Knopf, 1991).

11. The danger of engaging the state in places like Poland provided the impetus to create horizontal associations. This was the central idea behind the Polish "self-limiting revolution," which recognized the power of the state with its Soviet support and hence the improbability of toppling it. See Michnik (n. 10).

12. In 1992 the budgets of Greenpeace International and World Wildlife Fund were roughly $100 million and $200 million, respectively. UNEP's budget was roughly $75 million.

13. In 1994 both Greenpeace and World Wildlife Fund each had over six million members.

14. For a comprehensive study of environmental NGOs in the developing world, with important references to transnational ones, see Julie Fisher, *The Road from Rio: Sustainable Development and the Nongovernmental Movement in the Third World* (Westport, Conn.: Praeger 1993).

15. In 1967, for example, General Motors had production facilities in 24 countries and total sales of $20 billion. This total was greater than the GNP of all but 14 of the 124 members of the UN at the time. Also in 1967 Standard Oil of New Jersey had facilities in 45 countries and

total sales of $13.3 billion. See Gerald Sumida, "Transnational Movements and Economic Structures," in Cyril Black and Richard Falk (eds), *The Future of the International Legal Order* (Princeton: Princeton University Press, 1972), iv. 553.

16. See e.g. George Modelski, "The Corporation in World Society," *Year Book of World Affairs 1968* (New York: Praeger, 1968); Werner Feld, *Nongovernmental Forces and World Politics: A Study of Business, Labor and Political Groups* (New York: Praeger, 1972); Abdul A. Said and Luiz Simmons (eds), *The New Sovereigns: Multinational Corporations as World Powers* (Englewood Cliffs, NJ: Prentice-Hall, 1975).

17. Robert Angell, *Peace on the March: Transnational Participation* (New York: Van Nostrand Reinhold, 1969); Robert Keohane and Joseph Nye (eds), *Transnational Relations and World Politics* (Cambridge, Mass.: Harvard University Press, 1972), esp. essays by J. Bowyer Bell, Ivan Vallier, and Donald Warwock; Seyom Brown, *New Forces in World Politics* (Washington, DC: Brookings Institution, 1974); Richard Mansbach, Yale Ferguson, and Donald Lampert, *The Web of World Politics: Nonstate Actors in the Global System* (Englewood Cliffs, NJ: Prentice-Hall, 1976).

18. For discussions of the world political system with special emphasis on transnational activity, see Johan Galtung, *The True Worlds: A Transnational Perspective* (New York: Free Press, 1980).

19. For an overview of the debate, see Ray Maghroori and Bennett Ramberg (eds), *Globalism versus Realism: International Relations' Third Debate* (Boulder, Colo.: Westview Press, 1982); and Kalevi J. Holsti, *The Dividing Discipline: Hegemony and Diversity in International Theory* (Boston: Allen and Unwin, 1985).

20. Robert Gilpin, "The Politics of Transnational Economic Relations," in Keohane and Nye (n. 17).

21. Kenneth N. Waltz, *Theory of International Politics* (New York: Random House, 1979).

22. Michael Sullivan, "Transnationalism, Power Politics and the Realities of the Present System," in Maghroori and Ramberg (n. 19).

23. See e.g. Werner Feld and Robert Jordan, *International Organizations: A Comparative Approach* (New York: Praeger, 1983); and Harold Jacobson, *Networks of Interdependence: International Organizations and the Global Political System* (New York: Alfred Knopf, 1984).

24. The term "sovereignty at bay" comes from the title of the 1971 book by Raymond Vernon (New York: Basic Books). It is important to note that Vernon was not a proponent of the transnationalist challenge, even though the title of his book provided a catchphrase to encapsulate the host of arguments advanced by its proponents. See Raymond Vernon, "*Sovereignty at Bay*: Ten Years After," *International Organization*, 35 (Summer 1981).

25. In the words of John Ruggie, it could be said that the debate died down because scholars studied NGOs with an eye toward "institutional substitutability." If NGOs cannot substitute for the state as an institutional entity, they become politically irrelevant. Ruggie argues that such a mind-set bleaches out much of the phenomena responsible for long-term political change. See John Gerard Ruggie, "Territoriality and Beyond: Problematizing Modernity in International Relations," *International Organization*, 47 (Winter 1993), 143.

26. See K. J. Holsti, "Mirror, Mirror on the Wall, Which Are the Fairest Theories of All," *International Studies Quarterly*, 37 (September 1987); and Yosef Lapid, "The Third Debate: On the Prospects of International Theory in a Post-Positivist Era," *International Studies Quarterly*, 33 (September 1989). For one of the more provocative books to emerge from reflection on the third debate, see R. B. J. Walker, *Inside/Outside: International Relations as Political Theory* (Cambridge: Cambridge University Press, 1993).

27. James Rosenau, *Turbulence in World Politics* (Princeton: Princeton University Press, 1990).

28. R. B. J. Walker, *One World/Many Worlds* (Boulder, Colo.: Lynne Rienner, 1988).

29. Falk (n. 4).

30. The very term "nongovernmental organization" betrays a statecentric understanding of politics.

31. This is not to imply that studies of the influence of NGOs on states are unnecessary. There is still much to understand regarding the extent to which NGOs influence governments and the quality of their lobbying efforts. A focus on world civic politics, then, is not meant to supplant a statecentric notion of international politics so much as to augment it.

32. Michael Harwood, "Daredevils for the Environment," *New York Times Magazine*, 2 October 1988, 7. Also confirmed in private interviews at the time. See also Clive Davidson, "How Greenpeace Squeezed onto Satellite Link," *New Scientist*, 135 (July 1992), 20.

33. For discussions on the media-directed dimension of ecological political action, see Rik Scarce, *Eco-Warriors: Understanding the Radical Environmental Movement* (Chicago: Noble Press, 1990); David Day, *The Environmental Wars* (New York: Ballantine Books, 1989); Robert Hunter, *Warriors of the Rainbow: A Chronicle of the Greenpeace Movement* (New York: Holt, Rinehart and Winston, 1979); Walter Truett Anderson, *Reality Isn't What It Used to Be* (San Francisco: Harper and Row, 1990), chap. 7.

34. Bearing witness is a type of political action that originated with the Quakers. It requires that one who has observed a morally objectionable act (in this case an ecologically destructive one) must either take action to prevent further injustice or stand by and attest to its occurrence; one may not turn away in ignorance. For bearing witness as used by Greenpeace, see Hunter (n. 33); Michael Brown and John May, *The Greenpeace Story* (Ontario: Prentice-Hall Canada, 1989); Greenpeace, "Fifteen Years at the Front Lines," *Greenpeace Examiner*, 11 (October–December 1986).

35. Hunter (n. 33), 229.

36. Sociological perspectives on world politics have proliferated over the past few years. See e.g. Leslie Sklair, *Sociology of the Global System* (Baltimore: Johns Hopkins University Press, 1991); and David Jacobson, "The States System in the Age of Rights," Ph.D. diss. (Princeton University, 1991).

37. Joseph Gusfield, "Social Movements and Social Change: Perspectives on Linearity and Fluidity," in Louis Kriesberg (ed.), *Research in Social Movements, Conflicts and Change* (Greenwich, Conn.: JAI Press, 1981), iv. 326.

38. Paul Joseph, *Peace Politics* (Philadelphia: Temple University Press, 1993), 147–51; Johan Galtung, "The Peace Movement: An Exercise in Micro-Macro Linkages," *International Social Science Journal*, 40 (August 1989), 377–82.

39. Gusfield (n. 37), 326.

40. Blumer, "Social Movements," in Barry McLaughlin (ed.), *Studies in Social Movements: A Social Psychological Perspective* (New York: Free Press, 1969).

41. Linda Starke, *Signs of Hope: Working toward Our Common Future* (New York: Oxford University Press, 1990), 2, 105.

42. Mathew Wald, "Guarding the Environment: A World of Challenges," *New York Times*, 22 April 1990, A1.

43. George Gallup International Institute, "The Health of the Planet Survey," quoted in "Bush Out of Step, Poll Finds," *Terra Viva: The Independent Daily of the Earth Summit* (Rio de Janiero), 3 June 1992, 5. See generally Riley Dunlap, George Gallup, Jr., and Alec Gallup, "Of Global Concern: Results of the Health of the Planet Survey," *Environment*, 53 (November 1993).

44. David Day, *The Whale War* (San Francisco: Sierra Club Books, 1987), 157. For a critical view of Operation Breakout, see Tom Rose, *Freeing the Whales: How the Media Created the World's Greatest Non-Event* (New York: Birch Lane Press, 1989).

45. See Council on Economic Priorities, *Shopping for a Better World* (New York: Council on Economic Priorities, 1988); Cynthia Pollock Shea, "Doing Well by Doing Good," *World-Watch*, 2 (November–December 1989). According to a 1991 Gallup poll, 28 percent of the US public claimed to have "boycotted a company's products because of its record on the environment," and, according to Cambridge Reports, in 1990, 50 percent of respondents said that they were "avoiding the purchase of products by a company that pollutes the environment"—an increase of 18

percent since 1987. Quoted in Riley Dunlap, "Public Opinion in the 1980s: Clear Consensus, Ambiguous Commitment," *Environment*, 33 (October 1991), 36. See more generally Bruce Smart, *Beyond Compliance: A New Industry View of the Environment* (Washington, DC: World Resources Institute, 1992).

46. Jeremy Warford and Zeinab Partow, "Evolution of the World Bank's Environmental Policy," *Finance and Development*, no. 26 (December 1989).

47. US Bureau of the Census, *Statistical Abstract of the United States, 1993* (Washington, DC: Bureau of the Census, 1993), 227, table 372.

48. The average price per seal pup skin dropped from $23.09 in 1979 to $10.15 in 1983. See George Wenzel, *Animal Rights, Human Rights* (Toronto: University of Toronto Press, 1991), 124, table 6.12.

49. This led to a further drop in price. By 1985 the price per skin had dropped to $6.99. See n. 48.

50. Wenzel (n. 48), 52–3; idem, 'Baby Harp Seals Spared," *Oceans*, 21 (March–April 1988); see generally Day (n. 33), 60–4.

51. This example also demonstrates that environmental activists are not always accurate in assessing environmental threats and guaranteeing the ecological soundness of the sensibility they wish to impart. There is no evidence that harp seals were ever an endangered species. This is particularly troubling because the activities of Greenpeace, IFAW, and others produced severe social dislocation and hardship for communities as far away as Greenland, Iceland, and the Faroe Islands, as well as in the coastal communities of Newfoundland and Baffin Island. See Oran Young, *Arctic Politics: Conflict and Cooperation in the Circumpolar North* (Hanover, NH: University Press of New England, 1992), 128; J. Allen, "Anti-Sealing as an Industry," *Journal of Political Economy*, 87 (April 1979); Leslie Spence et al., "The Not So Peaceful World of Greenpeace," *Forbes*, 11 November 1991; Wenzel (n. 46).

52. On the issue of good conduct, see Gary Orren, "Beyond Self-Interest," in Robert Reich (ed.), *The Power of Public Ideas* (Cambridge, Mass.: Harvard University Press, 1988).

53. Bramble and Porter (n. 2), 238; Porter and Brown (n. 2), 61; Michael Parrish, "McDonald's to Do Away with Foam Packages," *Los Angeles Times*, 2 November 1990, A1.

54. "McDonalds Admits to Bowing to Ill-Informed Opinion on Polystyrene," *British Plastics and Rubber* (January 1991), 35; Phyllis Berman, "McDonald's Caves In," *Forbes*, 4 February 1991; Brian Quinton, "The Greening of McDonalds," *Restaurants and Institutions*, 100 (December 1990), 28; John Holusha, "Packaging and Public Image: McDonald's Fills a Big Order," *New York Times*, 2 November 1990.

55. Natural Resources Defense Council, "Intolerable Risk: Pesticides in Our Children's Food: Summary," *A Report by the Natural Resources Defense Council* (New York, 27 February 1989).

56. Timothy Egan, "Apple Growers Bruised and Bitter after Alar Scare," *New York Times*, 9 July 1991, A1.

57. Michael Fumento, *Science under Seige: Balancing Technology and the Environment* (New York: William Morrow, 1993), 20.

58. "Revenge of the Apples," *Wall Street Journal*, 17 December 1990, A8. See generally Allan Gold, "Company Ends Use of Apple Chemical," *New York Times*, 17 October 1990; Adrian de Wind, "Alar's Gone, Little Thanks to the Government," *New York Times*, 30 July 1991; Leslie Roberts, "Alar: The Numbers Game," *Science*, 24 March 1989, 1430. For criticisms of the Alar campaign, see Fumento (n. 57), 19–44; Bruce Ames, "Too Much Fuss about Pesticides," *Consumer's Research Magazine* (April 1990); and more generally idem, "Misconceptions about Pollution and Cancer," *National Review*, 42 (December 1990).

59. Dave Phillips, "Breakthrough for Dolphins: How We Did It," *Earth Island Journal*, 5 (Summer 1990); idem, "Taking Off the Gloves with Bumble Bee," *Earth Island Journal*, 6 (Winter 1991); "Three Companies to Stop Selling Tuna Netted with Dolphins," *New York Times*, 13 April 1990, A1, A14.

60. "Dolphin Dilemmas," *Environment*, 35 (November 1993), 21.

61. "US Law Bans Sale of Dolphin-UnSafe Tuna," *Earth Island Journal*, 9 (Summer 1994), 7.

62. See CERES Coalition, *The 1990 Ceres Guide to the Valdez Principles* (Boston: CERES, 1990); Valerie Ann-Zondorak, "A New Face in Corporate Environmental Responsibility: The Valdez Principles," *Boston College Environmental Affairs Law Review*, 18 (Spring 1991); Jack Doyle, "Valdez Principles: Corporate Code of Conduct," *Social Policy*, 20 (Winter 1990); Joan Bavaria, "Dispatches from the Front Lines of Corporate Social Responsibility," *Business and Society Review*, no. 81 (Spring 1992).

63. For an extended discussion of NGO corporate politics that provides additional examples, see Starke (n. 41), 89 ff.

64. See e.g. Jack Doyle, "Hold the Applause: A Case Study of Corporate Environmentalism," *Ecologist*, 22 (May–June 1992); David Beers and Catherine Capellaro, "Greenwash!", *Mother Jones*, March–April 1991. For sympathetic views, see Stephan Schmidheiny, *Changing Course: A Global Business Perspective on Development and the Environment* (Cambridge, Mass.: MIT Press, 1992); Smart (n. 45).

65. See e.g. Philip Hurst, *Rainforest Politics: Ecological Destruction in South East Asia* (Atlantic Highlands, NJ: Zed Books, 1990); H. Jeffrey Leonard (ed.), *Environment and the Poor: Development Strategies for a Common Agenda* (New Brunswick, NJ: Transaction Books, 1989).

66. The relationship between the world's poor and environmental destruction is a complicated one. See e.g. Robin Broad, "The Poor and the Environment: Friends or Foes?," *World Development*, 22 (June 1994); and Robert W. Kates and Viola Haarmann, "Where the Poor Live: Are the Assumptions Correct?," *Environment*, 34 (May 1992).

67. See World Wildlife Fund, *The African Madagascar Program* (pamphlet) (April 1994); Nyamaluma Conservation Camp Lupande Development Project, *Zambian Wildlands and Human Needs Newsletter* (Mfuwe) (March 1990); Gabrielle Walters, "Zambia's Game Plan," *Topic Magazine* (US Information Agency), no. 187 (1989); Roger Stone,

"Zambia's Innovative Approach to Conservation," *World Wildlife Fund Letter*, no. 7 (1989); *WWF Project Folder #1652*.

68. Proceedings of the workshop on Community Forest/Protected Area Management, Maumi Hotel, Yaounde, Cameroon, 12–13 October 1993, sponsored by the Cameroon Ministry of Environment and Forests; Roger Stone, "The View from Kilum Mountain," *World Wildlife Fund Letter*, no. 4 (1989); Michael Wright, "People-Centered Conservation: An Introduction," *Wildlands and Human Needs: A Program of World Wildlife Fund* (pamphlet) (Washington, DC: WWF, 1989); World Wildlife Fund, *1988–1989 Annual Report on the Matching Grant for a Program in Wildlands and Human Needs*, US AID Grant #OTR-0158-A-00-8160-00 (Washington, DC: WWF, 1989).

69. Roger Stone, "Conservation and Development in St. Lucia," *World Wildlife Fund Letter*, no. 3 (1988).

70. See Vandana Shiva, "North–South Conflicts in Global Ecology," *Third World Network Features*, 11 December 1991; John Hough and Mingma Norbu Sherpa, "Bottom Up vs. Basic Needs: Integrating Conservation and Development in the Annapurna and Michiru Mountain Conservation Areas of Nepal and Malawi," *Ambio*, 18: 8 (1989); Robin Broad, John Cavanaugh, and Walden Bellow, "Development: The Market Is Not Enough," *Foreign Policy*, no. 81 (Winter 1990); Hurst (n. 65).

71. Outside contact may also splinter traditional associations causing economic and social dislocation. See e.g. James Mittelman, *Out from Underdevelopment: Prospects for the Third World* (New York: St Martin's Press, 1988), 43–4.

72. Bratton, "The Politics of Government–NGO Relations in Africa," *World Development*, 17: 4 (1989), 574.

73. See "Whose Common Future," *Ecologist* (special issue), 22: 4 (July–August 1992); Robert McC. Adams, "Foreword: The Relativity of Time and Transformation," in B. L. Turner et al. (eds.), *The Earth as Transformed by Human Action* (New York: Columbia University Press with Clark University, 1990).

For how these pressures work in one particular area, see Susanna Hecht and Alexander Cockburn, *The Fate of the Forest: Developers, Destroyers and Defenders of the Amazon* (New York: Harper Perennial, 1990).

74. Hilary French, "Rebuilding the World Bank," in Lester Brown et al., *State of the World, 1994* (New York: W. W. Norton, 1994), 163.

75. See Bramble and Porter (n. 2); "Withdraw from Sardar Sarovar, Now: An Open Letter to Mr. Lewis T. Preston, President of the World Bank," *Ecologist*, 22 (September–October 1992); James Rush, *The Last Tree: Reclaiming the Environment in Tropical Asia* (New York: Asia Society, distributed by Boulder, Colo.: Westview Press, 1991).

76. Robert Livernash, "The Growing Influence of NGOs in the Developing World," *Environment*, 34 (June 1992), 15.

77. Such funding was evident in the preparatory meetings organized for the United Nations Conference on Environment and Development (UNCED). Organizations such as WWF spent thousands of dollars to bring Third World NGOs to Geneva, New York, and eventually to Brazil to attend the proceedings.

78. Michael Cernea, "Nongovernmental Organizations and Local Development," *Regional Development Dialogue*, 10 (Summer 1989), 117. One should note that although the overall trend is to fund local NGOs, the amount of money going to local NGOs decreased in 1987. It increased the following year, however.

79. Gernea (n. 78), 118, table 1. One should note that the reason for this shift in funding is a combination of the perceived failure of governments to promote development, the proved effectiveness of NGO responses to recent famines throughout Africa, and donors' preference for private sector development. See Anne Drabek, "Editor's Preface," *World Development*, 15, supplement (Autumn 1987).

80. Organization for Economic Cooperation and Development (OECD), *Development Cooperation in the 1990s: Efforts and Policies of the Members of the Development Assistance Committee* (Paris: OECD, 1989), 82.

81. See Fisher (n. 14).

82. For a discussion of the interface at the local level, see Philip Hirsch, "The State in the Village: The Case of Ban Mai," *Ecologist*, 23 (November–December 1993).

83. As a moment of social organization, civil society sits at an intermediate stage of collective development that finds its apex at the state. The state, however, does not supersede civil society but rather contains and preserves it in order to transform it into a higher level of social expression. The state's job, as it were, is to enable universal interest—in contrast to private interest—to prevail. In Hegelian terminology, it allows for the realization of ethical life in contrast to the abstract morality available in civil society. See *Hegel's "Philosophy of Right,"* trans. T. M. Knox (London: Oxford University Press, 1967).

84. More recent formulations of civil society, informed by new understandings of the public/private distinction, include the family as part of civil society. See Cohen and Arato (n. 5).

85. Alexis de Tocqueville, *Democracy in America*, ed. Jacob P. Mayer (Garden City, NY: Doubleday, 1969), 520.

86. David Held, "Introduction: Central Perspectives on the Modern State," in Held et al. (eds.), *States and Societies* (New York: New York University Press, 1983).

87. Gramsci (n. 6), 238 ff.

88. Timothy Mitchell, "The Limits of the State: Beyond Statist Approaches and Their Critics," *American Political Science Review*, 85 (March 1991).

89. There are, of course, many instances when activists *do* target the state, in which the interface of global civil society and the state system is critical to strategies pursued by TEAGs. For an extended discussion of this type of action, see Paul Wapner, *Environmental Activism and World Civic Politics* (Albany, NY: SUNY Press, forthcoming).

90. Cited in Sheldon Wolin, *Politics and Vision: Continuity and Innovation in Western Political Thought* (Boston: Little, Brown, 1960), 2.

91. Machiavelli was one of the first to recognize this conflation. It led to his "lowering

the sights" of politics—that is, removing such matters as salvation and morality from the domain of political life—insofar as he recognized the limited capacities of state apparatuses. See Niccolò Machiavelli, *The Prince* (Middlesex: Penguin Books, 1988); idem, *The Discourses* (New York: Cambridge University Press, 1988).

92. This point rests on the distinction between government and governance. See James Rosenau, "Governance, Order and Change in World Politics," in James Rosenau and Ernst-Otto Czempiel (ed.), *Governance without Government: Order and Change in World Politics* (Cambridge: Cambridge University Press, 1992); Oran Young, George Demko, and Kilaparti Ramakrishma, "Global Environmental Change and International Governance" (Summary and recommendations of a conference held at Dartmouth College, Hanover, NH, June 1991).

39 Networks and Mobile Arrangements: Organisational Innovation in the US Environmental Justice Movement

David Schlosberg

Over the last decade or so in the US, many grass-roots environmental groups have become increasingly alienated from the major environmental groups and the mainstream environmental lobby.[1] Criticisms have increased of a number of aspects of the major organisations, both in their everyday actions and their organisational form. There has been anger at the lacklustre and ineffective campaigns of the mainstream, disappointment at the lack of attention to the diversity of the grassroots, distrust of the professional atmosphere of organisations, frustration with control by the major funding organisations rather than memberships, and criticism of the centralised, hierarchical, professionalised organisations that are not accountable to memberships or local communities.[2]

In addition, and more specifically, the environmental justice community has been critical of the larger organisations for what they claim is their disregard of the wide variety of environmental hazards faced by people of colour, a paternalistic attitude toward low income and minority communities and grass-roots groups, and the lack of attention to diversity in the memberships, staffs, and boards of the Big Ten groups.[3]

Increasingly, grass-roots environmental movements have developed an entirely different *form* of organising. The environmental justice community, for example, has responded by organising a movement in a manner quite distinct from the Big Ten—in its model, its structure, and its tactics. Rather than constructing large Washington-based organisations, this movement has been networking and making connections, creating solidarity out of an understanding and a respect for both similarities and differences, and working from a variety of places with a wide array of tactics.

It has become popular to talk about networks in social movements generally and the environmental justice movement specifically. Indeed Diani argues (1995: xiii) that it has become the rule rather than the exception to talk about social movements as networks in recent years.[4] This trend began, one could argue, with the seminal work of Gerlach and Hines (1970) on the

From *Environmental Politics*, 6: 1 (1999), 122–48.

loose, dispersed networks of social movements in the 1960s. More recently, Bullard describes the environmental justice movement as a network of civil rights, social justice, and environmental groups.

My purpose here is twofold. First, I examine the *processes* that make up the network that is the environmental justice movement. What does it mean, and what does it look like, to be a social movement that is structured as a network? Secondly, I examine these structures as an *alternative* to the model used by the larger, major US environmental groups, which are structured more like the interest groups of conventional pluralist thinking and design. The argument here is that the environmental justice movement has recognised the limitations of past models of organising and eschews that conventional form and strategy.

I begin by exploring the value of difference in the movement, as the base of the newly developed network structures and processes lies in an acknowledgment of plurality, varied experiences, and diverse understandings of environmental problems. I continue by examining the bases of the environmental justice movement in a number of pre-existing social and political networks. I then turn to how networks link issues and establish alliances among diverse groups, and how networks form in order to deal with environmental issues of varying dimensions. I will also examine some of the reasons why this form of organising is a tactical strength, as it mirrors and maps itself onto the changing nature of the structures and practices of capital and politics. Finally, in an initial attempt to evaluate the network form, I examine some of the difficulties in, and criticisms of, networking as a social movement strategy.

The Value of Plurality

From William James's (1976 [1912]) understanding of radical empiricism to Donna Haraway's (1988) situated knowledges, a variety of theorists have insisted on acknowledging that diverse understandings are bred by varied experience. Such an acknowledgment, however, has had trouble making the crossover from theory to political action; numerous examiners of past social movements and attempts at democratic process have pointed this out.[5] But environmental justice takes difference seriously, and the recognition of diversity is really at the center of the movement.

While Capek (1993) writes of a singular Environmental Justice 'frame', she acknowledges that many environmental justice groups and networks incorporate ideas and themes outside of the frame she defines. This inability to completely frame the movement is crucial. In the various organisations and networks that make up the environmental justice movement, there is no insistence on one singular point of view, one policy that will solve all problems, or one tactic to be used in all battles. There is no one 'environmental justice,' 'minority', or 'grassroots' view of the environment. One study of social and environmental justice organisations found varied motivations for organising and a basic belief in the heterogeneous nature of the movement (ECO 1992: 35, 39). While there are obvious themes repeated throughout the movement—health, equity, subjugation, and the inattention of governmental agencies and representatives, for example—the particular experiences of these issues, and the formulation of understandings and responses, differ according to place. Rather than one particular frame, there is a coexistence of multiple beliefs as to the causes, situation of, and possible solutions for issues of environmental justice. The movement is constructed from differences such as these, and revels in that fact.

The environmental justice movement has an understanding of perspective and culture as grounded in the experiences of individuals and their communities. Knowledge is seen as situated, and hence the diversity of perspectives that emerge are seen as points of view located solidly in a particular place. The challenge of the movement is to validate this diversity in order to bring it into a network and add to its strength. As Barbara Deutsch Lynch argues:

If environmental discourses are culturally grounded, they will differ in content along class and ethnic lines. Where power in society is unequally distributed, not all environmental discourses will be heard equally. Thus, questions of environmental justice must address not only the effects of particular land uses or environmental policies on diverse groups in society, but the likelihood that alternative environmental discourses will be heard and valued. (1993: 110)

Environmental justice requires an understanding of the existence and importance of multiple perspectives and the validation of that variety. The cultural pluralism that forms the base of the movement, once recognised, opens opportunities for collaboration and the innovation of common action.

The processes that were present in the First National People of Color Environmental Leadership Summit of October 1991 serve as an example of the importance placed on plurality. Resisting a political process that many saw as built on keeping people of color divided, participants emphasized that all those coming to the table would be respected, that there would be equity in participation across race, ethnicity, gender, and region. Numerous participants noted the openness to difference, the listening to others, the mutual respect, solidarity, and trust that were both expressed and affirmed at the conference (see, for example, Grossman 1994; Lee 1992; Miller 1993). Organisers worked to make the experience, at its base, inclusive.

Participants affirmed that difference and plurality, forged with mutual respect into solidarity, add a strength to the movement. There were differences around race, gender, age, culture, and the urban/rural split, among others.[6] Dana Alston argued that the Summit brought a spirit of solidarity, and that the most important thing was the bonding that occurred across the differences (Di Chiro 1992: 104). Lee notes that the openness and inclusivity of the process showed that 'difference can be cooperative instead of competitive, that diversity can lead to higher harmony rather than deeper hostility' (Lee 1992: 52). What appeared through a respect for the many different stories, perspectives, and cultures, were some common themes. Difference was forged into unity, but a unity that kept diversity, rather than uniformity, at its base. Participants entered diverse; they left both diverse and unified.

The point here is that diversity is more than a slogan for environmental justice. There is attention paid to the many different experiences people have in their environments, the cultures that inform those experiences, and the various evaluations and reactions that emerge from them. Recognising and validating these differences is at the heart of environmental justice.

The Social Bases of Networks

The networks that make up the environmental justice movement differ from the organising of the Big Ten from the very base, and one of the key differences between the major organisations and grass-roots networks is where participants actually come from. Big Ten groups grew tremendously in the 1980s, and have become increasingly dependent on recruiting people from mailing lists—people who have no previous connections to the groups, but share basic interests. Conversely, local environmental justice and anti-toxics groups most often begin with people as real members of community social networks.

Solidarity originates in community relationships—pre-existing social networks around where people live, work, play, and worship. A number of sociologists (e.g. Fischer 1977: Wellman et al. 1988) have written about the importance of social and civic networks in creating community, and social movement theorists have picked up on the relationship between these networks and social action. As Tarrow (1994: 6) has argued, the magnitude and duration of much collective action 'depend[s] on mobilizing people through social networks and around identifiable symbols that are drawn from cultural frames of meaning'. Organisation emerges out of shared experiences and existing social networks around family, neighbourhood, school, work, religion, and racial and ethnic identity.[7]

Pre-existing relations and social networks have been crucial in the organisation of the environmental justice movement. Churches have played a major role: the United Church of Christ's Commission for Racial Justice did the first major study of the relationship between toxic wastes and race (United Church of Christ 1987) and was the major organiser of the First National People of Color Environmental Leadership Summit. The United Methodist Church's Department of Environmental Justice and Survival and the National Council of Church's Eco-Justice Working Group have also helped to bring religious networks into the development of the movement. Other pre-existing social networks, such as established social justice organisations, community organising centres, and historically black colleges, have added to the movement.

Two illustrations should suffice here. In the Southwest, the establishment of the Southwest Network for Environmental and Economic Justice (SNEEJ), came out of an original meeting and 'dialogue' that built on a decade of previous organising of groups working in issues such as police repression, immigration, food and nutrition, health care, campus issues, land and water rights, and worker/community issues of plant sitings (Moore and Head 1994, 192). One member group of SNEEJ, the Mothers of East Los Angeles (MELA), is a closely knit group of Mexican American women who organised in opposition to the siting of a prison, oil pipeline, and toxic waste incinerator in their neighbourhood (Pardo 1990). The mothers already had some contact with one another through traditional roles as the caretakers of the health and schooling of their children, and it was through these networks that they disseminated information about the numerous unfortunate plans for the neighbourhood. They also used the common experience of the church: weekly Monday marches would be organised through Sunday contacts (Schwab 1994: 56).[8]

The point here, and one that distinguishes the environmental justice movement from the major groups in the US, is that people become involved not through mailing lists, but from the variety of systems of pre-existing support.

People get to build support, friendship, camaraderie, goodwill, and fellowship with people they already know. If they have to form a coalition with others, it is not one person going cold turkey to deal with a group of unfamiliar people; it is a group of people who have already established some relationships with others whose interests might be similar, interfacing with another group. (Taylor 1992: 43)

At the base of networks are not simply shared interests, but more broadly shared experiences. Their origins demonstrate a politics of relations rather than a politics of isolated bodies of interest.

Linking Issues, Creating Networks

The environmental justice movement expands the notion of environment by defining it not just as external nature or the 'big outside', but as the places that people live, work, and play. Environment is community (Di Chiro 1995). The movement address 'environmental' issues as they relate to a broader agenda which includes employment, education, housing, health care, the workplace, and other issues of social, racial, and economic justice (Austin and Schill 1991). As Pulido has argued (1996: 192–3) environmental justice struggles are not strictly environmental. Instead, they challenge multiple lines of domination, and 'it is difficult to discern where the environmental part of the struggle begins and where it ends.' This linkage of issues is evident in surveys (ECO 1992: 35), and in much of the literature of the movement itself (e.g., Alston 1990: 13; Cole 1992: 641; Lee 1993: 50; Moore and Head 1993: 118). Richard Moore of SNEEJ argues, 'we see the interconnectedness between environmental issues and economic justice issues' (Moore quoted in Almeida 1994: 22). Lois Gibbs, of the Citizens Clearinghouse for Hazardous Waste (CCHW),[9] notes that 'environmental justice is broader than just preserving the environment. When we fight for environmental justice we fight for our homes and families and struggle to end economic, social and political domination by the strong and greedy' (CCHW 1990: 2).

This understanding of an environmentalism with diverse issues and an assertion of linkage calls for a broader movement—one that must necessarily forge a solidarity among a range of groups and movements. This type of networking across issues and groups is a key defining characteristic, and organising strategy, of the growing environmental justice movement. Examples of these issue linkages, and the concomitant networking, are numerous. Individual member organisations of SNEEJ often deal with the interrelationship of issues of race, class, and gender. Activists battling computer chip plants often have to deal not only with issues of contamination, but also with the politics of public subsidies of private corporations. Organisers working on health problems of strawberry pickers in California are inevitably brought into the contested terrain of immigration law.

While individual groups begin by working on specific issues, they often come to see not only the theoretical links between diverse problems, but usually begin to take on some of the other issues that affect them. As Peggy Newman, a past field organiser for CCHW, explains, '[i]nstead of seeing differences in our work for environmental justice and homelessness, health advocacy, worker rights, immigrant rights, community economic development, gay and lesbian rights, we must look for the common ground among the issues and be willing to assist in each others' efforts and coordinate our work' (Newman 1994: 94). Some see the linking of issues in the movement as a unifying phenomenon (Hofrichter 1993: 89).

But it is important here to note that this type of unity does not emphasise uniformity. Networks and alliances in the environmental justice movement depend as much on their differences and autonomy as they do on unity. In the formation of networks of solidarity, this is an important notion: that there is not necessarily one single unifying commonality, a single glue or mortar. Instead, a network holds itself together along the common edges of its pieces—where there is similarity or solidarity. The resulting mosaic itself—the movement—becomes the major commonality. Within a network, there remains both multiplicity and commonality.

Some networks or alliances are very conscious of this issue. Groups that share environmental concerns may still have radical differences. Yet the commonality of environmental experience serves as the mortar, even when there are differences in culture, style, ideology, or tactics. Respect for differences goes hand in hand with the building of an alliance.[10] SNEEJ, for example, is constantly working to keep Asian and African-American, Latino and Native American, urban and rural, and other differences, part of the network. When the women of South Central Los Angeles were battling a city-proposed incinerator, they were joined by white, middle-class women from two slow-growth groups across the city. Hamilton notes that '[t]hese two groups of women, together, have created something previously unknown to the City of Los Angeles—unity of purpose across neighborhood and racial lines' (Hamilton 1990: 11). Part of the crucial task of building networks is developing co-operation across numerous gaps—geographic, cultural, gender, social, ideological—and numerous organisations have come to see part of their task as the building of bridges between diverse communities and organisations (Anthony and Cole 1990: 16; Schwab 1994: 415; Williams 1993). The resulting alliances and networks span diverse issues, individuals, and groups, connecting them while continuing to recognize the numerous foundations those bridges are based on.

Rhizomes, Locality and the Breadth of Networks

Networks, in addition, have grown beyond the bounds of these examples of working together solely on the local level. Environmental problems do not limit themselves to the imposed boundaries of neighbourhood, city, state, or nation. Neither nature on its own, nor the environmental problems we construct through our interaction with it, confine themselves to a single level. Networks have developed along a number of lines that environmental problems and issues spread.

The metaphor of the rhizome is useful here. Rhizomes are a type of root system that does not send up just one sprout or stalk; rather, they spread underground and emerge in a variety of locations. Rhizomes connect in a way that is not visible—they cross borders and reappear in distant places without necessarily showing themselves in between.[11] The rhizome metaphor may be helpful in discussing situations that may be localised, but still shared by people in different places. Rhizomatic organising is based in making the connections—recognising patterns across both distance and difference. The conditions outside an oil refinery, municipal incinerator, or silicon chip manufacturer will be similar no matter where they are located, and so those communities will share environmental problems. Networks, then, may be built not only by people and organisations with differences coalescing around a particular local or regional problem, but also as people in distant areas respond to similar circumstances—toxic waste sites, types of manufacturing, particular toxins, shared health problems.

Local groups in the growing anti-toxics and environmental justice movement rarely remain isolated and unconnected. What makes environmental justice a *movement* are the linkages formed beyond the local. Most groups make links to other groups in their own locale, but, increasingly, groups make contact with outside organisations and existing networks which can provide resources, information, and solidarity. This 'translocality', as Di Chiro (1997) calls it, brings together groups and communities that would not otherwise have identified or developed a sense of commonality.

The first key large-scale network to develop came directly out of Love Canal and the Love Canal Homeowners Association (LCHA). Lois Gibbs and the LCHA were inundated with requests for information as the story of Love Canal and their fight with the local, state, and federal governments spread (Gibbs 1982). Gibbs and other volunteers began the Citizen's Clearinghouse for Hazardous Waste (CCHW) with the idea of helping other communities organise for environmental justice. By 1993, they had reported assisting over 8,000 groups (CCHW 1993: 3).

Networking at the CCHW happens in a number of ways. As a resource centre, the CCHW funnels information about key toxics, issues, industries, and companies to communities who are faced with these particular environmental problems. Communities share their experiences with the CCHW, enriching the resource base for other communities. The CCHW also distributes information about specific problems and issues in organising, such as fundraising, research, leadership, running meetings, legal issues, and the problems faced by women as they become increasingly involved in a political battle. They also send organisers to work with citizen groups on environmental and organisational issues. The organisation sponsors regional Leadership Development Conferences, where local leaders from various communities come together to share knowledge, experiences, and tactics. And CCHW holds a national gathering every year, which in addition to enabling networking, gives people the sense that their local battle is part of a larger, diverse movement.

In addition, the CCHW helps to bring individuals and communities together in a number of ways. Often, individuals or groups that call with a specific issue are put directly in touch with nearby groups that have had similar experiences. One of the unwritten rules of the CCHW is that if you get help, you are also expected to give it to others (CCHW 1989: 1). A local group that has been victorious, keeping a facility out of their community, will be encouraged to follow the story and see where a company is likely to try again. They then contact grassroots groups in these communities, warning them of the impending issue and offering assistance in organising.

The CCHW also focuses on the space between the local and the national, with an emphasis on 'larger than locals'. As local grassroots groups continually spring up, they need someone or group to turn to. The national group is there, but they cannot be continually everywhere and all-knowing. The larger than locals occupy the middle space. They are often state-wide organizations who know specific state laws and related battles, and are more accessible for help on a daily basis (S. Lynch 1993: 48–9). Larger than locals may develop and stay focused around specific issues, offering networking and assistance to groups dealing with these issues. Or they may expand either on the issues they deal with or on the tactics used.

One of the other most well-organised environmental justice organisations is the Southwest Network for Environmental and Economic Justice (SNEEJ). After its beginning in a dialogue of Latino, Asian American, African American, and Native American activists from over thirty community organisations in Oklahoma, Texas, New Mexico, Colorado, Arizona, Utah, Nevada, and California, the Network has become involved in campaigns around environmental justice in the EPA, the impact of high-tech industries on communities, justice on the US–Mexico border, sovereignty and toxic dumping on Native lands, and farmworker pesticide exposure. SNEEJ focuses on the importance of linkages, and has used networking to make a variety of connections.

Member groups of SNEEJ include those involved in struggles in both urban and rural communities, such as those fighting contamination from oil refineries in Richmond, CA, and those who live near the waste site in Kettleman City, CA, where toxic materials from the refinery are dumped. SNEEJ also has developed a network of communities that have dealt specifically with issues raised by the location of particular industries, such as the microelectronics industry. SNEEJ expanded this work in developing, with the Campaign for Responsible Technology (CRT), the Electronics Industry Good Neighbor Campaign (EIGNC). In its origins it tied together communities in Albuquerque, Austin, Phoenix, and San Jose; it has expanded to include groups in Portland and Eugene, Oregon, as well as groups across the border in Mexico.

The growing concern with networking and alliances, and the development of a rhizomatic movement, works against the NIMBY misnomer and the claim that local protests against environmental problems and undesirable land use comes from an 'enclave consciousness'. Plotkin (1990: 226, 229) argues that 'the place-bound confines of neighborhood constituted the relevant "environment" of community land-use protest ... Clearly the end result of the enclave consciousness is a policy of "beggar thy neighbor" as community groups regularly seek to export or exclude the perceived "bads" of urban life while fencing in the goods.' The only aims of these groups, he argues, are to avoid domination and be left alone (1990: 227). But the development of networks and alliances expands the understanding of community and locality. Numerous neighborhoods need protection, and the way to get that is not to be left alone, but to develop solidarity with others facing the same dangers in their neighborhoods. Activists celebrate the grass-roots links forged with other communities. As they argue, environmental justice is not about NIMBY, but rather the critical invention of new forms of coalition politics (Avila 1992).

The anti-toxics movement may have begun isolated, with communities fighting companies and local governments on their own. But after Love Canal, hundreds of citizen groups began to form, and they reached out to others. The EPA's own study on public opposition to the siting of hazardous waste facilities (US EPA 1979), notes that siting opposition before 1978 was done almost exclusively by groups on their own, while after 1978 more than half of the groups began to network in some way. Just as Love Canal became a focal point in 1978, resistance to PCB dumping in the majority African-American Warren County, North Carolina in 1982 became a focal point for further organising around environmental racism and environmental justice. Community groups are no longer isolated; far from NIMBY and enclave consciousness, connections are being made with an understanding that the concern is with 'Everyone's Backyard'.[12]

Network as Organisational Structure

The concept and practice of networks applies not only to pre-existing structures that evolve into political organisations, or the formation of groups around interrelated issues in various localities, but also to the very organisational structure of many of these groups. Previous ties in the neighbourhood, such as those that aided in the development of MELA, or previous social justice networks, which came together to form SNEEJ, become the basis of more formal organisation. But these networked organisations are quite distinct from a centralised, hierarchical, formal social movement organisation—what Zald and McCarthy (1987: 20) call an 'SMO'.

In fact, it is a critique of the SMOs, or major environmental organisations, that has driven the environmental justice movement to a more decentralised structure. The top-down, centralised managerial style and structure of the major groups has been criticised as disempowering, paternalistic, and exclusive. Organisers of the environmental justice movement have been conscious of the need to keep ownership of the movement in the hands of everyday participants, rather than in centralised organisations.[13] The key for organisers has been to create organisational models that are sufficient for networking purposes and strong enough to confront issues, but yet are both flexible and diverse enough to respond to changing circumstances at the local level.

Documents and discussions within the movement repeatedly stress the importance of decentralisation, diversification, and democratisation, as opposed to the centralised organisation with a singular leadership. When activists gathered for the regional dialogue that led to the development of SNEEJ, there were some that wanted a national organisation—but most argued for the importance of developing the network at the grassroots and regional levels (Almeida 1994: 30). The CCHW has also eschewed centralisation, arguing that 'it is empowered communities and local group autonomy that makes us strongest' (CCHW 1993: 3). Those gathering at the First National People of Color Leadership Summit also declined the temptation to develop a centralised organisation, and emphasised the importance of organising networks. Many activists noted that one of the most promising achievements of the summit was its commitment to an organisational model that stressed diversity and non-hierarchical principles, in contrast to the technocratic managerial style of the mainstream environmental groups (Di Chiro 1992: 105). Richard Moore of SNEEJ argued that the Summit was not about building an organisation, but rather 'building a movement. As a movement gets built, it starts from the bottom up. And those movements that we have seen develop from the top down are no longer there. So what we are about here is building a network, or building a net that works' (Lee 1992: 19).

Recognising, drawing on, and formalising the loose links among activists and other neighbourhood, familial, or occupational ties of solidarity, recent networks have developed a unique relationship between their center and base. As Tarrow (1994: 146) argues, 'the strategy of drawing on existing structures of solidarity may weaken the ties between center and base, but, when it succeeds, the resulting heterogeneity and interdependence produce more dynamic movements than the homogeneity and discipline that were aimed at in the old social-democratic model'. Brecher and Costello (1990: 333) note the importance of multiple organisations and levels of coordination in distinguishing between new networks and old forms of organizing. The heterogeneity and dynamism discussed by Tarrow, and multiplicity and coordination noted by Brecher and Costello, are apparent throughout the grass-roots environmental justice movement. Rather than a singular, centralised, and formal organisation, the movement has stressed a network structure—bottom-up, informal, spontaneous, and multiple. All of the qualities that supposedly destroy organisation have served, in fact, to build and sustain a movement.

Both SNEEJ and the CCHW have developed organisational and decision-making structures that take these lessons and principles seriously.[14] In SNEEJ, guidelines lay out the right of member organisations to be heard, respected, and involved in all aspects of the Network, including participation in committees and the coordinating council, in the decision-making process, and in resolutions for the annual gathering. SNEEJ guidelines insist that each individual and organisation that is part of the Network also has the right to self-control, autonomy, and self-determination (SNEEJ 1993). The ideals of the Network are based on the combination of decentralisation and solidarity.[15]

The CCHW has recently changed their organizing model to further emphasise community networking. The 'New Deal' replaced field offices with an 'Alliance of Citizen Organizers' (Brody 1994). CCHW trains local groups who volunteer to help other groups and leaders in their area. But the individual Alliance groups are responsible for organising with, and offering specific technical assistance to, groups in their region. Alliance members also participate as strategists for the CCHW, meeting in Roundtable format on specific issues such as dioxin, sludge, and economic development. This new model puts primary emphasis on direct networking between groups, further strengthening the network rather than the central CCHW office or staff.[16]

A network, then, is not simply the connection between issues and groups, but is a particular method and practice of that connection as well. Function, in this case, follows form.

Diversifying Tactics and Resources

One of the other key strengths of networking is the use of numerous, yet interlinked, strategies and tactics. Networking allows for two types of strategic diversity in the realm of tactics. First is the use of various points from which the movement addresses an issue, from the local level up through the national and international. Local groups have been involved in front line struggles at plant sites and waste dumps. Groups have coalesced regionally and statewide, bringing a number of groups into a focused attack. And the movement has addressed national issues, including government and industrial policy as well as the practices and policies of the national environmental groups.

In addition, at each of these levels the movement has used a variety of tactics and strategies, both legal and extralegal. People have circulated petitions and talked to neighbours; they have attended local government meetings and organised their own accountability sessions for local officials, candidates, agencies, and companies. There have been innumerable legal demonstrations, rallies, marches; a few picketed shareholder meetings and creative street theater actions; and a variety of organised illegal sit-ins and blockades.[17] There have also been numerous administrative complaints, citizen suits and tort actions (Cole 1994*a*, 1994*b*, 1994*c*). Finally, environmental justice groups and networks have pushed for changes in public policy, again from the local level up to the international.

All of these tactics are seen as useful to the progress and growth of the movement, and none is seen as an end in itself. Even those that focus on changing environmental policy and laws see the limitations of a focus on that singular strategy.[18] The key to the success of the networking strategy is the simultaneous use of a wide range of tactics. A movement organised as a network has an inherent organisational flexibility. Groups can use the types of tactics suited to their own local situation while coordinating these actions with others. And individual groups can themselves try a variety of tactics as their struggle continues. At the CCHW, this is understood, in part, as 'flexibility' (CCHW 1993: 36).

But it is also the respect for the importance of cultural and ideological diversity in the CCHW's network which leads to a respect for diverse tactical approaches:

Instead of trying to walk, talk and look the same we should celebrate how different cultures, ways of acting and approaches to fighting the issues have involved many more people in our struggle and brought about change ... Some communities protest in the streets and take over public meetings, while others hold prayer vigils outside public buildings and walks of concerns led by their religious leaders. It is allowing people to act in a manner in which they are comfortable, and retaining their cultural ways and values that keeps us moving forward. This diversity of people and cultures also keeps those in power from knowing what to expect and from controlling us. We should embrace our diversity as it is one of our most powerful tools. (CCHW 1993: 3)

In welcoming a variety of types of community participation in the movement, the CCHW demonstrates, once again, that inclusivity builds strength.

Networking also allows for a thorough and efficient pooling and mobilisation of resources. Local groups involved in a project, campaign, or action require a variety of resources. Groups need technical information, advice on, and analysis of specific issues. Assistance will be needed on organisational issues—structure, leadership, participation. Most will need either advice on finding funding or direct monetary support. More than likely groups will eventually have a need for legal advice and services. And there is always the issue of how to approach, use, and deal with the media. Networking makes for the possibility of the mobilisation of resources—both internally, by the sharing of the existing resources of the network, and externally, by linking with other groups or networks which can provide various resources.

The internal sharing of resources is one of the basic reasons for organising networks. The CCHW, for example, is seen as a 'support mechanism' that assists thousands of grass-roots groups around the country (Newman 1993). SNEEJ notes that part of its task is the provision of a broad base of support for local, state, and regional work. Both organisations provide education, technical assistance, training in leadership, assistance in obtaining funding from various sources, and help in attending and participating in actions and events from local to international. But resources flow not only from the centre of the network outward, for example, from the main offices of CCHW or SNEEJ, but from group to group within networks as well. One activist argues that the point of networking 'is that we can teach each other. And that is how you begin to pool resources, monetary, intellectual and strategy' (quoted in Lee 1992: 45). Groups use networks to build on local knowledge of a particular issue, and then pass that information along to other groups. Networks also help in the exchange of ideas and the pooling of resources by helping local groups get in touch with other networks or groups (experts in law, government processes, or particular areas of environmental research) who may specialise in a particular issue area. Grass-roots groups may also link up with larger, more established environmental groups, such as Greenpeace and the National Resources Defense Council (NRDC). Many activists argue that their campaigns would not have been possible without the resources of national organisations (e.g., Calpotura and Sen 1994: 255; Oliver 1994: 90–1). This networking greatly increases the resources available to any one group that might have worked in isolation.

Here it is important, and interesting, to note that even with the grass-roots critique of the major environmental organisations many local environmental justice groups network with, and use the resources of, those same organisations. There is a long history of this type of synergy and co-operation, going back to the Environmental Defense Fund's work with the United Farm Workers and California Rural Legal Assistance on the issue of DDT in the late 1960s. More recently, a number of national groups have assisted in the development of the national environmental justice networks even as they have been criticised for policies, or their presence in local communities has created problems. EDF, for example, has been thoroughly criticised for its well-known hijacking of the McDonald's styrofoam campaign (Dowie 1995: 139–40), and has been specifically accused of environmental racism in their support of pollution trading rights in the US (which gives permission, say critics, to older facilities in poor neighborhoods and communities of color to pollute over otherwise legal limits). Yet recently EDF has been of assistance to the National Oil Refinery Action Network (NORAN), which has filed an environmental racism suit against the California Air Resources Board for an emission trading scheme in Los Angeles (Cone 1997). Greenpeace has also been criticised by local groups in the past for being outsiders who hijack issues and campaigns, but the organisation has been active in key environmental justice battles in from the founding protest of the movement in Warren County, North Carolina to key victories in both Kettleman City and Los Angeles, California.[19]

The central issue in relationships such as these is *how* the groups are to work together. Again, it is the *process* that is crucial to grassroots groups, and it is not surprising that issues of process are central to grass-roots criticisms of the major organisations. Grass-roots groups in the environmental justice network have been willing to work with the major groups (especially given their resources), but the emphasis is on the *with*. The movement has welcomed tactical alliances and meaningful partnerships, but have insisted on retaining local control over issues and campaigns. The national organisations are respected parts of a network as long as they *assist* in an issue rather than attempt to *direct* local groups. I will come back to this issue in evaluating the network form.

Confronting Changes in Capital and Politics

There are many who argue that the US environmental movement must continue its liberal organisational strategy—that differences in the movement must be smoothed over in order to present a united front as an interest group pushing for plausible legislation (e.g., Norton 1991). And there is no shortage of environmental pundits attempting to push the movement in one direction or another, with one singular ideology or another. The argument here, on the other hand, is that a political strategy of networking strengthens the movement with a mobilisation of diversity. Networking gives a movement many points of attack, positions from which to argue, and tactics to use, while helping to pool resources efficiently. Networks are also a countermeasure against changes in the understanding of power, changes in political oversight, and, most importantly, changes in the nature of production and political economy.

First, many theorists have discussed the relationship among various forms of power or control and the value of a diverse, and linked response. Foucault (1978, 1979, 1980) has argued that power itself is a network that needs to be examined in its extremities. Laclau and Mouffe (1985) have also asserted that there are numerous forms of power and antagonisms in the social realm, and networks can develop in response. Haraway (1985, 1991: 170) argues that an understanding of the web-like structure of power may lead to new couplings and coalitions. Networks develop, then, not just out of pre-existing social relations and responses to environmental problems, but also out of an understanding of, and alliance around, how power links issues. This is illustrated most forcefully by the fact that most local environmental justice organisations may begin with a single issue in mind, but most often begin to relate issues and various forms of domination.

Second, and perhaps most obviously, capital itself has taken on a more rhizomatic form which poses a problem for previous interest group strategies. Capital's expanding strategy includes flexibility in production systems, a geographical division of labour, a geographical dispersal of production, and an ethic of mobility which enables companies to take advantage of capital and employment conditions they judge to be most advantageous (Harvey 1991). In response, a number of recent works on grass-roots environmentalism (e.g., Brecher and Costello 1994*b*; Gould et al. 1996; Karliner 1997) have focused on the need to revise and update the political strategy of the environmental movement in the face of the transnationalisation of political economy. On one level, individual localities and states have less control (in terms of environmental and labor laws) over such mobile capital—and the trend is increasingly to *reduce* such controls in order to attract industry (Gould 1991). On another level, neither national nor local organisations working alone can produce the pressure necessary to implement such controls. National environmental organisations simply do not have the political clout to impose restrictions on capital, and local groups working in isolation are up against the corporate promises of economic development (and political contributions). As Gould et al. (1996) describe, environmental protection is sacrificed in the face of the 'treadmill of production'. Increasing regimes of 'free trade' will continue this transition.

The necessary response to this treadmill, however, is the network. In that network organising makes it possible to respond in numerous areas simultaneously, it is a more formidable opponent to such structures and strategies. The response to transnational capital (and the translocal mobility of that capital) must, of necessity, be coordinated networks and coalitions.[20]

Finally, though obviously related, the third type of change that networks are suited for is the evolving nature of the political sphere, especially when it comes to environmental oversight. Political decisions are made on more than just the national level. At the state, county, and local level, decisions on issues of growth, environmental regulation, and corporate incentive packages are crucial to both industry and citizens. On the other hand, however, the globalisation of capital also minimises the decision-making realm of the nation state as the market seeks to take its place. If the major environmental groups continue their focus on the national government, then they miss a host of relevant political decisions. Citizen action is necessary on the regional and local level, because that is where much of the control remains lodged; it is necessary on the global level because the institutions of governance there are so limited (and undemocratic). And it is necessary to network across each of these levels, as political power flows through them simultaneously. In their respective analyses of grass-roots environmental organising, both Szasz (1994) and Gould, Schnaiberg and Weinberg (1996) stress the importance, and strength, of coalitions under current political-economic conditions. For the latter, this form of resistance is necessary to counter the 'transnational treadmill of production' (1996: 196).

Brecher and Costello (1994a, 1994b), have used the metaphor of Jonathan Swift's Lilliputians to describe the networking strategy. The little people used a web of hundreds of threads to capture Gulliver. Similarly, a variety of local actions, woven together, creates a network strong enough to tackle problems larger than those which any locality might be able to deal with on its own. The various threads that make up a powerful network come from numerous positions; the basis of network organising is to recognise, validate, and forge solidarity with these various positions. The emphasis is on both the importance of each and the strength in numbers of the numerous strands.

The argument here is that the environmental justice movement represents just such a Lilliputian, transnational, translocal, rhizomatic movement. It is a 'large' movement, but it is large because of the sheer number of local and small-scale groups that have interacted and intertwined as local concern with toxics, environmental inequity, and environmental racism has grown. Both the Movement, and its political success, have come with this linking.

The environmental justice movement is seen as a threat (Waxman 1992; USEPA 1991) because it merges both groups and issues. It brings environmental, economic, and democratic issues to the table, and refuses to break those issues down according to the lines of governmental authority—toxics issues to EPA, workplace issues to OSHA, participation issues to state legislators. Like the Lilliputians, the movement has worked together to combine forces, creating a network that shows numerous signs of success. The activities of the network have not only strengthened local groups and community resistance and attracted new grass-roots organisations, but they have been instrumental in identifying and addressing the larger problems that are shared, in numerous ways, across these diverse communities. In doing so, they have also affected environmental policy at both local and national levels. As Penny Newman argues (CCHW 1993: 21), '[w]hen the networks of women of color and poor communities of the US and the networks from around the world merge into a cooperative network the reverberations will be felt in every corporate board room and governmental stronghold worldwide'. Ambitious, maybe, but actions and responses to date point to its plausibility.

Evaluating the Strategy

Up to this point, I have tried to lay out the motivation, design, and workings of the networked organisational structure in the environmental justice movement, as well as show its possible promise and effectiveness. But it seems suitable at this point to ask a simple question of network organizing: is it a thoroughly workable form? It is possible to list the numerous victories of the US movement—the closure of waste dumps and incinerators, the prevention of others, the establishment of an Office of Environmental Justice in the EPA, President Clinton's Executive Order on Environmental Justice, and others.[21] But I want to evaluate the network strategy by examining three issues that may be the greatest weakness of the form: the problems of longevity, relationships over distance and difference, and the lack of an overall alternative vision.

First, networks by their very definition are mobile arrangements. Local groups often dissipate when their concern has run its course—after either victory or loss. Projects and campaigns begin and end, and individuals and groups burn out. Sustained resistance is rare. What happens when some of the Lilliputians drop their strings? The problem with this lack of staying power is that both governmental agencies and corporations are influenced by longevity; while they can often wait out sporadic protests, they have a much more difficult time ignoring community organisations and networks that have become established and coordinated.

But one strength of the network form is that the contact remains, even if informal. Groups which pull back, or even dissipate, will often be ready for new mobilisations. In one example, a local group in the Southwest US was very active in the Campaign for Responsible Technology (CRT) until it dropped out of the network in order to pursue more specific issues of the indigenous peoples of the region. One organiser of the CRT noted the sense of loss that came with this departure, and the effect of the loss of that one link in the larger network. But as the CRT developed a project on the water use of the high tech industry (SWOP/CRT 1997), the group which had dropped out offered input specific to the effects on indigenous populations.

In addition (and related) to the issue of longevity, networks must constantly keep up relations across both distance and difference. Difficulties of this sort come in a number of forms. When very different communities, or groups within communities, come together some may see themselves becoming part of a larger movement, while others remain most firmly associated with their most pressing particular issues. Within networks, solidarity is understood differently by different groups. Hence, a group working on indigenous issues might not see themselves completely aligned with a network which addresses the high tech industry, even if their respective foci overlap in numerous places.

Within a varied network like SNEEJ, other difficulties arise. Activists have complained that the resources of the network go to those groups or communities which 'cry loudest', which often happen to be the groups or communities which already have some resources at their disposal. And, of course, networks or coalitions that form within specific geographical areas, like a large city, face race and gender issues. A white member of an active group in a Western city told me that all the media, government, and foundation attention is paid to groups primarily of people of colour, which were, in his mind, neither as broad nor as effective as his own group. Elsewhere, some minority activists have pressured white activists and academics to leave the articulation of issues of environmental justice solely to people of colour (Epstein 1995: 7). Obviously, these attitudes—and it is difficult to determine whether they are minor or widespread—hamper the development and longevity of environmental justice networks.

Yet another tension in the development of network relations over distance and difference is the relation between the grassroots and the major and/or mainstream environmental organisations. As noted previously, while grassroots groups are often very critical of the major groups, they have often turned to these groups—and their resources—for alliances on specific campaigns and actions. Differences certainly remain between local groups, major organisations, and all that fall in between. The major groups often continue to ignore localised issues, and refrain from participating in them even when asked by locals. But a number of the major groups have learned that, while grass-roots groups and networks are suspicious of the mainstream, they *do* appreciate their assistance, as long as it is offered within a respectful process. Hence, the mainstream groups that work most successfully with the grassroots are those that work with the local groups, listen to their concerns, and do not make major moves without consultation with, and direction from, those locals. Generally, and as discussed by Gould et al. (1996: 195–6), the most successful efforts are made when alliances are formed between grassroots and larger regional or national organisations. Conversely, local mobilisations are often short and unsuccessful if the national groups 'countermobilize' against them.

Finally, it could be argued that any political struggle or movement that took on the rhizomatic form and decentralised functions of a network would simply become an amalgamation of numerous decentered struggles, incapable of dealing with the 'big pictures' of power, political economy, or the globalisation of many environmental issues. On the contrary, the assertion here has been that multiple, localised oppositions are a tactical strength. The key is the application of diverse critiques, approaches, and styles in various places of action.[22] Environmental degradation is not simply the singular product of a lone 'mega-machine' which can easily be unplugged in one place or with one singular changed practice. The targets of the environmental movement are varied; and so the movement itself is necessarily decentred and multiple. The issues and abuses that form the motivations for political action need to be targeted at the local level, in the multiplicity of places where they emerge. The multiplicity of experiences, issues, and resistances that have developed in the environmental justice movement call for and exemplify diverse approaches to change in varied venues. The basis of the movement is this composite character, and the plurality of levels of attack.

The criticism of all of this, of course, is that the focus is on resistance, and not on large-scale visions of global alternatives. On the contrary, the argument here is that solidarity across locally-based groups creates movements that reach and connect beyond the local and particular. Obviously, there are similarities among different communities and experiences. Issues of the power of capital, the market imprisonment of policy, the exclusion of effected populations from policy-making, the desire for participation and democratisation, and a focus on political process as a way to address both a lack of equity and recognition come up time and time again in the movement. Environmental justice networks, based even as they are on resistance, have shown themselves quite capable of flexing fairly large-scale—even global—muscles. Recent cross-border movements around NAFTA and GATT, World Bank policy in the Amazon, ozone policy, and the ownership of indigenous knowledge serve as examples.

In addition, it is important to recognise the politics and process of the environmental justice movement as a form of prefigurative politics (Epstein 1988). The form of the movement itself, and its development of this form out of critiques of past social movement organising, is a living articulation of an alternative form. Networks are not simply a means to an end—and a defensive end at that. They are an example of an attempt at an alternative political structure. In this sense, the movement counters many social movement theorists and left activists who argue that only a unified movement organised around a singular agenda can accomplish significant social change.

Conclusion

Networking and alliance-building have become a major tactic in environmental organising in the US, especially among grass-roots activists and groups. This move has been in response to the limitations of past models of organising as well as the changing nature of the structures and practices of capital and politics.

Networks begin at the level of the community, with bases in everyday relationships at home, church, work and play. The organisation of networks takes these local realities seriously, and continues the recognition and validation of diverse experiences, even as it links the multiplicity of peoples and issues into alliances. While they may restrict themselves to a local alliance around a local issues, these alliances may also take on a larger, and often more rhizomatic form. Networks expand the notion of environmental locality, as they expose the similarities shared by communities in disparate places.

Networking also goes beyond organisational form; it becomes the mode of organisational function. Decentralisation, diversification, and democratisation drive networks, as opposed to the centralised and hierarchical practices of past movements and present mainstream organising. Finally, these networks display a strength and resilience one might not expect from such a decentralised organisation. The plurality of a movement, its diverse tactics, and its numerous resources are understood as strategic advantages in organising.

What the development of networking shows, especially as it has been used in the environmental justice movement, is a new form of movement organising that is based on the strength of diversity. Dismissed is the conventional organising model, which sees difference as a hindrance. Instead, these networks and alliances have recognised the reality and importance of diverse experiences, validated multiplicity, and created a solidarity that has become a dynamic and effective environmental movement in the US.

Notes

1. Previous versions of this research have been presented at the Western Political Science Association conference in Portland, OR, March 1995; an on-line conference on Environmental Cultural Studies sponsored by the American Studies Department at Washington State University, June 1997; and *Environmental Justice: Global Ethics for the 21st Century*, University of Melbourne, Oct. 1997. The author is grateful to John Dryzek, David Carruthers, Irene Diamond, Dan Goldrich, Noel Sturgeon, Nathan Teske, and Doug Torgerson, in addition to editor Chris Rootes and two *Environmental Politics* referees, for comments on various incarnations of these ideas. An expanded version of this essay appears as a chapter in *Environmental Justice and the New Pluralism: The Challenge of Difference for Environmentalism* (Oxford University Press, 1999).

2. See Dowie (1991, 1995) and Gottlieb (1990, 1993) for discussions of these complaints. From within the movement, see Bullard (1994), Montague (1995), Cockburn and St. Clair (1994). For a fascinating account of the limits funding organisations put on the movement, see Rozek (1994).

3. The Big Ten consists of Natural Resources Defense Council, Environmental Policy Institute, National Wildlife Federation, Environmental Defense Fund, Izaak Walton League, Sierra Club, National Audobon Society, National Parks and Conservation Association, Wilderness Society, and Friends of the Earth. For criticisms from an environmental justice perspective, see various essays in the collections edited by Bryant (1995), Bullard (1993), and Hofrichter (1993). Numerous environmental justice organisations and activists signed two key letters to the mainstream leaders listing these complaints (Shabecoff 1990).

4. Diani's work, especially his definition of social movements as networks (1992), has certainly aided this trend in the sociological literature.

5. See Breines (1989) and Miller (1987) on the new left, and Freeman (1975) and Sirianni (1993) on the feminist movement.

6. Ruffins's (1992) account of the summit includes a discussion of the effect of bringing together Native American and Hawaiian activists with more urban-based African-American activists. After years of bitter feeling about the white environmental community's focus on wilderness and animals rather than the urban environment, indigenous activists helped him to experience, for the first time, 'the moral imperative of protecting animals and trees and land' (1992: 11).

7. Examples abound. Much has been written of the importance of extended families and community networks in the activism of working-class and African-American women (e.g., Haywood 1990; Krauss 1994; Naples 1992). The emergence of individuals in social networks also played a key role in determining participation in the civil rights movement (McAdam 1988). Churches have also been a source of activism around civil rights issues in African-American and Latino communities.

8. One of my favourite examples of the use of pre-existing social networks in environmental justice organising is the transition of the Newtown Florist Club, in Gainesville, Georgia, from a group that began by collecting money to buy flowers for ill residents to one organizing to learn about and fight against toxics released in the community (Kerr and Lee 1993: 13).

9. CCHW has recently revised its name to 'CHEJ: Center for Health, Environment, and Justice'; I will continue to refer to them as CCHW throughout this study.

10. One of the most impressive examples of such an alliance was built between Latinos and Hasidim in the Williamsburg section of Brooklyn, New York (Greider, 1993). El Puente and United Jewish Organisations worked together against a storage facility of low-level radioactive waste and a massive

garbage incinerator the city planned for the neighbourhood.

11. Deleuze and Guattari (1987) spawned the use of the rhizome metaphor. Their first three characteristics of a rhizome are the principles of connection, heterogeneity, and multiplicity (1987: 7–8). For other discussions of the metaphor in environmental politics, see LaChapelle (1994), and Kuehls (1995).

12. Appropriately, this is the name of the newsletter of the CCHW.

13. See, for example, the discussion by SNEEJ co-ordinator Richard Moore in Almeida (1994).

14. The environmental justice movement does not hold a monopoly on this type of organizing in US environmentalism. Bron Taylor (1995) discusses this type of 'solidarity activism' in both Earth First! and the Rainforest Action Network. For a thorough picture of networked solidarity in Earth First!, see Ingalsbee (1995).

15. This is not to assert that relations in the network actually work this way all of the time. The point here is the attention to these principles in the establishment of a grassroots network. I will return to a discussion of some of the limitations of the network form.

16. The model also, not coincidentally, conserves scarce resources.

17. For specific examples, see various issues of some of the newsletters of the movement, such as *Everyone's Backyard; Race, Poverty and the Environment; Crossroads; New Solutions*; and *Voces Unidas*.

18. Mililani Trask, an attorney active in environmental justice and sovereignty issues in Hawaii, argues that the legal realm is a valid one, but warns against a singular faith in the image of legal justice: '[D]o not put your eggs in the basket of the blind white lady. We must try other approaches' (Lee 1992: 38).

19. Greenpeace has recently imploded in the US, closing field offices, firing canvassers, and shutting down most of its active projects, including environmental justice.

20. The CCHW specifically suggests networking as a method of thwarting industry tactics. Waste companies looking for a site will choose a half-dozen or so communities that would be potentially suitable; they then sit back and watch how the communities react, moving into the one that is least resistant. In these cases, the CCHW suggests a meeting of groups from each target site to form a 'non-aggression pact' and unite around the principle of 'not in anyone's backyard' (Collette 1993: 5).

21. See the list of general successes compiled by Freudenberg and Steinsapir (1992).

22. This mirrors, for example, Foucault (1978: 96).

References

Almeida, Paul (1994), 'The Network for Environmental and Economic Justice in the Southwest: Interview with Richard Moore', *Capitalism, Nature, Socialism*, 5(1): 21–54.

Alston, Dana (1990), *Taking Back Our Lives: A Report to the Panos Institute on Environment, Community Development and Race in the United States* (Washington, DC: The Panos Institute).

Anthony, Carl and Luke Cole (1990), 'A Statement of Purpose', *Race, Poverty, and the Environment*, 1(1): 1–2.

Austin, Regina and Michael Schill (1991), 'Black, Brown, Red, and Poisoned: Minority Grassroots Environmentalism and the Quest for Eco-Justice', *Kansas Journal of Law and Public Policy*, 1: 69–82.

Avila, Magdelena (1992), 'David vs. Goliath', *Crossroads/Forward Motion*, Vol. 11, No. 2, pp. 13–15.

Brecher, Jeremy and Tim Costello (eds) (1990), *Building Bridges: The Emerging Grassroots Coalition of Labor and Community*. New York: Monthly Review Press.

—— (1994a), *Global Village or Global Pillage: Economic Reconstruction From the Bottom Up* (Boston, MA: South End Press).

_____ (1994b), 'The Lilliput Strategy: Taking on the Multinationals', *The Nation*, 259(21): 757–60.

Breines, Wini (1989), *Community and Organization in the New Left, 1962–1968: The Great Refusal*, 2nd edn (New Brunswick, NJ: Rutgers University Press).

Brody, Charlotte (1994), 'The New Deal: CCHW's New Organizing Model Takes Form', *Everyone's Backyard*, 13(4): 11–13.

Bryant, Bunyan (1995), 'Issues and Potential Policies and Solutions for Environmental Justice: An Overview', in Bunyan Bryant (ed.), *Environmental Justice: Issues, Policies, and Solutions* (Covelo, CA: Island Press).

Bullard, Robert D. (ed.) (1993), *Confronting Environmental Racism: Voices from the Grassroots* (Boston, MA: South End Press).

_____ (ed.) (1994), *Unequal Protection: Environmental Justice and Communities of Color* (San Francisco, CA: Sierra Club Books).

Calpotura, Francis and Rinku Sen (1994), 'PUEBLO Fights Lead Poisoning', in Robert D. Bullard (ed.), *Unequal Protection: Environmental Justice and Communities of Color* (San Francisco, CA: Sierra Club Books).

Capek, Sheila (1993), 'The "Environmental Justice" Frame: A Conceptual Discussion and an Application', *Social Problems*, 40(1): 5–24.

Citizens Clearinghouse for Hazardous Waste (CCHW) (1989), *Everybody's Backyard*, 7(2): 1.

_____ (1990), *Everybody's Backyard*, 8(1): 2.

_____ (1993), *Ten Years of Triumph* (Falls Church, VA: Citizens Clearinghouse for Hazardous Waste).

Cockburn, Alexander and Jeffrey St. Clair (1994), 'After Armageddon: Death and Life for America's Greens', *The Nation*, 259(21): 760–5.

Cole, Luke (1992), 'Empowerment as the Key to Environmental Protection: The Need for Environmental Poverty Law', *Ecology Law Quarterly*, 19: 619–83.

_____ (1994a), 'Environmental Justice Litigation: Another Stone in David's Sling', *Fordham Urban Law Journal*, 21: 523.

_____ (1994b), 'The Struggle of Kettleman City for Environmental Justice: Lessons for the Movement', *Maryland Journal of Contemporary Legal Issues*, 5: 67.

_____ (1994c), 'Civil Rights, Environmental Justice and the EPA: The Brief History of Administrative Complaints Under Title VI', *Journal of Environmental Law and Litigation*, 9: 309–98.

Collette, Will (1993), *How to Deal with a Proposed Facility* (Falls Church, VA: Citizens Clearinghouse for Hazardous Waste).

Cone, Marla (1997), 'Civil Rights Suit Attacks Trade in Pollution Credits', *Los Angeles Times* (23 July 1997): A1.

Deleuze, Gilles and Felix Guattari (1987), *A Thousand Plateaus: Capitalism and Schizophrenia* (Minneapolis, MN: University of Minnesota Press).

Diani, Mario (1992), 'The Concept of Social Movement', *Sociological Review*, 40: 1–25.

_____ Diani, Mario (1995), *Green Networks: A Structural Analysis of the Italian Environmental Movement* (Edinburgh: Edinburgh University Press).

Di Chiro, Giovanna (1992), 'Defining Environmental Justice: Women's Voices and Grassroots Politics', *Socialist Review*, 22(4): 93–130.

_____ Di Chiro, Giovanna (1995), 'Nature as Community: The Convergence of Environment and Social Justice', in William Cronon (ed.), *Uncommon Ground: Rethinking the Human Place in Nature* (New York: Norton).

_____ Di Chiro, Giovanna (1997), 'Local Actions, Global Expertise: Remaking Environmental Expertise', presented in the on-line conference on 'Cultures and Environments: On Cultural Environmental Studies,' June 1997; sponsored by the Washington State University American Studies Department.

Dowie, Mark (1991), 'American Environmentalism: A Movement Courting Irrelevance', *World Policy Journal*, 9: 67–92.

_____ Dowie, Mark (1995), *Losing Ground: American Environmentalism at the Close of the Twentieth Century* (Cambridge: MIT Press).

Environmental Careers Organization (ECO) (1992), *Beyond the Green: Redefining and Diversifying the Environmental Movement*

570 DAVID SCHLOSBERG

(Boston, MA: Environmental Careers Organization).

Epstein, Barbara (1988), 'The Politics of Prefigurative Community: The Non-Violent Direct Action Movement', in Mike Davis and Michael Sprinker (eds), *Reshaping the U.S. Left: Popular Struggles in the 1980s* (London: Verso).

—— (1995), 'Grassroots Environmentalism and Strategies for Social Change', *New Political Science*, 32: 1–24.

Fischer, Claude S. (1977), *Networks and Places: Social Relations in the Urban Setting* (New York: Free Press).

Foucault, Michel (1978), *The History of Sexuality. Vol. 1, An Introduction* (New York: Random House).

—— (1979), *Discipline and Punish: The Birth of the Prison* (New York: Random House).

—— (1980), *Power/Knowledge* (New York: Pantheon Books).

Freeman, Jo (1975), *The Politics of Women's Liberation* (New York: McKay).

Freudenberg, Nicholas and Carol Stensapir (1992), 'Not in Our Backyards: The Grassroots Environmental Justice Movement', in Riley E. Dunlap and Angela G. Mertig (eds), *American Environmentalism* (Philadelphia, PA: Taylor & Francis).

Gerlach, Luther P., and Virginia H. Hine (1970), *People, Power, and Change: Movements of Social Transformation* (Indianapolis, IN: Bobbs-Merrill).

Gibbs, Lois (1982), *Love Canal: My Story*, Albany, NY: State University of New York Press.

Gottlieb, Robert (1990), 'An Odd Assortment of Allies: American Environmentalism in the 1990s', *Gannett Center Journal* 4, No. 3, pp. 37–47.

—— (1993), *Forcing the Spring: The Transformation of the American Environmental Movement*, Washington, DC: Island Press.

Gould, Kenneth (1991), 'The Sweet Smell of Money: Economic Dependency and Local Environmental Political Mobilization', *Society and Natural Resources*, 4: 133–50.

——, Allan Schnaiberg, and Adam Weinberg (1996), *Local Environmental Struggles: Citizen Activism in the Treadmill of Production*, Cambridge: Cambridge University Press.

Greider, Katherine (1993) 'Against All Odds', *City Limits*, 18(7): 34–8.

Grossman, Karl (1994), 'The People of Color Environmental Summit', in D. Bullard (ed.), *Unequal Protection* (San Francisco, CA: Sierra Club Books).

Hamilton, Cynthia (1990), 'Women, Home and Community: The Struggle in an Urban Environment', *Race, Poverty, and the Environment*, 1(1): 3.

Haraway, Donna (1991 [1985]), 'A Cyborg Manifesto: Science, Technology, and Socialist-Feminism in the Late Twentieth Century', in *Simians, Cyborgs, and Women: The Reinvention of Nature* (New York: Routledge).

—— (1988), 'Situated Knowledges: The Science Question in Feminism as a Site of Discourse on the Privilege of Partial Perspective', *Feminist Studies*, 14(3): 575–99.

Harvey, David (1991), 'Flexibility: Threat or Opportunity?', *Socialist Review*, 21(1): 65–77.

Haywood, Terry (1990), 'Working Class Feminism: Creating a Politics of Community, Connection, and Concern', Ph.D. dissertation, Graduate School and University Center of the City University of New York.

Hofrichter, Richard (ed.) (1993), *Toxic Struggles: The Theory and Practice of Environmental Justice* (Philadelphia, PA: New Society).

Ingalsbee, Timothy (1995), 'Earth First!: Consciousness and Action in the Unfolding of a New-Social-Movement', Doctoral dissertation, Department of Sociology, University of Oregon.

James, William (1976 [1912]), *Essays in Radical Empiricism* (Cambridge, MA: Harvard University Press).

Karliner, Josh (1997), *The Corporate Planet: Ecology and Politics in the Age of Globalization* (San Francisco, CA: Sierra Club Books).

Kerr, Mary Lee, and Charles Lee (1993), 'From Conquistadores to Coalitions', *Southern Exposure*, 21(4): 8–19.

Krauss, Celene (1994), 'Women of Color on the Front Line', in D. Bullard (ed.), *Unequal Protection* (San Francisco, CA: Sierra Club Books).

Kuehls, Thom (1995), *The Space of Eco-Politics* (Minneapolis, MN: University of Minnesota Press).

LaChapelle, Dolores (1994), 'The Rhizome Connection', in David Clarke Burks (ed.), *Place of the Wild: A Wildlands Anthology* (Covelo, CA: Island Press).

Laclau, Ernesto, and Chantal Mouffe (1985), *Hegemony and Socialist Strategy: Toward a Radical Democratic Politics* (London: Verso).

Lee, Charles (1993), 'Beyond Toxic Wastes and Race', in D. Bullard (ed.), *Confronting Environmental Racism* (Boston, MA: South End Press).

—— (ed.) (1992), *Proceedings: The First National People of Color Environmental Leadership Summit* (New York: United Church of Christ Commission for Racial Justice).

Lynch, Barbara Deutsch (1993), 'The Garden and the Sea: U.S. Latino Environmental Discourses and Mainstream Environmentalism', *Social Problems*, 40(1): 108–24.

Lynch, Sue Greer (1993), 'Larger than Locals: The Critical Link', in Citizens Clearinghouse for Hazardous Waste, *Ten Years of Triumph* (Falls Church, VA: Citizens Clearinghouse for Hazardous Waste).

McAdam, Doug (1988), *Freedom Summer* (Oxford: Oxford University Press).

Miller, James (1987) *Democracy is in the Streets: From Port Huron to the Siege of Chicago* (New York: Simon & Schuster).

Miller, Vernice D. (1993), 'Building on Our Past, Planning for Our Future: Communities of Color and the Quest for Environmental Justice', in Hofrichter (ed.), *Toxic Struggles* (Philadelphia, PA: New Society).

Montague, Peter (1995), 'Big Picture Organizing, Part 5: A Movement in Disarray', *Rachel's Environment and Health Weekly*, No. 425.

Moore, Richard and Louis Head (1993), 'Acknowledging the Past, Confronting the Future: Environmental Justice in the 1990s', in Hofrichter (ed.) [1993].

—— (1994), 'Building a Net that Works: SWOP', in D. Bullard (ed.), *Unequal Protection* (San Francisco, CA: Sierra Club Books).

Naples, Nancy (1992), 'Activist Mothering: Cross-Generational Continuity in the Community Work of Women from Low-Income Urban Neighborhoods', *Gender and Society*, 6(3): 441–63.

Newman, Peggy (1993), 'The Grassroots Movement for Environmental Justice: Fighting for Our Lives', *New Solutions*, 3(4): 87–95.

—— (1994), 'Beyond the Neighborhood—Women Working for Multi-Ethnic, Multi-Issue Coalitionss', *The Workbook*, 19(2): 93–5.

Norton, Bryan G. (1991), *Toward Unity among Environmentalists* (Oxford: Oxford University Press).

Oliver, Patsy Ruth (1994), 'Living on a Superfund Site in Texarkana', in D. Bullard (ed.), *Unequal Protection* (San Francisco, CA: Sierra Club Books).

Pardo, Mary (1990), 'Mexican American Women Grassroots Community Activists: "Mothers of East Los Angeles" ', *Frontiers*, 11(1): 1–7.

Plotkin, Sidney (1990), 'Enclave Consciousness and Neighborhood Activism', in Joseph M. Kling and Prudence S. Posner (eds), *Dilemmas of Activism: Class, Community, and the Politics of Local Mobilization* (Philadelphia, PA: Temple University Press).

Pulido, Laura (1996), *Environmentalism and Social Justice: Two Chicano Struggles in the Southwest* (Tucson, AR: University of Arizona Press).

Rozek, Victor (1994), 'A Gathering of Warlords', *Wild Forest Review* (March): 22–5.

Ruffins, Paul (1992), 'Defining a Movement and a Community', *Crossroads/Forward Motion*, 11(2).

Schwab, Jim (1994), *Deeper Shades of Green: The Rise of Blue-Collar and Minority Environmentalism in America* (San Francisco, CA: Sierra Club Books).

Shabecoff, Philip (1990), 'Environmental Groups Told They Are Racists in Hiring', *New York Times* (1 Feb. 1990).

Sirianni, Carmen (1993), 'Learning Pluralism: Democracy and Diversity in Feminist Organizations', in John W. Chapman and Ian Shapiro (eds), *Democratic Community: NOMOS XXXV* (New York: New York University Press).

Southwest Network for Environmental and Economic Justice (SNEEJ) (1993), *Southwest Network for Environmental and Economic Justice* (Albuquerque, NM: SNEEJ).

Southwest Organizing Project (SWOP) and the Campaign for Responsible Technology (CRT) (1997), *Sacred Waters* (Albuquerque, NM: Southwest Organizing Project).

Szasz, Andrew (1994), *Ecopopulism: Toxic Waste and the Movement for Environmental Justice* (Minneapolis, MN: University of Minnesota Press).

Tarrow, Sidney (1994), *Power in Movement: Social Movements, Collective Action and Politics* (Cambridge: Cambridge University Press).

Taylor, Bron (ed.) (1995), *Ecological Resistance Movements: The Global Emergence of Radical and Popular Environmentalism* (Albany, NY: State University of New York Press).

Taylor, Dorceta (1992), 'Can the Environmental Movement Attract and Maintain the Support of Minorities?', in Bunyan Bryant and Paul Mohai (eds), *Race and the Incidence of Environmental Hazards: A Time for Discourse* (Boulder, CO: Westview Press).

United Church of Christ Commission for Racial Justice (1987), *Toxic Wastes and Race in the United States: A National Study of the Racial and Socioeconomic Characteristics of Communities with Hazardous Waste Sites* (New York: United Church of Christ).

United States Environmental Protection Agency (US EPA) (1979), *Siting of Hazardous Waste Management Facilities and Public Opposition* (SW-809) (Washington, DC: Government Printing Office).

—— (1991), 'Memorandum on Draft Environmental Equity Communication Plan'.

Waxman, Congressman Henry A. (1992), 'Environmental Equity Report is Public Relations Ploy: Internal Memoranda Reveal Report to be Misleading', Press release, 24 Feb. 1992.

Wellman, Barry, Carrington, Peter J. and Alan Hall (1988), 'Networks as Personal Communities', in Barry Wellman and S.D. Berkowitz (eds), *Social Structures: A Network Approach* (Cambridge: Cambridge University Press).

Williams, Michael (1993), 'Building Bridges . . . Plan the Span', *Everyone's Backyard*, 12(4): 18.

Zald, Mayer N. and John D. McCarthy (eds) (1987), *Social Movements in an Organizational Society* (New Brunswick, NJ: Transaction Books).

40 Green Parties in National Governments: From Protest to Acquiescence?

Thomas Poguntke

Introduction

Arguably, the degree of attention Green parties have attracted across publics and the global academic community alike far exceeds their real political impact. About 20 years after the first Green party deputies were elected to national parliaments in Western Europe (Rootes 1997; Richardson and Rootes 1995; Müller-Rommel 1990, 1993), some finally reached the highest echelons of power, that is, national governments. An important reason why it took them much longer than many other new parties (Mair 2001: 106) may be that many green activists did not think that national governments were the real loci of power. Governments and parliaments were believed to lack the power to address the most urgent issues relevant for the survival of mankind—pollution, the nuclear arms race, and the expansion of nuclear energy production. Why, then, try to get into government? While parliamentary representation might provide a suitable forum for making green ideas and demands known to a wider public, participation in government would at best change very little; at worst, it might merely serve to legitimise the continuation of the Old Politics of growth, militarism, exploitation of the third world and pollution (Doherty and de Geus 1996; Poguntke 1993).

While it is not the purpose of this concluding contribution to analyse these debates again, it is nevertheless useful to recall their intensity—and, some may say, far-sightedness—when trying to assess what the Greens have achieved in government. In other words, how much have Greens in government been able to change the course of national politics and how much has governmental incumbency changed the Greens? Conclusive answers are premature, of course, not least since we are dealing with a very recent phenomenon and the Greens may well improve their performance. Or they may come to the conclusion that their more radical supporters were, after all, right and that there is a real difference between being 'in government' and being 'in power'.

Nevertheless, a systematic comparison of the governmental record of Green parties in Belgium, Finland, France, Germany and Italy can provide tentative answers to these questions.

From *Environmental Politics*, 11: 1 (2002), 133–45.

An obvious point of departure for our analysis is provided in the comparison of their paths to power, which may have exposed individual Green parties to substantially different institutional pressures to streamline their party structures and moderate their ideological appeal. Once in power, the format of national party systems and the type of coalition may account for any substantial variation among their strategies within government and their concomitant policy achievements. Finally, what were the electoral payoffs of joining government? Did Green parties suffer at the polls, and could they maintain their links with the movements?

Paths to Power

Governmental incumbency on a lower level of the political system provides parties with valuable experience for their role in national government. Not all Green parties have been equally well prepared to meet the challenges of national government. Nor, because the institutional make-up of individual countries differs substantially, have they had equal chances to prepare themselves. To be sure, all parties have experienced the opportunities and constraints of being in local government to a greater or lesser extent. However, local politics is not politicised to the same degree as regional or national government. Frequently, personal contacts and reputations may be more important than party affiliation or ideology, and the small number of activists in a local party branch may have rendered many formal provisions of grass-roots democracy either superfluous or simply impractical (Poguntke 1994). Consequently, experience in local executives will normally not make parties fit for national government. The exigencies of regional government, on the contrary, resemble those of national governmental responsibility. We would therefore expect that parties would enter national government well prepared if they previously have held power at this intermediate level.

Yet, experience in regional government did not leave the German and Italian Greens better prepared for taking on the challenges of national government. Arguably, the German Greens should have been most familiar with handling the levers of executive power. After all, German federalism provides a unique opportunity structure in which new parties may acquire governmental experience at the intermediate level of governance provided in a truly federal system. However, the party certainly did not have a smooth start. It felt the need to reform its party structures twice (!) shortly after joining federal government in order to create a more efficient leadership structure that might provide the necessary institutional framework for coordinating party, parliamentary party and Green members of government (Raschke 2001: 40–55). Another indication of how unprepared the Greens were upon entering government was the debate as to whether or not Green members of government should be allowed to retain their parliamentary seats. While combining a cabinet post with a parliamentary mandate would violate the Green principle of separating office and mandate, the debate over this issue reflected a profound misunderstanding about the mechanics of party government in a parliamentary system (Lijphart 1992; Verney 1992). Revealingly, the example of French semi-presidentialism was frequently used in this debate.

Probably even more telling than the party's inability to enter government with organisational structures suited for governing was the fact that the Green Party's basic programme dated back to 1980. By 1998 it could at best serve as a source of entertaining, or sometimes even grotesque, quotations from the period when Green programmatic statements usually called for maximal solutions to be achieved over a minimal period of time. The basic programme, to give but one example, still called for the dissolution of NATO and the Warsaw Pact—the latter having been achieved, one is tempted to add, without much contribution by the German Greens (Poguntke 1993). It would be unfair, of course, not to mention that the Greens had modernised their programmes over the years by drafting a series of election manifestos and special programmes. However, the absence of an up-to-date basic programme, its revision delayed repeatedly in order to maintain the truce between factions, is indicative of the lack of reflection upon the role and function of a party in national government.

Similarly, the Italian Greens seem to have been unable to draw consistent conclusions from their experience in regional government. After all, their participation in national government resembles a roller-coaster ride between conflictual and consensual strategies within government, accompanied by similarly sharp turns in their approach to party organisation. This culminated in the 1999 relaunch of the party while it was still in government.

Experience in regional government is, however, but one important factor that may leave parties better prepared for national government. Equally important are parliamentary experience and, above all, parliamentary strength (see introductory contribution). Only parties that have had sizeable parliamentary delegations over a considerable period of time can hope to have acquired sufficient familiarity and expertise with the intricacies of national politics. Size is a particularly relevant variable here as politics is highly specialised and a small number of MPs would be overwhelmed by the multitude of tasks concomitant with modern parliamentary politics and the number of policy areas that need to be covered. In opposition, a small party may simply resort to concentrating on its core themes. Once in government, such self-limitation becomes untenable and may produce considerable problems. From this perspective, the uneven record of the Italian Greens appears less surprising, whereas the Belgian, Finnish and German Greens should have entered national government with a sufficient number of politicians familiar with a wide range of policy areas and the nuts and bolts of national parliamentary politics.

Organisational Change and Incumbency

Grass-roots democracy has been the hallmark of Green parties ever since they slowly (and sometimes painfully) grew out of the new social movements and established themselves as political parties. It was as much a normative concept aimed at reforming representative democracy as it was intended to be a safeguard against losing touch with the movements and becoming an established party (Frankland and Schoonmaker 1992; Poguntke 1989; 1993: 34–41). Moving from protest politics towards government meant that Green parties experienced a gradual shift of the relative importance of different relevant environments (Panebianco 1988: 12). While the movements remained important to mobilisation and ideological inspiration, an increasingly electoral (and eventually governmental) orientation meant that other relevant environments had to be given more attention. In other words, Green parties had to adapt to a changing environment

(Harmel and Janda 1982: 11; Katz and Mair 1992: 9) which was changing not least because they had chosen to play the game of electoral politics.

When analysing organisational change within Green parties on the path to power, two complementary patterns are identifiable. On the one hand, parties decide to adapt their structure to systemic constraints because they anticipate the need for centralisation should they eventually enter national government. On the other, they reform their organisation after joining government because they quickly realise that their 'reaction time' has been drastically reduced and they need more centralised leadership structures.

Anticipatory adaptation was widespread among successful European Green parties. The Italian Greens, for example, abolished collective leadership in 1993, at a time when the entire Italian party system was undergoing a fundamental transformation (Bull and Rhodes 1997; Newell and Bull 1997; Morlino 1998). The Flemish AGALEV strengthened its leadership after the experience of negotiations over entering government in 1991, and even the organisationally conservative German Greens introduced a 'Land council' as their co-ordinating body after they lost all their West German seats in the Bundestag elections of 1990.

However, virtually all Green parties experienced a further need to streamline their party structure after they had entered national government. As mentioned already, even parties that have had substantial experience with regional government (like the German and Italian Greens) realised that being in national government is an entirely different ball game. To a greater or lesser extent, all parties share the somewhat sobering experience that whatever was left of grass-roots democracy was hard to sustain under the pressures of participation in national government. Probably the most telling example of institutional constraints is that of the Finnish Greens who found it unsustainable not to allow their party chairperson to take up a post in government in a country where these positions are traditionally combined. Yet grass-roots democracy was not abandoned totally. ECOLO and the German Greens still maintain collective leadership and, while AGALEV allows ministers to hold party office, this is still very restricted (if highly disputed) in the German Green Party.

Equally significant as these abrupt changes were the gradual processes that resulted from adapting to the new role as a party of government (Harmel and Janda 1994: 275). Increased media exposure, the frequent need for quick decisions, the constraints of coalition politics and the increased resources that come with holding ministerial posts enhanced the power of party elites (and particularly members of government) at the expense of the rank-and-file. Consistently, linkages between new social movements and Green parties have played a secondary role once the latter were admitted to government. While the Italian Greens actively tried to reconnect with their extra-parliamentary roots towards the end of their term in government, party-movement relationships were not always easy. Military involvement in the Balkans was one of the major bones of contention in Italy and Germany, and the conflict over the transport of nuclear waste in Germany led to a passionate confrontation between a Green Minister for Environment and local protest groups trying to block those transports. At the same time, however, there have been many examples when Green members of government used their connections to the movements as a substitute for their lack of access to expertise and support from within the government apparatus.

Power within Government?

Greens in government means Greens in coalition government. Not only is coalition government the dominant mode of party government in democracies, but Green parties can only expect to play a relatively minor role in coalition government since their growth has had clear limits everywhere. However, as the example of the German FDP illustrates (Poguntke 1999), small parties may be capable of achieving disproportionate power, depending on the format of the party system and the nature of the coalition.

The power of a party within a coalition largely depends on its capacity to blackmail its coalition partners. First and foremost, this presupposes that the survival of government is at stake should the party decide to leave government. When assessing the governmental power of a party, our first criterion is therefore whether or not it is indispensable for the survival of government. However, while a particular coalition may not survive the exit of a small party like the Greens, the major coalition partner(s) may have attractive alternatives to which they can turn. While the German Greens, for example, were clearly needed for the survival of the first red-green federal government, they were in no position to remove Gerhard Schröder from the Chancellery. After all, he could have turned to the FDP, or even the Christian Democrats, instead.

Likewise, the credibility of a small party's threat to leave government depends on the range of its own available options. Again, Greens are in an uncomfortable strategic position. In three out of five countries, they are clearly part of the Left, in two cases even locked into an electoral alliance. Whereas coalition formulae follow a less clear-cut left-right logic in Belgium and Finland, Greens are still highly unlikely to side exclusively with the Right. In other words, Green parties suffer from a strategic disadvantage in that they are not pivotal parties that can turn to either side. On the contrary, they are clearly part of the left camp, maybe even adding to a bipolar pattern of party competition and coalition formation in several European countries (Mair 2002).

Arguably, the Belgian Greens were in a particularly strong position, because AGALEV was an indispensable coalition partner for the Flemish government and their exit would most likely have removed one of the larger coalition partners from power. Given the unique linkage between regional and federal coalitions, this clearly provided the Greens with a reasonably strong position within government. However the German Greens, frequently dubbed 'the most powerful Green party' in Western Europe, found themselves, as mentioned above, in a less than comfortable position. Modest policy achievements clearly reflect this.

From the perspective of blackmailing power, being a junior partner in an oversized coalition is certainly the least comfortable position to be in (Laver and Schofield 1990: 85; Sartori 1976: 122–5). The experience of the Greens in France, Italy, and Finland shows, however, that a purely numerical approach to evaluating the power of coalition partners is myopic. The examples demonstrate that its bargaining position within a coalition is not the sole power resource for a smaller coalition partner. Connecting to new social movements, appealing to public opinion, or simply implementing existing legislation are ways to achieve substantial policy goals in a situation where no credible exit option is available. After all, their position might not have been so different from that of other green parties in government: given their unambiguous anchorage in the Left, even in a minimum winning coalition, exit could only mean opposition—hardly an attractive option after 20 years on the road to power.

Last but not least an additional complication needs mentioning. The Italian and French Greens came to power as partners in an electoral alliance. Given the uncertainty about the 'real' electoral strength of each alliance partner that inevitably accompanies such arrangements, this may actually enhance the bargaining position of a smaller party within an alliance. After all, the larger parties can never be entirely sure whether it had not been the additional momentum that was provided by a small party that eventually tipped the balance in favour of their majority.

Overall, Green parties have been in a relatively unfavourable strategic position when they entered national governments for the first time. With the partial exception of the Flemish AGALEV, they were (numerically) not essential for keeping the other coalition partners in power. Arguably, much depended on how skilfully they exploited the structurally rather limited opportunities government would offer them. Again, the record is a mixed one.

Strategies in Government and Policy Impact

Next to deciding on the governmental programme, choosing portfolios is the most fundamental strategic decision upon entering government—albeit a highly constrained one, because it may involve clashes with coalition partners who claim the same ministry. Controlling the apex of the executive power responsible for a certain policy area gives a party the prerogative of formulating policy initiatives in that field, and it enables it to control and enforce the implementation of existing legislation. From this perspective, choosing the Environment portfolio was an obvious choice for all Green parties although it considerably limited their scope for broadening their appeal beyond environmental issues. To be sure, none of these ministries was restricted to environmental protection in a narrow sense.

However, when looking at the policy areas covered by Green ministers, it was only the German Greens who managed to obtain a so-called 'classical' portfolio, the Ministry for Foreign Affairs. Yet, another pattern is discernible. Green parties have attempted to expand into policy areas that can be regarded as natural extensions of ecological politics, such as Health and Agriculture, the latter now fashionably renamed in Italy and Germany as 'Ministry for Consumer Protection'. All parties attempted to shed their image of being a single-issue party. The Italian Greens made the most decisive attempt when they decided to trade the Ministry for the Environment for two other ministries (Agriculture, Community Policy) in the short-lived Amato government.

Clearly, selecting portfolios means choosing policy areas that will become (or remain) strongly associated with the Greens in the public mind. Equally important for a party's public image, however, is its general approach towards governing. Within the strategic constraints that have been discussed above, Green parties could still have chosen a conflictual approach that would have conveyed the message that they were, despite being in government, still calling for a more fundamental transformation of politics and policy. Somewhat surprisingly, none of the five Green parties has attempted such a double strategy. By and large, Green parties have been co-operative partners in government. The attempt of the leader of the Italian Greens, Carlo Ripa di Meana, to heighten the public profile of his party by publicly criticising coalition partners was soon met with strong disapproval from his own ranks. Eventually, the conflict led to his own exodus from the Greens and to the election of a party leader who was committed to a co-operative approach.

While the Greens decided to play by the rules and adopt a constructive approach to coalition government, this did not leave them without significant policy impact. It is in keeping with their rather limited blackmail potential that their most noticeable achievements are in policy areas that do not touch upon the core of vested socio-economic interests. All parties have had some success in modernising some of their country's legislation related to a libertarian agenda. More rights for illegal immigrants, an improved legal status for gay and lesbian couples, or a more liberal approach towards asylum seekers are relatively low-cost projects, and it is precisely here where the Greens scored points.

The picture is less convincing when it comes to ecological tax reform or the single most important issue for Green parties—nuclear power. While it is hardly an exaggeration to consider the conflict over nuclear power the essential launch pad for most Western European Green parties, their success in this policy area, which touches so much upon their core identity, has been very limited. Unsurprisingly, the French Greens achieved next to nothing in this respect, while their Finnish friends stopped a further expansion of nuclear energy but without a definite change of national policy. The German red-green government agreed on phasing out nuclear energy over two or three decades without providing a definite date as to when the last nuclear power station will have to be shut down. Compared to the original Green slogan of the early 1980s, which called for an immediate halt to all nuclear power generation in Germany, this is hardly a convincing victory.

Much Green success, however, does not meet the eye immediately. Given the considerable discretionary power of European administrations, much could be achieved by simply enforcing laws that already exist. Italy is a particularly telling example for this strategy which concentrated, often with the active support of experts from the movements, on implementing legislation that is already on the statute book but is not enforced seriously. Likewise, the French Greens could substantially increase the manpower and financial resources of the Ministry for the Environment.

The experience of German Greens in *Land* governments is another case in point. In many policy arenas, federal law takes precedence over *Land* legislation, but the administration is left to the *Länder*, where Green ministers of the environment could achieve much without conspicuous victories (Lees 1999: 179–81). The attempt of Green *Land* ministers to exploit their administrative discretion to further their causes has at times led to conflicts with the federal minister responsible for the same policy area. Confrontations between Green *Land* Ministers of the Environment and their Christian Democratic colleagues in Bonn gained much public attention and tended to end with an instruction by the federal minister that forced the reluctant *Land* minister to carry out federal policies. Obviously, being in federal government has also meant considerably more freedom of manoeuvre for Green *Land* ministers—an aspect that must not be forgotten when assessing the achievements of Green participation in national government.

Voters and Movement Activists: Equally Disappointed?

Given the lack of conspicuous success, particularly in the core area of nuclear power, a degree of disillusionment among Green voters may have been unavoidable. On the other hand, many studies have shown over the years that Green voters tended to be reformist and appreciative of the inherent limitations of governmental participation—not least because all Greens entered local governments during their years of electoral growth. This would suggest continued voter support for Green parties in government. Such contradictory expectations seem to be matched by inconclusive evidence when looking at how the Greens have fared after entering national governments. But exactly what evidence is there?

The electoral effects of incumbency are notoriously difficult to disentangle. This is the classic problem of an 'over-determined outcome' in that many other independent variables that have no relation to the fact that the party has just joined government may account for a change in a party's electoral fortunes (Müller and Strom 2000: 27; Rüdig and Franklin 2000). Our analysis is complicated by the fact that in some cases no national election has been held since the Greens joined government. Hence, there is no reliable standard of comparison. Survey results are equally problematic because they tend to report a 'mid-term effect', which means that governing parties usually experience a slump in their poll ratings halfway through their legislative term. Local, regional or European elections have been held in all countries after the Greens have joined national governments, and even though there are obvious problems of comparison involved here too, they can be used in an attempt to gauge the electoral effects of incumbency.

Overall, the picture is inconclusive. Those who have maintained that Green parties in national government were bound to lose support because they would inevitably disappoint (or even betray) the hopes and aspirations of their supporters have been proven wrong. The Finnish Greens managed to increase their share of the vote and were returned to government with an additional ministry for the first two years of the new government. The Italian Greens experienced both the worst European election result in their history and good returns in local and regional elections, though their 'true' electoral strength in the 2001 national elections is hard to determine because of the complications of the electoral systems which forces parties into electoral alliances. The Belgian and French Greens have performed reasonably well at the polls since they joined government, but the real test will be the next general election. This leaves us with the German Greens, who have suffered dramatic defeats at every single Land election since entering the national coalition with the SPD. To be sure, the extent of their decline in the polls tends to be inflated by the fact that these results are compared to a phase in German electoral politics when the Greens were considered to be something like the leading opposition party while the SPD was in shambles. Nevertheless, even when these distortions are taken into account, there is unambiguous evidence that the Greens have been penalised for entering national government.

Although evidence is still very patchy, the German Greens seem to represent almost a deviant case in that their record is so clearly negative. One possible explanation is that expectations were highest in a situation when a Green party was the sole (albeit not indispensable) coalition partner and when the new government represented—for the first time in the Federal Republic's history—a complete turnover of government.

It may be for these reasons that the German Greens suffered most from a strategic situation that is the inevitable consequence of joining national government, which (to a greater or lesser extent) has been the same for all parties considered in this volume. Incumbency has put Green parties at loggerheads with their own core constituency. Given the inevitably slow pace of policy change in national politics (frequently involving EU-wide changes), movement activists are bound to be disappointed. By their very nature, those who are active in new social movements tend to be single-issue oriented and to call for fast and radical change. This is the very antithesis to national coalition government constrained by European-wide regulations. Ironically, taking over the Ministry of the Environment is probably the most problematic (yet virtually inevitable) choice for a Green party because it involves the largest potential for confrontations with the very core of the Green constituency.

Again, the German example is instructive here. The dilemma of being a party of government was epitomised by the conflict over the transport of nuclear waste that led to a massive mobilisation of protest in Germany. Unenthusiastically committed to a policy of gradually phasing out nuclear energy production, Green politicians found themselves confronted by their formerly most loyal allies, the activists of the anti-nuclear movement, which is the nucleus of the ecology movement and the 'birthplace' of the Green party. Another highly conflictual issue for Green parties has been the conflict over the involvement of their countries in the Kosovo conflict, which touched upon the second element of Green identity, that is, their strong roots in the movement against the deployment of intermediate range nuclear missiles in the early 1980s. Although only parts of these movements were outright pacifist, acceptance of the Kosovo mission nevertheless represented a dramatic departure from previously held Green convictions that the use of military force should not be a means of foreign policy.

Inevitably, government incumbency required acceptance of the constraints of domestic and international policy-making even if this meant alienating a considerable portion of committed movement activists who no longer regarded the Greens as an adequate and trustworthy mouthpiece for their concerns and therefore withdrew their electoral support. One obvious reaction to this strategic dilemma was to broaden their appeal. All Green parties have attempted to free themselves from the image of a single-issue party and to acquire competence in other policy areas, not least by trying to occupy 'promising' portfolios like consumer protection. While this may pay off in the medium or long term, immediate electoral rewards are unlikely, because voters' perceptions of parties change very slowly. The almost universal weakness of parties on the Left when it comes to deciding who is to be trusted on economic policies is a case in point.

Furthermore, there is a danger of neglecting Green core competence by trying too hard to become a party concerned with a broader range of themes. After all, the only unmistakably Green issue is the concern with ecological politics, which goes beyond the mere concern with environmental protection now commonplace in modern democracies. Neglecting to emphasise what is distinct about the Green approach to the environment may lead to the electorally highly damaging feeling among the electorate that the Greens are no longer needed. The alternative option—'reconnecting' with the movements—has proven hardly more promising. After all, a posture of 'opposition in government' is barely tenable except for parties that hold the balance of power—a favourable but rare strategic position that has so far eluded the Greens everywhere.

In the end, Green party power within national coalition governments (and hence their electoral success) rests primarily on the skilful exploitation of a rather limited room for manoeuvre below the threshold of threatening or even exercising the exit option. Given the format of the respective party systems, normally this could only mean return to opposition on the radical fringes of the party system, including reconnecting with the movements. While this may win back some of the voters lost in the process of moderation, others, who are more moderately inclined, may defect instead. Obviously, self-limitation to opposition is hardly a viable and promising strategy for the majority of Green party activists. Instead, they may find that their performance in government (and at the polls) can be improved by treading a thin line between loyal co-operation within government and making it clear that Green policy objectives go far beyond the rather limited reforms that are possible under the constraints of coalition government.

References

Bull, Martin and Martin Rhodes (eds) (1997), 'Between Crisis and Transition: Italian Politics' in the 1990s, *West European Politics*. Special Issue.

Doherty, Brian and Marius de Geus (eds) (1996), *Democracy and Green Political Thought* (London: Routledge).

Frankland, E. Gene and Donald Schoonmaker (1992), *Between Protest and Power: The German Green Party* (Boulder, CO and Oxford: Westview).

Harmel, Robert and Kenneth Janda (1982), *Parties and their Environment: Limits to Reform?* (New York and London: Longman).

Harmel, Robert and Kenneth Janda (1994), 'An Integrated Theory of Party Goals and Party Change', *Journal of Theoretical Politics*, 6(4): 259–87.

Katz, Richard S. and Peter Mair (1992), 'Introduction: The Cross-National Study of Party Organizations', in Richard S. Katz and Peter Mair (eds), *Party Organizations: A Data Handbook on Party Organizations in Western Democracies, 1960–90* (London and Newbury Park, CA: Sage), 1–20.

Laver, Michael and Norman Schofield (1990), *Multiparty Government: The Politics of Coalition in Europe* (Oxford: Oxford University Press).

Lees, Charles (1999), 'The Red–Green Coalition', *German Politics*, 8(2): 174–94.

Lijphart, Arend (1992), 'Introduction' in Arend Lijphart (ed.), *Parliamentary versus Presidential Government* (Oxford: Oxford University Press), 1–27.

Mair, Peter (2002), 'The Green Challenge and Political Competition: How Typical is the German Experience?' in Stephen Padgett and Thomas Poguntke (eds), *Continuity and Change in German Politics. Beyond the Politics of Centrality? Festschrift for Gordon Smith* (London and Portland, OR: Frank Cass; first published as a special issue of *German Politics*, 10(2) (2001): 99–116.

Morlino, Leonardo (1998), *Democracy between Consolidation and Crisis. Parties, Groups, and Citizens in Southern Europe* (Oxford: Oxford University Press).

Müller-Rommel, Ferdinand (1990), 'New Political Movements and New Politics Parties in Western Europe', in Russell J. Dalton and Manfred Kuechler (eds), *Challenging the Political Order. New Social and Political Movements in Western Democracies* (New York: Oxford University Press/Cambridge: Polity), 209–31.

—— (1993), *Grüne Parteien in Westeuropa* (Opladen: Westdeutscher Verlag).

Müller, Wolfgang C. and Kaare Strom (2000), 'Coalition Governance in Western Europe. An Introduction', in Wolfgang C. Müller and Kare Strom (eds), *Coalition Governments in Western Europe* (Oxford: Oxford University Press), 1–31.

Newell, James L. and Martin Bull (1997), 'Party Organisations and Alliances in Italy in the 1990s: A Revolution of Sorts', *West European Politics*, 20: 81–109.

Panebianco, Angelo (1988), *Political Parties: Organization and Power* (Cambridge: Cambridge University Press).

Poguntke, Thomas (1989), 'The "New Politics Dimension" in European Green Parties', in Ferdinand Müller-Rommel (ed.), *New Politics in Western Europe: The Rise and Success of Green Parties and Alternative Lists* (Boulder, CO and London: Westview), 175–94.

—— (1993), *Alternative Politics: The German Green Party* (Edinburgh: Edinburgh University Press).

—— (1994), 'Basisdemokratie and Political Realities: The German Green Party', in Kay Lawson (ed.), *How Political Parties Work Perspectives from Within* (Westport, CT and London: Praeger), 3–22.

—— (1999), 'The Winner Takes it All: The FDP in 1982/1983—Maximizing Votes, Office and Policy?' in Kaare Strøm and Wolfgang C. Müller (eds), *Policy, Office, or Votes? How Political Parties Make Hard Decisions* (Cambridge: Cambridge University Press), 216–36.

Raschke, Joachim (2001), *Die Zukunft der Grünen. 'So kann man nicht regieren'* (Frankfurt and New York: Campus).

Richardson, Dick and Chris Rootes (1995), *The Green Challenge: The Development of Green Parties in Europe* (London and New York: Routledge).

Rootes, Christopher A. (1997), 'Environmental Movements and Green Parties in Western and Eastern Europe', in Michael Redclift and Graham Woodgate (eds), *The International Handbook of Environmental Sociology* (Cheltenham and Northampton, MA: Edward Elgar), 19–47.

Rüdig, Wolfgang and Mark N. Franklin (2000), 'Government Participation and Green Electoral Support: Comparative Analysis', paper presented at the Annual Conference of the UK Political Studies Association.

Sartori, Giovanni (1976), *Parties and Party Systems. A Framework for Analysis* (Cambridge: Cambridge University Press).

Verney, Douglas V. (1992), 'Parliamentary Government and Presidential Government', in Arend Lijphart (ed.), *Parliamentary versus Presidential Government* (Oxford: Oxford University Press), 31–47.

Section XIII: Ecological Democracy

Green movements press the liberal state in new and often uncomfortable directions. While liberal states are today almost all democratic, the kind of democracy they embody is limited. It is always constrained by the need above all to maintain the confidence of actual and potential investors in the economy; if environmental concerns clash with economic ones, then environmental concerns are compromised. While ecological modernization as dealt with in Section VII tries to get around this problem, that very attempt may stretch the liberal state into new kinds of post-liberal democracy. A further constraint on the capacity of the liberal democratic state in environmental affairs is its philosophical grounding in liberalism, which is (Wissenburg's protestations in Section IV notwithstanding) a generally individualistic and anthropocentric doctrine. Many greens believe that environmental issues demand holistic and ecocentric thinking. Finally, the liberal democratic state is a national state; given that many environmental issues and problems transcend state boundaries, we need to think about transnational democratic action that transcends these boundaries. Global civil society made an appearance in Section XII, but what does this mean for democratic institutions and practices more generally?

These sorts of concerns have led to an explosion in thinking and writing on democracy and the environment in recent years. This literature covers a spectrum from those who believe that modest reforms to liberal democracy are quite capable of producing effective solutions to environmental problems to those who think that a more radical overhaul is necessary (though only a few advocate transformation through revolution). Particular authors can be found at many points on this spectrum. The more moderate have already put in appearances in earlier sections; here we take a look at more radical proposals.

The essay by Ulrich Beck offers a critique and explanation of our current predicament, and the start of a democratic response. For Beck, we are moving from industrial society to a risk society, where everyday acts of being human, such as eating or even breathing, are fraught with risks. Decisions that in industrial society were made mostly by science and industry can now be contested, and issues of environmental risk can come to dominate the political sphere. In the risk society, new forms of democracy can enter if movements can push and engage 'subpolitics'. Beck argues for a more reflexive society that questions its own foundations, and in so doing moves democratic discourse and decision-making into areas previously immune to democratic control.

Andrew Dobson turns our attention to the individual, and offers specific suggestions for democratic and ecological citizenship. While Beck focuses on democratic participation as a way to change risky policies and practices, Dobson focuses on our responsibilities to each other as citizens. We have particular obligations and duties as *ecological* citizens. Unlike more traditional citizenship, these obligations and duties do not stop at the borders of our own state, or even the confines of our own generation.

If liberal democracy is currently not performing to an acceptable environmental standard, then the fault, according to our selection from leading ecofeminist Val Plumwood, is to be found in its liberalism rather than its democracy. Plumwood argues that liberalism is pervaded by mechanisms that suppress environmental concern: notably, dualism between reason and nature, celebration of the property-owning individual and associated denial of collective life, and consignment of many key environmental values to a private realm beyond the reach of politics. She argues for the cultivation of an alternative democratic culture informed by both ecological and feminist principles.

Building on notions that the essence of democracy is effective communication rather than voting or the representation of interests, the selection by John S. Dryzek anticipates democratic structures that embrace communication with the natural world. The kind of democracy without boundaries which he envisages does not fit well with existing liberal democratic states; but it is congruent with the kind of emerging order found in connection with transnational civil society. This conception of ecological democracy can inspire a search for institutions beyond the capitalist state.

Further Reading

A number of edited books explore the connections between environmentalism and democracy. Freya Mathews (ed.), *Ecology and Democracy* (1996) is a set of philosophically oriented essays on this theme. William Lafferty and James Meadowcroft (eds), *Democracy and the Environment* (1996) ranges widely over the performance of existing democratic institutions to more radical alternatives. Brian Doherty and Marius de Geus (eds), *Democracy and Green Political Thought: Sustainability, Rights and Citizenship* (1996) deals with issues of democracy as they arise in green politics and philosophy, with a view to movement beyond liberal democracy. Ben A. Minter and Bob Pepperman Taylor (eds), *Democracy and the Claims of Nature* (2002) is another good collection on these issues.

A good overview, with examples of environmental democracy from the local to the global, is Michael Mason, *Environmental Democracy* (2000). Graham Smith examines a particular form of environmental democracy in *Deliberative Democracy and the Environment* (2003). And for a picture of the potential of a 'civic environmentalism', see William Shutkin's *The Land that Could Be: Environmentalism and Democracy in the 21st Century* (2000). Ulrich Beck's many works on the risk society and reflexive modernization include *Risk Society: Towards a New Modernity* (1992) and *World Risk Society* (1999).

41 Politics of Risk Society

Ulrich Beck

Consider the intellectual situation in Europe after 1989. A whole world order had broken down. What an opportunity to adventure into the new! But we stick to old concepts and ideas, and make the same mistakes. There is even a kind of left protectionism and a switch of position. As Anthony Giddens has pointed out, radical socialism has become conservative and conservatism has become radical.[1] We have to rediscover this crazy, mad-cow disease world sociologically, and the script of modernity has to be rewritten, redefined, reinvented. This is what the theory of world risk society is about, and to give you a better idea of my 'mistakes', I will concentrate on three points.[2]

First, I shall return to the theory of risk society, to show how it conveys a new conception of a 'non-industrial' society and how it modifies social theory and politics. Secondly, I shall take the position of my critics and explore what I see as the theoretical issues which now limit the development of my ideas on risk. Thirdly, I shall point to the theoretical and political avenues that I should like to see explored, perhaps on a comparative and European level.

Britain is experiencing what *The Independent* has called 'beef-gate'—the shock of living in a risk society. Society has become a laboratory where there is absolutely nobody in charge. An experiment has been inflicted on us by the beef industries, and the most ordinary decision—to eat or not to eat beef—could be a life and death decision. Hamlet has to be reconsidered: to beef or not to beef, now is the question! Sociologically, there is a big difference between those who take risks and those who are victimized by risks others take. I shall point to a few epistemological principles which characterize the three main arguments of the theory of risk society.

Risk society begins where nature ends.[3] As Giddens has pointed out, this is where we switch the focus of our anxieties from what nature can do to us to what we have done to nature. The BSE crisis is not simply a matter of fate but a matter of decisions and options, science and politics, industries, markets and capital. This is not an outside risk but a risk generated right inside each person's life and inside a variety of institutions. A central paradox of risk society is that these internal risks are generated by the processes of modernization which try to control them.

Risk society begins where tradition ends, when, in all spheres of life, we can no longer take traditional certainties for granted. The less we can rely on traditional securities, the more risks we have to negotiate. The more risks, the more decisions and choices we have to make. There is an important line of argument which connects the theory of risk society, in this context, to

From Jane Franklin (ed.), *The Politics of Risk Society* (Cambridge: Polity, 1998), 9–22.

complementary processes of individualization in the spheres of work, family life and self-identity, which I have explored elsewhere.[4]

The theory of risk society interprets the ways in which these two states of interconnected processes, the end of nature and the end of tradition, have altered the epistemological and cultural status of science and the constitution of politics. In the age of risk, society becomes a laboratory with nobody responsible for the outcomes of experiments. The private sphere's creation of risks means that it can no longer be considered apolitical. Indeed, a whole arena of hybrid subpolitics emerges in the realms of investment decisions, product development, plant management and scientific research priorities. In this situation, the conventional political forces and representations of industrial society have been sidelined.[5] Let's look at these principles in more detail.

The notion of risk society clarifies a world characterized by the loss of a clear distinction between nature and culture. Today, if we talk about nature we talk about culture and if we talk about culture we talk about nature. When we think of global warming, the hole in the ozone layer, pollution or food scares, nature is inescapably contaminated by human activity. This common danger has a levelling effect that whittles away some of the carefully erected boundaries between classes, nations, humans and the rest of nature, between creators of culture and creatures of instinct, or to use an earlier distinction, between beings with and those without a soul.

We live in a *hybrid* world which transcends old theoretical distinctions, as Bruno Latour has convincingly argued.[6] Risks are *man-made hybrids*. They include and combine politics, ethics, mathematics, mass media, technologies, cultural definitions and precepts. In risk society, modern society becomes reflexive, that is, becomes both an issue and a problem for itself.

Many sociologists (including Foucault, or Adorno and Horkheimer, critical theorists of the Frankfurt School) pictured modernity as a prison house of technical knowledge. We are all, to alter the metaphor, small cogs in the gigantic machine of technical and bureaucratic reasons. Yet risk society, in opposition to the image of the term, captures a world which is much more open and contingent than any classical concept of modern society suggests—and is so precisely *because of* and not *in spite of* the knowledge that we have accumulated about ourselves and about the material environment.

As François Ewald argues,[7] risk is a way of controlling or, one could say, colonizing the future. Events that do *not* exist (yet) strongly influence our present affairs and actions. So risks are a kind of virtual, yet real, reality. The greater the threat (or to be more precise, the social definition and construction of the threat), the greater the obligation and power to change current events. Let us take 'globalization risk' as an example. It says, if you want to survive in the global capitalistic market, you have to change the basic foundations of modernity: social security, the nation-state, the power of the unions and so on. The greater the threat, the greater the change which has to be undertaken in order to control the future. This deeply politicizing meaning of the risk society argument can be used not only by environmentalists but also by global capital, and more effectively too. As Giddens and I have pointed out, there is another central paradox that we have to understand, which is that the more we try to colonize the future, the more likely it is to spring surprises on us. This is why the notion of risk moves through two stages.

In the first instance, risk seems no more than a part of an essential calculus, a means of sealing off boundaries as the future is invaded. Risk makes the unforeseeable foreseeable, or promises to do so. In this initial form, risk is a statistical part of the operation of insurance companies.[8] They know a lot about the secrets of risk which change society, even though nothing has yet happened. This is risk in a world where much remains as 'given', as fate, including external nature and those forms of social life coordinated by tradition. As nature becomes permeated by industrialization and as tradition is dissolved, new types of incalculability emerge. We move then into the second stage of risk, which Giddens[9] and I have called *manufactured uncertainty*. Here the production of risks is the consequence of scientific and political efforts to control or minimize them.

There are two aspects to this. There was once a time when a risk was something you indulged in for a bit of excitement. A bet on the Grand National, a spin of the wheel—it was all meant to add a bit of spice to an otherwise orderly and predictable life. Now manufactured uncertainty means that risk has become an inescapable part of our lives and everybody is facing unknown and barely calculable risks. Risk becomes another word for 'nobody knows.'[10] We no longer choose to take risks, we have them thrust upon us. We are living on a ledge—in a random risk society, from which nobody can escape. Our society has become riddled with random risks. Calculating and managing risks which nobody really knows has become one of our main preoccupations. That used to be a specialist job for actuaries, insurers and scientists. Now we all have to engage in it, with whatever rusty tools we can lay our hands on—sometimes the calculator, sometimes the astrology column. The basic question here is: how can we make decisions about a risk we know nothing about? Should we ignore it and possibly get hurt or killed? Or should we be alarmed and stop or exclude all likely causes? Which course of action is 'rational', the first or the second option?

On the other hand, manufactured uncertainty means that the source of the most troubling new risks we face is something most of us would regard as unequivocally beneficial—our expanding knowledge. It is partly because we know more about the brain that we now know that people in a persistent vegetative state may be conscious and so should not have their life support machines turned off. Yet, as scientific knowledge opens up new opportunities for us, it also makes the world more complex and unknowable, at least by any one individual, often for experts too. How many hamburgers do you need to eat to catch the deadly CJD? Fifty, a hundred, two hundred, a thousand? In what amount of time? Two of the first victims of CJD in Britain had been vegetarians for the five years before they caught it—before that, they had been addicted to hamburgers.

As knowledge and technology race ahead, we are left behind panting in ignorance, increasingly unable to understand or control the machines we depend on and so less able to calculate the consequences of their going wrong. Environmental science has encouraged us to be less short-term in our thinking. We now worry about the consequence of our actions for future generations in far-flung places. But this admirable long-termism also makes it more difficult to calculate the risks of our decisions. What is the risk that your grandchildren's environment will suffer if you use that aerosol or car too much?

Many believe that in the age of risk there can be only one authority left, and that is science. But this is not only a complete misunderstanding of science, it is also a complete misunderstanding of the notion of risk. It is not failure but success which has demonopolized science. One could even say that the more successful sciences have been in this century, the more they have reflected upon their own limits of certainty, the more they have been transformed into a source of manufactured reflexive uncertainty. Sciences are operating in terms of probabilities, which do not exclude the worst case.

This is even more true in identifying and managing risk. In the case of risk conflicts, politicians can no longer rely on scientific experts. This is so, first, because there are always competing and conflicting claims and viewpoints from a variety of actors and affected groups who define risks very differently.[11] So producing conflicting knowledge on risk is a matter of good and not bad experts. Secondly, experts can only supply more or less uncertain factual information about probabilities, but never answer the question: which risk is acceptable and which is not. Thirdly, if politicians just implement scientific advice, they become *caught in the mistakes, modes and uncertainties of scientific knowledge.* So the lesson of the risk society is this: politics and morality are gaining—have to gain!—priority over shifting scientific reasoning.

There used to be a clear division between research and theory, on the one hand, and technology, on the other. The logic of scientific discovery presupposes testing before putting into practice. This is breaking down in the age of risky technologies.[12] Nuclear technologies have to be built *in order* to study their functioning and risks. Test-tube babies have to be born *in order* to find out about the theories and assumptions of biotechnologies. Genetically engineered plants have to be grown *in order* to test the theory. The controllability of the laboratory situation is lost. This causes serious problems.

Scientists are becoming lay persons. They do not know what will happen before they begin their research. At the same time they need the support of the politicians and the public to finance their research and for this reason they have to claim that everything is under control and nothing can go wrong.

As Karl Popper once said, the basic rationality of science is that we should learn from our mistakes. In risk society, mistakes mean that nuclear reactors leak or explode, test-tube babies are born deformed, people are killed by CJD. So scientists cannot make mistakes any more, sorry. But they *do* make mistakes and more than ever they reflect upon them.

Society becomes a laboratory, but there is no one responsible for its outcomes. Experiments in nuclear energy and biotechnology, for example, become inconclusive in the dimensions of time, space and the number of people involved. There is, however, no experimenter in charge, no decision-maker to decide on the validity of the initial hypothesis with scientific authority.

So what is the role of politics? The fact is that no direct decisions are made about technology in the political system (with an exception of nuclear power plants). But on the other hand, if anything goes wrong, the political institutions are made responsible for decisions they didn't take and for consequences and threats they know nothing about.

In relation to the state and Parliament, industry possesses a double advantage. It has autonomy in investment decisions and a monopoly on the application of technology. Politicians are in a bad position, struggling to catch up with what is going on in technological development. Most MPs get their information about technological developments through the media; in spite of all the support for research, the political influence on the goals of technological development remains secondary. No votes are taken in Parliament on the employment and development of micro-electronics, genetic technology and the like. Most of the time, MPs vote in support of them in order to protect the country's economic future and jobs. Thus the division of power leaves the industries with the role of primary decision-maker without responsibility for risks to the public. Meanwhile, politics is assigned the task of democratically legitimizing decisions that it has not taken and doesn't know about, especially since the privatization of industries which were previously run by the state. What happens to the security standards of the privatized railway system? Of privately run nuclear power plants? Has the state really shed the responsibility in the eyes of the public?

So, risks are nobody's responsibility. Neurotechnologies and genetic engineering are reshaping the laws that govern the human mind and life. Who is doing this? Scientific experts? Politicians? Industries? The public? Ask any of them and the reply will be in each case: nobody. Risk politics resembles the 'nobody's rule' that Hannah Arendt tells us is the most tyrannical of all forms of power, because under such circumstances nobody can be held responsible. In the case of risk conflicts, bureaucracies are suddenly unmasked and the alarmed public becomes aware of what they really are: *forms of organized irresponsibility.*[13]

Given that risks are no longer attributable to external agency, industrial societies have developed institutions and rules for coping with unforeseen, unintended consequences and the risks they produce. The welfare state can be seen as a collective and institutional response to the nature of localized risks and dangers, based on principles of rule-governed attribution of fault and blame, legally implemented compensation, actuarial insurance principles and collectively shared responsibility. The classic example of this would be the creation of compensation and insurance schemes for accident and injury at work and unemployment.

However, under the impact of modern risks and manufactured uncertainties, these modes of determining and perceiving risk, attributing causality and allocating compensation have irreversibly broken down, throwing the function and legitimacy of modern bureaucracies, states, economies and science into question. Risks that were calculable under industrial society become incalculable and unpredictable in the risk society. Compared to the possibilities of adjudging blame and causality in classical modernity, the world risk society possesses no such certainties or guarantees.

In terms of social politics, the ecological crisis involves a systematic violation, or crisis, of basic rights, and the long-term impact of this weakening of society can scarcely be overestimated. For dangers are being produced by industry, externalized by economics, individualized by the legal system, legitimized by the sciences and made to appear harmless by politics. That this is breaking down the power and credibility of institutions only becomes clear when the system is put on the spot, as Greenpeace, for example, has tried to do. The result is the subpoliticization of world society.

In the second part of my paper, I shall switch sides to tell you about some of the refutations my risk society theory has provoked. In a conference in Cardiff in March 1996 Professor Hilary Rose said that she felt that risk society had a distinctly German background and that Britain could not afford to be a risk society. To her, the theory of risk society presumes a degree of wealth and security typical of postwar Germany. It is certainly one of the very few attempts to open up the social sciences and social theory to ecological questions, and it is the case that being 'green' is part of the German national identity. On the other hand, testing atomic weapons may be part of the French national identity, and eating roast beef on a Sunday lunchtime may be part of the British culture. Who knows? The important point to make here is that risk conflicts are not only intracultural conflicts. They cross cultural boundaries and are even more conflicts of contradictory certainties. People, expert groups, cultures, nations are having to get involved with each other whether they like it or not. It may not be completely wrong to say that a European public has been born, unintentionally and involuntarily, over the conflict over British beef. It is the 'mad-cow disease Europe' where everybody is quarrelling with everybody else, not only on a general technocratic level but also on an everyday level. If you visit, for example, a *Wirthaus* (a small local restaurant) in southern Bavaria and read the menu you will find a photograph of the local farmer and his family trying to build up trust in his 'good' beef which has nothing to do with the 'bad' British beef.

So, as Barbara Adams argues,[14] a distinction between knowledge and impact can be made which leads to a distinction between two phases of risk society. In the first phase, which we can call 'residual risk society', the impacts are systematically produced, are not the subject of public knowledge and debate and are not at the centre of political conflict. This phase is dominated by the self-identity of 'goods' of industrial and technological progress, which simultaneously intensifies and legitimizes as 'residual risks' hazards resulting from decisions. In the second phase, a completely different situation arises, when the hazards of industrial society dominate public and private debates. Now the institutions of industrial society produce and legitimize hazards which they cannot control. During this transition, property and power relationships remain constant and industrial society sees and criticizes itself *as* risk society. In the first phase, society still makes decisions and acts on the pattern of simple modernity. In the second phase, debates and conflicts which originate in the dynamic of risk society are being superimposed on interest organizations, the legal system and politics. So modernity becomes reflexive.

In all my books I try to demonstrate that the return to the theoretical and political philosophy of simple modernity, in the age of global risk, is doomed to failure. Those orthodox theories and politics remain tied to notions of progress and benign technological change, tied to the belief that the risks we face can still be captured by nineteenth-century, scientific models of hazard assessment and industrial notions of hazard and safety. Simultaneously, the disintegrating institutions of industrial modernity—nuclear families, stable labour markets, segregated gender roles, social classes—can be shored up and buttressed against the waves of reflexive modernization sweeping the West. This dominant attempt to apply nineteenth-century ideas to the late twentieth century is the *category mistake* of social theory, social sciences and politics. It is this point which I try to make in all my work. So let me sharpen this central idea and mention the core notions of *organized irresponsibility*, the *relations of definition*, and the *social explosiveness of hazards*.

The idea of *organized irresponsibility* helps to explain how and why the institutions of modern society must unavoidably acknowledge the reality of catastrophe while simultaneously denying its existence, cover its origins and preclude compensation or control. To put it another way, risk societies are characterized by the paradox of more and more environmental degradation, perceived and possible, and an expansion of environmental law and regulation. Yet at the same time no individual or institution seems to be held specifically accountable for anything. How can this be? To me the key to explaining this state of affairs is the mismatch that exists in risk society between the character of hazards, or manufactured uncertainties, produced by late industrial society and the prevalent *relations of definition*[15] which date in their construction and content from an early and qualitatively different epoch.

The notion of relations of definition is the parallel notion to the relations of production (Karl Marx) in the risk society. They include the rules, institutions and capacities that structure the identification and assessment of risks; they are the legal, epistemological and cultural matrix in which risk politics is conducted. I focus here on four relations of definition:

1 Who is to determine the harmfulness of products or the danger of risks? Is the responsibility with those who generate those risks, with those who benefit from them, or with public agencies?
2 What kind of knowledge or non-knowledge about the causes, dimensions, actors, etc., is involved? To whom does that 'proof' have to be submitted?
3 What is to count as sufficient proof in a world in which we necessarily deal with contested knowledge and probabilities?
4 If there are dangers and damages, who is to decide on compensation for the afflicted and on appropriate forms of future control and regulation?[16]

In relation to each of these questions, risk societies are currently trapped in a vocabulary that lends itself to an interrogation of the risks and hazards through the relations of definition of simple, classic, first modernity. These are singularly inappropriate not only for modern catastrophes, but also for the challenges of manufactured uncertainties. Consequently we have to face the paradox that at the very time when threats and hazards are seen to become more dangerous and more obvious, they simultaneously slip through the net of proofs, attributions and compensation with which the legal and political systems attempt to capture them.

Of course, everybody asks who is the *political subject* of risk society? I have put a lot of thought into answering this question, but my answer has not yet been acknowledged theoretically or politically.[17] My argument is as follows: nobody is the subject and everybody is the subject at the same time. It might not be very surprising to you that this answer has not been recognized. But there is more to it. What I propose comes very close to Bruno Latour's theory of quasi-objects.[18] To me the hazards themselves are quasi-subjects; this acting-active quality is produced by the *contradictions in which institutions get caught up in risk societies*. I use a metaphor to explain this idea: the *social explosiveness of hazard*. It explores the ways in which awareness of large-scale hazards, risks and manufactured uncertainties sets off a dynamic of cultural and political change that undermines state bureaucracies, challenges the dominance of science and redraws the boundaries and battle-lines of contemporary politics. So hazards, understood as *socially constructed and produced 'quasi—subjects'*, are a powerful uncontrollable 'actor' to delegitimize and destabilize state institutions with responsibilities for pollution control, in particular, and public safety in general.

Hazards themselves sweep away the attempts of institutional elites and experts to control them. Governments and bureaucracies, of course, exercise well-worn routines of denial. Data can be hidden, denied and distorted. The gap between knowledge and impact can be exploited. Counter-arguments can be mobilized. Expert-systems can be adjusted. Maximum permissible levels of acceptance can be raised. Human error, rather than systematic risk, can be cast as the villain of the piece and so on. And last but not least, Europe can be made responsible for the mad-cow disease crisis. However, states are fighting a battle where victories are temporary because they offer nineteenth-century pledges of security to the age of world risk society. We can see this happening all around us.

These ideas are, of course, bound to the notion of the *safety* or *provident* state, to be found in the work of François Ewald.[19] To me, his theory represents a basic shift in the interpretation of the welfare state. While the majority of social scientists have sought to explain the origins and construction of the welfare state in terms of class interests, the maintenance of social order or the enhancement of national productivity and military power, this argument understands the provision of services (health care), the creation of insurance schemes (pensions and unemployment insurance) and the regulation of the economy and the environment in terms of the creation of security. In relation to industries and technologies, of course, technical experts do play a central role in answering the question of how safe is safe enough. This model of the modern capitalist state as a provident state has been challenged. One of the critiques is that the notion of a safety state is much more closely correlated with the institutions and procedures of continental Western European states than with either the states of Anglo-American capitalism or the social democratic states of Scandinavia.

Finally, I should like to point to two implications of this thesis. The first is that risk society is not about exploding nuclear submarines falling out of the sky; it is not, as you might assume, one more expression of the 'German angst' at the millennium. Quite the opposite. What I suggest is a new model for understanding our times, in a not unhopeful spirit. What others see as the development of a postmodern order, my argument interprets as a stage of radicalized modernity. A stage where the dynamics of individualization, globalization and risk undermine modernity and its foundations. Whatever happens, modernity gets *reflexive*, that means concerned with its unintended consequences, risks and foundations.[20] Where most postmodern theorists are critical of grand narratives, general theory and humanity, I remain committed to all of these, but in a new sense. To me, Enlightenment is not a historical notion and set of ideas, but a process and dynamic where criticism, self-criticism, irony and humanity play a central role (the theme of my current research). Where for many philosophers and sociologists 'rationality' means 'discourse' and 'cultural relativism', my notion of 'reflexive modernity' implies that we do not have *enough* reason (*Vernunft*).

Secondly, previously depoliticized areas of decision-making are getting politicized through the perception of risk, and must be opened to public scrutiny and debate. Corporate economic decisions, scientific research agendas, plans for the development and deployment of new technologies must all be opened up to a generalized process of discussion, and a legal and institutional framework for their democratic legitimation must be developed.[21]

To me, technical (or ecological) democracy is the utopia of a responsible modernity, a vision of society in which the consequences of technological development and economic change are debated before the key decisions are taken. The burden of proof regarding future risks and hazards and current environment degradation would lie with the perpetrators rather than the injured party: from the polluter *pays* principle to the polluter *proves* principle. Finally, a new body of standards of proof, correctness, truth and agreement in science and law must be established. So what we need is nothing less than a *second Enlightenment* which opens up our minds, eyes and institutions to the self-afflicted endangerment of industrial civilization.

Many theories and theorists do not recognize the *opportunities* of risk society. Moreover, we have to recognize the ways in which contemporary debates of this sort—by which the nuclear and biotechnology industries, for example, have been forced to justify and defend their activities in the public domain[22]—are constrained by the epistemological and legal systems within which they are conducted.

So this could be one of the themes which I would like to see explored, maybe on a comparative and European level. It implies that we reconstruct the social definition of risks and risk management in different cultural frameworks; that we find out about the (negative) power of risk conflicts and definitions in contexts where people are forced together who do not want to speak to each other, but still have to. All this is familiar and already takes place. But to combine it with the questions of organized irresponsibility and the relations of definition in different European cultures and states might be worthwhile and a new adventure.

Notes

1. A. Giddens, *Beyond Left and Right* (Cambridge: Polity Press, 1994).
2. In this chapter, I shall attempt to summarize my argument on risk society; I have found it most stimulating to read the comments in David Goldblatt's chapter, 'The Sociology of Risk: Ulrich Beck', in D. Goldblatt, *Social Theory and the Environment* (Cambridge: Polity Press, 1996), 184–203.
3. U. Beck, *Risk Society* (London: Sage, 1992), 80–4.
4. Ibid., part 2, and U. Beck and E. Beck-Gernsheim, 'Individualization and Precarious Freedoms: Perspectives and Controversies of a Subject-Orientated Sociology', in P. Heelas, S. Lash and P. Morris (eds), *Detraditionalization* (Oxford: Blackwell, 1996), 23–48.
5. U. Beck, *The Reinvention of Politics* (Cambridge: Polity Press, 1997).
6. B. Latour, *Wir sind niemals modern gewesen* (Berlin: Academie Verlag, 1995).
7. F. Ewald, *L'État Providence* (Paris: Grasser & Fasquelle, 1987).
8. Ibid.
9. Giddens, *Beyond Left and Right*.
10. U. Beck, 'Misunderstanding Reflexivity', in Beck, *Democracy without Enemies* (Cambridge: Polity Press, 1998).
11. B. Wynne, 'May the Sheep Safely Graze?', in S. Lash, B. Szerszynski and B. Wynne (eds), *Risk, Environment and Modernity* (London: Sage, 1996).
12. U. Beck, *Ecological Politics in an Age of Risk* (Cambridge: Polity Press, 1995), 111–27.
13. Ibid. 92–106, 133–46.
14. B. Adams, 'Timescapes of Modernity', manuscript, Cardiff, 1997.
15. Beck, *Ecological Politics*, 116–18, 129–33, 136–7.
16. Goldblatt, *Social Theory*, 166f.
17. Beck, *Ecological Politics*, 96–110.
18. Latour, *Wir sind niemals modern gewesen*.
19. Ewald, *L'État Providence*.
20. U. Beck, A. Giddens and S. Lash, *Reflexive Modernization* (Cambridge: Polity Press, 1994).
21. Beck, *The Reinvention of Politics*.
22. E. Beck-Gernsheim, *The Social Implications of Bioengineering* (Atlantic Highlands, NJ: Humanities, 1995).

42 Ecological Citizenship

Andrew Dobson

Citizenship, as a concept, is about the rights and duties of individuals (usually) in a given political territory (e.g. the state).[1] In its participatory guises, it is normally associated with activity in the public sphere, and it may or not entail the cultivation and exercise of certain virtues. It is the specific design of this general architecture that gives us what we might call 'adjectival citizenships'—e.g. liberal citizenship, republican citizenship, cosmopolitan citizenship. Each of these types of citizenship interprets the architecture in different ways. So *liberal* citizenship tends to focus more on rights than on duties, *republican* citizenship speaks in the language of duty and of virtue, and *cosmopolitan* citizenship calls into question the territorial underpinnings of both these types of citizenship. *Ecological* citizenship is no exception to this general rule; that is, it works within the language of citizenship, but in ways that make it recognisably different from any of the three types of citizenship mentioned so far.

Environmental and Ecological Citizenship

Before I describe ecological citizenship, though, I want to contrast it with 'environmental citizenship'. I take *environmental* citizenship to refer to the way in which the environment–citizenship relationship can be regarded from a liberal point of view. This, then, is a citizenship that deals in the currency of environmental rights, that is conducted exclusively in the public sphere, whose principal virtues are the liberal ones of reasonableness and a willingness to accept the force of the better argument and procedural legitimacy, and whose remit is bounded political configurations modelled on the nation-state. For the most rough-and-ready purposes, it can be taken that environmental citizenship here refers to attempts to extend the discourse and practice of rights-claiming into the environmental context.

Ecological citizenship, on the other hand, deals in the currency of non-contractual duty, it inhabits the private as well as the public sphere, it refers to the source rather than the nature of duty in order to determine what count as citizenship virtues, it works with the language of virtue, and it is explicitly non-territorial. With this I do not mean to say that ecological citizenship is any more politically worthy or important than its environmental counterpart. From a political point of view, indeed, I regard environmental and ecological citizenship as complementary in that while they organise themselves on different terrains, they can both plausibly be read

Condensed by the author from his *Citizenship and the Environment* (Oxford: Oxford University Press, 2003), 83–140.

as heading in the same direction: the sustainable society. Enshrining environmental rights in constitutions, for example, is as much a part of realising the political project of sustainability as carrying out ecological responsibilities.

I do, though, regard ecological citizenship as more intellectually interesting than environmental citizenship from the point of view of citizenship itself. This is because environmental citizenship (understood, now, in the rather more specific sense I outlined above) leaves citizenship unchanged, in that the environment–citizenship encounter can be exhaustively captured and described by its liberal variant.[2] Ecological citizenship, on the other hand, obliges us to rethink the traditions of citizenship in ways that may, eventually, take us beyond those traditions. I have suggested that virtue is important for ecological citizenship, and in this regard it bears a family resemblance to civic republican citizenship. Ecological citizenship also shares a focus on the notion of the common good with its civic republican neighbour—environmental sustainability as a social objective is easily translatable into 'common good' language.

So both of the major citizenship traditions—liberal and civic republican—can be fruitfully connected with the 'project' of environmental sustainability. But I do not think that this project can be fully captured by these traditions, either together or in isolation. At the heart, I believe, of the tendency to overflow is the non-territorial nature of environmental sustainability as a social objective.

Ecological Non-Territoriality

It has become *de rigueur* to point out that many environmental problems are international problems—global warming, ozone depletion, acid rain—and that they are *constitutively* international in the sense that they do not, cannot, and will never respect national boundaries in their effects. If ecological citizenship is to make any sense, then, it has to do so outside the realm of activity most normally associated with contemporary citizenship: the nation-state.

It is crucial to see that as well as taking us beyond the nation-state, ecological citizenship also takes us beyond both a simple internationalism and a more complex cosmopolitanism. Ecological citizenship works with a novel conception of political space that builds in a concrete and material way on the 'historical' reasons for obligation outlined by Judith Lichtenberg. Lichtenberg distinguishes between what she calls 'moral' and 'historical' arguments for obligation. The moral view has it that 'A owes something positive to B . . . not in virtue of any causal role he has had in B's situation or any prior relationship or agreement, but just because, for example, he is able to benefit B or alleviate his plight' (Lichtenberg 1981: 80). In contrast, the historical view suggests that, 'what A owes to B he owes in virtue of some antecedent action, undertaking, agreement, relationship, or the like' (Lichtenberg 1981: 81). We might characterise the 'moral' view of obligation as that of the Good Samaritan, and the 'historical' view as that of the Good Citizen. What I want to show here is that there is a specifically ecological conception of political space, and that this gives rise to the kinds of obligations that lead to citizenship rather than Samaritanism.

Ecological citizens are not merely 'international' or even 'global'—but nor are they cosmopolitan, if by this we mean that they inhabit the space created in and by the unreal conditions of the ideal-speech situation, or in virtue of their being part of a 'common humanity'. The obligation space of ecological citizenship is 'produced' by the activities of individuals and groups with the capacity to spread and impose themselves in geographical [and] diachronic space. This produced space has no determinate size (it is not a city, or a state, and nor is it even 'universal') since its scope varies with the case.

Global Warming and Ecological Footprints

A good example of the kind of phenomenon that gives rise to citizenly rather than 'merely moral' obligations is global warming. Those individuals and communities that cause global warming are clearly in a different relationship to those harmed by it than the Good Samaritan to the poor unfortunate by the side of the road. The Good Samaritan was not responsible for the plight of the traveller, while global warmers are responsible for the rising sea levels that degrade lives on low-lying islands in the South Pacific. In Lichtenberg's terms global warmers owe obligations to those they harm by virtue of 'antecedent actions'—actions, in this case, that lead to global warming and its damaging effects.

In the ecological case the relevant space of citizenship obligation is best expressed via the earthy notion of the 'ecological footprint'. This, in considerable contrast to the nation-state, the international community, the globe, the world, or the metaphorical table around which cosmopolitanism's ideal-speakers are sat, is ecological citizenship's version of political space. Let me say something more, then, about the ecological footprint.

Nicky Chambers, Craig Simmons, and Mathis Wackernagel point out that, 'Every organism, be it a bacterium, whale or person, has an impact on the earth. We all rely upon the products and services of nature, both to supply us with raw materials and to assimilate our wastes. The impact we have on our environment is related to the "quantity" of nature that we use or "appropriate" to sustain our consumption patterns' (2000: xiii). Wackernagel and Rees then define the ecological footprint as 'the land (and water) area that would be required to support a defined human population and material standard indefinitely' (1996: 158).

The potentially asymmetric relationship between the space actually inhabited by a given human population and the ecological space required to sustain it is graphically illustrated by Wackernagel and Rees:

[I]magine what would happen to any modern city or urban region—Vancouver, Philadelphia or London—as defined by its political boundaries, the area of built-up land, or the concentration of socio-economic activities, if it were enclosed in a glass or plastic hemisphere that let in light but prevented material things of any kind from entering or leaving. . . . The health and integrity of the entire human system so contained would depend entirely on whatever was initially trapped within the hemisphere. It is obvious to most people that such a city would cease to function and its inhabitants would perish within a few days. (1996: 9)

In effect, Wackernagel and Rees's city borrows ecological space from somewhere else to enable it to survive. As long as ecological space is regarded as unlimited, this is an unremarkable fact. The 'ecological space debt' incurred by the city can be redeemed by drawing on the limitless fund of natural resources elsewhere in the world. But if we start thinking in terms of limits or thresholds, locally, regionally or globally, we encounter the possibility of unredeemable ecological space debt—unredeemable because the fund on which to draw is exhausted or degraded.

Another way of thinking about this is in terms of the relationship between the occupation of ecological space and environmental sustainability. In a world of thresholds and tolerances, environmental sustainability sets limits on the amount of ecological space that can be sustainably occupied. These limits might apply either to individuals or to communities. In principle it is possible broadly to determine the amount—or quota—of ecological space available to any individual or community, consistent with the sustainability objective. Again, this quota might apply either to a comprehensive package of environmental resources, or to one or some of them. Chambers and her colleagues outline the principle in the following way, and they offer the example of CO_2 emissions:

'Environmental space' is a methodology for achieving sustainability ... it is one of the few indicator approaches that not only documents the amounts of ecological capacity used by people, but also the amounts that could be used in a sustainable world. ... Once the 'environmental space' for those key resources has been defined, they are expressed as global per capita 'quotas' in line with a set of 'equity principles' of sustainable development. For example, assuming a global target of 11.1 gigatonnes CO_2 emissions is required to maintain climate stability by 2050, and assuming that global population in 2050 is 9.8 billion, the per capita 'environmental space' for energy is 1.1 tonnes per year. UK per capita production of CO_2 is in the region of 9 tonnes, thus implying a reduction in UK emissions by about 85 per cent. (2000: 21)

Two things should be noted in this quotation. First, there is a presumption that, absent qualifying conditions, ecological space should be divided equally among its potential recipients. Second, there is the observed fact that in connection with CO_2 emissions at least, ecological space is unequally distributed. All the evidence and calculations suggest, indeed, that this inequality of distribution across a whole range of environmental goods and services is systematically tipped in favour of wealthy countries and their wealthier inhabitants (Chambers et al. 2000: 122–3).

Whether the footprint is specific, calculable and inscribed in a limits to growth framework, or whether it is regarded merely as an expression of the unavoidable impact every individual has on the environment in the production and reproduction of human life, the footprint gives rise to the 'always already' community of obligation that I have adapted from Judith Lichtenberg.

The Production of Political Space

Another way of putting this is to say that the idea of the ecological footprint converts relationships we had thought to be 'Samaritan' into relationships of citizenship. And it does so not by some sleight of hand, but by pointing to 'antecedent actions and relationships' (in Lichtenberg's terms) where we had thought they did not exist. These actions and relationships give rise to the kinds of obligations that it is more appropriate to regard as obligations of citizenship than of Samaritanism. A key feature of this is to see that the 'space' of ecological citizenship cannot be understood in terms of contiguous territory. The effects that give rise to ecological citizenship are best captured in terms of 'action at a distance'. The contiguous territorial metaphors that are common to both liberal and civic republican citizenship are unhelpful here. Even cosmopolitan citizenship shares the idea of contiguous territory in the guise of 'one world'. In contrast, the key ecological citizenship point is that, 'the footprint is not usually a continuous piece of land or land of one particular type or quality. The globalization of trade has increased the likelihood that the bioproductive areas required to support the consumption—of the richer countries at least—are scattered all over the planet' (Chambers et al. 2000: 60). More pithily, Wackernagel and Rees write that, 'Bits of a population's Ecological Footprint can be all over the world' (1996: 53)

The 'space' of ecological citizenship is therefore not something *given* by the boundaries of nation-states or of supranational organisations such as the European Union, or even by the imagined territory of the cosmopolis. It is, rather, *produced* by the metabolistic and material relationship of individual people with their environment. This relationship gives rise to an ecological footprint which gives rise, in turn, to relationships with those on whom it impacts. We are unlikely to have met, or be ever likely to meet, those with whom we have these relationships. They may live near by or be far away, and they may be of this generation or of generations yet to be born. It is important to recognise too, of course, that they may live in our own nation-state. In this last case, though, I do not have ecological citizenly relations with them because they are fellow-citizens in the traditional nation-state sense, but because they (may) inhabit the territory created by my ecological footprint. By definition, then, ecological citizenship is a citizenship of strangers—as is, in a sense, all citizenship. The additional point of ecological citizenship, however, is that we are strangers not only to each other, but also to each other's place, and even time. The obligations of the ecological citizen extend through time as well as space, towards generations yet to be born. Ecological citizens knows that today's acts will have implications for tomorrow's people, and will argue that 'generationism' is akin to, and as indefensible as, racism or sexism.

This may be the best place to put down another marker: I regard ecological citizenship as a fundamentally anthropocentric notion. This is to say that while ecological citizenship obviously has to do with the relationship between human beings and the non-human natural world, as well as between human beings themselves, there is no need—either politically or intellectually—to express this relationship in ecocentric terms.

The underlying principle of this argument can be drawn from what we might call 'future generationism'. Its most articulate exponent, Bryan Norton, has written that:

introducing the idea that other species have intrinsic value, that humans should be 'fair' to all other species, provides no operationally recognizable constraints on human behaviour that are not already implicit in the generalized, cross-temporal obligations to protect a healthy, complex, and autonomously functioning system for the benefit of future generations of humans. (1991: 239)

Norton's basic idea is that the vast majority of environmentalists' demands regarding the protection of non-human nature can be met through attending to our obligations to future generations of human beings. These obligations, he says, amount to passing on a 'healthy, complex and autonomously functioning system', and so the sustaining of such a system is a by-product, as it were, of doing the right thing by future human beings. From this point of view there is no need for contentious and politically unpopular debates regarding either 'the rights of nature' or the 'ontological shift' favoured by deep ecologists. It is enough to recognise that we have obligations to future humans, and that these obligations include that of providing them with the means to life (broadly understood—I shall be more precise shortly). As I pointed out above, the ecological footprint extends into the future as well as across territories in the present, so the obligations of which Norton speaks can properly be thought of in terms of citizenship. So I regard ecological citizenship as anthropocentric, but anthropocentric in a 'long-sighted' way (Barry 1999: 223).

For all its superficial radical attractions, then, I do not endorse explicitly ecocentric accounts of ecological citizenship. The most fundamental reason I have for rejecting ecocentric eco-logical citizenship is that I regard the principal virtue of ecological citizenship to be that of justice, and I believe that justice can only very arguably be predicated of non-human natural beings—outside, at least, the family of great apes. Put differently, the community of justice is, for me, a human or human-like community, so if the community of ecological citizens is primarily a community of justice, the community must be a human, or human-like, one. While there is considerable metaphorical mileage in the idea that, 'Citizenship, in its fullest expression, must be understood as encompassing the more-than-human community' (Curtin 2002: 302), my view is that we can only have moral as opposed to citizenly relations with most non-human beings. I shall say more about justice as the principal virtue of ecological citizenship in a subsequent section.

The obligations of ecological citizenship are asymmetrical: they fall on those, precisely, with the capacity to 'always already' act on others. I suggested earlier that the ecological footprint gives rise to relationships with those '*on whom it impacts*'. Everything we have said about the differential size of ecological footprints suggests that these impacts will be asymmetrical. The relevant cleavage is that between 'globalising' and 'globalised' individuals, where the former is taken to refer to those whose action can 'impact at a distance', and the latter to those whose actions cannot. It is therefore not enough to say that, 'Individual citizens . . . owe a duty of care to the planet in terms of minimising resource consumption and pollution' (Steward 1991: 75), without specifying more carefully just *which* citizens have this duty of care. People who occupy less than their quota of ecological space have no such duty, except as a general injunction against wanton harm. The ecological footprint is key here. It is both an expression of the space of ecological citizenship and a way of framing decisions as to the direction of citizenship responsibilities.

Duty and Responsibility in Ecological Citizenship

I endorse Bart van Steenbergen's view that, 'There is one important difference between the environmental movement and other emancipation movements. This difference has to do with the notion of *responsibility* . . . citizenship not only concerns rights and entitlements, but also duties, obligations and responsibilities' (1994*b*: 146). But just what are these duties, obligations and responsibilities, and to whom or what are they owed? And whatever these duties, obligations and responsibilities are, and to whomever or whatever they are owed, can they be regarded as obligations of citizenship, properly speaking? Finally, should these obligations be expressed in terms of 'contract' and 'reciprocity', as they most often are in citizenship talk? I shall deal with each of these three issues in what follows.

First, then, what are the obligations of ecological citizenship? These follow very obviously from the discussion of ecological non-territoriality in the previous section. There I argued that the 'space' of ecological citizenship is the ecological footprint, and that the ecological footprints of some members of some countries have a damaging impact on the life chances of some members of other countries, as well as members of their own country. Simply put, then, the principal ecological citizenship obligation is to ensure that ecological footprints make a sustainable, rather than an unsustainable, impact. Exactly what this means in terms of individuals' daily lives is not something that can be discussed here, and I do not propose to outline a manifesto for 'green living'. To ask for such a manifesto, indeed, is to miss a key feature of the general ecological citizenship injunction. The obligation is evidently radically indeterminate. This does not make ecological citizenship meaningless, in the same way that recognising that 'democracy' or 'justice' or 'freedom' have various meanings neither makes discussion of them otiose, nor instantiation of them impossible. At the most general level, and with apologies to the Brundtland Commission whose definition of sustainable development has become the most widely cited, and which I adapt somewhat for present purposes, the ecological citizen will want to ensure that her or his ecological footprint does not compromise or foreclose the ability of others in present and future generations to pursue options important to them (World Commission on Environment and Development 1987: 43).

This formulation also offers an answer to the second question: to whom or to what are the obligations of ecological citizenship owed? Once again the answer flows from the 'ecological non-territoriality' of the previous section. Ecological footprints are an expression of the impact of the production and reproduction of individuals' and collectives' daily lives on strangers near and far. It is these strangers to whom the obligations of ecological citizenship are owed. Working out the exact extent of these obligations is not something that can be done here since there are many variables to consider (which individual? Which collection of individuals? Which category of consumption/production? What kind of impact—resource or waste? And so on). Whatever the specifics, this view of obligation contrasts with both the liberal and civic republican positions in which the scope of obligation is determined by the territorial boundaries of the polity—usually the state. Obligations might be owed either to fellow-citizens or to the state itself, but even in the former case the obligations of citizenship extend no further than those who are defined as citizens by the constituted political authority in question. Obligations of ecological citizenship, on the other hand, are due to anyone who is owed ecological space. Such people might inhabit the same politically constituted space, but they might not. Just as environmental problems cross political boundaries, so do the obligations of ecological citizenship.

But they do not cross them in the same way as they do for cosmopolitan citizens. In the world of cosmopolitan citizenship, obligations—and above all the obligation to acknowledge the force of the better argument—are owed by everyone to everyone. By contrast, the obligations of ecological citizenship are owed asymmetrically. Only those who occupy ecological space in such a way as to compromise or foreclose the ability of others in present and future generations to pursue options important to them owe obligations of ecological citizenship. This last formulation also reminds us that our discussion of the ecological footprint suggested that its impact is felt in the future as well as in the present. This, then, is another way in which the ecological answer to the 'to whom?' question of citizenship obligations differs from liberal, civic republican and cosmopolitan citizenships: such obligations are owed to the future as well as in the present. A critical implication of these types of obligation and to whom they are owed is that they contain no explicit expectations of reciprocity. If my ecological footprint is an unsustainable size then my obligation is to reduce it. It would be absurd to ask someone in ecological space deficit reciprocally to reduce theirs. The duty to reduce the size of an overlarge footprint is, however, driven by the correlative right to sufficient ecological space.

Earlier I referred to the distinction drawn by Judith Lichtenberg between 'moral' and 'historical' obligation, and argued that the latter can be regarded as a source of obligation of a citizenship type. Non-reciprocity is a common feature of both these kinds of obligation. Given the centrality of reciprocity to theories of citizenship, then, a question for us is whether the unreciprocated and asymmetrical obligations of ecological citizenship can be regarded as citizenship obligations at all. John Horton answers this question in the negative: 'The reason why reciprocal/contractual models of citizenship are attractive is precisely because they try to explain how the rights (and duties) of citizenship are circumscribed to citizens. The point about citizenship relations is that they only hold between citizens, and not, for example, between parents and children or peoples of one state and another' (1998). I agree entirely that we need to distinguish between the moral community and the community of citizens, but not that the best way of doing so is by determining who is actually or potentially capable of making contracts or responding to prompts of reciprocity. As an alternative, I have sought to show how the patterns and effects of globalisation have given rise to a series of material conditions within which the idea of transnational citizenship obligations can make sense. It is the *source* of these obligations that makes them citizenly, not whether they turn out to be reciprocally or non-reciprocally owed.

Ecological Citizenship and Virtue

The ecological citizen does the right thing not so much in reaction to incentives, but because it is the right thing to do. In this sense the idea of ecological citizenship is one of the resources on which a society might draw to make itself more sustainable. Ludvig Beckman captures this very effectively:

the fact that the sustainability of the consumerist and individualist lifestyle is put into question undoubtedly raises a whole range of questions about how to reconstruct our society. What new economic and political institutions are needed? What regulations and set of incentives are necessary in order to redirect patterns of behaviour in sustainable directions ... the question of sustainable behaviour cannot be reduced to a discussion about balancing carrots and sticks. The citizen that sorts her garbage or that prefers ecological goods will often do this because she feels committed to ecological values and ends. The citizen may not, that is, act in sustainable ways solely out of economic or practical incentives: people sometimes choose to do good for other reasons than fear (of punishment or loss) or desire (for economic rewards or social status). People sometimes do good because they want to be virtuous. (2001: 179)

But just what does 'being virtuous' mean in this context? In the first place ecological citizenship uncontroversially 'contains' the virtues of liberal and civic republican citizenship. As John Barry points out:

Citizenship, as viewed by green democratic theory, emphasizes the duty of citizens to take responsibility for their actions and choices—the obligation to 'do one's bit' in the collective enterprise of achieving sustainability. There is thus a notion of 'civic virtue' at the heart of this green conception of citizenship. A part of this notion of civic virtue refers to consideration of the interests of others and an openness to debate and deliberation. This implies that the duties of being a citizen go beyond the formal political realm, including, for example, such activities as recycling waste, ecologically aware consumption and energy conservation. (1999: 231)

Here Barry offers us explicit reference to both the liberal and civic republican traditions. The former is encapsulated in the reference to the virtue of 'an openness to debate and deliberation'. Civic republicanism is expressed through the idea of the 'collective enterprise' of achieving sustainability; this is a specific version of the 'common good' notion. So ecological citizenship contains the virtues typically associated with both liberal and civic republican citizenship.

But it also goes beyond them. It is not a matter of positing a series of virtues that are definitionally associated with such citizenship, but rather of attending to the conditions under which the obligations of citizenship are created, and via which, as a consequence, the virtues of such citizenship are called into play—whatever they may be. At this point the connections between this and two of the other dimensions of ecological citizenship we have discussed become apparent. I argued earlier in the 'ecological non-territoriality' section that the 'space' of ecological citizenship is created by the metabolistic relationship between individual human beings (and collections of them) and their non-human natural environment as they go about producing and reproducing their daily lives. This is the 'ecological footprint'. Building on this in the section on 'duty and responsibility in ecological citizenship' I suggested that the ecological citizen's responsibility is 'to ensure that her or his ecological footprint does not compromise or foreclose the ability of others in present and future generations to pursue options important to them'.

It will be apparent from this that the first virtue of ecological citizenship is justice. More specifically, ecological citizenship virtue aims at ensuring a just distribution of ecological space. In contrast, John Barry has argued that, 'It is relations of harm and vulnerability that underpin the community or network within which ecological stewardship and citizenship operate' (2002: 146). My view is that it is relations of systematic ecological injustice that give rise to the obligations of ecological citizenship. Vulnerability is a symptom of injustice rather than that which, in the first instance, generates networks of citizenship, and not all relations of vulnerability can be regarded as relations of citizenship. So my reference to a 'first' virtue of ecological citizenship is important and deliberate. With it, I intend to distinguish both between the foundational virtue of ecological citizenship and other virtues that may be instrumentally required by it, and also between virtue as Aristotelian 'dispositions of character' and *political* virtue. It is very common to see accounts of ecological virtue expressed in the Aristotelian idiom, but while this may be appropriate in broader contexts, I do not think it works in the specifically political context of citizenship.

Importantly, though, this leaves the possibility that sympathy, or other candidates such as care and compassion, might be regarded as secondary ecological citizenship virtues. This is to say that they might turn out to be important to the effective exercise of the first virtue, justice. Regarded in this way, as instruments in the service of ecological citizenship's principal virtue, Barry is absolutely right to point out that secondary virtues can be drawn from a variety of unlikely sources:

citizenship is a practice within which ecologically beneficial varies such as self-reliance and self-restraint can be learnt and practised. Although green citizenship is politically based, the activities, values and principles it embodies are not confined to the political sphere as conventionally understood. The virtues one would expect to be embodied in this green form of responsible citizenship, as a form of moral character, would be operative in other spheres of human action and roles. (1999: 228)

The Private Realm in Ecological Citizenship

In contrast to most articulations of citizenship, ecological citizenship operates in the private as well as the public sphere. This is so for two reasons. First, private acts can have public implications in ways that can be related to the category of citizenship. And second, some of the virtues of which we spoke in the previous section—care and compassion in particular, with their unconditional and non-reciprocal character—are characteristic of ideal-typical versions of private realm relationships.

In the specifically ecological context it should be clear how private acts have public implications of a citizenship sort. We know that the conception of space around which ecological citizenship is organised is the ecological footprint. This footprint, in turn, is an expression of the impact that individuals and groups of individuals make on their environment. This impact is a function of the production and reproduction of individuals' lives, both of which have a private as well as a public dimension. The private sphere itself can be understood either as the physical space within which people's lives are produced and reproduced (such as apartments, houses, mobile homes), or the realm of relationships usually regarded as 'private' (such as those between friends and family). In a rough-and-ready sense these dimensions of the private sphere correspond to the two ways in which the private realm can be related to ecological citizenship.

The private realm is important to ecological citizenship because it is a site of citizenship activity, and because some of the obligations it generates and the virtues necessary to meeting those obligations are analogously and actually present in the types of relationship we normally designate as 'private'. Although this is counter-intuitive in respect of the vast bulk of work done on citizenship in general, it is absolutely consistent with what political ecologists take citizenship to be about. Ecological citizenship is an encumbered citizenship, far removed, on one level at least, from gendered civic republicanism and its contemporary manifestations: 'the ideal citizen of classical republicanism ... was largely freed from the necessity to labour and to meet his bodily requirements ... unencumbered by the demands of everyday living' (Lister 1997: 32). Ecological citizenship, in contrast is *all about* everyday living. The 'sphere of necessity' cannot be transcended, since it is the sphere where much of the production and reproduction of human life takes place. The 'sphere of freedom' is an impossibilist sphere in which we live on thin air. In the terms I have deployed in this chapter, 'toiling to satisfy our material wants' amounts to the production of ecological footprints which, far from removing us from the realm of citizenship, actually generates the kinds of obligations peculiar to it.

Conclusion

While operating in the accepted language of citizenship—rights, obligations, virtue, territory, public and private spheres—ecological citizenship inflects this language in ways that entitle us to regard it as a different kind of citizenship. So what? Well, as well as being of intellectual interest, ecological citizenship should also be regarded as a practical tool for helping to achieve the widely-endorsed social objective of environmental sustainability. Governments overwhelmingly use fiscal sticks and carrots—or 'economic instruments'—as a mechanism for edging us towards more sustainable behaviour. And it seems to work. Road-pricing schemes, for example, have an almost immediate effect on people's behaviour.

Imagine, though, that these schemes were withdrawn tomorrow. The chances are that traffic levels would return to their pre-fine levels within a few weeks or months. No doubt some people would continue to take the bus into town, or to cycle or walk, having seen what a difference there is between a square empty of cars and one that is filled with them. But experience of car-less city days suggests that when cars are allowed back in, people fire up their engines and drive into town. The 'success' of road-pricing schemes, then, is bought at the cost of the signal failure to make anything other than a superficial impression on people's habits and practices. The change in behaviour lasts only as long as the incentives or disincentives are in place—and these are inevitably subject to the vagaries of fashion, experiment, and the direction of the political wind that happens to be blowing at the time.

Ecological citizenship addresses this problem at a different, deeper level—the level at which people do the right thing not in order to achieve some gain or avoid some harm to themselves, but because it is the right thing to do. Consumers react to superficial signals without caring about, understanding or being committed to the underlying rationale for the incentives to which they respond. Ecological citizens, on the other hand, would harbour a commitment to the principles and would 'do good' as a matter of justice rather than expediency.

Notes

1. This chapter is based on Dobson 2003: ch. 3.
2. The encounter between liberal and environmental citizenship throws up one interesting question, however: should the great apes be regarded as potential citizens in something like the way that human being (just a form of great ape, after all) are? See Dobson 2005.

References

Barry, J. (1999), *Rethinking Green Politics* (London, Thousand Oaks, New Delhi: Sage).

Barry, J. (2002), 'Vulnerability and Virtue: Democracy, Dependency, and Ecological Stewardship', in B. Minteer and B. Pepperman

Taylor (eds), *Democracy and the Claims of Nature* (Lanham, Boulder, New York, Oxford: Rowman and Littlefield).

Beckman, L. (2001), 'Virtue, Sustainability and Liberal Values', in J. Barry and M. Wissenburg (eds), *Sustaining Liberal Democracy: Ecological Challenges and Opportunities* (Houndmills: Palgrave).

Chambers, N., Simmons, C., and Wackernagel, M. (2000), *Sharing Nature's Interest: Ecological Footprints as an Indicator of Sustainability* (London and Stirling, VA: Earthscan).

Curtin, D. (2002), 'Ecological Citizenship', in I. Isin and B. Turner (eds), *Handbook of Citizenship Studies* (London: Sage).

Dobson, Andrew (2003), *Citizenship and the Environment* (Oxford: Oxford University Press).

Dobson, Andrew (2005), 'Citizenship', in A. Dobson and R. Eckersley (eds), *Political Theory and the Ecological Challenge* (Cambridge: Cambridge University Press).

Horton, J. (1998), Personal communication.

Lichtenberg, Judith (1981), 'National Boundaries and Moral Boundaries: A Cosmopolitan View', in Peter Brown and Henry Shue (eds), *Boundaries: National Autonomy and its Limits* (New Jersey: Rowman and Littlefield).

Lister, R. (1997), *Citizenship: Feminist Perspectives* (Basingstoke: Macmillan Press).

Norton, B. (1991), *Toward Unity Among Environmentalists* (New York and Oxford: Oxford University Press).

Steward, F. (1991), 'Citizens of Planet Earth', in G. Andrews (ed.), *Citizenship*, (London: Lawrence and Wishart).

van Steenbergen, B. (1994), 'Towards a global ecological citizen', in Bart van Steenbergen (ed.), *The Condition of Citizenship* (London: Sage).

Wackernagel, M. and Rees, W. (1996), *Our Ecological Footprint: Reducing Human Impact on the Earth* (British Columbia: New Society Publishers).

World Commission on Environment and Development (1987), *Our Common Future*, (Oxford and New York: Oxford University Press).

43 Inequality, Ecojustice, and Ecological Rationality

Val Plumwood

The Rationality of the EcoRepublic

I invite you to join me in imagining a future ecological and global version of Plato's great rationalist utopia, the EcoRepublic. A global scientist leader, notable for his rationality and brilliant scientific knowledge, establishes a major decision-making discipline of EcoGuardianship (called THE WAY) designed to generate a global bureaucratic-military class of rational decision-makers. Their skills, like those of Roman consuls, will be employed in the various national provinces, coordinating across world society to deal with the massive ecological problems a global capitalist economy has fathered on an injured and captive nature. The leader chooses the initial group of EcoGuardians, who go on to specify a perfectly objective, recursive process which will select their replacements and train them from infancy in every field of relevant knowledge, to become finally decision-makers in THE WAY. For this reproductive purpose they employ, not the Platonic method of selecting promising young rationalists from among the subordinated and devalued non-Guardian population, but the more rationally-appealing method of cloning themselves. This method, which they believe offers a higher degree of control over the chaotic and troublesome sphere of nature and the body, eliminates the need for any immediate affective community other than the EcoGuardians themselves. The EcoGuardians don't mix with the rest of the population, so as not to compromise by attachment their judgement, which often has to be harsh and punitive. They take a pledge to lead austere, Spartan lives, and always to put species survival and planetary health before every human desire.

We can further imagine that the EcoRepublic has come into existence because a working party of scientists and economists in 2099, faced with a severe global ecological crisis, have identified the conditions of compliance and flexibility as the two major political requirements needed to enable the human race to make the necessary sacrifices to survive into the next millenium.[1] Scientific reason must now be left to save the earth, and in the EcoRepublic, they reason, scientific reason will be in charge — perfect, objective, and uncontaminated by ridiculous prejudices and emotions, and constantly improving itself. Rational rulers must have a compliant world community, and lots of flexibility for dealing with environmental problems. They will require maximum freedom and speed, without cumbersome constituency or time-consuming

From Yeager Hudson (ed.), *Technology, Morality and Social Policy* (Lewiston: Edwin Mellen Press, 1998). Reprinted with permission.

debate. A topdown, military style autocratic decision-making chain will be maximally flexible and allow lightning changes in policy and direction to be sent down from the hyper-rational Scientist Commander and his team. In the perfectly eco-rationalist society this thinking gives rise to the EcoGuardians, a quasi-military as well as scientific order, who acquire total power to force compliance from the global population with the rules and quotas the EcoGuardians specify for every human community on earth.

At first, there is an improvement in some of the world's ecological problems, although mainly around THE WAY's headquarters where most EcoGuardians live, and at a horrendous price in human lives (by now very little non-human life remains). Many people hate THE WAY for its policies of random hostage taking and extermination of citizens from nations which do not meet their standards, the number executed being in exact rational proportion to their nation's degree of offence. Initially, the EcoGuardians stick to their mission of global coordination and of enforcing the global population's compliance with their eco-rational edicts. But after a time, things begin to get worse again after dissension begins to make itself felt among the EcoGuardians themselves. Many of the EcoGuardians seem to lose touch with THE WAY and the GREAT CRISIS it was their order's purpose to resolve. There are several attempts at reform by still committed Guardians, but a time eventually comes when it is clear that despite the austerity pledges, some of the EcoGuardians have become more interested in hedonism than in performing their guardian role. This group has taken to interpreting their pledges to mean spending most of their time supervising THE WAY's eugenic breeding festivals. This group is purged as heretics and replaced, but the remaining EcoGuardians increasingly merge religion and science. Their science was claimed to be the best available at the time THE WAY was set up, but now it seems to be turning out some seriously wrong predictions and is becoming increasingly ossified.

As ecological and human problems proliferate over time in what remains of the global market economy, the EcoGuardians increasingly turn inwards and confine themselves to their own protected planetary places. They avoid the degraded places, which increasingly join up to make large decaying patches on the face of the planet occupied by diseased, forgotten people. Those who are more in contact with what is happening in these places know things have gone badly wrong, and those who have not been too disabled by their situation have some ideas about what might be done. But these people have been cut off from theoretical knowledge and education, as well as decision-making competences, all of which have been monopolised by the remote elite of EcoGuardians. Despite this, some of these people have important knowledge, but they can't get any messages through to or motivate the decision-makers, because the society's formal structures are so one-way and authoritarian the arteries of communication and change from below are thoroughly blocked. "Complaining" carries a long prison term, and questioning an EcoGuardian's orders is punishable by death. The EcoGuardians themselves are well taken care of, and they lead such remote lives they don't seem to know or care about what is happening any more outside their specially protected, elite enclaves. Since there is no way for anyone to tell or engage them, their society proceeds towards alternatives of ecological collapse or major structural change.

The EcoRepublic is an extreme case, but the poor correctiveness and failure of ecological reflexivity and responsiveness to ecological deterioration it displays may be something it increasingly shares with contemporary forms of global capitalist society. The EcoRepublic illustrates what can happen when crucial reflexive and communicative feedback is undeveloped, disabled, or discounted. In a highly centralised society like the EcoRepublic it would be relatively easy to lose ecological correctiveness, since this is not linked across social spheres to other forms of social correctiveness, for example that of justice. Failure could be the consequence of the isolation of a ruling elite together with the silencing and disabling of other human groups who have key roles in providing ecological communication. It could result from communicative failure, or from the failure of decision-makers' motivation, even in the presence of good information networks, to use their power to maintain ecological relationships. We may imagine that, for the EcoRepublic, privilege and remoteness progressively erode the political and scientific elite's capacity to hear and to care about what is happening to degraded natural communities or their human inhabitants.

The initial EcoRepublic scenario represents a social structure not unlike that proposed by ecological oligarchs such as Garret Hardin and William Ophuls, and secretly dreamed of by many scientists. The EcoRepublic's privileging of groups seen as pre-eminent in rationality may be a dream of rationalism, but we can nevertheless imagine this society dying of a kind of rationalist arteriosclerosis. The EcoRepublic may have lots of rationalism, but rationalist solutions of this kind have very little ecological rationality. Institutions that encourage and express self-critical rationality are poorly developed in the EcoRepublic, which could reflect its generation from the least self-critical forms of current knowledge, dominant economics, and establishment science. As Beck, Giddens, and Lash (1994) argue, self-critical rationality, institutions and dispositions of knowledge are necessary conditions for dealing with postmodern and ecological crises. I shall argue that much more is required, including institutions which encourage speech from below and deep forms of democracy where communicativeness and redistributive equality are found across a range of social spheres.

Rationalism and the Crisis of Ecological Rationality

Several writers, especially John Dryzek (1987) have elaborated a concept of ecological rationality, initially defined as "the capacity of a system to maintain or increase the life supporting capability of ecosystems consistently" (Bartlett 1986; Dryzek 1987, 1990; Hayward 1994). In the context of the sorts of capacities for ecological damage now available to most human cultures, self-reflective and organised social capacities to correct human-induced ecological deterioration are required for human ecological survival. For modernist societies capable of very major and rapid ecological impacts, to lack adequate ecological correctiveness is rather like having a vehicle which is capable of going very fast but has a faulty or poorly developed brake and steering system. In the case of an organism, we could expect a similar imbalance between functions to lead to rapid death or extinction. For these high-impact contexts, ecological rationality must therefore be defined in more active terms than Bartlett's, as the capacity to correct tendencies to damage or reduce life-support systems. An ecologically rational society would be sustainable to the extent that its corrective capacities enable it to make consistently good ecological decisions that maintain its ecological relationships.

INEQUALITY, ECOJUSTICE, ECOLOGICAL RATIONALITY 611

Ecological rationality under this conception is a species of critical rationality, operating across a range of human spheres and relating them to the ecological communities in which human societies are embedded. The EcoRepublic demonstrates a failure of ecological rationality through the more general failure of critical rationality in the social and epistemological spheres. The EcoGuardians believe that their rational knowledge must save the world, and pour resources into knowledge, but resist adequate development of its self-critical functions. One reason for this failure is that the EcoGuardians are unable to recognise their own knowledge as politically situated knowledge, hence fail to recognise the need to make it socially inclusive, sensitive to its limitations, and actively engaged with its boundaries and others (Haraway 1991; Harding 1991). Relying on claims to objectivity to create a hegemonic 'we' whose truth claims dominion over all others, the EcoGuardians construct a form of knowledge that is insensitive in the very area in which the main ecological threats present themselves, the area given news of by marginal voices, in speech from below.

How does ecological rationality relate to rationalism and to other forms of rationality? As there are different forms of rationality, so there are different failures of rationality. Ecological rationality includes that higher-order form of prudential,[2] self-critical reason which scrutinises the match or fit between an agent's choices, actions, and effects and that agent's overall desires, interests, and objectives as they require certain ecological conditions for their fulfilment. Initially such an inquiry might aim at developing a balance between ecologically destructive capacities and corrective capacities, although a more sensible and ambitious objective would aim at phasing out destructive capacities and evolving a sympathetic partnership or communicative relationship with nature. A civilisation which lacks or underdevelops ecological rationality, which sets in motion massive processes of biospheric and ecological degradation which it cannot respond to or correct, does not match its actions to the survival aims it may be assumed it to have. Unless it has for good reasons chosen a path of self-extinction, its actions display a rationality failure in the ecological area in the same way that the actions of someone in the grip of a terminal addiction may be thought of as displaying a rationality failure, as contrary to their overall wishes and well-being.

The questions raised here under the rubric of rationality are those of the match between means and ends, the organisation and consistency of ends, whether some ends presuppose others, and whether subsidiary ends are overwhelming major ones, for example. In these terms there is a strong case for conceding a certain kind of priority (which I shall call basic priority) to ecological rationality; a certain level of ecological health, like individual health, is ultimately an essential precondition for most other projects. But also like individual health, it does not have to be expressed in a single specific form, but can be realised in relation to other projects and in terms of many different possible healthily organised lives. Conceding this kind of priority to ecological rationality is not however to assume any form of ecological reductionism, nor is it to assume a Malthusian approach giving automatic privilege to ecological factors in explanation and discounting or occluding social ones. Indeed I shall be arguing in this paper for a strong link between ecological rationality and social equality.

We had better not understand ecological rationality or, as I shall show, any of its main supporting concepts, in a rationalist way that links it to the doctrine of the separateness and supremacy of reason in human life. As the example of the EcoRepublic illustrates, the form of rationality involved in ecological rationality is in opposition to the form involved in rationalism, which elevates reason to Promethean status[3] and treats it as the ultimate value. A concept of ecological rationality should not repeat these mistakes by tying itself to traditional dualistic concepts of reason or by assuming that rationality has a monopoly of the capacities we need to mobilise for survival. Converging perspectives from feminist, postmodernist, and critical theory see the ecological crisis as an aspect and symptom of a more general crisis of the Western master concept of reason, whose project of rational colonisation of the inferiorised sphere of nature, rooted in antiquity, has come to flower in modernity in the domination of scientific reason and of impersonal rational mechanisms such as the global market. In the crises of limits which characterise postmodernity, we harvest the fruits of this limited and distorted form of rationality, whose bitterness gives the new era its characteristic rueful and self-critical stance which indicates a further, more fully reflexive stage of reason. The ecological wing of this new form critiques the ecological rationality of those rationalist and dualistic forms of reason that deny the social and ecological ground which supports our lives, and are unable to acknowledge their own insufficiency or the material and ecological conditions of their own production or continuation. If these over-elevated and dependency-denying forms of rationality can be traced to the historical alignment of dominant forms of reason with elite social formations (Plumwood 1993), ecological reason as a new and more fully self-critical form of reason must forge different political alliances (Harding 1991, 1993).

In these terms we can see the ecological crises of limits pressing us on multiple fronts—the oceans, the atmosphere, the forests, biodiversity loss, pollution, and human health—as indicators of rationality failures that bring up for question also our dominant systems of knowledge and decision-making. These questions about dominant forms of rationality are raised when, despite what we think of as sophisticated systems of ecology, information, and observation, few ecological limits have been anticipated sufficiently far in advance to avoid damage from human over-exploitation, when despite major existing levels of damage, more resources are poured into developing further exploitative capacities while corrective capacities remain seriously under-developed or are curtailed. If even where limit problems are identifiable in advance, as in the case of world fisheries, dominant forms of science have tended systematically to underestimate their seriousness and imminence, and to overestimate the resilience of the ecological systems in which we are embedded, questions must be raised about scientific rationality. In the sphere of global politics, the failures of the First Earth Summit and recent reversals in environmental regulation raise disturbing questions about the rationality of our present systems of national and global governance and their ability to stem escalating processes of ecological injury or to match constraining to destructive capacities. Ecological rationality then brings into question ordinary forms of rationality.

As a resting point for explanation, the concept of ecological rationality would have dubious strategic value. The tensions the concept flags rather invite further questions, especially about what kinds of societies would consistently make good ecological decisions.[4] As we increasingly press ecological limits, these are perhaps the most important questions of our time. As Dryzek's work shows, criteria of ecological rationality provide much political discriminatory power. They can help us critique the ecological irrationality of the EcoRepublic. It is clear that authoritarian political systems, especially the military systems organised around protecting privilege which still control so much of the planet, provide very few means or motivations for correctiveness and ecological feedback, especially those important kinds which come from below and register advanced ecological and social damage. This remains so where such systems are combined with the global market, which also provides a poor mechanism for registering such damage. Both political argument (Dryzek 1987) and general observation make a case for ruling out military and oligarchical systems as possible routes to solving environmental problems, contrary to the arguments of the authoritarian school of environmental thinkers who pin their hopes on ecological and scientific oligarchy.

Remoteness and Decision

Such oligarchies are said to be flexible, but as the EcoRepublic shows, care is needed in defining flexibility here: in the EcoRepublic, as increasingly in contemporary concepts of work flexibility (Martin 1995), the concept of flexibility is misleadingly one-way, going down but not up.[5] And even if we grant regimes of ecological oligarchy possession of both flexibility and powerful means to enforce compliance with environmental regulation (Thompson 1996), what is unexplained is how they can develop or maintain the political conditions for knowledge[6] or communication of this damage or for guaranteeing the ruler's motivation to use these powerful means for the purpose of protecting nature or ecological relationships. A major reason why the EcoGuardian structure is unsatisfactory for ecological decision-making is that their position as a privileged elite gives them a high level of remoteness from the consequences of their decisions, since the EcoGuardians themselves can largely escape being affected by ecological damage, and they have poor communicative and other motivating links to those who are affected. In oligarchical and authoritarian regimes there is a fatal lack of ecological correctiveness in part because the quality of decision-making suffers from forms of remoteness which dissociate decision-makers very strongly from consequent ecological damage and which can distort decision-makers' knowledge of and motivation to correct that damage.

Dryzek argues that an ecologically rational polity should meet various conditions which he believes point towards discursive democracy. It should be robust (capable of performing in different conditions), flexible (capable of adjusting to new situations), resilient (capable of correcting severe disequilibrium), and allow negative feedback ("react against human-induced shortfalls in life support capability"), coordinate responses and actions across different circumstances and boundaries, and match the scale of decision-making systems to the scale of ecological problems (Dryzek 1987, 1996). The EcoRepublic may fail on all these counts, but it fails perhaps most significantly in another important axis with major implications for democratic and ecological polities, which I shall term remoteness. Remoteness reduction is a good decision-making principle, because remoteness disturbs feedback and disrupts connections and balances between decisions and their consequences that are important for learning and for maintaining motivation, responsibility, and correctiveness. I will argue that Dryzek's conditions can usefully be supplemented by a further range of considerations about the effect of remoteness on the correctiveness of ecological decision-making and explore some of their implications for liberal democracy.

An understanding of the effect of remoteness may hold the key to making ecological rationality compatible with democracy and avoiding authoritarian or highly centralised approaches to securing it. There is a convergence between minimising remoteness in a decision-making system and maximising democracy in Mill and Dewey's sense that those who bear consequences in a democratic system must have a proportionate share in the relevant decision-making.[7] The concept of remoteness provides a way to focus on the kinds of political patterns that make some places better at the price of making other more distant places ecologically worse. Remoteness covers not only those direct consequential forms in which those who make decisions are enabled to avoid their adverse ecological consequences, but also communicative and epistemological forms of remoteness, in which they are remote from news or knowledge of these consequences. This kind of remoteness can involve communicative barriers or compartmentalisation both between decision-makers and damage to non-human nature, and also between decision-makers and those human beings associated with damaged nature. Remoteness principles thus confirm what the ecological behaviour of stratified and authoritarian systems also suggests, that an ecologically rational society is unlikely to be found where the kinds of political structures and culture necessary for human justice and communicativeness are also lacking. The same point applies to nature itself. As Hayward observes "only in a culture where humans are accustomed to listen to one another will there be any real prospect of heeding nature's protestations too" (Hayward 1994: 209).

The link between a society's incapacity to heed speech—warning or distress signals—from below in human society and ecological warning signals from non-human nature is especially significant in those cultural nodes of global capitalism whose culture is rationalist in flavour, drawn by a deep and strong-flowing historical current associating devalued humans and devalued forms or spheres of non-human nature (Plumwood 1993). Global market-based distributive systems augment these cultural systems in making a close association between vulnerable and abused places and vulnerable and abused people. Remoteness is a decision-making feature which links ecojustice and ecological rationality. The concepts of ecojustice and remoteness point to cyclical, positive feedback processes which enable the transfer of inequalities and harms from the social to the ecological sphere and back again, in much the same way that inegalitarian societies foster the transfer of harms across social spheres (Walzer 1983). When the remoteness from ecological harms of privileged groups most influential in decision-making systems meets a parallel silencing in the same decision-making systems of those most vulnerable to ecological harms, the social stage is set for major failures of ecological rationality. I will argue that remoteness is a rationality feature preventing contemporary liberal-capitalist societies, apparently the most promising candidates for ecologically rational societies, from dealing effectively with ecological problems, and that it has major implications for ecologically rational social structure. But first, I will look at the identification of remoteness with spatial remoteness characteristic of bioregionalism.

Remoteness, Autarchy and Spatial Scale

Bioregionalists have argued that small-scale autarchic communities which are designed specifically around recognition of their ecological relationships can best counter the adverse contemporary effects of remoteness on correctiveness and ecological decision-making (Sale 1980). In these types of communities, advocates think, a community's ecological relationships will be more clearly visible. People who are less epistemically remote from these relationships will be sensitive both to signals from nature and to the ecological harm done by their consumption and production decisions. Second, in autarchic bioregional communities, decision-makers will not be remote from decisions made about distant places and other peoples' lives, as centralised decision-making must be. Instead, when participatory decisions are made in a local community, decision-makers have to live with the ecological consequences of their decisions, including the ecological effects on themselves, their community, neighbours and direct descendents. And third, because democracy can only be truly participatory at the level of the small, face-to-face community, people will be in a position to have the knowledge and motivation as well as the democratic and communicative means to make good ecological decisions, decisions that reflect their own extended long-term and familiar interests as well as those of their local ecologically-defined communities. Indeed under such conditions these apparently divergent interests can be thought of as convergent and harmonious, if not identical. The democratic participation that societies on a human scale supposedly make possible would guarantee maximum feedback and correctiveness, exactly what is missing in the EcoRepublic.

These sorts of bioregional arguments seem to have succeeded in identifying an important set of decision parameters concerned with different kinds of remoteness, defining the boundaries of the ideal social community in terms of spatial remoteness conditions for good ecological decision-making. But remoteness is more than just spatial remoteness, and if we generalise these insights, we can see other relevant kinds of remoteness. They include consequential remoteness (where the consequences fall systematically on some other person or group leaving the originator unaffected), communicative and epistemic remoteness (where there is poor or blocked communication with those affected which weakens knowledge and motivation about ecological relationships), and temporal remoteness (from the effect of decisions on the future). One principle suggested by this implicit appeal to remoteness principles in bioregionalist thought might for example state that, other things being equal, an ecologically rational form of agency would minimise the remoteness of agents from the ecological consequences of their decisions (actions).[8] The principle aims to provide agents with the maximum motivation to reach responsible ecological decision, to correct bad ecological decisions, and to minimise the possibilities for ecojustice violations which systematically redistribute rather than eliminate adverse ecological consequences. Bioregionalism then proposes a participatory political structure which will empower those who bear the consequences,[9] or at least one which does not silence and disempower them.

Although the appeal of bioregionalism is often put down to nostalgia for the past, the remoteness conditions suggested by bioregionalism are in fact ways to maximise relevant ecological feedback and obtain the best conditions for ecologically benign decisions. The conditions that decision-makers should live in ways that make transparent the relevance to their own lives of the ecological relationships of their communities, and that they are minimally consequentially and epistemically remote from the ecological consequences of their consumption and production decisions, conduce to decision-making based on maximum relevant knowledge and motivation. Decision-makers who have little or no opportunity for remoteness from the ecological consequences of their decisions should, other things being equal, be well motivated to make decisions that are ecologically benign. But although bioregionalism is right to draw attention to the importance of spatial remoteness and points towards an important set of remoteness principles for good ecological decision-making, there are several problematic assumptions in its proposals. First, it tends to assume a reductionist rather than a basic form of ecological priority that privileges ecological relationships automatically over other kinds of relationships. Thus decision-making communities are to be formed to coincide exactly with important ecological boundaries, although there must on a non-reductionist view be other important components to community formation than ecological ones. Second, bioregionalism fails to consider adequately other causes and kinds of remoteness relevant to decision-making communities than spatial remoteness, and is mistaken, in my view, in identifying these remoteness principles as closely as it does with autarchy and smallness of scale.

A closer look suggests that the conditions of small-scale self-sufficiency assumed by bioregionalists to be the leading feature of ecological communities are neither necessary nor sufficient to guarantee that other important forms of remoteness are avoided. Observable small-scale communities (like the one I live in) suggest that proximity to local nature does little to guarantee the first condition of the bioregionalist, the transparency to inhabitants of ecological relationships and dependencies. The need to respect and maintain these relationships can still be obscured or overridden by other cultural factors, for example by the distorting and backgrounding force of anthropocentric cultural traditions, by the conditions of both general and ecological education, or by the intractability of local economic and social relationships. Many ecological impacts may still not be evident at the level of the local community, for example, the contribution of local animal waste to the global store of biospheric methane, and this would remain true for small self-sufficient communities. "Living close to the land" may under the right conditions help knowledge of and concern for ecological effects in a local community, but neither this closeness nor the local ecological literacy it might help generate is sufficient to guarantee knowledge of ecological effects and relationships in the larger global community or even a larger regional one; this requires a larger network, whose formation seems unlikely to be assisted by economic autarchy. Given that contemporary ecological effects are rarely likely to be contained within a single political community, autarchy is in general in conflict with the participatory principle that those most affected by decisions should have a proportionate share in making them. Similarly, small-scale communities, including self-sufficient ones, may have difficulty in meeting Dryzek's conditions of coordination across boundaries, flexibility, and matching scale (Dryzek 1996). Autarchy is not likely to be the best way of matching the scale of decision-making with the scale of impact to take responsibility for those wider ecological effects that are inevitably generated even by small-scale autarchic communities.

Nor does smallness of scale guarantee the absence of politically-based kinds of remoteness. Even face-to-face autarchic communities can make themselves epistemically and consequentially remote from ecological consequences through opportunities to redistribute ecological harms onto marginalised citizens, onto the future, and onto other less powerful communities. The extent to which this is possible within any given small-scale community depends on its political organisation, among other things, and especially on what sorts of opportunities for redistribution of ecological consequences these structures offer them. This would also be true of an economically self-sufficient community, unless we again make the question-begging and highly improbable assumption that it could be self-sufficient in its ecological impacts. The match between small scale and remoteness reduction is not as good as autarchy advocates have thought both because remoteness is more plural than they allow and because both human-scale and autarchy as such are much too politically and structurally underdetermined. This means that only under special conditions of political and cultural structure that are usually left unspecified would such a face-to-face community be likely meet optimum overall conditions for remoteness reduction.[10]

If remoteness has political as well as spatial conditions and expressions, this allows us to consider other crucial areas and ways to reduce remoteness than minimising the spatial scale of communities, ways that might bear on improving the ecological rationality of larger-scale societies (for example, by making ecological relationships more transparent in their economic and cultural systems). It is important to increase the range of options relating to size because, although smaller-scale communities certainly can reduce epistemic and responsive remoteness, and in some areas such as energy use can greatly reduce consequential remoteness, they can often also offer people fewer alternatives to damaging forms of economic activity, so that their benefits of reducing remoteness can be offset or cancelled out. This suggests that we should investigate remoteness reduction as a political and not only a spatial organising principle for ecological rationality.

Remoteness principles are consistently, blatantly and almost maximally violated by the dominant global order, but this is perhaps as much due to its political and other forms of organisation as it is to its global scale. Since laissez-faire market forms permit extreme levels of consequential, communicative and epistemic remoteness, and crusading neoliberalism is increasingly successful in maximising the social areas where this kind of market is used for decision-making, global neoliberalism may be close to maximising ecological remoteness. The present form of the global market economy creates very high levels of dissociation between consumption acts and production acts and their ecological consequences, actually encouraging remoteness as a form of comparative advantage, and so scores at a very high level on ecological irrationality. But social inequality is perhaps just as much of a factor here as geography. Inequality, whether inside the nation or out of it, is a major sponsor of remoteness, especially where it creates systematic opportunities and motivations to shift ecological ills onto others rather than to prevent their generation in the first place.

Inequality combines with geographical remoteness to generate excellent conditions for epistemic remoteness, creating major barriers to knowledge and offering massive opportunities for redistributing ecoharms onto others in ways that elude the knowledge and responsibility of consumers and producers along with concern for ecological consequences. Under conditions which allow both remoteness and rational egoism to flourish, such actions even emerge as mandatory for the rational self-maximiser, since the logic of the global market treats the least privileged as the most expendable, defining them as having "the least to lose" in terms of the low value of their health, land, and assets, and, by implication, of their lives.[11] This logic helps ensure that the least privileged are likely to feel the first and worst impacts of environmental degradation, as in the case of much global deforestation, pollution, waste dumping in poor and coloured communities, and environmentally hazardous working and living conditions for the poor. As it comes increasingly to dominate over other spheres, the global market systematically violates complex equality, enabling "one good or one set of goods [to be] dominant and determinative of value in all the spheres of distribution" (Walzer 1983), facilitating the positive feedback patterns adding ecological ills to social ills which are the mark of ecojustice violations. The next section draws out some implications of dominant forms of globalisation for an ecologically irrational distributive politics which permits those most influential in decision systems high levels of remoteness from ecological consequences and gives them a corresponding capacity to distribute ecoharms onto others.

Liberal Democracy and Ecological Rationality

Theoretically, it seems, a democracy where all have input into decisions should have a low level of remoteness and a maximum of ecological rationality. It should have a high level of correctiveness because it should maximise the informational base relevant to environmental degradation and should enable all affected citizens to be heard and have their problems addressed by responsive decision-makers.[12] But in actually existing liberal democracy, it doesn't seem to work quite like that, and it is commonly observed that liberal democracies are not performing well either in remedying ecological crises or in listening to disadvantaged citizens (Dowie 1995; Plumwood 1996b). Shallow forms of democratic politics provide only weak forms of ecological rationality, not well correlated with correctiveness on ecological or social matters, and their inequalities allow privileged groups many opportunities for remoteness. But we can draw few conclusions from this observation about the ecological rationality of deeper forms of democracy that may enable systematic reductions in remoteness.

Identifying the structural features that account for these rationality failures of liberal democracy is more difficult than noting the failures. Dryzek (1992) argues persuasively that the political and administrative spheres of liberal capitalism are unable to respond adequately to the complexity of the ecological problems generated by its imprisoning capitalist production systems. The interest group interpretation of liberal democracy is another feature which is highly problematic from the perspective of ecological rationality. It is increasingly apparent that the form of 'interest group' politics that flourishes in liberal democracy is unable to create stable measures for the protection of nature, or to recognise basic ecological priority,[13] that ecological well-being is not just another interest-group concern but ultimately a condition for most other interests. The conception of democracy and decision-making in terms of a central state mediating a multiplicity of competing (private) interest groups takes egoism, inequality and domination for granted, provides poorly for collective goods, and allows systematic redistribution of ecological ills to weaker groups.

The liberal-individualist model, as is well known, stresses a view of politics as the aggregation of self-interested individual preferences—increasingly market-weighted individual preferences. As Nancy Fraser notes, this means that "political discourse consists of registering individual preferences and bargaining, looking for formulas that satisfy as many private interests as possible.

It is assumed that there is no such thing as the common good over and above the sum of all the various individual goods, and so private interests are the legitimate stuff of political discourse" (1989: 80). The upshot of treating environmental interests this way is, at best, the process of progressive compromise between environmentalist interest groups and exploitative interests, and in this process, as it is easy to show in the case of forests and biodiversity, it is very difficult to maintain environmental values over the long haul.

For other ecological issues too, the liberal interest group model is highly problematic. Collective goods, which cover a major range of environmental cases, are not well treated. For many generalisable interests, the liberal interest group model faces the collective action problem in which an unquantifiable, highly diffused, generalisable, and perhaps not easily detectable ecological harm is pitted in a political contest against a quantifiable economic benefit accruing to a small (often very small) but highly concentrated and influential group. Interest group models tend to give poor results in this situation, while generating much community polarisation around environmental issues. (Both fisheries and forest issues exemplify this pattern.) Models stressing compromise between interest groups have a poor track record on many environmental problems, rarely stopping ecologically destructive activities as opposed to introducing ameliorative modifications which allow major damage to persist while also "giving something" to ecological interests.[14] These modifications sometimes represent worthwhile ecological gains in limited areas but rarely halt the overall progress of ecological damage.

However, a further major set of reasons for liberal capitalism's failures of ecological rationality derive from the structural features that generate both inequality and remoteness in systematic, large-scale, and connected ways. Liberal democracy as an interest group model, produces, not as a matter of accident, radical economic inequality, often in association with ethnic, gender, and other kinds of marginality and cultural subordination, which feed liberal capitalism's structural potential and need for the differential distribution of ecoharms, and generate failures of environmental justice. Environmental theory has mostly tended to assume that ecoharms are generalisable, affecting all people within an abstract national community more or less equally, and that ecological rationality should be approached therefore through a politics of the "common good". The appeal to many environmentalists of the small-scale communitarian ideal also tends to support the framing of ecological rationality issues in terms of the politics of the common good. While adherents of this approach are right to note that liberal democracy deals poorly with the politics of the common good, these perspectives also collude with the power-masking tendencies of liberal politics to create a widespread perception of ecoharms as innocent and accidental distributions of damage affecting everyone more or less equally. As a result many green theorists have been reluctant to take seriously questions of distribution of ecoharms.

Thus according to Ulrich Beck (1995), the politics of class conflict is mainly concerned with the distribution of social rewards, which is inequitable in class-differentiated societies. In contrast, he claims, in risk society ecological ills tend to be distributed more evenly, cutting across boundaries of class and power. This view is summed up in his aphorism: "Poverty is hierarchical, while smog is democratic" (1995: 60), a memorable and widely quoted statement. But unfortunately for Beck's theory, many ecological harms, including smog, are distributed just as unevenly as most commodities. A smog map of Sydney, for example, correlates the heaviest air pollution areas very closely with low socio-economic status. The veil of uncertainty Beck tries to throw over ecological harms is already thoroughly rent, by class, race, and gender as well as other forms of inequality.

The assumption of equality and generalisability in ecoharms holds good only for a certain range of ecoharms—those forms of degradation which have highly diffused or unpredictable effects not amenable to redistribution—and it holds even for many of those only very partially. It is hard to think of anything more likely to be generalisable than global warming, with its predictable outcome of increasingly extreme climatic events from which we all suffer in unpredictable ways. Events like the 1995 Chicago heatwave, where the 500 or more who died were mainly poor elderly people unable to afford air-conditioners, show that even these generalisable kinds of ecoharms tend to affect disproportionately those who already suffer from a social distribution deficit. So even in such apparently generalisable cases, what may mean discomfort for someone higher up the social scale may mean death to someone more marginal. For those kinds of degradation that are more localised and particularised in their impacts, such as exposure to toxins through residential and occupational area, much the same kind of politics of distribution can be played out as in the case of other societal goods.

For a range of environmental ills resulting from the institutions of accumulation, then, some considerable degree of redistribution and remoteness from consequences is possible along lines of social privilege. This is the basis of the ecojustice phenomenon known as "environmental racism" (which should often be termed, in my view, "environmental classism"). The socially privileged groups in a society can most readily make themselves remote from these easily perceived and particularised forms of environmental degradation; if their suburb, region or territory becomes degraded or polluted, they can buy a place in a more salubrious one. When local resources become depleted, they will be best placed to make themselves remote from local scarcities by taking advantage of wider supply sources and markets that continue to deplete distant communities in ways that elude knowledge and responsibility. They can buy expert help and remedies for environmental health and for other problems, and they are better able to mobilise in the public sphere for action on the ecological and other problems which concern them. Their working life is likely to involve a minimum of environmental pollution and disease compared to marginalised groups—for example compared to the US farm workers whose immediate life-expectancy is estimated to be twenty years below the national average (Jennings and Jennings 1993). At the same time, privileged groups are those who consume (both directly for their own use and indirectly for income generation) the greatest proportion of resources, and who have the strongest economic stake in the forms of accumulation which generate environmental harms. That is, the most socially privileged groups can make themselves relatively spatially, consequentially and epistemically remote from redistributable ecoharms, will usually have the most to gain and the least to lose from the processes that produce ecoharms, and their interests will often be better satisfied if ecoharms are redistributed rather than prevented. Some parallel conclusions can be drawn for ecological goods.

The situation is not much better for generalisable harms and damage to collective goods. Because socially privileged groups can most easily purchase alternative private resources (clean water for example), they have the least interest in maintaining in generally good condition collective goods and services of the sort typically provided by undamaged nature. In terms of their own experience, privileged groups are also likely to be more epistemically remote and distanced from awareness of both their own and nature's vulnerability and limits. For some very general forms of environmental degradation (such as nuclear radiation or biospheric degradation),[15] the ability of privileged groups to buy relief from vulnerability to environmental ills is ultimately an illusion. But for the key groups who are active in political decision-making it may still be the master illusion, fostered by their remoteness in other areas and sustained by their social privilege and influential in their choices and attitudes. The socially privileged also have a political opportunity to redistribute collective goods in their favour, via privatisation, which guarantees them superior access, and insulates them from many kinds of limits and scarcity. In short, the inequalities which thrive in liberal democracy provide systematic opportunities for consequential and epistemic remoteness in the case of both non-collective and collective goods.[16] Liberal capitalism thus provides a set of impersonal NIMBY mechanisms which guarantee that an important range of ecoharms, from both redistributable and collective sources, are redistributed to marginalised groups.

In a polity like this where the socially privileged have the main or central role in social decision-making, decisions are likely to reflect their relatively high level of consequential, epistemic, and communicative remoteness from ecological harms. From the perspective of ecological rationality then, these are among the worst groups therefore, to be allocated the role of decision-making. Yet in liberal democracies they are precisely the ones who have that role. The finding that it is socially privileged groups who are selected as politically active and effective in the liberal political structure is so well supported by empirical studies that Carole Pateman describes it as "one of the best attested findings in political science" (Pateman 1989: 163). That there is a complementary silencing of those marginalised citizens on whom most ecoharm falls is attested by the unresponsiveness of liberal systems to their redistributive deprivation and cultural subordination. Several indirect sources are available to provide information about the ecoharms of the marginalised and about prevalent ecological ills, including, in liberalism, the discourse of the public sphere and the market. If the market, considered as an information system about needs, registers information not equally but according to "market power" (income), information about the needs of those without "market power" registers very little. Bad news from below is not registered well by any of liberal democracy's information systems, hardly at all by the market, and often poorly by liberal democratic, electoral and administrative systems. Yet it is precisely this bad news from below that has to be heard if many crucial forms of ecological damage are to be socially registered and opened to political action.[17]

The epistemic remoteness of privileged groups from the kinds of ecoharms that fall on the marginal others impacts strongly on information and on the public sphere to the extent that privileged experience is hegemonic. This can create a general level of silence and epistemic distancing from these submerged kinds of ecoharms which can affect even those who suffer most from them. The consequential and epistemic remoteness of privileged groups from certain kinds of harms is reflected in what counts as ecological issue in the dominant public spheres.[18] The occupational health hazards of minority workers, the systematic poisoning of millions of migrant agricultural workers, and the dumping of toxic wastes on poor communities can pass unremarked while environmental attention is focused on consumer issues which impact on more privileged groups (Jennings and Jennings 1993) or on issues concerning "good nature". Again, socially privileged groups often aim to set themselves apart from otherised groups (in the process of hyperseparation (Plumwood 1993)) through overconsumption, and develop a culture celebrating consumption. Cultural and social values may be distorted in ways which inferiorise low consumers or "losers", for example in the West, those associated with bodily labour, materiality, and nature, and which give little attention to their ills. Cultural ideals will often tend to idealise the rich and successful and reflect their styles and standards of resource overconsumption, while portraying low consumption, satisficing lifestyles in negative or contemptuous terms (hooks 1994). If these consumerist values come to dominate in the public sphere, the cultural hegemony of social privilege can contribute to ecological damage as much as its economic domination.

There is clearly a serious problem about the ecological rationality of any system that allows those who have most access to political voice and decision-making power to be also those most relatively remote from the ecological degradation it fosters, and those who tend to be least remote from ecological degradation and who bear the worst ecological consequences to have the least access to voice and decision power. My argument implies not only that the inegalitarian power structure of liberalism is ecologically irrational, but also that the political and communicative empowerment of those least remote from ecological harms must form an important part of strategies for ecological rationality. There are many specific contextual forms this empowerment might take, such as access for community action groups to resources like public funding, but its general conditions surely require institutions which encourage speech and action from below and deep forms of democracy where communicative and redistributive equality flourish across a range of social spheres.

Beyond Liberal Democracy: Deliberative Modifications

The discussion above has suggested principles about who must be able to speak and participate effectively in the political process if the sorts of ecoharms suffered to a disproportionate degree by marginalised groups are to be subject to effective political action. As advocates of deliberative democracy note, the liberal interest group model which treats people as private political consumers provides little encouragement for the development of any public ecological morality, for collective responsibility or problem solving, or for people to transform their conception of their interests, their convictions or sympathies in response to social dialogue with affected groups (Young 1995; Dean 1996). To resolve conflicts over ecological harms through such means of reducing remoteness, we may need to create contexts in which both harming and harmed parties can communicate,[19] in which the harmed group is not disadvantaged as communicators and the harming group is neither remote (consequentially or epistemically), nor privileged in some other way in the decision-making process.[20] We can extend these conditions for equal dialogue and consensus to other matters. Ideally, to enable such transformation of interests to occur more readily, those who depend on producing the harms to earn a living should have a sufficient degree of confidence and social responsibility, overall access to economic flexibility, to social support and work reconstruction to be able make occupational and technological changes without incurring significant life penalties, that is, such penalties would need to be as far as possible socially borne. None of these conditions can be well realised in liberal forms of democracy; rather they point towards deliberative, participatory, or radical forms of democracy.

To some however the problems I have outlined suggest not that any major or general transformation of liberalism is required but rather that the problems can be resolved by adding minor and highly localised deliberative modifications to liberal democracy, such as stakeholder panels designed to address specifically ecological issues. Thus Denis Collins and John Barkdull (1995) argue that classical liberalism is the most ecologically rational system (although they consider only one source of comparison, the Soviet bloc), and that a solution to the kinds of ecological difficulties of liberal capitalism I have outlined can be found in the form of stakeholder panels that can operate within it to create dispute resolution dialogue between harming and harmed groups. Not only does this not involve any major repudiation of liberal thought, they argue, but this kind of intervention has a respectable pedigree in the thought of that father of liberal capitalist theory, Adam Smith.

As in the case of bioregionalism, the extent to which stakeholder panels can provide a solution depends upon many factors which are not specified in the model, which is radically underdetermined and ambiguous. It seems likely that the outcome will be partly dependent on how stakeholders are selected and how judicial functionaries are chosen, for example. But there is also a radical ambiguity in stakeholder panels as Barkdull and Collins describe them as between a judicial model (with an impartial judge), a voluntary interest group bargaining model, and a deliberative model attempting to arrive at a consensus about the common good. The first two return us to the liberal problems I have discussed above. To the extent that the third deliberative interpretation is intended, stakeholder panels may really represent a major modification and suspension of the interest group model, but they also provide an implicit admission that the classical liberal model Collins and Barkdull have set themselves the task of defending is inadequate for ecological rationality. My own experience of stakeholder panels suggests that, while there can be useful elements of social deliberation and consensus-seeking in the negotiation phase of the discussions, the interest group model which is so problematic for environmental issues tends to remain the basis upon which final political decisions are made. On such an interpretation, stakeholder panels will not only inherit the problems of liberal interest group bargaining, but will also inherit its difficulties in the ecojustice area and in representing adequately collective goods and public interests. Negotiation between harmed and harming parties must include advocates for and ways of representing more-than-human nature and also for the "public interest" or collective good. Both of these are among the potentially harmed parties, but they are omitted in many versions of the stakeholder panel and in Collins and Barkdull's discussion.

Collins and Barkdull concede that business is responsible for most ecoharms and that the poor or racially marginalised are the recipients of most ecoharms. But first, we are entitled to be puzzled as to why, if judicial panel-bargaining is so easily able to solve the kinds of ecological injuries Collins and Barkdull concede to be closely connected to social privilege, they are unable to solve the originating problems of social inequality they implicitly identify as at the source of the problem. Second, Collins and Barkdull do not explain how, in the situation of major, systematically produced, and strongly embedded inequalities they concede between the parties to the negotiation, stakeholder panels that bring them together to negotiate will overcome the problem that the harmed parties will often be in the same unequal position as they are in these other kinds of negotiations and contracts, such as the labour contract, and other kinds of speech contexts such as the liberal public sphere and the courts. The appearance of a solution here depends upon the assumption that such panels will be able successfully to bracket—set aside as irrelevant—social inequality. Third, they leave unexplained how the negotiation model will overcome the acute problems for the marginalised of silencing and political participation many theorists have identified as the failure of the liberal public sphere (Walzer 1983; Young 1990, 1995; Dean 1996). Unless stakeholder panels can somehow overcome pervasive social inequality to provide more than formal and assumed equality of voice, there is a danger that the panels would function in hegemonic ways to secure the appearance of consent from affected parties to solutions which may not truly represent their voice or interest in stopping the injury. In the context of "the wider failure in liberal democratic theory to distinguish free commitment and agreement from domination, subordination and inequality" (Pateman 1989: 83), it seems more likely that the panels would function to manufacture consent, by generating the hegemonic "we" which subsumes the marginal "I". In short, it is hard to see how stakeholder panels can meet the conditions for transformation of interests and deliberative process I have suggested above without a larger context of equality between the negotiating parties.

The same point holds for attempts to introduce veils of uncertainty. We might try to reinterpret Beck's thesis of risk society as a higher-order normative rather than a descriptive thesis, prescribing that effective political action to stem ecological harms is most likely if ecological risks are equally born and no group can be confident of escaping them. Beck's thesis is certainly more plausible in this form, which suggests a veil of uncertainty approach to involving those groups most influential in decision-making in reducing ecological harms (Young 1997). There is some apparent convergence between this strategy and the strategy of empowering the least remote, to the extent that a more equal society is likely to distribute ecological risks more equally, to have a thicker veil of uncertainty. But the converse does not hold, a veil of uncertainty strategy does not necessarily imply greater equality, since veils of uncertainty as limited devices for specific institutional uses are quite compatible with highly unequal and unjust social arrangements in the larger society. We can imagine the EcoRepublic simulating the uncertainty produced by equality by introducing some kind of stochastic ecological ordeal for decision-makers, for example assignment by lot to a highly polluted area, as a device to counter some of the dangers of remoteness. Yet it is hard to see what could motivate or maintain such measures in the context of the EcoRepublic. Similarly it is hard to see how such indirect strategies emphasising uncertainty could be made thorough or effective as general ways to deal with ecological damage without a larger context of equality which cannot be provided without major transformations of liberal capitalism.

Beyond Deliberative Democracy: The Public Sphere and the Ecological Rationality of Procedural and Participatory Democracy

We have seen that the radical inequality generated in liberal capitalism is a major remoteness factor that hinders the ability to respond both to collective forms of ecological degradation and also to those forms which impact differentially in terms mediated by privilege (ecojustice issues). Radical inequality acts as an incentive to redistribute rather than eliminate ecological harms, and to substitute private ecological goods for collective ecological goods. Inequality creates barriers to communication about ecoharms, both in the form of information and feedback on ecological degradation and its human impacts, and to responsiveness to this information as articulated need, as well as distorting information flows, public sphere knowledge and culture. Inequality is both itself a hindrance to ecological rationality and an indicator of other hindrances. The kind of society whose democratic forms open communication and spread decision-making processes as equally as possible should, other things being equal, offer the best chance of effective action on these significant kinds of ecoharms. Thus systems which are able to articulate and respond to the needs of the least privileged should be better than less democratic systems which reserve effective participation in decision-making for privileged groups.

In an ecologically rational society, ecoharms to marginalised groups as well as to other groups would be able to emerge as important issues in the public sphere, and those most subject to (potential) ecological harms would have an understanding of them and an effective political and public sphere voice. A strong and diverse public sphere not dominated by privileged groups and able to hear the bad news from below is essential to remoteness reduction. If the ability of all those who are injured as and with nature to have their needs considered is linked to their ability to participate in the political structure,[21] this suggests again that the elements of an ecologically rational and responsive democracy will have to be sought within the tradition which interprets democracy as widespread popular participation, choice, and involvement in decision-making, or which draws on the communicative or deliberative concepts of democracy which emphasise the public sphere.

Many of those dissatisfied with shallow interest group democracy have turned to the idea of a deliberative or communicative process to obtain a stronger account of democracy. In this model, democracy is envisaged variously as a process of participation, of deliberation, or of communication: the last two, it should be noted, somewhat narrowing the concept of participation in a potentially rationalist and inegalitarian direction. In my view, remoteness reduction requires us to go beyond these conceptions to a deep form of democracy that involves a justice dimension as redistributive equality (Fraser 1997), equality and plurality of communicative process (Young 1995), and complex equality (Walzer 1983). It requires not only a strong public sphere but perhaps more: communicative and participatory ideals and institutions that not only permit but actively solicit the voice from below. A strong case can also be made, I think, for solidarity and social citizenship, as well as robust collective life, as likely to reduce remoteness and increase ecological responsibility (Plumwood 1996b). And as I've argued elsewhere, it is also crucial to develop a democratic and non-anthropocentric culture which displaces reason/nature dualism in its various contemporary expressions (Plumwood 1993, 1996a, b), as a condition not only of greater human equality, but as the basis of more ecologically sensitive and communicative relationships with the natural world.

The notion that an ecologically rational society would need to take a participatory form derives some of its appeal from the idea that ecological harms are generalisable, so that, once these harms are recognised, general participation should be able to solve the problem of correcting them through consensus formation. If all are equally affected, and all are equally decision-makers in a participatory Rousseauian exercise of the general will, participatory democracy should be the obvious choice for a political framework to satisfy remoteness principles. But since, as we have seen, many ecological harms in modern large-scale societies have strong redistributive aspects based on various kinds of privilege, political structures, and ecological strategies premised on a "common good" framework will be insufficient to deal with them, since major parties are left out. As Iris Young notes "where some groups have greater symbolic or material privilege than others, appeals to a 'common good' are likely to perpetuate such privilege" (Young 1995: 141). Participatory projects that aim to form a "general will" through face-to-face decision-making are open to the objection that they assume simplistic, mystifying, or oppressive projects of unity (Young 1995). Thus too, communitarian and civic republican frameworks which posit a common good but lack any orientation towards recognising either difference or social equality will be correspondingly lacking in conceptual resources for tackling these redistributive features and will not foster ecological rationality in this area.

There are several more plausible recent refinements of the participation concept which replace the instrumental liberal concept of interest group bargaining by the concept of a partici- patory, communicative, or deliberative procedure which is not valued only instrumentally, in terms of the results it produces, but itself carries intrinsic value as democratic process: John Dryzek's discursive democracy and Iris Young's "communicative democracy" are two such refinements (both of Habermas's original communicative process idea). Dryzek describes discursive democracy as an attempt to "rescue communicative rationality from Habermas" (Dryzek 1990: 20). According to Habermas the liberal public sphere approximates the ideal speech situation of communicative rationality, constituting "a warning system with sensors that, though unspecialised, are sensitive to the entire gamut of society".[22] That is, the liberal public sphere is taken to represent a deliberative arena where everyone, despite other inequal- ities, has an equal opportunity to speak. This is just what we seem to need for ecological rationality.

Could such a strong public sphere come to the rescue and sufficiently counter the effects of remoteness elsewhere in a system? Not, I shall suggest, without larger transformative changes that are necessary to give a more adequate representation of the bad news from below. Once the formation of the public sphere in ways which reflect the cultural hegemony of privileged groups is recognised, its rescue potential appears much more contingent. Iris Young (1990, 1995) points up the exclusions produced by a model of critical deliberation which fails to recognise cultural specificity and other hegemonic baggage in the assumption of disengaged reason as the basis of deliberative process in the public sphere. Young's discussion shows how rationalist conceptions of speech distort and narrow both what is counted as legitimate speech and who is thought of as qualified to be a speaker. Since Western deliberative norms, Young argues, are hegemonic and agonistic, different "voices" and styles of communication need to be recognised and accorded equal legitimacy in any discussion-based process which aims to be open to all. Gendered and class or race-based norms of assertiveness and gendered speaking styles are signs and expressions of social privilege which exclude and silence. Dominant Western norms of deliberation follow the strongly entrenched cultural pattern of reason/nature dualism, privileging speech which is dispassionate and disembodied.

Young's analysis of cultural hegemony provides some illuminating philosophical confirmation for the empirical work confirming the domination of the public sphere by privileged groups (Pateman 1989). A communicative arrangement which aims to be non-exclusionary must be one which "attends to social difference, to the way power sometimes enters speech itself". But although Young's communicative democracy represents perhaps the most inclusive process account to date in terms of allowing for a multiplicity of voices, there are several remaining problems in her approach to communicative inequality as difference and the exclusive orientation to process. Young's account of silencing is based on a multicultural or ethnic recognition paradigm which aims at the expression of difference: "communicative democracy" she writes, "is better conceived as speaking across differences of culture, social position and need, which are preserved in the process" (p. 143). There are several problems here. First, this model is not appropriate for certain kinds of differences. If some differences are injuries, ways of incapacitating speech or expression even in the most favourable cultural paradigm, should our orientation be so exclusively to representing, expressing, and preserving difference, or do these kinds of differences demand also an orientation to healing action, to actively working for their elimination?[23] Should class differences and other disabling differences directly attributable to subordination be "preserved in the process" and viewed simply as a positive resource to be affirmed or represented? Those who are disabled by or in their difference cannot be empowered by affirming or preserving such differences. In the absence of distinctions between kinds of differences,[24] this formula disappears class differences and discounts the role of redistributive inequality in closing the public sphere to certain kinds of voices.

The hidden assumption here that social or redistributive inequality is irrelevant to political equality (a liberal version of mind/body dualism) and has no bearing on the ability to participate in the public sphere has been justly criticised by Carole Pateman and Nancy Fraser, among others. As Fraser (1997) states, to declare social inequalities, hierarchies, and status differentials bracketed or irrelevant to deliberation is not to make it so. If participatory or discursive democracy proliferates formal structures for participation and deliberation without considering and creating the material conditions necessary for equal participation, the result can only be what Carole Pateman calls "mini-liberalism". One source of the neglect of redistributive equality in liberal concepts of political equality are concepts of justice and equality defined in terms of reason and the state (Fraser 1997). These inherit the distortions of rationalist conceptions of reason which deny the conditions of reason's own production. To guarantee genuine equality of speech, discursive democracy has to attend to the conditions of social and cultural equality which will make equal participation in the public sphere more than a formal possibility.

A discursive form of democracy which permits the silencing of those groups most likely to bear ecological harms and continues to select privileged groups as major participants in the same way as liberal forms will have no obviously better claim to reduce remoteness or to be ecologically rational.

The second problem is related to the first but is more general, and turns on difficulties of adopting an exclusively procedural approach to hearing the bad news from below (whether the procedure is based on Habermas or Rawls). The idea that equality of access to social goods is entirely a matter of getting the right process for political communication has come to be widely accepted in the last twenty years. But an exclusive orientation to process neglects the other half of the process/product relationship, the redistributive outcome of the communicative process, and the relations of reciprocal corrigibility that must hold between process and product. For many activities, we may need to decide if a process is working well by seeing if it is turning out the right sort of product; the quality of a product can act as a test for the adequacy of the process, as the quality of the process can for the product in the democratic context. We can recognise this reciprocity of process and product even where the process is conceived as valuable in itself. A process of artistic expression, for example, may have value in its own right as an expressive process, but both we and the artist will still often want to assess that process, at least in part, in terms of the kinds of products it turns out. Although an artistic process, unlike an instrumental one, is not judged entirely in relation to its product, an artist will often attempt to keep a balance between attention to the process and attention to the product, modifying each in the light of the other. Where process and product are reciprocally corrigible, a choice between a concept of democracy driven exclusively by process and a concept which treats process in exclusively instrumental terms, as purely a means to some predetermined outcome, is a false one. If communicative processes are themselves, as Young suggests, imbued with power, communicative processes and democratic products must be among this "reciprocal" group, and we must seek ways to check and modify allegedly equal communicative processes, for example in terms of the kinds of distributive product which emerges from them.

To the extent that voices excluded by a flawed communicative process cannot proclaim or contest their own exclusion within the framework it offers (a version of the liar paradox), an illusion of adequacy and completeness of the process may be produced which cannot be corrected on a purely procedural level. To that extent also, external checks of fairness, such as that provided by the product, are required. Where the process of equal communication is revealed as politically problematic, as subject to all kinds of hegemonic modification, inflection, and interference (as Young's arguments do so reveal it), checking and modifying the communicative process by reference to the redistributive outcome is clearly essential. If a process of political communication is working well, if it is inclusive and open in a real and not just formal way to all, it should be producing a certain kind of distributive product. That product is substantive social and redistributive equality. Can we imagine a situation where a process whereby everyone has an equal opportunity to communicate needs and goals will result in a distributive outcome of serious social deprivation for some, and of substantial over-affluence for others? I believe that we would be entitled to conclude from the redistributive product that such a process is seriously flawed as a process of equal communication, and that the process has not yielded an adequate form of communicative democracy.

I want to draw out several points in conclusion. Ecologically rational societies would attend to various kinds of remoteness, including especially those consequential kinds based on social inequality. A society which aimed to reduce consequential remoteness and open ecojustice issues to effective political action would need, among other things, to be participatory and communicative, and it would need to be a society of substantial equality and democratic culture. Where we have good reason to believe that a hegemonic "we" has subsumed an excluded "I", and that existing inequalities will skew processes of communication and public sphere activity for a long time to come, we can't just hope that sufficient redistributive equality will emerge in the course of an apparently open communication process. A political structure that aimed to hear the bad news from below could not rely on somehow representing "below" in apparently fair communicative processes which were open to wide expressions of cultural difference, but would also need to adopt substantial social equality as a major redistributive and transformative objective (Fraser 1997). My argument has suggested that an ecologically rational society would need to be more ambitious in this direction than any society we now know, but that this may ultimately be the condition of our survival.

Notes

1. These conditions of compliance and flexibility are suggested in Thompson 1996.
2. Which is not to be identified with instrumental reason. See Plumwood 1996a. Indeed, since anthropocentric culture contributes in a major way to remoteness, such a prudential inquiry must go beyond concern with the arrangement of existing ends and extend to questioning the instrumental treatment of ecology and nature itself.
3. On Prometheanism, see Hayward 1994. For a feminist critique of rationalist interpretations of reason, see esp. Lloyd 1984.
4. Although culture, epistemology, ethics, and rationality itself are all implicated in questions of ecological rationality, and not only questions of political structure (contra Pepper 1993).
5. The interpretation of flexibility is plainly highly politically inflected and defined relative to larger political choices and parameters: thus an alternative interpretation of flexibility suitable for a democratic polity might see it as best realised in conjunction with features such as basic income security and democratic workplace responsibility.
6. An appeal to science will not solve the problem raised by ecological rationality. Unless we make the assumptions that the initial knowledge and judgement of the Scientist King is perfect, and that there is a method for perfectly reproducing and perfectly applying this body of knowledge, science itself cannot escape the need for epistemic, political, and social structures which enable good ecological correctiveness. To the extent that environmental oligarchy assumes that "objective science" can itself provide a reliable source of correctiveness, its proponents depend on ignoring the substantial body of work showing how power distorts conceptual frameworks and knowledges, and how science produces for the needs of the powerful. Recent work on the way such distortions in science are generated by forms of power and oppression includes Harding 1991.
7. Dewey 1961.
8. This formulation aims to avoid the ecological reductionism that haunts bioregionalism,

and the implication that ecological consequences are automatically privileged or are the only ones that must be considered.

9. It cannot without endorsing strong ecological priority empower those who bear the ecological consequences over those who bear other consequences, since ecological consequences are not the only kinds of consequences that will flow from a community's decisions. Not silencing and disempowering those who bear the consequences is a minimum condition, although some way might be found to supplement it by reflecting weak ecological priority.

10. Some theorists, for example, libertarian municipalists like Murray Bookchin, recognise that certain political conditions must be specified before we can decide whether or not a given small-scale autarchy is ecologically viable. But the question of how far the larger political networks they propose, such as federations, preserve remoteness principles remains to be considered.

11. This was the argument recently employed by World Bank officials to justify Third World waste dumping.

12. This is a bit narrow, of course, since not all ecological issues and areas of degradation or concern can be reduced to "ecoharms".

13. This is at least in part because it prioritises interests according to a completely different political logic than that involved in ranking ends according to whether they are preconditions for other ends.

14. This is the normal form of the lobbying contest between powerful economic interests and vocal green organisations the interest group model generates.

15. Many of these forms also impact on future people, who, in terms of exclusion from decisions which impact on their welfare, have to be considered highly disadvantaged.

16. So although we have the term "environmental racism" established to cover such issues of redistribution, these points provide reasons for thinking that, contra Beck, we still need concepts of class if we wish to understand them, and that we cannot work exclusively with the racialised "difference" discourses which are often used now as surrogates for suppressed concepts of class. Perhaps we can even regard class privilege as partly constituted by access to such forms of remoteness, and as having multiple determinants depending on the form at work.

17. Of course not all environmental issues have this association with marginality. Theorists of ecojustice have noted that those that have associations with more privileged groups, such as wilderness and biodiversity, tend to have a better public profile (Jennings and Jennings 1993). I do not intend to suggest that these more prestigious forms are less important or are negligible, but rather that the consequential remoteness of privileged groups is often reflected in what counts as an ecological issue in the public sphere. The divide coincides roughly with the difference between a concern about damage to 'good' nature versus a concern with repairing or avoiding further damage to 'bad' (already damaged) nature.

18. This is one among a number of reasons why the privileged may appear in opinion polls and the like as more environmentally concerned, a result which should clearly not be taken at face value.

19. I assume here neither that all ecoharms can be dealt with via party negotiation nor that these should take the form of "bargaining sessions," judicial or otherwise. Although consensus-oriented deliberation might deal better than liberalism with cases where there is agreement about what constitutes a collective ecological good, it will face problems in situations where there is no consensus about different conceptions of the ecological good, as in the case of different cultural conceptions of "the best state" of nature.

20. This condition seems to me to rule out individualist forms of capitalism and to point to community control of investment decisions, since the power to control these decisions so crucial to community well-being would tend to make entrepreneurial interests

sponsoring a polluting or damaging process highly privileged in any dispute resolution or communicative process.

21. See "The Civic Culture: A Philosophic Critique," in Pateman 1989.
22. Habermas, quoted in Dean 1996.
23. See also Phillips 1991, who argues that class differences require better parliamentary

representation, but does not discuss the paradox of making an allegedly equal political form complicit in representing differences of subordination.
24. Nancy Fraser has written insightfully of the need to discriminate among differences, only some of which are to be affirmed (Fraser 1995, 1997).

References

Bartlett, Robert (1986), "Ecological Rationality: Reason and Environmental Policy," *Environmental Ethics*, 8 (3): 221–39.

Beck, Ulrich (1995), *Ecological Enlightenment* (Atlantic Highlands, NJ: Humanities Press).

—— Giddens, Anthony, and Lash, Scott (1994), *Reflexive Modernisation* (Cambridge: Polity).

Collins, Denis, and Barkdull, John (1995), "Capitalism, Environmentalism, and Mediating Structures: From Adam Smith to Stakeholder Panels," *Environmental Ethics*, Fall: 227–324.

Dean, Jodi (1996), "Civil Society: Beyond the Public Sphere," in David M. Rasmussen (ed.), *Handbook of Critical Theory* (Cambridge, Mass.: Blackwell), 422–43.

Dewey, John (1961), *Democracy and Education* (London: Macmillan).

Dowie, Mark (1995), *Losing Ground* (Cambridge, Mass.: MIT Press).

Dryzek, John (1987), *Rational Ecology: Environment and Political Economy* (Oxford: Blackwell).

—— (1990), *Discursive Democracy: Politics, Policy and Political Science* (Cambridge: Cambridge University Press).

—— (1992), "Ecology and Discursive Democracy: Beyond Liberal Capitalism and the Administrative State," *Capitalism, Nature, Socialism*, 3 (2): 18–42.

—— (1996), "Political and Ecological Communication," in Freya Mathews (ed.), *Ecology and Democracy* (Portland, Ore: Frank Cass), 3–30.

Fraser, Nancy (1989), *Unruly Practices* (Cambridge: Polity Press).

—— (1995), "From Redistribution to Recognition? Dilemmas of Justice in a 'PostSocialist' Age," *New Left Review*, Sept./Oct., 68–95.

—— (1997), *Justus Interruptus* (Routledge: London).

Haraway, Donna (1991), "Situated Knowledges," in *Simians, Cyborgs and Women* (London: Free Association Books), 183–202.

Harding, Sandra (1991), *Whose Science, Whose Knowledge?* (Milton Keynes: Open University Press).

—— (1993) (ed.), *The Racial Economy of Science: Toward a Democratic Future* (Bloomington: Indiana University Press).

Hayward, Tim (1994), *Ecological Thought*, (Cambridge: Polity).

hooks, bell (1994), *Outlaw Culture* (London: Routledge).

Jennings, Cheri Lucas, and Jennings, H. Bruce (1993), "Green Fields/Brown Skin: Posting as a Sign of Recognition," in Jane Bennett and William Chaloupka (eds), *In the Nature of Things* (London: University of Minnesota Press), 173–96.

Lloyd, Genevieve (1984), *The Man of Reason* (London: Methuen).

Martin, Emily (1995), "Flexible Bodies: Health and Work in an Age of Systems," *Ecologist* 25 (6): 221–226.

Pateman, Carole (1989), *The Disorder of Women* (Cambridge: Polity).

Pepper, David (1993), *Eco-Socialism: From Deep Ecology to Social Justice* (London: Routledge).

Phillips, Anne (1991), *Engendering Democracy* (Cambridge: Polity).

Plumwood, Val (1993), *Feminism and the Mastery of Nature* (London: Routledge).

_____(1996a), "Anthrocentrism and Androcentrism: Parallels and Politics," *Ethics and the Environment*, 1 (2): 119–52.

_____(1996b), "Has Democracy Failed Ecology?," in Freya Mathews (ed.), *Ecology and Democracy* (Portland, Ore.: Frank Cass), 134–68.

Sale, Kirkpatrick (1980), *Human Scale* (London: Secker and Warburg).

Thompson, Janna (1996), "Towards a Green World Order: Environment and World Politics," in Freya Mathews (ed.), *Ecology and Democracy* (Portland, Ore.: Frank Cass), 32–48.

Walzer, Michael L. (1983), *Spheres of Justice* (New York: Basic Books).

Young, Iris (1990), *Justice and the Politics of Difference* (Princeton: Princeton University Press).

_____(1995), "Communication and the Other: Beyond Deliberative Democracy," in Margaret Wilson and Anna Yeatman (eds), *Justice and Identity* (Wellington: Allen and Unwin), 134–52.

Young, Oran (1997), "Fairness Matters: The Role of Equity in International Regimes," "Environmental Justice: Global Ethics for the 21st Century," Conference Melbourne, 1–3 October.

44 Political and Ecological Communication

John S. Dryzek

We can, I believe, best explore the prospects for an effective green democracy by working with a political model whose essence is authentic communication rather than, say, preference aggregation, representation, or partisan competition. The ecological context means that the kind of communicative democracy that ensues ought to take a particular shape or shapes. This shape depends not on the set of values through reference to which democrats have always justified their projects, though such values have an important place in any contemplation of appropriate political structure. It is, more importantly, a question of some political forms being better able to enter into fruitful engagement with natural systems than others, and so more effectively cope with the ecological challenge.

Why we Need Green Structures, not just Green Values

Inasmuch as there is a conventional wisdom on the matter of ecology and democracy, it would draw a sharp distinction between procedure and substance. As Robert Goodin (1992: 168) puts it, 'To advocate democracy is to advocate procedures, to advocate environmentalism is to advocate substantive outcomes'. And there can never be any guarantee that democratic procedure will produce ecologically benign substance. This distinction between procedure and substance forms the core of Goodin's (1992) treatment of green political theory. To Goodin, the green theory of value represents a coherent set of ends related to the protection and preservation of nature, whereas the green theory of agency addresses where and how these values might be promoted. Goodin argues that a green theory of agency cannot be derived from the green theory of value. Greens may still want to advocate, say, grassroots participatory democracy; but they should recognise that any such advocacy has to be on grounds separate from basic green values. This procedure/substance divide arises most graphically in the context of green advocacy of decentralisation and community self-control. Such decentralisation of political authority would have decidedly anti-ecological substantive consequences in many places with natural-resource-based local economies. Many counties in the Western United States are currently trying to assert their authority against federal environmental legislation (so far with little success in the courts) in order that mining, grazing on federal lands, and forest clearcutting can proceed unchecked.

Reprinted by permission from *Environmental Politics* 4:4 (1995), 13–30.

Decentralisation will only work to the extent that local recipients of authority subscribe to ecological values or, alternatively, the degree to which they must stay put and depend for their livelihoods solely on what can be produced locally.

On this kind of account, political structure obviously matters far less than the adoption of green values on the part of denizens in that structure, or the occupancy of key positions (such as membership in Parliament) in that structure by greens. Along these lines, Eckersley (1992) concludes that the key to green political transformation is the dissemination and adoption of ecocentric culture. In fairness, she also addresses the issue of political structure, though the kind of structure she advocates is quite close to what already exists in federal liberal democracies. Similarly, to Goodin the key to green politics is participation in electoral politics and coalition with other parties in an effort to ensure that governments in liberal democracies adopt, if only partially and incrementally, those parts of the green political agenda inspired by the green theory of value. As he puts it, 'we can, and probably should, accept green political prescriptions without necessarily adopting green ideas about how to reform political structures and processes' (Goodin 1992: 5).

The trouble with Goodin's position here is that it regards political agency as essentially unproblematical. In other words, all that has to be done is to convince people in positions of political authority that X should be pursued, and X will be pursued. Goodin's 'X' is in fact a rather large one: he considers (and I agree) that the green programme merits adoption on an all-or-nothing basis. But there are good reasons why dominant political mechanisms cannot adopt and implement that programme, or even substantial chunks of it, irrespective of the degree to which green values are adopted by participants in these mechanisms. For any complex system, be it economic, political, ecological, or social, embodies imperatives or emergent properties that take effect regardless of the intentions of the denizens of the system. Such imperatives constitute values that the system will seek. Other values will be downplayed or ignored.

To begin with the currently dominant order of capitalist democracy, all liberal democracies currently operate in the context of a capitalist market system. Any state operating in the context of such a system is greatly constrained in terms of the kinds of policies it can pursue. Policies that damage business profitability—or are even perceived as likely to damage that profitability—are automatically punished by the recoil of the market. Disinvestment here means economic downturn. And such downturn is bad for governments because it both reduces the tax revenue for the schemes those governments want to pursue (such as environmental restoration), and reduces the popularity of the government in the eyes of the voters. This effect is not a matter of conspiracy or direct corporate influence on government; it happens automatically, irrespective of anyone's intentions.

The constraints upon governments here are intensified by the increasing mobility of capital across national boundaries. So, for example, anti-pollution regulation in the United States stimulates an exodus of polluting industry across the Rio Grande to Mexico's *maquiladora* sector. Thus irrespective of the ideology of government—and irrespective of the number of green lobbyists, coalition members, or parliamentarians—the first task of any liberal democratic state must always be to secure and maintain profitable conditions for business.

Environmental policy is possible in such states, but only if its damage to business profitability is marginal, or if it can be shown to be good for business. Along these lines, Albert Weale

(1992: 66–92) discusses the ideology of 'ecological modernisation', which he believes has gained a toehold in German policy-making. More recently, United States Vice-President Albert Gore has pointed to the degree to which environmental protection can actually enhance business profitability. Yet it remains to be demonstrated that a systemic reconciliation of economic and ecological values is achievable here, as opposed to isolated successes on the part of green capitalists. If green demands are more radical, or 'all or nothing' in Goodin's terms, then 'nothing' remains the likely consequence in any clash with economic imperatives.

Even setting aside the economic context of policy determination under capitalist democracy, there remain reasons why the structure of liberal democracy itself is ultimately incapable of responding effectively to ecological problems. To cut a long story short, these problems often feature high degrees of complexity and uncertainty, and substantial collective action problems. Thus any adequate political mechanism for dealing with them must incorporate negative feedback (the ability to generate corrective movement when a natural system's equilibrium is disturbed), coordination across different problems (so that solving a problem in one place does not simply create greater problems elsewhere), coordination across actors (to supply public goods or prevent the tragedy of the commons), robustness (an ability to perform well across different conditions and contexts), flexibility (an ability to adjust internal structure in response to changing conditions), and resilience (an ability to correct for severe disequilibrium, or environmental crisis).[1]

One can debate the degree to which these criteria are met by different political-economic mechanisms, such as markets, administrative hierarchies, and international negotiations, as well as liberal democracies. My own judgment is that liberal democracy does not perform particularly well across these criteria. Negative feedback under liberal democracy is mostly achieved as a result of particular actors whose interests are aggrieved giving political vent to their annoyance, be it in voting for green candidates, lobbying, contributing money to environmentalist interest groups, or demonstrating. But such feedback devices are typically dominated by the representation of economic interests, businesses and (perhaps) labour. Coordination is often problematical because the currency of liberal democracy consists of tangible rewards to particular interests. Such particular interests do not add up to the general ecological interest. Further, complex problems are generally disaggregated on the basis of these same particular interests, and piecemeal responses crafted in each of the remaining subsets. The ensuing 'partisan mutual adjustment', to use Lindblom's (1965) term, may produce a politically rational resultant. But there is no reason to expect this resultant to be ecologically rational. In other words, interests may be placated in proportion to their material political influence, and compromises may be achieved across them, but wholesale ecological destruction can still result. Resilience in liberal democracy is inhibited by short time horizons (resulting from electoral cycles) and a general addiction to the 'political solvent' of economic growth (politics is much happier, and choices easier, when the size of the available financial 'pie' is growing).

Despite its inadequacies, I would argue that among the political mechanisms that have been tried by nations from time to time, liberal democracy is the most ecologically rational system (Dryzek 1987: ch. 9). But even setting aside the issue of the ecological adequacy of liberal democracy, and its relative merits compared to other systems, the fact remains that the way political systems are structured can make an enormous difference when it comes to the likelihood or otherwise of realising green values. And if this is true, then (to use Goodin's distinction) we should be able to derive a model of politics from the green theory of value, not just the green theory of agency. Let me now attempt such a derivation.

Biocentric and Anthropocentric Models, and their Inadequacies

What, then, might such a model look like? Would it be democratic? If so, in what sense of democracy? Presumably, what we are looking for is some kind of polity that could embed something more than short-term human material interests, and achieve more sustainable equilibria encompassing natural and human systems. Along these lines, Eckersley (1992) uses the term 'ecocentric' to describe her preferred kind of system. The term 'ecocentric' or 'biocentric' implies that intrinsic value is located in nature, and can connote an absence of regard for human interests, essentially shedding one 'centrism' in favour of another. But Eckersley herself is careful to say that she also wants the variety of human interests in nature to be sheltered under her ecocentric umbrella.

Does it make sense for us to speak in terms of ecocentric or biocentric democracy? In perhaps its most widely-used sense, 'ecocentric politics' refers only to a human political system that would give priority to ecological values. To advocate ecocentric politics in such terms is unremarkable, reducing as it does to advocacy of a biocentric ethic—one that accords intrinsic value to natural entities, irrespective of human interest in those entities. Beyond this ethical imperative politics is unchanged, and does not need to stand in any particular *structural* relation to nature. The problem with such a minimalist approach to ecocentric democracy is that it returns us directly to the position that was rejected in the previous section, where I tried to establish that we need green political structures as well as green values.

What more can ecocentric politics mean, beyond advocacy of biocentric values? A maximalist view here might emphasise the 'politics' created by and in nature, to which humans could adjust *their* politics. Now, Aristotle suggested long ago that what sets humans apart is that man is *zoon politikon*, the political animal. Primate ethology now suggests that there is something like politics that occurs in animal societies involving, for example, bargaining and trickery in the establishment of dominance hierarchies among males, though even here, one should be wary of anthropomorphising observed behaviour. Yet even if a quasi-politics can be found among primates or other animals, that kind of politics is one in which we humans cannot participate, just as animals cannot participate in our politics. Moreover, most of what goes on in the natural world (outside animal societies) would still be extremely hard to assimilate to any definition of politics.

The last century or so has seen the ascription of all kinds of political and social models to nature. Social Darwinists saw in nature a reflection of naked capitalism. Marx and Engels saw evolutionary justification for dialectical materialism. In 1915 the US political scientist Henry Jones Ford saw collectivist justification for an organic state. Nazis saw justification for genocide. Microeconomists see something like market transactions in the maximisation of inclusive fitness. Eco-anarchists from Kropotkin to Murray Bookchin see in nature models only of co-operation and mutualism. Roger Masters (1989) has recently suggested that liberal democracy is 'natural' in its flexibility in responding to changing environments. Ecofeminists see caring and nurturing, at least in female nature. And so forth. In short, just about every human political ideology and political-economic system has at one time or another been justified as consistent with nature, especially nature as revealed by Darwinism.

But this sheer variety should suggest that in nature we will find no single blueprint for human politics. And even if we did, that model would only prove *ecologically* benign to the extent that it could demonstrate that cross-species interactions were universally mutualistic and benign, rather than often hostile and competitive. Following Kropotkin, Murray Bookchin (1982) propounds exactly such a mutualistic, co-operative view of nature, to which he suggests human social, economic, and political life should be assimilated. But Bookchin's position here is, to say the least, selective in its interpretation of nature, and no more persuasive than all the other selective interpretations which have been used to justify all manner of human political arrangements. So a maximalist notion of ecocentric politics of the sort advocated by Bookchin should be rejected.

Yet nature is not devoid of political lessons. What we *will* find in nature, or at least in our interactions with it, is a variety of levels and kinds of communication to which we might try to adapt. The key here is to downplay 'centrism' of any kind, and focus instead on the kinds of interactions that might occur across the boundaries between humanity and nature. In this spirit, the search for green democracy can indeed involve looking for progressively less anthropocentric political forms. For democracy can exist not only among humans, but also in human dealings with the natural world—though not *in* that natural world, or in any simple *model* which nature provides for humanity. So the key here is seeking more egalitarian interchange at the human/natural boundary; an interchange that involves progressively less in the way of human autism. In short, ecological democratisation here is a matter of more effective integration of political and ecological communication.

On the face of it, this requirement might suggest that the whole history of democratic theory—and democratic practice—should be jettisoned, and that a truly green programme of institutional innovation should be sought under a different rubric than 'democracy'. For democracy, however contested a concept, and in however many varieties it has appeared in the last two and a half thousand years, is, if nothing else, anthropocentric. One way to substantiate this point would be to go through all the major models of democracy (for example, as presented in Held (1987)), and test them for anthropocentrism. Obviously I have not the space to do that. But let me just note that inasmuch as democratic theory has been taken under the wing of liberalism in the last few hundred years (and most of it has been), then its anthropocentrism has been guaranteed. As Freya Mathews (1991*b*: 158) notes, 'liberalism as it stands is of course anthropocentric: it takes human interest as the measure of all value'. Liberalism does so because only reasoning entities are accorded political standing. The members of a liberal democracy might, of course, choose to enact positive measures for environmental protection, for example by granting legal rights to natural objects. Guardians for those objects might then make claims on political and legal systems. But any such representation might simply *down*grade nature to another set of interests, disaggregating and isolating these interests by assigning them to identifiable natural objects, thus ignoring their intrinsically ecological (interconnected) character.

If we take the major alternative to liberalism, we find that Marxism (and so its associated models of democracy) is equally materialistic and anthropocentric, seeking human liberation in part through more effective domination and control of nature (Eckersley 1992: 75–95).[2]

The Communicative Rationality of Ecological Democracy

To attempt to move in a different direction here, let me return to the issue of the connection between democracy and reason, as highlighted in Mathews's mention of liberalism. Without wishing to get too involved in the various debates surrounding democracy and rationality (Spragens 1990; Dryzek 1990*a*), let me suggest that the best or most fruitful approach to the issue of how we might rescue rationality and perhaps democracy from anthropocentrism begins with Jürgen Habermas's analysis of the dialectics of rationalisation attendant upon modernity. To Habermas (notably, 1984, 1987), modernisation connotes two kinds of rationalisation. The first is instrumental: instrumental rationality may be defined in terms of the capacity to devise, select, and effect good means to clarified and consistent ends. The second is communicative: communicative action involves understanding across subjects, the coordination of their actions through discussion, and socialisation. Communicative rationality is the degree to which these processes are uncoerced, undistorted, and engaged by competent individuals. On Habermas's account, instrumental rationalisation has so far come out ahead, and with it the domination of money and power in political and social life, especially through bureaucracy and capitalism. One can imagine a democracy of instrumental or strategically rational individuals, and this kind of democracy is modelled in great detail by public choice analysis but, as public choice has itself shown, such a democracy is an incoherent mess, producing unstable and arbitrary outcomes (Dryzek 1992). Thus some degree of communicative rationality is crucial to *any* democracy. More important for present purposes, communicative rationality constitutes the model for a democracy that is deliberative rather than strategic in character; or at least one where strategic action is kept firmly in its place.

But could such a democracy be green? Eckersley (1992: 109–17) for one argues that it cannot. And in the terms in which she argues, she is entirely correct. She points out that for Habermas (just as for most liberals) the only entities that matter are ones capable of engaging as subjects in dialogue—in other words, human beings. In a belief carried over from his earlier work on the philosophy of science, Habermas considers that the only fruitful human attitude toward the natural world is one of instrumental manipulation and control. Indeed, the whole point of communicative rationalisation is to *prevent* human interactions with one another becoming like human interactions with the natural world (Alford 1985: 77). Human liberation is bought at the expense of the domination of nature, and so Habermas is as anthropocentric as orthodox Marxists here. And for this reason Eckersley dismisses Habermas as having any possible relevance to the search for an ecocentric politics.

Let me suggest that it would be more appropriate here to try to rescue communicative rationality from Habermas. The key would be to treat communication, and so communicative rationality, as extending to entities that can act as agents, even though they lack the self-awareness that connotes subjectivity. Agency is not the same as subjectivity, and only the former need be sought in nature. Habermas treats nature as though it were brute matter. But nature is not passive, inert, and plastic. Instead, this world is truly alive, and pervaded with meanings.[3]

Minimally, a recognition of agency in nature would underwrite respect for natural objects and ecological processes. Just as democrats should condemn humans who would silence other humans, so should they condemn humans who would silence nature by destroying it. But there are implications here for politics, as well as morality. For this recognition of agency in nature means that we should treat signals emanating from the natural world with the same respect we accord signals emanating from human subjects, and as requiring equally careful interpretation. In other words, our relation to the natural world should not be one of instrumental intervention and observation of results oriented to control. Thus communicative interaction with the natural world can and should be an eminently rational affair (Dryzek 1990*b*). Of course, human *verbal* communication cannot extend into the natural world.[4] But greater continuity is evident in non-verbal communication—body language, facial displays, pheromones, and so forth (Dryzek 1990*b*: 207). And a lot goes on in human conversation beyond the words, which is why a telephone discussion is not the same as a face-to-face meeting. More important than such continuities here are the ecological processes which transcend the boundaries of species, such as the creation, modification, or destruction of niches; or cycles involving oxygen, nitrogen, carbon, and water. Disruptions in such processes occasionally capture our attention, in the form, for example, of climate change, desertification, deforestation, and species extinction.

The idea that there may be agency in nature might seem to fly in the face of several hundred years of Western natural science, social science, and political theory. But perhaps the suggestion is not so far-fetched. Accounts of the actual practice of biological science often emphasise not manipulation and control, but rather understanding and communication. Examples here are especially prominent in work on animal thinking (notably by Donald Griffin), ethology (as in the work of Jane Goodall on chimpanzees), ecology (Worster 1985), and even genetics (see Keller's (1983) discussion of the 'feeling for the organism' in the work of Barbara McClintock).

Agency in nature on a grand scale is proposed in James Lovelock's Gaia hypothesis, which suggests that the biosphere as a whole acts so as to maintain the conditions for life. Lovelock does not suggest that Gaia has awareness, and so it cannot be described as a subject (still less a goddess). Rather, Gaia consists of a complex, self-regulating intelligence. But taking the hypothesis to heart 'implies that the stable state of our planet includes man as a part of, or partner in, a very democratic entity' (Lovelock 1979: 145). Let me suggest that Lovelock's words here may be taken more literally than perhaps he intends, and that his hypothesis can indeed help us conceptualise a non-anthropocentric democracy.[5]

All of these suggestions of agency in nature have their critics, especially among philosophers, probably less frequently among natural scientists. And it may often be hard to prove these positions scientifically. But that may not be the point. No democratic theory has ever been founded on scientific *proof* of anything, and there is no reason to seek an exception here. When it comes to the essence of *human* nature, political theorists can only disagree among themselves. To some, a utility-maximising *homo economicus* captures the essence of human nature; to others (mostly sociologists), it is a plastic, socialised conception of humanity in which there are no choices to be made, let alone utilities to be maximised; to others (such as critical theorists) a communicative and creative self; to others (such as civic republicans) a public-spirited and reflective self. In the present context, the idea of an ecological self (Mathews 1991*a*) is perhaps more appropriate than these established paradigms of personhood. My general point here is that when it comes to an ecological democracy that opens itself toward non-human nature, we should not apply standards of proof which no other democratic theory could possibly meet.

I have tried to show that it is conceivable that processes of communicative reason can be extended to cover non-human entities. Communicative reason can underwrite a particular kind of democracy in purely human affairs—one that is discursive or deliberative in character, whose essence is talk and scrutiny of the interests common to a group of people, or of particular interests of some subset of that group. But of course non-human entities cannot talk, and nor should they be anthropomorphised by giving them rights against us or preferences to be incorporated in utilitarian calculation, still less votes. However, as I have suggested, there are senses in which nature can communicate. So what kind of politics or democracy can be at issue here?

Democracy without Boundaries

To approach an answer, we first need to clear away some of the underbrush that has accumulated with the pervasiveness of liberal discourse in the last few centuries. In a liberal conception of democracy, the essence of democracy is preference aggregation (Miller 1992: 54–5). Liberals themselves might disagree as to what mechanisms for preference aggregation work best, or whose preferences should be aggregated, or to what extent aggregated preferences should be restrained by other considerations (such as basic human rights). But on one thing they all agree: preferences need to be aggregated, and if so, then a basic task is to define the population (society, or citizenry) whose preferences are to be taken into account. In practice, this can be done very precisely, with electoral registers and so forth. The liberal model of democracy requires a hard-and-fast boundary between the human and non-human world (not to mention a boundary between public and private realms, now challenged by feminists). For non-human entities cannot have preferences that we could easily recognise, or be at all confident in attributing to them. Thus ecological democracy cannot be sought in the image of preference aggregation in liberal democracy.

This liberal ideal of democracy as preference aggregation also presupposes the notion of a self-contained, self-governing community. But in today's world, that notion is becoming increasingly fictional, as political, social, and especially economic transactions transcend national boundaries. In which case, it might be productive to start thinking about models of democracy in which the boundaries of communities are indeterminate. Burnheim's proposals for demarchy can be interpreted as interesting moves in this direction. To Burnheim (1985), democracy and democratic legitimacy are not to be sought in geographically-bounded entities like nation states, but rather in functional authorities of varying geographical scope, run by individuals selected by lot from among those with a material interest in the issue in question. Now, Burnheim's functional authorities arguably establish different boundaries: between functional issue areas, rather than geographical territories. But the trouble here is that there are of course major interactions across issue areas. So interactions across issue areas, no less than interactions across state boundaries, force us to look for the essence of democracy not in the mechanical aggregation of the preferences of a well-defined and well-bounded group of people (such as a nation-state, or set of persons with a material interest in an issue), but rather in the content and style of interactions. Some styles may be judged anti-democratic (for example, the imposition of a decision without possibility for debate or criticism), some relatively democratic (for example, wide dissemination of information about an issue, the holding of hearings open to any interested parties, and so on).

A focus on the style and content of interactions fits well with the communicative rationality grounding for democracy to which I have already alluded. Now, some critics of deliberative democracy and its grounding in communicative rationality argue that it privileges rational argument, and effectively excludes other kinds of voices. But the solution to any such exclusion is obvious: the deliberative model should be extended so as to make provision for such alternative voices.[6] A similar extension may be in order to accommodate non-human communication.

Along with a recognition of the indefinite nature of boundaries of the political community, such extension means that we are now well-placed (or at least better-placed than liberal democrats) to think about dismantling what is perhaps the biggest political boundary of them all: that between the human and the non-human world. This is indeed a big step, and no doubt some people would still believe that it takes us out of the realm of politics and democracy altogether, at least as those terms are conventionally defined. Yet there is a sense in which human relationships with nature are *already* political. As Val Plumwood points out in her contribution to this collection, politicisation is a concomitant of the human colonization of nature. Such colonization connotes an authoritarian politics; democratisation would imply a more egalitarian politics here.

Democracy is, if nothing else, both an open-ended project and an essentially contested concept; indeed, if debates about the meaning of democracy did not occur in a society, we would hesitate to describe that society as truly democratic. All I am trying to do here is introduce another—major—dimension of contestation.

At one level, it is possible to propose ecological democracy as a regulative ideal. This is, after all, how the basic principles of both liberal and deliberative democracy can be advanced (Miller 1992: 55–6). For liberals, the regulative ideal is fairness and efficiency in preference aggregation: the various institutional forms under which preference aggregation might proceed are then a matter for investigation, comparison, and debate. Similarly, for deliberative democrats, the regulative ideal is free discourse about issues and interests; again, various institutional forms might then be scrutinised in the light of this ideal. For ecological democrats, the regulative ideal is effectiveness in communication that transcends the boundary of the human world. As it enters human systems, then obviously ecological communication needs to be interpreted. However, unlike the situation in liberal democracy (or for that matter in Burnheim's demarchy), this communication does not have to be mediated by the material interests of particular actors.

The content of such communication might involve attention to feedback signals emanating from natural systems; in which case, the practical challenge when it comes to institutional design becomes one of dismantling barriers to such communication. With this principle in mind, it is a straightforward matter to criticise institutions that try to subordinate nature on a large scale. Think, for example, of the development projects sponsored by the World Bank, which until recently did not even pretend to take local environmental factors into account (now they at least pretend to). Yet it is also possible to criticise approaches to our dealings with the environment that do exactly the reverse, and seek only the removal of human agency. On one of his own interpretations, Lovelock's Gaia can do quite well without people. And a misanthrope such as David Ehrenfeld (1978) would prefer to rely on natural processes left well alone by humans.

With this regulative ideal of ecological democracy in mind we are, then, in a position both to criticise existing political-economic arrangements and to think about what might work better. I am not going to offer a blueprint for the institutions of such a democracy. The design of such a democracy should itself be discursive, democratic, and sensitive to ecological signals. Moreover, idealist political prescription insensitive to real-world constraints and possibilities for innovation is often of limited value. And variation in the social and natural contexts within which political systems operate means that we should be open to institutional experimentation and variety across these contexts (though, as I noted earlier, an ability to operate in different contexts may itself be a highly desirable quality for any political-economic mechanism).

When it comes to criticism of existing political (and economic) mechanisms, it is reasonably easy to use the ecological communicative ideal to expose some gross failings. Perhaps most obviously, to the degree that any such mechanism allows internal communication to dominate and distort signals from the outside, it merits condemnation. So, for example, a bureaucracy with a well-developed internal culture may prove highly inattentive to its environment. And bureaucratic hierarchy pretty much ensures distortion and loss of information across the levels of hierarchy. Indeed, these are standard criticisms of bureaucracy as a problem-solving device, though such criticisms are usually couched in terms of a human environment, not a natural one. Markets can be just as autistic, if in different ways. Obviously, they respond only to *human, consumer* preferences that can be couched in *monetary* terms. Any market actor trying to take nonpecuniary factors into account is going to have its profitability, and so survival chances, damaged (this is not to gainsay the possibility of green consumerism). Conversely, the positive feedback of business growth (and the growth of the capitalist market in general) is guided by processes entirely internal to markets.

Above all, existing mechanisms merit condemnation to the extent that their size and scope do not match the size and scope of ecosystems and/or ecological problems. Under such circumstances, communications from or about particular ecological problems or disequilibria will be swamped by communications from other parts of the world. Here, markets that transcend ecological boundaries, which they increasingly do, merit special condemnation. The internationalisation and globalisation of markets make it that much easier to engage in local despoilation. It may be quite obvious that a local ecosystem is being degraded and destroyed, but 'international competitiveness' is a good stick with which to beat environmentalist critics of an operation. For example, they can be told that old growth forests must be clearcut, rather than logged selectively. Obviously, some ecological problems are global, as are some markets. This does not of course mean that effective response mechanisms to global ecological problems can be found in global markets. Market autism guarantees that they cannot.

Turning to the desirable scope and shape of institutions suggested by the ideal of ecological democracy, the watchword here is 'appropriate scale'. In other words, the size and scope of institutions should match the size and scope of problems. There may be good reasons for the predispositions toward small scale in ecoanarchism and 'small is beautiful' green political thought. Most notably, feedback processes in natural systems are diffuse and internal (Patten and Odum 1981), and do not pass through any central control point. Highly centralised human collective choice mechanisms are not well-placed to attend to such diffuse feedback. Moreover, the autonomy and self-sufficiency advocated by green decentralisers can force improved perception of the natural world. To the degree that a community must rely on local ecological resources, it will have to take care of them. It does not follow that local self-reliance should be taken to an extreme of autarky. Rather, it is a matter of degree: the more the community is politically and economically self-reliant, then the more it must take care of its local ecosystems. Presumably the degree of self-reliance necessary to secure adequate care here depends a great deal on the level of environmental consciousness in the community in question. To the extent that environmental consciousness is lacking, then economic consciousness has to do all the work, so there are many places (such as resource-dependent local economies in the American West) where only autarky would do the trick.

But obviously not all ecological problems and feedback signals reside at the local level. Some of them are global, and hence demand global institutional response. There is no need in this scheme of things to privilege the nation-state, and every reason not to; few, if any, ecological problems coincide with state boundaries. There is only slightly greater reason to privilege bioregions. Bioregions are notoriously hard to define, and again many problems transcend their boundaries. For example, an airshed will not necessarily correspond with a watershed, and a single watershed may contain several radically different types of ecosystems. (I lived in the Columbia river basin, which contains both mid-continent deserts and coastal forests.)

Coordination through Spontaneous Order

An ecological democracy would, then, contain numerous and cross-cutting *loci* of political authority. The obvious question here is: how does one coordinate them, given that one cannot (for example) resolve air pollution problems while completely ignoring the issue of water pollution, or deal with local sulphur dioxide pollution while ignoring the long-distance diffusion of sulphur dioxide in acid rain? The way this coordination is currently accomplished is by privileging one level of political organisation. In unitary political systems, this will normally be the national state, though matters can be a bit more complicated in federal systems. The state (national or sub-national) will of course often contain an anti-pollution agency which (nominally, if rarely in practice) coordinates policy in regard to different kinds of pollutants. But, as I have already noted, this is an entirely artificial solution, and no more defensible than privileging the local community, or for that matter the global community.

The main conceivable alternative to privileging the state is to rely on the emergence of some spontaneous order that would somehow coordinate the actions of large numbers of bodies. One example of such an order is the market, especially as celebrated by von Hayek (Goodin

1992: 154). But markets, as noted, are not exactly an ecological success story. Nor are they much good at coordinating the activities of *political* authorities. Within decentralised political systems, coordination is achieved largely through the spontaneous order of partisan mutual adjustment, which to Lindblom (1965) is at the core of collective decision in liberal democracies. Such regimes may contain more formal and consciously-designed constitutions, but partisan mutual adjustment proceeds regardless of the content of such formalisms. This adjustment involves a complex mix of talk, strategy, commitment, and individual action devised in response to the context created by the actions of others. As I noted earlier, this kind of spontaneous order under liberal democracy leaves much to be desired when scrutinised in an ecological light.

Ecosystems, including the global ecosystem, are also examples of spontaneous order, so one might try to devise an imitation which included humans. Along these lines, Murray Bookchin (1982) attempts to develop a naturalistic justification for human political organisation. His ecoanarchist prescriptions might make some sense at the local level. But he can develop no *naturalistic* justification for the kinds of political order that would be needed to transcend localities, beyond relying on the spontaneous generation of structures whose specification is completely indeterminate (which is really no answer at all).

Let me suggest that there is a kind of spontaneous order which might perform the requisite coordinating functions quite well. Discussions in democratic theory are normally directed toward how the state, or state-analogues such as local governments and intergovernmental authorities, shall be constructed. What this focus misses is the possibility of democratisation *apart from* and *against* established authority (Dryzek 1996). This latter kind of democratisation is associated with the idea of a public sphere or civil society. Public spheres are political bodies that do not exist as part of formal political authority, but rather in confrontation with that authority. Normally, they find their identity in confrontation with the state (think, for example, of Solidarity in Poland in the early 1980s), though authority constituted at levels both higher and lower than the state can also be the object of their ire. Resistance here is often 'local' in the sense of being issue-specific. Such local resistance is celebrated by Michel Foucault, though he would not be interested in the constructive role for public spheres intimated here. The internal politics of public spheres is usually defined by relatively egalitarian debate, and consensual modes of decision making. Contemporary examples are afforded by new social movements, especially on behalf of feminism, ecology, and peace. Indeed, the green movement may be conceptualised in these terms—at least the parts of that movement that do not seek entry into the state through electoral politics.

Such public spheres fit well with communicative and deliberative models of democracy. But what do they have to do with coordination across geographical jurisdictions or functional issue area boundaries? The answer is that scope in these terms is unbounded and variable, possibly responding to the scope of the issue in question. To take a simple example, the environmental movement is now international, and organisations such as Greenpeace or Friends of the Earth International can bring home to particular governments the international dimension of issues, such as the consequences to Third World countries of toxic wastes exported by industrialised countries. Along these lines, Goodin (1992: 176–7) notes that green parties can assist in the 'coordination of international environmental policies', though as a green 'Realo' he appears to have only conventional party political participation in state politics in mind, rather than public spheres. To take another example, international public spheres constituted by indigenous peoples and their advocates can bring home to boycotters of furs in London or Paris the resulting economic devastation such boycotts imply for indigenous communities in the Arctic, which rely for cash income on trapping. A public sphere on a fairly grand scale was constituted by the unofficial Global Forum which proceeded in parallel with the United Nations Conference on Environment and Development in Rio in 1992. The point is that the reach of public spheres is entirely variable and not limited by formal boundaries on jurisdictions, or obsolete notions of national sovereignty. And they can come into existence, grow, and die along with the importance of particular issues. So, for example, it is entirely appropriate that the West European peace movement declined as cold war tensions eased in the 1980s.

Conclusion

In contemplating the kinds of communication that might ensure more harmonious coordination across political and ecological systems, there is an ever-present danger of lapsing into ungrounded idealism and wishful thinking. Yet green democracy is not an all-or-nothing affair, and it can constitute a process as well as a goal. As a goal, any such green democracy might appear very distant, given the seeming global hegemony of profoundly anti-environmental liberal democratic and capitalist ideas, celebrated by Francis Fukuyama (1992) as the end of history. But if the 'grow or die' system of capitalist democracy is ultimately unsustainable in the light of ecological limits, green democrats are well-placed to both hasten its demise and intimate political alternatives. This might not be a bad way to see history moving again.

Notes

For helpful comments, the author would like to thank the other participants in the Melbourne *Democracy and the Environment* Working Group, especially Robyn Eckersley, Freya Mathews, and Val Plumwood; Robert Goodin; David Schlosberg; and audiences at Griffith University's School of Australian Environmental Studies, Australian National University's Research School of Social Sciences, and the Ecopolitics VII conference.

1. Greater detail on these requirements may be found in Dryzek (1987).
2. Curiously enough, Fascism may do better than either liberalism or Marxism in the anti-anthropocentrism stakes; as Anna Bramwell (1989: 195–208) notes, the first green 'party' in Europe was actually a strand in Hitler's

Nazi Party. But Fascism obviously takes us quite a long way from democracy, and the arguments of eco-authoritarians such as Robert Heilbroner and Garrett Hardin have been too thoroughly discredited to warrant any attention here.
3. This point should not be confused with the green spirituality advocated by deep ecologists, goddess worshippers, and others who see divinity in nature. The choice here is not between an inert nature on the one hand and a nature populated by wood nymphs, sprites, and goddesses on the other. Nor does a recognition of agency in the natural world imply that its entities should be treated like human subjects.
4. Prince Charles may talk to his rhododendrons, but they do not talk back.

5. The Gaia hypothesis bears some resemblance to superorganismic and teleological treatments of ecosystem development, which have long been abandoned by most academic ecologists (except Eugene Odum), who are committed to more reductionist and stochastic models. But the superorganismic view lives on in the pages of *The Ecologist*.

6. Iris Marion Young points to the equal validity of greeting, rhetoric, and storytelling.

References

Alford, C. Fred (1985), *Science and the Revenge of Nature: Marcuse and Habermas* (Gainesville, FL: University Press of Florida).

Bookchin, Murray (1982), *The Ecology of Freedom: The Emergence and Dissolution of Hierarchy* (Palo Alto, Calif.: Cheshire).

Bramwell, Anna (1989), *Ecology in the 20th Century: A History* (New Haven: Yale University Press).

Burnheim, John (1985), *Is Democracy Possible?* (Cambridge: Cambridge University Press).

Dryzek, John S. (1987), *Rational Ecology: Environment and Political Economy* (Oxford: Basil Blackwell).

—— (1990a), *Discursive Democracy: Politics, Policy, and Political Science* (Cambridge: Cambridge University Press).

—— (1990b), 'Green Reason: Communicative Ethics for the Biosphere', *Environmental Ethics*, 12: 195–210.

—— (1992), 'How Far Is It from Virginia and Rochester to Frankfurt? Public Choice as Critical Theory', *British Journal of Political Science*, 22: 397–417.

—— (1996), *Democracy in Capitalist Times: Ideals, Limits, and Struggles* (Oxford: Oxford University Press).

Eckersley, Robyn (1992), *Environmentalism and Political Theory: Toward an Ecocentric Approach* (Albany, NY: State University of New York Press).

Ehrenfeld, David (1978), *The Arrogance of Humanism* (New York: Oxford University Press).

Fukuyama, Francis (1992), *The End of History and the Last Man* (New York: Free Press).

Goodin, Robert E. (1992), *Green Political Theory* (Cambridge: Polity).

Habermas, Jürgen (1984), *The Theory of Communicative Action*, i. *Reason and the Rationalization of Society* (Boston: Beacon).

—— (1987), *The Theory of Communicative Action*, ii. *Lifeworld and System* (Boston: Beacon).

Held, David (1987), *Models of Democracy* (Cambridge: Polity).

Keller, Evelyn Fox (1983), *A Feeling for the Organism: The Life and Work of Barbara McClintock* (San Francisco: W. H. Freeman).

Lindblom, Charles E. (1965), *The Intelligence of Democracy: Decision Making Through Mutual Adjustment* (New York: Free Press).

Lovelock, James (1979), *Gaia: A New Look at Life on Earth* (Oxford: Oxford University Press).

Masters, Roger D. (1989), *The Nature of Politics* (New Haven: Yale University Press).

Mathews, Freya (1991a), *The Ecological Self* (Savage, Md.: Barnes & Noble).

—— (1991b), 'Democracy and the Ecological Crisis', *Legal Service Bulletin*, 16 (4): 157–9.

Miller, David (1992), 'Deliberative Democracy and Social Choice', *Political Studies*, 40 (special issue): 54–67.

Patten, Bernard C., and Odum, Eugene P. (1981), 'The Cybernetic Nature of Ecosystems', *American Naturalist*, 118: 886–95.

Spragens, Thomas A., Jr. (1990), *Reason and Democracy* (Durham, NC: Duke University Press).

Weale, Albert (1992), *The New Politics of Pollution* (Manchester: Manchester University Press).

Worster, Donald (1985), *Nature's Economy: A History of Ecological Ideas* (Cambridge: Cambridge University Press).

Bibliography

Abbey, Edward (1975), *The Monkey Wrench Gang* (Philadelphia, PA: J. B. Lippincott).

Ackerman, Bruce A, and William T. Hassler (1981), *Clean Coal, Dirty Air: or How the Clean Air Act became a Multibillion-Dollar Bail-Out for High-Sulfur Coal Producers and What Should Be Done About It* (New Haven, CT: Yale University Press).

Ageyman, Julian, Bullard, Robert, and Evans, Bob (2003) (eds), *Just Sustainabilities* (Cambridge, MA: MIT Press).

Amy, Douglas J. (1987), *The Politics of Environmental Mediation* (New York: Columbia University Press).

Anderson, Terry L., and Leal, Donald R. (1991), *Free Market Environmentalism* (Boulder, CO: Westview).

Andruss, V., Plant, C., Plant, J., and Wright, E., (1990) (eds), *Home! A Bioregional Reader* (Philadelphia: New Society).

Arrow, Kenneth J. et al.(1995), 'Economic Growth, Carrying Capacity, and the Environment', *Science*, 268 (28 April): 520–1.

Barnett, Harold J. and Morse, Chandler (1963), *Scarcity and Growth: The Economics of Natural Resource Availability* (Baltimore: Johns Hopkins University Press for Resources for the Future).

Beck, Ulrich (1992), *Risk Society: Towards a New Modernity* (London: Sage).

—— (1999), *World Risk Society* (Cambridge: Polity).

Beckerman, Wilfred (1974), *In Defence of Economic Growth* (London: Cape).

—— (1995), *Small is Stupid: Blowing the Whistle on the Greens* (London: Duckworth).

—— (2002), *A Poverty of Reason: Sustainable Development and Economic Growth* (Oakland, CA: The Independent Institute).

Bookchin, Murray (1980), *Toward an Ecological Society* (Montreal: Black Rose).

—— (1982), *The Ecology of Freedom: The Emergence and Dissolution of Hierarchy* (Palo Alto, CA: Cheshire).

—— (1986), *The Modern Crisis* (Philadelphia, PA: New Society).

—— (1988), 'Social Ecology Versus Deep Ecology', *Socialist Review*, 18(3): 9–29.

—— (1990). *Remaking Society: Pathways to a Green Future* (Boston, MA: South End Press).

—— (1990). *The Philosophy of Social Ecology* (Montreal: Black Rose).

—— and Dave Foreman (1991), *Defending the Earth* (Boston, MA: South End Press).

Braithwaite, John, and Drahos, Peter (2000), *Global Business Regulation* (Cambridge: Cambridge University Press).

Bryant, Bunyan (1995) (ed.), *Environmental Justice: Issues, Policies, and Solutions* (Covelo, CA: Island Press).

—— and Mohai, Paul (1992) (eds), *Race and the Incidence of Environmental Hazards: A Time for Discourse* (Boulder: Westview Press).

Bullard, Robert D. (1993) (ed.), *Confronting Environmental Racism: Voices from the Grassroots* (Boston: South End Press).

—— (1994) (ed.), *Unequal Protection: Environmental Justice and Communities of Color*. San Francisco: Sierra Club Books.

_____ (2000), *Dumping in Dixie: Race, Class, and Environmental Equity*, 3rd edn (Boulder, CO: West-view Press).

Camacho, David (1998) (ed.), *Environmental Injustices, Political Struggles* (Durham, NC: Duke University Press).

Catton, William R. (1980), *Overshoot: The Ecological Basis of Revolutionary Change* (Urbana, IL: University of Illinois Press).

Christoff, Peter (1996), 'Ecological Modernisation, Ecological Modernities', *Environmental Politics*, 5: 476–500.

Churchhill, Ward (2002), *Struggle for the Land: Native North American Resistance to Genocide, Ecocide, and Colonization* (San Francisco: City Lights Books).

Clark, John (1990), *Renewing the Earth: The Promise of Social Ecology: A Celebration of the Work of Murray Bookchin* (London: Green Print).

Cole, Luke, and Foster, Sheila (2000), *From the Ground Up: Environmental Racism and the Rise of the Environmental Justice Movement* (New York: New York University Press).

Cole, S. D. (1973), *Models of Doom: A Critique of the Limits to Growth* (New York: Universe Books).

Daly, Herman E. (1973) (ed.), *Toward a Steady-state Economy* (San Francisco: W. H. Freeman).

_____ (1992), 'Free Market Environmentalism: Turning a Good Servant into a Bad Master', *Critical Review*, 6: 171–83.

_____ and Townsend, Kenneth E. (1993) (eds), *Valuing the Earth: Economics, Ecology, Ethics* (Cambridge, MA: MIT Press).

Devall, Bill and Sessions, George (1985), *Deep Ecology: Living as if Nature Mattered* (Salt Lake City, UT: Peregrine Smith).

Diamond, Irene and Orenstein, Gloria Feman (1990) (eds), *Reweaving the World: The Emergence of Ecofeminism* (San Francisco, CA: Sierra Club Books).

Diani, Mario and McAdam, Doug (2003), *Social Movements and Networks* (Oxford: Oxford University Press).

DiZerega, Gus (1993). 'Unexpected Harmonies: Self-Organization in Liberal Modernity and Ecology', *The Trumpeter*, 10: 25–32.

Dobson, Andrew (1998), *Justice and the Environment: Conceptions of Environmental Sustainability and Social Justice* (Oxford: Oxford University Press).

Doherty, Brian (2002), *Ideas and Actions in the Green Movement* (London: Routledge).

_____ and de Geus, Marius (1996) (eds), *Democracy and Green Political Thought: Sustainability, Rights, and Citizenship* (London: Routledge).

Doyle, Timothy, and Kellow, Aynsley (1995), *Environmental Politics and Policy Making in Australia* (South Melbourne: Macmillan).

Dryzek, John, Downes, David, Hunold, Christian, and Schlosberg, David (2003), *Green States and Social Movements* (Oxford: Oxford University Press).

Easterbrook, Gregg (1995), *A Moment on Earth: The Coming Age of Environmental Optimism* (New York: Penguin).

Eckersley, Robyn (1995) (ed.), *Markets, the State and the Environment: Towards Integration* (Melbourne: Macmillan).

Ehrlich, Paul (1968). *The Population Bomb* (New York: Ballantine).

Ehrlich, Paul and Ehrlich, Anne (1996), *The Betrayal of Science and Reason* (Washington, DC: Island Press).

Faber, Daniel (1998) (ed.), *The Struggle for Ecological Democracy: Environmental Justice Movements in the United States* (New York: Guildford).

Ferry, Luke (1995), *The New Ecological Order* (Chicago: University of Chicago Press).

Fischer, Frank and Black, Michael (1995) (eds), *Greening Environmental Policy: The Politics of a Sustainable Future* (New York: St. Martin's Press).

Foreman, Dave and Davis, John (1991), *The Earth First Reader: Ten Years of Radical Environmentalism* (Salt Lake City, UT: Peregrine Smith).

Foster, John Bellamy (2000), *Marx's Ecology: Materialism and Nature* (New York: Monthly Review Press).

——— (2002), *Ecology Against Capitalism* (New York: Monthly Review Press).

Fox, Warwick (1990), *Toward a Transpersonal Ecology: Developing New Foundations for Environmentalism* (Boston, MA: Shambhala).

Georgescu-Roegen, Nicholas (1976), *Energy and Economic Myths: Institutional and Analytical Economic Essays* (New York: Pergamon Press).

Goldsmith, Edward, and the editors of *The Ecologist* (1972), *Blueprint for Survival* (Boston: Houghton Mifflin).

Goodwin, Jeff and Jasper, James M. (2003) (eds), *The Social Movements Reader: Cases and Concepts* (Oxford: Blackwell).

Gore, Al (1992), *Earth in the Balance: Ecology and the Human Spirit* (New York: Penguin).

Gorz, Andre (1980), *Ecology as Politics* (Boston: South End).

Guha, Ramachandra (2004), *The Ramachandra Guha Omnibus* (Oxford: Oxford University Press).

——— and Martinez-Alier, Juan (1997), *Varieties of Environmentalism: Essays North and South* (London: Earthscan).

Gundersen, Adolf (1995), *The Environmental Promise of Democratic Deliberation* (Madison, WI: University of Wisconsin Press).

Hajer, Maarten A. (1995), *The Politics of Environmental Discourse: Ecological Modernization and the Policy Process* (Oxford: Oxford University Press).

Hardin, Garrett (1993), *Living Within Limits: Ecology, Economics, and Population Taboos* (New York: Oxford University Press).

Harvey, David (1996), *Justice, Nature, and the Geography of Difference* (Oxford: Blackwell).

Hay, Peter (2002), *Main Currents in Western Environmental Thought* (Bloomington: Indiana University Press).

Hays, Samuel P. (1987), *Beauty, Health, and Permanence: Environmental Politics in the United States, 1955–1985* (Cambridge: Cambridge University Press).

Heilbroner, Robert (1991), *An Inquiry into the Human Prospect: Looked at Again for the 1990s* (New York: Norton).

Jacobs, Michael (1991), *The Green Economy: Environment, Sustainable Development and the Politics of the Future* (London: Pluto).

Jänicke, Martin and Weidner, Helmut (1996) (eds), *National Environmental Policies: A Comparative Study of Capacity-Building* (Berlin: Springer).

Johansen, Bruce E. (2003), *Indigenous Peoples and Environmental Issues: An Encyclopedia* (Westport, CT: Greenwood Publishing).

Katz, Eric, Light, Andrew, and Rothenberg, David (2000) (eds), *Beneath the Surface: Critical Essays on the Philosophy of Deep Ecology* (Cambridge, MA: MIT Press).

Kaufman, Herbert (1960), *The Forest Ranger: A Study in Administrative Behavior* (Baltimore: Johns Hopkins University Press).

Kelman, Steven (1981), *What Price Incentives? Economists and the Environment* (Boston: Auburn House).

Light, Andrew (1998), *Social Ecology After Bookchin* (New York: Guilford Press).

Laduke, Winona (2002), *The Winona Laduke Reader* (Stillwater, MN: Vayageur Press).

Lafferty, William and Meadowcroft, James (1996) (eds), *Democracy and the Environment: Problems and Prospects* (Cheltenham, UK: Edward Elgar).

——— (2000), *Implementing Sustainable Development: Strategies and Initiatives in High Consumption Societies* (Oxford: Oxford University Press).

Langhelle, Oluf (2000), 'Why Ecological Modernization and Sustainable Development Should Not be Conflated', *Journal of Environmental Policy and Planning*, 2(4): 303–22.

Lappe, Frances Moore and Collins, Joseph (1977), *Food First: Beyond the Myth of Scarcity* (Boston: Houghton-Mifflin).

Lee, Kai N. (1993), *Compass and Gyroscope: Integrating Science and Politics for the Environment* (Washington, DC: Island Press).

Lester, James P. (1995) (ed.), *Environmental Politics and Policy: Theories and Evidence*, 2nd edn (Durham, NC: Duke University Press).

Lipschutz, Ronnie D. (1995), *Global Civil Society and Global Environmental Governance: The Politics of Nature from Place to Planet* (Albany: State University of New York Press).

Lomborg, Bjørn (2001), *The Skeptical Environmentalist: Measuring the Real State of the World* (Cambridge: Cambridge University Press).

Luke, Timothy (1995), 'Sustainable Development as a Power/Knowledge System: The Problem of Governmentality', in Fischer and Black (eds), *Greening Environmental Policy: The Politics of a Sustainable Future* (New York: St. Martin's Press).

——— (1997), *Ecocritique* (Minneapolis: University of Minnesota Press).

Martinez-Alier, Joan (2003), *Environmentalism of the Poor: A Study of Ecological Conflicts and Valuation* (Cheltenham, UK: Edward Elgar).

Mason, Michael (2000), *Environmental Democracy* (London: Earthscan).

Mathews, Freya (1996) (ed.), *Ecology and Democracy* (Portland, OR: Frank Cass).

Mayer, Margit and Ely, John (1998), *The German Greens* (Philadelphia: Temple University Press).

McGinnis, Michael (1998) (ed.), *Bioregionalism* (London: Routledge).

Meiners, Roger E., and Yandle, Bruce (1993) (eds), *Taking the Environment Seriously* (Lanham, MD: Rowman and Littlefield).

Melucci, Alberto (1989), *Nomads of the Present* (Philadelphia: Temple University Press).

Merchant, Carolyn (1980), *The Death of Nature: Women, Ecology, and the Scientific Revolution* (San Francisco: Harper and Row).

——— (1989), *Ecological Revolutions: Nature, Gender, and Science in New England* (Chapel Hill: University of North Carolina Press).

Mies, Maria, and Shiva, Vandana (1993), *Ecofeminism* (London: Zed).

Minteer, Ben A. and Taylor, Bob Pepperman (2002) (eds), *Democracy and the Claims of Nature* (Lanham, MD: Rowman and Littlefield).

Mol, Arthur P. J. and Sonnenfeld, David (2000) (eds), *Ecological Modernisation Around the World* (London: Frank Cass).

Myers, Norman and Simon, Julian L. (1994), *Scarcity or Abundance: A Debate on the Environment* (New York: Norton).

Naess, Arne (1989), *Ecology, Community and Lifestyle* (Cambridge: Cambridge University Press).

O'Connor, James (1997), *Natural Causes: Essays in Ecological Marxism* (New York: Guildford).

Ostrom, Elinor (1990), *Governing the Commons* (Cambridge: Cambridge University Press).

Paehlke, Robert, and Torgerson, Douglas (2004) (eds), *Managing Leviathan: Environmental Politics and the Administrative State*, 2nd edn (Peterborough, Ontario: Broadview).

Pearce, David, Markandya, Anil and Barbier, Edward R. (1989), *Blueprint for a Green Economy* (London: Earthscan).

_____ and Barbier, Edward R. (2000), *Blueprint for a Sustainable Economy* (London: Earthscan).

Plumwood, Val (1993), *Feminism and the Mastery of Nature* (London: Routledge).

_____ (2002), *Environmental Culture: The Ecological Crisis of Reason* (London: Routledge).

Press, Daniel (1994), *Democratic Dilemmas in the Age of Ecology: Trees and Toxics in the American West* (Durham, NC: Duke University Press).

Redclift, Michael (1987), *Sustainable Development: Exploring the Contradictions* (London: Methuen).

Rootes, Chris (1999) (ed.), *Environmental Movements: Local, National, and Global* (London: Frank Cass).

_____ (2004) (ed.), *Environmental Protest in Western Europe* (Oxford: Oxford University Press).

Rosenbaum, Walter A. (1985), *Environmental Politics and Policy* (Washington, DC: Congressional Quarterly Press).

Sagoff, Mark (1988), *The Economy of the Earth* (Cambridge: Cambridge University Press).

Sale, Kirkpatrick (1985), *Dwellers in the Land: The Bioregional Vision* (San Francisco, CA: Sierra Club Books).

Salleh, Ariel (1998), *Ecofeminism as Politics: Nature, Marx, and the Postmodern* (London: Zed Books).

Scarce, Rik (1990), *Eco-Warriors: Understanding the Radical Environmental Movement* (Chicago: Noble).

Schlosberg, David (1999), *Environmental Justice and the New Pluralism: The Challenge of Difference for Environmentalism* (London: Oxford).

Schmidheiny, Stephan (1992), *Changing Course: A Global Business Perspective on Development and the Environment* (Cambridge, MA: MIT Press).

Schnaiberg, Allan (1980), *The Environment: From Surplus to Scarcity* (Oxford: Oxford University Press).

Seed, J., Macy, J., Fleming, P., and Naess, A. (1988), *Thinking Like a Mountain: Towards a Council of All Beings* (Philadelphia: New Society).

de-Shalit, Avner (2000), *The Environment Between Theory and Practice* (Oxford: Oxford University Press).

Shiva, Vandana (1997), *Biopiracy: The Plunder of Knowledge and Nature* (Boston: South End Press).

_____ (1999), *Stolen Harvest: The Hijacking of the Global Food Supply* (Boston: South End Press).

_____ (2002), *Water Wars: Pollution, Profits, and Privatization* (Boston: South End Press).

Shutkin, William (2000). *The Land that Could Be: Environmentalism and Democracy in the 21st Century* (Cambridge, MA: MIT Press).

Simon, Julian (1981), *The Ultimate Resource* (Princeton: Princeton University Press).

Simon, Julian (1995) (ed.), *The State of Humanity* (Oxford: Blackwell).

___ and Herman Kahn (1984) (eds), *The Resourceful Earth: A Response to Global 2000* (New York: Basil Blackwell).

Smith, Graham (2003), *Deliberative Democracy and the Environment* (London: Routledge).

Snyder, Gary (1974), *Turtle Island* (New York: New Directions).

Spaargaren, Gert, Mol, Arthur P. J., and Buttel, Frederick (2000) (eds), *Environment and Global Modernity* (London: Sage).

Stretton, Hugh (1976), *Capitalism, Socialism, and the Environment* (Cambridge: Cambridge University Press).

Stroup, Richard L. and Meiners, Roger E. (2000), *Cutting Green Tape: Toxic Pollutants, Environmental Regulation, and the Law* (Oakland, CA: The Independent Institute).

Torgerson, Douglas (1999), *The Promise of Green Politics: Environmentalism and the Public Sphere* (Durham, NC: Duke University Press).

Taylor, Bron (1995) (ed.), *Ecological Resistance Movements* (Albany: State University of New York Press).

Tokar, Brian (1987), *The Green Alternative* (San Pedro, CA: R. & E. Miles).

United States Council on Environmental Quality and the Department of State (1981), *The Global 2000 Report to the President, Entering the 21st Century* (Charlottesville, VA: Blue Angel, Inc.).

Vogel, David (1986), *National Styles of Regulation: Environmental Policy in Great Britain and the United States* (Ithaca, NY: Cornell University Press).

von Weiszäcker, Ernst, Lovins, Amory B., and Lovins, L. Hunter (1997), *Factor Four: Doubling Wealth, Halving Resource Use* (London: Earthscan).

Wall, Derek (1999), *Earth First and the Anti-roads Movement: Radical environmentalism and Comparative Social Movements* (London: Routledge).

Wapner, Paul (1996), *Environmental Activism and World Civic Politics* (Albany: State University of New York Press).

Weale, Albert (1992), *The New Politics of Pollution* (Manchester: Manchester University Press).

Weaver, Jace (1996) (ed.), *Defending Mother Earth: Native American Perspectives on Environmental Justice* (Maryknoll, NY: Orbis Books).

Wildavsky, Aaron (1995), *But Is It True? A Citizen's Guide to Environmental Health and Safety Issues* (Cambridge, MA: Harvard University Press).

Williams, Bruce A. and Matheny, Albert R. (1995), *Democracy, Dialogue, and Environmental Disputes: The Contested Languages of Social Regulation* (New Haven, CT: Yale University Press).

Wissenburg, Marcel (1998), *Green Liberalism: The Free and the Green Society* (London: UCL Press).

Yaffee, Steven Lewis (1994), *The Wisdom of the Spotted Owl: Policy Lessons for a New Century* (Washington, DC: Island Press).

Young, Stephen (2000) (ed.), *The Emergence of Ecological Modernisation: Integrating the Environment and Economy* (London: Routledge).

Index